CONSUMER
BEHAVIOR

ninth edition

Harcourt College Publishers

Where Learning Comes to Life

TECHNOLOGY

Technology is changing the learning experience, by increasing the power of your textbook and other learning materials; by allowing you to access more information, more quickly; and by bringing a wider array of choices in your course and content information sources.

Harcourt College Publishers has developed the most comprehensive Web sites, e-books, and electronic learning materials on the market to help you use technology to achieve your goals.

PARTNERS IN LEARNING

Harcourt partners with other companies to make technology work for you and to supply the learning resources you want and need. More importantly, Harcourt and its partners provide avenues to help you reduce your research time of numerous information sources.

Harcourt College Publishers and its partners offer increased opportunities to enhance your learning resources and address your learning style. With quick access to chapter-specific Web sites and e-books . . . from interactive study materials to quizzing, testing, and career advice . . . Harcourt and its partners bring learning to life.

Harcourt's partnership with Digital:Convergence™ brings :CRQ™ technology and the :CueCat™ reader to you and allows Harcourt to provide you with a complete and dynamic list of resources designed to help you achieve your learning goals. Just swipe the cue to view a list of Harcourt's partners and Harcourt's print and electronic learning solutions.

C 62 00 00 00 00 00 25 20

http://www.harcourtcollege.com/partners/

CONSUMER BEHAVIOR

ninth edition

Roger D. Blackwell
The Ohio State University

Paul W. Miniard
Florida International University

James F. Engel
Eastern College

HARCOURT COLLEGE PUBLISHERS

Fort Worth   Philadelphia   San Diego   New York   Orlando   Austin   San Antonio
Toronto   Montreal   London   Sydney   Tokyo

PUBLISHER	Mike Roche
ACQUISITIONS EDITOR	Bill Schoof
MARKETING STRATEGIST	Beverly Dunn
DEVELOPMENTAL EDITOR	Bobbie Bochenko
ART DIRECTOR	Van Mua
PROJECT MANAGER	Angela Williams Urquhart

ISBN: 0-03-021108-5
Library of Congress Catalog Card Number: 00-033520

Address for Domestic Orders
Harcourt College Publishers, 6277 Sea Harbor Drive, Orlando, FL 32887-6777
800-782-4479

Address for International Orders
International Customer Service
Harcourt College Publishers, 6277 Sea Harbor Drive, Orlando, FL 32887-6777
407-345-3800
(fax) 407-345-4060
(e-mail) hbintl@harcourtbrace.com

Address for Editorial Correspondence
Harcourt College Publishers, 301 Commerce Street, Suite 3700, Fort Worth, TX 76102

Web Site Address
http://www.harcourtcollege.com

Harcourt College Publishers will provide complimentary supplements or supplement packages to those adopters qualified under our adoption policy. Please contact your sales representative to learn how you qualify. If as an adopter or potential user you receive supplements you do not need, please return them to your sales representative or send them to: Attn: Returns Department, Troy Warehouse, 465 South Lincoln Drive, Troy, MO 63379.

Printed in the United States of America

1 2 3 4 5 6 7 8 9 048 9 8 7 6 5 4 3 2

Harcourt College Publishers

The Dryden Press Series in Marketing

Reedy
Electronic Marketing

Rosenbloom
Marketing Channels: A Management View
Sixth Edition

Sandburg
Discovering Your Marketing Career CD-ROM

Schaffer
Applying Marketing Principles Software

Schaffer
The Marketing Game

Schellinck and Maddox
Marketing Research: A Computer-Assisted Approach

Schnaars
MICROSIM

Schuster and Copeland
Global Business: Planning for Sales and Negotiations

Sheth, Mittal, and Newman
Customer Behavior: Consumer Behavior and Beyond

Shimp
Advertising and Promotions: Supplemental Aspects of Integrated Marketing Communications
Fifth Edition

Stauble
Marketing Strategy: A Global Perspective

Talarzyk
Cases and Exercises in Marketing

Terpstra and Sarathy
International Marketing
Eighth Edition

Watson
Electronic Commerce

Weitz and Wensley
Readings in Strategic Marketing Analysis, Planning, and Implementation

Zikmund
Exploring Marketing Research
Seventh Edition

Zikmund
Essentials of Marketing Research

HARCOURT BRACE COLLEGE OUTLINE SERIES
Peterson
Principles of Marketing

ABOUT THE AUTHORS

Roger D. Blackwell is a Professor of Marketing at The Ohio State University. He is also president of Roger Blackwell Associates, Inc., a consulting firm in Columbus, Ohio, through which he works with many of America's most successful companies.

Roger Blackwell was named "Outstanding Marketing Educator in America" by Sales and Marketing Executives International and "Marketer of the Year" by the American Marketing Association. He also received the "Alumni Distinguished Teaching Award," the highest award given by The Ohio State University. After thirty years at the university and recently receiving two additional teaching awards, his depth of knowledge and enthusiasm for teaching still make him a favorite among students.

Dr. Blackwell received his B.S. and M.S. degrees from The University of Missouri and his Ph.D. from Northwestern University. He also received an honorary doctorate degree from The Cincinnati College of Mortuary Science. He resides in Columbus, Ohio, and serves on numerous boards of both privately and publicly held corporations including Airnet Systems, Applied Industrial Technologies (formerly Bearings, Inc.), The Banc Stock Group, Checkpoint Systems, Flex-Funds, Max & Erma's Restaurants, Intimate Brands, and Anthony and Sylvan Pools. In addition, Roger is on the board of several start-up technology and internet firms.

Paul W. Miniard earned his B.S., M.A., and Ph.D. at the University of Florida and is currently the BMI Professor of Marketing at Florida International University and Director of the College of Business Administration's Ph.D. program. Previously, he was a tenured member of the faculties at the University of South Carolina and The Ohio State University.

Dr. Miniard is well known through his published research in the areas of advertising and consumer behavior. His research has appeared in a number of leading journals, including *Journal of Advertising, Journal of Advertising Research, Journal of Business Research, Journal of Consumer Psychology, Journal of Consumer Research, Journal of Experimental Social Psychology, Journal of Marketing Research,* and *Journal of Public Policy & Marketing.* He has received a number of honors and awards for his research, service, and teaching at both the undergraduate and graduate levels. He also serves as a consultant and expert witness in areas involving advertising and consumer behavior. In 1992, Dr. Miniard visited the University of International Business and Economics in Beijing, China, to help set up a course in consumer behavior.

James F. Engel earned his B.S. at Drake and obtained his Ph.D. at the University of Illinios, Urbana. Professor Engel has a distinguished name in the study of consumer behavior. He was honored by his peers in 1980 as the founder of the field when he was named one of the first two Fellows of the Association for Consumer Research. He received a similar citation with the prestigious Paul D. Converse Award of the American Marketing Association. These honors were given in recognition of his pioneering research that first appeared in 1960, his role as senior author of this textbook, and other forms of leadership.

He presently is Distinguished Professor of Marketing and Director of the Center for Organizational Excellence at Eastern College, St. Davids, Pennsylvania, where he moved in 1990. Professor Engel has shifted his emphasis from consumer goods marketing to the application of nonprofit marketing principles to religious organizations worldwide. He has served as a consultant and management development specialist with hundreds of organizations in more than 60 countries.

PREFACE

"Consumer behavior is everything and everything is consumer behavior" might well be the motto for this book. This may not be a surprising statement, given that stellar organizations around the world have adopted a "customer is king" orientation to succeed in the crowded marketplace and that this is indeed a consumer behavior text. Yet, at its core, this statement reflects accurately the strides made in the field of consumer behavior over the years. The study of consumer behavior has its roots in examining people for the sake of understanding and gaining insight. It focused on questions such as, "Why do people spend their time and money on activities, such as enjoying meals together with family or friends, participating in sports, donating blood and body organs, and visiting restaurants and stores for something other than food and functional necessities?" However, it didn't take long to realize that marketers could apply this type of research to influence people's store and product choices.

Today, studying and understanding consumer behavior is prerequisite for the success of firms in the marketplace and individuals in the workplace. It provides insights into product, pricing, retail, advertising, and communication strategies. Accordingly, this text focuses on *how* and *why* consumers make specific decisions and behave in certain ways—what motivates them, what captures their attention, and what retains their loyalty? To answer such questions, we examine the individual and group characteristics that influence consumers' decisions and behaviors, such as demographics, lifestyles, personality, values, culture, and family. Whether you become the director of a human services agency, account manager at an advertising agency, or marketing manager at an industrial firm, you will learn many concepts that can later be applied to your specific job responsibilities. Similarly, we believe there are many topics discussed in this text that you can apply to your own consumer activities, making you a wiser consumer.

Thirty Years in the Making, with an Eye to the Future

In the ninth edition of *Consumer Behavior,* as with preceding editions, we incorporate information from every discipline that contributes to understanding consumers. Since the first edition, published in 1968, we have borrowed from all the social sciences helpful in understanding consumers—psychology, economics, sociology, anthropology, and the few consumer-behavior-oriented marketing studies that existed at that time. Sans a blueprint to guide the development and organization of the first text, we turned to the model we had developed to analyze consumer decision making, which became known as the EKB model—named after James Engel, David Kollat, and Roger Blackwell. Refined in the second edition, it soon became the organizing framework for most books in consumer behavior and for marketing programs in many organizations. When Paul Miniard joined the team to replace David Kollat, the model became the EBM model to reflect his contributions. You'll still find the seven-stage model (comprised of need recognition, search, pre-purchase evaluation of alternatives, purchase, consumption, post-consumption evaluation, and divestment) in its latest version in the ninth edition of *Consumer Behavior*, referred to as the Consumer Decision Process (CDP) model.

Although *Consumer Behavior* is still entrenched in its tried-and-true theoretical foundation, it has always been a goal of the authors to anticipate where the field is going in the future, and this edition carries on that forward-thinking goal. We address new applications of consumer behavior theory by addressing Internet buying and Internet-assisted decision making where relevant. We also try to inject a global perspective whenever possible, with international examples of theory in practice.

We also introduce briefly new areas of influence that expand the scope and relevance of consumer behavior beyond affecting the sale of a product or the patronage of a store. New to this edition is the concept of comprehensive consumer orientation—a step beyond the marketing orientation most firms have adopted today. It focuses on the need for a unified consumer orientation for all members of the supply chain. This requires shared information in the channel and a common consumer-oriented goal. It also focuses on the role of consumers in shaping all aspects of societies, which given the drive toward market-driven economies is becoming a popular topic in popular press. Imagine the effects of cellular telephones on the lives of people in a small village in India. Beyond seeing this group of individuals as a new market segment for phones, a comprehensive consumer analysis examines the changes in society that might result from the exposure to technology and its acceptance by villagers.

There are other emerging areas of consumer behavior research at which we can only hint in this edition. One of those is the influence of inherited or genetic determinants of consumer behavior. The U.S. government funded the Human Genome Project for over $3 billion, and it is possible that basic research of this nature will be discussed in your classes. This research and other areas of scientific inquiry will probably lead to the evolution of the dynamic study of consumer behavior and perhaps provide content for future editions of *Consumer Behavior*. We hope this edition will help you understand the state of knowledge about consumers that currently exists, but also stimulate you to become one of the researchers that will create the knowledge needed for tomorrow.

Eight Times Improved

Over the years, we have searched for ways to improve each new edition of *Consumer Behavior*—leading to eight editions of improvements and innovations. For those of you familiar with its previous editions, you'll find many changes throughout this text. Our approach was to make the book easier and more enjoyable to read. At the same time, we streamlined the text without excluding information that students need for a thorough rather than superficial understanding of the topic. Some chapters and topics lend themselves better to this process than others, as you will see the further you read.

The ninth edition also reflects changes in the marketplace. This edition, more than any previous one, uses examples from marketers in Europe, Asia, Africa, and Australia as well as the Americas, reflecting the interests of our adopters throughout the world, who use the book in one of its various translations, including Russian, Portuguese, Japanese, Korean, French, and Spanish. The Internet, of course, is a revolutionary force in consumer behavior and is discussed throughout the book. We encourage students to research the companies we describe in the Consumer In Focus examples to obtain updates on their strategies and practices. Several examples go beyond how consumers buy products to analyze how they use products and how organizations are using this type of information and analysis to develop new marketing strategies.

Those who are familiar with the prior edition of this text will notice a major change in our coverage of psychological processes. Previously, chapters in the "Psychological Processes" section focused on various theories and processes, followed by a consideration of their practical relevance and business implications. In this edition, we have shifted the focus by centering on the business requirements for influencing consumer behavior before introducing the theories that provide guidance to those seeking to do so. Accordingly, we have renamed this section (now called "Influencing Consumer Behavior"), which contains three new chapters that are markedly different from their predecessors.

Another major innovation in this edition is the addition of seven cases at the end of the text, most of which can be applied to global strategic situations. The cases (Amazon.com, Avon, Pick 'n Pay, Service Corporation International, National Pork Producers Council, Manco, and DYB.com) are designed to encourage students to apply some of the concepts developed in this text to a variety of organizations. The focal topics are only guidelines to the topics that can be discussed in conjunction with the cases. Visuals relating to the cases are provided for instructors to enhance in-class discussions.

Finally, we recognize the efforts of our colleagues around the world with a new feature called suggested readings. Following each Part of the book is a list of recent academic articles on topics discussed in that section. This list is not designed to be a complete guide to literature for these topics, but it is designed to provide students with a short list of recent references should they desire more information.

Practicing What We Preach

In *Consumer Behavior*, we describe the need to develop products, services, and strategies based on what consumers want. And that's what we've tried to do in this edition—listen to our customers and adapt accordingly. We give many thanks to our colleagues who have taken the time to write us over the years and tell us what they would like to see in future editions, and thanks also to the many friends who have contributed to the success and evolution of this book in a more formal way.

In an ongoing effort to be customer friendly and marketing oriented, we encourage you to submit questions or comments to either author about his respective chapters. Paul Miniard was the primary author of Chapters 4, 6, 8, 9, 10, 14, 15, and 16, and Roger Blackwell was the primary author of Chapters 1, 2, 3, 5, 7, 11, 12, and 13. Please feel free to write, email, or call us.

To Accompany the Main Text

The new edition of *Consumer Behavior* includes a comprehensive set of supplements designed to enhance student learning and comprehension as well as instructor presentation of text materials.

Instructor's Manual   This manual includes extensive chapter outlines and teaching suggestions along with answers to text review and discussion questions. Transparency Masters are also included to help illustrate key text figures.

Test Bank   Thoroughly revised and updated to accompany the ninth edition, this test bank contains questions to help you gauge student comprehension through a selection of true/false, multiple choice, and essay questions. Each question is classified according to type, and the correct answer is given.

Computerized Test Bank Available as a CD-ROM for Windows, the computerized version of the printed test bank enables instructors to preview and edit test questions, as well as add their own. Questions can be scrambled and printed in various formats.

Lecture Presentation Software in Microsoft PowerPoint® **New to this edition!** Classroom lectures and discussions come to life with this innovative presentation tool. This program allows instructors to customize multimedia classroom presentations through this instructor-friendly presentation. Organized by chapter, this program includes key material from each chapter along with ads, figures, and tables from the text.

Videos Closely tied to the text, this video package features real-world organizations and events related to *Consumer Behavior*. Segments featuring concepts directly from chapter materials are included.

Web page A Web site, dedicated to this new edition, can be found at *www.harcourtcollege.com/marketing*. This site includes information for both instructors and students that includes consumer-behavior-related links, along with links to business sites and other resources of interest to people who are learning about or teaching a consumer behavior course.

Distance Learning For professors interested in supplementing classroom presentations with online content or who are interested in setting up a distance learning course, Harcourt College Publishers, along with WebCT, can provide the industry's leading online courses. WebCT provides tools to help you manage course content, facilitate online classroom collaboration, and track your students' progress. In conjunction with WebCT, Harcourt College Publishers also offers information on adopting a Harcourt online course, WebCT testing service, free access to a blank WebCT template, and customized course creation. For more information on this service, please contact your local sales representative. To view a demo of any of our online courses, go to *webct.harcourtcollege.com*.

Our Hats Go off To . . .

We owe a great intellectual debt to James Engel whose name is retained on this edition to recognize his role as senior author in the earlier editions. David Kollat left the academic world to shape retail strategy at The Limited, but his influence on understanding consumer decisions was monumental and also greatly appreciated.

This text is a culmination of efforts, assistance, research, and guidance from colleagues around the world. Foremost in importance are the thousands of researchers whose labors provide the essential content of knowledge about consumers and whose works are cited throughout the book. Our colleagues in The Association for Consumer Research have shaped our thinking about all aspects of consumer behavior. We are particularly fortunate to have outstanding colleagues at The Ohio State University and Florida International University to stimulate our intellectual and pedagogical endeavors. We appreciate the assistance and helpful suggestions of Professors Greg Allenby, Mike Barone, Jim Burroughs, Robert Burnkrant, Peter Dickson, Leslie Fine, Curt Haugtvedt, William Lewis, and Deepak Sirdeshmukh with this edition.

Our thanks go to the following colleagues who participated in an important pre-revision survey that helped shape the new edition: Barry Babin, The University of Southern Mississippi; Sue O'Curry, DePaul University; Kim Robertson, Trinity University; Larry Seibert, Indiana University Northwest; Ekkehard Stephan, University of Cologne; Gail Tom, California State University; and Linda Wright, Mississippi State University.

A special thanks goes to Professor Steve Burgess, who gave detailed critiques and suggestions (for Chapters 1, 2, 3, 7, and 11), and Kristina Blackwell, who assisted in gathering materials for Roger Blackwell's chapters and in preparing the cases for this edition. Jennifer Weinbach spent numerous hours collecting materials and proofing Paul Miniard's chapters. We received outstanding support from Bobbie Bochenko and Bill Schoof of The Dryden Press and many others from Harcourt College Publishers including Angela Urquhart, Van Mua, Lisa Kelley, and Linda Blundell. Thanks to Tonia Grubb at York Production Services for her efforts and support. We especially appreciate the help we received from many executives and staff of the business organizations described in the book, many who provided their valuable time and knowledge to be sure we "got it right" for the future leaders of the world.

On a personal note, we would like to thank the people in our lives who support and assist us in all that we do. Roger Blackwell especially acknowledges Kristina Blackwell, his partner and confidant in all of life and the one who makes it all worthwhile. He is also blessed with a father who taught him the joy of being a teacher and a mother who taught him the insights of a businessperson. Thank you also to Kelley Hughes and Mary Hiser who kept the office functioning efficiently while he was chained to the computer writing this text. Paul Miniard extends his appreciation to his fiancée, Jennifer, and his daughter, Crystal, for their patience and understanding during the many months he lived in the office working on this revision. And he is eternally grateful to his parents who taught him the value of education and who supported him during his nine years as an undergraduate and graduate student at the University of Florida. Finally, he wishes to acknowledge the life-long influence of Professor Joel Cohen, his mentor and exemplar, and Professor Peter Dickson, his best friend.

A Motto to Market By

The time a student spends studying at a university is a mere moment in the course of a lifetime of learning. We hope this text helps make learning about consumer behavior a great experience and that it will serve as a reference guide once you have entered the workplace. This brings us back to the motto we have embraced—consumer behavior is everything and everything is consumer behavior. This simple phrase has come to reflect the beliefs of many professors who teach this subject and practitioners who use the theories and facts represented in this book to guide firms from size small to extra large. We hope that the dedication of researchers and practitioners worldwide reflected in this ninth edition of *Consumer Behavior* will make you want to adopt this motto as well.

BRIEF CONTENTS

CONTENTS

CONSUMER BEHAVIOR

ninth edition

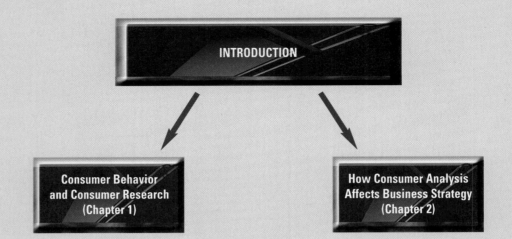

PART I

Introduction to Consumer Behavior

Each and every day, all of us are confronted with a myriad of consumer behavior issues. Whether you are deciding which television show to watch, driving by billboard advertisements, listening to the radio, or surfing the Internet, you are interfacing with topics of relevance to the study of consumer behavior.

Laying the foundation for studying how consumers make purchase decisions is the goal of Chapter 1. It focuses on identifying the activities included in consumer behavior and how consumer analysts monitor consumer trends. Various methods of consumer research allow all of us, whether we are consumer analysts or marketing students, to observe, record, and analyze a variety of consumer reactions, behaviors, and characteristics. Whether you take this information and learn how to be a smarter consumer or how to become a marketing professional, studying consumer behavior can affect many areas of your life.

Chapter 2 focuses on incorporating consumer behavior into strategic planning for nonprofit firms and for-profit corporations. In today's hypercompetitive business environment, satisfying consumers is required to remain competitive—regardless of the size or scope of the organization. Moreover, identifying consumers' needs, formulating strategies to fulfill those needs, and monitoring changing trends through consumer research and analysis have kept consumer behavior at the top of most executives' list of priorities. At the forefront of implementation is the concept of segmentation—the reality that though people may share some similarities, we are not all alike.

As you read this text, ask yourself how the content speaks to your life and career. You will find that more than most fields you will study, consumer behavior may touch and mirror your daily life. Welcome to what we hope will be a great adventure and a life-long topic of interest.

CHAPTER 1

Consumer Behavior and Consumer Research

OPENING VIGNETTE

It's 8:00 a.m. and a sudden blare of hip-hop radiates from the Sony clock radio through the bedroom. A hand reaches out from beneath a sea of Polo flannel sheets and fumbles for the alarm's off button—just as a Pizza Hut jingle begins on the radio. Another day in the life of Julie, a 20-year-old university student, has begun.

She races downstairs to see her younger brother and sister fighting over the last Pop-tart, and her mother stuffing Oscar Mayer Lunchables into their backpacks. Julie lives with her family in a suburb close to campus; she has decided to save the money she makes from her part-time job at a campus copy-shop rather than spend it on rent. As is the case for many consumers of any age, Julie is in a hurry to get to campus and decides to pick up a quick cup of coffee and a bagel once she's on campus rather than take the time to eat breakfast at home.

After attending classes, she heads to Kinko's, where her job is to assist customers, primarily other college students, with their printing and copying needs. Although sometimes she'd rather be exercising with her friends or spending time with her boyfriend, she decides that gaining work experience during her college career is more important; besides, earning spending money has its advantages. Suddenly, she remembers that her mother's birthday is tomorrow and she hasn't yet bought anything for her. During her break, she calls 1-800-FLOWERS and orders a birthday flower bouquet to be delivered the next morning. She knows her mother needs a lot of practical items, like a new desk lamp for her home office, but she wants to splurge on something special and indulgent instead. She knows her mother likes flowers and would not spend money on herself for something so frivolous. The sales associate who helps her place this order describes in detail what the arrangement will look like and gives her confidence that she's made a good selection.

Before heading home, Julie's pager goes off—it's her mother asking her to stop and get some milk on the way home. Instead of dealing with a crowded parking lot, big grocery store, and long lines, she stops at the Shell station close to home where she can order a gallon of skim milk to be delivered to the pump while she fills her tank. Even though it costs a little more, the time and convenience are worth it—especially after a long day.

She arrives home hours after the rest of her family has already eaten. Hungry and tired, she remembers the jingle playing on the radio when she woke up and decides to order a pizza (no meat because she's recently become a vegetarian), which, once it arrives, she takes up to her room to eat. She turns on the TV for background noise and checks her e-mail, hoping to get a message from her French cyber-friend whom she met in a global chat-room. She then checks the progress of the stocks in which she has invested through E-Schwab. (Monitoring and trading stock has become a hobby of hers, and she believes so many older

5

people will be on the social security welfare program when she and her friends retire that social security will provide very little security for retirement.) Finally, she logs onto the Internet to search the *Journal of Marketing* and the *International Journal of Research in Marketing* for information on consumer research, the topic of a report she must prepare for one of her classes. Just before midnight, Julie turns out the light, turns on the radio, and goes to sleep.

It's just another day in the life of a typical American consumer in her age group and life stage.

From the time we learn to walk and talk, we are all involved in consumer behavior on a daily basis. Whether we go to a retail store, shop via catalog or on the Internet, or sit at home eating breakfast, we are functioning as living, breathing consumers. Just like Julie, all of us face a myriad of consumer decisions each day, from deciding which brands to use and buy, where and how to buy them, and how to spend time and resources.

If you consider all the encounters we have each day with products, brands, and advertisements, not to mention people and time expenditure choices, you begin to understand something about the scope of the subject called *consumer behavior.* Far more than just a specialized area of marketing, consumer behavior affects nearly every aspect of life.

What Is Consumer Behavior?

Consumer behavior is defined as *activities people undertake when obtaining, consuming, and disposing of products and services.* Simply stated, consumer behavior has traditionally been thought of as the study of "why people buy"—with the premise that it becomes easier to develop strategies to influence consumers once a marketer knows why people buy certain products or brands.

There are several activities included in the definition of consumer behavior— obtaining, consuming, and disposing.

- **Obtaining** refers to *the activities leading up to and including the purchase or receipt of a product.* Some of these activities include searching for information regarding product features and choices, evaluating alternative products or brands, and purchasing. Consumer behavior analysts examine these types of behaviors, including how consumers buy products—do they shop specialty stores, shopping malls, or the Internet? Other issues might include how consumers pay for products (with cash or credit cards), whether they buy products as gifts or for themselves, whether consumers transport products or have them delivered, where they get information about product and store alternatives, and how brands influence their product choices.

- **Consuming** refers to *how, where, when, and under what circumstances consumers use products.* For example, issues relating to consumption might include decisions about whether consumers use products at home or at the office. Do they use products according to instructions and as intended or do they find their own unique ways of using products? Is the experience of using the product pleasurable or purely functional? Do they use the entire product before disposing of it or is some of it never consumed?

- **Disposing** includes *how consumers get rid of products and packaging.* In this instance, consumer analysts might examine consumer behavior from an ecological standpoint—how do consumers dispose of product packaging or product remains (are products biodegradable or can they be recycled)? Consumers might also choose to reuse some products by handing them down to younger children. Or they may resell them in resale shops, swap them on the Internet or classified ads, or sell them again at garage sales or flea markets.

These activities are depicted in Figure 1.1, which also shows how many variables affect the process of consumer behavior. Each of these influences will be discussed throughout the text, but are introduced here to show how "individual and unique" a consumer's behavior can be.

Consumer behavior also can be defined as a *field of study, focusing on consumer activities.* As the study of consumer behavior has evolved, so has its scope. Historically, the study of consumer behavior focused on buyer behavior or "why people buy." More recently, researchers and practitioners have focused on **consumption analysis,** *why and how people consume* in addition to *why and how they buy.* Analysis of consumption behavior represents a broader conceptual

---

Figure 1.1 Consumer Behavior

CONSUMER INFLUENCES

Culture	Ethnicity
Personality	Family
Life-stage	Values
Income	Available Resources
Attitudes	Opinions
Motivations	Past Experiences
Feelings	Peer Groups
Knowledge	

ORGANIZATIONAL INFLUENCES

Brand	Product Features
Advertising	Word of Mouth
Promotions	Retail Displays
Price	Quality
Service	Store Ambiance
Convenience	Loyalty Programs
Packaging	Product Availability

OBTAINING
- How you decide you want to buy
- Other products you consider buying
- Where you buy
- How you pay for product
- How you transport product home

CONSUMING
- How you use the product
- How you store the product in your home
- Who uses the product
- How much you consume
- How product compares with expectations

DISPOSING
- How you get rid of remaining product
- How much you throw away after use
- If you resell items yourself or through a consignment store
- How you recycle some products

CONSUMER BEHAVIOR

framework than buyer behavior does because it includes issues that arise after the purchase process occurs.

Successful organizations understand that consumer behavior should be the primary focus of every aspect of the firm's marketing program. This is described as the **marketing concept**—*the process of planning and executing the conception, pricing, promotion, and distribution of ideas, goods, and services to create exchanges that satisfy individual and organizational objectives.* The key element in this definition is the *exchange* by the marketer of something of such value that the customer will pay the price that meets the needs and objectives of the organization. From the consumer's standpoint, the satisfaction with the exchange depends on satisfaction with *consumption* of the product as well as the exchange. Consumers will only want to pay for products and services that satisfy their needs, but that is unlikely to occur unless the firm thoroughly understands how buyers *consume* or *use* a particular product. Unless a product is used as intended, it is likely that consumer satisfaction with the product will suffer. That is why marketers spend time and money developing specific use and care instructions for products.

As an example of how consumption analysis affects marketing, consider what Procter & Gamble did to make its laundry detergent fit the usage patterns of consumers. Warehouse marts, such as Sam's Club and Costco, allow consumers to save money by buying large quantities of products—in this example, giant packages of laundry detergent. This seems to be a win-win situation for the manufacturer (who is able to sell larger quantities of product) and the consumer (who can save money). Yet when consumers tried to *use* these large boxes, many consumers found their laundry shelves would not accommodate the height of the package, causing some consumers to discontinue purchase of the brand. To address the problem revealed through consumption analysis, Procter & Gamble redesigned the boxes to be shorter and wider. The new boxes contained the same amount of detergent but now fit the consumption realities of consumer kitchens and laundry rooms. By understanding how consumers use the product, P&G was able to solve consumption problems, thereby increasing customer satisfaction and loyalty.

Why Study Consumer Behavior?

People study consumer behavior for a variety of reasons. You may be a university student completing this course because it is required for your degree, or a business executive gaining insight into consumer trends. Whatever the reason, studying consumer behavior is rising in popularity among university students and others as well.

What questions are answered by studying consumer behavior? The list is unlimited, but consider the breadth of areas involved in the following questions:

1. Why did you choose the school at which you are now studying?
2. Why did you buy your clothes from Abercrombie & Fitch, Old Navy, JCPenney, Benetton, C&A, or any of the thousands of other retail stores?
3. How do you allocate the 24 hours of each day between studying, working, watching TV, sleeping, working out in a gym, watching a sport, or participating in a sport?
4. Do you usually cook your food from scratch, microwave it, or buy it

already cooked in a restaurant to eat there or take home? Why do you eat certain types or brands of food most often?

5. If you had the choice of attending a sports event, visiting a museum, attending a concert, or spending the evening with games and Internet chats on your computer, which would you choose?

6. When you graduate and buy a car, do you plan on buying a new or used car? Which model or make will you most likely choose?

7. Which ads do you like and which do you dislike? How do they influence your purchase decisions?

8. Did you donate blood this year? Do you give time or money to help people with medical or economic problems, or do you leave those problems for other people to solve?

9. Did you vote in the last election? For whom and why?

10. Compared to other people earning the same income as you, do you save more or less than they do? Do you make financial decisions based on what pleases you now or what will provide the biggest payoff later?

Although you might find it relatively easy to answer these questions as they apply to you, understanding the reasons that cause you and others to answer them differently is more difficult. Therein lies the challenge that consumer analysts and marketers face when chasing the ever-precious consumer. A firm's ability to attract consumers, satisfy and retain them, and sell more to them affects greatly a company's profitability. Consider question 6. If you were an executive at Nissan or Volkswagen, how much would you pay to know how the millions of buyers in the market for new cars each year would answer? Beyond corporate bottom lines, look at question 9 and consider how valuable it would be for a political party or politician to know why large numbers of citizens have voted as they have.

The relevance and importance of each of these questions vary from one organization to another. Retail executives would be interested in knowing how millions of consumers would answer question 7, but this type of consumer information can also help nonprofit organizations better serve the public. Knowing how consumers would prefer to spend their time, as indicated in question 5, might help ballet companies and arts organizations better promote and position their offerings. Or if a health agency's mission focuses on increasing the nation's blood supply or reducing the incidence of AIDS, it could concentrate its study of consumer behavior on finding answers to question 8.

Collectively, the issues identified in this list of questions represent the breadth of issues included in the study of consumer behavior and in this text. It also serves as a good starting point to begin examining this more-important-than-ever subject.

Consumer Behavior Helps Analyze Consumers' Increasing Influence

Every day, in every country around the globe, an election is held. The election is not about who or which political party will be leading that nation. Consumers are the ones casting their votes, and they do it with their dollars, euro, or yen. With their money, consumers elect the retailers and other organizations they want to survive and be profitable enough to provide jobs for a nation's citizens. With their votes, consumers determine which people will have good jobs or bad jobs, and which will have no jobs at all. Ultimately, consumers determine which companies will have rising share prices (which attract capital and improved technology) and which companies will be attractive acquisitions for other companies. On a macro-economic level, when consumers "vote" with their money, they determine which nations are able to sell their goods to other nations for needed foreign currency and investment, which yield jobs and prosperity.

"The Consumer Is King"

Today, businesses around the world recognize that "the customer is king." Knowing why and how people consume products helps marketers understand how to improve existing products, what types of products are needed in the marketplace, or how to attract consumers to buy their products. In essence, consumer behavior analysis helps firms know how to *please the king* and *directly impact company revenues*. In the long run, one is not possible without the other. Without customer satisfaction, organizations are unlikely to increase their sales and revenues. And without increased revenues, organizations do not have the resources to invest in customer service centers, special sales promotions, or sales training—all of which are important components of even the most elementary customer satisfaction programs. The most successful organizations develop marketing programs that are under the influence of the consumer instead of programs that attempt to place consumers under the influence of marketing.

In general, those who study consumer behavior include those who desire to influence or change the behavior of consumers in some way. Some marketers, such as business organizations, want to use marketing to influence brand choice and purchase, whereas others, such as health organizations or governments, use demarketing to influence people to stop smoking or practice safe sex. In these instances, consumers are the recipients of attempts at influence. This *consumer influence perspective* is the concern of many, including those in marketing, consumer education and protection, and public policy.

Consumer behavior also includes the study of consumers as *sources of influence* on organizations. Instead of influencing consumers, effective organizations increasingly are adopting a total marketing approach to product development, innovation, research, and communication. By seeking methods to allow consumers to influence the organization to have the products, prices, promotions, and operations that consumers will buy, organizations are more likely to satisfy customers, create brand loyalty, and increase revenues. Marketing-oriented firms of the 21st century will be focused more on allowing customers to influence them rather than on how they can influence consumers.

As a practical philosophy of managing successful organizations, **marketing** is *the process of transforming or changing an organization to have what people will buy* (at a profit, in the case of for-profit organizations). And if marketing is working well in an organization, which entity is being influenced? The *organization is influenced by the needs and wants of the market* instead of the consumer being influenced by the desires of the firm.

"Only the Customer Can Fire Us All"

When Sam Walton, founder of the world's largest retail organization, was alive, he used to visit each store every year and talk with the store's associates and customers, gathering information and formulating ideas on how to improve his stores. It was a strategy that took him from one small store in Arkansas to a chain large enough to challenge and eventually beat Sears and Kmart at the retailing game they helped invent. Even after Wal*Mart became a public corporation and

Sam Walton became a billionaire, he continued to walk through his stores and talk to his associates. He would remind everyone from the cashiers to the senior executives that "the only person who can fire us all is the customer."

He spoke the truth. Walton believed that consumers ultimately determine which organizations thrive and which ones fail. He understood the power of consumers as an entity—when they make their choices in the marketplace, they vote for the candidates they want to survive in today's hypercompetitive retail marketplace.

The power of the consumer is immense, and the desire of global firms, such as Carrefour (a French-based hypermarket), to understand consumers is huge. The most successful entrepreneurs will tell you how costly and challenging it has become to recruit new customers; therefore, *the thrust in recent years has been on keeping customers*. The strategy of some of the best retailers around the globe has been to create a relationship with customers so that they don't even consider "going anyplace else." Whether the strategy is offering special services and special products or a customer loyalty card, the goal is the same: *recruit and keep customers*. Yet, in order to reach this goal, firms must understand their customers and potential customers.

Consumer Behavior Educates and Protects Consumers

Many people care about the study of consumer behavior because they want to help consumers act or buy more wisely. Through education, consumers can be taught how to detect deception and other abuses and be made aware of opportunities for redress. Further, anyone can benefit from money-saving strategies and tips on how to be "better shoppers." Educational programs must be based on research into motivation and behavior if they are to be relevant in the real world of consumer life. Consumer economists, home economists, and specialists in consumer affairs are among the leading researchers of how and why people consume products.

Public policy leaders and social commentators study a variety of societal issues from a consumer behavior standpoint, such as the problems of overconsumption and underconsumption. Compulsive eating, overspending, drug usage, and excessive gambling are behaviors that many agencies and individuals wish to minimize, whereas exercising, reading, and eating nutritional foods are encouraged by health organizations and social agencies. Understanding these issues from a consumer perspective helps policy makers, consumer interest groups, and businesses develop the best methods to reach consumers with information and assistance.

Figure 1.2a provides an example of this type of educational activity from Georgia Pacific, producer of bath and kitchen paper products, and the Department of Health and Human Services. Georgia Pacific introduced its Health Institute campaign in 1999 to educate consumers on the dangers of bacteria and germs in their bathrooms and how to protect against them. Figure 1.2b shows a similar campaign for American Cancer Society.

Consumer Behavior Helps Formulate Public Policy

Organizations and individuals interested in public policy need to know the needs of the public to formulate policy relating to economics, social welfare, family planning, or most any other area of public policy. They also need to know how to predict behavior when policy changes occur. When the Federal Reserve changes

Figure 1.2a   **Consumer Education Activity**

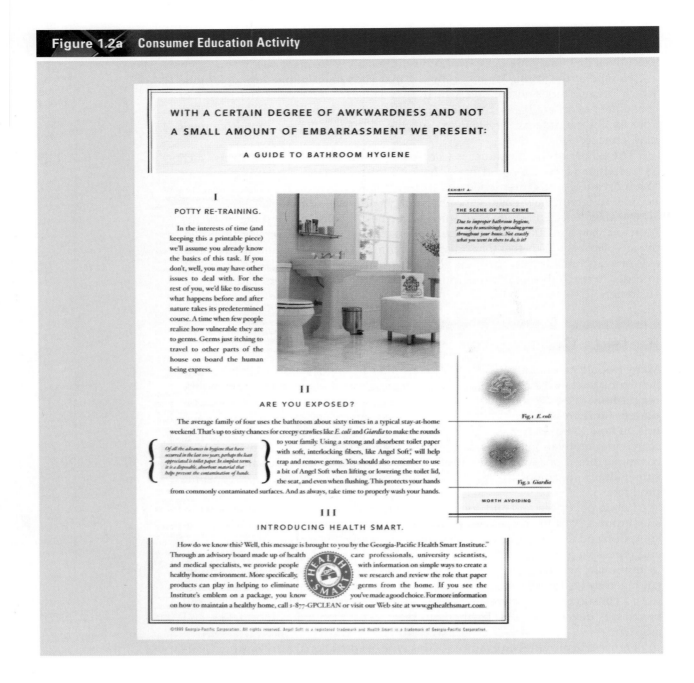

interest rates, what will be the effect on demand for homes, cars, investments, and other products? Will government-mandated warnings on labels cause consumers to buy less or more of the product? For years, economic policy has recognized the importance of such questions, but the amount of research in this area has been limited. In recent years, public policy has changed to emphasize a shift *from* government protection and education to guarantee consumer welfare *to* protection resulting from competitive markets.

The cornerstone of a market-driven economy is the right of any consumer to make an informed and unrestricted choice from an array of alternatives. When this right is curtailed because of business abuse, governments are expected to influence consumer choice by curbing deception and other unfair trade practices.

Figure 1.2b **Consumer Education Activity**

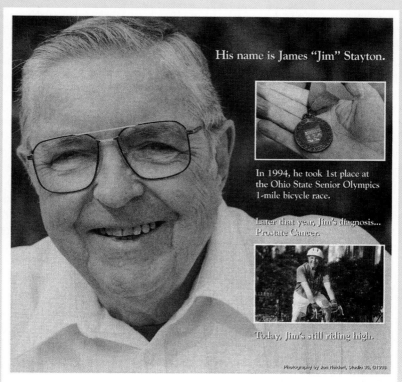

His name is James "Jim" Stayton.

In 1994, he took 1st place at the Ohio State Senior Olympics 1-mile bicycle race.

Later that year, Jim's diagnosis... Prostate Cancer.

Today, Jim's still riding high.

Photography by Jon Heidert, Studio 35, ©1998

His name is James "Jim" Stayton. He is a cancer survivor.

Because of incredible breakthroughs in research, early detection and education of cancer, men like Jim Stayton are winning the fight against prostate cancer. In fact, just five short months after his surgery, Jim was on his bike, competing once again. And the number of success stories, like Jim's, have never been higher. But until every man wins the fight against prostate cancer, the research and education can't stop. They can't slow down until we find a cure. Because until then, there will be a man who won't survive. A life lost. A grandpa. A father. A friend. Help keep the American Cancer Society's research and educational programs. Contribute to the cure. Call your local American Cancer Society office today at 1-800-ACS-2345. Or visit our web site at www.oh.cancer.org.

Contribute To The Cure.

AMERICAN CANCER SOCIETY
Ohio Division, Inc.

Consumer Behavior Affects Personal Policy

From an individual standpoint, possibly the most important reason you should be interested in consumer behavior is the effect it will have on your own life. Personal policy includes how you behave (toward others and in buying situations), your values and beliefs, and how you live your life. Will you marry and have children or remain single? And will you spend your income on material goods or on charity causes to help the underprivileged?

A person's economic quality of life is also determined by personal policy. Here's a bold statement: what you have in life will not be determined by how much you earn as much as it will be by how you spend and save. How and where consumers buy products can also influence consumers' lifestyles in the long run. Consumer in Focus 1.1 features two consumers with different views on spending and saving behaviors.

Consumer in Focus 1.1

Ahmed and James are about to graduate from college with business degrees and have secured jobs paying approximately $35,000 a year. They both want and need to buy a car. They opt for a new Volkswagen Jetta costing around $20,000 with a modest down payment and monthly payments of $600 for four years. Ahmed obtains information from *Consumer Reports* and other sources when buying the car and follows advice on maintaining it properly, changing oil and performing maintenance at specified times, and keeping the car clean inside and outside. James, on the other hand, does none of these and, by the end of four years, owns an unreliable, dirty, and dented car, and decides to buy or lease another car, continuing the $600 monthly payments. Because Ahmed takes care of his car, it is reliable and attractive at the end of four years. Instead of buying a new car, he invests the $600 per month in a mutual fund for the next six years, knowing that most any car that is well maintained will last for 10 years and 100,000 miles.

At the end of six more years, Ahmed's investment has increased to well over $50,000 with which he can buy a new $20,000 car and still have a $30,000 investment to multiply. Even if both consumers earn the same amount of income throughout life, Ahmed will likely amass a greater amount of assets due to his consumption behaviors. How these consumers spend, save, and consume will determine how much healthcare they can buy when they are older, how much they can invest in the stock market, and what kinds of cars and homes they can buy in the future. By saving the $600 per month on car payments (and applying this type of consumption behavior to other areas as well), Ahmed might choose to retire earlier, buy a house, or eventually buy a Porsche—without earning more than James.

Retailers appeal to different consumers with different spending and saving behaviors. Grocery stores, such as Kroger and Minnesota-based Byerly's, offer consumers a wide variety of produce, meats, gourmet foods, and prepared entrees in attractive stores with good lighting and wide aisles. Though a consumer may spend an average of $130 to $150 per cart of groceries in this type of grocery store, others may choose to shop at another type of store, such as Aldi (the German-based, global grocery giant that caters to lower-income consumers). Instead of paying $3.69 for a box of a leading national brand of cereal at the posh grocery store, the Aldi shopper pays $1.69 for the Aldi private brand. Although quality is not sacrificed (the cereal comes from the same manufacturer, is made with the same formula, and is packaged in a box similar to the national brand's), this consumer has limited brand choices and less ambiance. However, when the Aldi shopper checks-out at the cash register, the total bill is $70 to $80.

Similar to the consumers featured in Consumer in Focus 1.1, shopping and spending patterns can help consumers save money. At first glance, you might conclude that Kroger's and Byerly's target and attract middle- and upper-income consumers, whereas Aldi caters to low-income consumers. Even though this may be true, since consumers have choices on how and where they spend their incomes, these stores appeal to consumers' spending and savings policies. Even upper-income consumers might choose to sacrifice selection, national brands, ambiance, and some services to save hundreds or thousands of dollars on groceries per year. The Aldi shopper may choose to save this money or spend it on healthcare, childcare, or other items. When it comes to categories such as casual clothing, housewares, and small appliances, consumers often choose mass retailers, such as Wal*Mart and Target, over traditional department stores, such as Macy's and Burdines. The cost savings and convenience of one-stop-shopping have swayed consumers to shop at discount retailers even though they might have given up some extras like carpeting, warm lighting, and individual attention. Think about it. If you had a choice of making 30 percent additional income by working longer hours or taking on a second job or decreasing your expenses by 30 percent with smarter consumer decisions, which would you prefer?

Personal policy also affects how individuals define success. For many people, success means income and wealth, and perhaps a wide array of possessions such as cars, clothing, and homes. As you study consumer behavior, keep in mind that is not the definition everyone uses. In his book, *Courage Is Contagious*,[1] former congressman John Kasich describes Albert, a mentally retarded man who shines shoes two days a week at the Children's Hospital of Pittsburgh and gives his tips to the hospital's Free Care Fund. Over the last four decades, Albert has raised and donated over $40,000 to help the children in the hospital. His definition of success may differ from yours, but it serves as a model just as do those of more famous individuals, such as Nelson Mandela, Margaret Thatcher, or Bill Gates. As a student, you might define success as graduating from college and taking a job with a Fortune 500 company or perhaps starting your own firm. Success is also defined in personal terms, such as having a family, contributing time and money to not-for-profit organizations, or physical and emotional well-being.

By understanding success in consumer behavior terms, marketers can begin to understand how to appeal to specific consumers. For example, Mercedes has enjoyed positioning its cars as an "attainment" of economic success, thereby attracting consumers who either have achieved monetary success or want to be perceived as having done so.

Evolution of Consumer Behavior

Look at the myriad of products available to consumers on the shelves and screens of today's retailers and marketing organizations, and you quickly realize that choices face consumers every hour of the day and night. Red blouses or blue shirts? Music by SmashMouth or Garth Brooks? Compact cars, pick-up trucks, or sports utility vehicles? Shares of stock in Home Depot, Ford Motor, or Dell Computer, bought from a broker, an employer, on-line, or a bank? Heinz ketchup or Picante Salsa, bought from a supermarket, a super Wal*Mart, or a super-convenient online service such as Peapod or Streamline? Consumers face an almost infinite number of possibilities, but who determines the final selection of what is available for consumers to snatch off retail shelves? In this section, we examine how the entity responsible for making those determinations has changed, which mirrors the changes that have occurred in business and in the study of consumer behavior.

Who Determines What Consumers Can Buy?

All the organizations involved in determining what consumers are able to buy are included in the **retail supply chain,** defined as *all the organizations involved in taking a product from inception to final consumption.* These organizations typically include *manufacturers* (who manage the raw materials and produce the products); *wholesalers* (or other forms of distributors who procure products, house them, and distribute them to point of sale); *retailers* (who sell them to final users through stores or direct sales); and *consumers* (who buy and consume the products). The supply chain also includes many *facilitating organizations* such as advertising and research firms, financial institutions, and transportation or logistics firms. As with any structure, the focus and power within the supply chain to determine what is offered to consumers has shifted throughout history, as summarized in Figure 1.3.

In the early days of the American Colonies until the U.S. Civil War, traders— a type of wholesaler—served as the connector between European products and U.S. markets. It was these distributors who determined whether consumers were

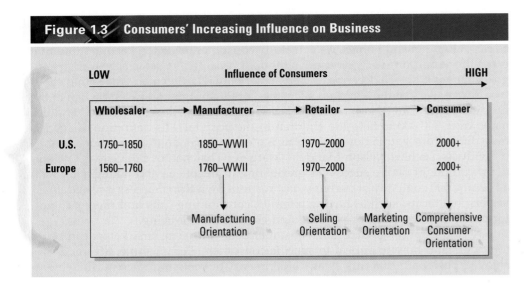

offered red dresses or blue shirts or barrels containing shovels or sugar. Consumers had little if any influence on the process.

Manufacturing emerged in the mid-1800s and blossomed during the U.S. Civil War, giving rise to the power of manufacturers in the supply chain in the late 1800's until the latter part of the 20th century. Manufacturers such as Procter & Gamble had the ability to decide what types of products should be made, what colors and sizes the packages should be, how they should be advertised, and where retailers should place them on shelves. Whether the product was soap, shoes, cars, or banking services, manufacturers dominated what was produced and ultimately made available for consumers to buy.

Power began to shift again soon after World War II, when retailers began to take more control in the supply chain. Mega-retailers such as Wal*Mart, Ikea, Home Depot, and Toys R Us were not only larger than many of the manufacturers and wholesalers; they were closer to the increasingly elusive consumer. Retailers began to enforce their views about what products to manufacture, how they should be packaged, where they should be inventoried, and how they should be priced and sold. Retailers dominated other members of the supply chain because they could provide the essential connection between production and consumption.

By the end of the 20th century, the power had shifted again, fueled much by the formalization of the study of consumer behavior and implementation of consumer research. Increased competition and slowing population growth in the United States created an environment in which many companies were chasing fewer new customers, who were bombarded with time pressures and thousands of advertisements per day. The new millennium brought with it a new boss that would determine what products and services would be available to consumers, ruling such giants as Procter & Gamble, General Electric, and Microsoft. The same boss gives orders to retailers as large as Wal*Mart, Carrefour Pick'n Pay, C & A, Printemp, The Body Shop, or Home Depot. Even wholesalers as respected as Cardinal Health (pharmaceuticals) or Ingram Micro (computers and books) and integrated producers and distributors such as Shell Oil must take orders from the boss. The boss, of course, is the *consumer*—thus making the study of consumers and consumer behavior more important than ever.

Just as the consumer is the focus and basis of marketing strategy, so too is the consumer the focal point for building a new fangled supply chain, called a demand chain.[2] Rather than building and operating their supply chain from manufacturer to market, the best firms are creating chains based on consumers' needs, wants, problems, and lifestyles. Consumer behavior is a driving force in the formation of cutting-edge supply chains, whether the chain is supplying consumer goods such as grocery and apparel, healthcare services from physicians and hospitals, cultural experiences at a performance or art gallery, or financial services from a bank or broker.

With each shift in power along the supply channel came an associated shift in business orientation. As a result of the convergence of changing market forces, including increased competition, changing consumer lifestyles, power shifts within the supply chain, and the influence of the consumer, business orientation changed from a *manufacturing focus* to a *marketing focus*. Apple rejuvenated its sales and its brand by adopting a marketing focus and creating a new design and ad campaign, as seen in Figure 1.4. The new focus differentiated the brand with emotional appeal and personality.

Manufacturing Orientation

Imagine if you will, the challenges facing Henry Ford in the early 1900s when the Model T swept the market. It was during that time of great demand, when Ford was selling all the cars that it could make, that Mr. Ford made the famous statement about variations in the Model T: *"you can get it in any color as long as it is black."* That statement accurately reflected the focus of that time—the producer

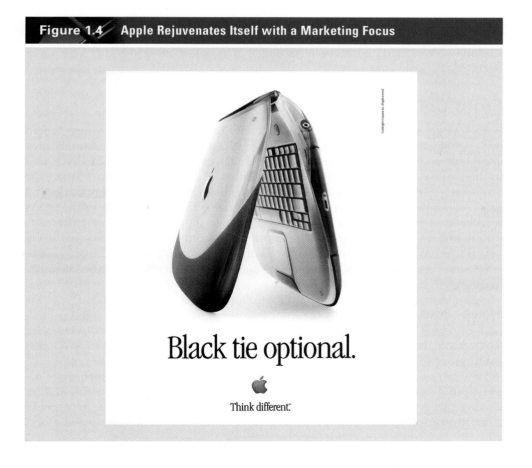

Figure 1.4 Apple Rejuvenates Itself with a Marketing Focus

Black tie optional.

Think different.

dictated what was sold—showing that the manufacturing orientation was centered primarily on *how to make products.* Today's consumer researcher wasn't needed back then, and Mr. Ford's approach would certainly mean defeat in today's marketplace. Today's auto marketers face marketing pressures from a variety of competitive challenges, including automotive superpowers, such as Daimler-Chrysler, and a greatly segmented market that demands variety, from Range Rover and Honda SUVs to Corvette and Dodge convertibles, just to name a few. Henry Ford's management skills and understanding suited an earlier era, but today he would need, among other things, a crash course in consumer behavior to compete effectively with the recent image and marketing programs of Volkswagen.

From Manufacturing to Selling

The earliest contributions to consumer behavior occurred in the 1920s when production capacity began to outrun demand, and the challenge shifted from *how to manufacture goods* to *how to sell them.* As competition intensified, advertising agencies emerged as important institutions, and universities began offering courses on selling, advertising, and other marketing areas. Advertising agencies and universities relied on the accumulated wisdom of experience rather than behavioral science to influence consumers, with the one exception of *behaviorism.*

Learning theorist John B. Watson applied the practical aspects of this psychological approach to advertising and highlighted the importance of repetitive advertising to build awareness and brand preference. Using this principle, the Ted Bates advertising agency devised the phrase USP (unique selling proposition) to describe the importance of selecting a benefit of the product and repeating that phrase so often that consumers uniquely associate that benefit with a particular brand. Diet Coke was one of the first diet products to assert taste rather than low calories as its USP. This USP appeared in its U.S. campaign "Just for the Taste of It" and was repeated internationally, as seen in the German ad in Figure 1.5 ("Calories are out; Taste is in.")

From Selling to Marketing

For a few years after World War II, it was easy to predict what consumers would buy—anything firms could produce. They were catching up from the scarcity they experienced during the Depression and the war years. The age of scarcity ended in the United States and Canada by the 1950s and in most of Europe during the 1960s and 1970s, and with its exit came a transition to a new era—the **marketing era.** During this time, *productive capacity far exceeded demand,* requiring the study of consumer behavior to grow beyond its economic roots. Although price once dominated the study of consumer behavior by economists, modern-day marketers began to focus on many other dimensions affecting consumer choice, such as quality, convenience, image, and advertising, aiding the transition of organizations to *having what consumers would likely buy.*

Ask Wal*Mart executives what they sell in their stores, and you may get the answer, "Nothing." According to senior management, Wal*Mart is not in the business of *selling things to* consumers; it's in the business of *buying what people need* to consume. Its positioning as a purchasing agent for consumers led to its success throughout the end of the 20th century.

Switching from a sales to a marketing orientation required a much more sophisticated set of tools to understand consumers and what they might buy. During this era, marketing activities expanded with the speed and force of a nuclear mushroom cloud throughout the most successful firms around the globe.

Figure 1.5   Coca-Cola Advertising Worldwide

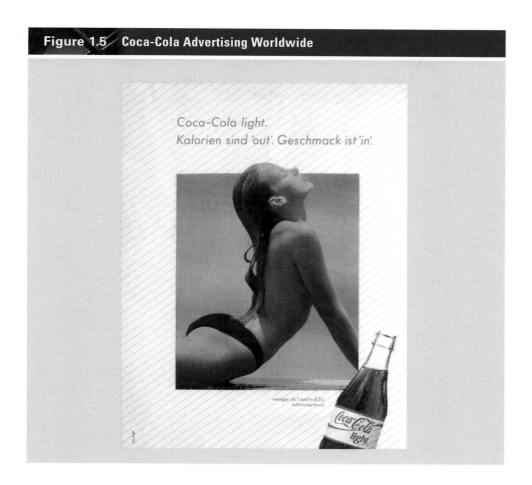

Coca-Cola light.
Kalorien sind 'out'. Geschmack ist 'in'.

Behavioral sciences took center stage and provided a toolbox of theories and methodologies borrowed by innovative marketing organizations, including:

- **Motivation research:** Marketers were hungry for new insights, and one of the tastiest theories was motivation research, derived from psychoanalytic theories of Sigmund Freud. Led by its chief proponent, Ernest Dichter,[3] the world of Freud and psychoanalysis found its way to the marketplace during the 1960s, with publications such as Vance Packard's *Hidden Persuaders*.[4] The goal of motivation researchers was *to uncover hidden or non-recognized motivations through guided interviewing.* One widely reported finding from the motivation research era was that *women bake cakes out of the unconscious desire to give birth.* Yes, you read this correctly. Thus, Pillsbury created the dough boy icon with the appeal of a cuddly baby (Figure 1.6) that appears in ads and on merchandise to build its brand.

- **Positivism:** Positivism refers to the *process of using rigorous empirical techniques to discover generalizable explanations and laws.* In other words, it takes the view that if it can't be proven in the laboratory, the data are not useful, and that only information derived from scientific methods should be used in decision making. The goals are twofold: (1) to understand and predict consumer behavior, and (2) to discover cause-and-effect relationships that govern persuasion and/or education. Until recently, most published consumer research embraced the research paradigm of positivism.

Figure 1.6   "Nothin' Says Lovin' Like Somethin' from the Oven"

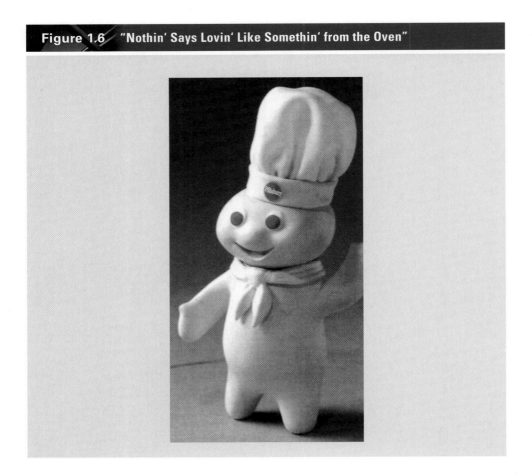

- **Post-modernism:** Post-modernism is a complementary approach to positivism, which gained popularity in the 1980s. Different in its goals and methods,[5] **post-modernism,** *uses qualitative and other research methods to understand consumer behavior.* It may include understanding the emotion involved in choosing a brand. Post-modern research led to ethnographic and other research methods to describe how people consume products, as featured in the following pages.

Comprehensive Consumer Orientation

Whereas a **marketing orientation** focuses on *how an organization adapts to consumers,* a comprehensive **consumer orientation** extends this focus to *how all organizations in a demand chain adapt to changing consumer lifestyles and behaviors.* Additionally, it recognizes the role of consumers in shaping aspects of society, including government, societal organizations, and all areas of life. Such an understanding of consumers is valuable as nations move from centrally planned economies toward free-market systems. Whether working together in a supply chain or in society, the key is cooperation between entities to work toward the comprehensive good of all members. For example, a market orientation views the Internet as a tool for marketing products or reaching consumers, but a comprehensive consumer approach focuses on how the Internet builds communities and affects life around the world in the 21st Century.

Much of the remainder of this text focuses on the issues affecting firms with a marketing and/or comprehensive consumer orientation. In order to succeed during this era, firms will need to sharpen their skills in areas such as information technology, customer retention programs, consumption research, consumer purchase decision making, branding, and Internet strategies. And they will have to hone their already developed skills in advertising, communication, and marketing. All these areas will be emphasized throughout this text.

How Do You Study Consumers?

As competition among firms around the globe increases, management searches for marketing strategies to combat the new challenges they face in the marketplace. At the foundation lies the need for valid, accessible, and practical information about consumer motivation and behavior. The question is how to obtain that information. Marketing research is concerned with the application of theories, problem-solving methods, and techniques to identify and solve marketing problems.[6] To get help in planning and strategy, marketers have turned to behavioral sciences to collect and interpret information about consumers. Today, technology aids and accelerates the comprehensive collection of consumer information. Regardless of method, the goal is to understand how to study consumer behavior and implement a strategy that is best for specific situations.

A Foundation in the Sciences

Studying consumer behavior is much like studying medicine. Medicine is an applied science using knowledge from chemistry, biology, psychology, engineering, and other disciplines. If you are a runner suffering from pain in your knee, your physician might try to research and diagnose the problem with an X-ray. However, if the problem is with cartilage rather than with bones, the X-ray will not suffice, and the physician may order an MRI for more information. Before deciding how to fix the problem, the physician will also do additional research, including taking a medical history and blood work.

Similarly, consumer behavior is an applied science drawing from economics, psychology, sociology, anthropology, statistics, and other disciplines. To understand consumer behavior, you need to know what is going on inside a consumer's mind just as thoroughly as a surgeon understands what is going on inside your knee. But understanding why consumers behave the way they do is just the beginning. You must also have the skill of a surgeon in applying that knowledge to product development, advertising, retailing, and all the other areas of marketing programs. Getting inside the minds of consumers requires the theoretical and methodological equivalents of X-rays, blood analyses, and MRIs.

Methods of Studying Consumer Behavior

The issue that even the best marketers are addressing is how to research consumer behavior most effectively. And there is no single solution. Consumer analysts are turning to a variety of effective techniques to "get into the minds of consumers." These methods might include conducting experiments to determine changes in buyer behavior based on special product offers and coupons or asking questions through interviews and focus groups. Many organizations today are borrowing liberally from anthropology and sociology to approach research from a less formal, more natural setting.[7] These methods might include exploring peoples' homes, cars, closets, and offices in order to understand better how consumers use products or invent ways to solve problems. Such methods can be classified into three major methodological approaches: (1) observational, (2) interviews and surveys, and (3) experimentation.

Observation

An **observational approach** to consumer research consists primarily of *observing consumer behaviors in different situations.* Sometimes researchers monitor behaviors in their natural settings, such as watching consumers use products and eat foods in their homes, whereas in other instances, they monitor behaviors prompted in artificial settings. This might include observing how consumers react to different advertisements, packaging, or colors in a research facility.

In recent years, marketers have searched for ways to tap into the powerful $165 billion children's market. In order to create products, messages, and advertisements to connect effectively with kids, marketers have conducted research and sought input from children. Watching children in their natural surroundings, including at home, in shopping malls, in skating rinks, and at playgrounds, gives marketers information about their preferences and lifestyles, in real time, without having to rely on written or oral communication, which can be difficult for children, especially young ones. Marketers can watch children's subconscious responses to products and displays through observational research.[8]

In-home observation *gets marketers inside peoples' homes to example exactly how products are consumed.* The observation may be done with personal interviews and surveys, video cameras, or other technologies that measure actual experience with a product. For example, a major cereal manufacturer seeks volunteer families that agree to have video cameras installed in their kitchens that are activated by motion detectors. When a family member enters the kitchen, the camera begins recording the events. From these tapes, the manufacturer can observe how much milk is used in a cereal bowl, whether the milk is whole or skim, whether consumers drink the milk afterward, what other items are consumed with the cereal, and other consumption details that lead to improved products or packaging. Perhaps crunchier cereal needs to be developed for skim milk households, an example of adapting an existing product to fit better the changing tastes and consumption patterns. Children might also have difficulty pouring milk or preparing their own breakfasts. One cereal manufacturer now packages a carton of milk with a plastic "bowl" of cereal to make consumption easier for children and portability of a cereal breakfast easier for adults. Eating in the car on the way to work has made Kellogg's NutriGrain cereal bars very popular in the United States. In fact, Breakaway Foods recently began marketing "meals on a stick," which allow consumers to microwave frozen meals (pastas) and eat them on the go.

Shadowing is a *method in which a researcher accompanies or "shadows" consumers through the shopping and consumption processes,* asking questions about each step of the process. Usually answers are transcribed with a video or audio recorder. For example, a retailer might choose to shadow consumers as they shop. By understanding why and how consumers move through the shopping process, marketers can begin to identify ways to solve the problems encountered by consumers. The result is more satisfied customers, who in turn develop brand or store loyalty.

Interviews and Surveys

Consumer analysts also gather information from consumers by conducting surveys and interviews. **Surveys** are an *efficient way of gathering information from a large sample of consumers by asking questions and recording responses.* They can be conducted by mail, telephone, via Internet, or in person, with each method having some advantages and disadvantages. Many surveys done in person are *mall intercepts*—conducted in shopping malls. The advantage of this method is that researchers can ask consumers more complex questions, show product samples or different ads, and ask opinions. Yet, this method may be expensive and subject to **interviewer bias,** in which *responses are influenced by the interviewer's characteristics* (age, gender, etc.) *or by a desire to please the interviewer. Telephone surveys* also allow researchers to obtain a lot of information quickly from consumers; however, the questions and topics covered must be fairly simple. Consumers who choose not to answer questions or are not home when the call is made can complicate the research process. *Mail questionnaires* allow consumer researchers to gather a lot of information, without interviewer bias; however, this approach takes the most time to complete because of the time it takes to send out the surveys and then receive them from consumers. *Internet surveys* are conducted using questionnaires that might be the same as used with telephone, mall intercept, or mail surveys. Internet surveys have the advantage of speed in completion, ease of data entry, and the possibility for complexity in questionnaire design since interactivity between consumers and researchers is included. These traits, combined with the decline in response to telephone surveys, lead some researchers to believe this method could replace telephonic research in the next 25 years.[9] The major disadvantage is the question of whether Internet users who respond to questionnaires are representative of a broader group of consumers who may be the market target.

Focus groups are frequently used to delve into a variety of consumer and consumption issues. Focus groups usually *consist of 8 to 12 people involved in a discussion led by a moderator skilled in getting consumers to discuss a subject thoroughly,* focused on the topic of interest to the researcher. Compared to large-scale telephone or mail surveys, focus groups can probe in depth the very specific aspects of how consumers prepare to buy, decide to purchase, and use products.

Longitudinal studies involve *repeated measures of consumer activities over time to determine changes in their opinions, buying, and consumption behaviors.* A common method of collecting data is through membership or customer loyalty programs, such as those operated by airlines and some grocery chains. An airline, for example, can measure trips by its frequent fliers to study their consumption behaviors in terms of overseas versus domestic travel, repeated trips to the same city, special meal requests, and seat preferences, just to name a few. These data create profiles of the consumption styles/profiles of key market segments, which can be used with targeted communication, improved product and service offerings, and perhaps cooperative marketing programs with hotels or food companies.

There are many other types of longitudinal studies designed to understand consumer behavior over time. Many of these are provided by research organizations such as Information Resources Institute. It maintains a representative panel of consumers who agree to set up a scanner at home to record the UPC code of every product purchased at the end of each day, as well as, the outlet at which it was purchased. This method makes it possible to measure changes in consumption of all major product categories, as well as market share shifts by brand and retail outlet.

Experimentation

Experimentation, as a research methodology, *attempts to understand cause-and-effect relationships by carefully manipulating <u>independent variables</u>* (such as number of advertisements, package design, methods of communication) *to determine the effects of changes on <u>dependent variables</u>* (such as purchase intent or behavior). A typical **laboratory experiment** is described in Consumer In Focus 1.2.[10] A **field experiment** *takes place in a natural setting such as a home or a store.* An example is a retailer that mails several versions of a coupon with variations in price, presentation, and copy to measure the most effective combination.

Consumption Research

Consumption research builds on the three primary research methods to examine how people buy and use products. Consumption analysis sometimes uses ethnographic tools, borrowed from anthropology, to understand how values and culture influence usage of products and other behaviors.

Consider the problem facing a marketing manager who has to submit a sales forecast for dishwashers to his boss. How much can sales of this product increase in the U.S. market when a very high proportion of U.S. families who can afford a dishwasher already own one? How can a company such as Whirlpool increase its sales in industrialized markets when the sales growth potential for this product category seems limited? Traditional marketers might turn to the ever-popular strategy of price cutting to increase the number of households that can afford to buy a dishwasher, or they might sell in other countries where the need for dishwashers is increasing. Although both of these are reasonable and useful approaches to understanding and influencing consumer buying decisions, consumption analysis approaches the solution differently and identifies different strategies for different markets.

The next time you are in your kitchen, observe how the appliance is used and how consumers compensate for product shortcomings. Researchers might find that many households contain kitchens with dishwashers full of clean dishes and sinks full of dirty dishes. Ask most consumers what the biggest problem with their dishwashers is and they will say, "It doesn't unload itself." They can load a

Consumer in Focus 1.2

Inclusive Versus Partitioned Pricing: Should Shipping Costs Be Included in Prices?

When you order a new outfit from a catalog, do you know how much you are spending on the product and how much you are spending on the shipping and handling? Most retailers usually divide a product's price into two mandatory parts, the base price of a product and the surcharge for shipping and handling, rather than charging an all-inclusive price. Defined by the authors of this study as partitioned pricing, firms presumably use this pricing technique to increase demand and profits, but there is little empirical support to show that these prices increase demand or theoretical explanation for why this should occur. Professors Morwitz, Greenleaf, and Johnson implemented an experiment to test hypotheses of how consumers process partitioned prices and how partitioned pricing affects their processing and recall of total costs. Finally, they measured consumers' purchase intentions to estimate potential product demand.

The professors conducted an experiment in which they studied consumers' reactions to different pricing strategies for a product available from both a catalog and a store. The subjects (233 undergraduate business students) were asked to choose between two brands of telephones: a control telephone (Sony brand) sold at a store and a target telephone

(AT&T brand) sold through a catalog. Subjects were split into three groups who saw the AT&T phone price expressed three different ways: (1) combined price of $82.90, including shipping and handling, (2) base price of $69.95 and surcharge of $12.95, and (3) base price of $69.95 with a surcharge of 18.5 percent. In each situation, the control phone was quoted at one all-inclusive price.

Subjects read the descriptions and prices of the two different phones and were asked to identify their purchase intentions on a ten-point bipolar scale with (1) labeled "I would definitely buy the Sony" and (10) labeled "I would definitely buy the AT&T phone." These responses were used to estimate the impact of partitioned pricing on demand. Then the subjects were asked to recall the total price of the AT&T phone without turning back to the description.

The results of the experiment suggest that consumers exposed to the partitioned prices recall significantly lower total prices and exhibit greater intent to buy (or demand). The manner in which the surcharge is presented and consumers' preference for the brand name also influence how they react to partitioned prices.

Source: Vicki G. Morwitz, Eric A. Greenleaf, and Eric J. Johnson, "Divide and Prosper: Consumers' Reactions to Partitioned Prices," Journal of Marketing Research 35 *(November 1998), 453–463.*

few dishes at each meal until they finally get it full and turn it on. But their lifestyles are so busy, they don't have time to empty them, so their sinks end up full of dirty dishes. Additional analysis of middle- to high-income consumers reveals that they often live in "time poverty."

What does this mean if you are the marketing manager at Whirlpool trying to prepare a five-year strategic plan for dishwashers? It means you've just discovered a way to increase dramatically the total size of the market for dishwashers—sell consumers (in certain segments) two dishwashers! The people with time constraints are usually the ones with the money to spend on a second dishwasher.

Here's how the two-dishwasher concept works. After running the first load of dishes in one dishwasher, the clean dishes are not put away into kitchen cupboards. They remain housed in the "clean" dishwasher. Consumers use the clean dishes as they are needed and just load them when they become soiled into the empty dishwasher. Once this dishwasher is full (and the other one is probably empty), it is run and the process is repeated—but in reverse. One dishwasher is used as a storage cabinet for clean dishes while the other is the receptacle for dirty dishes. Not only does the consumer save time (for more valuable activities), but the marketer has also found a way to increase demand for dishwashers.

Sound far-fetched? Actually, this consumption-driven growth is happening to dishwasher sales today. High-income, time-impoverished consumers are building new houses and refurbishing old ones to include two dishwashers. Kitchen designers report it is a major trend—one that consumer researchers could have predicted based on analysis of consumption patterns.

Ethnographic research often involves a variety of research methods. Understanding the consumer may begin with a focus group; extend the knowledge with a large-scale survey by mail, telephone, or in person; and end with an intimate research approach, such as shadowing. Some firms even hire "spies" (researchers posing as customers) to shop their stores, eat at their restaurants, or stay in their hotels, as seen in Consumer in Focus 1.3. From these methods, preliminary knowledge may be used to develop marketing programs. Hypotheses may also be developed for further testing with experiments in laboratory settings or in the marketplace. All these may be combined with data collected longitudinally from scanner checkouts or other methods to develop predictions and models that explain how consumers buy and use products. Though this process leads to good information for management and researchers to use in marketing strategy, the research cycle time needs to be reduced because of the rapid pace at which the environment is changing.[11]

The Underlying Principles of Consumer Behavior

Before reading the remainder of this book, it is important to outline and review a few underlying principles that have shaped this text. They have become mottoes for some of the most successful organizations. They might seem basic, but they are often misunderstood or ignored.

The Consumer Is Sovereign

Peter Drucker, world-renowned professor and perhaps the most influential writer among business executives, said it well, "There is one valid definition of business purpose: *to create a customer*."[12] And marketing executives agree that it is much easier to create a customer if you have what the consumer wants to buy.

Consumer in Focus 1.3

Undercover Research

J. C. Schaefer arrives at The Windsor Court hotel in New Orleans just before noon and heads to the hotel bar to have lunch while the hotel readies his room. Neither the staff nor the manager knows that Mr. Schaefer is there to "spy" on the hotel and prepare a report on his experiences and findings. Over the next two days, he will employ a variety of tests to see if The Windsor Court, a member of Preferred Hotels & Resorts Worldwide and recipient of *Conde Nast Traveler* magazine's award for best hotel in the world, is as good as its reputation. Preferred requires all of its hotels to meet at least 80 percent of its standards in an annual test conducted by Richey International, the creation of Mr. Richey, alias Mr. Schaefer.

As soon as he arrives at the hotel, the testing begins. Preferred Hotels requires that all guests be greeted within 30 seconds of their arrival. The doorman at the Windsor makes it in 12 seconds—a good beginning to the 50 different standards he will test before he is done checking in. Rather than dining in the five-star (highest possible rating) dining room, Mr. Richey dines in the hotel bar and orders crab cakes with french fries, an item not listed on the menu. After receiving his special request, he discreetly dictates his observations into a small tape recorder hidden in his coat pocket. He notes the good food and friendly service, but notes the waiter's lack of eye contact and the oversight of leaving the ketchup at the table after the french fries were removed from the table.

During his stay, Mr. Richey will photograph his room, noting overall cleanliness, condition of curtains, bedspreads, and bathroom facilities. He checks the sink and bath drains and floor for hair, and in 40 percent of all cases will find some in any of these three areas. In the Windsor Court, he finds none, but does note that one baseboard is scuffed. Before leaving for dinner, he tests the housekeeping staff, which will enter his room to turn down the bed, by leaving magazines askew in the magazine rack, disabling a light bulb in the lamp by the bed, and unscrewing the cap of a bottle of lotion provided by the hotel. When he returns a few hours later, the bed is neatly turned down, but the light bulb is not replaced and the room has not been tidied up to his satisfaction. More tests follow the next day.

After the research is completed, Mr. Richey calls Mr. Hansjorg Maissen, the hotel manager, to tell him he has completed his "review" and is ready to report his findings. Following the report, Mr. Maissen, who is generally pleased with the findings, takes the specific information and prepares memos reporting the shortcomings to the appropriate staff members.

Although there are other methods to get information on performance, such as customer satisfaction surveys, Mr. Richey's "agents" give insight into real experiences customers might have during their stay. Richey's agents are trained like cameras—to observe and record their findings without bias, opinions, or apprehension.

Source: Neal Templin, "Undercover With a Hotel Spy," The Wall Street Journal *(May 12, 1999), B1–B12.*

Consumer behavior, as a rule, is purposeful and goal oriented. Products and services are accepted or rejected on the basis of the extent to which they are perceived as relevant to needs and lifestyles. The individual is fully capable of ignoring everything the marketer has to say. It all comes down to the simple point: *consumers are much more adept at forcing changes within firms to meet the consumption preferences of consumers than marketers are adept at getting consumers to buy (at least more than once) a product that does not meet the needs and usage preferences of consumers.* Understanding and adapting to consumer motivation and behavior is not an option—it is an absolute necessity for competitive survival. Firms that survive and thrive learn that the consumer reigns.

The Consumer Is Global

"The world is our marketplace" might be declared as the new creed for consumers and organizations in the next century. As people throughout the world strive for economic development and greater self-sufficiency, achieving higher standards of living becomes a dominant motivation in offering attractive business opportunities in new markets. Organizations can reach more consumers, and consumers can access products from foreign countries, especially on the World Wide Web. Astute entrepreneurs everywhere are discovering the gains that can be made when a concerted effort is made to understand prospective consumers and meet their needs with culturally relevant products. It is accurate to state that basic consumer needs and decision processes are universal.

The new global consumer buys the same brands promoted in global as well as local media, from the same types of retailers, and for the same reasons in many countries throughout the world. Nevertheless, there are major cultural differences in the ways in which motivation and behavior are carried out in practice. Whether it is South Africa, Taiwan, China, Russia, Holland, or Australia, researchers are using the same methods and theories to conduct research and analyze consumer behavior. And an enhanced mode of global sharing of knowledge is disseminating information at lightning speed across geographical and cultural borders. Even though there are differences between cultures, today, as consumers become more global, the similarities are much greater.

Consumers Are Different; Consumers Are Alike

As children in school, we learned to focus on the *differences* (primarily outward in appearance) that distinguish people around the world. As marketing practitioners, we must dive deeper into understanding consumer behavior to identify market segments and niches, both within and spanning specific geographical boundaries. **Segmentation** *focuses on the* similarities *within a group of consumers, while recognizing the differences between groups;* intermarket segmentation occurs when this is done across national boundaries.[13] Figure 1.7a and b shows how the French version of *Cosmopolitan,* though different in language, is similar in style and content to the American *Cosmopolitan.* Although differences between French and American women exist, *Cosmopolitan* cuts across those differences and markets to the similarities among consumers.

The Consumer Has Rights

Consumer needs are real. They are expressed in the purchases consumers make and in the purchases they choose to forego. Leo Bogart, a well-known marketing strategist, stated that the combined effect of the thousands of advertisements consumers face each year is a constant reminder of material goods and services they don't have. Individuals are motivated toward more consumption, acquisition, and upward mobility, and society is driven to produce and innovate.[14] Sometimes, however, fraud and manipulation occur, and in response to such events, the Consumer Bill of Rights was written,[15] as shown in Figure 1.8.

Rights are absolute, inviolable, and nonnegotiable. Outright deception, poor product quality, nonresponse to legitimate complaints, pollution, and other actions are nothing less than violation of legitimate rights. There has been a shift in national consciousness, leading to urgent demands for moral and ethical behavior in business and professions, even in the face of violations of such standards by political leaders. Manufacturers and retailers are increasingly faced with vigorous protest when actions go against social consensus.

The right way to think about consumer behavior includes high standards concerning deception, fraud, or lack of consumer information. What do you think— do firms generally increase their profits by deceiving or cheating consumers?

Figure 1.7a   Similar Segments, Different Countries

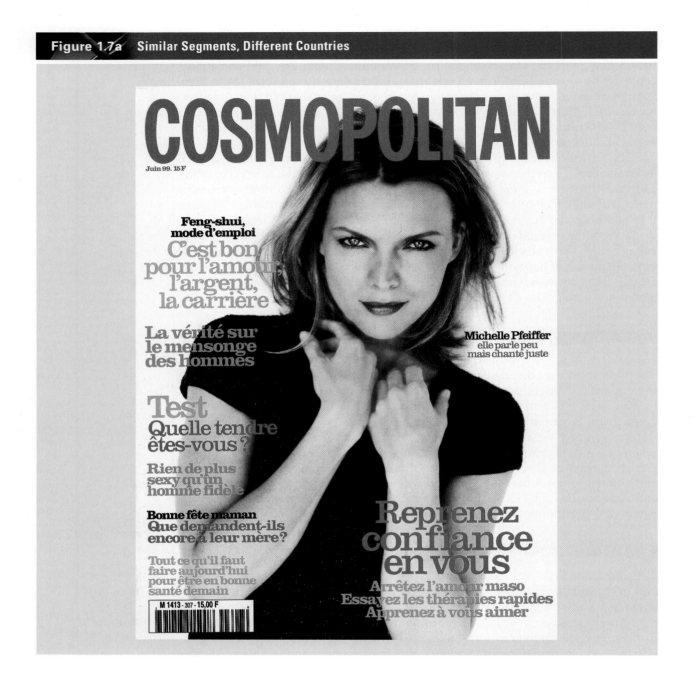

Though high standards for consumer information and prevention of consumer deception are justifiable for personal and moral reasons, they also help the long-term profitability of organizations. Research indicates that firms with clear, visionary standards of right and wrong are the ones that earn the highest profits and have the best performing stock.[16]

Dr. James Collins and Dr. Jerry Porrous, authors of the best-selling book *Built To Last*[17] document in great detail the values of some of the most profitable companies that have enjoyed long-term growth in earnings and stock appreciation. Although General Electric and Westinghouse were both strong firms in their industries, there is a significant difference in their long-term financial performances. And although both companies sold good products, employed good technology,

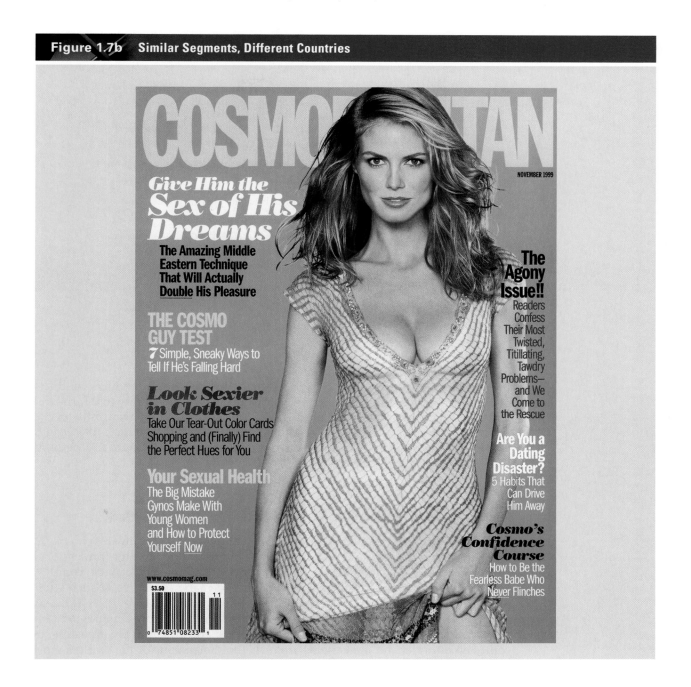

Figure 1.7b   Similar Segments, Different Countries

and satisfied consumer needs, a significant difference existed—the *values* of the company. Even though Westinghouse was the technology leader and positioned as the leader in the electric industry, GE dominated in the long run because of its visionary values. Call it values or call it ethics, the best firms are those with their customers' safety and social and physical well-being in mind.

Sometimes skeptics criticize companies for advertising, accusing them of trying to persuade consumers to buy products or services that they might not need. Some call it social irresponsibility. However, in actuality, there are times when *not* advertising a product or service could be considered socially irresponsible. If a company develops a product to help consumers quit smoking, consumers would be worse off if they didn't know about the product or were withheld the right to

Figure 1.8 Consumer Bill of Rights

The Consumer Bill of Rights

1. The Right to Safety—protection against products or services that are hazardous to health and life.

2. The Right to be Informed—provision of facts necessary for an informed choice; protection against fraudulent, deceitful, or misleading claims.

3. The Right to Choose—assured access to a variety of products and services at competitive prices.

4. The Right to be Heard (Redress)—assurance that consumer interests receive full and sympathetic consideration in formulation and implementation of regulatory policy, and prompt and fair restitution.

5. The Right to Enjoy a Clean and Healthful Environment.

6. The Right of the Poor and Other Minorities to Have Their Interests Protected.

buy the product. More generally, any company that believes it produces products or services that consumers either need or desire has a responsibility to inform and educate consumers about that product. Failure to do so may also result in the failure of the firm. In contrast, if a firm produces a bad product, it will find that effective advertising only accelerates the demise of the product and perhaps the firm.

Everyone Needs to Understand Consumers

Firms of all sizes are "getting to know" their customers and consumers who might one day become customers. At times, it is necessary to involve professional researchers and develop formal research investigations that can be complex and costly to accomplish this task. You will read many examples of such studies throughout this book. But some of the best research, however, is done as managers move outside their executive suites and into the stores, homes, and offices of consumers. When this is done sensitively and perceptively, research becomes an attitude, and the benefits are real. Tom Peters, one of the world's most influential business consultants, says marketers should be obsessed with learning from and listening to their customers. Peters recommends successful executives spend at least 25 percent of their time in the field—where the customers are!

Challenges for the Future

It has been more than 30 years since the field of consumer research was born, evolving from various disciplines in behavioral sciences. More than ever before, the need to understand consumers and consumer behavior has become a hot topic around the globe, from boardrooms and executive suites to universities and hospitals. Now, we find ourselves with new challenges:

1. Gathering and interpreting correctly the information that organizations need to meet the sophisticated needs of organizations in the 21st century

2. Developing effective consumer research methods to keep abreast of the rapid changes in consumer trends and lifestyles

3. Understanding consumer behavior from a broader perspective as an important part of life in its own right

Fasten your seatbelt as we fly into the midst of a sophisticated base of theory and methodology highlighted in the remainder of this text. Consumer behavior is dynamic and exciting, and one thing is for sure—the rate at which consumers are changing and at which marketing is adapting will only accelerate in the next century. Mastering this subject will require a long-term commitment to the study of consumers—how their lifestyles and needs are changing, how family structures and relationships are changing, and how purchase behaviors and consumption patterns are changing. Although this book is designed to make you a better marketer by illustrating how firms use consumer research to enhance marketing strategies, mastery of this subject can help make you a better consumer as well.

Summary

Research into consumer motivation and behavior has assumed significance in contemporary societies worldwide. In the past 30 years, a large and growing multidisciplinary field of study has emerged. A concern of businesses, consumer economists, and others is to find more effective strategies to influence and shape behavior. And the best firms are searching for ways to gather and analyze consumer information to help direct their firms. As a result, consumer research is of premier importance in this applied world.

Just as business orientation evolved throughout the years (from a manufacturing orientation to consumer orientation), so has the study of consumer behavior evolved, sometimes fueling and sometimes keeping pace with the changes in organizations. One thing is for certain, consumer behavior is more important than ever in today's consumer-focused world, making consumer analysts valuable to any type of organization. Some consumer analysts have a more holistic perspective referred to as *post-modernism* and are focusing efforts on studies of consumption to understand how humans think and behave in this important life activity. When we factor in the more recent expansion of inquiry across cultural borders, the result is a rich and growing field of research. In addition to exploring why people buy certain products, consumer behavior also focuses on the study of how consumers use products. Consumption research provides marketers with insights to guide new product development and communication strategies.

The perspective of this book is primarily, although not exclusively, that of the field of marketing. As a result, our central concern is the practical relevance of principles and findings to business strategies. Once you accept the premise that it is important to study consumers, the question of how best to study them arises. Various research methods are used today to get into the minds of people to understand why they behave in certain ways. These methods include observational research, interviews and surveys, and experimentation. Although research provides insight into marketing planning and corporate strategy, it also serves as the basis for consumer education and protection, and furnishes important information for public policy decisions.

Review and Discussion Questions

1. Discuss the statement made by Sam Walton, "only the customer can fire us all." Do you agree with this statement, and how do you relate consumer behavior to this statement?

2. Which of the following decisions should be considered legitimate topics of concern in the study of consumer behavior: (a) selecting a college, (b) purchasing a life insurance policy, (c) smoking a cigarette, (d) selecting a church to join, (e) selecting a dentist, (f) visiting an auto showroom to see new models, or (g) purchasing a college textbook. Explain the importance or potential application of each.

3. Think of a product you recently bought and used. Using a consumption analysis approach, describe what product or packaging features could be improved based on an examination of how it is consumed.

4. Examine current advertisements for consumer products and select one for a new product. Will this product succeed in the long run in the consumer marketplace? What factors determine success?

5. A family has just come into the local office of a lending agency, asking for a bill consolidation loan. Payments for a new car, television, stereo, bedroom set, and central air conditioning have become excessive. The head of the family does not have a steady source of income, and real help is now needed. Is this an example of purposeful consumer behavior, or has this family been manipulated into making unwise purchases?

6. If it is true that motivations and behavior can be understood through research, is it also true that the marketer now has greater ability to influence the consumer than would have been the case in an earlier era?

7. What contributions does the analysis of consumer behavior make to the fields of finance, production, insurance, and top management administration?

8. Would it be equally necessary to understand consumer behavior if the economic system were not one of free enterprise? In other words, is the subject matter of this book only of interest to those in capitalistic systems, or does it also have relevance for socialism and for communism where they still exist?

9. Review Consumer in Focus 1.3. What areas would you encourage a research "spy" to test if you were the manager of this hotel, and how would you use the information?

Endnotes

1. John Kasich, *Courage is Contagious* (New York: Doubleday, 1998).

2. Roger Blackwell, *From Mind To Market* (New York: Harper Business, 1997).

3. Ernest Dichter was a prolific writer. Perhaps the most representative of his contributions is *The Strategy of Desire* (New York: Doubleday, 1960).

4. Vance Packard, *The Hidden Persuaders* (New York: Mackay, 1957).

5. The most definitive source on this subject is John F. Sherry, "Post-modern Alternatives: The Interpretive Turn in Consumer Research," in Thomas S. Robertson and Harold J. Kassarjian, eds., *Handbook of Consumer Behavior* (Englewood Cliffs, NJ: Prentice Hall, 1991), 548-591.

6. Naresh Malhotra, *Marketing Research: An Applied Orientation*, 3rd ed. (Upper Saddle River, NJ: Prentice Hall, 1999).

7. Joshua Macht, "The New Market Research," *Inc.* (July 1998), 88–94.

8. Tom McGee, "Getting Inside Kids' Heads," *American Demographics* (January 1997), 53.

9. Seymour Sudman and Edward Blair, "Sampling in the Twenty-First Century," *Journal of the Academy of Marketing Science* 27 (Spring 1999), 269–277.

10. Vicki G. Morwitz, Eric A. Greenleaf, and Eric J. Johnson, "Divide and Prosper: Consumers' Reactions to Partitioned Prices," *Journal of Marketing Research* 35 (November 1998), 453–463.

11. Naresh K. Malhotra, Mark Peterson, and Susan Bardi Kleiser, "Marketing Research: A State of the Art Review and Directions for the Twenty-First Century," *Journal of the Academy of Marketing Science* 27 (Spring 1999), 160–183.

12. Peter E Drucker, *The Practice of Management* (New York: Harper & Row, 1954), 37.

13. Salah Hassan and Roger Blackwell, *Global Marketing Perceptives and Cases* (Dryden Press, 1994), 53.

14. Leo Bogart, "Where Does Advertising Research Go from Here?" *Journal of Advertising Research* 9 (March 1969), 10.

15. For a fascinating history, see Robert J. Lampman, "JFK's Four Consumer Rights: A Retrospective View," in Scott E. Maynes, *The Frontier of Research in Consumer Interest*, 19–36.

16. James Collins and Jerry Porrous, *Built to Last* (New York: Harper Business, 1997).

17. Ibid.

CHAPTER 2

How Consumer Analysis Affects Business Strategy

OPENING VIGNETTE

What is the world's largest corporation? The answer lies in the small midwestern town of Bentonville, Arkansas. Wal*Mart , the U.S.-based mega-retailer, with sales rapidly approaching $200 billion and with well over 1 million employees, has built a retail business that serves consumers throughout the world. The more difficult question is what are the underlying strategies that catapulted a small, rural store to a world-class giant? Believe it or not, most of the strategies employed by Wal*Mart are found in most every marketing and management textbook. They include market segmentation, a focus on customer service, monitoring consumer trends, database management, and global marketing. Wal*Mart's implementation of these concepts in the marketplace makes up its strategy: understand what consumers need and want to buy; meet those needs better than competitors (at lower prices when possible); and when consumer behavior changes, change with it.

Wal*Mart was built upon a strategy of market segmentation. Rather than enter large metropolitan areas, Wal*Mart's strategy in the 1970s and 1980s focused on *rural* market segments. Its competitors were small hardware and general merchandise stores just like itself. If Wal*Mart had entered the larger, "more attractive," city markets, it would have faced crushing competition from K-Mart and Sears. With a military-inspired, flanking-action approach, "General" Sam Walton began to surround his giant competitors from smaller, outlying areas, and by the 1990s, Wal*Mart became the superior force—bigger than Sears and K-Mart combined. To appeal to *urban* segments of the population, Wal*Mart also developed Sam's Club, a new form of retailing known today as the warehouse format. Sam's Club, which reached $1 billion in sales in just five years, appealed to consumers in urban and suburban areas where there were few stores larger or more powerful.

Much of Wal*Mart's success can be attributed to the values and vision of founder Sam Walton, who thrived on change, whether it was trends in consumer behavior or technology. Eventually, he led Wal*Mart to a position of superiority in data warehousing, data mining, and logistics. And today, it has the largest database in the world (more than twice as large as the U.S. government's), designed to track what consumers are buying, cut costs, offer lower prices to consumers, and increase customer satisfaction.

When a Wal*Mart customer buys a box of Pampers baby diapers (or "nappies"), the "cha-ching" of its NCR cash register is heard all the way in Bentonville, thanks to rapid and sophisticated EDI transmission of data to a 101-terabyte data warehouse. It is also heard in the Cincinnati factory of Procter & Gamble, the manufacturers of Pampers. Cooperation occurs through RetailLink, Wal*Mart's system of sharing data with its supply chain partners to schedule manufacturing and delivery more efficiently. Not only does this process reduce stockouts and costs for consumers, it greatly increases consumer satisfaction and loyalty to a store.

Sam Walton got his ideas from everywhere—employees, competitors, books, and most of all, consumers. And this practice continues today as Wal*Mart expands to global markets. With nearly 3,000 stores found in many countries, including Canada, Mexico, Germany, the United Kingdom, China, Indonesia, and Brazil, retail analysts project Wal*Mart may reach sales volume of $1 trillion in about 15 years, an amount higher than the current GDP of most nations.

Sources: Sam Walton, "Made In America," *Doubleday (1992).* Mass Market Retailers *(September 1999).* Wal-Mart Annual Reports *(1998 and 1999).*

The Century of the Consumer

The new millennium has given birth to a global century of the consumer, requiring new skills for consumer analysts who want to formulate and implement marketing strategies for organizations. Developing consumer-based corporate strategy requires a thorough understanding of *consumer trends, global consumer markets, models to predict purchase and consumption patterns, and communication methods to reach target markets most effectively.* This chapter focuses on the concepts, methods, and skills that you, as an individual involved in understanding how to formulate and implement consumer-driven strategies, will need to develop marketing strategies in the future. They include market segmentation and consumer-based strategies, customer retention programs, and global marketing and communication strategies.

From Market Analysis to Market Strategy: Where Does Consumer Behavior Fit?

The collective battle cry from retailers, wholesalers, and manufacturers alike during the next century is "Serve the Customer!" Superior market-driven strategies and execution in the marketplace are important in times of intense competition and high consumer expectations. The characteristics of market-driven strategies include:

1. Developing a shared vision about the market and how it is expected to change in the future
2. Selecting avenues for delivering superior value to customers
3. Positioning the organization and its brands in the marketplace using distinctive competencies
4. Recognizing the potential value of collaborative relationships with customers, suppliers, distribution channel members, internal functions, and even competitors
5. Reinventing organizational designs to implement and manage future strategies.[1]

The goal of any organization is to provide consumers with more *value* than its competitors do. **Value** is the *difference between what consumers give up* (pay with time, money, or other resources) *for a product and the benefits they receive.* Value is the total bundle of utilities received by customers compared to the total bundle of *dis*utilities they must pay. In today's value-conscious environment, sellers must stress the overall value of their products.[2]

Quality, often thought to be synonymous with value, is not enough to sustain competitive advantage in today's environment,[3] but the combination of other components of value, such as brand, image, price, and product features, does provide advantage. It is not clear, however, how these components communicate value to customers.[4] For example, both Nike and Reebok athletic shoes provide the same basic functions and quality; however, Nike might have a special cushioning feature in the sole of the shoe and the famous swoosh on the outside of the shoe. It is also the brand endorsed by Michael Jordan. And Reebok might feature a nighttime reflector and cost a bit less. Consumers choose the product that provides them the best value—not necessarily in terms of cost savings, but in terms of overall benefits, which might include, in this example, the approval of consumers' peers.

Marketing strategy involves *the allocation of resources to develop and sell products or services that consumers will perceive to provide more value than competitive products or services.* The process includes *market analysis, market segmentation, market strategy,* and *implementation,* with the study of consumers at the core. As seen in Figure 2.1, the consumer relates directly with each of these areas of strategy formulation and implementation. In order to reap the rewards of consumer

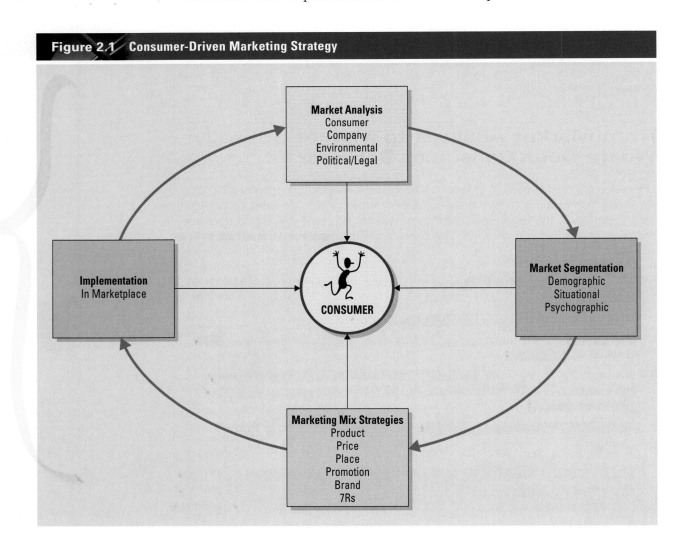

Figure 2.1   Consumer-Driven Marketing Strategy

research and market planning, it is important to understand how consumer behavior fits into the marketing process. What roles do consumers and consumer behavior have in market analysis, marketing strategy, and the entire marketing process? Figure 2.1 shows four major steps of marketing any product or service and introducing it to the marketplace.

Market Analysis

Market analysis is the *process of analyzing changing consumer trends; current and potential competitors; company strengths and resources; and the technological, legal, and economic environments.* All these factors add dimension and insight into the potential success of a plan for a new product or service.

Consumer Insight and Product Development   When marketers attempt to get consumers to buy their products, most of the time they fail. Kuczmarski & Associates studied the success rates for 11,000 new products launched by 77 different companies and found that only 56 percent were still on the market 5 years later.[5] Group EFO Ltd. reports even more discouraging figures. Only 8 percent of new product concepts offered by a group of 112 leading manufacturers and retailers reached the market, and 83 percent of those that did failed to meet marketing objectives.[6]

Why is this failure rate so high? The answer is simple and straightforward— *a new product must satisfy customers' needs, wants, and expectations, not those of a management team.* Although formal analyses might point to product life cycles, poor performance, or failed communication plans, often the bottom-line issue is lack of understanding of the intended market. For instance, many firms don't understand how targeted consumers are likely to react to new products—different consumers possess different levels of innovativeness, which affect which advertising and positioning strategies will be most effective. For example, highly innovative consumers attach more importance to stimulation, creativity, and curiosity,[7] characteristics that marketers can use to target product offerings and advertising to specific segments.

Organizations around the world are spending billions of dollars each year on product concepts that would never be introduced to the marketplace if they were more closely tested against consumer insight. **Consumer insight** can be defined as *an understanding of consumers' expressed and unspoken needs and realities that affect how they make life, brand, and product choices.*[8] It combines *facts* (either from primary or secondary research, sales data, or customer information) with *intuition*, resulting in an *insight* that can lead to a new product, existing product innovation, brand extension, or revised communication plan. As companies turn to consumer feedback for new product guidance and ideas, researchers and marketers search for ways to channel the ideation process to allow consumers to be more focused and productive, and provide better information to marketers.[9]

In an era of consumer-focused marketing, marketers need close access to reality through action research or at least participant observation.[10] Anyone in the firm can conduct research, including the CEO. Eastman Kodak executive Raymond H. DeMoulin was in a Tokyo fish market early one morning when he observed a photographer trying to pry open a film container with his teeth while holding his camera. This observation quickly gave rise to a product change so that it now is possible to open containers of Kodak film with one hand.[11] DeMoulin was doing consumer research that morning, even though he had no clipboard with him and engaged in no computerized analysis of data. He made enlightened use of observation, which then was blended with experience and intuition (creative insight) to build practical, workable marketing strategy. As with other corporate initiatives, the greater perceived importance placed on consumer

"New + improved"
↑
6 mos.

insight by top management, the more likely it is to affect product development strategies.

Consumer Environment   When marketers study the *consumer environment*, they may look at a number of issues, including demographic trends, personal and group influences, motivation, attitudes, consumer knowledge, changing consumer needs and wants, consumption patterns, and consumer lifestyles. The relationship between the consumer in the middle of the model in Figure 2.1 and the market analysis stage is an important one. Understanding changes in the consumer environment can lead to new product ideas, product adaptations, new packaging, or even new services to help consumers meet their changing needs.

Consumers work more hours per day than in the past, on average, and their lifestyle in a mobile society also causes them to spend more time commuting. Feeling the stress of time constraints and deadlines, consumers want flexibility. Appealing to these market trends, Figure 2.2 shows an ad from Mitsubishi touting its Amity CN Mini-Notebook computer and Mobileaccess cellular smartphone (which doubles as a wireless modem). Mitsubishi recognized that consumers sometimes can't or don't want to work only in their offices—portability of computers and other work-related items is important to them. The company saw an opportunity in the marketplace for adapting a product to meet different consumer needs. The tagline at the bottom of the ad, "We see the big picture," refers to the vision of the company—it understands consumer behavior and is building technology and products to fulfill consumers' needs and wants.

Figure 2.2   Mitsubishi Addresses Consumption Needs

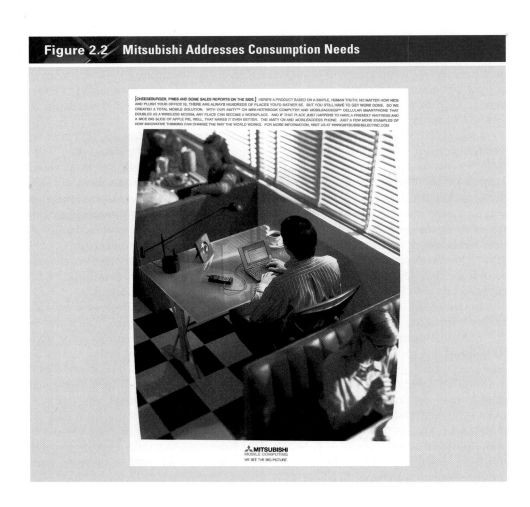

Corporate Strengths and Resources   Firms must also analyze their *corporate strengths and resources* to understand whether, in the case of Mitsubishi, developing the Amity and Mobileaccess is feasible. This would include examining the financial stability and resources of the company, as well as its personnel, managerial, production, research, and marketing abilities. How much can the company invest of these various resources into the development and marketing of this product? What resources does the company lack, and how might it find the right solutions to overcome those weaknesses—whether it be financial grants or loans, or strategic partners to develop special product components? And since this is a technology-based product, further consideration must be given to the technology itself—does it even exist, or must Mitsubishi or another company develop it first?

Current and Potential Competitors   A thorough market analysis also examines *current and potential competitors.* A traditional approach to this type of analysis focuses strategic thinking on staying ahead of the competition, which might include looking at existing competitive products and figuring out how to add a feature that might make it "just a little better" than the competitive product in the mind of the consumer. Other, more innovative firms, pay less attention to matching or beating their rivals, but focus on how to make their competitors irrelevant in the marketplace with innovation.[12] Has Mitsubishi innovated enough to make its competitors irrelevant or at least less powerful in the marketplace? How will current competitors of Mitsubishi react to the introduction of this new product? How easy will it be for them to enter the market, or if they are already marketing a similar product, how will they react to this new brand?

Firms have to anticipate various reactions of their current competitors, such as advertising blitzes, price cuts, product giveaways, and other sales and promotion strategies. And they must anticipate which firms, though they might not be competitors at this time, might enter the marketplace with similar products. Are they inherently positioned better to market and sell this type of specialty computer?

Market Environment   Marketers must also examine the condition of the overall *market environment* into which the product or service will be introduced. Factors such as the state of the economy, government regulations, physical conditions, and technology play an important role in the potential success of a product or service in the marketplace. If the economy is not good—unemployment is high, inflation is high, or wages are declining—introducing a relatively expensive specialty computer to the mass market may fail. Although there may be segments of the market that will buy this type of product regardless of the overall economic conditions, volume may be too small to justify introduction, or price and distribution strategies may need to be changed. Legal and governmental considerations, especially when selling in global markets, must be examined to understand import restrictions and other legal issues. And finally, physical conditions, such as the condition of the environment or of a country's infrastructure, are also important considerations.

Market Segmentation

The next step in creating market strategy is **market segmentation,** the *process of identifying a group of people similar in one or more ways,* based on a variety of characteristics and behaviors, highlighted in Figure 2.3. The goal is to identify these groups of people with similar behavior so that product or packaging adjustments or communication strategies can be adapted to meet their specific needs, thereby increasing the possibility of sale to this target group. A **market segment** is a *group of consumers with similar needs and behavior that differ from those of the entire mass market.*

Figure 2.3   Consumer-Driven Marketing Strategy

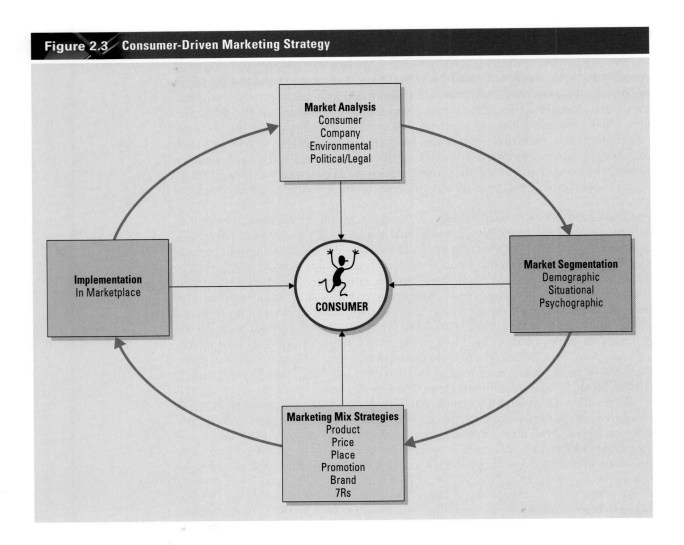

The need for segmentation results from the differences between people. If all humans were identical in their preferences and behaviors, market segmentation would not be needed because every product could be the same. Because people differ so much in their motivations, needs, decision processes, and buying behaviors, products ideally would be custom-tailored to each user to give maximum satisfaction to consumers.

The goal in measuring market segments is to allocate consumers into categories that minimize variance within groups and maximize variance between groups. By identifying market segments that are similar in their behavior, products can be developed that are closely matched to the preferences of that group. By maximizing variance between segments, a differential advantage is obtained that, ideally, will be so appealing that it will command a premium price greater than the cost of catering to the specialized preferences of a particular segment. But the more individualized the product and the smaller the segment for which it is designed, the greater the likelihood that the costs to the marketer will increase. Adaptation to the need of a specific segment may require a higher price than consumers in that segment are willing to pay. For example, custom-tailored clothing and custom-designed homes meet the needs of individual customers, but they carry with them higher price tags, making it difficult to compete with the lower prices of mass-produced products.

The opposite of market segmentation is **market aggregation** or **mass marketing**—*when organizations choose to market and sell the same product or service to all consumers.* This strategy may be effective in developing economies where there exists pent-up demand for basic products. These markets want functional benefits at the lowest possible prices. That usually means a standardized product, produced at low cost, in long, homogeneous production runs, and sold through basic distribution channels with few added services or extras.

Although some firms still choose a market aggregation approach, the reality is that mass markets are going the way of the dinosaur in most industrially advanced countries. In North American and European markets, it may not be too bold to say that there are no more mass markets, only variations in the size of market segments. This is due to several factors:

- Affluence—consumers can afford products that are more customized to suit their individual tastes, needs, and lifestyles.

- Consumer databases—product designers have the information needed to address variations in consumers' consumption and behavior patterns, and marketers have the information needed to advertise and communicate with individual consumers.

- Manufacturing technology—production processes can be computer controlled and tailored to smaller production runs without corresponding cost increases.

- Multiple distribution channels—multiple methods of retailing, including direct sales and Internet retailing, allow distribution to be closely related to the needs and desires of specific segments.

Identifying Segments In marketing strategy applications, one principle is that segmentation is based on identifying and appealing to *consumers with similar behavior, not necessarily similar characteristics.* Consumer analysts use consumer characteristics for segmentation because they are correlates, or "proxies," for behavior and not because the characteristics are determinants of why people buy. For example, market segments that buy a stereo priced at $3,000 are much different from those that buy a stereo priced at $300. Not only will the product and price be different, based upon different music-listening behavior, but the distribution channels and promotional components of the marketing mix will also likely be different. At first glance, one might conclude (falsely) that the segments buying the $3,000 stereo would all be high income and the segments buying the $300 stereo would be low income. In fact, a few low-income students might buy the expensive stereo, and some high-income consumers might buy the lower priced stereo.

It is difficult to measure behavior for the purpose of developing a targeted marketing mix. It is relatively easy, however, to measure consumer characteristics such as income, age, or gender. Therefore, the basis for developing marketing strategy often relies on these types of consumer characteristics because they indicate probable consumer behaviors. Figure 2.4 summarizes variables used to segment populations. Demographics, psychographics, purchase and consumption behaviors, geographical characteristics, and situational factors are the variables typically used to define segments of potential customers with similar behavior. These variable-based segments sometimes overlap, as Figure 2.5 discloses, yielding a better-defined segment. Often this improves the predictability and sensitivity of how segments will respond to specific types of advertising, promotions, product variations, and distribution channels.

Addressing the Needs of Market Segments Consumers are becoming more sophisticated and are demanding more customized products to fit their individual

---

Figure 2.4 **How to Segment Consumer Markets**

Consumer Characteristics

Demographics

Age	Education	Marital status
Gender	Family size	Occupation
Ethnicity	Nationality	Religion
Income	Life stage	Living arrangements

Psychographics

Activities	Interests	Opinions

Purchase and Consumption Behaviors

Shopping location preferences	Brand loyalty
Frequency of purchase	Benefits sought
Media used	How used
Price sensitivity	Rate of use

Values

Culture

Personality

Geographical Characteristics

National boundaries
State and regional boundaries
Urban versus rural
Zip code

Situational Characteristics

Work versus leisure usage
Time
Where used

---

needs, preferences, and tastes. The goal to be consumer-driven has caused many successful firms to offer different products or services to different market segments, a costly and complex undertaking, especially as customers and their needs grow increasingly diverse. **Mass customization,** *customizing goods or services for individual customers in high volumes and at relatively low costs,* is one way for firms to offer unique value to customers with efficiency. The key to making mass customization pay off in terms of value to the company is understanding what type of customization customers value the most, which varies in different situations.[13] An organization can obtain this type of information by researching its customer base and offering incentives to customers who give information.

Some firms practice the ultimate form of market segmentation and customization—creating and marketing to segments of one. This process was identified in marketing journals in recent years and popularized in the best-selling book, *The One To One Future.*[14] In that book, Rogers and Pepper describe a flower store in Bowling Green, Ohio, that specializes in selling flower arrangements and small gifts—just as most flower stores of similar size. But instead of waiting for customers to come into the store or call to place an order, this store relies on its database for proactive marketing. When a customer places an order, the contact and billing information is recorded along with what was ordered, for whom, and for which occasion. If a customer sends yellow roses for her mother's birthday on October 13, the flower store contacts the customer a few weeks prior to that date the following year and asks if they should send a similar bouquet this year.

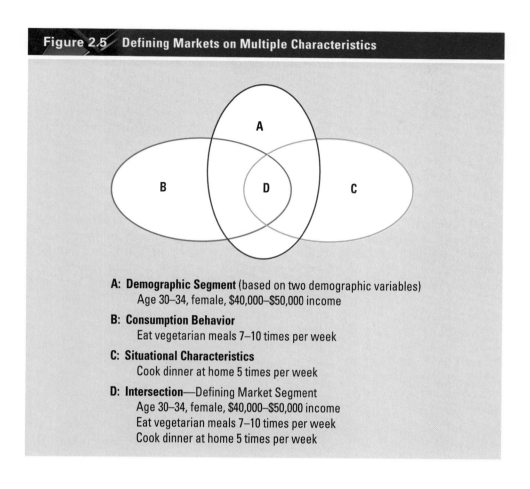

Figure 2.5 Defining Markets on Multiple Characteristics

A: **Demographic Segment** (based on two demographic variables)
   Age 30–34, female, $40,000–$50,000 income

B: **Consumption Behavior**
   Eat vegetarian meals 7–10 times per week

C: **Situational Characteristics**
   Cook dinner at home 5 times per week

D: **Intersection**—Defining Market Segment
   Age 30–34, female, $40,000–$50,000 income
   Eat vegetarian meals 7–10 times per week
   Cook dinner at home 5 times per week

Although they sell flowers, they really sell solutions and simplicity. With this style of individual-based marketing, this store creates loyal and delighted customers. Does this same process work for larger than one-to-one, but still highly individualized, segments in a product as complex as auto manufacturing? See Consumer in Focus 2.1 for the answer.

Profitability of Market Segmentation   The ultimate goal of segmentation is increased customer satisfaction and profitability. Increased profitability occurs when the economic value to consumers is higher than the cost of creating the value. For example, a computer program might be adapted to the special needs of some users and positioned based on benefits most desired by this specific segment.[15] If the costs of adaptation were expensive but caused the program to be worth hundreds or even thousands of dollars of value to many users, the higher price that could be charged compared to a standardized product might yield millions of dollars of additional profitability. Adding value by identifying profitable market segments is a process that created fortunes for Michael Dell and Bill Gates in the computer industry.

Segmentation can increase profitability by decreasing marketing expenses. BalletMet, a nationally recognized ballet company based in Columbus, Ohio, reduced its promotional expenses and increased its response rate by targeting specific audiences for specific performances. It tracks its subscribers and regular attendees and analyzes which types of performances they prefer. BalletMet performs three major ballets each year—popular and well-known productions such

Consumer in Focus 2.1

Design Your Own Car

Customized cars have always been popular with some consumers. Usually they relied on a "chop shop" to take a new car and literally cut (or chop) the cars to customize them to a buyer's taste, apply new paint, and perhaps redo the interiors. During the 1950s and 1960s, Chevrolets, Fords, and Plymouths, with chopped front windshields, flared fenders, and other variations on basic models usually created on a do-it-yourself basis, were the envy of young drivers. Many who could not afford them in that era are today members of the Street Rod Association, recreating the past for folks who missed the customized cars of the 1950s.

The 21st century brought with it a new breed of car driver who also subscribes to the mass customization process, but now can order these cars directly from the factory. Want a unique paint color or interior for your Porsche? It's available from the factory and very popular—over half of Porsche's buyers choose from one of the manufacturer's custom programs. BMW and Audi also offer similar options.

Mercedes-Benz takes the customized approach further with its Designo program, the automotive equivalent of made-to-measure clothing. For about 10 percent extra of the car's normal price, the customer can design his or her own blend of special colors and interiors. You can order your SLK special edition convertible in copper, electric green, slate blue, espresso, or metallic black. Everything from wood choice (charcoal maple, natural maple, natural elm) to floor mats will be custom according to the way you design it. Mercedes discovered that though consumers want more choices to express their personal style, they don't want to spend a lot of time flipping through paint chips and talking about carpet fiber. The Designo package answers this need with a set palette of radical colors and trim combinations that are designed into the manufacturing process. Last-minute delivery and assembly-line integration of green steering wheels and slate blue fenders keep costs down and allow the buyer to get behind the wheel quickly with a car custom-designed to individualized tastes.

Source: Based partially on Morgan Murphy, "The Chop Shop in Stuttgart," Forbes (March 22, 1999), 172.

as *Swan Lake* and *The Nutcracker*—and an entire series of smaller ballets, which vary from very contemporary to traditional. Instead of sending promotional pieces to everyone in the database for the series ballets, BalletMet sends special promotions to those patrons most likely to attend. It doesn't lose potential patrons by limiting its direct mail promotions to everyone because performance reviews and articles appear in targeted news publications. It does, however, lower promotion costs—it can produce fewer mail pieces and cut mailing costs. It also uses visual design to promote its performances differently depending on the theme of the ballet and the feeling of the performances. Figure 2.6a and b shows the promotional piece sent for *Swan Lake* (traditional ballet) and that used for a contemporary performance. For any given performance, BalletMet can change the picture on the direct mail piece depending on whether it is targeting women, men, athletes, families, or other segments. If directed toward male patrons, the featured dancer might be female rather than male.

Criteria for Choosing Segments   How does a firm choose which segment it should target when many potential segments have been identified? Determining the attractiveness of a market segment involves analyzing segments based on four criteria:

- **Measurability** refers to the *ability to obtain information about the size, nature, and behavior of a market segment.* Consumers may behave in similar ways, but those behaviors must be able to be measured directly or with close correlates in order to formulate and implement marketing mix strategies.

Figure 2.6a   BalletMet Adapts Promotions to Audience

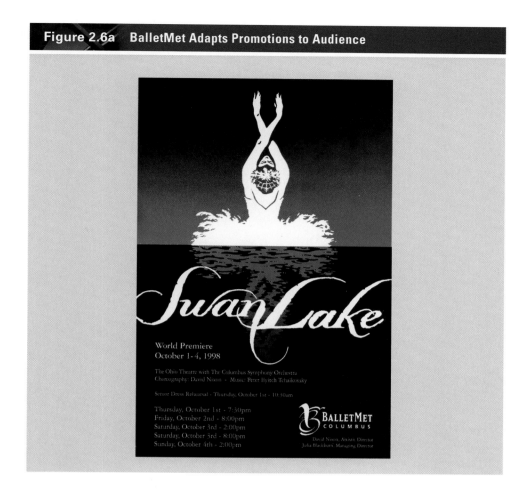

- **Accessibility** (or reachability) is the *degree to which segments can be reached,* either through various advertising and communication programs or through various methods of retailing.

- **Substantiality** refers to the *size of the market.* Small segments may not generate enough volume to support development, production, and distribution costs that would be involved in satisfying these segments. Generally, the more substantial the segment, the better it will serve as a market target.

- **Congruity** refers to *how similar members within the segment are in behaviors or characteristics that correlate with behavior.* The more congruous a segment is, the more efficient are product offerings, promotion, and distribution channels directed specifically to that segment.

On a final note, segmentation methods and strategies continue to be refined by marketers. In an era characterized by increasing market diversity resulting in market fragmentation,[16] segmentation strategy, based on data mining, and customized manufacturing technology, allows firms to reach smaller but potentially more profitable segments.

Marketing Mix Strategies

Marketing strategy (highlighted in Figure 2.7) involves a plan to meet the needs and desires of specific target markets by providing value to that target better than competitors. Such a plan must specify the essential components of the marketing

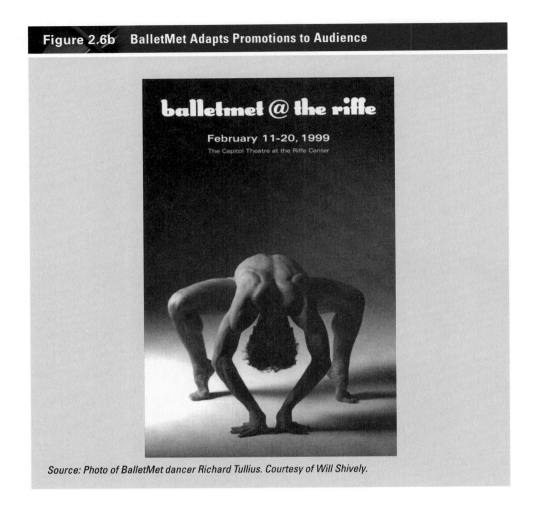

Figure 2.6b   BalletMet Adapts Promotions to Audience

Source: Photo of BalletMet dancer Richard Tullius. Courtesy of Will Shively.

mix, often described as the four P's (product, place, price, and promotion issues). Consumer research is critically important in developing segmentation strategy as well as formulating the marketing mix, and both are also affected by the decision process of consumers, as you will see in Chapter 3.

The first element of the marketing mix is **product,** which includes the *total bundle of utilities* (or benefits) *obtained by consumers in the exchange process.* Products include both goods and services as well as both tangible and intangible attributes. Products may be purchased for a variety of reasons ranging from satisfying a basic need (food) to indulging in something that just feels good (massage). Internally, a firm analyzes its capabilities and the costs associated with producing, distributing, and selling the product. Externally, however, the focus in product development is on how consumer behavior will affect the product. What form of the product best serves consumption patterns for the target segment? What packaging will best attract consumers and satisfy their transportation, usage, and disposal of the product? How will consumers compare this product to competitive or substitute products? Marketers must answer these questions and monitor consumption patterns, with product innovations following consumption trends closely.

The next element of the marketing mix is **price,** or the *total bundle of disutilities* (costs) *given up by consumers in exchange for a product.* Disutility usually refers to money (or a credit card) paid for the product, but includes other disutilities such as time, inconvenience, and psychological risk that add to the "price" of a

Figure 2.7   Consumer-Driven Marketing Strategy

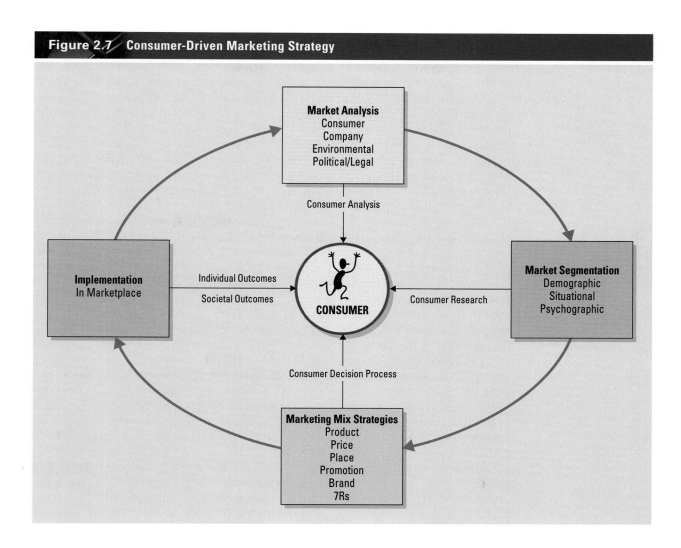

product. For BalletMet, the primary product is the performance, but it includes other utilities such as the social experience with others. The "price" includes the cost of the ticket and the time spent at the ballet, which might be spent on competitive products such as sports or with family members.

Consumer research is needed for many aspects of determining price policies. How important do consumers consider price compared to other aspects of a marketing mix? Will consumers respond best to a policy of "everyday low prices" (used by firms such as Wal*Mart), or will consumers prefer stores with promotional pricing (sometimes called "hi-low" or "loss leader")? Can raising the price of a product improve a consumer's perception of the product's quality? (The answer often is yes.) How important is it to have the lowest price among competitors?

Having the lowest price is not as important as having the price fall in the range consumers expect to pay for the product, according to a recent study conducted for the International Mass Retail Association.[17] In that study, consumers indicated it is more important for the price of a product to fall in the range they expect to pay for that product than to be the "absolute lowest priced" product in the category. For example, if a consumer expects to pay between $25.00 and $28.00 for a blouse, the exact price of the product, as long as it falls in the range, is not as important in the decision to buy the product as other product features such as fabric, fit, and style.

Consumer research about price can show how to communicate price most effectively. Research indicates that the ending of the price (the pennies after the dollar figure) affect consumer perception of the product. For example, consumers perceive a product labeled $25.00 as higher quality than a product with a $24.98 price tag. In a study, on price and quality, researchers[18] found that consumers perceive products with prices ending in round numbers and $.00 to be of higher quality. Consumers relate prices that end in numbers such as $.99 to discount items. From an operations standpoint, firms must price products to cover their costs and required profit margin. From a consumer standpoint, firms must anticipate the reactions consumers might have to certain prices and the image associated with different price points—if a product is priced too low, it might be perceived as lower quality than a higher priced item.

The next element of the marketing mix is *promotion,* including advertising, public relations, sales promotion, and personal sales. In much of the rest of this text, you will see how understanding consumers helps organizations communicate with and promote to their target markets most effectively. Organizations must determine what message they want to send to which consumers, which forms of communication will best reach specific segments, what type of communication should occur during the various stages of the purchase and consumption processes, and how different product attributes should be positioned through different forms of media.

The final element of the marketing mix is *place* (or distribution). In this phase, firms decide the most effective outlets through which to sell their products and how best to get them there. Where will consumers expect and want to buy this product—through mass retailers, electronic retailing, direct selling, or catalogs? A product might sell better in an outlet in which consumers receive personal assistance with product choice and operations instructions, whereas other products might sell better in mass retail outlets.

No marketing strategy would be complete without discussion of *brand strategy.* Brands are critically important to successful marketing strategies and influenced by many areas of consumer behavior. That is why you will find them discussed throughout this text, but they warrant mention here because brand is a company asset that needs to be managed like any other asset. The more consumers equate a brand with their personal preferences, the more of the company's products they are likely to buy and probably for a premium price. And if a product benefit is conveyed in a brand name (for example, PicturePerfect television), consumers are more likely to recall the advertised benefit claim.[19] Brands are sometimes defined as *promise*—a promise to consumers that the attributes they desire most will be obtained when they buy the preferred brand.

Marketers who fail to build and maintain their brands are playing *marketing roulette.* Failure to invest in product quality, advertising development, and customer satisfaction reduces a company's primary competitive strategy to little more than a price war, a dangerous game unless a firm is the low-cost producer. Even for low-cost producers, failure to build brands usually results in low margins and profitability, and probably a declining market share. Consumers want brands they know and trust. Brand equity is created for a firm when it develops a favored position in targeted segments that command prices higher than the costs of building the brand.

Implementation

All these areas of the marketing mix merge to create a consumer-based plan to market and sell products to target markets. If the marketing function is done well, selling becomes much easier. The key is in *implementation.* The best strategies are rendered worthless if they are not executed well in the marketplace—the point at which interaction with the consumer transforms strategy into reality.

The characteristics of the 21st century are likely to present the marketing profession with major opportunities and threats that have important implications for strategy implementation.[20] The outcome can be profits or problems with results that can affect individuals and organizations alike, and society in the long run. For example, the widespread acceptance of e-mail has changed the way people communicate. Grandparents can communicate efficiently with their grandchildren in other countries, hearing-impaired people can "talk" and respond more freely with others, and business partners can exchange ideas instantaneously, changing the dynamics of friends and family relationships dramatically. Businesses run more efficiently, as do relationships. Although the telephone has not been replaced, individuals, businesses, and society have changed dramatically with the successful marketing and consumer acceptance of e-mail.

The Seven R's of the Marketing Mix

Organizations of all sizes are looking to consumer behavior analysis for answers on how to perform well in the marketplace. Marketers are expanding on the four P's of the marketing mix to include seven R's—research, rate, resources, retailing, reliability, reward, and relationship. Figure 2.8 summarizes the seven R's and what each factor means from the organization's and the consumer's point of view.

Figure 2.8   The Seven R's of the Marketing Mix

	Organization	Consumer
Research	Formulate methodology Conduct research Analyze research	Participate in research Provide information and access to mind of the market
Rate	Speed to market	Speed through shopping process Usage rates of products

Resources	Commitments to project:
	  financial, personnel, etc.
	Cost: effect on pricing
		Payment for product: money,
		  time, attention, energy, and emotions
		Scarcity of resources

Retailing	Which outlets to sell products?
	Location in store and shelf
	  position
		Where they expect to buy product and
		  where they like to shop

Reliability	Dependency on supply chain
	  members
	Avoiding product recalls
		Product quality and consistency
		Reliability of retailer
		Access to company for questions
		  or product problems

Reward	Program to increase purchases and loyalty	Reward from using product Reward programs
Relationship	Relationships within supply chain Relationships with customers Customer satisfaction	Loyalty to brand and store Feeling valued and special Customer satisfaction

When the seven R's are addressed in marketing plans and in implementation, the result can be customer satisfaction of skyscraper proportions. The bulk of the evidence shows that sustainable market share comes primarily from an ongoing focus on customer satisfaction and retention, leadership in quality, and superior service.

Customer Loyalty and Retention Strategies

Many marketing strategists are placing more attention on customer retention than new customer solicitation because it is generally less expensive to hold onto present customers than to attract new ones. In the industrialized countries of North America, Europe, and Japan, customer loss can be disastrous because there are fewer new consumers to replace lost customers. Therefore, customer loyalty based on genuine and ongoing satisfaction is one of the greatest assets a firm can develop. At the same time, many consumers are becoming more fickle, choosing to try new products featured in special promotions or a new retailer entering a market rather than remaining brand loyal to a product or retailer.

What is causing this decline in loyalty, and what does it mean to organizations? As consumers are given more choices, distinctions between brands fade, and people try new things.[21] They feel a sense of entitlement to try new brands, especially if they don't feel "rewarded" for remaining loyal, and they perceive many brands to be equal in terms of quality and value received. As a result, switching behavior increases (otherwise known as defection from a given brand or product), as do complaints, cynicism toward the concept of loyalty, and litigious activities.[22] To address the problem of customer defection, researchers are beginning to use changes in customer transaction patterns as a basis for identifying likely defectors (even before defection occurs)[23] and gearing promotions or special incentives to them.

Customer Loyalty Programs

In an effort to increase loyalty toward a brand of product, service, or retailer, organizations have implemented a variety of loyalty or reward programs, which by definition, acknowledge and reward consumers' "good behavior"—in this case, behaving the way the organization wants them to behave. Many of you may have a "frequent flyer" card, which allows you to accumulate "miles" when you travel on the airline. After you reach a specified number of miles, you can cash in your miles for a free airline ticket. The most frequent fliers are given "elite" status with gold or platinum cards and are rewarded with perks, such as upgrades, special (shorter) check-in lines, and priority status on standby lists. Many hotels, retailers, and restaurants also offer frequent purchase cards to encourage consumers to buy from them and build a relationship with them. However, it is often unclear from just monitoring purchase behavior if consumers repeat behavior because of habit and convenience or because of deeper attachment to the brand.[24]

Several years ago, grocery stores sought ways to differentiate themselves from their competitors, in an industry experiencing thin margins and fierce competition. A glut of vendor-driven promotions meant that a majority of stores in a given area would have the same promotion at the same time.[25] Many of them adopted frequent shopper cards, trying to pass on special savings to their most loyal customers, rather than rewarding customers that only came to the store to shop the weekly specials, known as *cherry-pickers.* Shoppers joined these loyalty programs, primarily to take advantage of member specials.[26] Though these programs worked well to differentiate grocery retailers, today almost 50 percent of all grocery stores have adopted this type of program, according to *Chain Store Age,* evening the playing field once again.

Loyalty programs have the distinct opportunity of providing rewards to consumers and information to retailers. Unfortunately, many firms have invested millions of dollars in systems to collect consumer data, but few have invested in the interpretation of the data and fewer in the implementation of data into strategy. And data collection without analysis creates little more than overhead. At the top of loyalty program managers' success stories is Tesco's U.K. program, featured in Consumer in Focus 2.2.

Customer loyalty programs help organizations identify customer segments that can be targeted with special offers or perks more likely to be of value to them.[27] Travelodge, a U.S.-based economy hotel chain, segmented its market based on type of travel (vacation versus business) and offered different rewards to different groups. For example, for years the primary customer was a leisure customer, whom the hotel enticed with a "stay 10 nights and get an 11th night free" offer. After researching the business segment, Travelodge began offering business customers an airline mileage reward, along with the service of being able to get an update on program points upon arrival at the hotel.[28]

Strengthening Customer Relationships

Regardless of type of loyalty program and how it is executed in the marketplace, the ultimate goal is to strengthen the relationship with the customer. The following list highlights some strategies to accomplish this:

Consumer in Focus 2.2

Loyalty Programs that Start with the Customer

Tesco's performance in the United Kingdom places it at the top of the list of loyalty program success stories. Designed and managed by Clive Humby, chairman of Dunnhumby Ltd., a database consulting and management company, the program focuses on managing Tesco's customers rather than just its loyalty program.

When shoppers sign up to join this frequency program, they benefit from two distinct Tesco's programs—*reward* and *incentive* programs. The reward program is designed to reward consumers for a particular behavior, such as increasing total purchases, shopping in a new department, or whatever behavior the store wants its customers to continue doing. On the other hand, Tesco's incentive program helps the organization to alter customers' behaviors, by enticing them with special prices or other financial and personal incentives. For example, program members may receive a 5 percent cost reduction if they shop during specified hours, shifting some of the demand from peak hours to slower retail times. They may also receive a benefit if they bring their own shopping bags to the store or recycle bottles. The Tesco incentive program is designed to help change consumers' behaviors in some way.

These programs differ from many of those found in the United States, where all customers are rewarded in the same way, regardless of their behavior. Just by possessing the card, they get a reward—the same reward goes to the retailer's best and worst member customers, which defeats to some degree the purpose of the program. Rather than viewing its program members as a single segment of customers, Tesco uses data analysis of its 11 million cardholders to create more than 37,000 customer segments and provide different rewards and incentives to each of those segments, based on the goals of specific promotional programs. Some receive rewards; some receive incentives; and some receive either both or neither.

Some skeptics might still feel inclined to ask, "Do loyalty programs really work?" If Tesco is an indicator, the answer is yes. It recently surpassed long-time rival Sainsbury to become number one in food store sales in the United Kingdom. The key is not just in having the right programs, but also in managing and implementing them well and using the resulting data.

Source: Excerpted and based on: Don E. Schultz, "Manage Customers, Not Loyalty Programs," Marketing News (January 4, 1999), 35–36.

- *Make individualized marketing a reality.* Pizza Hut operates a system that contains electronic profiles of nine million customers who have received deliveries of pizza in the past making it possible to target relevant messages to individual customers.[29] Loyalty programs are a critical foundation of what has become known as one-to-one marketing.

- *Institute a total quality control policy.* Total quality control (TQC) or total quality management (TQM) is an operating philosophy that has its roots in the late 1970s when the Japanese took seriously the teachings of W. Edwards Deming.[30] He called for a total commitment to excellence from top management exemplified by an effective system of quality circles (groups of employees regularly meeting to help solve problems), an employee suggestion system, wide use of statistical quality control principles, a goal of "zero defects," and constant training programs. A commitment to quality helps ensure that the products a firm produces will satisfy its customers and therefore foster trust among the parties and promote repeat sales.

- *Introduce an early warning system to identify problems.* By the time a customer shows up as a cancellation in a system, it normally is too late for retention measures to work. Early warning systems identify customers who buy less and prompt marketing efforts to reach them before they are lost customers. The system identifies potential defectors with behavior analysis and surveys, knowing that monitoring quality and performance must occur through the eyes of the consumer.[31] In its simplest form, learning what the customer expects in quality and performance and monitoring customer response continually, through focus groups, regular surveys, or salespeople,[32] provide information needed for firms to strengthen customer relationships.

- *Build realistic expectations.* Remember that satisfaction is based on an assessment of how consumers' expectations about a product are met. A consumer purchasing a cellular phone based on its offer of "clearest reception in the entire metropolitan area," who later finds geographical limits on the phone's range, will be unhappy with the purchase, the product, and the brand because of the unrealistic advertising claim. Exaggeration, which often leads to dissatisfaction, undermines other organizational programs designed to enhance loyalty and promote repeat purchase.

- *Provide guarantees.* Product guarantees have grown robustly through the years taking some of the perceived risk out of buying a particular brand or product. Although there is evidence that guarantees have greater effects on evaluations of new brands,[33] all companies can use them to encourage a sale and begin a relationship with a customer.

- *Provide information on product use.* Consumers must be given information on how products should be used (to ensure the best possible performance), while product designers should anticipate how consumers may try to adapt its use to fit into their lifestyles or actual usage conditions. For example, buyers often stretch the description of an electric toaster's intended use for sliced bread to include bagels, English muffins, rolls, and other types of baked goods. Since these items are often thicker than the product the toaster was designed to handle, dissatisfaction and frustration occur, leading to a tarnished relationship with the customer. Providing accurate information about correct usage for bread not only enhances satisfaction with the toaster but may create opportunities for the manufacturer to sell additional, specialized ovens or toasters for other products.

- *Solicit customer feedback.* If an organization wants to foster customer loyalty and repeat purchase behavior, it needs to know how it is performing in the eyes of the customer. A customer feedback system—as simple as a 1-800 number to a more complex proactive customer satisfaction survey—allows firms to capture this information. Feedback must reach all levels of management and serve as input for constant improvement in terms of sales methods, advertising and communication programs, and product design.

- *Acknowledge, address, and rectify consumer complaints.* Some organizations employ a person (and on a grander scale a consumer affairs department) to hear customer complaints and cool down irate customers. Key to the success of this process is the acknowledgment of the problem and ability of the company representative to fix the problem. If a complaint is voiced but the person hearing the complaint isn't empowered to rectify the problem, frustration with the product, brand, and company increases. Organizations also become frustrated in the complaint process; unfortunately for consumers, a company's willingness to listen and respond tends to decrease as the number of complaints increases.[34]

  Sometimes large-scale problems due to product defects occur, as was the case with tainted hamburger meat at the U.S. fast-food chain Jack-In-The-Box and with Coke in Belgium in the summer of 1999. Fatalities and illness resulting from product use or misuse can devastate a company's reputation, acceptance, and profits. Moreover, how the company handles these tragedies can affect long-term performance in the marketplace as much as the actual events. Denying a problem without substantial support of "no corporate wrongdoing" or blaming the consumer (for misuse) can destroy customer relations that may have taken years to build. Often, an immediate and apologetic recognition of a serious problem accompanied by a recall might fend off consumer outrage, panic, and defection.

- *Reinforce customer loyalty.* Based on learning theory—behaviors that are rewarded are repeated—customer loyalty programs can help influence purchase behaviors. Ranging from simple letters reminding customers that their insurance company is still interested in them to offering special promotions for very loyal or frequent buyers, these programs have evolved into valuable tools for building and maintaining customer relationships.[35]

When marketing programs are implemented well, they deliver a superior consumer experience. Consumers tend to repeat their purchase behavior and develop loyalty to a company and its brands or outlets, leading to increased sales and profits and invaluable information on how to improve existing strategies. This information flow feeds the never-ending process of marketing strategy and the improvement of all parts of its implementation.

Global Marketing Strategy

Perhaps no manager should be promoted to a position of major responsibility in a contemporary organization if that individual cannot "think globally." Corporations such as Coca-Cola, IBM, Gillette, Nestle, Sony, and Unilever derive more than 50 percent of their sales outside their country of origin, making a global perspective a necessity in strategic planning today. Thinking globally involves the ability to understand markets beyond one's own country of origin with respect to:

1. Sources of demand: selling to markets throughout the world

2. Sources of supply: sourcing materials, expertise, and management from the world

3. Methods of effective management and marketing: learning from firms around the world how best to manage and market globally[36]

Growth-oriented firms, striving for enhanced shareholder value (ESV), have increasingly looked to global expansion as a way to achieve growth objectives, especially once they have reached market share dominance in their own countries. Some countries, and therefore firms that are domiciled within them, have more experience in global practices. The Netherlands has a history of global trading and operations stretching over 400 years. The Dutch East India Co. dominated the world economically for many years, and Holland was the second largest owner of U.S. investments until recently. Although U.S. firms were able to survive for many years serving their country's markets because of sheer size, European firms had to learn to trade across national borders if they wanted to grow substantially. This history has positioned corporate giants, such as Unilever, Shell, KLM, and Phillips, for global competition and success.

Globalization is not limited, however, to large firms. The growing world population, which reached six billion people in October 1999, represents an intriguing possibility for growth and profitability for large and small firms alike. Small, relatively obscure companies with specialized "niches" or market segments that transcend national boundaries are likely to export and be successful. In fact, 80 percent of the 100,000 U.S. companies that export are small businesses.[37] Because of their size, small firms tend to be flexible and adapt to local markets well. Small organizations are expected to continue fueling growth in global business as they use the Internet to reach global markets.

Global Market Analysis and Strategy

Global market analysis starts with understanding markets on a global basis in terms of people. What are their needs, ability and authority to buy, and willingness to spend? How do they differ from consumers to whom we already sell? As highlighted in Consumer in Focus 2.3, today's consumers have the opportunity to buy from a myriad of foreign-made and globally branded products found in stores from London to Sao Paulo or on the Internet. But consumers also must choose from ideas, advertisements, and friends representing a diversity of nations and cultures. Cultural, ethnic, and motivation variables affect how consumers make purchase decisions, thus increasing the need for consumer analysts and researchers to help design global marketing strategies. Firms look to consumer analysts to help identify growing populations and segments of consumers economically able to buy products, and strategies for how to reach them effectively. Although this chapter discusses global marketing and consumer behavior from a strategy standpoint, Chapter 7 focuses on global consumer and population trends, and Chapter 11 focuses on cultural and ethnic variables.

Can Marketing Be Standardized?

Though many firms have adopted a global perspective, in which all areas of the world provide possible markets to which to sell or from which to source, is it possible to use one marketing program in all target countries? Or must marketing programs be modified for each country? There are many strategic considerations in terms of cost, brand image, advertising message and methods, and effectiveness that must be evaluated before deciding the best solution for a particular product. If marketing programs must be modified to each culture, firms will fail if they do not develop specific products, promotions, and organizations for each country.

Consumer in Focus 2.3

A Snapshot of Global Retailing

Walk down Oxford Street in London—the definitive form of "High Street Retailing"—and a new marketplace is evident on every block. You can choose from a myriad of retail concepts, including some of the most famous traditional English retailers, such as Boots, Selfridge's, and Marks and Spencer. Step inside Selfridge's, however, and you step into a global market featuring merchandise from all over the world with brands ranging from Sony (Japan) to Miele (Germany) in the household goods department, and Lindt (Switzerland) to Mars (United States) in the food court. When you shop in Boots, which now sells far more than the traditional pharmaceutical products of a "chemist," you will be served with cash registers and computer software that is among the most technologically advanced in the world, designed and produced in several different countries. And when you shop at Marks and Spencer, you can find popcorn, tortilla chips, or other salty snacks, which in fact, were probably produced in Marion, Ohio.

Venture further into the High Street shopping scene of London and you likely will see store signage, not only in English but frequently appearing in Arabic or Japanese as well, and hear other shoppers speaking in French, Yiddish, Afrikaans, German, and nearly every other language of the world. With the removal of double-decker buses and replacement of black taxis with yellow ones, this shopping experience could occur in New York City along famed Fifth Avenue. Except for variations in proportion, consumers can scan Manhattan's shopping district and find many of the same stores (or, at least, types of stores), brands, and Babylonic collection of languages. Even more important—from the perspective of this book—chances are you would find some of the same consumers.

Enormous economies of scale and advantages of unified brand image are achieved, however, if the marketing program is standardized.

At the most basic level, marketers must ask which of the following they believe is greater: the differences between or similarities among consumers of different countries and different cultures. If you agree that consumer behavior is subject to cultural universals, then you might agree with the position that advertising can be standardized. This position has intrigued marketers ever since Erik Elinder first raised it in 1965,[38] and the debate over its validity intensified with a controversial article by Ted Levitt describing the globalization of the marketplace.[39] In either instance, the reality exists that there are inherent cultural differences between consumers from different cultures that must be addressed at some level of the marketing plan.

Cross-cultural analysis is the *comparison of similarities and differences in behavioral and physical aspects of cultures.* Included are "meaning systems" of consumers in a nation that are intelligible within the cultural context of that country. Marketing practitioners need cultural empathy in order to predict how consumers will buy and use new products and to avoid "blunders" when entering a new market. **Cultural empathy** refers to *the ability to understand the inner logic and coherence of other ways of life and refrain from judging other value systems.*

Communication with consumers can occur at different stages of the purchase process, including at the time of sale. **Ethnographics** can help analyze *the subtle ways buyers and sellers interact in the marketplace and can be useful in business negotiation processes.* The more that is known about the cultures of the parties involved in the transaction (different styles and habits), the greater the likelihood of successful negotiation.[40] Communication prior to sale, in the form of advertising, is also affected by cultural variables. These variables shed light on various issues, including which attributes of a new product are likely to be more valued than others, which language should be used in the ads, and who might be an effective spokesperson for the brand or product.

How will cultural analyses change over time as consumers in Asia and Africa watch more U.S. television shows and movies, and communicate with people in

Canada and Europe on the Internet? Will they adopt some of the characteristics of these cultures? And can they, therefore, be targeted effectively with ads and communication pieces used in the United States or in Europe? Or will they still maintain their own unique cultural identities and characteristics, and require the formulation of specialized communication programs? These represent the types of questions consumer analysts will have to address in the future as the marketplace experiences increased globalization.

Intermarket Segmentation

Whether targeting European consumers or consumers around the globe, many successful global marketers identify and reach consumers through **intermarket segmentation**—*the identification of groups of customers who transcend traditional market or geographic boundaries.* Intermarket segments consist of people who have similar patterns of behavior regardless of where they live. When intermarket segmentation is adopted at a strategic level, marketing strategies focus on similar customer behavior wherever it is found in the world rather than on national boundaries as definitions of markets.[41]

Intermarket segmentation plays a key role in understanding the similarities as well as the differences between consumers and countries that become the foundation of marketing standardization—an international marketing strategy more organizations are adopting.[42] A study of 27 multinational enterprises (MNES), including companies such as General Foods, Nestle, Coca-Cola, Procter & Gamble, Unilever, and Revlon, found that 63 percent of the total marketing programs could be rated as "highly standardized."[43] These marketers have built successful strategies on the principle that "people are basically the same around the globe" even though they may vary in specific traits often influenced by structural elements such as economic resources, urbanization, and population age. *The challenge is to build the core of the marketing strategy on the universals rather than on the differences.*

An example of this strategy would be the focus on the desire to be beautiful. In a sense, young women in Tokyo and in Berlin are sisters not only "under" the skin but "on" their skin, lips, fingernails, and even in their hair styles. Consequently, they are likely to buy similar cosmetics that are promoted with similar appeals.[44] Appeals to universal images, such as mother and child, freedom from pain, and glow of health, may cut across many boundaries.

Hugo Boss, a high-quality apparel company, accomplishes intermarket segmentation by appealing to affluent, design-conscious consumers. Men who buy Boss can be found in the same types of stores, reading the same types of advertisements in globally distributed magazines, expecting the same type of fit and service, and buying at the same price points, whether they live in Munich, London, New York, Mexico City, or Hong Kong. Furthermore, the behavioral differences between men buying Boss suits and men buying Sears suits in New York are probably greater than the behavioral differences between men buying Boss in New York and men buying Boss in Hong Kong. These men are similar enough to constitute an intermarket segment. Similarly, Escada, a women's apparel and accessories label, markets to a segment of women around the world (Figure 2.9a and b).

Localization Based on Differences

As the European Union (EU) continues to fine-tune functioning as a single market, with the introduction of the euro in 1999, firms are increasingly defining market segments to consist of similar types of customers and cultures throughout Europe rather than groups within a specific country. But as more businesses treat the EU as one common market, will the cultural identities of each country

Figure 2.9a   Intermarket Segmentation of Fashion

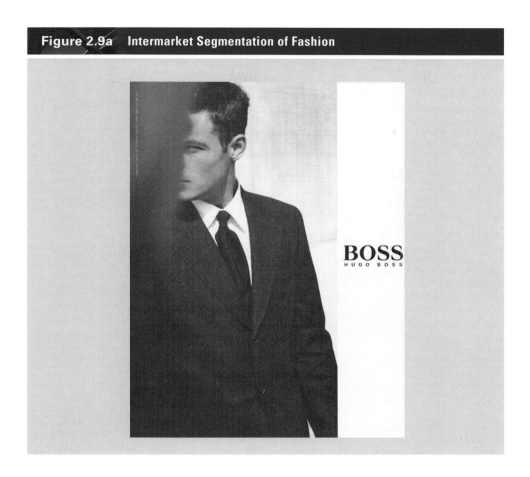

disappear? Will the French become more or less French if treated as a generic European? The answer depends on whether a firm's implementation of marketing strategies is based on the similarities among consumers or the differences between consumers.

True localization of marketing strategies would argue for different products and ads in every country of the world. Although this is economically inefficient and impractical, it is necessary to examine the needs and wants of specific markets and to adapt products, packaging, and advertising based on the differences between markets and the consumer behavior patterns of the target markets. Therefore, going global and acting local has become the choice of many marketers.

Before Japanese cars were introduced in the United States, the cars had to be redesigned so that the steering wheels were on the left side of the car. How many Americans would have bought Hondas had the steering wheel been on the "wrong" side? You might think that medicines would be the same around the world because they are used for the same human species. Yet, it is not uncommon to see the same medicine dispensed according to local preferences: capsules in the United States and Canada, tablets in England, injections in Germany, and suppositories in France.

Global Advertising Effectiveness

In a global business environment, many firms turn to advertising to communicate with new consumers around the world. This can be done through either globalized or localized advertising campaigns. Global campaigns focus on sending

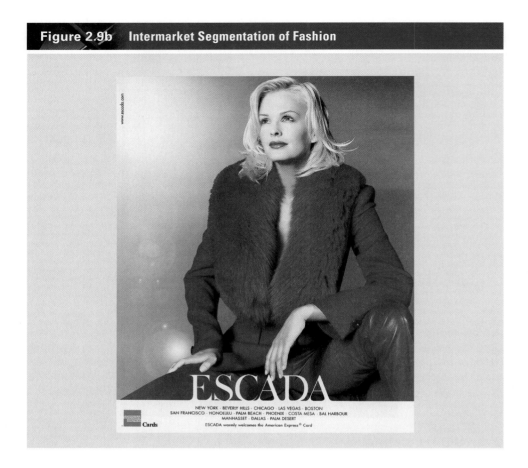

Figure 2.9b   Intermarket Segmentation of Fashion

the same message to consumers around the world. Localized campaigns adapt messages to the norms of the different cultures addressed in a particular market.

Global advertising agencies can be efficient in implementing globalized advertising campaigns that relay the same message to each market regardless of geographical location. At first, Nestle found difficulties in promoting its Nescafe line to consumers in different cultures because the definition of coffee is different for many people. Japan has a tea culture; France, Germany, and Brazil like ground coffee; the United Kingdom has embraced instant coffee. Nestle decided to sell "coffeeness" around the world rather than selling coffee. By selling the aroma and feelings associated with coffeeness and allowing consumers to decide what coffee means to them, Nescafe has overcome cultural differences and linked Nescafe advertising in 50 countries.

Some advertising messages and specific product characteristics tend to be suited better than others for a globalized advertising approach. These characteristics are summarized as follows:

1. The communications message is based on similar lifestyles.
2. The appeal of the ad is to basic human needs and emotions.
3. The product satisfies universal needs and desires.[45]

Although global advertising campaigns might be effective for some products and firms, others need to recognize cultural differences and adapt their campaigns accordingly.[46] McCain Foods, the distributor of a highly successful brand of frozen french-fried potato, decided to adapt its advertising to the local tastes and norms of specific markets. Television commercials seen in Germany show the potatoes served at the dinner table with a glass of beer nearby. If the same ad were shown in France, it would be less effective because wine is the usual drink with meals.

Global marketers are faced with the tradeoff between the efficiencies of standardized advertising and the effectiveness and cultural sensitivity of localized campaigns. Some global advertising, though uniform in its message throughout the world, uses language or stereotypes to keep the feeling associated with the product distinctive. Using words from another language in an ad violates the reader's grammar expectations, and attracts attention.[47] Although foreign text may catch the attention of a reader, it might also cause miscommunication if the words are not understood.

Regardless of advertising approach, implementation of the campaign in a new market can be successful only if the strategic landscape of that market is understood. For example, firms in the United States typically spend about 3 percent of sales on advertising. In Australia, the advertising to sales ratio is typically between 7 and 8 percent, in Sweden about 5 percent, in Mexico a little more than 5 percent, and in Canada between 4 and 5 percent.[48] An American company entering Australia may underbudget for advertising according to local practices, which could decrease the effectiveness of the campaign because of lower levels of exposure. In Japan, comparative advertising is not permitted by the Advertising Code, which explains, "Let us avoid slandering, defaming and attacking others."[49] Marketing programs in Japan are strongly influenced by Confucianism, which places high value on self-esteem, reciprocity, and harmony. Values are also derived from Buddhism, leading to a need for simplicity and a dominant aesthetic sense as well as loyalty and satisfaction in interpersonal relationships.[50]

Overcoming Language Problems

Language problems must be overcome to standardize marketing programs and avoid blunders such as these: In a Paris hotel, a sign requests that guests "Please leave your values at the desk." In Bangkok, a dry cleaner's advertising suggests that customers "Drop your trousers here for best results." In a Norwegian cocktail lounge, the message may have been a bit confused by a sign that says, "Ladies are requested not to have children in the bar." A Coors slogan in English, "Turn it Loose," in Spanish, became "Suffer from Diarrhea."[51] Linguistic techniques borrowed from cross-cultural methodologies are helpful to marketers in overcoming such problems.

A useful technique for overcoming language problems is **back-translation.** In this procedure, *a message* (word or a series of words) *is translated from its original language to the translated language and then back to the original by several translators.* The purpose of the iterations is to attempt to achieve conceptual equivalency in meaning by controlling the various translation biases of translators.[52]

Brand Names

Brand names should be evaluated from a cross-cultural perspective even if currently used only in domestic markets. "Thinking globally" includes considering the possibility that the brand will someday be extended to other countries, as well as making it more appealing to diverse cultures within the current country. Coined names are increasing in popularity among Fortune 500 companies because they do not need to be translated. This makes names like Exxon and Xerox very effective in a global market.

Among the questions that need to be answered before settling on an English brand name are the following:

1. Does the English name of the product have another meaning, perhaps unfavorable, in one or more of the countries where it might be marketed?

2. Can the English name be pronounced everywhere? For example, Spanish and some other languages lack a "k" in their alphabets, an initial letter in many popular U.S. brand names.

3. Is the name close to that of a foreign brand, or does it duplicate another product sold in English-speaking countries?

4. If the product is distinctly American, will national pride and prejudice work against the acceptance of the product?[53]

Global brands can have substantial advantages for creating awareness for a product or brand worldwide. As consumers travel between countries, global brands are easily recognized and often trusted. Global brands often have helpful associations as well. The image of being global often adds legitimacy to the brand in addition to the association of being competitive and having staying power. A country association to a brand occurs frequently. Grey Poupon is French mustard, Steiff is German stuffed animals, and Levi's is American jeans.[54] If a country has the perception in the mind of consumers to produce the best product in a specific category, a distinct country-of-origin association and advantage is created. Figure 2.10 shows how advertisers have used the country of origin or country association to appeal to new furniture buyers.

Figure 2.10   Country of Origin as an Advertising Appeal

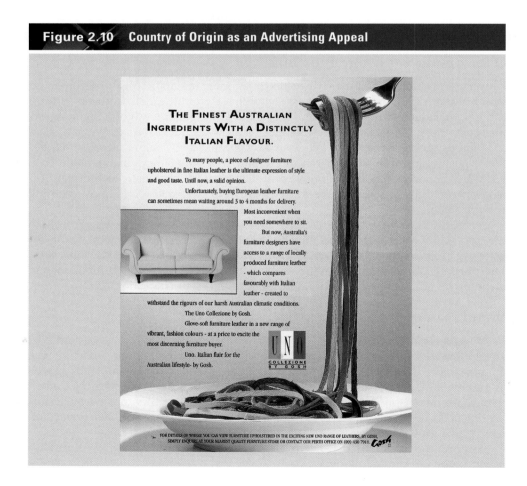

Although global brands often work well, many companies are realizing that globalization is not an all-or-nothing proposition. There are many parts to a brand: the name, symbol, slogan, and associations. Many marketers, including Coca-Cola, are finding that although they have a global brand, not all portions of the brand are global. Diet Coke is sold in the United States, whereas the same product is sold as Coca-Cola Light in Europe because of restrictions on using the word *diet* when no medicinal connotation is intended. Many marketers globalize those elements for which there is a payoff in cost or impact but let other elements of a product's brand equity be customized to local markets.

Summary

You have seen in the previous pages that consumer focus, a bedrock premise of marketing, has become even more a driving force in the contemporary economy. Marketing that works well in the long run results from a series of win–win exchanges with consumers, sometimes known as relationship selling. In order for marketing and sales to generate a strong foundation for corporate growth, both parties involved need to be satisfied during the exchange.

As we see it, several key factors will determine success or failure of consumer-based marketing strategies: (1) getting close to the consumer, (2) individualized marketing, (3) priority commitment to customer satisfaction and retention, and (4) a focus on global marketing strategy. And at the center of market analysis, market segmentation, and marketing mix strategies is the consumer.

For students of consumer behavior, a new era has emerged. The easy times of the 20th century (growth populations, high levels of demand and need for products, slower pace of society, lower expectations from consumers, vast labor pools) that characterized success in most industrialized nations have changed, leaving many academics and executives examining the fundamental assumptions and guidelines underlying strategy formulation.[55] What was once a competitive environment in which many good players could, and did, win is evolving into one best characterized as "hypercompetitive." Intense competition has sparked the popularity of customer retention programs (loyalty programs) among firms in a variety of industries. Customer retention can be enhanced through such tactics as creating realistic expectations, ensuring that product and service quality meet expectations, monitoring satisfaction and customer-retention levels, offering guarantees, and meeting dissatisfaction head-on by quick and appropriate response.

Consumer behavior analysts are increasingly required to understand buying and consumption decisions on a global basis. Cross-cultural analysis, the systematic comparison of similarities and differences in the behavioral and physical aspects of cultures, provides an approach to understanding market segments both across national boundaries and between groups within a society. The process of analyzing consumers on a cross-cultural basis is particularly helpful in deciding which elements of a marketing program can be standardized in multiple nations and which elements must be localized.

Review and Discussion Questions

1. Why does market segmentation exist? Is the use of market segmentation strategies by organizations harmful or helpful to consumers and to society?

2. What are some of the most common bases used for market segmentation?

3. What criteria for selecting segments should be used by an organization in deciding which segments to target?

4. Using the concept of consumer insight and marketing mix, choose a product that has been introduced to the market in the last two years and explain why you think it has succeeded.

5. Suppose you are the marketing manager for a new Ford sports car. How would you use intermarket segmentation to develop marketing strategies for Ford?

6. In reference to your answer to question 5, how would you best communicate to the target audience? Describe your promotion campaign for Ford.

7. Suppose you are the owner and operator of a small specialty store selling breads and pastries. How would you build a loyalty program to maximize customer loyalty and retention?

Endnotes

1. David Cravens, Gordon Greenley, Nigel Piercy, and Stanley Slater, "Integrating Contemporary Strategic Perspectives," *Long Range Planning* (August 1997), 493–506.

2. Dhruv Grewal, Kent B. Monroe, and R. Krishnan, "The Effects of Price-Comparison Advertising on Buyers' Perceptions of Acquisition Value, Transaction Value, and Behavioral Intentions," *Journal of Marketing* 52 (April 1988), 46–59.

3. Robert Woodruff, "Customer Value: The Next Source for Competitive Advantage," *Journal of the Academy of Marketing Science* 25, 2 (Winter 1998), 139–153.

4. A. Parasuraman, "Reflections on Gaining Competitive Advantage Through Customer Value," *Journal of the Academy of Marketing Science* 25, 2 (Spring 1997), 154–161.

5. "Flops," *Fitness Week* (August 16, 1993), 79.

6. Cyndee Miller, "Survey: New Product Failure Is Top Management's Fault," *Marketing News* (February 1, 1993), 2.

7. Jan-Benedict E. M. Steenkamp, Frenkel ter Hofstede, and Michel Wedel, "A Cross-National Investigation into the Individual and National Cultural Antecedents of Consumer Innovativeness," *Journal of Marketing* 63, 2 (April 1999), 55–69.

8. Kristina Blackwell and Roger Blackwell, *Consumer Insight,* prepared for Kodak, Inc., (September 1999).

9. Jacob Goldenberg, David Mazursky, and Sorin Solomon, "Toward Identifying the Inventive Templates of New Products: A Channeled Ideation Approach," *Journal of Marketing Research* 36, 2 (May 1999).

10. Evert Gummersson, "Implementation Requires a Relationship Marketing Program," *Journal of the Academy of Marketing Science* 26 (Summer 1998), 242–249.

11. "Shoot Out at the Check-Out," *The Economist* (June 5, 1993), 69.

12. W. Chan Kim, Renee Mauborgne, "Value Innovation: The Strategic Logic of High Growth," *Harvard Business Review* (January/February 1997), 103–114.

13. James H. Gilmore and B. Joseph Pine II, "The Four Faces of Mass Customization," *Harvard Business Review* (January/February 1997), 91–102.

14. Martha Rogers and Bill Pepper, *The One To One Future* (Bantam, Doubleday, 1997).

15. Frenkel Ter Hofstede, Jan-Benedict E. M. Steenkamp, and Michel Wedel, "International Market Segmentation Based on Consumer-Product Relations," *Journal of Marketing Research* 36 (February 1999), 1–17.

16. Jagdish Sheth and Rajendra Sisodia, "Revisiting Marketing's Lawlike Generalizations" *Journal of the Academy of Marketing Science* 27, 1 (Winter 1999), 71–87.

17. Roger Blackwell and Kristina Blackwell, "Changing Consumption Trends," *International Mass Retail Association* (1997).

18. Mark Stiving, Greg Allenby, and Russell Winter, "An Empirical Analysis of Price Endings with Scanner Data," *Journal of Consumer Research* 24 (June 1997), 57–67.

19. Kevin Lane Keller, Susan E. Heckler, and Michael J. Houston, "The Effects of Brand Name Suggestiveness on Advertising Recall," *Journal of Marketing* 62, 1 (January 1998).

20. Nigel Piercy, "Marketing Implementation: The Implications of Marketing Paradigm Weakness for the Strategy Execution Process," *Journal of the Academy of Marketing Science* 26, 2 (Spring 1998), 222–236.

21. Steve Schriver, "Customer Loyalty: Going, Going . . ." *American Demographics* (September 1997), 20–21.

22. Ibid.

23. Michael M. Pearson and Buy H. Gessner, "Transactional Segmentation to Slow Customer Defections," *Marketing Management* 8, 3 (Summer 1999).

24. Mark P. Pritchard, Mark E. Havitz, and Dennis R. Howard, "Analyzing the Commitment-Loyalty Link in Service Contexts," *Journal of the Academy of Marketing Science* 27, 3 (Summer 1999), 333–348.

25. Matt Nannery, "Disloyalty Programs," *Chain Store Age* (March 1999), 126.

26. Marcia Mogelonsky, "Supermarket Loyalty," *American Demographics* (November 1997), 36.

27. C. B. Bhattacharya, "When Customers Are Members: Customer Retention in Paid Membership Contexts," *Journal of the Academy of Marketing Science* 26, 1 (Winter 1998), 31–44.

28. Doroty Dowling, "Frequent Perks Keep Travelers Loyal," *American Demographics* (September 1998), 32–36.

29. Power, "How to Get Closer to Your Customers," 44–54.

30. For a valuable summary of Deming's methods, see Mary Walton, *The Deming Management Method* (New York: Dodd, Mead, & Company, 1986). See, for example, Frank Rose, "Now Quality Means Service Too," *Fortune* (April 22, 1991), 98–110; and Gilbert Fuchsberg, "Gurus of Quality Are Gaining Clout," *The Wall Street Journal* (November 27, 1990), B1.

31. William Band, "Performance Metrics Keep Customer Satisfaction Programs on Track," *Marketing News* (May 28, 1990), 12.

32. Lawrence A. Crosby, Kenneth R. Evans, and Deborah Cowles, "Relationship Quality in Services Selling: An Interpersonal Influence Perspective," *Journal of Marketing* 54 (July 1990), 68–81.

33. Daniel E. Innis and H. Rao Unnava, "The Usefulness of Product Warranties for Reputable and New Brands," in Holman and Solomon, *Advances,* 317–322.

34. Claes Fornell and Robert A. Westbrook, "The Vicious Cycle of Consumer Complaints," *Journal of Marketing* 48 (Summer 1984), 68–78.

35. Blaise Bergiel and Christine Trosclair, "Instrumental Learning: Its Application to Consumer Satisfaction," *Journal of Consumer Marketing* 2 (Fall 1985), 23–28.

36. Salah Hassan and Roger Blackwell, *Global Marketing Perspectives and Cases* (Forth Worth, TX: The Dryden Press, 1993), 3.

37. "Three Small Businesses Profit by Taking on the World," *The Wall Street Journal* (November 8, 1990), B2.

38. Erik Elinder, "How International Can European Advertising Be?" *Journal of Marketing* 29 (April 1965), 7–11.

39. Theodore Levitt, "The Globalization of Markets," *Harvard Business Review* 61 (May/June 1983), 92–102. For the contrasting perspective, see Yoram Wind, "The Myth of Globalization," *Journal of Consumer Marketing* 3 (Spring 1986), 23–26.

40. Brian Mark Hawrysh and Judith Lynne Zaichkowsky, "Cultural Approaches to Negotiations: Understanding the Japanese," *European Journal of Marketing* 25 (1991), 51–60.

41. Salah Hassan and Roger Blackwell, *Global Marketing Perspectives and Cases* (Fort Worth, TX: The Dryden Press, 1993), 53–57.

42. Robert D. Buzzell, "Can You Standardize Multinational Marketing?" *Harvard Business Review* 46 (November/December 1986), 102–113; Theodore Levitt, "The Globalization of Markets," *Harvard Business Review* 61 (May/June 1983), 92–102; "Multinationals Tackle Global Marketing," *Advertising Age* (June 25, 1984), 50ff. Also see "Marketers Turn Sour on Global Sales Pitch Harvard Guru Makes," *The Wall Street Journal* (May 11, 1988), 1.

43. Ralph Z. Sorenson and Ulrich E. Wiechmann, "How Multinationals View Marketing Standardization," *Harvard Business Review* 53 (May/June 1975), 38–56. Also see William H. Davidson and Philippe Haspeslagh, "Shaping a Global Product Organization," *Harvard Business Review* 60 (July/August 1982), 125–132.

44. Arthur Fatt, "The Danger of 'Local' International Advertising," *Journal of Marketing* 31 (January 1967), 60–62.

45. Roger Blackwell, Riad Ajami, and Kristina Stephan, "Winning the Global Advertising Race: Planning Globally, Acting Locally," *Journal of International Consumer Marketing* 3 (1991), 108, 120.

46. H. Simon, "Lessons from Germany's Midsize Giants," *Harvard Business Review* (March/April 1992), 115–123.

47. Hassan and Blackwell, *Global Marketing Perspectives and Cases.*

48. Charles E. Keown, Nicolas Synodinos, Laurence Jacobs, and Reginald Worthley, "Can International Advertising Be Standardized?" World Congress of the Academy of Marketing Sciences, Barcelona, 1987. For a macroeconomic perspective on this issue, see Seymour Banks, "Cross-National Analysis of Advertising Expenditures," *Journal of Advertising Research* 26 (April/May 1986), 11–23.

49. This section abstracted from Dentsu Incorporated, *Marketing Opportunity in Japan* (London: McGraw-Hill, 1978), 84–114. Dentsu is one of the largest advertising agencies in the world.

50. Walter A. Henry, "Impact of Cultural Value Systems on Japanese Distribution Systems," in Pitts and Woodside, *Personal Values and Consumer Psychology,* 255–270.

51. Kevin Lynch, "Adplomacy Faux Pas Can Ruin Sales," *Advertising Age* (January 15, 1979), S–2ff; and "When Slogans Go Wrong," *American Demographics* (February 1992), 14.

52. Richard W. Brislin, "Back-Translation for Cross-Cultural Research," *Journal of Cross-Cultural Psychology* 1 (September 1970); Oswald Werner and Donald T. Campbell, "Translating, Working through Interpreters and the Problems of Decentering," in Raoul Naroll and Ronald Cohen, eds., *A Handbook of Method in Cultural Anthropology* (Garden City, NY: National History Press, 1970), 298–420.

53. Walter P. Margulies, "Why Global Marketing Requires a Global Focus on Product Design," *Business Abroad* 94 (January 1969), 22–34.

54. David A. Aaker, *Managing Brand Equity* (New York: The Free Press, 1991), 263–269.

55. David Cravens, "Implementation Strategies in the Market-Driven Strategy Era," *Journal of the Academy of Marketing Science* 26, 3 (Summer 1998), 237–241.

Suggested Readings for Part I

Narsh K. Malhotra, Mark Peterson, and Susan Bardi Kleiser, "Marketing Research: A State of the Art Review and Directions for the Twenty-First Century," *Journal of the Academy of Marketing Science* 27, 2 (Spring 1999), 160–183.

Kendra Parker, "How Do You Like Your Beef?" *American Demographics* (January 2000), 35–37.

Kendra Parker, "Got Questions? All You Have to Do Is Ask," *American Demographics* (November 1999), 36–39.

Kevin Lane Keller, "The Brand Report Card," *Harvard Business Review* (January/February 2000), 147–157.

Frenkel Ter Hofstede, Jan-Benedict E. M. Steenkamp, and Michel Wedel, "International Market Segmentation Based on Consumer-Product Relations," *Journal of Marketing Research* 36 (February 1999), 1–17.

Ruth N. Bolton, P. K. Kannan, and Matthew D. Bramlett, "Implications of Loyalty Program Membership and Service Experiences for Customer Retention and Value," *Journal of the Academy of Marketing Science* 28, 1 (Winter 2000), 95–108.

Nancy Shepherson, "Holding All the Cards: Grocers want frequent-shopper programs to get up closer and very personal," *American Demographics* (February 2000), 35–37.

Mark P. Pritchard, Mark E. Havitz, and Dennis R. Howard, "Analyzing the Commitment-Loyalty Link in Service Contexts," *Journal of the Academy of Marketing Science* 27, 3 (Summer 1999), 333–348.

Bernard Jaworski, Ajay K. Kohli, and Arvind Sahay, "Market-Driven Versus Driving Markets," *Journal of the Academy of Marketing Science* 28, 1 (Winter 2000), 45–54.

Jagdish N. Sheth, Rajendra S. Sisodia, Arun Sharma, "The Antecedents and Consequences of Customer-Centric Marketing," *Journal of the Academy of Marketing Science* 28, 1 (Winter 2000), 55–66.

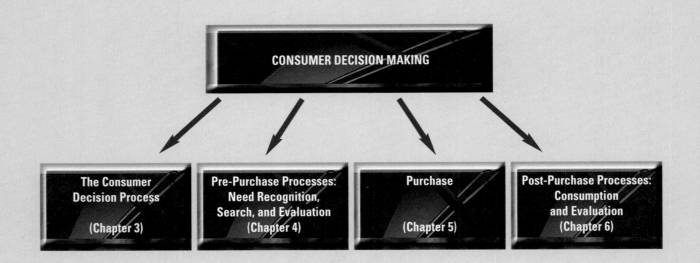

PART II

Consumer Decision Making

Because what we buy and use is ultimately the result of some decision we have made, understanding consumer behavior requires appreciating how people make their purchase and consumption decisions. Part II of the text is designed to give you such an appreciation.

Chapter 3 introduces a model of the consumer decision process, which features the seven major stages of decision making and the variables that affect activities in these stages. The model shows how consumers purchase products to solve problems and highlights the activities that occur before, during, and after the purchase of a product. Take special time to understand this model as it is presented—it has served as a point of study in the field of consumer behavior, and it provides the structure for the remainder of this book.

Chapter 4 focuses on the *pre-purchase* stages of the decision process model—need recognition, information search, and alternative evaluation. It begins with need recognition and what causes consumers to begin searching for a product, service, or solution to fulfill their needs and wants. The focus then shifts to the internal and external search for information. Where do consumers get information about how to satisfy their needs? How long do they search for information needed to make decisions before they are ready to evaluate their alternatives? This leads to the next topic of the chapter: pre-purchase alternative evaluation. As you'll see, there are many different ways in which consumers can evaluate choice alternatives during decision making.

Chapter 5 focuses on purchase—how and where consumers buy products, and what factors influence their purchase behaviors. This chapter examines the various retail options available to consumers and the strategies successful retailers are implementing to compete for consumer patronage.

Chapter 6 explores the *post-purchase* stages in the consumer decision process—consumption and post-consumption evaluation. Consumption consists of how and when consumers use products, including whether or not they use them as instructed and intended, and whether they use them soon after purchase or store them for later use. Decision making does not stop with consumption, however, because there is likely to be continued evaluation of the product or service leading to a response of satisfaction or dissatisfaction, which has significant implications for customer retention.

The Consumer Decision Process

OPENING VIGNETTE

Procter & Gamble wants to increase the proportion of clothing you clean with its products. Although you might already wash your clothes with Tide and Bounce fabric softener, most consumers have additional cleaning needs not fulfilled by existing P&G products. To identify consumers' unmet clothing care needs, the company turned to consumption research in which marketers interviewed thousands of consumers about their current cleaning methods and products. P&G found that consumers tend to wear their "dry-clean-only" garments more often without cleaning than they do their washable clothing. Why? Many reasons were discovered, including high dry cleaning costs, wear-and-tear on the garments of commercial dry cleaning, and lack of time to take and retrieve clothing from the dry cleaner.

All these consumer *problems* led to the introduction of Dryel to the marketplace in 1998. Dryel is a garment-cleaning kit designed to let consumers do their own dry cleaning at home in their dryers—a new *alternative* to buying services from a retail dry cleaner. Consumers can remove stains and refresh their clothing by placing them in special applicator bags that release a solvent during the process.

P&G tested the at-home dry cleaning alternative, and consumers responded favorably. They were pleased with the quality of the product, the ease of *consuming* or *using* the product, and how their clothes looked and smelled after cleaning. They also liked the convenience of *purchasing* Dryel at grocery stores and discount retailers. All these factors contributed to the overall *satisfaction* consumers felt with the product and the at-home cleaning process. By studying closely how consumers used and reacted to the product, P&G was able to anticipate overall satisfaction ratings and the likelihood of repurchase, leading to its decision to introduce the product.

To disseminate *information* about the new product to consumers, the company introduced a set of television commercials—each one highlighting a different consumer problem solved by Dryel. One ad features a woman racing to her local dry cleaner, jumping over obstacles, to retrieve a garment she needs that evening. She reaches the store only to see the "closed" sign hanging on the front door. The ad goes on to explain how to use the product and where to purchase it.

The manufacturer and marketer of some of the world's best-known brands, including Pampers, Head & Shoulders, and Folger's, used consumption research to identify a problem unmet by its current product line. P&G marketers formulated their product development and marketing strategies based on the consumer decision process model and entered the dry cleaning business.

In order to thrive in the hypercompetitive climate of the future, firms of all sizes and types must focus on the first order of any business transaction—namely,

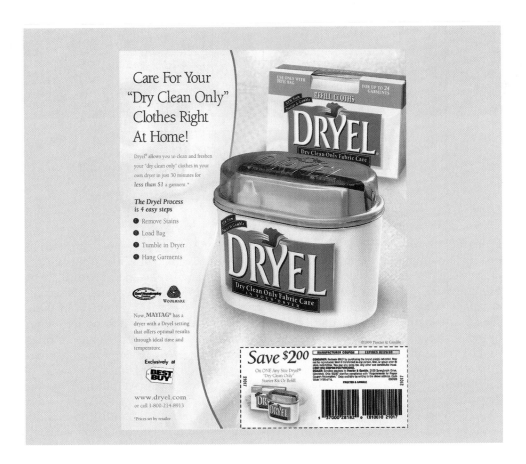

understanding how consumers make product and purchase decisions. Quite simply, businesses and nonprofit organizations alike have to analyze and understand the minds of the end users of every product that is made and every service that is offered in order to formulate strategies to keep existing customers and entice new ones. This Dryel example illustrates that, by understanding why consumers buy certain products instead of others, how they buy them, and how lifestyle, demographic, and environmental factors affect their choices, marketers can determine how to meet customers' needs and wants. Sometimes meeting these needs means introducing new products, reformulating existing ones, or altering communication strategies to reach new consumer segments. And sometimes it results in removing products from retailers' shelves.

The Consumer Decision Process Model

You've just arrived at the airport in a strange city and have rented a car to get to your hotel. If you don't know how to get there, you have two choices—use a set of directions detailing the roads you need to take (left at High Street, left at second light onto Glenco Rd., and so forth) or study a road map. Directions seem much easier at first glance, but what happens when you hit a detour, need to go to a different destination, or simply get lost along the way? A list of streets is fairly useless in this scenario, but a roadmap can guide you to where you want to go.

In the disruptive, discontinuous markets of contemporary and future business environments, a "road map" of how consumers make purchase decisions is

Figure 3.1 **How Consumers Make Decisions for Goods and Services**

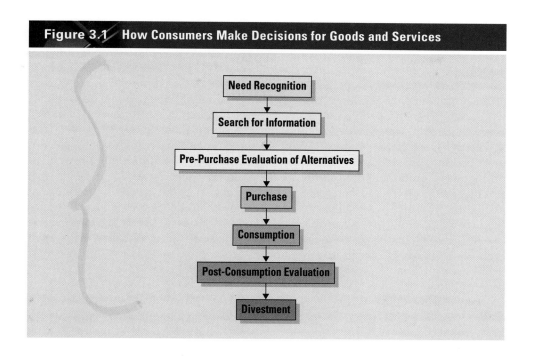

much more reliable than a set of "directions." The **Consumer Decision Process (CDP) model,** a simplified version of which is shown in Figure 3.1, represents a *roadmap of consumers' minds that marketers and managers can use to help guide product mix, communication, and sales strategies.* The model captures the activities that occur when decisions are made in a schematic format and shows how different internal and external forces interact and affect how consumers think, evaluate, and act.

No one buys a product unless they have a problem, a need, or a want, and the CDP model shows how people solve the everyday problems in life that cause them to buy and use products of all kinds. The CDP model, in its earliest state, was developed by Professors Engel, Kollat, and Blackwell at The Ohio State University, and was known as the EKB model. It served as the foundation for earlier editions of this textbook. As the textbook evolved, so did the model, which was renamed the EBM model to acknowledge the work of Professor Paul Miniard, who joined the team as co-author of the text. The goal in creating this model was to analyze how individuals sort through facts and influences to make decisions that are logical and consistent for them.

As the model shows, consumers typically go through seven major stages when making decisions: need recognition, search for information, pre-purchase evaluation, purchase, consumption, post-consumption evaluation, and divestment. Though marketing textbooks and consumer researchers sometimes employ slightly different terminology for each of the stages, the study of consumer behavior focuses primarily on these seven stages and how various factors influence each stage of consumers' decisions. By understanding the stages in the consumer decision-making roadmap, marketers can discover why people are or are not buying products and what to do to get them to buy more or from a specific supplier.

The first half of this chapter focuses on each stage of the Consumer Decision Process model. Pay special attention to how Figures 3.2 through 3.8 build upon one another to create the complete CDP model. To make these concepts more understandable, below each figure is a "running example" of how a college student in need of a car might move through each stage.

Stage One: Need Recognition

The starting point of any purchase decision is a customer need (or problem). **Need recognition** occurs when *an individual senses a difference between what he or she perceives to be the* ideal *versus the* actual *state of affairs*. Consumers don't just walk into a store and say, "I notice you have things to sell. I have some extra money I would like to spend so just pick something out and charge it to my credit card." Consumers buy things when they believe a product's ability to solve a problem is worth more than the cost of buying it, thereby, making recognition of an unmet need the first step in the sale of a product. Need recognition, sometimes called problem recognition, shown in Figure 3.2 is one of the focal topics of Chapter 4.

In addition to needs, consumers have desires, as is the case with the student in Figure 3.2. But realistically, marketers must examine desires under a microscope of constraints, including ability and authority to buy. While marketers strive to fulfill the desires of their consumers, they must keep costs in line with what their target markets can afford. Consumers are willing to sacrifice some of their desires for affordable products that meet their needs though they might still aspire to their desires.

Marketers must *know consumers' needs*—if they know where consumers "itch," they have a better idea of where to "scratch" with new and improved products, more effective communication programs, and more user-friendly distribution channels. Firms sometimes make the mistake of developing new products based

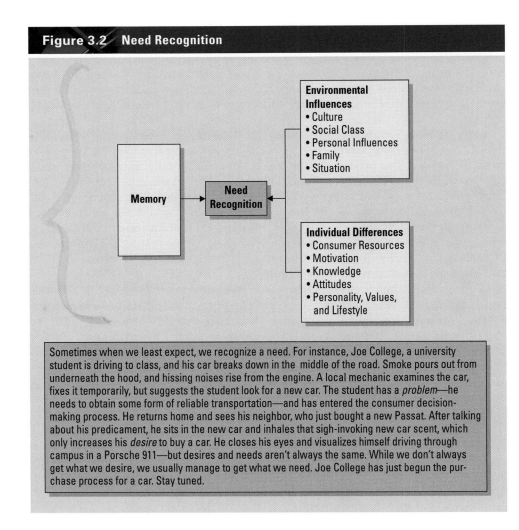

Figure 3.2   Need Recognition

Sometimes when we least expect, we recognize a need. For instance, Joe College, a university student is driving to class, and his car breaks down in the middle of the road. Smoke pours out from underneath the hood, and hissing noises rise from the engine. A local mechanic examines the car, fixes it temporarily, but suggests the student look for a new car. The student has a *problem*—he needs to obtain some form of reliable transportation—and has entered the consumer decision-making process. He returns home and sees his neighbor, who just bought a new Passat. After talking about his predicament, he sits in the new car and inhales that sigh-invoking new car scent, which only increases his *desire* to buy a car. He closes his eyes and visualizes himself driving through campus in a Porsche 911—but desires and needs aren't always the same. While we don't always get what we desire, we usually manage to get what we need. Joe College has just begun the purchase process for a car. Stay tuned.

on what they are able to manufacture or sell rather than based on what consumers want to buy. Products and services that don't solve consumer problems fail, no matter how dazzling the technology or how much is spent on advertising aimed at convincing consumers to buy them.

Even stellar manufacturers like Procter & Gamble have made the mistake of flooding the market with unnecessary product variations. In the 1980s, P&G experienced slowed sales growth because of a major consolidation among retailers and a deluge of competitive knock-off products. The company fought back by introducing hundreds of slightly new but not-so-different products, such as 35 varieties of Bounce fabric softeners. In its defense, the company said its goal was to offer consumers more choices, but unfortunately, the choices didn't address any unmet needs. After years of confusing consumers and encouraging retailers to stock products that consumers didn't want to buy, Durk Jager, P&G president and CEO, began slashing the number of product variations to meet consumer desires more closely based on interviews and sales reports.

Pottery Barn fell into the category of retailers that added too many SKUs (stock keeping units) and expanded the size of the stores so much that they became unprofitable. Over-inventoried in many product categories, Pottery Barn slashed its SKUs by 30 percent. The new look? Cleaner, simpler, and more consumer-friendly stores that carry what consumers want. Before understanding purchase behavior, Pottery Barn followed the lead of other retailers that simply put more products on their shelves, hoping that someone would find something he or she needed and buy it. That's why the best retailers limit the SKUs with "category management" programs that focus on fewer SKUs and faster inventory "turns."

Retailers and manufacturers alike must monitor consumer trends because as consumers change, so do their problems and needs. Some influences most likely to alter the way consumers look at problems and the ways to solve them are *family, values, health, age, income,* and *reference groups.* Spotting *changes* in these variables is often the key to new marketing opportunities. Thirty-year-old consumers with families need to buy more detergent and shampoo (usually in larger quantity packages) than do consumers in their seventies, who may be living alone and in smaller homes with less storage space. As consumers move through different *life stages,* their needs and buying habits for many items can be expected to change. Desire also increases with the *expectation of rising income;* that's why Ford and other car manufacturers send new car information to graduating university seniors anticipating their first substantial jobs.

Marketers often communicate a need, thereby raising consumers' awareness of unperceived needs or problems. Many years ago, Listerine mouthwash used advertising to increase the awareness of "halitosis" and in the process dramatically increased mouthwash sales. Listerine did not create the problem of bad breath; it simply raised awareness of the problem. And Scope still does today with ads that make people more aware of "morning breath." Can marketers create needs? Not really, but they can show how a product meets unperceived needs or problems consumers may not have considered before.

Stage Two: Search for Information

Once need recognition occurs, consumers begin searching for information and solutions to satisfy their unmet needs. Search may be **internal,** *retrieving knowledge from memory or perhaps genetic tendencies,* or it may be **external,** *collecting information from peers, family, and the marketplace,* as shown in Figure 3.3. Sometimes consumers search passively by simply becoming more receptive to information around them, whereas at other times they engage in active search behavior, such as researching consumer publications, paying attention to ads, searching the Internet, or venturing to shopping malls and other retail outlets.

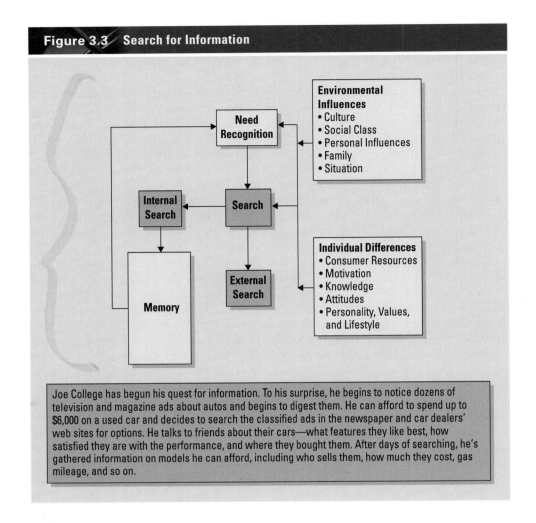

Figure 3.3 Search for Information

Joe College has begun his quest for information. To his surprise, he begins to notice dozens of television and magazine ads about autos and begins to digest them. He can afford to spend up to $6,000 on a used car and decides to search the classified ads in the newspaper and car dealers' web sites for options. He talks to friends about their cars—what features they like best, how satisfied they are with the performance, and where they bought them. After days of searching, he's gathered information on models he can afford, including who sells them, how much they cost, gas mileage, and so on.

Sometimes consumers are thrust unexpectedly into the search process, prompted by situational factors, often out of their control. When a car suddenly breaks down or a refrigerator stops running, consumers must search for information just as they would for planned purchases. But these types of situational factors might place limits on the amount of time available to search. When a refrigerator breaks suddenly, consumers need a replacement quickly—they can't afford to search as extensively as they would if they were planning the purchase.

The length and depth of search is determined by variables such as personality, social class, income, size of the purchase, past experiences, prior brand perceptions,[1] and customer satisfaction. If consumers are delighted with the brand of product they currently use, they may repurchase the brand with little if any search behavior, making it more difficult for competitive products to catch their attention. That's why victorious firms place a high priority on keeping customers satisfied. When consumers are unhappy with current products or brands, search expands to include other alternatives.

Sources of Information   As in the case of the student car buyer, consumers search a variety of sources to obtain the information they need to make product choices with which they are comfortable. These sources can be categorized as (1) marketer-dominated or (2) nonmarketer-dominated, as shown in Figure 3.4. By marketer dominated, we refer to anything that the supplier does for purposes

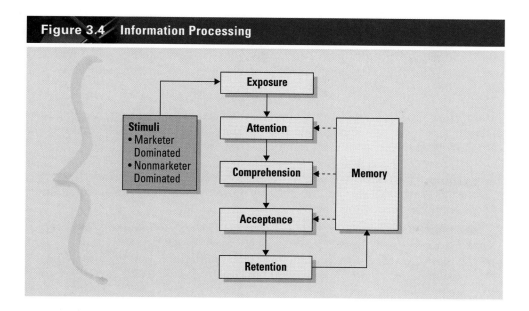

Figure 3.4 Information Processing

of information and persuasion, such as using advertising, salespersons, infomercials, web sites, and point-of-sales materials.

Search is not limited to these marketer-dominated sources. Consumers also seek information from sources over which marketers have little control, yet are critically important to consumers. Nonmarketer-dominated sources include friends, family, opinion leaders, and media. Many of these influences come in the form of word-of-mouth; others come from having consulted objective product rating sources such as *Consumer Reports,* government and industry reports, or news stories in the mass media.

Increasingly, information search is occurring on the Internet. Although some searches on the Internet may take a fairly long time, others are much speedier, depending on how the web site is designed.[2] Some researchers indicate that if on-line retailing decreases the cost of searching for price information, consumers will become more price sensitive.[3] Other studies have shown that by altering web design and making it easier to search for and compare quality information, consumers will become less price sensitive and more likely to purchase quality products.[4] It is the execution of the web site that influences how consumers will use it in the consumer decision process.

Some consumers prefer the "old-fashioned" approach to search, called shopping. Many consumers think walking and browsing through malls is fun, whereas others think it is a chore. Understanding when search is fun and when it is a chore provides valuable information for retailers. For example, the search for microwave oven information and alternatives probably doesn't excite many consumers. The most effective marketing channel in this instance minimizes the time and effort required to obtain information. That is why Best Buy, a major appliance retailer, scatters video kiosks throughout its stores; the kiosks provide in-depth information *quickly.* The search for an evening dress might be different, however. Browsing, trying on different styles, and experiencing the store's ambiance may bring pleasures of fantasy, association, and anticipation. In this case, the experience is more important than the speed with which the dress is identified and purchased.

While in-store information search is appealing to some consumers, others prefer catalog shopping—a simplified version of the traditional shopping experience. One of the reasons for the increased popularity of catalogs among consumers is that the typical catalog page provides more information for less effort than does the typical retail store. Victoria's Secret, which dominates the catalog field, allows consumers to scan hundreds of fabric, style, and color alternatives quickly without leaving home or turning on a computer. Searching its catalogs, filled with pictures of beautiful models in interesting settings, is also an entertaining way to identify the latest fashion designs.

Information Processing   As a consumer is exposed to information resulting from external search, he or she begins to process the stimuli. Figure 3.4 highlights the steps involved in processing information. They include:

1. *Exposure.* First, information and persuasive communication must *reach* consumers. Once exposure occurs, one or more of the senses are activated and preliminary processing begins.

2. *Attention.* After exposure, the next step is to allocate (or not allocate) information-processing capacity to the incoming information. The more relevant the message and its content, the more likely attention will be attracted. Consumers frequently ignore commercial persuasion at this stage and engage in selective attention.

3. *Comprehension.* If attention is attracted, the message is further analyzed against categories of meaning stored in memory. The marketer hopes that accurate comprehension will occur.

4. *Acceptance.* Once comprehension occurs, the message can be either dismissed as unacceptable (a common outcome) or accepted. The goal of the message is to modify or change existing beliefs and attitudes, but the message must be accepted before this can happen. There is a good chance of at least some change occurring if acceptance within the system or structure occurs.

5. *Retention.* Finally, the goal of any persuader is for this new information to be accepted *and* stored in memory in such a way that it is accessible for future use.

Everyone is exposed to a barrage of messages competing for their attention, but each comprehends, accepts, and retains only a few. Brand equity and favorable brand image in the minds of consumers help firms get their messages into this subset. Information processing is discussed in detail in Chapters 14–16.

Stage Three: Pre-Purchse Evaluation of Alternatives

The next stage of the consumer decision process is evaluating alternative options identified during the search process, as shown in Figure 3.5. In this stage, consumers seek answers to questions such as "What are my options?" and "Which is best?" when they compare, contrast, and select from various products or services. Consumers compare what they know about different products and brands with what they consider most important and begin to narrow the field of alternatives before they finally resolve to buy one of them.

Consumers use new or pre-existing evaluations stored in memory to select products, services, brands, and stores that will most likely result in their satisfaction with the purchase and consumption. Different consumers employ different **evaluative criteria**—*the standards and specifications used to compare different products and brands.* How individuals evaluate their choices is influenced by both individual and environmental influences, as shown in Figure 3.5. As a result, evaluative criteria become a product-specific manifestation of an individual's

[handwritten margin notes:]
Inept set
won't buy - not acceptable

Evoked set
will buy

Inert set
alternate if evoked not avail.

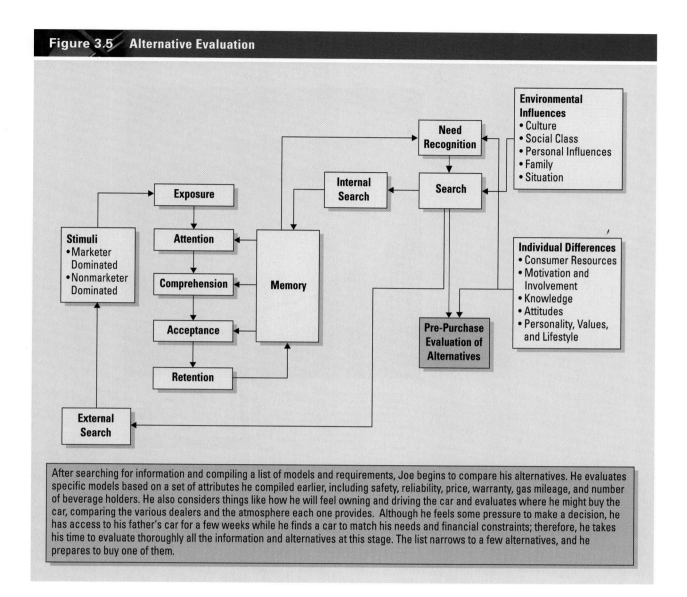

Figure 3.5   Alternative Evaluation

After searching for information and compiling a list of models and requirements, Joe begins to compare his alternatives. He evaluates specific models based on a set of attributes he compiled earlier, including safety, reliability, price, warranty, gas mileage, and number of beverage holders. He also considers things like how he will feel owning and driving the car and evaluates where he might buy the car, comparing the various dealers and the atmosphere each one provides. Although he feels some pressure to make a decision, he has access to his father's car for a few weeks while he finds a car to match his needs and financial constraints; therefore, he takes his time to evaluate thoroughly all the information and alternatives at this stage. The list narrows to a few alternatives, and he prepares to buy one of them.

needs, values, lifestyles, and so on. But consumers must also evaluate *where* they are going to purchase the desired product, and they apply relevant evaluative criteria to the retail outlets from which they will buy.

Some attributes upon which alternatives are evaluated are *salient*, and some are *determinant*, yet both affect marketing and advertising strategy. Consumers think of **salient attributes** as potentially the most important. In the case of buying a car, these would include price, reliability, and factors believed to vary little between similar types of cars. How alternatives differ on **determinant attributes** (details such as style, finish, and type of cupholders) usually *determine which brand or store consumers choose*, especially when they consider the salient attributes to be equivalent. Why do consumers prefer one brand of dishwasher over another? Dishlex, an Australian manufacturer, appeals to individuals' desire for "quietness" and strength by highlighting these attributes (see Figure 3.6).

Consumers often monitor attributes such as quantity, size, quality, and price; further, changes in these attributes can affect their brand and product choices. If consumers recognize a price increase in a brand that they prefer, they often

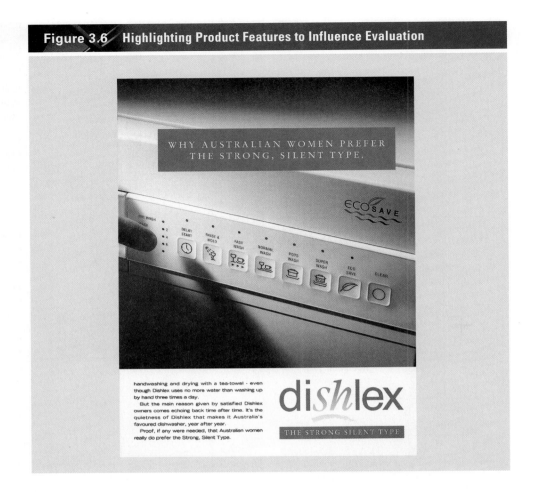

Figure 3.6   Highlighting Product Features to Influence Evaluation

evaluate the *motive* (the degree to which consumers perceive the company increasing profits is directly correlated with how "unfair" the increase is perceived)[5] of the price increase to determine whether the price change is fair or not. Perceived unfairness leads to lower shopping intentions.[6]

Recent research has focused on the elements affecting the choice process for experience goods, such as entertainment. Movies serve as a good category to research since they are experience goods that are hard to evaluate prior to viewing.[7] Although variables, such as word-of-mouth and critic reviews, have been identified as critical influencers on consumer choice of movies,[8] other psychological variables, such as emotional expectations and latent product interest, also play an important role in choice. The finding that new movie choice is influenced by emotional expectations, not by cognitive assessment of product attributes, recognizes the role of emotions in certain areas of consumer behavior.[9] In fact, when evaluating alternatives and making tradeoffs between product attributes, emotion-laden tradeoffs complicate how tradeoffs are made and what value is assigned to various attributes during the choice process.[10]

From the perspective of where to purchase, consumers may evaluate purchasing from one store over another based on consumer traffic within the store, cleanliness of the store, how often the store is out of stock of the needed item, and how many checkout lanes are available. When retailers achieve equivalence on salient attributes such as price and quality, consumers make choices based on "the details" such as ambiance or personal attention given to the customer.

Stage Four: Purchase

The next stage of the consumer decision process is purchase, shown in Figure 3.7. After deciding whether or not to purchase, consumers move through two phases. In the first phase, consumers choose one retailer over another retailer (or some other form of retailing such as catalogs, electronic sales with the aid of a TV or PC, or direct sales). The second phase involves in-store choices, influenced by salespersons, product displays, electronic media, and point-of-purchase (POP) advertising.

A consumer might move through the first three stages of the decision process according to plan and intend to purchase a particular product or brand. But consumers sometimes buy something quite different from what they intended or opt not to buy at all because of what happens during the purchase or choice stage. A consumer may prefer one retailer but choose another because of a sale or a promotional event at a competitor's store, hours of operation, location, or traffic-flow problems. Inside the store, the consumer may talk with a salesperson who changes

Figure 3.7   Purchase

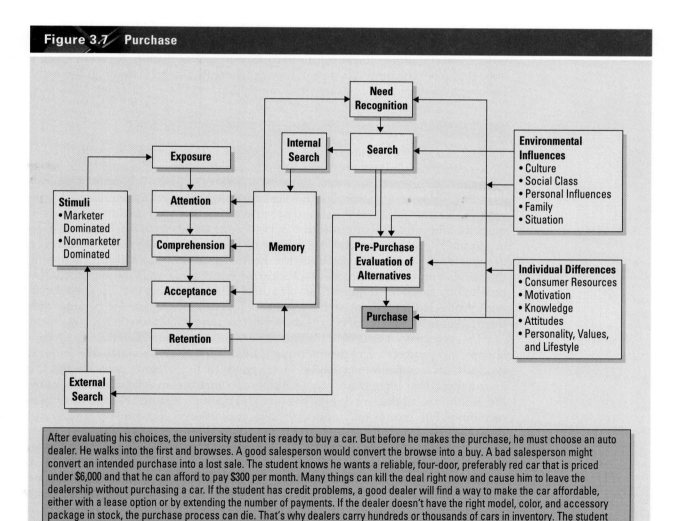

After evaluating his choices, the university student is ready to buy a car. But before he makes the purchase, he must choose an auto dealer. He walks into the first and browses. A good salesperson would convert the browse into a buy. A bad salesperson might convert an intended purchase into a lost sale. The student knows he wants a reliable, four-door, preferably red car that is priced under $6,000 and that he can afford to pay $300 per month. Many things can kill the deal right now and cause him to leave the dealership without purchasing a car. If the student has credit problems, a good dealer will find a way to make the car affordable, either with a lease option or by extending the number of payments. If the dealer doesn't have the right model, color, and accessory package in stock, the purchase process can die. That's why dealers carry hundreds or thousands of cars in inventory. The student finds a used VW Jetta that he likes and can afford, and he buys the car.

his or her decision, see an end-of-aisle display that switches his or her brand preference, use a coupon or price discount, fail to find the intended product or brand, or lack the money or right credit card to make the purchase. The best retailers manage the overall attributes and image of the store to achieve preferred patronage among the market target and to manage, in micro detail, all aspects of the in-store shopping experience.

Stage Five: Consumption

After the purchase is made and the consumer takes possession of the product, consumption can occur—the point at which consumers use the product. Figure 3.8 highlights both the consumption and post-consumption evaluation stages. Consumption can either occur immediately or be delayed. For example, if a consumer sees a sales promotion for frozen entrees, he or she may "stock up" on the item, buying more than can be used in the normal time frame of consumption. This requires consumers to "warehouse" products in freezers or on their pantry shelves. How consumers use products also affects how satisfied they are with the purchases and how likely they are to buy that particular product or brand in the future. How carefully they use or maintain the product may also determine how long the product will last before another purchase is needed. Figure 3.9 shows how Volvo highlights the consumption stage in one of its ads. Not only does it appeal to the "consumption" of safety (a salient feature), but it also highlights the hedonic benefit of consumption (thrilling feeling).

Stage Six: Post-Consumption Evaluation

The next stage of consumer decision making is post-consumption evaluation, in which consumers experience a sense of either satisfaction or dissatisfaction. *Satisfaction* occurs when consumers' expectations are matched by perceived performance; when experiences and performance fall short of expectations, *dissatisfaction* occurs. The outcomes are significant because consumers store their evaluations in memory and refer to them in future decisions, as shown by the feedback arrows in Figure 3.8. If the consumer is highly satisfied, subsequent purchase decisions become much shorter. Competitors, for the most part, have a hard time accessing the minds and decision processes of satisfied customers because these customers tend to buy the same brand at the same store. But consumers that are dissatisfied with products they buy or stores from which they buy are ripe for picking with the marketing strategies of competitors who promise something better.

The most important determinant of satisfaction is consumption: how consumers use products. The product might be good, but if consumers don't use it properly, dissatisfaction may occur. Increasingly, firms develop good care and use instructions, and offer warranties, service, and instruction programs. For example, if the student doesn't change the oil in his car, or take it in for tune-ups when recommended, the car may not perform as well as expected, causing him to feel disappointed with the outcome.

Even if the product works well, consumers often "second-guess" their purchase decisions, especially with big-ticket items, causing them to ask, "Have I made a good decision?" "Did I consider all the alternatives?" "Could I have done better?" This type of questioning is called *post-purchase regret* or *cognitive dissonance*—and the higher the price, the higher the level of cognitive dissonance. In response, successful firms have 1-800 numbers to answer questions, provide hang-tags or brochures for consumer reference, or follow up with a phone call a day or so after the sale. These tactics confirm that customers are satisfied, but more importantly, they provide information to comfort consumers.

Figure 3.8   Consumption and Post-Consumption Evaluation

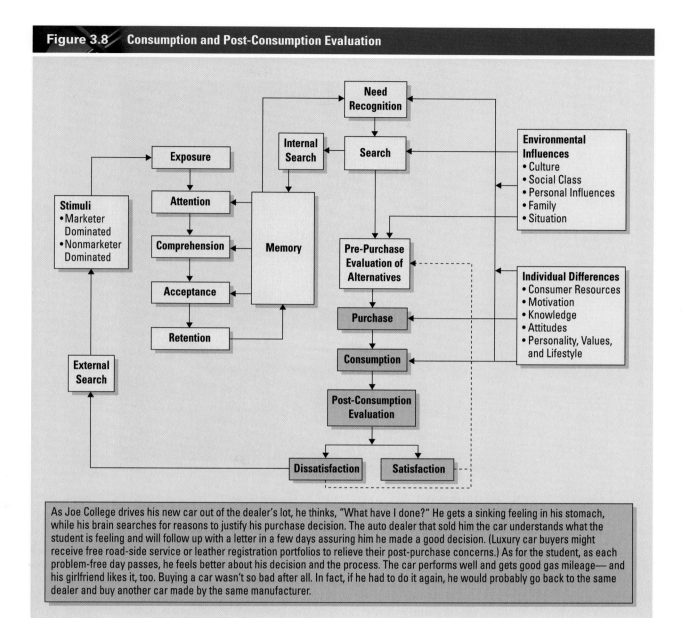

As Joe College drives his new car out of the dealer's lot, he thinks, "What have I done?" He gets a sinking feeling in his stomach, while his brain searches for reasons to justify his purchase decision. The auto dealer that sold him the car understands what the student is feeling and will follow up with a letter in a few days assuring him he made a good decision. (Luxury car buyers might receive free road-side service or leather registration portfolios to relieve their post-purchase concerns.) As for the student, as each problem-free day passes, he feels better about his decision and the process. The car performs well and gets good gas mileage— and his girlfriend likes it, too. Buying a car wasn't so bad after all. In fact, if he had to do it again, he would probably go back to the same dealer and buy another car made by the same manufacturer.

Emotions also play a role in how someone evaluates a product or transaction. An emotion can be defined as a reaction to a cognitive appraisal of events or thoughts; is accompanied by physiological processes; is often expressed physically (for example, in gestures, posture, or facial expressions); and may result in specific actions to cope with or affirm the emotion.[11] For example, satisfaction with a car has been found to be dependent on a combination of attribute satisfaction and dissatisfaction and positive (joy) and negative (anger, guilt, or contempt) effects or emotions.[12]

Just as consumers compare price and evaluate the fairness of exchange in the alternative evaluation stage, so do they revisit these issues during post-purchase evaluation. Some research indicates that how consumers view the fairness of the exchange *over time* affects current and future usage behavior. Price and usage also affect their overall evaluations of the fairness of the exchange. In turn, these evaluations affect overall satisfaction and future usage.[13]

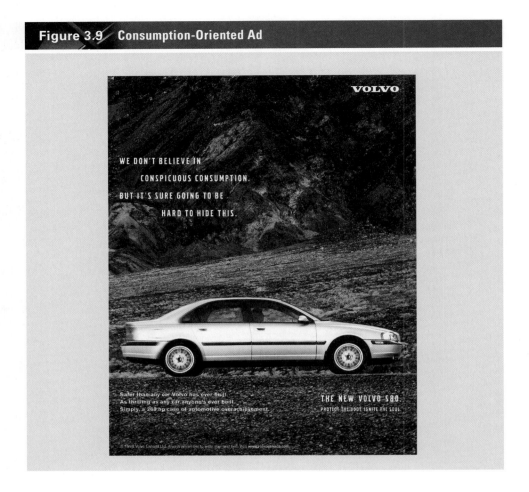

Figure 3.9   Consumption-Oriented Ad

Stage Seven: Divestment

Divestment is the last stage in the Consumer Decision Process model (Figure 3.10). Consumers have several options, including outright disposal, recycling, or re-marketing. When the student in the example is finished using the car he purchased, he has to dispose of it somehow. He can choose to sell (remarket) it to another consumer, trade it in on another vehicle, or take it to the junkyard. With other products, consumers find themselves having to dispose of packaging and product literature as well as the product itself. In these situations, recycling and environmental concerns play a role in consumers' divestment methods.

How Organizations Use the CDP Model

One of the goals of the CDP model was to help marketers, consumer analysts, and researchers study consumers and customers. Managers of firms can examine how their customers proceed through the decision model (adapted for the product or service they sell) and ask questions, such as those at the end of the chapter in Figure 3.15. Manufacturers such as P&G and General Motors, large and small retailers, and nonprofit organizations use the CDP model to:

1. Identify relationships between variables that affect consumer decision making
2. Identify topics for additional research
3. Develop and implement marketing mix strategies

Figure 3.10   Divestment

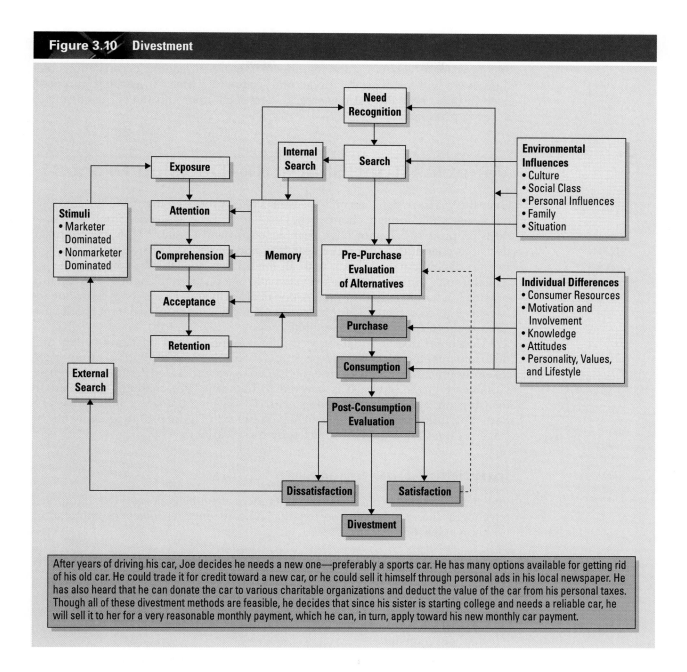

After years of driving his car, Joe decides he needs a new one—preferably a sports car. He has many options available for getting rid of his old car. He could trade it for credit toward a new car, or he could sell it himself through personal ads in his local newspaper. He has also heard that he can donate the car to various charitable organizations and deduct the value of the car from his personal taxes. Though all of these divestment methods are feasible, he decides that since his sister is starting college and needs a reliable car, he will sell it to her for a very reasonable monthly payment, which he can, in turn, apply toward his new monthly car payment.

In the past, retailers succeeded without really trying to influence consumers at any stage of the decision process except purchase. Retailers generally left concern about the first three stages to manufacturers who developed new products, advertised brands, set the level of each attribute in products, and generally took the lead in marketing activities outside the store. Today, retailers focus on the early stages of consumer decision making as well, while manufacturers take on more responsibility for what happens in-store. They offer programs to train salespeople, store fixtures, and POP materials. Together, retailers and manufacturers work to link retail sales data to problem recognition, search, and alternative evaluation, helping each other succeed. Persuading consumers to buy a specific brand of product from a specific retailer increasingly requires the cooperative strategic efforts of the manufacturer *and* the retailer focused on *all* stages of consumer decisions.

The remainder of this text is organized around the CDP model. You will learn the theoretical foundations for the various consumer behaviors in these stages and how these behaviors are shaping marketing in leading organizations. Although we will focus on the model one section at a time for learning purposes, keep in mind how the various stages affect each other and the entire consumer decision process.

Variables That Shape the Decision Process

Over the years, researchers and specialists have produced many studies and theories regarding human choice behavior—John Dewey's conceptualizations of decision process behavior have been especially influential.[14] How people make decisions continues to interest researchers and strategists because of its complexity and dynamic nature. Even with all the options available to them, people are usually quite rational and make systematic use of the information, and usually consider the implications of their actions before they decide to engage or not engage in a given behavior.[15] In this section, we summarize information about variables that can influence decision making.

Consumer decision making is influenced and shaped by many factors and determinants that fall into these three categories: (1) individual differences, (2) environmental influences, and (3) psychological processes. A summary of these variables follows, but each is covered in depth in later chapters, with Part III focusing on individual differences, Part IV on environmental influences, and Part V on influencing consumer behavior. Refer to Figure 3.10 to see how all the stages of the CDP model are affected by these variables.

Individual Differences

Five major categories of individual differences affect behavior: (1) demographics, psychographics, values and personality; (2) consumer resources; (3) motivation; (4) knowledge; and (5) attitudes.

- **Demographics, psychographics, values, and personality** How people differ affects decision processes and buying behavior. You will read about these influences in depth in Chapter 7. These variables include what has come to be known as *psychographic research* to probe into those individual traits, values, beliefs, and preferred behavior patterns that correlate with behavior in market segments.

- **Consumer resources** Each person brings three primary resources into every decision-making situation: (1) time, (2) money, and (3) information reception and processing capabilities (attention). Generally, there are distinct limits on the availability of each, thus requiring some careful allocation. Chapters 5 and 7 provide guidelines to help you assess the implications of limited resources on consumer motivation and behavior.

- **Motivation** Psychologists and marketers alike have conducted a wide variety of studies to determine what takes place when goal-directed behavior is energized and activated. Chapter 8 discusses motivation thoroughly.

- **Knowledge** Knowledge is defined in Chapter 9 as information stored in memory. It encompasses a vast array of items such as the availability and characteristics of products and services; where and when to buy; and how to use products. One main goal of advertising and selling is to provide relevant knowledge and information to consumers so as to assist them with decision making, especially in extended problem solving.

- **Attitudes** Behavior is strongly influenced by attitudes toward a given brand or product. An attitude is simply an overall evaluation of an alternative, ranging from positive to negative. Once formed, attitudes play a directive role on future choice and are difficult to change. Nevertheless, attitude change is a common marketing goal, as you will see in Chapter 10.

Environmental Influences

Consumers live in a complex environment. In addition to individual variables, their decision process behavior is influenced by environmental factors, including (1) culture, (2) social class, (3) family, (4) personal influence, and (5) situation.

- **Culture** Culture, as used in the study of consumer behavior, refers to the values, ideas, artifacts, and other meaningful symbols that help individuals communicate, interpret, and evaluate as members of society. Chapter 11 provides a comprehensive overview of cultural issues from both a global and an ethnic perspective.

- **Social class** Social classes are divisions within society that comprise individuals sharing similar values, interests, and behaviors. You will also see this discussed in Chapter 11. Socioeconomic status differences may lead to differing forms of consumer behavior (for example, the types of alcoholic beverages served, the make and style of car driven, and the styles of dress preferred).

- **Family** Since the field of consumer research was founded, the family has been a focus of research. You will learn in Chapter 12 that the family often is the primary decision-making unit, with a complex and varying pattern of roles and functions. Cooperation and conflict often occur simultaneously with interesting behavioral outcomes.

- **Personal influence** As consumers, our behaviors are often affected by those with whom we closely associate. This is referred to as *personal influence* and is discussed in Chapter 13. Consumers often respond to perceived pressure to conform to the norms and expectations provided by others—seeking and taking their counsel on buying choices, observing what others are doing as information about consumption choices, and comparing their decisions to those of others.

- **Situation** Behaviors change as situations change. Sometimes these changes are erratic and unpredictable, such as a job layoff, and at other times, they can be predicted by research. Situation is treated as a research variable in its own right and is discussed in various chapters.

Psychological Processes Influencing Consumer Behavior

Finally, those who wish to understand and influence consumer behavior must have a practical grasp of three basic psychological processes: (1) information processing, (2) learning, and (3) attitude and behavior change.

- **Information processing** Communication is a bottom-line marketing activity. Therefore, consumer researchers have long been interested in discovering how people receive, process, and make sense of marketing communications.

Information processing research, discussed in Chapter 14, addresses ways in which information is retrieved, transformed, reduced, elaborated, stored, recovered, and retrieved.

- **Learning** Anyone attempting to influence the consumer is trying to bring about learning—the process by which experience leads to changes in knowledge and behavior. Learning theory (Chapter 16) is relevant, especially for those products and services bought on the basis of relatively little reflection and evaluation.

- **Attitude and behavior change** Changes in attitude and behavior are an important marketing objective that reflects basic psychological influences and have been the subject of decades of intensive research. Chapter 15 reviews this literature from the perspective of designing effective promotional strategies.

Types of Decision Process

The extent to which each of the stages in Figure 3.10 is followed in the precise form and sequence suggested can vary from one situation to the next. Sometimes consumers undertake a complex decision process requiring substantial amounts of time and energy. More common, however, are rather simplistic processes in which relatively little time and effort are devoted to the decision.

Decision Process Continuum

One way to think about these variations is to imagine a continuum of decision-making complexity ranging from high to low (Figure 3.11). In situations in which consumers are making a decision for the first time, actions must be based on some form of problem solving. When this process is very complex, it is called **extended problem solving** (EPS). **Limited problem solving** (LPS), however, represents a lower degree of complexity. For convenience, we refer to the process along the middle of the continuum as **midrange problem solving.**

In Figure 3.11, we allow for the fact that most consumer purchases are made on a repeated basis. When this is the case, the individual may engage in problem solving once again. Alternatively, he or she may greatly simplify the decisions by foregoing any deliberation of purchase alternatives and simply choose the same brand purchased previously. This represents **habitual decision making,** the least complex of all decision processes.

Initial Purchase

When the initial decision is made by EPS, enduring buying patterns based on brand loyalty are often established. However, LSP leads to inertia-based habits—it's easier to do the same thing over again than switch. The reasons for these distinctions will be discussed in this section.

Extended Problem Solving   When the decision process is especially detailed and rigorous, EPS often occurs. EPS is commonly used by consumers purchasing automobiles (as in our student example), expensive clothing, stereo equipment, and other major products or services for which the costs and risks of a wrong decision are high. Sometimes EPS is fueled by doubts and fears; other times it is based on lack of experience and information about an expensive, significant, or high-involvement purchase. Regardless of the reason, these consumers are open to

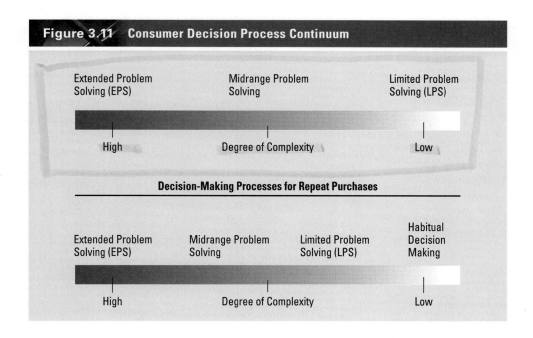

Figure 3.11 Consumer Decision Process Continuum

information from various sources and are motivated to undertake the effort to make "the right choice."

When EPS is activated, all seven stages in the decision process are likely to be followed, although not necessarily in exact order. Consumers engaging in EPS generally evaluate many alternatives, consult a wide variety of product information sources, and research options on how and where to make the purchase.

In short, *thought and evaluation usually precede the act of purchase and use because of the importance of making the right choice.* The process of analysis and reflection, however, does not cease after purchase and use. If the item purchased is perceived as falling short of expectations, the outcome can be substantial, and often vocal, dissatisfaction. The desired outcome is satisfaction, expressed as positive recommendations to others and the intention to repurchase should the occasion arise.

Limited Problem Solving   The other extreme of the decision-making continuum is limited problem solving (LPS).[16] In most situations, consumers have neither the time, the resources, nor the motivation to engage in EPS. It is far more common to simplify the process and sharply reduce the number and variety of information sources, alternatives, and criteria used for evaluation. Consumer in Focus 3.1 features dialog from a focus group about toothpaste.

Several of the men in the focus group express sentiments such as "buy a brand that I recognize" or "buy the cheapest brand,"[17] both examples of "simple rules" that may drive consumers' choices. One focus group member squeezes the very last out of his toothpaste tube, makes a mental note to stop at the supermarket on the way home, happens to see a special on a new brand that he recognizes, picks up a large tube, and goes on his way.

With LPS, there is little information search and evaluation before purchase. In other words, *need recognition leads to buying action; extensive search and evaluation are avoided because the purchase does not assume great importance.* Yet, any supplier offering a competitive distinction, no matter how small, can gain temporary advantage; and a "why not try it" attitude often will lead to trial of a new brand as seen in the comments by Greg, Bill, and Fred in Consumer in Focus 3.1.

Consumer in Focus 3.1

Buying Toiletries—Get It over with Fast

Eleven men younger than the age of 40 years are participating in a focus group on a topic that no one thinks is too exciting—brand preferences for bath soap and toothpaste. Our moderator has just asked, "Which brand of toothpaste do you prefer to buy?" Six different brands were mentioned. Then he asked, "Would you buy another brand if your favorite is not available?"

Ed: "Yes. There are a couple of other brands that are just as good. All I care is that it has fluoride."

Brad: "What difference does it make? Toothpaste is toothpaste."

Sam: "Yeah, I'd buy something else, but there's no way that I would pay more, no matter what it is."

Rick: "Sure. I like to shift brands once in awhile just to try something new. I get tired of the same old thing."

Moderator: "OK, what if a new brand is available two-for-one at the same price of the other brands? Would you be likely to try it?"

Greg: "Sure, as long as it isn't some weirdo thing from Mars."

Bill: "I agree with that. I would probably try it if I recognize the company or brand name. Why not?"

Fred: "You bet—low price is what I want."

Moderator: "What I am hearing is that low price is probably the most important thing and that you are willing to try different brands."

Everyone: Many expressions of agreement.

For example, a brand that is recognized at point of sale is more likely to be tried, indicating the importance of winning the battle of advertising recognition in the war for market share. Further, heavy point-of-sale sampling, display, couponing, and other devices can be effective in triggering brand trial.

Midrange Problem Solving EPS and LPS, as you probably observed, are extremes on a decision process continuum, but many decisions range somewhere in between. Think of deciding which movie to see. It usually takes a minimum amount of information to know what is playing, where it is playing, and at what time. Because several options look promising, there is a need to evaluate them, often by consulting the reviews in the newspaper or recommendations of a friend. All this can be accomplished quickly with only moderate deliberation.

Repeat Purchases

Most purchases are repeated over time. When repeat purchases occur, there are two possibilities: (1) repeated problem solving, and (2) habitual decision making.

Repeated Problem Solving Repeat purchases often require continued problem solving. Several factors can lead to this outcome, including dissatisfaction with a previous purchase (often resulting in brand switching) and retail stockouts (when the retailer doesn't have product available). In this type of purchase behavior, the buyer must weigh the consequences of investing time and energy in finding another alternative.

Habitual Decision Making It is far more likely that repeat purchases will be made on the basis of habits or routines that "simplify" life for the consumer.

Habitual behavior takes different forms, depending on the decision process followed in the initial purchase: (1) brand or company loyalty, or (2) inertia.

- *Brand or company loyalty* Consumers have certain expectations about the products they buy and the retailers from whom they purchase. The satisfaction that consumers experience when their expectations are met or exceeded often results in loyalty to that product or retailer. For the most part, consumers want to reward these companies with continued use over time—that is, brand or company *loyalty*, which can be highly resistant to change.

Marketers covet high loyalty and often do everything possible to maintain it. Anyone who tries to dislodge loyal purchasers of a brand of 35mm film such as Fuji could face a tough challenge. This loyalty is often based on both the high involvement nature of photography to consumers who take their photography seriously and their belief that Fuji offers the brightest color and picture quality. Such buyers have no incentive to change unless there is a demonstrable competitive breakthrough. In fact, many firms reward customers for their continued patronage with loyalty programs, as Fuji does with coupons applicable to future purchases. Other loyalty programs reward consumers with a free dinner after their tenth visit to a restaurant or the accumulation of points in an airline program.

- *Inertia* Toothpaste is a product category in which there is limited brand loyalty. Where any degree of loyalty does exist, it mostly consists of several brands, all of which are about equal. Buying habits of this type are based on *inertia* and are unstable. Although there is no incentive to switch, this may occur quite readily when prices are lowered with a coupon or another brand is promoted as offering something new.

Impulse Buying

The so-called impulse purchase (an unplanned, spur-of-the-moment action triggered by product display or point-of-sale promotion)[18] is the least complex form of LPS but differs in some important ways. Here are its characteristics:[19]

1. A sudden and spontaneous desire to act accompanied by urgency
2. A state of psychological disequilibrium in which a person can feel temporarily out of control
3. The onset of conflict and struggle that is resolved by an immediate action
4. Minimal objective evaluation exists—emotional considerations dominate
5. A lack of regard for consequences

Although there is an absence of the careful reasoning characteristic of EPS, there is not the indifference that accompanies LPS. A high sense of emotional involvement and urgency, in effect, short-circuits the reasoning process and motivates immediate action.

Variety Seeking

Consumers often express satisfaction with their present brand but still engage in brand switching. The motive is variety seeking, which occurs most often when there are many similar alternatives, frequent brand shifts, and high purchase frequency.[20] It can occur simply because someone is bored with his or her current brand choice, or it can be prompted by external cues such as store stockouts or

Figure 3.12   Categories of Purchase Behaviors

		Number of Brands Purchased in a Given Time Period	
		Single	**Multiple**
Consumer Committment	**High**	Brand loyalty	Variety seeking
	Low	Repeat purchase behavior	Derived varied behavior

Source: Hans C. M. Van Trijp, Wayne D. Hoyer, and J. Jeffrey Inman, "Why Switch? Product Category—Level of Explanations for True Variety-Seeking Behavior," Journal of Marketing Research *(August 1996), 281–292.*

coupons that promote switching. Figure 3.12 presents four categories of purchasing patterns, ranging from brand loyalty to variety seeking. It incorporates factors such as consumer commitment (loyalty) to brands and the number of brands purchased in a particular time period.[21] When variety seeking seems likely, there is merit in appeals such as the one illustrated in Figure 3.13, which advertises a different dessert for every day of the week.

Figure 3.13   Variety Is the Spice of Life

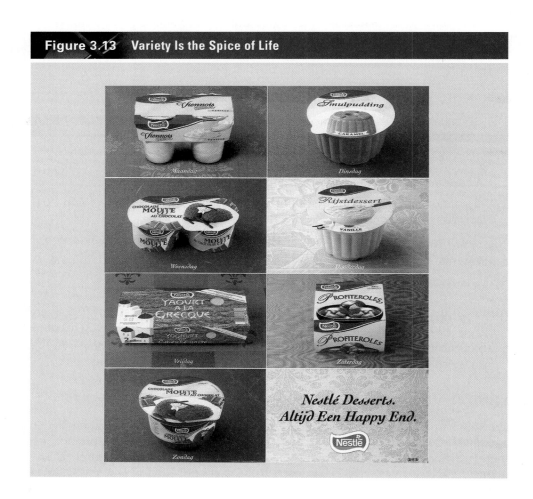

Factors Influencing the Extent of Problem Solving

The extent of the problem-solving process consumers undergo in different purchase situations depends on three distinctive factors: (1) degree of involvement, (2) degree of differentiation between alternatives, and (3) amount of time for deliberation.

Degree of Involvement

The degree of *personal involvement* is a key factor in shaping the type of decision process that consumers will be followed. **Involvement** is the *level of perceived personal importance and/or interest evoked by a stimulus within a specific situation.*[22] To the extent that it is present, the consumer acts with deliberation *to minimize the risks* and *to maximize the benefits* gained from purchase and use.

Involvement ranges from low to high. The degree of involvement is determined by how important consumers perceive the product or service to be. Simply stated, the more important the product or service to a consumer, the more motivated he or she is to search and be involved in the decision. Involvement becomes activated and felt when intrinsic personal characteristics (needs, values, self-concept) are confronted with appropriate marketing stimuli within a given situation.[23] Furthermore, it seems to function in comparable ways across cultures although the specific products and modes of expression will vary somewhat.[24]

How involved are consumers in their purchase decisions for a product such as multivitamins? Several decades ago, when multivitamins were being advertised fairly heavily in mainstream media, consumers were introduced to the idea of taking their vitamins "once-a-day." They were given information on the importance to their health and the convenience of taking one vitamin per day. Over time, choosing and purchasing multivitamins went from being a medium to high involvement purchase to a low involvement decision. But various factors, such as the interest in herbal medicines and the evolution of self-medication sparked the opportunity for One-A-Day vitamins to provide new information to consumers and increase the degree of involvement in the decision to purchase, as seen in Figure 3.14. One-A-Day now has a variety of herbal additives available to consumers—ranging from Ginkgo (for memory) to Ginseng (for energy)—involving consumers more in their purchase decisions.

Several factors exist that determine the degree of involvement consumers have in making a decision. Research on the factors that generate high or low involvement is extensive and is summarized in the following section. Take time to review the factors and understand how they play a role in the various purchase decisions you make.

Personal Factors   The degree of involvement tends to be higher when the outcome of the decision affects the person directly. Personal factors include self-image, health, beauty, or physical condition. Without activation of need and drive, there will be no involvement, and it is strongest when the product or service is perceived as enhancing self-image.[25] When that is the case, involvement is likely to be enduring and to function as a stable trait, as opposed to being situational or temporary.[26] For example, the purchase of cosmetics tends to be a high involvement decision because it affects directly a consumer's self-image and looks. A consumer's physical handicap may also affect how involved he or she is in buying a home. Are there steps leading up to the house? Is there a bedroom on the first floor, and are doorways wide enough to accommodate a wheel chair?

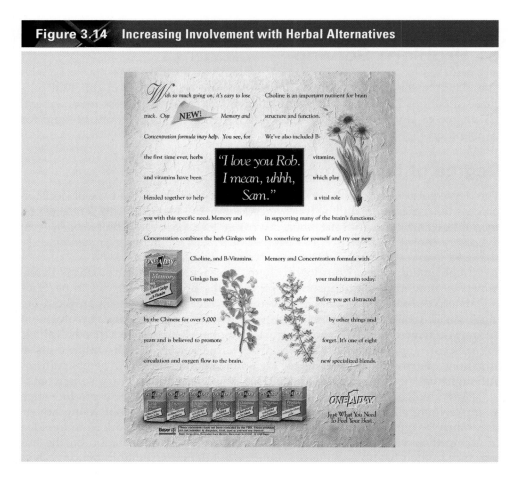

Figure 3.14   Increasing Involvement with Herbal Alternatives

Product Factors   Products or brands also become involving if there is some perceived risk in purchasing and using them. Many types of perceived risk have been identified, including physical (risk of bodily harm), psychological (especially, a negative effect on self-image), performance (fear that the product will not perform as expected), and financial (risk that outcomes will lead to loss of earnings).[27]

As one would logically expect, the greater the perceived risk, the greater the likelihood of high involvement. When perceived risk becomes unacceptably high, there is motivation either to avoid purchase and use altogether or to minimize risk through the search and prepurchase alternative evaluation stages in extended problem solving. For example, consumers may become highly involved in the choice and purchase of a physician, especially when surgery is required, because of the high perceived risk.

Situational Factors   Situational (or instrumental) involvement includes factors such as whether the product is purchased for personal use or as a gift, and whether it is consumed alone or with others. Situational involvement changes over time: it may be strong on a temporary basis and wane once purchasing outcomes are resolved.

This is often the case with fads such as trendy clothing items in which involvement is high initially but quickly diminishes once the item is worn and fashions begin to change. There also are times when an otherwise uninvolving product takes on a different degree of relevance because of the manner in which it will be used.[28] For example, there can be a big difference in the perceived importance between a brand of bath gel purchased for home use and that given as a gift.

Finally, involvement can increase when social pressures are felt. For example, research indicates that consumers react quite differently when purchasing wine for ordinary personal consumption than when serving it at a dinner party.[29] Consumers may feel pressure to buy a more expensive or well-recognized wine when entertaining with friends than when eating alone.

Perceptions of Difference Among Alternatives

Marketers find that, EPS is more probable when choice alternatives are seen as differentiated.[30] The more similar choices are perceived to be, however, the greater the likelihood that consumers will spend less time on problem solving. An application of this is, if a consumer is shopping and finds that Bounce fabric softener is out of stock and perceives the Snuggle brand to be similar, she will spend less time choosing the available alternative than if she perceives the difference between the two to be great.

Time Availability

Two time-related factors also affect the degree of involvement in a decision—how much time a consumer has to devote to solving the problem and how quickly the decision needs to be made. Returning to our car buyer, he spent a lot of time evaluating various cars because he had access to his father's car and didn't need to make a purchase right away. But if he hadn't had access to an alternative form of transportation, he may have had to make a much quicker decision. In this case, the situation places a time constraint upon the decision. Another consumer might want a new car but does not have much time to read brochures, talk with friends, and test-drive various brands because of job and family-related time constraints. That consumer may be less involved in the decision because of the time constraints that he or she brings to the situation. As a general rule, therefore, EPS is followed when time pressures are low.

Consumer's Mood State

Consumer mood can strongly influence information processing and evaluation.[31] Consumer mood state, how people feel at a particular moment is discussed in Chapter 8. For example, if consumers are in a good mood and look forward to shopping for a Christmas gift, they may spend more time in the shopping mall looking for the perfect gift. Whereas others may dislike holiday shopping and spend as little time as possible in the shopping process.

At times, a positive effect on mood can cause consumers to reduce the length and complexity of the decision process,[32] but at other times, mood can have exactly the opposite effect.[33] Look at the decision process of purchasing funeral services. If purchased before the need occurs (as is the case with prearranged funerals), consumers may spend more time looking at alternative choices; whereas if purchased at the time of need, the family may feel distraught and emotional, and may choose to shorten the decision process. Though it is not always clear *how* mood will affect consumer behavior, it could affect it in some way, as you will read in Chapter 10.

Diagnosing Consumer Behavior

The primary focus of this chapter has been the consumer decision process, with an emphasis on the CDP model as a framework for examining how consumers

Figure 3.15 Diagnosing the Consumer Decision Making Process

Need Recognition

1. What needs and motivations are satisfied by product purchase and usage? (i.e., What *benefits* are consumers seeking?)
2. Are these needs dormant or are they presently perceived as felt needs by prospective buyers?
3. How involved with the product are most prospective buyers in the target market segment?

Search for Information

1. What product- and brand-related information is stored in memory?
2. Is the consumer motivated to turn to external sources to find information about available alternatives and their characteristics?
3. What specific information sources are used most frequently when search is undertaken?
4. What product features or attributes are the focus of search when it is undertaken?

Pre-Purchase Evaluation of Alternatives

1. To what extent do consumers engage in alternative evaluation and comparison?
2. Which product and/or brand alternatives are included in the evaluation process?
3. Which product evaluative criteria (product attributes) are used to compare various alternatives?
    a. Which are most salient in the evaluation?
    b. How complex is the evaluation (i.e., using a single attribute as opposed to several in combination)?
4. What are the outcomes of evaluation regarding each of the candidate purchase alternatives?
    a. What is believed to be true about the characteristics and features of each?
    b. Are they perceived to be different in important ways, or are they seen as essentially the same?
5. What kind of decision rule is used to determine the best choice?

Purchase

1. Will the consumer expend time and energy to shop until the preferred alternative is found?
2. Is additional decision-process behavior needed to discover the preferred outlet for purchase?
3. What are the preferred models of purchases (i.e., retail store, in the home, or in other ways)?

Consumption

1. How is the consumer using the product?
    a. For intended purpose?
    b. As recommended in usage/care instructions?
    c. To solve some problem the product was not designed for?
2. What other products are used in conjunction with the product?
3. Where is the product stored when not in use?
4. What is normal frequency of usage and duration of consumption?
5. In relationship to purchase, where and when does the consumption occur?
6. How are household members, peers, and others involved in consumption?

Post-Consumption Evaluation

1. What degree of satisfaction or dissatisfaction is expressed with respect to previously used alternatives in the product or service category?
2. What reasons are given for satisfaction or dissatisfaction?
3. Has perceived satisfaction or dissatisfaction been shared with other people to help them in their buying behavior?
4. Have consumers made attempts to achieve redress for dissatisfaction?
5. Is there an intention to repurchase any of the alternatives?
    a. If no, why not?
    b. If yes, does intention reflect brand loyalty or inertia?

Divestment

1. When does the consumer divest of the product?
    a. When the product is either completely consumed or used?
    b. When the consumer tires of it?
    c. When a better alternative comes along?
2. How does the consumer dispose of the product?
    a. Does he or she throw away the product at home or somewhere else?
    b. Does the consumer recycle the product or resell it?
    c. Does the consumer donate the product to a nonprofit organization or give it to a friend?
3. How does the consumer dispose of the packaging?
4. What role does concern for the environment play in the divestment choice?

make decisions. Figure 3.15 features a guide for strategic thinking that incorporates the materials covered in this chapter, including the consumer decision process, types of decisions, and degree of involvement. It is a list of questions that will help in formulating diagnostic marketing research and developing communication and marketing strategies.

Summary

The purpose of this chapter has been to introduce you to the nature of consumer decision making and the influences on this process. The Consumer Decision Process (CDP) model provides a "roadmap" of how consumers find their way in a world of consumption decisions.

Consumer decisions, analyzed with the aid of the CDP model, move through the following stages: (1) need recognition, (2) search for information, (3) pre-purchase evaluations of alternatives, (4) purchase, (5) consumption, (6) post-purchase alternative evaluation, and (7) divestment. As consumers move through these stages, marketers have an opportunity to react to and influence behavior with effective communication and marketing strategies that address each of these stages and the variables that affect each stage. Purchase and consumption are affected by a complex set of factors that influence and shape decision process behavior, including *individual differences* and *environmental influences.*

Decision processes can range from extended problem solving (which can be viewed as one end of a problem-solving continuum) to limited problem solving (the opposite end of the spectrum). EPS is characterized by intensive search for information and complex evaluation, whereas LPS represents far less motivation to search widely for information and engage in alternative evaluation.

When the occasion arises for repeat purchases, many consumers quickly develop habitual decision processes. On occasion, they are brand loyal and stay with their initial choice. This often occurs when there is high perceived involvement. When not true, habits are likely to be built on loyalty or inertia. If a consumer has no reason to switch, a repurchase will be made. But the consumer also is prone to switch if there is incentive to do so. This frequently occurs when there is low involvement and little commitment to prefer one alternative to another.

Several factors influence decision process behavior in terms of degree of involvement. Determinants of involvement include (1) personal factors, (2) product factors, (3) situational factors.

Review and Discussion Questions

1. There are some who argue that consumers really do not pursue any kind of decision process but make their selections more or less randomly without any apparent reasoning. What is your position on this issue? Why?

2. Define the terms *extended problem solving* and *limited problem solving*. What are the essential differences? What type of decision process would you expect most people to follow in the initial purchase of a new product or brand in each of these categories: toothpaste, flour, men's cologne, carpeting, toilet tissue, bread, light bulbs, a 35mm camera, a sports car?

3. Referring to question 3, is it possible that the decision process could differ widely from one consumer to another in purchasing each of these items? Explain.

4. How might a manufacturer of automatic washers and dryers use a decision process approach to better understand how consumers purchase these products?

5. Which of the following types of products do you think are most likely to be purchased on the basis of brand loyalty and on the basis of inertia: laundry detergent, motor oil, lipsticks, shoe polish, soft drinks, lawn care products (fertilizers, and so on), and spark plugs?

6. Assume you are responsible for marketing a new digital camera. You are up against Kodak and Nikon, which have built substantial brand loyalty. What strategies could you suggest to make market inroads?

7. Assume you have been called in as a marketing consultant to suggest an advertising strategy for a new brand of dry cat food. Which of the types of decision processes discussed in this chapter do you believe is likely with most prospective buyers? Why do you say this? What difference will this make in marketing strategy?

Endnotes

1. Sridhar Moorthy, Brian T. Ratchford, and Debabrata Talukdar, "Consumer Information Search Revisited: Theory and Empirical Analysis," *Journal of Consumer Research* 23, 4 (1997), 263–277.

2. Abeer Y. Hogue and Gerald Lohse, "An Information Search Cost Perspective for Designing Interfaces for Electronic Commerce," *Journal of Marketing Research* 36 (August 1999), 387–394.

3. J. Alba, J. Lynch, B. Weitz, C. Janisqewski, R. Lutz, A. Sawyer, and S. Wood, "Interactive Home Shopping: Consumer, Retailer, and Manufacturer Incentives to Participate in Electronic Marketplaces," *Journal of Marketing* 61 (July 1997), 38–53.

4. John Lynch and Dan Ariely, "Interactive Home Shopping: Effects of Search Cost for Price and Quality Information on Consumer Price Sensitivity, Satisfaction with Merchandise Selected and Retention," working paper, Marketing Department, Duke University (1999).

5. Robert Franciosi, Praveen Kugal, Roland Michelitsch, Vernon Smith, and Gang Deng, "Fairness: Effect on Temporary and Equilibrium Prices in Posted-Offered Markets," *The Economic Journal* 105 (July 1995), 938–950.

6. Margaret C. Campbell, "Perceptions of Price Unfairness: Antecedents and Consequences," *Journal of Marketing Research* (May 1999), 187–199.

7. Mohanbir Sawhney and Jehoshua Eliashberg, "A Parsimonious Model for Forecasting Gross Box Office Revenues of Motion Pictures," *Marketing Science* 15 (1996), 113–131.

8. Jehoshua Eliashberg and Steven Shugan, "Film Critics: Influencers or Predictors?" *Journal of Marketing* 61 (April 1997), 68–78.

9. Ramya Neelamegham and Dipak Jain, "Consumer Choice Process for Experience Goods: An Econometric Model and Analysis," *Journal of Marketing Research* 36 (August 1999), 373–386.

10. Mary Frances Luce, John W. Payne, and James R. Bettman, "Emotional Trade-Off Difficulty and Choice," *Journal of Marketing Research* 36 (May 1999), 143–159.

11. Richard P. Bagozzi, Mahesh Gopinath, Prashanth Nyer, "The Role of Emotions in Marketing," *Journal of the Academy of Marketing Science* 27, 2 (Spring 1999), 184–206.

12. Richard Oliver, "Cognitive, Affective, and Attribute Bases of the Satisfaction Response," *Journal of Consumer Research* 20 (December 1993), 418–430.

13. Ruth N. Bolton and Katherine N. Lemon, "A Dynamic Model of Customers' Usage of Services: Usage As an Antecedent and Consequence of Satisfaction," *Journal of Marketing Research* 36 (May 1999), 171–186.

14. John Dewey, *How We Think* (New York: Heath, 1910).

15. Icek Ajzen and Martin Fishbein, *Understanding Attitudes and Predicting Social Behavior* (Englewood Cliffs, NJ: Prentice-Hall, 1980).

16. Harold E. Kassarjian, "Consumer Research: Some Recollections and a Commentary," in Richard J. Lutz, ed., *Advances in Consumer Research* 13 (Provo, Utah: Association for Consumer Research, 1986), 6–8.

17. Wayne D. Hoyer, "Variations in Choice Strategies across Decision Contexts: An Examination of Contingent Factors," in Lutz, *Advances,* 23–26.

18. Francis Piron, "Defining Impulse Purchasing," in Rebecca H. Holman and Michael R. Solomon, eds., *Advances in Consumer Research* 18 (Provo, Utah: Association for Consumer Research, 1991), 512–518.

19. Dennis W. Rook and Stephen J. Hoch, "Consuming Impulses," in Elizabeth C. Hirschman and Morris B. Holbrook, eds., *Advances in Consumer Research* 12 (Provo, Utah: Association for Consumer Research, 1985), 23–27.

20. Itamar Simonson, "The Effect of Purchase Quantity and Timing on Variety-Seeking Behavior," *Journal of Marketing Research* 27 (May 1990), 150–162; Wayne D. Hoyer and Nancy M. Ridgway, "Variety Seeking as an Explanation for Exploratory Purchase Behavior: A Theoretical Model," in Thomas C. Kinnear, ed., *Advances in Consumer Research* 11 (Provo, Utah: Association for Consumer Research, 1984), 114–119.

21. Hans C. M. Van Trijp, Wayne D. Hoyer, and J. Jeffrey Inman, "Why Switch? Product Category—Level of Explanations for True Variety-Seeking Behavior," *Journal of Marketing Research* 33 (August 1996), 281–292.

22. John H. Antil, "Conceptualization and Operationalization of Involvement," in Kinnear, *Advances,* 204.

23. Richard L. Celsi and Jerry C. Olson, "The Role of Involvement in Attention and Comprehension Processes," *Journal of Consumer Research* 15 (September 1988), 210–224.

24. See James Sood, "A Multi Country Research Approach for Multinational Communication Strategies," *Journal of International Consumer Marketing* 5 (1993), 29–50; Dana L. Alden, Wayne D. Hoyer, and Guntelee Wechasara, "Choice Strategies and Involvement: A Cross-Cultural Analysis," in Thomas K. Srull, ed., *Advances in Consumer Research* 16 (Provo, Utah: Association for Consumer Research, 1989), 119–125.

25. Meera P. Venkatraman, "Investigating Differences in the Roles of Enduring and Instrumentally Involved Consumers in the Diffusion Process," in Michael J. Houston, ed., *Advances in Consumer Research* 15 (Provo, Utah: Association for Consumer Research, 1988), 299–303.

26. Robin A. Higie and Lawrence E. Feick, "Enduring Involvement: Conceptual and Measurement Issues," in Srull, *Advances,* 690–696.

27. See George Brooker, "An Assessment of an Expanded Measure of Perceived Risk," in Kinnear, *Advances,* 439–441; John W. Vann, "A Multi-Distributional, Conceptual Framework for the Study of Perceived Risk," in Kinnear, *Advances,* 442–446.

28. Russell W. Belk, "Effects of Gift-Giving Involvement on Gift Selection Strategies," in Andrew Mitchell, ed., *Advances in Consumer Research* 9 (Ann Arbor, MI.: Association for Consumer Research, 1981), 408–411.

29. Judith L. Zaichkowsky, "Measuring the Involvement Construct," *Journal of Consumer Research* 12 (December 1985), 341–352.

30. Giles Laurent and Jean-Noel Kapferer, "Measuring Consumer Involvement Profiles," *Journal of Marketing Research* 22 (February 1985), 41–53.

31. Consumer research was strongly influenced in 1980 by the finding that feelings and mood (affective responses) operate independently from cognitive responses. See Robert Zajonc, "Feeling and Thinking: Preferences Need No Inferences," *American Psychologist* 35 (February 1980), 151–175. This was followed by an influential article by Mitchell and Olson. See Andrew Mitchell and Jerry Olson, "Are Product Attribute Beliefs the Only Mediator of Advertising Effects on Brand Attitudes?" *Journal of Marketing Research* 18 (August 1981), 318–322.

32. Meryl Paula Gardner, "Mood States and Consumer Behavior: A Critical Review," *Journal of Consumer Research* 12 (December 1985), 281–300.

33. Haim Mano, "Emotional States and Decision Making," in Marvin E. Goldberg, Gerald Gom, and Richard W. Pollay, eds., *Advances in Consumer Research* 17 (Provo, Utah: Association for Consumer Research, 1990), 577–589.

34. Hoyer, "Variations in Choice Strategies across Decision Contexts," 23–26.

35. J. Craig Andrews, "Motivation, Ability, and Opportunity to Process Information: Conceptual and Experimental Manipulation Issues," in Houston, *Advances*, 219–225.

36. Richard E. Petty, John T. Cacioppo, and David Schumann, "Central and Peripheral Routes to Advertising Effectiveness: The Moderating Role of Involvement," *Journal of Consumer Research* 10 (September 1983), 135–144.

CHAPTER 4

Pre-Purchase Processes: Need Recognition, Search, and Evaluation

OPENING VIGNETTE

American households buy about $825 million of plastic storage products each year, but it is a low-growth category. Rubbermaid, a leading manufacturer of such products, hopes to change this. After a five-year absence from national television advertising, Rubbermaid is ready to launch a new advertising campaign that pitches its products as problem solvers in a variety of areas: homes, offices, backyards, gardens, and playgrounds.

The four 30-second TV spots show before-and-after household images with Rubbermaid products coming to the rescue of overcrowded refrigerators, messy laundry rooms, and overflowing bedrooms, with the voice-over "one of the many thousands of solutions we have to make life a little easier." These new ads represent a major departure from Rubbermaid's focus on the product and its price that marked much of its earlier marketing.

Rubbermaid is reinforcing its ad campaign by offering an 89-page booklet, "1,001 Solutions for Better Living," that offers tips on how its products could help consumers deal with problems in their homes and office spaces. Some of the booklet's tips are practical, such as putting Rubbermaid Ultra Grip plastic liner under a computer keyboard to prevent it from slipping, or keeping a Rubbermaid ice cream scoop to fill cupcake tins with cake or muffin batter. Others are more blatantly aimed at increasing sales, such as a suggestion to use different-colored laundry baskets for sorting whites, darks, and delicate clothing.

Source: Excerpted from Raju Narisetti, "Rubbermaid Ads Pitch Problem Solving," The Wall Street Journal *(February 4, 1997), B6.*

The future of all goods and services ultimately depends on whether consumers perceive them as fulfilling consumption needs. Recognition of these needs leads consumers into a decision-making process that determines what they buy and what they consume. We label the first stage of the decision-making process as **need recognition,** defined as *the perception of a difference between the desired state of affairs and the actual situation sufficient to arouse and activate the decision process.* We begin the chapter with this initial stage of decision making.

Need Recognition

Figure 4.1 illustrates what happens during need recognition. Need recognition depends on how much discrepancy exists between the actual state (the consumer's

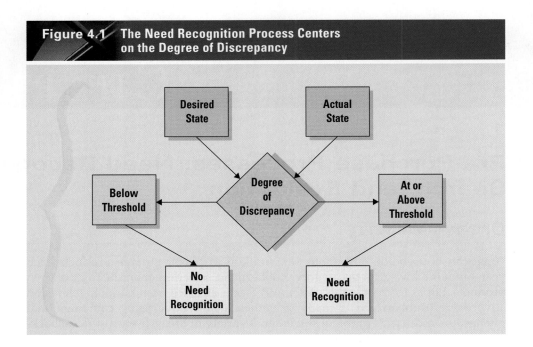

Figure 4.1   The Need Recognition Process Centers on the Degree of Discrepancy

current situation) and the desired state (the situation the consumer wants to be in). When this difference meets or exceeds a certain level or threshold, a need is recognized. For example, a consumer currently feeling hungry (actual state) and wanting to eliminate this feeling (desired state) will experience need recognition when the discrepancy between the two states is of sufficient magnitude. However, if the difference is below the threshold level, need recognition will not occur.

Thus, need recognition will occur when changes in either the actual or desired state cause the two to be noticeably out of alignment. As anyone who has gone too long since his or her last meal knows, the simple passage of time can lead to an unpleasant deterioration in the actual state. Similarly, a need may be recognized simply because consumers have depleted their existing product inventory. The last slices of bread were toasted for breakfast, and more bread will be needed for tonight's dinner. In this instance, need recognition is triggered by an anticipated need in the immediate future resulting from a change in the current situation.

Consumers' desired states also change. What we desire in our younger years may not be the same as when we grow older. Whereas today many male baby boomers get a haircut as soon as their hair starts touching their ears, in their younger days need recognition never crossed their mind even though their hair was touching their shoulders! Consider the childless couple that has little need for the products necessary for raising children. However, after discovering that they will soon be parents, they will experience a change in their desired state. Products that previously were irrelevant to them now become essential.

As indicated by these examples, need recognition often occurs for reasons outside a company's control. Nonetheless, it is possible for businesses to influence need recognition. Activating need recognition is often an important business objective that, when neglected, can have unfavorable consequences for individual companies and entire industries. In the following sections, we discuss the practical value of understanding need recognition and describe some of the ways in which companies attempt to influence it.

Why Businesses Need to Understand Need Recognition

One potential benefit of understanding need recognition is that it may reveal potential opportunities that a business may wish to exploit. Identifying a market segment with unsatisfied desires (i.e., the actual state falls substantially short of the desired state) provides businesses with new sales opportunities. Such is the case for female motorcycle riders, many of whom are less than thrilled with the riding gear currently available for women. "Either I buy men's clothes or I have to have something custom-made," says one female rider. "It can get very expensive."[1]

The existence of unsatisfied needs and desires today lays the foundation for the new businesses and product innovations of tomorrow. To see just how "far out" these unfulfilled needs may take us, read Consumer in Focus 4.1.

An analysis of need recognition may also reveal existing barriers to a firm's success. Consider the furniture industry.[2] During the 1970s, Americans bought dinettes once every 12 to 13 years. In the 1990s, the average replacement rate is every 21 years. Between 1987 and 1997, American households reduced their spending on furniture by 13 percent.

Consumer in Focus 4.1

Unfilled Needs Represent Business Opportunities

Would you like to travel into outer space? If you answered yes, you are not alone. One survey reports that around 60 percent of Americans and 70 percent of Japanese are interested in space travel. Another indication of consumers' fascination with outer space is that within three months of the Pathfinder landing on Mars, NASA received 500 million hits on its web page!

Unfortunately, consumers currently lack the means for fulfilling their desires for an out-of-this-world experience. But plans are already on the drawing board for making space tourism a reality. Pete Conrad, the man who made the first pinpoint landing on the surface of the moon, wants to make history again—this time by starting the first space airline. And the Japanese are talking about building a hotel off this planet.

"I predict that people will be flying to space routinely for vacations," says Conrad. At the same time, however, he realizes that a space airline won't be flying anytime soon. He estimates that, in a few decades, average consumers may get to space as easily as they travel from coast to coast. To encourage private construction of space vehicles, the X Prize Foundation of St. Louis is offering $10 million to the builder of a craft able to carry at least three people to an altitude of 62 miles and return to fly again within two weeks. One member of the X Prize Foundation is Erik Lindbergh, grandson of legendary aviator Charles Lindbergh.

One company, Space Adventures, is counting on builders to deliver the goods. It's booking reservations for suborbital flights, which it says will depart in three to five years. A $6,000 deposit is required for reserving a seat and goes toward the overall cost of tickets, estimated at $75,000 to $100,000 each. Space Adventures already takes travelers on zero-gravity airplane flights, such as those used to simulate space flight for the movie *Apollo 13*, as well as for a ride on a Russian MiG-25 military jet that soars 70,000 feet above the earth. Prices start at $5,500 per person.

Not everyone, however, is optimistic about the future of space tourism. John Pike of the Federation of American Scientists believes that safety and cost issues make space tourism a risky, if not impossible, venture. The odds of getting killed are 1 in 100 on the space shuttle and 1 in a million on a passenger airplane, he said. "The problem is trying to figure out who's going to fly it for the first several thousand times in order to get it safe enough and cheap enough to get tourists," says Pike. "I don't see how we can get there from here."

Source: Excerpted from Dina Elboghdady, "Far-out: Former Astronaut Wants to Start a Space Airline," Miami Herald (August 7, 1997), 9A; Robin Stansbury, "Space Tours No Longer Are Sci-fi," Miami Herald (April 12, 1998), 1J, 4J; "Cheick Diarra," Fast Company (September 1999), 136; "Like Grandpa, Like Grandson," Miami Herald (July 1, 1999), 2A.

What is responsible for this state of affairs? Although it would be overly simplistic to point the finger at a single culprit, there is no denying that the industry's failure to adequately stimulate need recognition is a major reason. Says one industry executive, "The auto industry has convinced Americans to buy $25,000 cars that they throw away every three years, but the furniture industry still sells bedroom sets that people pass down to their kids." "We haven't done a great job of attracting the consumer," adds another industry observer.

Until the furniture industry can motivate consumers to redecorate more often, the industry's future does not look rosy. Stop for a moment and think about the basic strategies that might be pursued in this situation. In particular, what implications are suggested by viewing need recognition as depending on whether consumers perceive a meaningful difference between their current and ideal states? More generally, how can companies stimulate need recognition?

How Companies Can Activate Need Recognition

To illustrate some of the options for activating need recognition, let's stay with the furniture example. Apparently, many consumers are rather content with keeping the same set of furniture for many years, even decades. What they currently own is deemed sufficient. They do not experience a strong desire for something new and different.

One way of activating consumers' needs for new furniture is to change their desired state. That is, offer them something to die for! Develop and promote new styles, designs, and fabrics. Show consumers how much more attractive and enjoyable their homes will be when refurbished with new furniture.

Product innovations may cause need recognition. This was certainly the case when Reebok came out with its pump athletic shoe. This innovation, in which the user could adjust the air cushion in the shoe's sole, changed the ideal or desired state of many teenagers. The same thing is happening today with the advent of on-board navigation systems for automobiles. These navigational systems provide drivers with a computerized voice that guides them block by block to their selected destination. The success of such innovations largely depends on their ability to satisfy previously unfulfilled needs.

Another option is available to the furniture industry, one that must be handled very delicately so as not to offend consumers. Under this strategy, emphasis is placed on influencing how consumers perceive their actual state. The objective would be to undermine consumers' perceptions about the adequacy of their existing furniture. Advertising could suggest, perhaps in a humorous way, the possibility that one's present furniture is in greater need of retirement than recognized previously. To the extent that such advertising was successful in causing consumers to question the adequacy and attractiveness of their existing furniture, consumers would experience greater need recognition.

One example of using advertising to alter consumers' perceptions of the actual state of things appears in Figure 4.2. Many women may not recognize that they suffer from a calcium deficiency. Instead, they may incorrectly perceive their actual state as being healthier than it truly is. For these women, the ad in Figure 4.2, if believed, should cause them to recognize a discrepancy between their actual and desired states.

Simply reminding consumers of a need may be sufficient to trigger need recognition. Consumers browsing a retailer's aisles may encounter a display that reminds them of a previously recognized but since forgotten purchase need. Dentists send patients due for a checkup and cleaning a simple reminder in the mail that it's time to schedule an appointment. Advertisements, such as the one in Figure 4.3, are another way of reminding consumers of their needs. And some

Figure 4.2   This Ad Activates Need Recognition by Educating Consumers about the Actual State

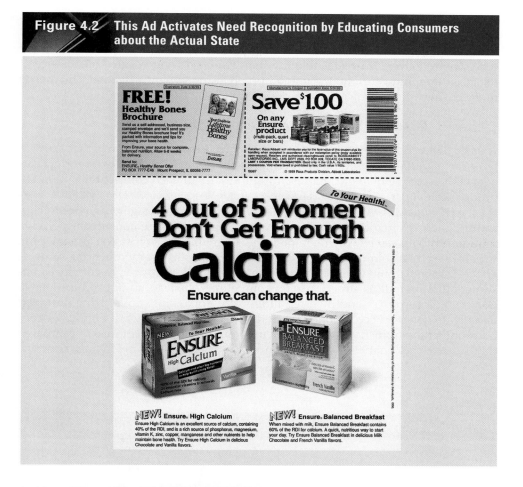

Figure 4.3   Reminding Consumers of Their Needs Can Activate Need Recognition

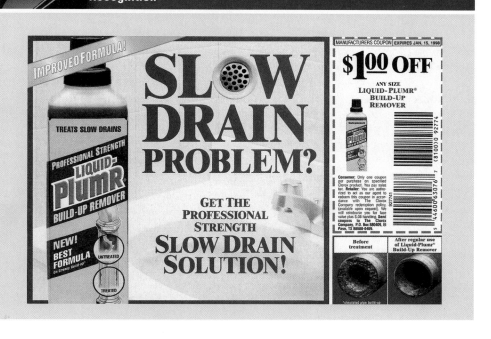

manufacturers have modified their products in order to stimulate need recognition. Although most toothbrushes wear out in three months, consumers typically replace them only once a year. Toothbrush maker Oral-B introduced a patented blue dye in the center bristles that gradually fades during usage. The absence of the blue dye indicates that the toothbrush is no longer effective and needs replacement.[3]

Generic Versus Selective Need Recognition

A basic distinction among efforts to activate need recognition is whether they attempt to stimulate primary demand (representing the total sales of a product category) or selective demand (representing the sales of each competitor within the product category). Companies seeking to *grow the size of the total market for a product (i.e., stimulate primary demand)* are attempting to elicit to **generic need recognition.** Such is often the case for product categories where consumers perceive minimal differences between competitors. Take milk. For most consumers, milk is perceived as a commodity product. One brand tastes pretty much the same as another. It is extremely difficult for a particular milk producer to convince consumers that its milk is superior to its competitors. Instead, milk producers have pooled their resources and invested millions of dollars into advertising designed to activate generic need recognition and build primary demand. Figure 4.4 contains one of the industry's advertisements from its current "got milk?" campaign that started back in 1994.[4] We will return to this campaign in Chapter 6 as one

Figure 4.4   **The Milk Industry Focuses on Generic Need Recognition**

example of the potential benefits offered by understanding consumers' product consumption.

The potential value of growing a product market need not be limited to product categories comprised of relatively undifferentiated brands. According to Jack Trout, a well-known marketing consultant, "If you are the leader, it is a lot better to broaden the category even though that might help the other guys who are nibbling away at you. What you want to do is build a market as big as you can and then defend it with a vengeance, like Coke and Hertz do."[5] Thus, even in product markets containing differentiated brands, the market leader may find it profitable to stimulate primary demand. This ultimately depends on whether the leader attracts and keeps a sufficient share of the new business.

Selective need recognition occurs when the *need for a specific brand within a product category (selective demand) is stimulated.* Marketing efforts now focus on persuading consumers that their needs will be satisfied by a particular brand. In this regard, comparative advertising that describes the advantages of one brand over its competition may be particularly effective. The comparative ad appearing in Figure 4.5 is intended to make parents perceive that Drypers are a better choice for satisfying their baby's diaper needs.

Search

Simply because consumers have experienced need recognition does not necessarily mean that they will proceed through the decision process. This depends on the importance of the need at the time it is activated. A hungry consumer, for instance, may not think that the rumblings in his or her stomach merit immediate action. It also depends on whether consumers believe that a solution to the need is within their means. Many consumers desire owning an expensive automobile, but lack the money necessary for satisfying this desire.

Figure 4.5   Comparative Advertising Is a Good Way to Activate Selective Need Recognition

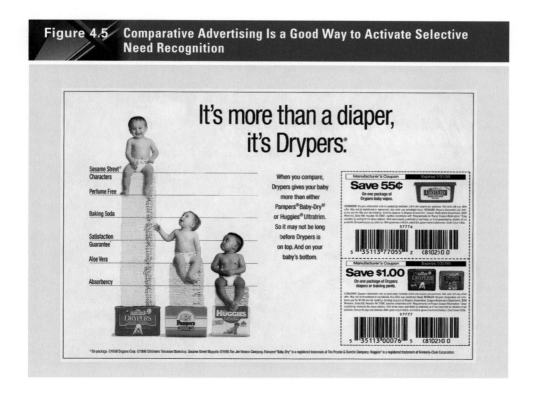

Nonetheless, consumers will often proceed through the decision-making process following need recognition. **Search,** the second stage of the decision-making process, represents the *motivated activation of knowledge stored in memory or acquisition of information from the environment concerning potential need satisfiers.* As this definition suggests, search can be either internal or external. **Internal search** involves *scanning and retrieving decision-relevant knowledge stored in memory.*[6] **External search** consists of *collecting information from the marketplace.*

Internal Search

As indicated by Figure 4.6, consumers experiencing need recognition begin their search internally. Many times a past solution is remembered and implemented. For this reason, consumers often have little need for undertaking external search before a purchase, even for major expenditures such as furniture, appliances, and automobiles.[7] More than half of the consumers participating in one study reported relying solely on their existing knowledge when choosing an auto repair service.[8]

Consumers' reliance on internal search will depend on both the adequacy or quality of their existing knowledge as well as their ability to retrieve this knowledge from memory. First-time buyers obviously lack the necessary information for making a decision based solely on internal search. Even experienced buyers may need to undertake external search. Experienced buyers may find their knowledge to be inadequate for product categories characterized by large interpurchase times (the amount of time between purchase occasions) during which there are significant product changes in prices, features, and new brands and stores. Even if product changes have been minimal, internal search is hindered by large interpurchase times due to problems of forgetting.

The degree of satisfaction with prior purchases also determines the consumer's reliance on internal search. If the consumer has been satisfied with the results of previous buying actions, internal search may suffice.[9]

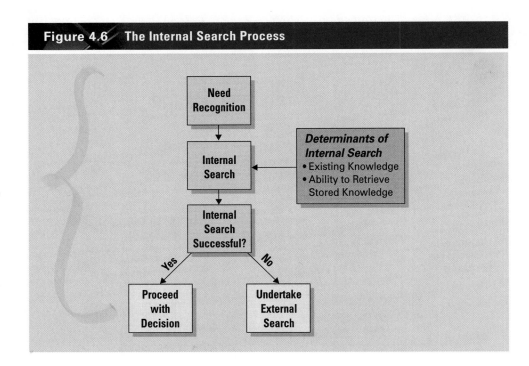

Figure 4.6   The Internal Search Process

External Search

When internal search proves inadequate, the consumer may decide to collect additional information from the environment. *External search motivated by an upcoming purchase decision* is known as **pre-purchase search.** This type of external search can be contrasted with another type called **ongoing search,** in which *information acquisition takes place on a relatively regular basis regardless of sporadic purchase needs.*[10] The car enthusiast who enjoys reading automotive magazines for their own sake would be engaging in ongoing search. Consumers who read the same magazines because of a forthcoming purchase would be engaging in pre-purchase search.

The primary motivation behind pre-purchase search is the desire to make better consumption choices. Similarly, ongoing search may be motivated by desires to develop a knowledge base that can be used in future decision making. Ongoing search also occurs simply because of the enjoyment derived from this activity.[11] Consumers may browse through a mall, without having specific purchase needs, simply because it is "fun" to them.

How Much Do Consumers Search?

The answer to this question is, "It depends." Sometimes we invest substantial amounts of time and effort into collecting information for a pending purchase decision. Take, for example, buying a home. Few, if any, of the purchase decisions made during our lifetime will exceed the amount of search undertaken while shopping for a new home. One of the authors of this book recently completed searching for a new house. He devoted hundreds of hours over several months to searching the housing market. With the aid of his real estate agent, a list of existing homes for sale that met certain criteria (location, price, size, and so on) was developed. A day or two was then spent visiting these homes. This process was repeated several times.

Eventually, after examining dozens of existing homes, he reluctantly decided to build a new home. He had heard many complaints from others that had gone through this experience, including his own parents. He also realized that this would greatly complicate matters. Numerous decisions unique to building a new home must be made. Should you hire an architect to draft plans for the home? Perhaps it would be better to find a builder that offers a variety of models that can be customized. Should one builder do everything? Or should certain parts of the home (e.g., flooring, pool, landscaping) be handled by subcontractors? What about options and upgrades? Builders offer options for certain features that must be decided upon (e.g., the color of the kitchen tile). And nearly anything can be upgraded for the right price.

Fortunately, many purchase decisions are more easily made than the decision to buy a home. Think about your last trip to the grocery store. If you are like most grocery shoppers, the time you spent making each individual purchase decision can be measured in seconds! Consumers have little patience in locating what they want. According to Anthony Adams, vice president of marketing research at Campbell Soup, "After about 45 seconds, we find that consumers just give up."[12] Even less time is taken once the shopper arrives at the proper location. On average, around 12 seconds passes from the moment a consumer stops where the product sits on the shelf and places the chosen item in his or her grocery cart.[13]

Why do we engage in greater search for some products instead of others? According to a **cost versus benefit** perspective, *people search for decision-relevant information when the perceived benefits of the new information are greater than the perceived costs of acquiring this information.*[14] A major benefit is making better purchase decisions. The time and effort that must be expended represent search costs. Consumers will search until the benefits no longer outweigh the costs.

Search costs vary directly with how easily information can be acquired. Making it easier for consumers can lead to greater search. Such was the case for the unit price information available in grocery stores.[15] Unit price information is typically presented on separate tags along the grocer's shelf. Acquiring this information becomes much easier when it is consolidated and presented on a single list. For this reason, consumers' purchases reflected greater search and use of unit price information presented on a list than on separate tags.

One reason the Internet is dramatically changing consumer behavior is that it helps us search much more easily and efficiently than ever before. With a few clicks on the computer screen, we're driving down the information highway. And to make life easier, technology has been developed that does most of the work for us. Just indicate what you are looking for, and the software searches the Internet for you.

As noted earlier, making better purchase decisions is the primary benefit of prepurchase search. This benefit depends on **perceived risk,** representing *consumers' uncertainty about the potential positive and negative consequences of the purchase decision.* Generally speaking, as the perceived risk of a purchase decision increases, so does search. By searching more, consumers hope to reduce the chances of making a purchase they'll regret. It is little wonder that 40 percent of auto buyers searched the Internet in 1999 before making their purchase.[16]

When consumers perceive significant differences between products but are uncertain about which product is best for their needs, search becomes more likely.[17] Similarly, as potential consequences become more important, perceived risk increases, thereby leading to greater search. A poor choice is easier to live with when the price is cheap, but not so when you are spending thousands of dollars. Consequently, consumers invest more effort into search as the price of the product increases.[18]

The Value of Understanding Consumer Search

Companies benefit from an understanding of consumer search in many ways. When, as noted earlier, Campbell Soup realized the unwillingness of consumers to devote more than 45 seconds in locating what they want, the company streamlined its soup selections so that shoppers could locate what they want as quickly as possible.[19] In this instance, the company modified the breadth of its product line in response to understanding consumer search.

Pricing decisions may also benefit. Companies want to know how much they should charge in order to maximize their profitability. They also need to know how much attention they should give to the prices charged by competitors in setting their own prices.

As a rule of thumb, a company should pay as much attention to the prices of its competitors as do consumers in its target market. Consider the retailer that competes with a couple of other retailers in its area. If consumers typically compare the prices charged by retailers, this would highlight the need to pay particular attention to the competition's prices. In this situation, the retailer would be unable to sell items comparable to those offered by its competitors at a less than competitive price. For this reason, grocery executives are more likely to respond to a competitor's price cuts for "high-visibility" items (soda, milk, bananas) when consumers engage in more price comparison shopping.[20]

In contrast, reduced levels of price comparison search offer the company more flexibility in setting prices. It is not uncommon for consumers to visit a single retailer before making their purchase decisions. When this is the case, the retailer can more easily get away with charging higher prices. Thus, by understanding the emphasis given to price by consumers during search, a company can better appreciate consumers' price sensitivity.

Consumer search also carries important implications for promotional strategy. Ideally, a firm should focus its promotional efforts on those areas most likely to be searched by target consumers. Companies can feel more confident about the potential payoff of their investments in advertising and in-store promotional materials if these represent important sources of information used during decision making. These investments would be wasted on consumers that rely solely on internal search.

Sometimes other people serve as critical sources of information. The opinions of a pharmacist about the product best suited for relieving certain symptoms often leads to selecting the recommended product. Friends' opinions may be instrumental, particularly when they are perceived as being well-informed about the product. Promotional efforts would be focused on gaining a favorable opinion among those serving as valued information sources.

Because what happens during search may determine what happens during purchase, it is also important for companies to understand the relationship between various search activities and the particular brand purchased. That is, beyond understanding the frequency and nature of different activities, we also need to understand if and how each activity influences consumers' choices. Each time a company discovers that search of a particular kind enhances the odds of its product being purchased, it has uncovered another opportunity for gaining more customers.

One way to do this would be to survey recent product buyers about their search behaviors. Respondents could be classified into different search segments based on the amount and/or nature of their search. The percentage of consumers choosing the company's brand within each search segment would be identified. They would then test whether this percentage differs significantly across the search segments.

To illustrate, suppose that a company discovered that consumers who consulted a pharmacist during search were much more likely to buy the company's product (e.g., 35 percent of this search segment buys from the company) than those who did not acquire information from this source (e.g., only 10 percent of this segment buys from the company). If so, clearly it's in the company's best interest to encourage this search activity. One example of using advertising to encourage consumer search of a particular nature appears in Figure 4.7. Notice how the ad asks the reader to talk to a pharmacist or dermatologist. The wisdom of this request ultimately depends on whether consumers are more likely to purchase the advertised brand after talking to these sources.

On the other hand, suppose that the company finds that consumers are much less likely to buy the company's product if they engage in a specific search activity. When this happens, clearly there is substantial incentive for the company not to encourage this type of search. Less defensible, however, are attempts to discourage search. As described in Consumer in Focus 4.2, such efforts may actually backfire.

Pre-Purchase Evaluation

Ultimately, the likelihood of a product being purchased depends on whether it is evaluated favorably by consumers. In deciding which products and brands to buy, consumers will rely heavily on their evaluations of the alternatives available for

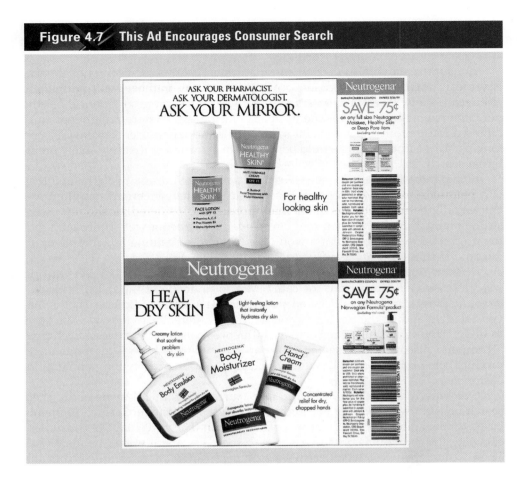

Figure 4.7   This Ad Encourages Consumer Search

Consumer in Focus 4.2

How One Company's (Unintentional?) Efforts to Reduce Consumer Search Backfired

Ibiley School Uniforms, a retailer in Miami, Florida, was the focus of an article appearing in the local newspaper. This article described how the retailer's recent advertising was receiving a less than warm reception from consumers. Of particular concern was the sales pitch, "Hey, school uniforms are never on sale, and you have to go to Ibiley anyway!"

The problem is that consumers don't have to go to Ibiley. School board policy allows parents to buy uniform components anywhere. Yet this is not how consumers interpreted Ibiley's advertising. As one consumer explained, "Listening to that I believed I *had* to buy the uniforms there. When I called Kendale Lakes Elementary, they told me that that wasn't true, that I could go to Target or any other store.

They're misleading people with that ad."

Ibiley president Eddy Barea stood by his advertising technique. "It's not misleading, it's true. They have to come to Ibiley because we're the best company to go to. That's just my way of advertising, telling them we're the best company with the best quality."

It might also be a way of discouraging consumers from shopping with the competition. And it's easy to see why the company wouldn't mind if it did. The newspaper article contained numerous comparisons between the prices charged by Ibiley and its competitors for a variety of boys' and girls' garments. For the overwhelming majority, Ibiley charged more than the competition.

Source: Excerpted from Maria A. Morales, "It Pays to Shop around for Uniforms," Miami Herald (July 20, 1997), 1B, 2B.

choice. Disliked alternatives are quickly rejected, if not ignored completely. Liked alternatives may be considered and compared, with the one receiving the most positive evaluation being chosen.

The manner in which choice alternatives are evaluated is the focus of our third stage of the consumer decision-making process, **pre-purchase evaluation.** Although we have presented search and prepurchase evaluation as "separate" stages for pedagogical reasons, you should recognize that the two stages are intricately intertwined during decision making. The acquisition of product information from the environment, for instance, will normally lead to some evaluation (e.g., "these prices are too high") that may then guide subsequent search (e.g., "let's check the store across the street").

Before deciding what to purchase, consumers have other decisions to make. Should all possible offerings in the marketplace be considered, or should consideration be restricted to some subset of the offerings? Of those alternatives deemed worthy of consideration, how should they be evaluated? These fundamental aspects of the pre-purchase evaluation process are represented in Figure 4.8, which provides a roadmap of where we are going in this section.

Determining Choice Alternatives

When making purchase decisions, we normally have a number of possibilities from which to choose. Yet we may not consider all alternatives that are available to us. It is highly unlikely that, the next time you decide to eat out, you will consider all the restaurants in your area. Instead, you will probably make a choice after considering only a subset of available restaurants.

Those alternatives considered during decision making compose what is known as the **consideration set** (also known as the **evoked set**).[21] As suggested by the information presented in Table 4.1, the consideration set typically contains only a subset of the total number of alternatives available to the consumer. Recognize that these results represent the average size of the consideration set. Some consumers have even larger consideration sets. For others, the consideration set is

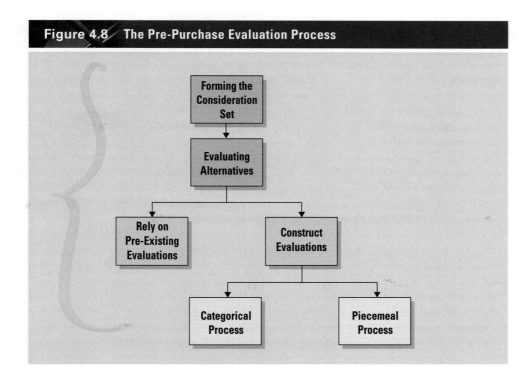

Figure 4.8   The Pre-Purchase Evaluation Process

Forming the Consideration Set

Evaluating Alternatives

Rely on Pre-Existing Evaluations

Construct Evaluations

Categorical Process

Piecemeal Process

Table 4.1	Average Size of Consumers' Consideration Sets by Product Category		
Product Category	**Average Consideration Set Size**	**Product Category**	**Average Consideration Set Size**
Analgesic	3.5	Frozen dinners	3.3
Antacid	4.4	Insecticides	2.7
Air freshener	2.2	Laundry detergent	4.8
Bar soap	3.7	Laxative	2.8
Bathroom cleaner	5.7	Peanut butter	3.3
Beer	6.9	Razors	2.9
Bleach	3.9	Shampoo	6.1
Chili	2.6	Shortening	6.0
Coffee	4.0	Sinus medicine	3.6
Cookies	4.9	Soda	5.1
Deodorant	3.9	Yogurt	3.6

Source: John R. Hauser and Birger Wernerfelt, "An Evaluation Cost Model of Consideration Sets," Journal of Consumer Research 16 (March 1990), 393–408.

smaller. Consumers extremely loyal to a particular brand will have only this brand in their consideration set.

Because failure to gain entry into the consideration set means that a competitor's offering will be purchased, gaining consideration for one's product is essential. The importance of gaining consideration is well appreciated by Jim Ivey, the CEO at Savin Corporation, a manufacturer of office copiers. "With all the competitors and all the brands, making sure you are on the consideration list is most important," he says. Increasing consideration is also important for the horse racing industry, as discussed in Consumer in Focus 4.3.

Fortunately, companies have at their disposal a variety of ways for gaining consideration from their target customers. One way is to simply ask. How many times have you ordered a hamburger at a fast-food restaurant only to be asked if you would also like some fries? Shoppers having just decided on which suit to purchase are likely to be asked by the salesperson if they want to consider accessory items. Simply requesting consideration is common in the marketplace.

Gaining consideration may often require making changes in one of the four P's—product, price, promotion, and physical distribution. If consideration sets are constructed based on what is available at the local store, failure to have the company's products present at the point of purchase eliminates consideration. The company's distribution strategy would then need to be adjusted. An expensive price tag may preclude consideration of the product by many consumers. The desirability of price cuts could be explored. Promotional activities can encourage consideration. Automobile manufacturers sometimes offer gifts or money to simply test-drive their cars. Coupons can play essentially the same role. Notice how the ad in Figure 4.9 encourages consideration by offering consumers $100 if they buy from a competitor after considering the company's offering.

Consumer in Focus 4.3

Getting Thoroughbred Racing Back in the Saddle

The Sport of Kings has stumbled in the far turn and is looking to marketing to help put it at the front of the pack. For years, steep declines in thoroughbred racetrack attendance have meant most parks are scrambling just to salvage existing customer relationships and revenues, let alone attract new spectators. This sport faces low interest and rapidly growing competition from other forms of gaming, such as reservation and riverboat casinos.

In 1998, the industry formed the National Thoroughbred Racing Association (NTRA). The NTRA plans to market this sport extensively to raise its profile and popularity, using a nationwide branding campaign and increased television coverage. According to Rick Baedeker, the association's vice president of marketing, "The industry has never been marketed as a whole, and never means never. We paid a price for that. Each track has done its own marketing and advertising, which by necessity had been of a retail nature to flip the turnstiles, and we slipped in the mind of the consumer. It's not that they think badly of us. They just don't think of us."

The NTRA plans on spending around $150 million over a four-year period to overcome this lack of consideration. In the manner of the NBA's "I love this game!" the industry already has adopted a slogan—"Go, Baby, Go!"—a reference to cheers heard in the racetrack stands. Consumers in the 25- to 54-year-old age group are the primary target. The existing fan base is disproportionately older, and the aging of these fans has been cause for further concern about the industry's attendance problems.

Source: Excerpted from Maricris G. Briones, "And They're Off!" Marketing News *(March 30, 1998), 1, 14.*

In some instances, a company may find it beneficial to encourage consumers to consider not only its brand, but competitive brands as well. This possibility is suggested by what is known as the **attraction effect.** The attractiveness of a given alternative and its odds of being chosen are enhanced when a clearly inferior alternative is added to the set of considered alternatives.[22]

Constructing the Consideration Set

Suppose you were hungry and decided to eat out tonight. In this instance, there are at least two ways you could go about constructing a consideration set. You could undertake external search, such as scanning the restaurants listed in the yellow pages, mentally noting those worth further consideration. A more likely scenario, however, would involve an internal search through memory, which will probably yield several possibilities. In the latter situation, the consideration set would depend on your *recall of choice alternatives from memory* (known as the **retrieval set**).[23]

Not all the alternatives retrieved from memory or available at the point of purchase will necessarily receive consideration. When there are preexisting evaluations, consumers may screen the alternatives based on how favorable they are about each one. After all, if you know that your taste buds are terrified by a particular restaurant's cuisine, there's no sense giving it a moment's thought. Instead, consumers will largely limit their consideration to those alternatives toward which they are favorably predisposed.

Obviously, consumers cannot construct a consideration set based on an internal search of memory without prior knowledge of at least some alternatives. Yet, particularly for first-time buyers in the product category, consumers may lack knowledge about what alternatives are available to choose from. When this occurs, the consideration set may be developed in any one of several ways. The consumer might talk to others, search through the yellow pages, consider all brands available at the store, and so on. Thus, external factors such as the retail

Figure 4.9   Offering Incentives to Gain Purchase Consideration

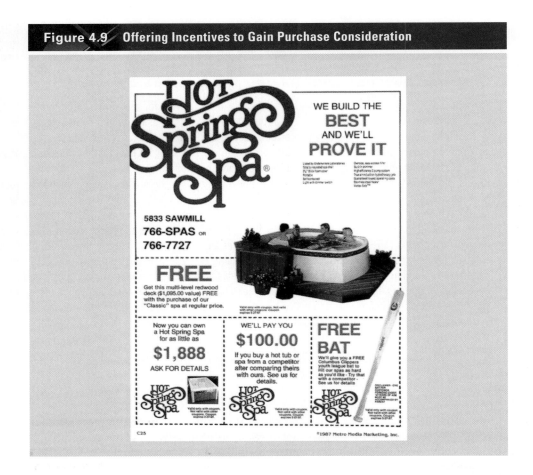

environment have a greater opportunity to affect the consideration set of less knowledgeable consumers.[24]

The manner in which the consideration set is constructed can shape marketing strategy. Consider those situations in which consumers construct a consideration set based on an internal memory search. When this occurs, the odds of a given offering being chosen depend on its being recalled from memory. Accordingly, when consideration sets are based on internal search, it is very important that consumers are able to *recall* the company's offering.

At other times, *recognition* rather than recall becomes more important in determining the consideration set. Take the consumer who quickly scans the shelf at a grocery store to determine what is available and makes a choice among those brands that he or she recognizes, ones that look familiar. Recognition of alternatives available at the point of purchase would therefore determine the consideration set. Beyond making sure its offering is available at the store, a company would also want to teach consumers about what its product packaging looks like so that it can be easily recognized.[25]

Deciding How to Evaluate the Choice Alternatives

As indicated earlier in Figure 4.8, determining the consideration set is only part of the prepurchase evaluation. In addition, consumers must decide how these considered alternatives will be evaluated. There are basically two options for doing this: (1) rely on pre-existing product evaluations stored in memory, or (2) construct new evaluations based on information acquired through internal or external search.

Relying on Pre-Existing Evaluations

Which do you prefer, Coke or Pepsi, McDonald's or Burger King, Colgate or Crest? Most American consumers would find it rather easy to answer this question. This is because their prior consumption of these products has led to the formation of evaluations that are stored in memory. If the relevant evaluations are retrieved during internal search, then each can be compared to determine which considered alternative is most liked.

Obviously, consumers' ability to use this decision strategy depends on the existence of pre-existing evaluations. These pre-existing evaluations may be based on prior purchase and consumption experiences with a product. At other times, they may be based on indirect or secondhand experiences, such as the impressions we might form after hearing our friends talking about a product.

The extent to which these pre-existing evaluations are based on direct versus indirect experiences is important. Because consumers are more confident in evaluations derived from actual product usage, they'll be more likely to use these pre-existing evaluations when making their purchase decisions. Such is the case for many of the purchase decisions we make while grocery shopping. It is for this reason that consumers are able to make many of their selections in only a few seconds.

Constructing New Evaluations

In many circumstances, consumers may be unable or unwilling to rely on their pre-existing evaluations for making a choice. Unless you are more than a casual bowler, it is unlikely that you hold any preferences concerning urethane versus reactive resin bowling balls. Inexperienced consumers making a first-time purchase decision will typically lack pre-existing evaluations.

Even experienced consumers possessing pre-existing evaluations may elect not to use these evaluations. After decades of purchasing and driving automobiles, older consumers are likely to hold rather strong feelings about different automobile makers. Nonetheless, if considerable time has elapsed since they made their last purchase, they may question whether they are adequately informed about today's offerings.

There are two basic processes by which consumers can construct evaluations. According to a **categorization process,** *evaluation of a choice alternative depends on the particular category to which it is assigned.* In contrast, under a **piecemeal process,** *an evaluation is derived from consideration of the alternative's advantages and disadvantages along important product dimensions.* We discuss each process next.

The Categorization Process One aspect of human knowledge is the existence of mental categories. Categories can be very general (motorized forms of transportation). They can be very specific (Harley-Davidson motorcycles). Typically, these categories are associated with some degree of liking or disliking. Moreover, the evaluation attached to a category may be transferred to any new object assigned to the category.[26]

This same process can be used when consumers are forming their initial evaluations of a product.[27] To the extent that the product can be assigned membership to a particular category, it will receive an evaluation similar to that attached to the category. If consumers perceive a new product they encounter at the grocery store as just another health food, then they may simply evaluate it based on their liking of health foods in general.

Accordingly, when consumers rely on a categorization process, a product's evaluation depends on the particular category to which it is perceived as belonging. Given this, companies need to understand whether consumers are using categories that evoke the desired evaluations. Indeed, how a product is categorized can strongly influence consumer demand. For example, what products come to mind when you think about the "morning beverages" category? To the soft drink industry's dismay, far too few of us include sodas in this category. Several attempts have been made at carving out a place for soft drinks at the breakfast table, but with little success.[28]

Brand extensions, in which a *well-known and respected brand name from one product category is extended into other product categories,* is one way companies employ categorization to their advantage. Through consumer research, it was discovered that the Dole brand name, although traditionally associated with the fresh and canned fruit sections of a supermarket, could work in the frozen section as well. This led to the launch of Dole Fruit & Juice Bars.[29] The company's hope is that consumers' favorable opinions toward the Dole name will transfer to its new brand extensions. Disney holds similar aspirations for its recent entry into the cruise line industry.

That consumers' evaluations of a brand extension may depend on their liking of the core brand is well established. However, the effectiveness of this strategy is lessened as the product categories of the extension and core brand become more dissimilar.[30] Extending the Disney name into the cruise line industry makes sense. Extending its name into other product categories (e.g., beer or cigarettes) does not.

The Piecemeal Process A piecemeal process essentially involves constructing an evaluation of a choice alternative using bits and pieces. First, consumers must determine the particular criteria or product dimensions to be used in evaluating choice alternatives. In deciding which automobile to purchase, consumers may consider such criteria as safety, reliability, price, brand name, country of origin (where it is made), warranty, and gas mileage. They may also consider the feelings that come from owning (such as prestige and status) and driving (such as exhilaration and excitement) the car.

Decisions involving "noncomparable" alternatives may require the consumer to use more abstract criteria during evaluation.[31] Consider the consumer faced with choosing between a refrigerator, a television, and a stereo. These alternatives share few concrete attributes (price is an exception) along which comparisons can be made directly. Comparisons can be undertaken, however, using abstract dimensions such as necessity, entertainment, and status.

Next, consumers need to evaluate the strength or weakness of each considered alternative along the particular criteria deemed important in making their choice. Is the product's price acceptable? Does the product provide the desired benefits? Is the warranty strong enough?

In many cases, consumers already have stored in memory judgments or beliefs about the performance of the choice alternatives under consideration. The ability to retrieve this information may strongly affect which alternative is eventually chosen.[32] However, consumers lacking such stored knowledge will need to rely on external information in forming beliefs about an alternative's performance.

In judging how well an alternative performs, consumers often use cutoffs.[33] A **cutoff** is simply a *restriction or requirement for acceptable performance.* Consider price. Consumers usually have an upper limit for the price they are willing to pay. A price that exceeds this limit will be viewed as unacceptable.[34] Similarly, consumers may reject a food item because it exceeds the number of calories they are prepared to consume.

Consumers may rely on certain signals when judging product performance. **Signals** are *product attributes that are used to infer other product attributes.* Attributes such as brand name, price, and warranty may be interpreted as signals of product quality. Many of us would perceive the quality of a watch much differently depending on whether it carries the Rolex or Timex brand name. Higher prices are often interpreted as an indicator of higher quality.[35] A strong warranty may be interpreted in a similar fashion.[36] Companies that fail to recognize the signaling power of certain attributes may unnecessarily sell themselves short. Read Consumer in Focus 4.4 for an example of this.

The final step in a piecemeal process involves using one's judgments about the performance of the considered alternatives to form an overall evaluation of each alternative's acceptability. Consumer researchers have identified a number of ways in which consumers may do this. A fundamental distinction between these evaluation strategies is whether they are compensatory or noncompensatory.

Noncompensatory Evaluation Strategies   Common to this set of evaluation strategies is that a product's weakness on one attribute *cannot* be offset by its strong performance on another attribute. Consider snack foods. Manufacturers have the capability of meeting consumers' desires for healthier snacks by cutting the amount of oil and salt in the products. But eliminate too much of these ingredients and the snacks taste lousy. Although the reformulated product will score high marks on nutritional considerations, this strength cannot overcome the

Consumer in Focus 4.4

Is Whirlpool Missing the Signal?

Which brand of washing machines is best? To answer this question, *Consumer Reports* rated 16 brands along numerous dimensions: load capacity, water and energy efficiency, how well the machine could handle unbalanced loads, and so on. As reported in the February 1991 issue, products of the Whirlpool Corp. received the best ratings. In addition to selling washers that carry the Whirlpool name, the company also makes the washers that sell under the Sears' Kenmore and KitchenAid brand names. All three brands were at the top of the ratings.

But what if consumers are unaware of the *Consumer Reports* ratings? How might they go about judging quality? As

we noted in the chapter, a product's warranty can serve as a signal of quality. And this is where Whirlpool may be missing the signal. Consider the warranty information shown below based on a fact sheet developed by the manufacturer of the Amana brand that rested upon its washers being displayed by the retailer.

Based on this information, consumers may come to very different conclusions about which brand is best than implied by the *Consumer Reports* ratings. One can only wonder about how many sales Whirlpool lost because of the weak signal conveyed by its warranty.

	Transmission		Nontransmission		Cabinet Rust
	Labor	Parts	Labor	Parts	
Amana	5 Years	10 Years	1 Year	2 Years	5 Years
Frigidaire	1 Year	5 Years	1 Year	1 Year	1 Year
GE/Hotpoint	1 Year	5 Years	1 Year	1 Year	1 Year
Kenmore	1 Year	5 Years	1 Year	1 Year	1 Year
Maytag	1 Year	10 Years	1 Year	2 Years	5 Years
Whirlpool	1 Year	5 Years	1 Year	1 Year	1 Year

Source: "Washing Machines," Consumer Reports *(February 1991), 112–117.*

weakness in the product's taste. According to Dwight Riskey, a psychologist and vice president of market research at Frito-Lay, "Consumers won't sacrifice taste for health in snacks."[37]

Noncompensatory evaluation strategies come in many different forms.[38] According to a **lexicographic strategy,** *brands are compared initially on the most important attribute.* If one of the brands is perceived as superior based on that attribute, it is selected. If two or more brands are perceived as equally good, they are then compared on the second most important attribute. This process continues until the tie is broken.

The **elimination by aspects strategy** resembles the lexicographic approach. As before, brands are first evaluated on the most important attribute. Now, however, the *consumer imposes cutoffs.* The consumer may, for example, use cutoffs such as "must be under $2" or "must be nutritious."

If only one brand meets the cutoff on the most important attribute, it is chosen. If several brands meet the cutoff, then the next most important attribute is selected and the process continues until the tie is broken. If none of the brands are acceptable, the consumer must revise the cutoffs, use a different evaluation strategy, or postpone choice.

Cutoffs also play a prominent part in the **conjunctive strategy.**[39] Cutoffs are established for each salient attribute. *Each brand is compared, one at a time, against this set of cutoffs.* Thus, processing by brand is required. If the brand meets the cutoffs for *all* the attributes, it is chosen. Failure to meet the cutoff for any attribute leads to rejection. As before, if none of the brands meet the cutoff requirements, a change in either the cutoffs or the evaluation strategy must occur. Otherwise, choice must be delayed.

To illustrate the operation of these strategies, consider the information presented in Table 4.2. This table contains attribute-performance ratings (from excellent to poor) for four different brands of food and attribute-importance rankings (where 1 is most important). Which brand would be chosen if a lexicographic strategy were used? The answer is brand A. A comparison on the most important attribute, taste, produces a tie between brands A, B, and D. This tie is broken on the next most important attribute, price, because brand A has the highest rating of the three brands. Notice, however, what would happen if the attribute-importance rankings were slightly different. For instance, if price were more important, brand C would then be chosen.

Choice based on elimination by aspects would depend on the particular cutoff values imposed by the decision maker. Suppose the minimum acceptable values for taste and price were "excellent" and "very good," respectively. Brand A would again be chosen. But if the cutoff for taste was lowered to "very good" and the cutoff for price was raised to "excellent," then brand C would be selected.

Table 4.2	Hypothetical Brand Ratings				

Attribute	Importance Ranking	Brand Performance Ratings			
		Brand A	Brand B	Brand C	Brand D
Taste	1	Excellent	Excellent	Very Good	Excellent
Price	2	Very Good	Good	Excellent	Fair
Nutrition	3	Good	Good	Poor	Excellent
Convenience	4	Fair	Good	Good	Excellent

To illustrate the conjunctive strategy, assume that the consumer insists that the brand receive a rating of at least "good" on each attribute. In Table 4.2, brand A is rejected because of its inadequate rating (i.e., does not meet the cutoff requirement of "good") on convenience, whereas brand C is inadequate on nutrition. Brand D is eliminated by the unacceptable price rating. Only brand B meets all the cutoff requirements and therefore would be evaluated as an acceptable choice.

Compensatory Evaluation Strategies   Did you notice the plight of poor brand D in Table 4.2? Despite its excellent ratings in three of the four salient attributes (including the most important attribute), brand D never emerged as the top brand. Why? Because of its poor price performance. Indeed, none of the noncompensatory strategies permitted the brand's poor rating on price to be offset by its otherwise excellent performance.

This is not the case for compensatory evaluation strategies. Now a perceived weakness of one attribute may be offset or compensated for by the perceived strength of another attribute. Two types of compensatory strategies are the simple additive and weighted additive.

Under **simple additive,** the *consumer simply counts or adds the number of times each alternative is judged favorably in terms of the set of salient evaluative criteria.* The alternative having the largest number of positive attributes is chosen. The use of simple additive is most likely when consumers' processing motivation or ability is limited.[40]

A more complex form of the compensatory strategy is the **weighted additive.** *The consumer now engages in more refined judgments about the alternative's performance than simply whether it is favorable or unfavorable. These judgments are then weighted by the importance attached to the attributes.* In essence, a weighted additive rule is equivalent to the multiattribute attitude models described later in Chapter 10.

At this point, it is useful to stop and consider what all this means for the practitioner. What value does knowledge about the particular evaluation strategy used during decision making have for the development of marketing strategies?

Fundamentally speaking, marketers need to understand evaluation strategies because they affect consumer choice. An understanding of the strategy (or strategies) used by a company's customers, which is the strategy that leads to the choice of the company's product, may suggest actions that maintain or facilitate customers' use of this strategy. For instance, if customers use a lexicographic strategy with product quality being the most important attribute, the company may find it profitable to implement an advertising campaign stressing the importance of product quality and the quality of the company's product.

Understanding evaluation strategies is also important for identifying the appropriate actions for improving consumers' product evaluations.[41] To illustrate, suppose that brand C in Table 4.2 improved its taste perception from "very good" to "excellent." This change makes considerable sense if consumers use a lexicographic strategy because it would lead to brand C being chosen. Suppose, however, that consumers use a conjunctive strategy with cutoffs of "good." Improving the product's taste would be of little value because its nutritional rating of "poor" is unacceptable. Instead, it would be critical to enhance the brand's nutritional performance.

Changing consumers' evaluation strategies provides marketers with another mechanism for influencing choice. In some cases, this might involve changing the importance of product attributes. For instance, assuming a lexicographic strategy, the maker of brand C in Table 4.2 might try to alter the importance consumers attach to taste and price. A lexicographic strategy with price being the most important attribute would lead to the selection of brand C, whereas this strategy would lead to brand A being chosen when taste is most important.

Changing the cutoffs is another mechanism for altering choice. As illustrated by the example in the prior discussion of elimination by aspects, changes in the minimum acceptable values for taste and price resulted in the selection of different brands from Table 4.2.

How Good Are We at Evaluating Alternatives?

Numerous examples indicate that consumers have little to brag about when it comes to evaluating which alternative is best for them. A classic demonstration of this involved offering grocery shoppers the opportunity to win a sizable amount of money if they could choose accurately which of two brands was the best buy.[42] Doing this requires shoppers to calculate each brand's unit price and choose the lowest. To complicate matters, the brand having the higher unit price was described as being on sale (though even at the sale price, its unit price was still greater). Apparently, many shoppers interpreted this sale as a signal that the inferior brand was a better buy. In this instance, the signal was misleading, and they made the wrong choice.

Such mistakes are commonplace. Consumers unable to afford buying the product outright but wishing to avoid the high interest rates of buying it on credit often opt for what is known as "rent-to-own." The consumer pays a weekly or monthly fee to lease the product with an option to buy. And pay they do! By the time the customer exercises the option to buy and completes all the required payments, the average interest rate is 100 percent and ranges as high as 275 percent.[43]

Consumers' ability to accurately evaluate choice alternatives is important for their own welfare as well as society's. Every time we make a poor decision, we pay the price, although often we may not even be aware of this. Take credit insurance that covers the borrower's financial obligation if he or she becomes disabled or dies. According to Consumers Union, publisher of *Consumer Reports,* a magazine devoted to providing consumers with impartial evidence concerning product performance, consumers overpay for the coverage they receive by $2 billion a year![44]

Nor is it in society's best interests for its members to consume inefficiently. Consequently, public policy makers are very interested in helping consumers make better purchase decisions. For this reason, the U.S. Congress required cigarette packages to carry warning labels. The nutritional labels on today's food packaging were mandated by legislation.

Summary

The decision process begins when a need is activated and recognized because of a discrepancy between the consumer's desired state and actual situation. Understanding need recognition may reveal unfulfilled desires, thereby indicating potential business opportunities. Sometimes businesses influence need recognition as a way of stimulating product purchase.

Search for potential need satisfiers will occur following need recognition. If an internal search of memory provides a satisfactory solution to the consumption problem, it is unnecessary for consumers to seek information from their environment. Often, however, some degree of external search is needed. Consumers will search so long as the perceived benefits of the collected information outweigh the costs of acquiring it. To the extent that consumer search of a particular nature enhances the odds of product purchase, efforts to enhance such search may be warranted.

Prepurchase alternative evaluation represents the decision-making stage in which consumers evaluate considered alternatives to make a choice. Sometimes preexisting evaluations are retrieved from memory and acted upon. At other times, consumers have to construct new evaluations in order to make a choice. Understanding how these evaluations are made may reveal a number of opportunities for businesses to influence consumer behavior.

Review and Discussion Questions

1. What are the basic strategies available for companies seeking to influence need recognition?

2. Discuss how need recognition triggered your last soft drink purchase. Was this different from need recognition leading to the purchase of new shoes? What role, if any, do you feel marketing efforts played in both situations?

3. Explain how each of the following factors might affect consumer search: (a) brand loyalty, (b) store loyalty, (c) uncertainty about which brand best meets consumers' needs, and (d) the importance consumers place on paying a low price.

4. Consider two alternative target segments that differ only in their propensity for information search. One segment undertakes a substantial amount of external search during decision making. In contrast, consumers in the remaining segment are far less active in their search behaviors. Which segment, if either, would be a better target market? Assuming both were targeted, how should marketing activities differ in pursuing each segment?

5. A recent study has classified consumers into one of three segments based on the amount of search they did when making their purchase decisions. For each segment, the percentage buying your brand versus competitive brands was examined. The results are as follows:

	Percentage Buying	
Amount of Search	**Your Brand**	**Competitors' Brands**
Minimal	3	97
Moderate	9	91
Extensive	17	83

What implications do these results carry for marketing strategy?

6. The results of a consumer research project examining whether target consumers' brand preferences at the time of need recognition carried over to actual purchase has just arrived on your desk. Consumers just beginning their decision process were asked about their preferences for the company's brand and two competitors' brands. These results, as well as each brand's share of purchases, are as follows:

Brand	Consumers' Preference at Time of Need Recognition	Share of Purchases
Company's brand	50%	30%
Competitor A	30%	50%
Competitor B	20%	20%
Total	100%	100%

What conclusions would you reach from this information?

7. In the chapter, we indicate that offering incentives is one way for a product to gain consideration during consumer decision making. How else might a product try to enter the consideration set?

8. A restaurant is trying to decide on the appropriate method for assessing consumers' consideration set when they are deciding where to eat out. One person has argued for a recall method in which consumers are asked to remember the names of restaurants without any memory cues. Another person recommends a recognition method in which consumers are given a list of local restaurants and asked to circle the appropriate names. Which method would you recommend? Would your answer change if consumers normally consulted the yellow pages in making the decision?

9. A company that currently offers a product warranty quite similar to the warranties offered by competitors is considering the merits of increasing the warranty's coverage. A market study was undertaken to examine consumer response to an improved warranty. College students were shown the product accompanied by either the original warranty or the improved warranty. Students perceived the improved warranty as much better. Moreover, the product's quality was rated higher when it was paired with the improved warranty. Although the company viewed these results as very encouraging, concerns were raised about the appropriateness of using college students, most of whom have yet to make a purchase in the product category. Consequently, the study was replicated using older consumers possessing greater purchase experience. As before, the improved warranty was seen as providing much better coverage. However, quality judgments were unaffected by the warranty. How can you explain this difference between the two studies' findings concerning the warranty's influence on perceived product quality? Further, do you believe that the company should offer the improved warranty?

Endnotes

1. Faye Penn, "Motorcycle Mamas: Women Bikers Ride Down Stereotypes," *Miami Herald* (August 7, 1997), 1G, 5G.

2. This discussion of the furniture industry is drawn from the following sources: Cheryl Russell, "The New Consumer Paradigm," *American Demographics* (April 1999), 50–58; Jennifer Steinhauer, "Traditions Hurting Some Big Names in Furniture Industry," *Miami Herald* (September 14,

1997), 8F; Teri Agins, "Furniture Firms Try Show Biz to Woo Public," *The Wall Street Journal* (November 12, 1993), B1, B6.

3. Ian MacMillan and Rita Gunther McGrath, "Discovering New Points of Differentiation," *Harvard Business Review* (July/August 1997), 133–145.

4. Paula Mergenhagen, "How 'got milk?' Got Sales," *Marketing Tools* (September 1996), 4–7.

5. Raju Narisetti, "Rubbermaid Ads Pitch Problem Solving," *The Wall Street Journal* (February 4, 1997), B6.

6. Internal search has received relatively little attention in the consumer behavior literature. For exceptions, see James R. Bettman, *An Information Processing Theory of Consumer Choice* (Reading, MA: Addison-Wesley, 1979), 107–111; Gabriel J. Biehal, "Consumers' Prior Experiences and Perceptions in Auto Repair Choice," *Journal of Marketing* 47 (Summer 1983), 87–91. For research on how internal search may affect external search, see Girish Punj, "Presearch Decision Making in Consumer Durable Purchases," *Journal of Consumer Marketing* 4 (Winter 1987), 71–82.

7. John D. Claxton, Joseph N. Fry, and Bernard Portis, "A Taxonomy of Prepurchase Information Gathering Patterns," *Journal of Consumer Research* 1 (December 1974), 35–42; David H. Furse, Girish N. Punj, and David W. Stewart, "A Typology of Individual Search Strategies Among Purchasers of New Automobiles," *Journal of Consumer Research* 10 (March 1984), 417–431; David E. Migley, "Patterns of Interpersonal Information Seeking for the Purchase of a Symbolic Product," *Journal of Marketing Research* 20 (February 1983), 74–83; Joseph W. Newman, "Consumer External Search: Amount and Determinants," in Arch G. Woodside, Jagdish N. Sheth, and Peter D. Bennett, eds., *Consumer and Industrial Buyer Behavior* (New York: North Holland, 1977), 79–94.

8. Biehal, "Consumers' Prior Experiences and Perceptions in Auto Repair Choice."

9. Geoffrey C. Kiel and Roger A. Layton, "Dimensions of Consumer Information Seeking Behavior," *Journal of Marketing Research* 18 (May 1981), 233–239.

10. Peter H. Bloch, Daniel L. Sherrell, and Nancy M. Ridgway, "Consumer Search: An Extended Framework," *Journal of Consumer Research* 13 (June 1986), 119–126.

11. Ibid.

12. Patricia Braus, "What Is Good Service?" *American Demographics* (July 1990), 36–39.

13. Peter R. Dickson and Alan G. Sawyer, "The Price Knowledge and Search of Supermarket Shoppers," *Journal of Marketing* 54 (July 1990), 42–53. Also see Wayne D. Hoyer, "An Examination of Consumer Decision Making for a Common Repeat Purchase Product," *Journal of Consumer Research* 11 (December 1984), 822–829.

14. Joel E. Urbany, "An Experimental Examination of the Economics of Information," *Journal of Consumer Research* 13 (September 1986), 257–271. Also see Narasimhan Srinivasan and Brian T. Ratchford, "An Empirical Test of a Model of External Search for Automobiles," *Journal of Consumer Research* 18 (September 1991), 233–242.

15. J. Edward Russo, "The Value of Unit Price Information," *Journal of Marketing Research* 14 (May 1977), 193–201; J. Edward Russo, Gene Krieser, and Sally Miyashita, "An Effective Display of Unit Price Information," *Journal of Marketing* 39 (April 1975), 11–19.

16. David Altaner, "Dot-com Deals," *Sun-Sentinel* (February 13, 2000), 1F, 7F.

17. Urbany, "An Experimental Examination of the Economics of Information." Also see Joel E. Urbany, Peter R. Dickson, and William L. Wilkie, "Buyer Uncertainty and Information Search," *Journal of Consumer Research* 16 (September 1989), 208–215; Calvin P. Duncan and Richard W. Olshavsky, "External Search: The Role of Consumer Beliefs," *Journal of Marketing Research* 19 (February 1982), 32–43.

18. Kiel and Layton, "Dimensions of Consumer Information Seeking Behavior."

19. Braus, "What Is Good Service?"

20. Joel E. Urbany and Peter R. Dickson, "Consumer Information, Competitive Rivalry, and Pricing in the Retail Grocery Industry," working paper, University of South Carolina (1988).

21. For research on consideration sets, see Joseph W. Alba and Amitava Chattopadhyay, "Effects of Context and Part-Category Cues on Recall of Competing Brands," *Journal of Marketing Research* 22 (August 1985), 340–349; Juanita J. Brown and Albert R. Wildt, "Consideration Set Measurement," *Journal of The Academy of Marketing Science* 20 (Summer 1992), 235–243; John R. Hauser and Birger Wernfelt, "An Evaluation Cost Model of Consideration Sets," *Journal of Consumer Research* 16 (March 1990), 393–408; Frank R. Kardes, Gurumurthy Kalyanaram, Murali Chandrashekaran, and Ronald J. Dornoff, "Brand Retrieval, Consideration Set Composition, Consumer Choice, and the Pioneering Advantage," *Journal of Consumer Research* 20 (June 1993), 62–75; Prakash Nedungadi, "Recall and Consumer Consideration Sets: Influencing Choice Without Altering Brand Evaluations," *Journal of Consumer Research* 17 (December 1990), 263–276; John H. Roberts and James M. Lattin, "Development and Testing of a Model Consideration Set Composition," *Journal of Marketing Research* 28 (November 1991), 429–440.

22. Joel Huber, John W. Payne, and Christopher Puto, "Adding Asymmetrically Dominated Alternatives: Violations of Regularity and the Similarity Hypothesis," *Journal of Consumer Research* 9 (June 1982), 90–98; Joel Huber and Christopher Puto, "Market Boundaries and Product Choice:

Illustrating Attraction and Substitution Effects," *Journal of Consumer Research* 10 (June 1983), 31–44; Barbara Kahn, William L. Moore, and Rashi Glazer, "Experiments in Constrained Choice," *Journal of Consumer Research* 14 (June 1987), 96–113; Sanjay Mishra, U. N. Umesh, Donald E. Stem, Jr., "Antecedents of the Attraction Effect: An Information-Processing Approach," *Journal of Marketing Research* 30 (August 1993), 331–349; Yigang Pan and Donald R. Lehmann, "The Influence of New Brand Entry on Subjective Brand Judgments," *Journal of Consumer Research* 20 (June 1993), 76–86; Srinivasan Ratneshwar, Allan D. Shocker, and David W. Stewart, "Toward Understanding the Attraction Effect: The Implications of Product Stimulus Meaningfulness and Familiarity," *Journal of Consumer Research* 13 (March 1987), 520–533; Itamar Simonson, "Choice Based on Reasons: The Case of Attraction and Compromise Effects," *Journal of Consumer Research* 16 (September 1989), 158–174.

23. Alba and Chattopadhay, "Effects of Context and Part-Category Cues on Recall of Competing Brands."

24. Joseph W. Alba and J. Wesley Hutchinson, "Dimensions of Consumer Expertise," *Journal of Consumer Research* 13 (March 1987), 411–454.

25. Wayne D. Hoyer and Stephen P. Brown, "Effects of Brand Awareness on Choice for a Common, Repeat-Purchase Product," *Journal of Consumer Research* 17 (September 1990), 141–148.

26. Carolyn B. Mervis and Eleanor Rosch, "Categorization of Natural Objects," *Annual Review of Psychology* 32, 89–115.

27. Mita Sujan, "Consumer Knowledge: Effects on Evaluation Strategies Mediating Consumer Judgments," *Journal of Consumer Research* 12 (June 1985), 31–46.

28. Robert M. McMath, "The Perils of Typecasting," *American Demographics* (February 1997), 60.

29. Elinor Selame and Greg Kolligian, "Brands Are a Company's Most Important Asset," *Marketing News* (September 16, 1991), 14, 19.

30. For research on brand extensions, see David A. Aaker and Kevin Lane Keller, "Consumer Evaluations of Brand Extensions," *Journal of Marketing* 54 (January 1990), 27–41; Michael J. Barone, Paul W. Miniard, and Jean B. Romeo, "The Influence of Positive Mood on Brand Extension Evaluations," (1999) working paper; David M. Boush and Barbara Loken, "A Process-Tracing Study of Brand Extension Evaluation," *Journal of Marketing Research* 28 (February 1991), 16–28; Kevin Lane Keller, "Conceptualizing, Measuring, and Managing Customer-Based Brand Equity," *Journal of Marketing* 57 (January 1993), 1–22; Kevin Lane Keller and David A. Aaker, "The Effects of Se-

quential Introduction of Brand Extensions," *Journal of Marketing Research* 29 (February 1992), 35–50; Barbara Loken and Deborah Roedder John, "Diluting Brand Beliefs: When Do Brand Extensions Have a Negative Impact?" *Journal of Marketing* 57 (July 1993), 71–84; C. Whan Park, Sandra Milberg, and Robert Lawson, "Evaluation of Brand Extensions: The Role of Product Feature Similarity and Brand Concept Consistency," *Journal of Consumer Research* 18 (September 1991), 185–193.

31. James R. Bettman and Mita Sujan, "Effects of Framing on Evaluation of Comparable and Noncomparable Alternatives by Expert and Novice Consumers," *Journal of Consumer Research* 14 (September 1987), 141–154; Kim R. Corfman, "Comparability and Comparison Levels Used in Choices among Consumer Products," *Journal of Marketing Research* 28 (August 1991), 368–374; Michael D. Johnson, "Consumer Choice Strategies for Comparing Noncomparable Alternatives," *Journal of Consumer Research* 11 (December 1984), 741–753; Michael D. Johnson, "Comparability and Hierarchical Processing in Multialternative Choice," *Journal of Consumer Research* 15 (December 1988), 303–314; Michael D. Johnson, "The Differential Processing of Product Category and Noncomparable Choice Alternatives," *Journal of Consumer Research* 16 (December 1989), 300–309; C. Whan Park and Daniel C. Smith, "Product-Level Choice: A Top-Down or Bottom-Up Process?" *Journal of Consumer Research* 16 (December 1989), 289–299.

32. Gabriel Biehal and Dipankar Chakravarti, "Information Accessibility as a Moderator of Consumer Choice," *Journal of Consumer Research* 10 (June 1983), 1–14; Gabriel Biehal and Dipankar Chakravarti, "Consumers' Use of Memory and External Information in Choice: Macro and Micro Perspectives," *Journal of Consumer Research* 12 (March 1986), 382–405; John G. Lynch, Jr., Howard Marmorstein, and Michael R Weigold, "Choices from Sets Including Remembered Brands: Use of Recalled Attributes and Prior Overall Evaluations," *Journal of Consumer Research* 15 (September 1988), 169–184.

33. For research on cutoff usage, see Barton Weitz and Peter Wright, "Retrospective Self-Insight on Factors Considered in Product Evaluations," *Journal of Consumer Research* 6 (December 1979), 280–294; Peter L. Wright and Barton Weitz, "Time Horizon Effects on Product Evaluation Strategies," *Journal of Marketing Research* 14 (November 1977), 429–443.

34. Susan M. Petroshius and Kent B. Monroe, "Effects of Product-Line Pricing Characteristics on Product Evaluations," *Journal of Consumer Research* 13 (March 1987), 511–519.

35. William B. Dodds, Kent B. Monroe, and Dhruv Grewal, "Effects of Price, Brand, and Store Information on Buyers' Product Evaluations," *Journal of Marketing Research* 28 (August 1991), 307–319; Gary M. Erickson and Johnny K. Johansson, "The Role of Price in Multi-Attribute Product Evaluations," *Journal of Consumer Research* 12 (September 1985), 195–199; Michael Etgar and Naresh K. Malhotra, "Determinants of Price Dependency: Personal and Perceptual Product Evaluations," *Journal of Consumer Research* 8 (September 1981), 217–222; Zarrel V. Lambert, "Product Perception: An Important Variable in Price Strategy," *Journal of Marketing* 34 (October 1970), 68–76; Irwin P. Levin and Richard D. Johnson, "Estimating Price-Quality Tradeoffs Using Comparative Judgments," *Journal of Consumer Research* 11 (June 1984), 593–600; Kent B. Monroe, "The Influence of Price Differences and Brand Familiarity on Brand Preferences," *Journal of Consumer Research* 3 (June 1976), 42–49; Akshay R. Rao and Kent B. Monroe, "The Effect of Price, Brand Name, and Store Name on Buyers' Perceptions of Product Quality: An Integrative Review," *Journal of Marketing Research* 26 (August 1989), 351–357.

36. William Boulding and Amna Kirmani, "A Consumer-Side Experimental Examination of Signaling Theory: Do Consumers Perceive Warranties as Signals of Quality?" *Journal of Consumer Research* 20 (June 1993), 111–123.

37. Robert Johnson, "In the Chips," *The Wall Street Journal* (March 22, 1991), B1–B2.

38. For a discussion of other forms of noncompensatory evaluation strategies, see James R.

Bettman, *An Information Processing Theory of Consumer Choice* (Reading, MA: Addison-Wesley, 1979), 181–182.

39. For a study of the conjunctive decision rule, see David Grether and Louis Wilde, "An Analysis of Conjunctive Choice: Theory and Experiments," *Journal of Consumer Research* 10 (March 1984), 373–385.

40. Joseph W. Alba and Howard Marmorstein, "The Effects of Frequency Knowledge on Consumer Decision Making," *Journal of Consumer Research* 14 (June 1987), 14–25.

41. Peter L. Wright, "Use of Consumer Judgment Models in Promotion Planning," *Journal of Marketing* 37 (October 1973), 27–33.

42. Noel Capon and Deanna Kuhn, "Can Consumers Calculate Best Buys?" *Journal of Consumer Research* 8 (March 1982), 449–453. Also see Catherine A. Cole and Gary J. Gaeth, "Cognitive and Age-Related Differences in the Ability to Use Nutritional Information in a Complex Environment," *Journal of Marketing Research* 27 (May 1990), 175–184.

43. Melanie Eversley, "Interest Rising in Regulations on Rentals," *Miami Herald* (August 21, 1997), 1C, 3C.

44. Marcy Gordon, "Groups Urge Consumers to Pass on Credit Insurance," *Miami Herald* (March 18, 1999), 19A.

CHAPTER 5

Purchase

OPENING VIGNETTE

A series of focus group interviews was held throughout the United States on behalf of the International Mass Retail Association to discuss consumers' views on shopping, primarily at mass merchandisers, price clubs, big box stores, and grocery stores. The entire shopping process, including traveling to the store, experiences in the store, purchase influencers (such as advertising and POP displays), and checkout, was discussed thoroughly. Some of the reasons consumers choose one retailer over another are as follows:

- "I choose the store that I know the best inside—I can shorten my visit that way. I wish stores would put up a board that shows where products have been moved to so that I can find them. When Kroger [a grocer] changes where the salsa is, just tell me so that I don't have to hunt the store to find it."

- "I'm a buyer, not a shopper. I go where I can get in, buy what I need, and get out the fastest. I've always liked the Target checkout system because you seem to move through it quicker."

- "I go to the store with the least amount of stuff in the aisles. I don't like bumping my cart into displays of products I don't want to buy."

- "I used to go to large stores where I could buy everything from socks to steaks. But now that I'm older, I have a hard time getting through these stores. I actually go to several stores that are smaller and break up my shopping through the week."

- "I want the advertising to tell me something about the store. Tell me you've widened the aisles or that you open more checkout lanes, and I'll go."

- "I won't go to a store that doesn't show me clearly what I'm paying for a product. I like Target because you can scan a product and it tells you what price is in the computers."

- "Visual presentation to me in a store is a big part. It's like soup. . . you think if it looks good, it must taste good. No matter how good it tastes, if it looks like crap, I'm not going to buy it."

- "I don't like to go to a store with salespeople that don't know what they are talking about. At Lowes [a building supply store], everyone is polite and they can help you find what you need. But at Home Depot, they actually know how to work the product you're looking for and know about its features. I'd rather pay more for the help and advice."

In general, consumers focused on speed through the store, cleanliness, assortment of product, checkout, and availability of products when deciding where to purchase products. Overall, consumers' store choices were most influenced by convenience, how the store performed on the details, and perceptions they had about the store.

Source: Based on "Consumer Logistics: A Qualitative Look at the Shopping Process," Understanding Your Customer II, *Roger Blackwell and Kristina Blackwell, for the International Mass Retail Association (1998).*

To Buy or Not to Buy

To buy or not to buy? That is the question answered in stage four of the CDP model—purchase. In the *purchase decision process,* consumers decide:

1. Whether to buy
2. When to buy
3. What to buy (product type and brand)
4. Where to buy (type of retailer and specific retailer)
5. How to pay

As you read in the opening vignette, many factors influence these shopping decisions, including in-store promotions, store cleanliness, level of service, price, value, and overall retail experience. Retailers compete with each other on these various attributes to win the patronage of consumers. Consumers, in turn, must sift through the options made available to them and decide not just which product and brand to buy, but where and how to buy it. The possibility has also increased that a consumer might never enter a store, making a purchase instead from the Internet, a catalog, or a direct sales person.

The first hurdle is actually to decide to make the decision to purchase. Consumers always face the option of aborting the process for many reasons, including changed motivations and circumstances, new information, or lack of available products, thereby deferring the decision.[1] Once the decision to buy has been made, various outcomes can occur. For example, a consumer may enter the Abiyuki District in Tokyo with the intention of buying a Sony television set but leave with a Panasonic television *and* a Bosch dishwasher. The decision to buy can lead to a *fully planned purchase* (both the product and brand are chosen in advance), a *partially planned purchase* (intent to buy the product exists but brand choice is deferred until shopping), or an *unplanned purchase* (*both* the product and brand are chosen at point of sale).

Fully Planned Purchase   Marketers promote brand and store loyalty with advertising and other programs that encourage consumers to plan their purchases. Research indicates purchase planning is more likely to occur when involvement with the product is high[2] (as with autos) but can occur with lower involvement purchases (groceries) as well. Whether or not purchasing occurs as planned is affected by in-store factors, such as knowledge of store layout and design, and time pressures that restrict browsing and in-store decision making.[3] Planned purchasing may also be interrupted or diverted by marketing tactics that might switch consumers from their preferred brand, including *sampling of products, price reductions, coupons, point-of-purchase displays, or other promotional activities.* How marketing efforts affect purchase depends on loyalty. Studies indicate that coupon ads that provide useful product information work well with consumers who are interested in switching brands, but attractive pictures are more effective with consumers who are loyal to a competitive brand.[4]

Partially Planned Purchase   Consumers may plan the products they intend to purchase but delay choice of brand or specific styles or sizes of the product until they are in the store or on a web site. When involvement is low, consumers often resort to buying "one of the brands I know and like." The final brand or style decision may be influenced by price reductions or special displays and packaging.[5]

Unplanned Purchase   Studies indicate that 68 percent of items bought during major shopping trips and 54 percent on smaller trips are unplanned.[6] These "impulse" sales, bought by consumers in an often whimsical manner, can be prompted by POP displays, a sale price on a related product,[7] or just by seeing a new product in the store. They also show that consumers use in-store influences to guide product and brand choices made within the store.[8] Shoppers often intentionally use product displays and materials from catalogs as a surrogate shopping list. In other words, a display can remind a consumer of a need and trigger a purchase.

Purchase Factor   When and if a purchase occurs is affected by *timing factors* such as seasonality; thus, a demand chain must be able to provide products such as air conditioners, snow blowers, umbrellas, and seasonal apparel when consumers need them, or the purchase may never occur. Similarly, retailers increase their profits by predicting, promoting, and supplying the right amount of inventory for Christmas, Hanukkah, Cinco de Mayo, and other holiday purchase needs. Further, some promotions that offer refunds or other future benefits in exchange for "effort" by the consumer (such as saving receipts or collecting UPC codes) seem attractive at the time of brand choice but not as attractive later, when they have to complete the required tasks.[9] These promotions may accelerate the timing of purchase.

Timing also affects the price, and therefore the likelihood, of a purchase. For example, a student who intends to purchase an airline ticket to visit family members during semester break may not be able to purchase the ticket if he or she waits too long to secure a reservation at an affordable price. Timing factors were a primary driver behind the birth and success of convenience stores, such as Seven-Eleven and United Dairy Farmers, which recognized that consumers want to buy milk, beer, gas, and other products whenever they want. A key to the success of e-tailers, such as E-Trade and Amazon.com, is their ability to offer 24-hour-per-day shopping opportunities.

When making a purchase, a consumer must also decide *how to pay*. Although cash and checks are still important for many purchases, many consumers pay with credit cards—often influenced by the availability of delayed payments or easy access to credit. Marketers often prefer consumers to use credit cards or checks from which they can *create a database of names for developing continuous communications and relationships with the consumer*, a process called **data-based marketing** or **data mining**.[10] The largest retailer credit card database belongs to Sears, Roebuck & Co., which has the astonishing figure of 44 million household accounts in its customer database, or nearly half of the households in the United States. Sears earns more profit from its credit card operations than all $30 billion of its sales in its retail stores.[11]

In this chapter, you will learn more about purchase, specifically, retail applications and strategies. Think carefully about how you and other consumers make purchase decisions. You may find that you understand your own purchases better, allowing you to receive more value for your purchase dollars. If you work for a retailer, you obviously are interested in how the purchase and retail processes occur and how to influence consumers to buy from your store.

Retailing and the Purchase Process

Retailing can be described as the process of uniting consumers and markets. It is usually the culmination point of the efforts of the supply chain partners to meet the demands of consumers. The purchase process, carried to completion, requires consumers to react with retailers of some type.

Why People Shop

Whether consumers buy from bazaars, flea markets, or department stores, the most basic question to answer when examining purchase behaviors is "why do people shop?" The most obvious answer is "in order to acquire something," but there exists a myriad of personal and social reasons that consumers shop, as described in Figure 5.1. For some consumers, shopping alleviates loneliness, dispels boredom, provides escape and fantasy fulfillment, and relieves depression. Others view shopping as a sport (with the goal of beating the system) or a modern form of the primal "hunt" (with the shopper acting as "the great provider").

There also are consumers that, to put it mildly, don't like to shop, with about 20 percent of the population avoiding the marketplace whenever possible.[12] These consumers are largely oblivious and unresponsive to marketing efforts positioning retailing as a "fun experience," but they may embrace Internet buying or direct marketing that promises to make shopping quicker, easier, and less personally involving.

When planning retail strategies for their stores or their products, many marketers determine how their core customers think of shopping—*is it fun for them or is it a chore they must complete?* If consumers shop for social interaction or some of the other reasons highlighted in Figure 5.1, they are more likely to enjoy shopping than consumers who just "buy" products. If shopping is considered to be work, marketers should strive to make the shopping process easier—with quicker checkout lines, easy-to-read store guides and maps, easy to navigate aisles, and

---

Figure 5.1   Why Do People Shop?

Personal Motives	**Social Motives**
Role Playing Diversion Self-Gratification Learning about New Trends Physical Activity Sensory Stimulation	Social Experiences Outside the Home Communication with Others Who Have Similar Interests Peer Group Attraction Status and Authority Pleasure of Bargaining

Source: Excerpted from Edward M. Tauber, "Why Do People Shop?" Journal of Marketing 36 (October 1972), 46–59

conveniently located staple products. If shopping is considered fun, however, the goal is to provide more reasons to visit the store and stay in it longer. For many consumers, shopping is both, depending on the product and the retailer. The challenge to consumer analysts is to know which consumers and in which situations shopping is one or the other.

You can begin to analyze whether Internet retailing will replace grocery stores, apparel retailers, bookstores, and most other location-based retailers based on this principle. If consumers fully plan their food shopping and consider it work, and if electronic shopping is less work, without significantly higher prices, electronic shopping services such as Peapod, Webvan, Home Grocer, and Streamline might gain substantial market share. If, however, consumers consider grocery shopping fun—as a social occasion to walk with a companion through pleasant smelling and appearing stores in order to see products, compare labels, get ideas, obtain information,[13] and perhaps sample products—then electronic retailing will have difficulty taking market share from effective location-based retailers.

The Purchase Decision Process

A great deal of research and the experience of successful retailers provide clues to understanding how consumers decide where to buy products. In a consumer's choice process, consideration of *which type of retail concept* (Internet, direct mail, catalog, or location-based retailers) usually precedes choosing *which type of store* (mass retailer, hypermarket, department store, specialty store, and so on) and *which specific retailer to patronize* (Wal*Mart versus K-mart). Figure 5.2 shows how consumers usually decide whether to buy from a discount store or a department store before choosing between Wal*Mart and Target or between Bloomingdale's and Marshall Field's. In reality, however, retail choice is often an interactive process in which *type* of outlet and *specific retailer* affect each other.

The process of choosing a specific store involves the matching of consumer characteristics and purchase characteristics with store characteristics. An individual may use different criteria to evaluate which store best meets his or her needs depending on the type of purchase. Consumers compare retail and store options based on how they perceive each will perform on the various criteria.

But consumers don't always go through the entire series of choices, from retail concept to competitive retailers to specific store choice. Past experience and store image might take consumers right to the specific store choice. If you've purchased jeans at the Gap in the past and like the product and the experience, you may proceed from purchase need to store selection immediately. But if you are buying something for the first time or had a bad experience previously, then you may evaluate more alternatives.

Consumers in different market segments form images of stores based on their perceptions of the attributes they consider important. Research indicates that *customers can quickly name a store* (that is, retrieve from long-term memory) *when asked what store comes to mind for specific attributes* such as "lowest overall prices" and "most convenient."[14] These top-of-mind responses are described as **automatic cognitive processing** and are associated strongly with customers' primary store choices, within each segment of the market. So much of the store choice process shown in Figure 5.2 is explained by automatic cognitive processing that it becomes very important to understand how images of retailers develop to place a store at the "top of the mind" within each consumer segment.

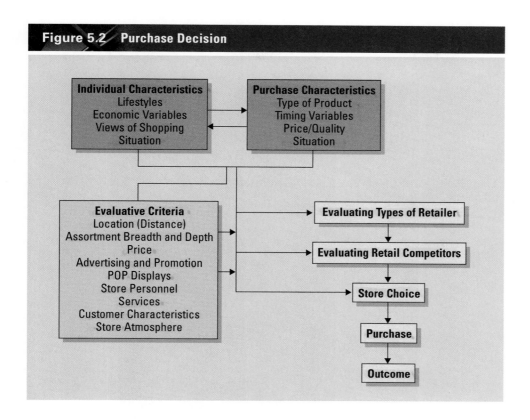

Figure 5.2 **Purchase Decision**

Retail Image

Consumers rarely know all the facts about all the stores they might shop. To make choices, *consumers rely on their overall perception of a store,* referred to as **store image.** Although this concept has been defined in various ways,[15] the idea of store personality is best described as "the way in which a store is defined in the shopper's mind, partly by its functional qualities and partly by an aura of psychological attributes."[16] The image of a retailer, on certain key variables, influences whether or not and in which stores consumers purchase products. Because image is the perceptual reality on which consumers rely when making choices, image measurement is an important tool for consumer analysts. It is measured across several dimensions reflecting salient attributes. Not surprisingly, almost the entire gamut of attitude research methods is used, from semantic differentials to multidimensional scaling.[17]

Another aspect of the retail setting that may affect shopping behavior is the perceived level of crowding within the store. Large crowds can lead to reductions in shopping time, postponement of unnecessary purchases, and less interaction with sales personnel.[18] However, for some consumer segments, especially younger consumers, crowded stores can connote popularity of the store and its products, giving teens a feeling of "fitting in" with their peers if they shop there. Abercrombie & Fitch, an apparel retailer, has developed a brand and an image appealing to its consumers (rebellious, trendy, cool), as shown in Figure 5.3, but the image would not be as successful if the image of excellent quality were not met in the products it sells.

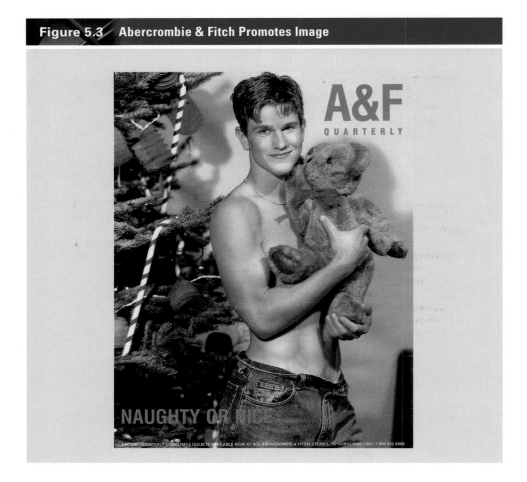

Figure 5.3   Abercrombie & Fitch Promotes Image

Determinants of Retailer Success or Failure

Although determinants of store choice may vary by market segment and by product class, the most important attributes determine which retailers succeed and which ones fail. These determinants fall into the following categories noted in Figure 5.2: (1) location, (2) nature and quality of assortment, (3) price, (4) advertising and promotion, (5) sales personnel, (6) services offered, (7) physical store attributes, (8) nature of store clientele, (9) store atmosphere, and (10) post-transaction service and satisfaction. Each of these variables is important in determining consumer choice although the weight given them varies by market segment.

Location

For most consumers, location is perceived in terms of time and hassle as well as actual distance. Consumers generally overestimate both functional (actual) distance and functional time. In some markets, location may include the ability to walk to the location or the availability of public transportation. In Japan, for example, retailers are sometimes called "railroad retailers" because they are clustered near major rail stations that nearly all consumers use for commuting to work.

Cognitive maps or consumer perceptions of store locations and shopping areas are more important than actual location.[19] They represent the distance and time consumers perceive they have to travel to reach and shop at the store. Variations between cognitive and actual distance are related to factors such as ease of parking in the area, quality of merchandise offered by area stores, checkout procedures, display and presentation of merchandise, and ease of driving to an area. Other factors affecting the cognitive maps of consumers include the price of merchandise and helpfulness of salespeople.[20]

Nature and Quality of Assortment

Depth, breadth, and quality of assortment are important determinants of store choice. This is especially true for stores in shopping centers.[21] One reason specialty stores such as the Gap, bebe, and the Limited have been so successful is their ability to assemble and present dominant assortments, whether defined on the basis of classification, end use, or lifestyle.[22] These specialty stores have narrow but deep assortments, usually appealing to a specific niche or segment of consumers.

Dominant assortment of merchandise is also critical to the success of mass merchandisers known as "category killers," which specialize in one category of merchandise. An example is Toys 'R' Us, with hundreds of stores spread from Germany to Hong Kong. Other category killers include Virgin mega-stores, Circuit City (electronics), Lenscrafters (eyeglasses), Home Depot and Wickes (home care), and Staples (office supplies). Category killers and niche retailers compete effectively with department stores because department stores typically have slower inventory turns along with higher operating expenses, lower sales per square foot, and larger inventory losses.

Price

The importance of price as a determinant of store patronage varies by type of product. Supermarkets have placed great emphasis on price since the 1930s when King Kullen on Long Island, New York, pioneered the concept. The importance of price depends on the nature of the buyer. Some customers preferring factors such as convenience will, in effect, trade off that consideration against higher prices.[23] Keep in mind that it is the consumer's perception of price that is usually more important than actual price.[24]

Price may be the most misunderstood variable in retailing. When Wal*Mart overtook Sears as the largest retailer in the United States, Sears cut its prices in a failed attempt to win back customers. What Sears failed to understand is that Wal*Mart not only has the policy of "Everyday Low Prices (EDLP)," it also has highly effective employee relations policies to enforce the policy "Treat every customer as a guest." It was only after Sears embraced a policy of making its stores more customer-friendly, symbolized by the slogan "Come to the Softer Side of Sears," did it regain some of its former success. Do not confuse "lowest price" with "acceptable range of price" as a determinant of store choice. Table 5.1 shows that consumers prefer prices that are within an acceptable range (combined with other attributes that consumers prefer) to prices that are always lowest. A common mistake of retailers is to use a strategy that emphasizes lowest price in order to appeal to the minority of consumers who value lowest price the most at the expense of losing the majority of consumers who prefer other attributes to lowest price.

For many years, retailers often relied on price to build patronage, a strategy whose efficiency is increasingly questioned, despite its widespread use.[25] Price promotion may only shift demand from one time period to another for a store, or from one brand to another within the store without increasing a store's total sales.

Table 5.1 The Importance of Price in Product Decisions

How Consumers React to the Importance of Paying the Lowest Price Versus Paying a Price in the Range They Expect to Pay* in Brand Choice

Product Category	Lowest Price(%)			Price Range(%)		
	Total	Female	Male	Total	Female	Male
Television	57	55	59	80	84	74
Prescriptions	63	64	60	58	62	53
Sweatshirts	58	60	56	75	79	70
Jeans	59	59	60	74	79	68

*Research indicated that women evaluate products more on expected price range and men evaluate more on lowest price.

Source: Roger Blackwell and Tina Blackwell, Understanding Your Customer, Part I *(International Mass Retail Association, 1997), 24.*

Nevertheless, price advertising is frequently used to maintain competitive parity, based on a belief that market share between competing retailers is influenced by advertising the lowest price. Although a segment of consumers is affected by price advertising, loyalty may last only until the next set of advertised prices attracts that segment elsewhere. Detailed scanner data on sales and changes in price are now available for all types of consumer goods, making it easier for marketers to discover what works[26] and turn information into strategic customer-focused actions.[27]

Marketers need to address how market segments respond to short-term changes in brand prices and promotions.[28] Questions about the relative effectiveness of price promotions, advertising, sales promotion, and so forth are increasingly analyzed with scanner data.[29] Research indicates that price promotions, and to a lesser degree, in-store displays have brand substitution effects but also store substitution effects on a retailer and its competitors. Ultimately, consumers rely on their overall image of a retailer to filter the effects of price advertising.[30]

Advertising and Promotion for Positioning of the Retail Brand

Advertising and other forms of promotion are important tools to create a retail brand—a summary of consumer perceptions about the store and overall image. Advertising to create a retail brand includes image and information. When a retailer creates its initial image in a market or attempts to position itself differently than in the past, the advertising should emphasize "image." **Image advertising** uses *visual components and words that help consumers form an expectation about their experience in the store and what kinds of consumers will be satisfied with the store's experience.* You can see that as an objective in the Abercrombie & Fitch ad in Figure 5.3 and in the Target ad in Figure 5.4a. **Information advertising,** on the other hand, *provides details about products, prices, hours of store operation, locations, and other attributes that might influence purchase decisions,* as seen in the Bauhaus ad in Figure 5.4b.

Figure 5.4a   Retail Brand Building and Marketing at Target

Retail advertising appears to be evolving to an emphasis on image advertising and nonprice information instead of the price advertising that was often the practice of retailers in the past. If consumers need specific information about locations or hours of operation and perhaps prices, such information is often available in more detail at the retailer's web site. This frees funds for "brand building" or positioning advertising in broadcast and print media.

The focus of retailing has also evolved to focus on marketing. Historically, retail firms emphasized merchandising—buying the right merchandise, displaying and stocking it correctly, and pricing and taking markdowns at the right time.

Figure 5.4b   Retail Brand Building and Marketing at Bauhaus

Most retailers gave little attention to marketing activities outside the store, except for price advertising. Today, in an effort to change perceptions of the store and attract consumers, retailers are adding marketing activities, such as special hours and services for "preferred customers" and communicating with segments through computerized databases.

Sales Personnel

You Win with People! is the title of Woody Hayes's book on winning. College football coach Hayes's philosophy is as true in retailing as it is in football. Although much of retailing is characterized today by self-selection without the intervention of a salesperson, knowledgeable and helpful salespeople are still important when choosing a store or shopping center.[31] European stores recognize the importance of personal selling and hire individuals who attend apprentice programs and complete specific educational and test requirements. In the United States, low unemployment rates have caused retailers to be staffed with personnel who frequently do not match consumer expectations.

What makes a salesperson effective? Research shows that although personal characteristics (such as personality, temperament, age, and appearance of salespeople) have some relationship to performance, skill levels and motivation are even more important.[32] These characteristics can be influenced through increased training and experience, visionary leadership, and corporate culture.

What this means is that sales success is determined by two factors: (1) the relationship during the transaction, and (2) the persuasion strategies used.[33] The salesperson's ability to win a buyer's confidence and successfully complete a negotiation process are affected by:

- *Perceived knowledge and expertise.* A salesperson's ability to exert persuasive influence is affected by his or her perceived expertise. When salespeople are seen as knowledgeable, consumers are more likely to buy a product based on their trust and confidence in the associate.[34]

- *Perceived trustworthiness.* A buyer's prior beliefs about a seller's trustworthiness affect the entire negotiation process. Buyer–seller agreements, as well as buyer willingness to make concessions, are enhanced when high levels of perceived trustworthiness are present. Bargaining toughness is viewed more positively when trust is strong.[35]

- *Customer knowledge.* Several recent studies have shown that the more familiar a salesperson is with his or her customer, the more likely he or she is to close a sale.[36] Knowledgeable sales associates can describe and classify different types of customers (including knowledge about traits, motives, and behavior) and have information about other sales experiences to guide them in similar situations.

- *Adaptability.* A sophisticated customer knowledge structure, in turn, seems to be related to adaptability. With this structure in place, a salesperson is able to respond to changing and individual customer needs and expectations.

Even though consumer confidence in retail salespeople is often low, some stores find ways to recruit, train, and motivate high quality sales personnel. Home Depot has become a successful do-it-yourself, home improvement store partly because of its policy of training salespeople to walk the floors and help consumers. Salespeople are expected to learn about every item in their aisle and in two aisles adjacent. Salespeople, often recruited from the ranks of carpenters and electricians, are encouraged to spend all the time needed with customers, even if it takes hours.[37]

People are also at the center of the strategy of Starbucks, the mega-star of the world of coffee and snacks, and one of the world's fastest growing specialty retailers. The firm provides stock options, even for its part-time workers, and tremendous training programs. The result? Employee turnover that is half or less than that of other food operations. CEO Howard Schultz explains, "Our only sustainable competitive advantage is the quality of our work force. We're building a national retail company by creating pride in—and a stake in—the outcome of our labor."[38]

Services Offered

Convenient self-service facilities, ease of merchandise return, delivery, credit, and overall good service have all been found to be considerations affecting store image. This varies depending on the type of outlet and consumer expectations. For instance, Marshall Field's and other upscale department stores provide personal shoppers to assist customers in assembling complete outfits, including accessories and shoes. A personal shopper will also proactively call a customer when the store receives merchandise that may coordinate well with his or her existing wardrobe. Harrod's and Selfridge's in the United Kingdom; Coles-Meyer in Australia; and C & A in Europe, Brazil, and Argentina are just a few of the firms focusing on providing excellent service to attract consumers. Consumer in Focus 5.1 discusses how Loblaw's, Canada's largest supermarket chain, has become a leader and innovator in providing services to consumers.[39]

Consumer in Focus 5.1

Loblaw Supermarkets Wow Customers with Extras

When you enter its front doors, Loblaw's wants you to shed all of your views on what a grocery store should or shouldn't be. Of course, Canada's largest supermarket chain sells all the grocery and produce items found in grocery stores throughout the world, but the extras it offers wow consumers and industry experts alike. *The* leader in the ancillary service arena, Loblaw's rents store space to dry cleaners, liquor shops, and coffee shops, and it offers in-store pharmacies and banking centers to its customers. Though other stores have followed suit, Loblaw's upped the ante by offering video-game and cell-phone sales outlets in some of its stores and leasing space to Club Monaco Inc. (a clothing chain).

In a bold move, Loblaw's raised the bar of service extras even higher in late 1999 by including a 7,000-square-foot fitness club in its new 80,000-square-foot superstore. Loblaw's GoodLife Fitness Club lets consumers work out, take aerobics classes, sauna, leave their children in the daycare center, and buy their groceries for the day or week in one visit. And time-pressured, female consumers, who look for creative ways to juggle a multitude of responsibilities and pressures, like the concept so much that the company plans to roll-out ten more GoodLife Fitness clubs throughout Canada.

Loblaw's strategy is to build customer loyalty and sales with superior ancillary services in addition to great products. And the strategy is working. Even as U.S. giants Costco Wholesale (a bulk food discounter) and Wal*Mart seem to be taking some share of the Canadian grocery market, Loblaw's continues to post 20 percent annual growth rates.

Source: Based partly on: Joel A. Baglole, "Loblaw Supermarkets Add Fitness Clubs to Offerings," The Wall Street Journal *(December 27, 1999), B4.*

Physical Store Attributes

Elevators, lighting, air conditioning, convenient and visible washrooms, layout, aisle placement and width, parking facilities, carpeting, and architecture affect store image and choice. *The physical properties of the retail environment designed to create an effect on consumer purchases* are often referred to as **store atmospherics.**[40] From the marketer's perspective, a store's atmospherics can help shape both the direction and duration of consumers' attention, and increase the odds that a consumer will purchase products that otherwise might go unnoticed. The retail environment can also express character and image of the store to consumers. Finally, the store setting can also elicit particular emotional reactions, such as pleasure and arousal, that can influence the amount of time and money consumers spend while shopping.[41]

Supermarkets such as Byerly's in Minneapolis delight customers with lavish chandeliers and warm, inviting carpeting on the floors, while Hard Rock Cafés throughout the world stimulate consumers' imaginations by displaying records, instruments, and clothing of famous musicians. Consumer in Focus 5.2 shows how Sephora attracts customers with its unique store atmosphere.

Atmospherics can involve multiple senses to attract consumer purchase behavior. Music can affect purchase.[43] Music played in a store at a low volume may encourage more social interaction between shoppers and sales staff. Faster or slower music may affect perceptions of time spent in the store, and classical music may give a more upscale or higher-priced image than other music.[44] Music tempo (slow versus fast) also affects shopping. Research indicates that slow-tempo music increases both shopping time and expenditures compared with fast-tempo music in grocery stores.[45] In restaurants, patrons spent nearly 25 percent more time and nearly 50 percent more on bar purchases when the tempo was slow.[46]

Consumer in Focus 5.2

Sephora: Using Physical Attributes and Interactivity to Influence Purchase Decisions

Sephora, the latest cosmetic and beauty product mega-star, is striving to change the face of retailing. The French-based retailer, formed in 1993 and acquired by LVMH Moet Hennessy Louis Vuitton in 1997, takes merchandising a step further by combining color, scent, and design to create a feast for the senses. The result is that consumers can't walk by the stores—rather, they feel an urgency to walk inside. Once inside, Sephora focuses on how consumers buy beauty products rather than on how retailers sell them.

A young woman approaches a sleek, black-and-red case inside a Paris Sephora store featuring 365 different shades of lipstick—literally a different shade for every day of the year. She tries on different colors, from green and purple to shades of yellow and pink. In most cosmetic stores, this would be inappropriate,[42] but at Sephora it is an expected part of the experience. Arranged by product category, rather than by brand name, consumers can experiment with all types of products throughout the store.

Sephora currently operates over 230 stores throughout Europe, the United States, and Asia. In addition to opening its 21,000-square-foot U.S. flagship store at Rockefeller Center, it recently opened its first store in Japan to tap into the Asian market—the second largest beauty and cosmetic market in the world. The self-serve atmosphere, bright colors, contemporary design, and extravagant three-story building are expected to bring a new sense of luxury to the cosmetic shopping experience in Japan.

Source: Based partly on: www.sephora.com and Phyllis Berman and Katherine Bruce, "Makeover at the Makeup Counter," Forbes (April 19, 1999).

Colors within the store can also influence consumers' perceptions and behavior. Consumers have rated retail interiors using cool colors as more positive, attractive, and relaxing than those using warmer colors, which are sometimes most suitable for a store's exterior or display windows to draw customers into the store.[47] Although color does not affect perceptions of merchandise quality, it does affect how up to date consumers believe merchandise displays are.

Store Clientele

The type of person who shops in a store affects consumer purchase intention because of the tendency to match one's self-image with that of the store. One West Coast computer store is known for its rude sales personnel and junky appearance, but millions of technology buffs throng to the store because of its wide selection of merchandise and the perception that it is the preferred store of techies.[48]

Some customers may also avoid stores because they do not want to associate with or be associated with the store. Some people may prefer department stores over mass marketers, such as K-mart and Wal*Mart, for that reason, although it appears that the number of consumers who consider it "smart" to shop at retailers that provide value is increasing. Young consumers may avoid a retailer because it has "too many old people there," and some older consumers may avoid stores that attract "too many young people." Restaurants frequently reflect a trendy belief about what type of people are likely to be the clientele and thus, offer positive or negative reasons for patronage. Some consumers may avoid restaurants that are believed to attract children, whereas other market segments are attracted to restaurants that are "kid-friendly."

Point-of-Purchase Materials

Point-of-purchase (POP) displays and signs can increase the odds of capturing consumers' attention, and thereby stimulate purchase and increase sales.[49] Some reports indicate that up to 70 percent of purchase decisions in grocery and drug stores are made in store aisles, often aided by the prompt of a POP attention grabber.[50]

Times are lucrative for agencies specializing in creating POP displays and campaigns for several reasons. First, they are inexpensive compared to other forms of promotion; second, they reach people where they buy the products; and third, they add atmosphere to retail stores. Moreover, informative and easy-to-use POP materials can partly help offset declines in the quantity and quality of retail salespeople.[51] This is when a YES (which stands for "Your Extra Salesman") POP unit might come in handy. This unit, which hangs on the shelf, works like a window shade. Product information is printed on a self-retracting shade that rolls down from a canister unit.[52] POP designers are pushing the envelope of creativity even further to create massive cardboard displays, figures, and a myriad of other attention-grabbers described in Figure 5.5.

Consumer Logistics

Consumption analysis focuses on more than what people buy; it examines how people shop at stores. **Consumer logistics**[53] is the *speed and ease with which consumers move through the retail and shopping process*—from the time they begin the shopping process to the time they take products home. It examines store characteristics (such as signage, lighting, customer service, and checkout), keeping peoples' shopping behaviors in mind. It contains seven primary consumer stages:

Figure 5.5 POP Lingo	
Aisle Interrupter	Cardboard sign that juts into the middle of the aisle to break visual pattern
Dangler	Sign hanging down from a shelf that sways when shoppers pass
Dump Bin	Box-shaped display holding products loosely dumped inside making it easy to refill and easy for consumers to touch and put back
Glorifier	Small plastic "stage" that elevates one product above others
Wobbler	A jiggling sign that catches the eye with movement
Lipstick Board	Plastic surface on which messages are written in crayon (and which can be changed easily)
Necker	Coupon hanging on a bottle-neck
YES unit	"Your extra salesperson," a fact sheet that pulls down like a shade
Ceiling Breakthrough	A sign that hangs from the ceiling, causing the appearance that something has broken through to the other side

Source: Based on Ymiko Ono, "Wobblers and Sidekicks Clutter Stores, Irk Retailers," The Wall Street Journal (September 8, 1998), B1 and B4

(1) preparation to shop; (2) arriving at and (3) entering the store; (4) movement through the store; (5) checkout; (6) travel home and home-warehousing; and (7) inventory stockouts, which prompt repurchase. These stages, as seen in Figure 5.6, cover location of stores, store layouts, aisle width, POP displays, checkouts, traffic in the store, customer service and personnel, payment methods, signage, and safety of stores from the consumer's perspective. Retailers can use this list to segment and organize research they have done on these topics and how they affect store sales and consumer satisfaction.

The purchase process is facilitated, positively or negatively, by consumer logistics. For example, in-store traffic flow can affect sales. Crowding in a store often causes people to be less satisfied, and widening aisles may help to increase consumer willingness to buy, especially in shopping situations that require shopping carts. If this is not physically possible, allowing consumers to have some choice about handling the crowded conditions may cause them to be more positive about the store.[54] Offering an express checkout lane for small purchases is an option, with Safeway in Britain and Meijer's in the United States offering self-checkout lanes, as seen in Consumer In Focus 5.3. Stores can also reorganize, putting staple items, such as milk and bread, in the front of the store so as to attract small purchases, which are often lost to convenience stores.

In general, stores are adding technology, personnel, and training to increase service and decrease the time consumers spend waiting in the store and at checkout. Target (and more recently Wal*Mart) positions scanners throughout the

Figure 5.6 **Stages of Consumer Logistics**

1. Preparation	2. Arriving at Store	3. Enter Store	4. Moving through the Store	5. Checkout	6. Going Home and Storage	7. Inventory Replenishment
• Coupons • Advertising • Shopping circulars brands • Lists—getting products and stores on list • Planning route to travel • Point of departure • Bundling of stops • Hours of operation • Perception of how busy it will be • Needs of products • Looking at catalog from store if available • Perceptions about store	• Outstore environment • Parking lot • Safety—patrol on duty • Signage • Lighting • Clientele • Crowded • Weather	• Greeters • Getting and separating carts • Entry—cluttered or clean • Cameras • First stops • Comfort with size • Familiarity • Ability to see through store	• Layout of products • Changes in product locations • Signage for sections • Lighting • Music • Store personnel • Assistance/help mechanisms • Product selection • Carts • Aisles • Promotions or POP • Price evaluations • Brand evaluation • Who shopping with them • Size of store • Handicaps • Reading labels • Traffic in store	• Amount of time in line • Number of people in lane • Choosing "best" line • Size of aisles • Self-checkout • Payment methods • Loading on belt • Monitoring prices • Price checks/ accuracy • Redeeming coupons • Bagging • Scanning prices • Security hairpins	• Getting out to car • Ease of exiting parking lot • Products in car • Where put items at home • Pantry loading • Disposal problems	• Needed to start process again • Satisfaction/ dissatisfaction with product, brand, store

store for shoppers who need to check prices. If a product is not marked or is on sale, consumers may take the item, scan the barcode, and get a reading on the price of the product and decide whether to buy or not before they reach the checkout lane. Waiting in line is a frustrating experience for consumers, especially when they see unused resources, such as empty tables in a restaurant or closed checkout lanes in a grocery store.[55] Offering some sort of distraction while people wait (such as small impulse items and magazines to read) or moving personnel from the back of the store to open more checkout lanes when needed makes the shopping experience more satisfactory and increases likelihood of repeat patronage. You can see how many of the items discussed in this section affect the consumer logistics process.

What consumers expect and demand from a purchase situation changes depending on what type of store they are visiting. For example, as time pressures on consumers increase, they search for ways to increase the efficiency of their shopping patterns.[56] Let's now take a look at *where* consumer purchases are occurring around the world and how retailers are adapting their strategies to meet changing consumer behaviors.

Consumer in Focus 5.3

Check This Out

Although self-checkout might have first been tried in the Netherlands and in the United States, Britain's Safeway stores were the first retailer to roll it out on a mass level. By early 1998, self-checkout scanners were installed in over 150 U.K. Safeway stores in order to ease consumers' frustrations with waiting in long checkout lines.

Here's how it works. When consumers enter the store, they use their magnetic loyalty card to free one of the 96 available handheld scanners from its cradle and begin the shopping process. They record their purchases as they shop the store and fill their baskets. When they return the scanner to its cradle, a receipt is generated, and they pay at a dedicated checkout counter. To monitor people's honesty, Safeway conducts occasional "re-scans" in which a checkout person will rescan the items to compare totals. This is likely to happen 1 out of every 16 visits. Other stores, like Meijers in the United States, are experimenting with a system that has the consumer scan each item as it is unloaded from the cart at checkout. This system also allows consumers to pay for their purchases when they scan with credit or debit cards. One person is stationed in front of the six units to monitor any problems that may occur.

Initial reactions from consumers and retailers are positive. Consumers like the convenience of the speedy checkout process, whereas retailers have experienced good return on their investments in terms of satisfaction and labor savings. In an effort to be more competitive in the convenience arena, retailers, such as Kroger (United States) and Tengelmann (Germany), have followed the footsteps of Royal Ahold's Albert Heijn division, which has rolled out the technology to several of its Dutch stores.

Source: Based partly on: Matt Nannery, "Britain's Safeway Expanding Self-Checkouts to 150 Stores," Chain Store Age *(January 1997), 150–155.*

The Changing Retail Landscape

Today, consumers want to purchase goods and services from a variety of retailing formats; therefore, the most successful marketers are turning to **multi-channel retailing**—*reaching diverse consumer segments through a variety of formats based on their lifestyles and shopping preferences.* Multi-channel retailing includes many alternatives: location-based retailing, direct selling, direct marketing, and electronic retailing. Even for the same market segment, consumers demonstrate a desire to buy from multiple channels, depending on the situation. Successful marketers find it easier to change their retail format to fit the lifestyles of consumers than trying to change the lifestyles and behavior of consumers to fit existing or emerging formats. Traditional retailers rely on merchandising techniques and markdowns to move goods rather than a good understanding of what consumers want.[57]

Location-Based Retailing

Consumers generally buy most products from retailers that have a physical location—a store—housed in either a mall, strip center, central market, or CBD (central business district). Location-based formats include specialty stores, grocery and drug stores, and convenience stores. But in recent years, value-oriented retailers, such as discount stores, superstores, hypermarkets, and "big-box" stores, have experienced the greatest growth.

Value-Oriented Retailers

Value retailers usually offer consumers lower prices than other forms of retailing because of their large economies of scale and high volume turns.[58] Many consumers also find them convenient because they can buy many different types of products in one store or see a large selection of items, in the case of the big-box stores. Figure 5.7 defines the various value retailers and summarizes their advantages to consumers.

One form of location-based retailing that thrives in nations other than the United States is the **hypermarket.** These stores *incorporate breakthrough technology in materials handling in a warehouse-operating profile that provides both a warehouse feel for consumers as well as strong price appeal.* Examples include Carrefour, based in France and found in nations throughout the world, Cara in Benelux, Pick 'n Pay in South Africa, and Big W in Australia. Although the United States does not have true hypermarkets, many of the principles of this form of retailing have been incorporated by Meijer, BigK, Home Depot, Lowes, and Wal*Mart Superstores.

The Shopping Mall

On average, U.S. consumers are visiting malls less often than they used to, and when they do, they visit about half the stores they used to—3.5 stores per trip as opposed to seven.[59] Diminished leisure time, traffic congestion, increased stress levels, economic fears, concerns about security, and Internet shopping are some of the causes of the decline.

Figure 5.7 Value-Oriented Retailers

Type of Retailer	Description	Advantages to Consumers	Characteristics
Big Box store Home Depot Circuit City Best Buy	Specialize in specific product category	Product depth, many brands, related products Lower prices Easier shopping process	Large market presence and volume Range of services Often "expert" in category
Discount/Mass retailer Wal*Mart Target Kmart	General merchandise, organized in store areas, such as auto, apparel and home décor and furnishings	Product breadth, national brands, lower prices, convenience, consistency between stores Easier buying process	High turn products in 100,000+ sq. ft. stores Negotiated advantages from national and private suppliers Good merchandising of products Large backrooms (but becoming more efficient with logistics)
Super Store BigK Meijer	Mass retail store with the addition of groceries	Addition of groceries means true one-stop shopping	Same as above Large turn of groceries
Hypermarket Pick'nPay Carrefour Vertkauf	Similar to a superstore (soft goods, grocery, and apparel) with addition of items such as appliances Items displayed in pallets	Low prices compared to area retailers Product breadth Convenience of one-stop shopping	Up to 200,000 sq. ft. Manufacture-direct-to-retail palletized packaging and display Decrease labor cost of shelving products by using forklift Verticalization of space (stack to ceiling to eliminate back room)

Yet this has not stopped U.S. developers from building new retail space. In the 1970s, there existed 8 square feet of retail space per person, and today that has increased to more than 20 square feet. Similar trends are occurring in Europe and Australia—though the amount of retail space per person is much lower in other nations than in the United States.

Regional shopping malls have progressed dramatically since J. C. Nichols built the first one, Country Club Plaza, in Kansas City in 1922. Today, there are more than 28,500 shopping centers in the United States, compared with only 2,000 in 1957, far more than any other nation.

Although the Plaza still offers one of the most exciting collections of upscale retailers in North America, the ultimate mall today is found in Edmonton, Alberta, Canada. The West Edmonton Mall, generally recognized as the largest in the world, was the first mega-mall, with 5.2 million square feet and 800 stores and services. It features a 5-acre World Waterpark (the largest indoor water park in the world), 19 movie theaters, a hotel, 110 food outlets, dozens of amusement rides, an ice rink, a miniature golf course, a chapel, a car dealership, and a zoo. Consumers arrive from all over North America to shop and play for a few days in this "destination shopping center."

Others have followed suit. Bluewater, Europe's new crown jewel of shopping centers, can be found 17 minutes outside London and two hours from Paris, once the chunnel-tunnel rail link opens in 2003.[60] Another giant, The Mall of America, in suburban Minneapolis, boasts 400-plus stores, including Bloomingdale's, Macy's, and Nordstrom's. The 4.2-million-square-foot mall is undergoing an expansion phase, expecting to almost double its size. Perhaps the newest version of the mega-mall is Easton in Columbus, Ohio. It features almost 4 million square feet of retail space built around a "Town Center" designed to act as a gathering place for shoppers, and where children can play in the large outdoor fountains. Easton celebrates the traditional shopping patterns found in small towns across North America a century earlier. Instead of enclosed malls that control consumer activities and traffic patterns, Easton incorporates an outdoor shopping district, in which pedestrians and vehicles "live together," with a "retailtainment" mall. The mall features innovative local restaurants and stores such as Ocean Club and The Modern Object, and national chains such as Cheesecake Factory, Potterybarn, and Nordstrom. It also includes value retailers as perimeter stores in addition to an ice-skating rink, soccer fields, and fitness center. Easton, as other contemporary malls, strives to be more than just a place to shop; it strives to be "*the* place to *be*."

Direct Marketing

A growing percentage of consumers' shopping and buying activities now occur in some other place than a store. Strategies used to reach consumers in the home, office, or airplane, instead of relying on consumers to visit stores, are referred to as direct marketing. Direct marketing is growing in the United States and in most developing countries of the world, including some countries in Africa, China, and India. Compared with the general population, in-home shoppers are somewhat younger with slightly higher household incomes, have above average education and income, and are more likely to live in a smaller town or rural areas. Most are active retail shoppers who shop at home for reasons other than deliberate avoidance of the store or shopping mall.[61] Yet direct marketing is also of interest to older consumers, home-bound or disabled consumers, and other special segments of the population. The items most frequently ordered are apparel, magazines, home accessories, home maintenance and kitchen equipment, and home office supplies.

There are six methods of direct marketing: (1) direct selling; (2) direct mail ads; (3) direct mail catalogs; (4) telemarketing; (5) direct response ads; and (6) interactive electronic media, including notably, the Internet. Direct marketing, in all its forms, involves direct contact with consumers. Although credit cards, loyalty programs, and scanner data are increasingly making it possible for stores to collect data about consumers, direct marketing offers the possibility of selecting specific target markets through the use of specialized mailing lists, databases, or media. This permits customized appeals and creative strategy based on the lifestyles and needs of the target market segments.

Direct Selling   **Direct selling** is defined as *any form of face-to-face contact between a salesperson and a customer away from a fixed retail location.* Although accurate statistics are hard to come by, direct personal selling now accounts for about 2 percent of all general merchandise sales and mostly takes place in a home, a workplace, or some other location outside a retail store. Avon's door-to-door selling method might seem like a blast from the past, but the company still relies on its sales force for about 98 percent of its sales.[62] However, it will spend up to $90 million in global advertising to promote its website.[63] The Longaberger Company relies on its 37,000-plus sales consultants to sell its up-scale, handmade baskets and home furnishings to customers through in-home parties. Headquartered in a giant basket-shaped building near Dresden, Ohio, Longaberger sales are approaching $1 billion. A key to its long-term success is the collectability of its baskets and other products. When consumers "invest" in Longaberger products, they become a part of the Longaberger family network, which sponsors trading and sales opportunities during the year.

Direct Mail Ads   Shopping in response to direct mail appeals has been shown to meet real consumer needs, such as availability of merchandise, convenience, low price, and better quality. Although many individuals often assume wrongly that direct mail is an unwanted invasion into the home, polls consistently show that well over half of consumers welcome direct mail, open it, and read it—though this declines as education and income increase.

Direct Mail Catalogs   Catalog buying has experienced dramatic growth in recent years, averaging about 7 percent per year growth in sales (at least twice as high as location-based retailers). According to studies, more women than men shop via catalogs; more than two-thirds of catalog shoppers have attended college; they are technology savvy; and they spend more time and money on leisure events. In North America, catalogs currently appeal to upscale consumers, whereas in many countries, the catalog is preferred more by downscale consumers.

Telemarketing   Nearly 20 percent of direct response orders now are triggered by a telephone call (referred to as outbound telemarketing). Homes can be targeted with great demographic precision using census data available within geographic zip codes. Further, real personalization can be achieved if the caller is skillful and sensitive. **Inbound telemarketing,** on the other hand, refers to the *use of a 1-800 number* (or 1-888 number) *to place orders directly.* The heaviest users are younger, better-educated families with higher incomes and children at home.[64] Telemarketing works much better with present customers (where a customer database indicates prospects' interests and preferences) rather than cold calls.

Direct Response Ads   About 20 percent of in-home purchases are stimulated each year by newspaper, magazine, and yellow pages ads that call for a direct response such as return of an order form. But big growth in this category is occurring in TV home shopping both in the United States and abroad. The "on-screen sell" seems to work well with a variety of products, especially when there is a need for demonstration. Eastman Kodak Co. introduced its new Cameo zoom lens camera on the QVC shopping network, and 9,700 were sold in just 70 minutes.[65] Kodak also benefited from pitching some related company products at the same time.

Purchase Behavior in the E-Commerce Revolution

The glamour child of direct marketing today is e-commerce. Just as the industrial revolution radically changed the nature of work, created enormous wealth, altered family structure, spawned new lifestyles, and eventually affected even the primary form of government throughout the world, the e-commerce revolution can be expected to bring about changes no less profound. Consumer analysts must be equipped to understand and interpret these changes and their effects both on society and marketing strategies.

The winners in "clicks and order" retailing, like their predecessors in "bricks and mortar" retailing, will be those who know how to take care of the customer better than competitors and provide better solutions than were available to consumers in the past. The technology of electronic retailing determines what can be offered to consumers, but only consumers determine which of those technologies will be accepted. The challenge for consumer analysts is to make sense of this form of retailing. Figure 5.8 applies the first four stages of the CDP Consumer Decision model to e-commerce retailing and purchasing.

When examining how consumers make purchase decisions, one shortcoming of the Internet is ability to touch and experience the product before purchase. At Le Printemps in France, one of the world's most famous department stores, consumers can go online and talk with a salesperson at the store. The salespersons—called "Webcamers"—are equipped with ultra-lightweight laptop computers, wireless networking gear, and video cameras. They also wear rollerblades, which allow them to move quickly throughout Le Printemps' 1.5-million-square-foot flagship store (located on 24 floors, in 3 buildings).[66] Consumers talk online with salespeople who show consumers the exact garment, perhaps enlisting another person to model the garment. It even has a global wedding and gift registry (www.printemps.fr) available to its global customer base. The department store is experimenting with other innovations, such as fashion shows, 24-hour shopping, and hosts that would make special presentations of merchandise similar to TV's Home Shopping Network.

Of the thousands of consumers who visit the web site of an e-tailer, only a few actually purchase goods on the site. Even among consumers who make a decision to buy a product, enter product and personal information into a "shopping cart" on the site, and enter their credit and shipping data, most terminate the process without completing a transaction. Although the reasons are not yet clear, but are an area of research today, the consequence is that many early e-tailers have failed to make a profit from transactions. Some of the e-tailers project their future growth more on advertising revenues than actual transactions.

Figure 5.8   A Consumer Analysis of E-Commerce

Problem Recognition

Which parts of shopping cause consumers problems that can be solved better on the Internet or through an e-tailer?
• Not being able to go to a store when the store is open
• Store location is far away (either other city or country)
• Need special products that are not carried by many retailers (special sizes, out-of-print materials, personal preferences, or products for special medical needs)
Example   A consumer might have difficulty buying size 14 shoes from a traditional retailer that cannot afford to carry inventory of specialized products that don't turn quickly. An e-tailer or shopping directly from the manufacturer solves the problem better for the consumer than the existing retail channel. E-tailers may have a major advantage in solving problems for these consumers *by selling products that appeal to segments too small for location-based retailers.*
Limitations   Trying on the shoes for fit and comfort, an important part of buying, is a problem that e-tailing does not solve very well. Even when consumers are attracted to apparel and order it, the return rate is so high that location-based retailers may have lower costs than e-tailers.

Search

In which instances is the search process enhanced or simplified by the Internet?
• Searching a wide variety of sources of information, perhaps on a global basis
• Identifying a specific product title, name, or brand and retailer selling the item
• Searching for information on competitive brands or on a topic of interest
• Ability to "shop" various retailers for products and prices
Example   In the past, if consumers were looking for a specific book or music CD, they might have to travel to several stores to find the title. The search process could involve several phone calls or trips to various stores. With the Internet, however, consumers can search on-line for the inventories of location-based retailers and choose to buy from the store or buy on-line. Also, accessing information about products or interests can be done from home rather than in the library.
Limitations   If consumers are not exactly sure what they are looking for, the search may be complicated if help is not available to narrow the search process. The search will lead to purchasing in countries where the postal service or commercial services can deliver the products easily and cheaply, especially if issues such as transportation charges, shipping damages, and customs and duties are not solved satisfactorily.

Pre-Purchase Evaluation of Alternatives

In which instances is the evaluation process enhanced or simplified by the Internet?
• When comparing product prices across retailers (especially global locations)
• When comparing features of products
Example   E-tailing offers consumers advantages in comparing attributes of products offered by competitors, especially price. Numerous search programs and Web sites are available to compare prices after consumers have defined other attributes or brands that are in their consideration set.
Limitations   Two major issues make it difficult for consumers to evaluate alternatives on variables other than price. First, many of the data for such comparisons are not retrievable from the databases of competitors, who may actively avoid the disclosure of such data. The second problem is that many of the most important attributes cannot be compared digitally.

Purchase

When is purchasing on the Internet more efficient and preferred to other forms of purchase?
• When you can't physically go to the store
• When calling is difficult or not convenient
• When the same order is repeated
• When the consumer is familiar with the products being ordered
• When the consumer doesn't need the product immediately
Example   Consumers who have purchased shirts from L.L.Bean in the past, might find it convenient to visit the website and order additional shirts. The advantage is that this can be done anytime, day or night, without fear that the size will be wrong. Some similarities exist for nonperishable, staple items found in grocery stores.
Limitations   When a consumer walks through a grocery store to buy the average purchase of 18 items, the consumer uses about 21 minutes to search the store, select products, check out, and load the car. Can grocery e-tailing compare in time and assistance? Only if the e-tailer provides information about product selections and availability, provides "time utility," and offers a similar or lower price. If it is easier and more convenient to use an e-tailer, then consumers may be willing to absorb the higher costs of home delivery and a "hired shopper."

Consumer Resources: What People Spend When They Purchase

Regardless of how or what consumers purchase, they have several budgets from which they spend to obtain products and services. Consumers spend money, time, and attention when they buy products. Therefore, all products can be viewed as having economic, time, and cognitive prices that consumers have to pay in the purchase process.

Money and Time Budgets

Basic economics tell us that the more money a person earns, the more he or she has to spend in the marketplace. Chapter 7 will highlight income trends for consumers around the world, but here we want to focus on how consumers use their resources to make purchases. Studies show that the more money people make, the busier they are, thus increasing the value of their time. Although people can make an infinite amount of money (at least in theory), they can have only 24 hours per day to "spend" on activities as basic as sleeping and eating to playing sports, working, and shopping.[67] How consumers allocate that time depends on their **timestyles.**

Consumer time budgets, which people spend on life activities, used to be divided into two components: work and leisure. It assumed that all time spent outside work was leisure. In contrast, a contemporary view of time, as indicated in Figure 5.9, divides it into three blocks: paid time, obligated time, and discretionary time. **Discretionary time** is **leisure time**[68]—*when individuals feel no sense of economic, legal, moral, social, or physical compulsion or obligation.* In recent years, as people work more hours and find themselves obligated to do more work or family activities, the amount of leisure time in American time budgets has decreased significantly. **Nondiscretionary time** includes *physical obligations* (sleeping, commuting, personal care, and so forth), *social obligations* (which increase with urbanization and the rising proportion of professional and white-color occupations), *and moral obligations.* Physical and social obligations increase with increasing income.

Harried American consumers cope with time-crunched lifestyles in many ways. Many people just cut back on sleep. Others spend less time doing what they really want to do or choose activities that take less time. Consumer decision making also takes time, as shown in Figure 5.10. The amount of time consumers are willing to spend on shopping activities often decreases as the amount of money

---

Figure 5.9   Concepts of Consumer Time Budgets

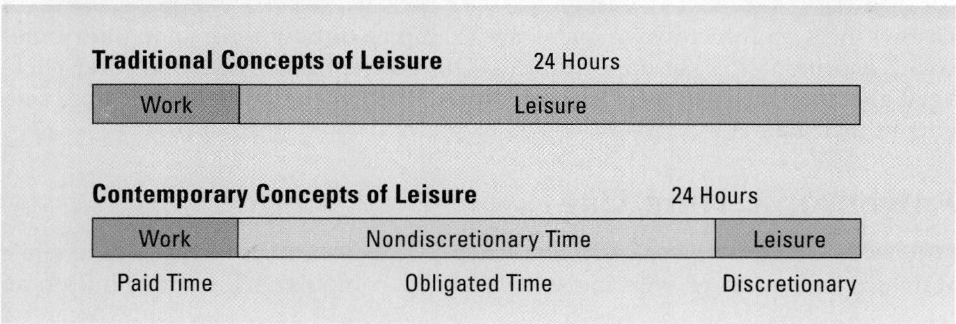

Traditional Concepts of Leisure   24 Hours

Work	Leisure

Contemporary Concepts of Leisure   24 Hours

Work	Nondiscretionary Time	Leisure
Paid Time	Obligated Time	Discretionary

| Figure 5.10 | Consumer Purchase Activities Involving Expenditure of Time |

Pre-Purchase
- Information gathering
  - Conversation
  - Misc. media use (e.g., *Consumer Reports*)
  - Browsing, window shopping
  - Other advertising (e.g., billboard)
- Search for "time-saving" features
- Comparison shopping

Purchase
- Buying
  - By mail/telephone
  - In the store
  - Form of payment (e.g., cash, check, credit card)
- Related travel time and waiting in line

Post-Purchase
- Information gathering and learning on how to use product
- Filling out warranty forms
- Repairs and maintenance
- Actual use of the product and continued use of the product
- Disposing of product (presorting aluminum and plastic, driving to the city dump, etc.)

Source: John P. Robinson and Franco M. Nicosia, "Of Time, Activity, and Consumer Behavior: An Essay on Findings, Interpretations, and Needed Research," Journal of Business Research 22 (1991), 171–186.

they make increases. This makes brands an important part of the buying process. If a consumer trusts a brand, he or she can spend less time repurchasing the product. Factors such as enjoyment of shopping may also influence the amount of time consumers are willing to devote to buying activities.[69]

Time-Using Goods   Some products and services require the use of time. Examples would be watching television, skiing, fishing, golfing, and playing tennis. How likely consumers are to purchase time-using goods depends on their time usage in a typical 24-hour day. As consumers make more money, they are willing to spend more money on the precious time they do have. This has increased the market for travel, extreme sports, and eating out. For example, some consumers choose to play tennis rather than golf. In addition to taking less time, tennis is more physically challenging.[70]

Time-Saving Goods   Consumers can gain leisure time by decreasing nondiscretionary time expenditures with goods and services. Hiring either a neighborhood teenager or ChemLawn to mow the lawn may free a consumer for either more work (which might increase income) or more leisure. Childcare, housecleaning, restaurants, and a wide array of other services are direct substitutes for time obligations and are among the fastest growing markets in industrialized economies. Dishwashers and microwave ovens are examples of how time-saving attributes create enormous market opportunities. This concept holds for foods and packaged goods. In fact, Minute Rice and Minute Maid even highlight their time benefits in their names.

Polychronic Time Use

Polychronic time involves *combining activities simultaneously,* such as eating while watching television or working with a laptop computer while traveling on an airplane. By combining activities, individuals use their time resources to accomplish several goals at the same time. This concept has also been called "dual time usage" and contrasts with *performing only one activity at a time* (**monochronic time use**). Computers make some of these things possible.

Many products are marketed to enrich the time budgets of consumers through polychronic time usage. Drive-through cleaners, prepared meals bought at a supermarket, the addition of racks to facilitate reading while using exercise bikes, and beepers for dental patients who want to shop in nearby stores while waiting for appointments are just a few innovations driven by polychronic time trends.[71] Cellular phones were accepted rapidly in part because they let people commute, walk, and talk on the phone simultaneously. Spinner.com allows people to listen to their favorite music while working on their computers.

Time Prices

Products have economic prices as well as "time prices," which are often featured as a product benefit in an ad. Such ads may state that the product requires only two hours to install. Some stores advertise wider aisles and more checkout lanes to tell consumers that it will take less time to shop than it did in the past. Harried consumers—those who feel rushed and pressured for time—visit fewer stores and make few comparisons by considering fewer brands and attributes than those who are relaxed shoppers.[72] Product attributes may communicate the ability to reduce the time price of a product. Examples include new "dry" deodorants, quick-dry paint, and higher-horsepower lawn mowers.

Cognitive Resources

Walking through a supermarket, you may see a lot of consumers looking up and down the aisles, scanning shelves, picking up products and comparing labels, spending minutes or even hours in the store, and often looking a bit confused. This is not a new form of ritual shopping behavior; it is an illustration that consumers have another resource from which they must spend to buy products and services—cognitive resources, highlighted here and examined further in Chapter 14.

Cognitive resources represent the *mental capacity available for undertaking various information-processing activities.* Just as marketers compete for consumers' money and time, so do they compete for cognitive resources or the attention of consumers. **Capacity** refers to the *cognitive resources that an individual has available at any given time for processing information.*

The *allocation of cognitive capacity* is known as **attention.** Attention consists of two dimensions: direction and intensity.[73] *Direction* represents the focus of attention. Because consumers are unable to process all the internal and external stimuli available at any given moment, they must be selective in how they allocate this limited resource. Some stimuli will gain attention; others will be ignored. **Intensity,** however, refers to the *amount of capacity focused in a particular direction.* Consumers will often allocate only the capacity needed to identify a stimulus before redirecting their attention elsewhere. On other occasions, consumers may pay enough attention to understand the gist of the ad. Sometimes consumers may give the ad their complete concentration and carefully scrutinize the message, such as a consumer in the market for a new car who is reading an automobile ad.

Gaining the consumer's attention represents one of the most formidable challenges a marketer may face. Consumers are bombarded continually by many stimuli that compete for their limited capacity. Consumers encounter hundreds of ads in a typical day, bombarded with radio, TV, magazine, newspaper, billboard, and Internet advertising. And the number is expected to increase as marketers develop new avenues for reaching consumers (for example, the use of ads in rental videos, or video displays in shopping carts or at checkout). A major determinant of an ad's success, then, is its effectiveness in gaining consumer attention.

Gaining attention at the point of purchase can be equally important. The use of eye-catching POP displays, as described earlier, can be instrumental in helping a product stand out from the clutter of brands squeezed onto a retailer's shelf. Packaging can serve a similar function. Achieving a "louder voice on store shelves" was a major consideration in designing the cans for the various Coca-Cola brands. Pringles also gained attention by putting potato chips in a tall canister rather than in a bag.

Shallow Attention   Many products are simply not important enough to consumers to warrant a "large" investment of their limited cognitive resources, as is the case with low-involvement products. In many respects, consumers are "cognitive misers," as they attempt to find acceptable rather than optimal solutions for many of their consumption needs. This same barrier occurs for marketing communications. Even if an ad can grab consumers' attention, consumers may not devote a lot of attention to it, which can reduce learning and retention. Studies suggest that stimuli—whether advertising, POP displays, or communication messages—that fail to receive a sufficient amount of capacity are unlikely to leave a lasting impression on the consumer.

Danger of Exceeding Cognitive Capacity   Because capacity is limited, it is possible to provide too much information and exceed capacity.[74] What happens when information overload occurs? Some have speculated that too much information on packaging can cause confusion and cause consumers to make poorer choices, even though the information may make them feel better about their decisions.[75] Critics, however, disagree.[76] They maintain that information overload, though possible, is unlikely because consumers will stop processing information before they are overloaded.[77] However, one study suggests that consumers may be unable to stop short of overloading when in an information-rich environment.[78]

The amount of attention a consumer gives to a product or specific purchase choice depends on factors such as involvement, situation, personality, and other variables. A group of consumers may spend a lot of time at a new and exciting product display in a supermarket—some consumers might be reading the labels because they are interested in nutrition and fat content; others might be reading about a contest associated with buying the product; and yet others might be reading preparation instructions. The reasons that people spend their time, money, and attention budgets on products vary depending on the characteristics of the individual.

Communicating with Consumers: Integrated Marketing Communications

The final step in promoting purchase and taking retail strategy to consumers is developing an integrated marketing communications (IMC) program,[79] which differs from traditionally programmed communications in several ways:

1. IMC programs are comprehensive. Advertising, web sites, personal selling, retail atmospherics and in-store programs, behavioral modification programs, public relations, investor relations programs, employee communications, and other forms are all considered in the planning of an IMC.

2. IMC programs are unified. The messages delivered by all media, including such diverse influences as employee recruiting and the atmospherics of retailers, are the same or supportive of a unified theme.

3. IMC programs are targeted. The public relations program, advertising programs, in-store and point-of-purchase programs all have the same or related target markets.

4. IMC programs have coordinated execution of all the communications components of the organization.

5. IMC programs emphasize productivity in reaching the designated targets when selecting communication channels and allocating resources to marketing media.

Studies indicate that only half of all promotions generate economic benefits to the advertisers, making the need for integrated advertising and promotion efforts important.[80] E-tailing provides opportunities to *build brands on the Internet*, as well as provide specific information showing consumers where to find that brand at a local dealer or retail outlet. Burton Snowboards, for example, has developed a very effective marketing program involving its web site, snowboarding "events" and sponsorships, as well as conventional media. Click on www.Burton.com for an example.

Advertising on the Internet has become a major medium, competing with television, radio, newspapers, magazines, outdoor and other direct media that have been the preferred ways for consumers to search for information and products in the past. Web surfers are well aware of the millions of banners at the top of each page (which are more effective at attracting consumers than at the bottom of the page), and most everywhere else. These banners invite consumers to "click here" to hyperlink to another web site or buy a product from the current one. In case you are worried that traditional media will disappear, it is useful to know that e-tailers spend most of their advertising budget on traditional media to attract consumers to their web site.

Summary

Attracting consumers to buy more from a particular store includes performing well on the attributes that consumers think are most important—location, nature and quality of assortment, price, advertising and promotion, sales personnel, services offered, physical attributes, store clientele, store atmosphere, and post-transaction service.

Increasingly, retailers are reaching consumers through a variety of formats. Multichannel retailing includes in-store and nonstore retailing. In-store retailing includes traditional stores, specialty stores, mass merchants, and factory direct stores, whereas out-of-store formats include direct selling, direct marketing, and electronic retailing. Even though many formats promote self-selection of products, consumers still rely on personal sales assistance when available. The factors that differentiate successful salespersons from their counterparts are (1) perceived knowledge and expertise, (2) perceived trustworthiness, (3) knowledge of their customer, and (4) adaptability.

When consumers do make a purchase, they have several budgets from which to spend: time, money, and attention. The more money individuals earn, the more valuable their time becomes. Products and services classified by their time properties may be called time goods. Time-using goods require the use of time, whereas time-saving goods allow consumers to increase their discretionary time.

Consumers also allocate attention to various activities in life. Because this capacity is limited, people must be selective in what they pay attention to and how much attention is allocated during information processing. Gaining consumers' attention can be challenging for marketers, especially when the product is of limited importance. To gain consumer attention, marketers design IMC programs that communicate similar messages and images through various media in an effort to increase the bang for their promotional buck.

Review and Discussion Questions

1. Define the term *store image* and explain why it is important as a concept for retail management. Choose one retailer and evaluate its image and how that image is portrayed in its advertising.

2. You are the marketing manager for a manufacturer of specialty watches designed for runners. Would you sell these items through retail stores, or would you try direct marketing (either alone or in combination with retail distribution)? Why?

3. Many contend that interactive electronic media will revolutionize consumer buying patterns. What is your opinion? What advantages are offered? Will traditional retail shopping become largely obsolete?

4. Choose a retailer you frequent often. Evaluate the store based on the elements of consumer logistics. How would you change the store?

5. How might the relationship between time budgets and economic budgets affect the marketing strategy of a major retailer?

6. What are some of the trends affecting time budgets for most Americans? How do you think these trends will be changing in the future?

7. Create an IMC strategy for a specific brand of clothing. What promotional elements would you include, and what would be the look and feel and message?

Endnotes

1. Ravi Dhar, "Consumer Preference for a No-Choice Option," *Journal of Consumer Research* 24 (September 1997), 215–231.

2. Alain d'Asdtous, Idriss Bensouda, and Jean Guindon, "A Re-Examination of Consumer Decision Making for a Repeat Purchase Product: Variations in Product Importance and Purchase Frequency," in Thomas K. Srull, *Advances in Consumer Research* 16 (Provo, Utah: Association for Consumer Research, 1989), 433–438.

3. C. Whan Park, Easwar S. Iyer, and Daniel C. Smith, "The Effects of Situational Factors on In-Store Grocery Shopping Behavior: The Role of Store Environment and Time Available for Shopping," *Journal of Consumer Research* 15 (March 1989), 422–433.

4. France Leclerc and John D. C. Little, "Can Advertising Copy Make FSI Coupons More Effective?"

Journal of Marketing Research 4 (November 1997), 473–484.

5. For a careful analysis of the impact of retail promotions, see Rodney G. Walters, "Assessing the Impact of Retail Price Promotions on Product Substitution, Complementary Purchase, and Interstore Sales Displacement," *Journal of Marketing* 55 (April 1991), 17–28.

6. J. Jeffrey Inman and Russell Winer, "Impulse Buying," *The Wall Street Journal* (April 15, 1999), A1.

7. Pradeep K. Chintagunta and Sudeep Haldar, "Investigating Purchase Timing Behavior in Two Related Product Categories," *Journal of Marketing Research* 35 (February 1998), 43–53.

8. David I. Kollat and Ronald P. Willett, "Customer Impulse Purchasing Behavior," *Journal of Marketing Research* 4 (February 1967), 21–31.

9. Dilip Soman, "The Illusion of Delayed Incentives: Evaluating Future Effort-Money Transactions," *Journal of Marketing Research* 35 (November 1998), 427–437.

10. Laura Loro, "Data Bases Seen as 'Driving Force,'" *Advertising Age* (March 18, 1991), 39.

11. Joseph B. Cahill, "Sear's Credit Business May Have Helped Larger Retailing Woes," *The Wall Street Journal* (July 6, 1999), A1.

12. James U. McNeal and Daryl McKee, "The Case of Antishoppers," in Lusch et al., eds., *1985 AMA Educators' Proceedings,* 65–68.

13. Jack A. Lesser and Sanjay Jain, "A Preliminary Investigation of the Relationship Between Exploratory and Epistemic Shopping Behavior," in Robert E. Lusch et al., eds., *1985 AMA Educators' Proceedings* (Chicago: American Marketing Association, 1985), 75–81.

14. Arch G. Woodside and Randolph J. Trappey III, "Finding Out Why Customers Shop Your Store and Buy your Brand: Automatic Cognitive Processing Models of Primary Choice," *Journal of Advertising Research* 32 (November-December 1992), 59–78.

15. See Jay D. Lindquist, "The Meaning of Image," *Journal of Retailing* 50 (Winter 1974/1975), 29–38; Robert A. Hansen and Terry Deutscher, "An Empirical Investigation of Attribute Importance in Retail Store Selection," *Journal of Retailing* 53 (Winter 1977/1978), 59–72; Leon Arons, "Does Television Viewing Influence Store Image and Shopping Frequency?" *Journal of Retailing* 37 (Fall 1961), 1–13; Ernest Dichter, "What's in an Image," *Journal of Consumer Marketing* 2 (Winter 1985), 75–81.

16. Pierre Martineau, "The Personality of the Retail Store," *Harvard Business Review* 36 (January/February 1958), 47.

17. For semantic differential, see: G. H. G. McDougall and J. N. Fry, "Combining Two Methods of Image Measurement," *Journal of Retailing* 50 (Winter 1974/1975), 53–61. For customer prototypes, see: W. B. Weale, "Measuring the Customer's Image of a Department Store," *Journal of Retailing* 37 (Spring 1961), 40–48. For Q-sort, see: William Stephenson, "Public Images of Public Utilities," *Journal of Advertising Research* 3 (December 1963), 34–39. For Guttman scale, see: Elizabeth A. Richards, "A Commercial Application of Guttman Attitude Scaling Techniques," *Journal of Marketing* 22 (October 1957), 166–173. For multidimensional scaling, see: Peter Doyle and Ian Fenwick, "How Store Image Affects Shopping Habits in Grocery Chains," *Journal of Retailing* 50 (Winter 1974/1975), 39–52. For psycholinguistics, see: Richard N. Cardozo, "How

Images Vary by Product Class," *Journal of Retailing* 50 (Winter 1974/1975), 85–98. For multiattribute approach, see: Don L. James, Richard M. Durand, and Robert A. Dreves, "The Use of a Multi-Attribute Model in a Store Image Study," *Journal of Retailing* 52 (Summer 1976), 23–32.

18. Gilbert D. Harrell, Michael D. Gutt, and James C. Anderson, "Path Analysis of Buyer Behavior under Conditions of Crowding," *Journal of Marketing Research* 17 (February 1980), 45–51. See also Michael K. Hui and John E. G. Bateson, "Perceived Control and the Effects of Crowding and Consumer Choice on the Service Experience," *Journal of Consumer Research* 18 (September 1991), 174–184.

19. David B. Mackay and Richard W. Olshavsky, "Cognitive Maps of Retail Locations: An Investigation of Some Basic Issues," *Journal of Consumer Research* 2 (December 1975); and Edward M. Mazze, "Determining Shopper Movements by Cognitive Maps," *Journal of Retailing* 50 (Fall 1974), 43–48.

20. R. Mittelstaedt et al., "Psychophysical and Evaluative Dimensions of Cognized Distance in an Urban Shopping Environment," in R. C. Curhan, ed., *Combined Proceedings* (Chicago: American Marketing Association, 1974), 190–193.

21. Hansen and Deutscher, "An Empirical Investigation"; Lindquist, "The Meaning of Image"; Gentry and Burns, "How Important"; and John D. Claxton and J. R. Brent Ritchie, "Consumer Prepurchase Shopping Problems: A Focus on the Retailing Component," *Journal of Retailing* 55 (Fall 1979), 24–43.

22. Walter K. Levy, "Department Stores: The Next Generation," *Retailing Issues Letter* 1 (1987), l.

23. Robert H. Williams, John J. Painter, and Herbert R. Nicholas, "A Policy-Oriented Typology of Grocery Shoppers," *Journal of Retailing* 54 (Spring 1978), 27–42.

24. Kent B. Monroe, "Buyers' Subjective Perceptions of Price," *Journal of Marketing Research* 10 (February 1973), 73–80.

25. Joseph N. Fry and Gordon H. McDougall, "Consumer Appraisal of Retail Price Advertisements," *Journal of Marketing* 38 (July 1974); V. Kumar and Robert P. Leone, "Measuring the Effect of Retail Store Promotions on Brand and Store Substitution," *Journal of Marketing Research* 25 (May 1988), 178–185.

26. Alan L. Montgomery and Peter E. Rossi, "Estimating Price Elasticities with Theory-Based Priors," *Journal of Marketing Research* 36 (November 1999), 413–423.

27. John Roberts, "Developing New Rules for New Markets," *Journal of the Academy of Marketing Science* 28, 1 (Winter 2000), 31–44.

28. Randolf E. Bucklin, Sunil Gupta, and S. Siddarth, "Determining Segmentations in Sales Response Across Consumer Purchase Behaviors," *Journal of Marketing Research* 35, 2 (May 1998) 189–197.

29. Greg Allenby, "Reassessing Brand Loyalty, Price Sensitivity, and Merchandising Effects on Consumer Brand Choice," working paper, 1993.

30. Stephen K. Keiser and James R. Krum, "Consumer Perceptions of Retail Advertising with Overstated Price Savings," *Journal of Retailing* 452 (Fall 1976), 27–36.

31. "Service: Retail's No. 1 Problem," *Chain Store Age Executive* (January 1987), 19.

32. Gilbert A. Churchill, Jr., Neil M. Ford, Steven W. Hartley, and Orville C. Walker, Jr., "The Determinants of Salesperson Performance: A Meta-Analysis," *Journal of Marketing Research* 22 (May 1985), 103–118.

33. This categorization has its roots in Peter H. Reingen and Arch G. Woodside, *Buyer-Seller Interactions: Empirical Research and Normative Issues* (Chicago: American Marketing Association, 1981).

34. Arch G. Woodside and William Davenport, Jr., "The Effect of Salesman Similarity and Expertise on Consumer Purchasing Behavior," *Journal of Marketing Research* 11 (May 1974), 198–203. Also see Paul Busch and David T. Wilson, "An Experimental Analysis of a Salesman's Expert and Referent Bases on Social Power in the Buyer-Seller Dyad," *Journal of Marketing Research* 13 (February 1976), 3–11.

35. Paul H. Schurr and Julie Ozanne, "Influences on Exchange Processes: Buyers' Preconceptions of a Seller's Trustworthiness and Bargaining Toughness," *Journal of Consumer Research* 11 (March 1985), 939–953.

36. Siew Meng Leong, Paul S. Busch, and Deborah Roedder John, "Knowledge Bases and Salesperson Effectiveness: A Script-Theoretic Analysis," *Journal of Marketing Research* 26 (May 1989), 164–178; Harish Sujan, Mita Sujan, and James R. Bettman, "Knowledge Structure Differences Between More Effective and Less Effective Sales People," *Journal of Marketing Research* 25 (February 1988), 81–86; and David M. Syzmanski, "Determinants of Selling Effectiveness," *Journal of Marketing* 52 (January 1988), 64–77.

37. "Customer Rapport," *Direct Marketing* (January 1994), 46.

38. Howard Schultz and Dori Yang, "Pour Your Heart Into It: How Starbucks Built A Company One Cup at a Time," *Hyperion* (January 1999).

39. Joel A. Baglole, "Loblaw Supermarkets Add Fitness Clubs to Offerings," *The Wall Street Journal* (December 27, 1999), B4.

40. Philip Kotler, "Atmospherics as a Marketing Tool," *Journal of Retailing* 49 (Winter 1973/1974), 48–63. Also see: Robert J. Donovan and John R. Rossiter, "Store Atmosphere: An Environmental Psychology Approach," *Journal of Retailing* 58 (Spring 1982), 34–57; Elaine Sherman and Ruth Belk Smith, "Mood States of Shoppers and Store Image: Promising Interactions and Possible Behavioral Effects," in Melanie Wallendorf and Paul Anderson, eds., *Advances in Consumer Research* 14 (Provo, Utah: Association for Consumer Research, 1987), 251–254.

41. Peter Doyle and Ian Fenwick, "How Store Image Affects Shopping Habits in Grocery Chains," *Journal of Retailing* 50 (Winter 1974/1975), 39–52.

42. Phyllis Berman and Katherine Bruce, "Makeover at the Makeup Counter," *Forbes* (April 19, 1999).

43. For a review and analysis of music's usefulness to marketers, see Gordon C. Bruner II, "Music, Mood, and Marketing," *Journal of Marketing* 54 (October 1990), 94–104.

44. Richard Yalch and Eric Spangenberg, "Effects of Store Music on Shopping Behavior," *Journal of Consumer Marketing* 7 (Spring 1990), 55–63.

45. Ronald E. Milliman, "Using Background Music to Affect the Behavior of Supermarket Shoppers," *Journal of Marketing* 46 (Summer 1982), 86–91.

46. Ronald E. Milliman, "The Influence of Background Music on the Behavior of Restaurant Patrons," *Journal of Consumer Research* 13 (September 1986), 286–289.

47. Joseph A. Bellizzi, Ayn E. Crowley, and Rondla W. Hasty, "The Effects of Color in Store Design," *Journal of Retailing* 59 (Spring 1983), 21–45.

48. Rick Brooks, "Alienating Customers Isn't Always a Bad Idea, Many Firms Discover," *The Wall Street Journal* (January 7, 1999), A1, A12.

49. V. Kumar and Robert P. Leone, "Measuring the Effect of Retail Store Promotions on Brand and Store Substitution," *Journal of Marketing Research* 25 (May 1988), 178–185; Gary E. McKinnon, J. Patrick Kelly, and E. Doyle Robison, "Sales Effects of Point-of-Purchase In-Store Signing," *Journal of Retailing* 57 (Summer 1981), 49–63; Arch G. Woodside and Gerald L. Waddle, "Sales Effects of In-Store Advertising," *Journal of Advertising Research* 15 (June 1975), 29–33.

50. Ymiko Ono, "Wobblers and Sidekicks Clutter Stores, Irk Retailers," *The Wall Street Journal* (September 8, 1998), B1, B4.

51. John A. Quelch and Kristina Cannon-Bonventre, "Better Marketing at the Point of Purchase,"

Harvard Business Review 61 (November/December 1983), 162–169.

52. Howard Schlossberg, "P-O-P Display Designer Wants to Keep Shoppers Shopping Longer," *Marketing News* (November 11, 1991), 15.

53. As defined in Roger Blackwell and Tina Blackwell, *Understanding Your Customer; Consumer Logistics,* International Mass Retail Association (1998).

54. Michael K. Hui and John E. G. Bateson, "Perceived Control and the Effects of Crowding and Consumer Choice on the Service Experience," *Journal of Consumer Research* 18 (September 1991), 174–184.

55. Julie Baker and Michaelle Cameron, "The Effects of the Service Environment on Affect and Consumer Perception of Waiting Time: An Integrative Review and Research Proposition," *Journal of the Academy of Marketing Science* 24, 4 (Summer, 1996), 338–349.

56. Benedict Dellaert, Theo Arentze, Michel Bierlaire, Aloys Borgers, and Harry Timmermans, "Investigating Consumers' Tendency to Combine Multiple Shopping Purposes and Destinations," *Journal of Marketing Research* 35, 2 (May 1998).

57. Roger D. Blackwell and Wayne Talarzyk, "Lifestyle Retailing: Competitive Strategies for the 1980's," *Journal of Retailing* 59 (Winter 1983), 7–27.

58. Frederick E. Webster, "Understanding the Relationships Among Brands, Consumers and Resellers," *Journal of The Academy of Marketing Science* 28, 1 (Winter 2000), 17–23.

59. "The Changing Face of Retail," *The Retailer* (Winter 1994), 6–15.

60. Mary Beth Knight, "The New Crown Jewel," *Chain Store Age* (March 1999), 177–179.

61. See, for example, Peterson and Albaum, "Nonstore Retailing in the United States"; Martin P. Block and Tamara S. Brezen, "A Profile of the New In-Home Shopper," in Rebecca Holman, ed., *Proceedings of the 1991 Conference of the American Academy of Advertising* (New York: Rebecca H. Holman, D'Arcy Masius Benton & Bowles, Inc., 1991), 169–173; Paul I. Edwards, "Home Shopping Boom Forecast in Study," *Advertising Age* (December 15, 1986), 88.

62. Erin White, "Ding-Dong, Avon Calling (on the Web, Not Your Door)," *The Wall Street Journal* (December 28, 1999), B4.

63. Ibid.

64. "Behavior and Attitudes of Telephone Shoppers," *Direct Marketing* (September 1987), 50.

65. Riccardo A. Davis, "QVC Clicks for Kodak Cameras," *Advertising Age* (January 17, 1994), 17.

66. Kevin J. Delaney, "Where the E in E-Shopping Stands for 'Extreme,'" *The Wall Street Journal* (October 14, 1999), B1ff and company web sites, www.printemps.fr and www.webcamer.com.

67. This conceptual framework is developed originally in Justin Voss and Roger Blackwell, "Markets for Leisure Time," in Mary Jane Slinger, ed., *Advances in Consumer Research* (Chicago: Association for Consumer Research, 1975), 837–845; and Justin Voss and Roger Blackwell, "The Role of Time Resources in Consumer Behavior," in O. C. Ferrel, Stephen Brown, and Charles Lamb, eds., *Conceptual and Theoretical Developments in Marketing* (Chicago: American Marketing Association, 1979), 296–311.

68. Justin Voss, "The Definition of Leisure," *Journal of Economic Issues* 1 (June 1967), 91–106.

69. Howard Marmorstein, Dhruv Grewal, and Raymond P. H. Fishe, "The Value of Time Spent in Price-Comparison Shopping: Survey and Experimental Evidence," *Journal of Consumer Research* 19 (June 1992), 52–61.

70. Douglass K. Hawes, W. Wayne Talarzyk, and Roger D. Blackwell, "Consumer Satisfaction from Leisure Time Pursuits," in Mary J. Slinger, *Advances* 822.

71. Carol Felker Kaufman, Paul M. Lane, and Jay D. Lindquist, "Exploring More than 24 Hours a Day: A Preliminary Investigation of Polychronic Time Use," *Journal of Consumer Research* 18 (December 1991), 392–401.

72. Aida N. Rizkalla, "Consumer Temporal Orientation and Shopping Behavior: The Case of Harried vs. Relaxed Consumers," in Robert L. King, ed., *Retailing: Its Present and Future* 4 (Charleston, SC: Academy of Marketing Science, 1988), 230–235.

73. Scott B. MacKenzie, "The Role of Attention in Mediating the Effect of Advertising on Attribute Importance," *Journal of Consumer Research* 13 (September 1986), 174–195.

74. James R. Bettman, "Issues in Designing Consumer Information Environments," *Journal of Consumer Research* 2 (December 1975), 169–177.

75. Jacob Jacoby, Donald Speller, and Carol Kohn Berning, "Brand Choice Behavior as a Function of Information Load," *Journal of Marketing Research* 11 (February 1974), 63–69.

76. Jacob Jacoby, Donald Speller, and Carol Kohn Berning, "Brand Choice Behavior as a Function of Information Load: Replication and Extension," *Journal of Consumer Research* 1 (June 1974), 33–42; J. Edward Russo, "More Information Is Better: A Reevaluation of Jacoby, Speller, and Kohn," *Journal of Consumer Research* 11 (November 1974),

467–468; William L. Wilkie, "Analysis of Effects of Information Load," *Journal of Marketing Research* 11 (November 1974), 462–466; Jacob Jacoby, Donald E. Speller, and Carol A. K. Beming, "Constructive Criticism and Programmatic Research: Reply to Russo," *Journal of Consumer Research* 1 (September 1975), 154–156; Jacob Jacoby, "Information Load and Decision Quality: Some Contested Issues," *Journal of Marketing Research* 15 (November 1977), 569–573. Also see Debora L. Scammon, "Information Load and Consumers," *Journal of Consumer Research* 4 (December 1977), 148–155; Naresh K. Malhotra, "Information Load and Consumer Decision Making," *Journal of Consumer Research* 8 (March 1982), 419–430; Naresh K. Malhotra, Arun K. Jain, and Stephen W. Lagakos, "The Information Overload Controversy: An Alternative Viewpoint," *Journal of Marketing* 46 (Spring 1982), 27–37; Naresh K. Malhotra, "Reflections on the Information Overload Paradigm in Consumer Decision Making," *Journal of Consumer Research* 10 (March 1984), 436–440.

77. Jacob Jacoby, "Perspectives on Information Overload," *Journal of Consumer Research* 10 (March 1984), 432–435.

78. Kevin Lane Keller and Richard Staelin, "Effects of Quality and Quantity of Information on Decision Effectiveness," *Journal of Consumer Research* 14 (September 1987), 200–213.

79. This section is based on Roger D. Blackwell, "Integrated Marketing Communications," in Gary L. Frazier and Jagdish N. Sheth, eds., *Contemporary Views on Marketing Practice* (Lexington, MA: Lexington Books, 1987), 237–250.

80. Marnik G. Dekimpe and Dominique M. Hanssens," Sustained Spending and Persistent Response: A New Look at Long-Term Marketing Profitability," *Journal of Marketing Research* 36 (November 1999), 397–412.

CHAPTER 6

Post-Purchase Processes: Consumption and Evaluation

OPENING VIGNETTE

Champagne makers have become a victim of their own success. They have done a wonderful job in positioning their product as an essential part of celebration activities. More than 50 percent of annual champagne sales take place at year-end, the season of Christmas and New Year's parties.

However, after reaching a peak in the mid-1980s, champagne consumption in the United States has been flat for several years. In order to stimulate sales, champagne makers are trying to expand consumption outside of the holiday season. One market leader, Korbel, has been at the forefront of these efforts. It has tried a number of promotions to boost sales throughout the year, including sponsoring a boat in the America's Cup yacht race and becoming an official licensed product of the 1996 Summer Olympics. These promotional activities helped Korbel steal market share. Nonetheless, as noted by Andrew Varga, the senior brand manager for Korbel, "we weren't bringing in new users and we weren't getting consumption of champagne up every day."

Korbel is now pinning its hopes on an entirely new product: chardonnay champagne. The drink is packaged in a green chardonnay-type glass bottle and tastes more like a table wine than traditional champagne. Korbel has persuaded major retailers to display the product on the chardonnay shelves, as well as with other sparkling wines.

Korbel hopes consumers will view the new product as something that can be consumed everyday, with meals. But it also knows that this will not be easy. As Mr. Varga explains, "One of the toughest things in the champagne category is changing the deep-seated imagery of the product directly tied to celebration."

Source: Excerpted in part from Elizabeth Jensen, "Champagne Makers Are Hoping Chardonnay Adds Fizz to Sales," The Wall Street Journal (March 21, 1997), B5.

Selling more of one's product does not necessarily require selling to more people. Another option for increasing sales is to enhance the amount of consumption per customer. This may involve getting consumers to use more of the product per consumption occasion (e.g., when the order taker at a fast-food restaurant prompts you to change your french fries order from regular size to extra large). Or it may involve increasing the number of times consumption occurs. As described in the chapter vignette, Korbel certainly hopes that its new chardonnay champagne will be consumed more frequently than its traditional champagne.

This chapter starts with the consumption stage of the consumer decision process. In many ways, consumption represents the most important part of the decision process. For it is here that we usually can best evaluate what the product has to offer. How did the product perform? Did it deliver what was expected? Depending on the answers to such questions, consumers will develop more or less favorable evaluations of their consumption experiences. These post-consumption evaluations represent the final stage of the consumer decision process and are discussed in the latter part of the chapter.

Consumption

Consumption represents consumers' usage of the purchased product. Although this definition is simple, understanding consumption is much more complex. Indeed, there are a number of different ways to think about consumption. Let's start with consumption behavior itself.

Consumption Behaviors

When is the last time you ate frozen pizza? Have you attended a professional football game in the past year? Do you watch the *Ally McBeal* TV program? Have you ever taken a cruise on an ocean liner? Are you currently a member of a bowling league?

Your answers to the preceding questions reveal whether or not you are a consumer of these products. **User** and **nonuser** are terms often used to distinguish between *those who consume the product* and *those who do not.* The number of people that fall into the user and nonuser categories is important to businesses in a couple of ways. Knowing the number of current users in a product category is one indicator of the market's attractiveness to the company. Generally speaking, the larger the market (i.e., as the number of users increases), the greater its attractiveness.

The size of the nonuser market segment speaks to future growth opportunities. Converting nonusers into users is not a viable option for increasing sales when the market contains few nonusers. But as the number of nonusers increases, the potential payoff from courting nonusers becomes greater. Consider hair-growth products such as Rogaine. Around three million American men use these products. But this is only a small fraction of the 40 million men in the United States that have hereditary hair loss.[1] As hair-growth products improve, there is substantial opportunity for increasing the size of the user market. Similarly, there is an enormous nonuser market for cruise ships since around 90 percent of North Americans have yet to come on board.[2]

An understanding of consumption behaviors requires more than simply distinguishing between those who consume and those who don't. Indeed, consumption behaviors can be characterized along a number of important dimensions that are represented in Figure 6.1 and discussed subsequently.

When Does Consumption Occur?

One fundamental characteristic of consumption behaviors involves when usage occurs. In many cases, purchase and consumption go hand in hand. That is, in making the purchase, we have committed ourselves to when consumption will occur. Buying tickets for a concert or sporting event, eating at a restaurant, and taking your car to the local car wash fall into this category. At other times, purchases are made without knowing precisely when consumption will occur. Food items bought during your last trip to the grocery store sit on a shelf or in the refrigerator until you decide to consume them.

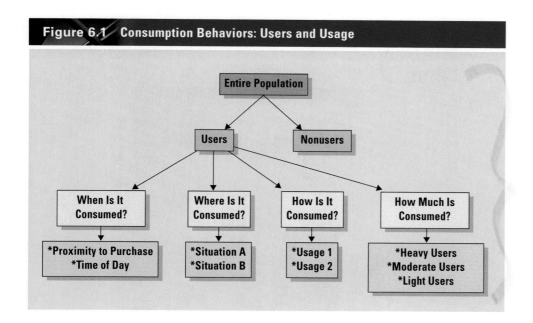

Figure 6.1 Consumption Behaviors: Users and Usage

When consumption decisions are made independently of prior purchase decisions (such as when you are choosing something to munch on from your pantry), it may be worthwhile for a company to consider putting some of its efforts into encouraging consumption rather than focusing exclusively on encouraging purchase. This was so for one food manufacturer that discovered many people left its product sitting in their pantries long after purchase had occurred. This discovery prompted the company to develop an advertising campaign that aired late at night encouraging consumers to consume the food as a late-night snack. Another example of encouraging consumption is provided by the wine industry. In response to declining wine consumption, a new multimedia advertising campaign was launched in 1999 featuring the slogan: "Wine. What are you saving it for?"[3]

The time of day at which usage occurs is another component of understanding the "when" of consumption behaviors. Food consumption depends very heavily on the time of day. We rarely eat spaghetti for breakfast or cereal for dinner. Orange juice is usually consumed at the breakfast table. In years past, the orange juice industry attempted to break out of this restriction with its famous advertising campaign slogan, "It isn't just for breakfast anymore." A similar theme is reflected in the Pop-Tarts ad shown in Figure 6.2. In contrast, pizza makers have been marketing "breakfast pizzas" in the hope that they can gain a share of the breakfast table.

When consumption occurs can be especially important for those taking certain medications. Read Consumer in Focus 6.1 to learn about how a medication's effectiveness may depend on the time it is taken.

Sometimes it is beneficial to segment the market based on when consumption occurs. Those promoting the Florida Keys have discovered important differences between tourists who visit during the summer versus those visiting during the more expensive winter months. Winter visitors typically are older and wealthier, enjoy sightseeing, and are more likely to be white non-Hispanics. Summer visitors tend to stay for shorter amounts of time (around four days on average) and are more likely to be found snorkeling in the reefs. Hispanics and blacks are more likely to be visiting during the summer. Information such as this allows one to target the appropriate segments more effectively and efficiently.[4]

Figure 6.2   Kellogg's Wants More Than Just Breakfast Consumption of Its Product

Consumer in Focus 6.1

The Effectiveness of Medications May Depend on When They're Consumed

Our bodies have internal rhythms that make certain diseases worse at certain times of the day. Consider blood pressure, which in the majority of people surges in the early mornings, just when they're awakening. For hypertension patients, that surge is dangerous. Heart attacks and strokes occur most frequently during those morning hours.

Chronotherapy involves using people's internal biological rhythms to treat disease more effectively, and even minimize side effects. Asthma attacks often occur at night and usually are more severe at night. Some asthma patients have cut nighttime attacks in half by taking formulations of theophylline in the early evening, timed to provide enough medication to get them through the night. One type of cholesterol medicine, the "statin" drugs, works better when given in the evening because it targets a cholesterol-affecting liver enzyme that is most active at night. And the Food and Drug Administration recently approved a hypertension drug specially coated so it won't reach peak strength until around 6 a.m., when it's most needed.

Unfortunately, knowledge about chronotherapy is not as extensive as it could be. "Most doctors are not completely familiar with the fact that when we take medicines is critical" to how well they work, says chronobiology expert Michael Smolensky of the University of Texas-Houston Health Science Center.

Source: Excerpted from Lauran Neergaard, "Research Finds Internal Clock Important in Drug Effectiveness, Health," Miami Herald (May 1, 1999), 11A.

Where Does Consumption Occur?

In addition to when, it is useful to understand where consumption takes place. Beer sales are quite sensitive to whether consumption happens inside or outside the home. The majority of sales for domestic brews are generated by in-home consumption. In contrast, import beers obtain the majority of their sales "on premise" (in bars and restaurants).[5] Apparently, many believe that drinking import beers projects a more favorable social image to those present during consumption.

Failure to understand where consumption occurs can be a costly mistake. This was the lesson learned by Wendy's when it offered a drive-through breakfast containing scrambled-egg platters, made-to-order omelets, French toast and pancakes. "Customers raved about the product, but said, 'I can't travel with it,' and didn't buy it," says communications vice president Denny Lynch.[6] In contrast, Burger King avoided this problem by offering French Toast sticks and miniature pancakes that could be easily held and dipped into maple syrup.

How Is the Product Consumed?

Different people may purchase the same product but consume it in different ways. Consider rice. Sometimes rice is used as an ingredient that is mixed with other food items (e.g., a casserole). Sometimes it is served by itself as a side dish. The particular brand of rice that is purchased often depends on how it will be used. When users intended to serve the rice as a side dish, they were more likely to buy a well-known brand despite its more expensive price. If, however, rice was to be used as an ingredient, they more often opted for a cheaper competitor. Do you know why these differences would occur?

Apparently, many consumers believed that the higher-priced brand tasted better than the less expensive competition. And if they intended to serve the rice by itself, they were willing to pay the higher price in order to enjoy the better taste. But when rice is mixed with other ingredients, its taste becomes less noticeable. For this reason, consumers did not feel justified in spending the additional money for something that goes unnoticed. Thus, a change in how the product was to be consumed led to a change in what was purchased.

Understanding how consumers use milk was an essential element in the development of the "got milk?" advertising campaign. Prior advertising by the industry depicted milk as something that was consumed alone. Yet milk is a product that typically is digested along with something else, such as cookies, brownies, cereal, or a sandwich. Consequently, the "got milk?" campaign reflected this reality by showing people suffering from a lack of milk while consuming certain food items. In one commercial, a ruthless businessman dies and fears that he has gone to hell. To his relief, he finds a plate of giant chocolate chip cookies and a refrigerator full of milk cartons. After munching on the cookies, he reaches for some milk, only to discover that all the cartons are empty. Commercials such as this have helped the milk industry hold per capita consumption steady after many years of declining consumption.[7]

Understanding how the product is used may also lead to uncovering new business opportunities. Sometimes companies discover consumers using their products in new and innovative ways. Such was the case for a soap manufacturer. It realized that its sales in one rural region vastly exceeded what would be expected based on the population living in that area. After further investigation, it found that many of the local farmers were using the soap to protect their fruit trees from preying insects and animals. Simply hanging the soap from the limbs deterred the pests without harming the fruit.

Sometimes it is in a company's best interest to change how its product is consumed. Read Consumer in Focus 6.2 for an illustration of this.

Consumer in Focus 6.2

Changing How Russians Consume Vodka

In a large second-floor room of the Rossiya movie theater in Uglich, Russia, Vladimir Shabalin teaches people how to drink vodka. "Smell it first," he tells visitors clasping murky antique shot glasses. They do. "Take a sip, and hold it in your mouth for just a bit. Swallow, and then have a mild snack."

As director of a new vodka "library" in Uglich that will eventually allow visitors to sample from 800 different vodka brands, Shabalin and his partners are part of a scattered effort to create a new, upscale culture of drinking the ancient spirit. Why? Because businesses that depend on vodka sales are worried that Russians are moving away from vodka to what are viewed as more refined drinks, including gin, whiskey, and expensive wine. "People are afraid of alcoholism, and vodka is strongly associated in their minds with

alcoholism," says Natalya Karchazhkina, a senior analyst with Qualitel Data Services, a Moscow market research firm.

These concerns over alcoholism are quite understandable. The Russian Health Ministry estimates that domestic hard-liquor consumption is 3.7 gallons per capita. The World Health Organization considers 2.1 gallons per capita highly dangerous, which is reflected in the declining average life expectancy of Russian men, now about 58 years.

The vanguard of the new drinking culture hopes to refurbish vodka's reputation by teaching people to drink it for taste rather than its punch. "You can't ban vodka, so you have to teach people how to drink it properly," says Viktor Minayev, a partner in the Uglich vodka library.

Source: Excerpted from Neela Banerjee, "Russia Learns to Savor Its 'Spirit,'" Miami Herald *(June 5, 1999), 1C, 9C.*

How Much Is Consumed?

Although a group of consumers may share a common bond in terms of engaging in the same consumption behavior (e.g., wine drinkers), they may differ substantially in the amount of consumption. Some may have only an occasional glass of wine; some may drink wine nearly every day but only at the dinner table; and some may drink it every day, all day long.

These differences in the amount of consumption provide one basis for segmenting the user market. This form of segmentation, called **usage volume segmentation,** typically *divides users into one of three segments: heavy users, moderate users, and light users.* Heavy users are those exhibiting the highest levels of product consumption. In the United States, 16 percent of adult consumers account for 88 percent of all wine consumption.[8] Light users are those who consume rather small amounts of the product. Moderate users fall in between these two extremes. All else being equal, heavy users are typically a primary target market. In most cases, the profit potential gained from selling to a heavy user greatly exceeds that realized from moderate and light users.

Changing the amount of consumption is often an important business objective. Consider the ad shown in Figure 6.3. Notice how the copy appearing at the bottom of the ad ("Murphy's Once A Week") explicitly calls for a level of usage greater than that currently exhibited by many users. The current "got milk?" advertising campaign aims to increase consumption among current milk drinkers rather than focusing on nonusers.[9]

Businesses will sometimes try to encourage consumption by modifying their product offerings. As noted earlier, champagne makers are hoping that their new offering will increase consumption. Camera film manufacturers have similar hopes for the new, smaller-sized cameras, some of which are no larger than a credit card. Consumers may be more likely to carry these tiny cameras around with them, thereby leading to more opportunities to snap pictures.[10]

Figure 6.3   This Product Wants Weekly Consumption

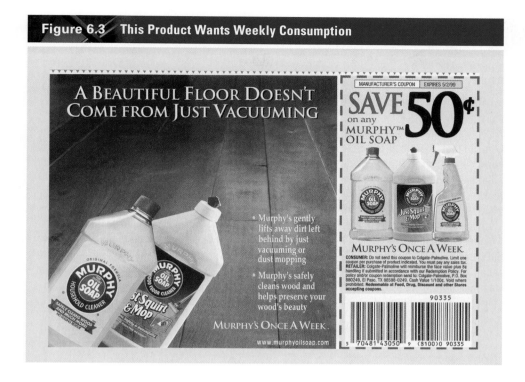

Those interested in consumer welfare often find themselves trying to change the amount of consumption. In recent years, substantial efforts have been undertaken to reduce the consumption of such things as cigarette smoking, illegal drug usage, and underage drinking. Similarly, nutritionists try to get us to eat less junk food while including more nutritionally balanced foods in our diet. For this reason, legislation was passed that required food labels describing a product's nutritional properties. Similarly, as discussed in Consumer in Focus 6.3, toothpaste manufacturers have been required to include warning labels about the potential health risks of overconsumption to small children.

Consumption Experiences

In the preceding section, we focused on particular behavioral characteristics of consumption, such as when and where it takes place. We now turn to the consumption experience itself.

How Does It Feel?

A critical characteristic of many consumption behaviors is the particular feelings experienced during consumption.[11] How do you feel when you are eating your favorite candy? The last time you visited a dentist, how did you feel? What (if any) feelings do you experience when pouring laundry detergent into the washing machine?

Feelings come in many different shapes and sizes. They can be positive (e.g., excitement, pleasure, relief, sentimental); they can be negative (e.g., angry, bored, guilty, regretful). Sometimes they are overwhelming. More often they are experienced with much less intensity.

One of the most intense and inspiring things that I have experienced personally was during my first helicopter ride while vacationing in the Hawaiian Islands. I floated above an extinct volcano, lush with the vegetation that comes from

Consumer in Focus 6.3

Curbing Toothpaste Consumption

Because children under 6 years old are unable to control their swallowing reflex, they typically swallow toothpaste when brushing their teeth. A study at the Medical College of Georgia School of Dentistry found that about half the children this age don't spit out or rinse out. Instead, they swallow the toothpaste. Making matters worse, they tend to use too much toothpaste on their own, especially when they use flavored children's toothpastes.

So what's the problem? Too much fluoride. If ingested in large quantities, fluoride can be deadly, especially for small children. "The fluoride in toothpaste is considered a drug," says Regina Miskewitz, director of research and development for Church & Dwight, maker of Arm & Hammer products. "When I receive the fluoride here, it has a skull-and-bones on it."

To minimize the dangers of overconsumption, the following directions and warnings have been added to the toothpaste tube: "Do not swallow. **Children under 6 yrs.:** To minimize swallowing use a pea-sized amount and supervise brushing until good habits are established. **Keep out of the reach of children under 6 years of age.** If you accidentally swallow more than used for brushing, seek professional help or contact a poison control center immediately."

However, some perceive the warning to be unnecessary. "Our position was that they went a little too far," says Clifford Whall, director of product evaluations for the American Dental Association's Council on Scientific Affairs. "We didn't think you needed a label like that because it could unnecessarily scare consumers into not using toothpaste."

Source: Excerpted from Don Oldenburg, "How Safe Is Toothpaste? FDA Orders Warning Labels with Chilling Message," Miami Herald *(June 20, 1997), 4F.*

growing in an area that receives the greatest amount of rainfall on our planet. I hovered next to spectacular waterfalls scattered in remote pockets throughout the island. I saw cliffs magnificently sculptured by the ocean winds. At one point, I found myself holding back tears of joy as I marveled at the wonders of nature before me.

Unfortunately, such consumption experiences are the exception rather than the rule. Many consumption behaviors are rather ordinary and experienced with little feeling. Pouring laundry detergent into the washing machine, taking vitamin pills, and pumping gas into a car are activities usually performed without much feeling.

Of course, even an ordinary consumption activity can evoke strong feelings when things go wrong. Have you ever had the dry cleaner lose your clothes? What about having a trash bag filled with garbage break open, spilling its contents everywhere? Negative feelings, such as disappointment and regret, perhaps even anger, may arise whenever the consumption experience fails to measure up to what was expected.

Typically, negative feelings during product usage are undesirable from both the customer's and company's perspective. Although they may sometimes be an inherent part of the consumption experience (such as the nervousness and anxiety that accompanies getting a tooth pulled), often they are the result of failing to deliver what the customer wants and expects. Feelings such as disappointment, regret, frustration, and anger are clear indicators of a problem. Implementing corrective actions requires identifying the reasons for these negative feelings.

Depending on the nature of the consumption experience, companies may find it beneficial to position their products based on the feelings experienced during consumption. There are two basic approaches for positioning the product in terms of consumption feelings. One approach is to focus on the positive feelings that consumption provides. Consider the ad for York Peppermint Pattie shown in

Figure 6.4. The ad tells consumers to "Get the sensation," thereby emphasizing the feelings experienced during product consumption. Automobile manufacturers often promote the thrills of driving their sports cars. Sometimes they emphasize the feelings of being able to own a status symbol. This was so in one newspaper ad for Jaguar that read, "Want to feel good about yourself? Try repeating, 'I drive a Jaguar.'"

What do you think is the second approach to feeling-based positioning? If you believe that it involves emphasizing how the product reduces or eliminates negative feelings, you are correct. One car rental company promotes itself through advertising showing the frustration and irritation consumers may experience when renting from the competition—feelings that are of course avoided when renting from its company. Similarly, many consumers experience tremendous guilt when eating food, especially if the food is less than healthy. As shown in Figure 6.5, one food manufacturer responds to these concerns by positioning its product as "guilt free."

How Rewarding or Punishing Was the Experience?

Consumption experiences differ in terms of whether consumers find them to be rewarding or punishing. From this perspective, consumption experiences can be characterized by whether they provide positive reinforcement, negative reinforcement, or punishment. Each type of experience is diagrammed in Figure 6.6.

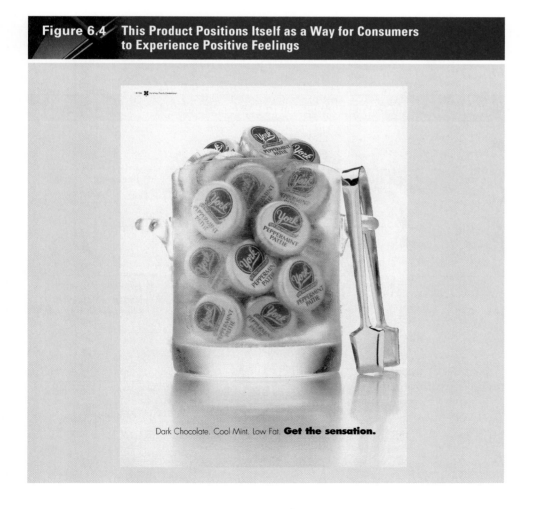

Figure 6.4 **This Product Positions Itself as a Way for Consumers to Experience Positive Feelings**

Dark Chocolate. Cool Mint. Low Fat. **Get the sensation.**

Figure 6.5 This Product Positions Itself as Avoiding Negative Feelings That May Arise During Consumption

Great Taste Without Guilt.
Sara Lee Reduced Fat Baked Goods
Sara Lee
55¢
REDUCED FAT
POUND CAKE
55¢
REDUCED FAT
APPLE PIE
55¢
REDUCED FAT
RASPBERRY COFFEE CAKE
55¢
REDUCED FAT
CHEESECAKE

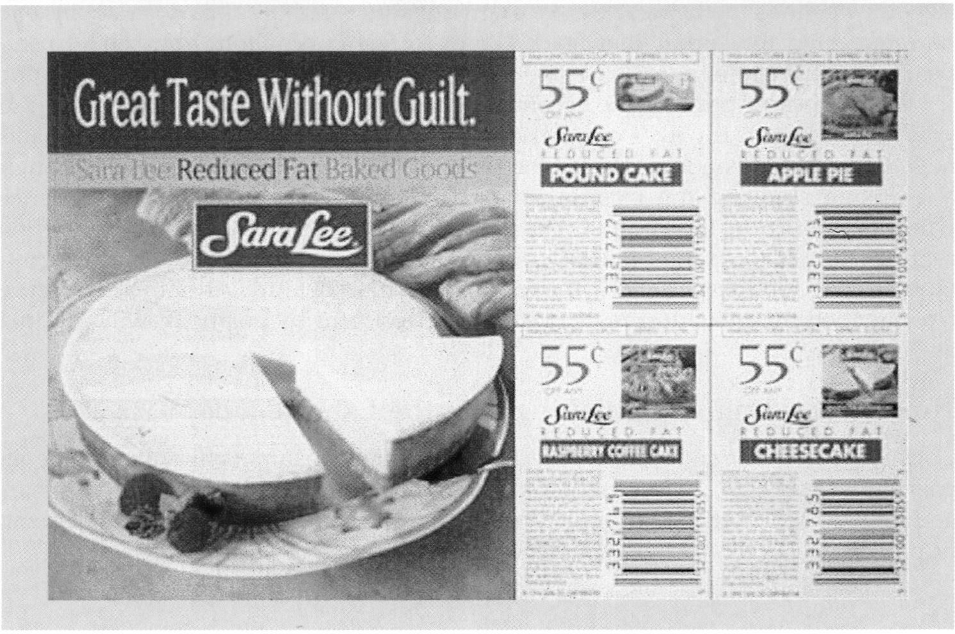

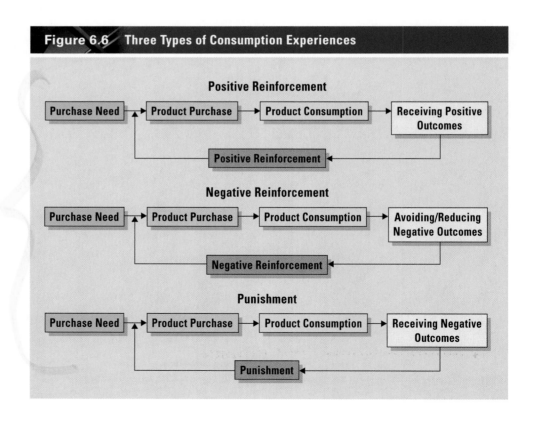

Figure 6.6 Three Types of Consumption Experiences

Positive Reinforcement
Purchase Need
Product Purchase
Product Consumption
Receiving Positive Outcomes
Positive Reinforcement
Negative Reinforcement
Purchase Need
Product Purchase
Product Consumption
Avoiding/Reducing Negative Outcomes
Negative Reinforcement
Punishment
Purchase Need
Product Purchase
Product Consumption
Receiving Negative Outcomes
Punishment

A consumption experience provides **positive reinforcement** when the *consumer receives some positive outcome from product usage.* For example, many of us love to visit amusement parks because of the thrills and exhilaration experienced while riding certain attractions. **Negative reinforcement** occurs when *consumption enables consumers to avoid some negative outcome.* Eye drops, for instance, are used to remove the negative feelings caused by burning, irritated eyes. Sometimes both positive and negative reinforcement can happen during consumption. An air freshener can replace odors (negative reinforcement) with a refreshing smell (positive reinforcement).

Ideally, companies want their products to provide as much reinforcement as possible. Doing so means that customers are much more likely to become repeat buyers. Unfortunately, there are times when the consumption experience brings punishment. **Punishment** occurs when *consumption leads to negative outcomes.* Cosmetic surgeries that leave the person in worse shape than before the surgery are punishing indeed. A punishing consumption experience is unlikely to be tried again, particularly if the negative outcomes experienced during consumption outweigh any reinforcement that may have also been received.

Consumers are less likely to enjoy buying and using negative reinforcement products than positive reinforcement products.[12] Consequently, they will often spend less time and effort when buying these products. This, in turn, limits a product's opportunity to break through the clutter of competitive brands and gain the consumer's consideration.

Companies offering negative reinforcement products should recognize the existence of three distinct market segments for their products. Obviously, consumers currently experiencing the problem solved by the product are the primary target. Consumers who formerly suffered from the problem compose another market segment that may be receptive to appeals that encourage product use to ensure that the problem will not recur. Even consumers who have not faced the problem may be a viable segment. It may be possible to encourage product consumption as a means of reducing the odds that consumers would ever experience the problem. One commercial currently running on TV features a young father talking about his family's history of hair loss. He explains that although he currently doesn't have a problem, he uses the advertised product to reduce the chances of future hair loss.

Did It Confirm or Disconfirm Expectations?

Another way to think about consumption experiences involves the degree to which the expectations carried by consumers into purchase and consumption are confirmed or disconfirmed. Consider the following comments from a person who had just completed a canoe trip around Biscayne Bay, Florida: "I was enticed into coming on this trip. I was told it would be easy and it was not. I was told it would be cool and it was not. I was told I would see lots of wildlife and I saw very little. I'm just glad it is over."[13] Obviously, the consumption experience did not live up to this person's expectations.

The extent to which the consumption experience confirms or disconfirms expectations typically has a powerful influence on consumers' evaluations following product consumption. We discuss this influence later in the chapter when we consider postconsumption evaluations.

Consumption Norms and Rituals

Consumption norms represent *informal rules that govern our consumption behavior.* A suit and tie are the expected garb for businessmen. Gifts representing expressions of love are exchanged on Valentine's Day. A corsage is a fundamental part of a prom date.

Many consumption activities are ritualized. **Consumption rituals** are defined as "a type of expressive, symbolic activity constructed of multiple behaviors that occur in a fixed, episodic sequence, and that tend to be repeated over time. Ritual behavior is dramatically scripted and acted out and is performed with formality, seriousness, and inner intensity."[14] At the time this chapter is being written, it's almost Thanksgiving, so let's use this U.S. national holiday to illustrate consumption rituals.[15]

The origins of Thanksgiving go back to 1621 when the Pilgrims invited the local Indians to a feast celebrating a good harvest. It has since become one of the most widely observed holidays in America. The script is all too familiar. Family and close friends converge to a single location for a day of relaxation, conversation, and of course, eating. Turkey, mashed potatoes, stuffing, cranberries, and pumpkin pie will be found on many dining tables. Although most people think of Thanksgiving as a day of family togetherness, it also represents symbolically a celebration of material abundance. The table is loaded with a greater variety of foods than found at nearly any other time during the year; plates are filled until they are overflowing, and the hostess often isn't happy until at least some of the participants announce that they have eaten too much!

Companies sometimes try to reinforce their products' place in consumption rituals. Two advertising examples are shown in Figure 6.7. Notice how each ad positions the product as a part of the family tradition.

Holiday rituals are but one of many different types of consumption rituals. Most of us perform certain grooming rituals that are followed routinely when getting ready in the morning.[16] Gift-giving behavior can also be characterized as ritual.[17]

Compulsive Consumption

Consumption behavior can take forms and directions that are decidedly counterproductive. The term **compulsive consumption** refers to *those practices that, though undertaken to bolster self-esteem, are inappropriate, excessive, and disruptive to the lives of those who are involved.*[18] Often, consumers experience a lack of control over their own actions. The gratification received usually is temporary, and common outcomes include profound guilt and helplessness.

For many people, gambling is a common form of compulsive consumption.[19] According to the National Gambling Impact Study Commission, over five million Americans have a gambling problem. This problem is not limited to adults. More than one million American adolescents ranging in age from 12 to 17 are compulsive gamblers. Estimates of the economic cost of problem gambling are in the billions of dollars.[20]

Shopping addiction is another form of compulsive consumption. The so-called shop-a-holic finds release in this behavior in much the same ways as alcoholics or drug addicts.[21] The unique element here, however, is that the addiction is to the *process of buying* and not the possession of the items. Shopping addicts often report that the purchased items do not serve any useful purpose.

The Internet has given birth to a new type of compulsive consumption: web dependency. Web dependents average nearly 40 hours a week on the Internet. Nearly half are homemakers and unemployed college students. They spend most of their time in "chat rooms" where they often assume different identities. Letters seeking advice from columnists Ann Landers and Abigail Van Buren about web dependency are common. And one mother was arrested for child endangerment after police discovered her children in a feces-littered playroom while she sat nearby in a spotless computer room.[22]

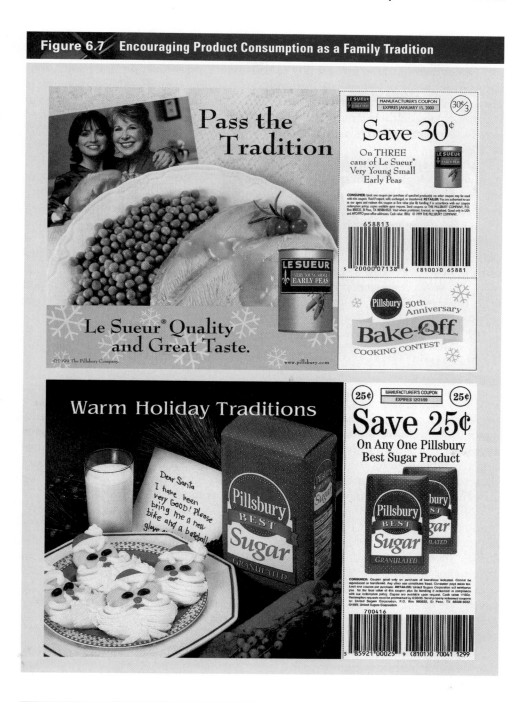

Figure 6.7   Encouraging Product Consumption as a Family Tradition

Post-Consumption Evaluations

As discussed in Chapter 4, evaluating choice alternatives is a fundamental part of the pre-purchase phase of the decision-making process. Evaluation of the chosen alternative is a fundamental part of the post-purchase stages of the decision-making process. During and following consumption, consumers form evaluations of the product and the consumption experience. These post-consumption evaluations may strongly resemble those evaluations held prior to purchase, particularly when the consumption experience is a satisfying one. At other times, however, they may have little resemblance to the evaluations held prior to consumption. A favorable pre-purchase evaluation may easily dissolve away with a disappointing or unsatisfactory consumption experience.

One indicator of the favorability of consumers' post-consumption evaluations is the American Customer Satisfaction Index (ACSI). Over 50,000 U.S. consumers are surveyed about their level of satisfaction with major companies and government services. Table 6.1 reports the findings for those receiving the highest and lowest satisfaction scores of the 190 companies and services included in the 1997 ACSI survey.[23]

Mercedes-Benz, with an average satisfaction score of 87 out of a possible 100, received the highest rating. The rest of the top 10, largely consisting of companies that compete in the supermarkets of America, were close behind, with scores ranging from 86 to 84. By comparison, those in the bottom 10 received scores of 65 or lower. For the fourth straight year, the Internal Revenue Service was rated as the least satisfying entity. The Internal Revenue Service's average score of 54 placed it at the very bottom, a distinction it has held for the past four years. Without the IRS, McDonald's would have occupied last place.

Why should these companies worry about whether consumers are satisfied with their products? The answer to this question can be found in the following section.

The Importance of Customer Satisfaction

It Influences Repeat Buying

Probably the most obvious reason companies must pay attention to customer satisfaction is that it influences whether consumers will buy from the same company again. Positive post-consumption evaluations are essential for retaining customers. Those holding negative evaluations of the product following consumption are unlikely to buy again. Typically, it is cheaper to retain an existing customer than to recruit a new one.[24] Companies have therefore become very focused on ensuring that their customers have satisfactory consumption experiences.

Nonetheless, the relationship between customer satisfaction and customer retention is not perfect.[25] According to an article published by the *Harvard Business Review,* "In business after business, 60% to 80% of lost customers reported on a survey just prior to defecting that they were satisfied or very satisfied. Most automakers . . . still see 90% of their customers claiming to be satisfied and 40% coming back to buy again."[26] Yet it should not be too surprising that many of the customers satisfied today take their business elsewhere tomorrow. After all, there are typically many competitors dangling attractive incentives as bait to lure away one's customers.

Although a satisfactory consumption experience does not guarantee loyalty, the likelihood that customers will remain loyal depends on their level of satisfaction. The Xerox Corporation discovered that customers reporting to be "totally satisfied" were six times more likely to repurchase its products than customers who reported simply being "satisfied."[27] For this reason, businesses have begun to realize that simply satisfying customers may not be enough. Rather, they should strive for "customer delight" that comes when customers are satisfied completely.[28]

It Shapes Word-of-Mouth Communication

Beyond influencing consumers' future purchase behaviors, post-consumption evaluations affect other behaviors as well. Discussing one's consumption experiences with other people is a common activity. How many times have you heard people talking about their last vacation, seeing the latest movie, dining at some

Table 6.1 The Top and Bottom 10 of the 1997 American Customer Satisfaction Index			
Company/Service	**Ranking**	**Score***	**Change from 1996**
Mercedes-Benz	1	87	none
H.J. Heinz (food processing)	2	86	− 4.4%
Colgate-Palmolive (pet foods)	3	85	NA
H.J. Heinz (pet foods)	4	85	NA
Mars (food processing)	5	85	− 1.2%
Maytag	6	85	+ 2.4%
Quaker Oats	7	85	+ 3.7%
Cadillac	8	84	− 4.5%
Hershey Foods	9	84	− 4.5%
Coca-Cola	10	84	− 3.4%
Wells Fargo	181	65	− 8.5%
Continental Airlines	182	64	− 3.0%
Northwest Airlines	183	64	− 4.5%
Ramada	184	64	− 8.6%
Pizza Hut	185	63	− 4.5%
Police (central cities)	186	63	+ 6.8%
American Airlines	187	62	− 12.7%
Unicom	188	62	− 8.8%
McDonald's	189	60	− 4.8%
Internal Revenue Service	190	54	+ 8.0%

*Maximum score is 100.

Source: Ronald B. Lieber, "Now Are You Satisfied? The 1998 American Customer Satisfaction Index," Fortune (February 16, 1998), 161–164.

restaurant, or getting ripped off by some unscrupulous company? For many, conversations concerning consumption experiences are a daily occurrence.

Obviously, the favorability of such word-of-mouth communication directly depends on the favorability of the consumption experience.[29] Negative consumption experiences not only reduce the odds of repeat buyers, they also lead consumers to say unflattering things when discussing their experiences with others. Dissatisfied consumers sometimes go to great lengths to share their negative opinions with others, even complete strangers. Consider the unhappy renter who, at his own expense, copied and distributed hundreds of copies of the flyer appearing in Figure 6.8.

Note, then, that a company's ability to deliver a satisfying consumption experience will affect its success in retaining current customers as well as recruiting new ones. Disappointed customers may not only take their business elsewhere, but they may spread the word to others, thereby undermining the company's recruitment efforts. Satisfied customers become repeat buyers and are valuable messengers for reaching new prospects.

Figure 6.8 Dissatisfaction Often Leads to Negative Word-of-Mouth

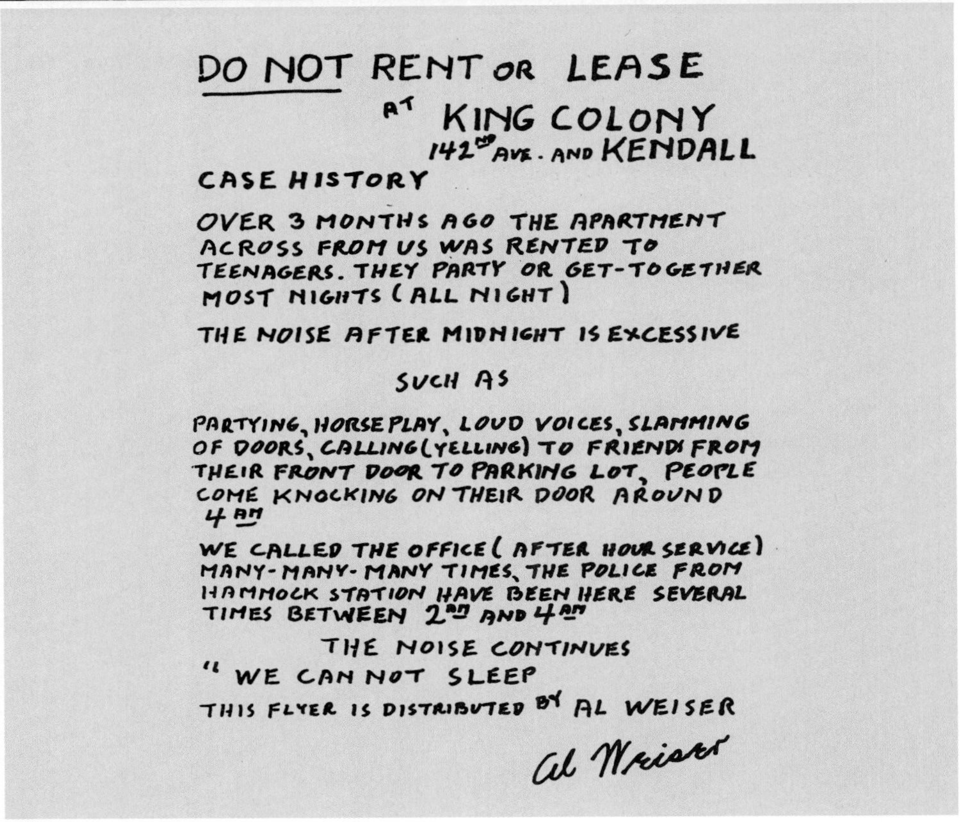

DO NOT RENT OR LEASE
AT KING COLONY
142ND AVE. AND KENDALL
CASE HISTORY
OVER 3 MONTHS AGO THE APARTMENT ACROSS FROM US WAS RENTED TO TEENAGERS. THEY PARTY OR GET-TOGETHER MOST NIGHTS (ALL NIGHT)
THE NOISE AFTER MIDNIGHT IS EXCESSIVE
SUCH AS
PARTYING, HORSEPLAY, LOUD VOICES, SLAMMING OF DOORS, CALLING (YELLING) TO FRIENDS FROM THEIR FRONT DOOR TO PARKING LOT, PEOPLE COME KNOCKING ON THEIR DOOR AROUND 4 AM
WE CALLED THE OFFICE (AFTER HOUR SERVICE) MANY-MANY-MANY TIMES, THE POLICE FROM HAMMOCK STATION HAVE BEEN HERE SEVERAL TIMES BETWEEN 2 AM AND 4 AM
THE NOISE CONTINUES
" WE CAN NOT SLEEP
THIS FLYER IS DISTRIBUTED BY AL WEISER
Al Weiser

Dissatisfaction Leads to Complaints

Beyond spreading negative word-of-mouth, dissatisfied customers may also file formal complaints and lawsuits against the company. This, in turn, may generate negative publicity and absorb the time and resources required for defending the company in the courtroom and in the press.

Although dissatisfaction is an essential prerequisite for complaint behavior, not every dissatisfied customer will complain.[30] Yet without knowing the customer's reasons for being unhappy, the task of taking corrective actions in order to avoid or minimize future unhappiness becomes all the more challenging. In addition, dissatisfied customers who don't voice their complaints are more likely to take their business elsewhere.[31] For these reasons, companies should take steps that enable unhappy customers to easily voice their concerns.[32] One car rental company advertises a 1-800 number for just this purpose.

Why do so few complain? Sometimes consumers do not hold the product directly responsible for their dissatisfaction. Instead, they may attribute a dissatisfying consumption experience to themselves (e.g., "I used it improperly") or to external circumstances that are beyond control (e.g., "Bad weather caused my flight to be delayed").[33] Even if consumers hold the product or retailer responsible, complaint behavior still may not occur when consumers don't believe it's worth their time and effort.[34]

For those who do take the time and effort to register their complaints, a sincere attempt to rectify problems can alleviate the dissatisfaction and potentially lead to even stronger intentions to repurchase.[35] The speed of response by the company to a complaint is important. Customers feel more satisfied when the response is quicker.[36] And, of course, the nature of the company's response is critical. For complaints involving monetary losses, customers' satisfaction with the company's response becomes greater as does the percent of the loss repaid by the company.[37]

Implications for Competitive Strategy

Beyond understanding the post-consumption evaluations of their own customers, companies may also find it useful to understand these evaluations of their competitors' customers. Doing so provides valuable guidance to the development of customer recruitment strategies. Efforts to steal business away from the competition are unlikely to succeed when competitors' customers are happy with their current company. Instead, there is usually a greater return from attacking the competitor serving a rather unsatisfied customer base. Unhappy customers are more willing to consider alternative offerings. And in mature markets where few nonusers become users, a company's growth heavily depends on attracting the dissatisfied customers of the competition.

Of course, the recruitment of dissatisfied customers is important even for vibrant, growing markets. Consider what happened a few years ago when America Online (AOL) made a change in its pricing strategy. AOL shifted from hourly fees to unlimited access for a flat rate. Customer usage increased so much that it became nearly impossible to gain access. Stories about frustrated customers, some of whom had taken their business elsewhere, became commonplace. AOL's competitors moved quickly to take advantage of the situation. A 1997 Super Bowl ad for CompuServe started off with a blank screen and the sound one hears when trying unsuccessfully to log onto the Internet. It closed by telling the viewer: "Looking for dependable Internet access? CompuServe. Get on with it."[38]

Companies that are successful in satisfying their customers often find it advantageous to advertise this success. Doing so reinforces the attitudes of current customers. It also can enhance the pre-purchase evaluations of consumers who the company wishes to recruit. One example of such advertising appears in Figure 6.9. This ad for the BellSouth telephone company informs consumers that it is ranked number one in customer satisfaction with their local residential phone service. This ranking is based on a survey conducted by J.D. Powers and Associates, a market research firm that built its reputation on measuring customer satisfaction. Revenues at J.D. Powers were nearly $65 million in 1998, making it the 13th largest market research organization in the United States.[39] The company surveys more than one million people worldwide about their satisfaction with various product categories and companies.

So What Determines Satisfaction?

Obviously, a critical determinant of satisfaction is consumers' perceptions of the product's performance during consumption. Poor performance and unfavorable consumption experiences usually guarantee that consumers will be dissatisfied with the product unless there are extenuating circumstances. In general, the more favorable a product's performance, the greater the customer's satisfaction.

Yet even good performance does not ensure satisfied customers. This is because customer satisfaction typically depends on more than actual performance. According to Richard Oliver's **expectancy disconfirmation model,** *satisfaction depends on a comparison of pre-purchase expectations to actual outcomes.*[40] To illustrate, suppose that when you go for your doctor's appointment you are told that

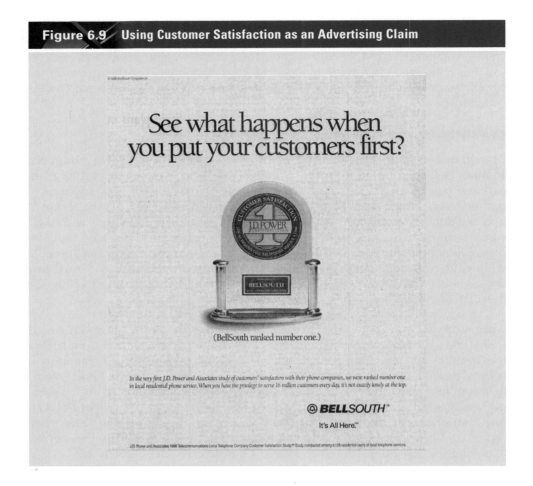

Figure 6.9   Using Customer Satisfaction as an Advertising Claim

the doctor is running behind schedule and that you will be seen in a few minutes. A half-hour later, you finally see the doctor. Would you be very happy about waiting this long, especially after expecting a much shorter wait? Now suppose that you were initially told that it would be an hour before you would see the doctor. Would you feel any differently about having to wait a half-hour? Chances are you would. In this instance, your expectations were exceeded. Most of us would feel better about waiting a half-hour after expecting to wait an even longer time.

Thus, even a product that provides relatively good performance may lead to a dissatisfying consumption experience when this performance falls short of what the consumer expected. Unfortunately, failing to meet customers' expectations is a common business problem. A prime example involves the airline industry. Read Consumer in Focus 6.4 to learn more about this.

When comparing what is expected to what is received, there are three possible outcomes. If the *product delivers less than expected,* **negative disconfirmation** occurs. **Positive disconfirmation,** on the other hand, exists when the *product provides more than expected.* Finally, **confirmation** takes place when the *product's performance matches expectations.* Confirmation produces greater satisfaction than exists following negative disconfirmation. Positive disconfirmation evokes the highest levels of satisfaction.

The fact that satisfaction may depend on what is expected and what is received poses a dilemma when marketing products. Companies often encourage consumers to hold very high expectations about what they will receive from the

Consumer in Focus 6.4

Customer Dissatisfaction Takes Off in the Airline Industry

Oversold flights, frequent flier miles that are hard to redeem, mishandled baggage and horror stories about passengers being trapped on planes are fueling a wave of complaints about the airline industry. The number of passenger complaints to the Transportation Department increased by 25 percent between 1997 and 1998.

"Airlines got freedom with deregulation, and frankly a lot of them exploited that freedom unfairly," explains Sen. Ron Wyden of Oregon. "It seems to me you have a situation where airline profits are going through the roof and passenger service is being left at the gate." Major U.S. carriers posted net profits of $5.1 billion in 1998, down just slightly from their all-time record of $5.2 billion in 1997. The nation's largest carrier, United Airlines, had net earnings of $1.34 billion.

United officials have acknowledged their customer service has fallen short of what is desired by top business travelers. "It would be disingenuous of me to say that we weren't already aware of the fact that air travelers were unhappy," says United chairman Gerald Greenwald. "What shocked us was the depth of the dissatisfaction we uncovered."

One way the company is responding to the situation involves changing its advertising. As far back as 1965 the company's advertising had encouraged consumers to "come fly the friendly skies of United." But in today's environment of late flights, lost luggage and ill-tempered personnel, friendly is not the word that would be used by many passengers. In 1997 United scrapped its old campaign in favor of a new $125 million advertising campaign that claims its service is "rising." According to Greenwald, "It tells our customers that we are working hard to improve our products to meet their needs." Yet in a recent survey of consumers' opinions concerning airline quality, United finished last among the nation's 10 major carriers. Apparently, United has not risen very far.

Source: Excerpted from Glen Johnson, "Vexed With the Airlines? So Are Washington Lawmakers," Sun-Sentinel *(February 14,1999), 1J, 4J; Glen Johnson, "U.S. Airways Tops Quality Survey,"* Miami Herald *(April 20, 1999), 3C; "New United Ads Take Off from the Crowd,"* Miami Herald Business Monday *(May 19, 1997), 10.*

product. Such is the case for the Softsoap ad in Figure 6.10 that promises "showering will never be the same again." By setting high expectations, companies hope that consumers will be more likely to make a trial purchase.

However, in setting such high expectations, companies increase the risk of consumers being less than satisfied. Unless the product is able to deliver what has been promised, the likelihood of negative disconfirmation increases as expectations increase. The resulting dissatisfaction reduces the odds of repeat buying. In sum, higher expectations should help encourage trial purchasing but may do so at the expense of repeat purchasing. Setting expectations at a sufficiently high level in order to get that initial purchase without sacrificing future purchases because of the disappointment consumers experience when the product fails to deliver what was anticipated represents a marketing challenge.

One approach to this challenge is exemplified by Levenger, a mail-order catalog company specializing in "tools for serious readers" (writing instruments, items for a study, and so on). The company's motto: "under promise and over deliver." In essence, the company seeks to exceed the expectations it creates among its customers. By adopting a conservative approach when setting expectations (the "under promise" part), the company improves its chances of evoking positive disconfirmation.

As illustrated in Figure 6.10, advertising is one way for companies to influence consumers' expectations. But it is far from being the only method for doing so. Different brand names may evoke different expectations (consider Rolex versus Timex). Product packaging creates expectations.[41] Expectations may also depend on the product's price. Higher price usually leads to greater expectations about how the product will perform. One computer manufacturer substantially

Figure 6.10   Does This Ad Set Reasonable Expectations?

reduced the number of features offered by its product, thereby enabling it to also reduce the product's price. As a result, product returns declined from about 12 to 5 percent. Apparently, consumers expected less and became less demanding when the computer cost less money.[42]

Beyond influencing satisfaction through its impact on confirmation or disconfirmation, expectations may directly affect satisfaction. This is because expectations may color or bias the interpretation of the consumption experience itself. A classic study illustrating this basic principle involved getting consumers to taste and rate different brands of beer. When the consumed brands were unlabeled (i.e., consumers tasted the brands without knowing their brand identities), consumers did not differentiate between the brands; they rated all the brands essentially the same. This was not the case when consumers tasted the brands and knew their brand identities (i.e., the brands were labeled). For some brands, consumers' ratings increased dramatically when the label was present during consumption. Thus, the expectation created by the brand label was powerful enough to alter consumers' interpretation of what their taste buds were telling them.[43] Findings such as these underscore the added benefits companies receive from having strong brand names for their products.

Expectations do not always bias post-consumption evaluations. It depends on the *ambiguity* of the consumption experience. Can consumers truly determine whether they are benefiting from taking vitamins? How do we know whether the person who repaired our car or TV took advantage of us by unnecessarily replacing parts that were in working condition? For many consumption experiences, it is virtually impossible for consumers to determine whether the product performs as expected. And in these instances, post-consumption evaluations may be particularly susceptible to initial expectations. In contrast, unambiguous consumption experiences provide better grounds for evaluating the consumed item, thereby reducing the opportunity for expectations to affect evaluations directly.

To illustrate how expectations' influence on post-consumption evaluations depends on the ambiguity of the consumption experience, consider the following study.[44] Some people are shown an ad emphasizing the qualities and virtues of the polo shirt being advertised; others are not shown the ad. In essence, the ad creates an expectation of product quality. Participants then judge the quality of the advertised shirt based solely on a visual inspection. This visual inspection yields rather ambiguous evidence concerning product quality (e.g., what looks good to the naked eye may feel rather thin and flimsy to the touch). Those exposed to the ad creating a quality expectation reported higher quality ratings for the polo shirt than participants not given the ad. Thus, in the presence of ambiguous evidence concerning product quality, the expectation created by advertising biased the participants' quality judgments.

This study also included a second product category: paper towels. People were allowed to actually test the towel's ability to absorb water. This water test yielded clear evidence of product quality. Apparently this unambiguous evidence nullified expectation's influence since participants provided the same product ratings whether or not they had seen an ad promoting product quality prior to conducting the water test.

Finally, we talked earlier in the chapter about how consumption may lead to a variety of feelings of differing favorableness and intensity. The feelings experienced during consumption may also be important in determining satisfaction.[45] Positive feelings enhance satisfaction; negative feelings reduce it.

Summary

This chapter examines the last two stages in the consumer decision process—consumption and post-consumption evaluation. A fundamental part of market segmentation for many products involves distinguishing between users (those who consume) and nonusers (those who do not). It is also important to understand the dynamics of consumption: When does consumption occur? Where does it occur? How is the product consumed? How much is consumed? Beyond answering these questions, a thorough understanding of the consumption stage of the decision-making process further requires focusing on the consumption experience itself. This involves considering the types of feelings experienced during consumption, the extent to which consumption provides positive versus negative reinforcement, and whether pre-purchase expectations are confirmed.

Just as consumers form pre-purchase evaluations to help them decide which product should be purchased and consumed, they also form post-consumption evaluations about the consumed product. Typically, companies examine these post-consumption evaluations in terms of customer satisfaction. Understanding satisfaction is essential for several reasons. The level of satisfaction or dissatisfaction influences repeat buying, word-of-mouth communication, and complaint behavior. Further, an understanding of the satisfaction or dissatisfaction of competitors' customers enables a company to more effectively and efficiently steal business from the competition.

Consumers' satisfaction with a product heavily depends on its performance. But beyond this, it may further depend on what consumers expect. Companies must be careful that customers do not expect too much. Otherwise, they end up being dissatisfied. If consumers expect too little, they may underappreciate what the product has to offer and, consequently, buy something else. Walking the line between promising too much and selling the product short is one of marketing's toughest challenges.

Review and Discussion Questions

1. In the chapter, we discussed how one rice manufacturer discovered that many of its customers switched to a lower-priced competitor when using the rice as an ingredient. What suggestions do you have for this manufacturer concerning how it could encourage consumers to buy its brand when using rice as an ingredient?
2. Describe the different ways a company could segment a market based on consumption.
3. Consider fast-food restaurants. Now apply the concepts presented in the "Consumption Behaviors" section to this product category. What implications might this analysis carry in developing business strategy for a particular restaurant?
4. The chapter indicates that satisfaction may depend on consumers' expectations of product performance and the feelings experienced during consumption. How important do you believe each of these might be in determining satisfaction with the following products: scissors, an amusement ride, vitamin pills.
5. A business is interested in throughly understanding the opinions held by its customers following product consumption. Given this objective, what suggestions do you have about what should be examined?
6. "Come to White Fence Farm where we offer the world's best chicken." This claim has been heard for many years on Chicago radio. Would you recommend its continuation from the perspective of consumer satisfaction? What are the possible dangers?
7. Why are consumers' expectations important?

Endnotes

1. Yumiko Ono, "Pharmacia Bets New Rogaine Grows Sales," *The Wall Street Journal* (August 4, 1997), B6.
2. Gregg Fields, "Vessels Revamp Cruise Industry," *Miami Herald* (November 12, 1999), 1C.
3. Robert P. Libbon, "How Popular Is Wine These Days?" *American Demographics* (September 1999), 25.
4. Marika Lynch, "Keys Might Be Losing Allure," *Miami Herald* (January 31, 1997), 1A.
5. Kevin T. Higgins, "Beer Importers Upbeat about Future, Despite Warning Signs," *Marketing News* (October 25, 1985), 1ff.
6. Judith Weinraub, "Breakfast! The Drive-through Phenomenon," *Miami Herald* (February 6, 1997), 1E, 3E.
7. Paula Mergenhagen, "How 'got milk?' Got Sales," *Marketing Tools* (September 1996), 4–7.
8. Libbon, "How Popular Is Wine These Days?"
9. Mergenhagen, "How 'got milk?' Got Sales."
10. Emily Nelson, "Camera Makers Focus on Tiny and Cute," *The Wall Street Journal* (March 14, 1997), 1B.
11. Richard L. Oliver, "Cognitive, Affective, and Attribute Bases of the Satisfaction Response," *Journal of Consumer Research* 20 (December 1993), 418–430; Robert A. Westbrook, "Product/Consumption-Based Affective Responses and Postpurchase Processes," *Journal of Marketing Research* 24 (August 1987), 258–270; Robert A. Westbrook and Richard L. Oliver, "The Dimensionality of Consumption Emotion Patterns and Consumer Satisfaction," *Journal of Consumer Research* (June 1991), 84–91.
12. Stanley M. Widrick, "Concept of Negative Reinforcement Has Place in Classroom," *Marketing News* (July 18, 1986), 48–49.
13. Geoffrey Tomb, "Parks Offer a 2-hour Glide to Serenity," *Miami Herald* (September 10, 1996), 1B, 6B.
14. Dennis W. Rook, "The Ritual Dimension of Consumer Behavior," *Journal of Consumer Research* 12 (December 1985), 251–264.

15. For a classic article on this subject, see Melanie Wallendorf and Eric J. Arnould, "'We Gather Together': Consumption Rituals of Thanksgiving Day," *Journal of Consumer Research* 18 (June 1991), 13–31.

16. Rook, "The Ritual Dimension of Consumer Behavior."

17. Russell W. Belk, Melanie Wallendorf, and John F. Sherry, Jr., "The Sacred and the Profane in Consumer Behavior: Theodicy on the Odyssey," *Journal of Consumer Research* 16 (June 1989), 1–38.

18. Ronald J. Faber, Thomas C. O'Guinn, and Raymond Krych, "Compulsive Consumption," in Melanie Wallendorf and Paul Anderson, eds., *Advances in Consumer Research* 14 (Provo, Utah: Association for Consumer Research, 1987), 132–135.

19. Alvin C. Burns, Peter L. Gillett, Marc Rubinstein, and James W. Gentry, "An Exploratory Study of Lottery Playing, Gambling Addiction and Links to Compulsive Consumption," in Gerald A. Gorn and Richard W. Pollay, eds., *Advances in Consumer Research* 17 (Provo, Utah: Association for Consumer Research, 1990), 298–305.

20. "Report for Congress on Gambling Addiction Stirs Debate with Gaming Industry," *Miami Herald* (March 19, 1999), 3A.

21. Thomas C. O'Guinn and Ronald J. Faber, "Compulsive Buying: A Phenomenological Explanation," *Journal of Consumer Research* 16 (September 1989), 151–155.

22. Thomas G. Watts, "Caught in the Web: 'Dependents' Studied," *Miami Herald* (August 16, 1997), 10A.

23. Ronald B. Lieber, "Now Are You Satisfied? The 1998 American Customer Satisfaction Index," *Fortune* (February 16, 1998), 161–164.

24. Claes Fornell and Birger Wernerfelt, "Defensive Marketing Strategy by Customer Complaint Management: A Theoretical Analysis," *Journal of Marketing Research* 24 (November 1987), 337–346.

25. Richard L. Oliver, "Whence Consumer Loyalty?" *Journal of Marketing* 63 (Special Issue 1999), 33–44; Thomas A. Stewart, "A Satisfied Customer Isn't Enough," *Fortune* (July 21, 1997), 112–113.

26. Quoted from page 59 of Frederick F. Reichheld, "Learning from Customer Defections," *Harvard Business Review* (March/April 1996), 56–69.

27. Thomas O. Jones and W. Earl Sasser, Jr., "Why Satisfied Customers Defect," *Harvard Business Review* (November/December 1995), 88–99.

28. Kevin T. Higgins, "Coming of Age: Despite Growing Pains, Customer Satisfaction Measurement Continues to Evolve," *Marketing News* (October 27, 1997), 1, 12; Jones and Sasser, "Why Satisfied Customers Defect"; Steve Lewis, "All or Nothing: Customers Must Be 'Totally Satisfied,'" *Marketing News* (March 2, 1998), 11–12; Richard L. Oliver, Roland T. Rust, and Sajeev Varki, "Customer Delight: Foundations, Findings, and Managerial Insight," *Journal of Retailing* 73 (Fall 1997), 311–336; Benjamin Schneider and David E. Bowen, "Understanding Customer Delight and Outrage," *Sloan Management Review* 41 (Fall 1999), 35–45.

29. For research concerning word-of-mouth activity by consumers, see Marsha L. Richins, "Negative Word-of-Mouth by Dissatisfied Consumers: A Pilot Study," *Journal of Marketing* 47 (Winter 1983), 68–78.

30. Richard L. Oliver, "An Investigation of the Interrelationship between Consumer Dissatisfaction and Complaint Reports," in Melanie Wallendorf and Paul Anderson, eds., *Advances in Consumer Research* 14 (Provo, Utah: Association for Consumer Research, 1987), 218–222.

31. Claes Fornell and Nicholas M. Didow, "Economic Constraints on Consumer Complaining Behavior," in Jerry C. Olson, ed., *Advances in Consumer Research* 7 (Ann Arbor, Mich.: Association for Consumer Research, 1980), 318–323.

32. Fornell and Wernerfelt, "Defensive Marketing Strategy by Customer Complaint Management: A Theoretical Analysis." Perhaps surprisingly, efforts to encourage one's customers to complain ultimately may cause companies to become less responsive to this form of customer feedback. Evidence indicating this possibility is reported by Claes Fornell and Robert A. Westbrook, "The Vicious Circle of Consumer Complaints," *Journal of Marketing* 48 (Summer 1984), 68–78.

33. For research on the role of attributions as a determinant of complaint behavior, see Valerie S. Folkes, "Consumer Reactions to Product Failure: An Attributional Approach," *Journal of Consumer Research* 10 (March 1984), 398–409; Valerie S. Folkes and Barbara Kotsos, "Buyers' and Sellers' Explanations for Product Failure: Who Done It," *Journal of Marketing* 50 (April 1986), 74–80; Valerie S. Folkes, Susan Koletsky, and John L. Graham, "A Field Study of Causal Inferences and Consumer Reaction: The View from the Airport," *Journal of Consumer Research* 13 (March 1987), 534–539.

34. Ralph L. Day, "Modeling Choices among Alternative Responses to Dissatisfaction," in Thomas C. Kinnear, ed., *Advances in Consumer Research* 11 (Provo, Utah: Association for Consumer Research, 1984), 496–499.

35. Mary C. Gilly and Betsy D. Gelb, "Post-Purchase Consumer Processes and the Complaining

Consumer," *Journal of Consumer Research* 9 (December 1982), 323–328; Denise T. Smart and Charles L. Martin, "Manufacturer Responsiveness to Consumer Correspondence: An Empirical Investigation of Consumer Perceptions," *Journal of Consumer Affairs* 26 (Summer 1991), 104–128.

36. Gilly and Gelb, "Post-Purchase Consumer Processes and the Complaining Consumer"; Chow-Hou Wee and Celine Chong, "Determinants of Consumer Satisfaction/Dissatisfaction Toward Dispute Settlements in Singapore," *European Journal of Marketing* 25 (1991), 6–16.

37. Gilly and Gelb, "Post-Purchase Consumer Processes and the Complaining Consumer."

38. Jared Sandberg, "CompuServe Will Mock AOL's Woes in Super Bowl Ad," *The Wall Street Journal* (January 24, 1997), B16; David Poppe, "AOL's Still Busy-Taking Cancellations," *Miami Herald* (January 31, 1997), 1C, 3C.

39. "Honomichl Top Fifty," *Marketing News* (June 7, 1999), H1–H39.

40. Richard L. Oliver, "A Cognitive Model of the Antecedents and Consequences of Satisfaction Decisions," *Journal of Marketing Research* 17 (November 1980), 460–469. Also see Ruth N. Bolton and James H. Drew, "A Multistage Model of Customers' Assessments of Service Quality and Value," *Journal of Consumer Research* 17 (March 1991), 375–384; Gilbert A. Churchill, Jr., and Carol Suprenant, "An Investigation into the Determinants of Customer Satisfaction," *Journal of Marketing Research* 19 (November 1983), 491–504; Ernest R. Cadotte, Robert B. Woodruff, and Roger L. Jenkins, "Expectations and Norms in Models of Consumer Satisfaction," *Journal of Marketing Research* 24 (August 1987), 305–314; Richard L. Oliver and Wayne S. DeSarbo, "Response Determinants in Satisfaction Judgments," *Journal of Consumer Research* 14 (March 1988), 495–507;. David K. Tse and Peter C. Wilton, "Models of Consumer Satisfaction Formation: An Extension," *Journal of Marketing Research* 25 (May

1988), 204–212; Robert B. Woodruff, Ernest R. Cadotte, and Roger L. Jenkins, "Modeling Consumer Satisfaction Using Experience-Based Norms," *Journal of Marketing Research* 20 (August 1983), 296–304. Whether expectations always play a role in determining satisfaction has been questioned recently. See Susan Fournier and David Glen Mick, "Rediscovering Satisfaction," *Journal of Marketing* 63 (October 1999), 5–23.

41. Jennifer Lach, "The Price Is Very Right," *American Demographics* (April 1999), 44–45.

42. Herbert M. Myers, "Packaging Must Keep Promises Made to Buyers," *Marketing News* (July 6, 1998), 11–12.

43. Ralph I. Allison and Kenneth P. Uhl, "Influence of Beer Brand Identification on Taste Perception," *Journal of Marketing Research* 1 (August 1964), 36–39.

44. Stephen J. Hoch and Young-Won Ha, "Consumer Learning: Advertising and the Ambiguity of Product Experience," *Journal of Consumer Research* 13 (September 1986), 221–233.

45. Laurette Dube and Bernd H. Schmitt, "The Processing of Emotional and Cognitive Aspects of Product Usage in Satisfaction Judgments," in Rebecca H. Holman and Michael R. Solomon, eds., *Advances in Consumer Research* 18 (Provo, Utah: Association for Consumer Research, 1991), 52–56; Laurette Dube-Rioux, "The Power of Affective Reports in Predicting Satisfaction Judgments," in Martin E. Goldberg, Gerald A. Gorn, and Richard W. Pollay, eds., *Advances in Consumer Research* 17 (Provo, Utah: Association for Consumer Research, 1990), 571–576; Richard L. Oliver, "Cognitive, Affective, and Attribute Bases of the Satisfaction Response"; Robert A. Westbrook, "Product/Consumption-Based Affective Responses and Postpurchase Processes"; Westbrook and Oliver, "The Dimensionality of Consumption Emotion Patterns and Consumer Satisfaction."

Suggested Readings for Part II

Akshay R. Rao, Mark E. Bergen, and Scott Davis, "How to Fight a Price War," *Harvard Business Review* (March/April), 107–116.

Mark Stiving, Greg Allenby, and Russell Winter, "An Emperical Analysis of Price Endings with Scanner Data," *Journal of Consumer Research* 24 (June 1997), 57–67.

Leonard L. Berry, "Cultivating Service Brand Equity," *Journal of the Academy of Marketing Science* 28, 1 (Winter 2000), 128–137.

Mary Jo Bitner, Stephen W. Brown, and Matthew L. Meuter, "Technology Infusion in Service Encounters," *Journal of the Academy of Marketing Science* 28, 1 (Winter 2000), 138–149.

Bart J. Bronnenberg, Vijay Mahajan, and Wilfried R. Vanhonacker, "The Emergence of Market Structure in New Repeat-Purchase Categories: The Interplay of Market Share and Retailer Distribution," *Journal of Marketing Research* 37 (February 2000), 16–31.

Duncan I. Simester, John R. Hauser, Birger Wernerfelt, and Roland T. Rust, "Implementing Quality Improvement Programs Designed to Enhance Customer Satisfaction: Quasi-Experiments in the United States and Spain," *Journal of Marketing Research* 37 (February 2000), 60–71.

Adrian J. Slywotzky, Clayton M. Christensen, Richard S. Tedlow, and Nicholas G. Carr, "The Future of Commerce," *Harvard Business Review* (January/February 2000), 39–47.

Charles S. Areni, Dale F. Duhan, and Pamela Kiecker, "Point-of-Purchase Displays, Product Organization, and Brand Purchase Likelihoods," *Journal of the Academy of Marketing Science* 27, 4 (Fall 1999), 428–441.

Roland T. Rust and Richard L. Oliver, "Should We Delight the Customer?" *Journal of the Academy of Marketing Science* 28, 1 (Winter 2000), 86–94.

David Glen Mick and Susan Fournier, "Paradoxes of Technology: Consumer Cognizance, Emotions and Coping Strategies," *Journal of Consumer Research* 25 (September 1998), 123–143.

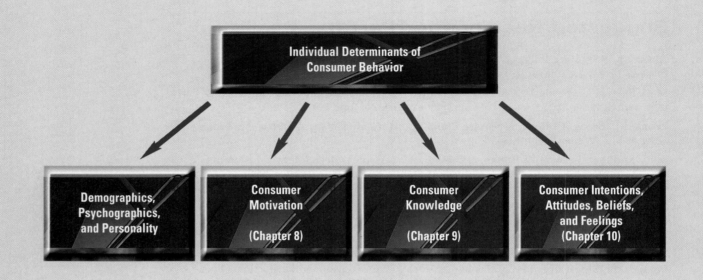

PART III

Individual Determinants of Consumer Behavior

Consumers are like fingerprints. No two are exactly the same. One person may have lots of time but little money, while the next person may have lots of money but little time. One buyer may have years of experience in purchasing and using the product. Another may know very little and lack prior experience. And what motivates one individual to buy need not be the same reason that leads the next individual to do so.

The existence of these individual differences makes life a bit more complicated for those wishing to influence consumers and their behaviors. After all, what works when selling to Jim may be ineffective when selling to Jennifer. Consequently, when developing a business strategy, it is important to understand the key characteristics of target consumers.

In this section of the text, we focus on some of the individual characteristics that are particularly useful for analyzing consumer behavior. Traditionally, companies have paid close attention to the demographic characteristics (e.g., age, income, marital status) of their target consumers. Chapter 7 discusses demographics as well as other psychographic and personality variables useful in understanding consumer behavior. In Chapter 8 we consider consumer motivation and the diversity of needs that motivate purchase behavior. Consumers also differ in what they know and how they feel about products. Chapter 9 focuses on consumer knowledge. This knowledge, along with feelings, ultimately determines consumers' attitudes and intentions. Chapter 10 discusses the importance of understanding consumers' beliefs, feelings, attitudes, and intentions.

CHAPTER 7

Demographics, Psychographics, and Personality

OPENING VIGNETTE

Started in 1990 by brothers Andrew and Thomas Parkinson, Peapod delivers groceries to consumer homes for a five percent delivery surcharge and a monthly membership fee. Peapod grew from a 400-home test to a full fledged company, with about 100,000 member-households in eight metropolitan markets in the United States. Using customized software, the consumer logs onto the Internet and accesses the Peapod website. There, the customer is presented with a menu of choices, such as "view last order," "comment," "select list," and of course "order." Peapod offers grocery products for home delivery—ranging from meats, seafood, and dairy to frozen, baby items, and alcohol. After selecting the desired type of product, Peapod lists various sizes, brands, and prices for each item. Customers simply click on the item, and it is placed in their shopping cart.

The target market for Peapod, "time starved" dual income families has not complained, so far, about the cost of the service. In fact, for parents who would rather spend time at home with their families or single, career-minded individuals who do not have time to shop, this service might seem like a convenient alternative. For them, the extra costs and the tip given to the driver are worth the convenience. But for most consumers, the extra charges are prohibitive to using the service very often. They would rather take the time to shop in the store than pay extra to have someone else do it. Many lower-income families also do not have computers at home to buy electronically. But even for some consumers who might not have a lot of disposable income, some consumers like to be the first to try things. Their personalities affect their purchase decisions. Other consumers are swayed by their values—such as valuing the social activity of going to a store and seeing friends and neighbors.

Peapod's revenues reached $69 million in 1998, yet the company has not made a profit since its inception. The company predicts that around twenty percent of all grocery purchases will be made online by 2005—what do you think? Only consumers will decide.

Source: www.peapod.com and Roger Blackwell and Kristina Blackwell, "The More Retailing Changes, The More It Stays The Same," Discount Merchandizer (June 2000).

Analyzing and Predicting Consumer Behavior

How is the population makeup changing? How do people spend time, choose friends, allocate financial resources to products or retailers, and support social programs? These issues involve the study of **demographics,** defined as *the size, structure, and distribution of a population.* According to Canadian demographer, David Foot, "Demographics explain 2/3rds of everything. They help predict which products will be in demand and what school enrollments will be in the future. They also help forecast which drugs will be in fashion ten years down the road and which types of crime can be expected to increase."[1] Global demographics give a summary view of the world's population, as seen in Figure 7.1. Some of the facts in this chart might surprise you.

Demographic analysis is used in two ways—as *market segment descriptors* (as you read in Chapter 2) and in *trend analysis.* To create *descriptors of market segments,* marketers match demographic and psychographic profiles of a segment with its consumer behaviors. The demographic variables that correlate sufficiently with specific consumer behaviors are then used to describe that segment. In this sense, demographics are used as a proxy for how consumers will behave, based on characteristics such as age, income level, and ethnicity. When marketers do not have primary research or during initial stages, demographic information can be used to guide new product development, product repositioning, brand extension, distribution strategies, or media and creative appeals in communications programs. When marketers need more information than can be gleaned from demographics, personal values and psychographics allow them to identify and describe in more detail the specific market segment and its individual members.

Consumer analysts use demographic trends to predict changes in demand for, and consumption of, specific products and services by monitoring which population groups will be growing in the future. Nonprofit agencies and businesses alike monitor demographic, technological, and lifestyle environment changes to alter product and service offerings and how they communicate to consumers.

It is not enough, however, to consider demographics alone. People in similar situations buy many of the same products as do others in the same age, geographic, or income category, yet this is not always the case. People act differently because of basic traits and social-psychological makeup that reflect their personality, personal values, and lifestyles. Marketing, focuses on what people will buy in the future. Consumer analysts turn to demographics, psychographics, and lifestyles to help predict the answers. These are the variables analyzed in Chapter 7.

Figure 7.1   Demographic Analysis

If the Earth's population were to shrink to a village of 100 people, with all existing human ratios remaining the same, it would look like this

- There would be 57 Asians, 21 Europeans, 14 from Western Hemisphere, and 8 Africans.
- 51 would be female; and 49 would male.
- 70 would be non-white; 30 would be white.
- 70 would be non-Christian; 30 would be Christian.
- 50% of the entire world's wealth would be in the hands of only 6 people—and all 6 would be US citizens.
- 80 would live in sub-standardized housing.
- 70 would not be able to read.
- 50 would be malnourished.

Source: Based on a presentation given by Mr. George F. Fussell, Jr., Chairman, Frank Russell Company, Tacoma, Washington (March 22, 1999).

Demographic Analysis and Social Policy

Demographic analysis also provides helpful information for policy questions related to **macromarketing,** *the aggregate performance of marketing in society.* Macromarketing analysis evaluates marketing from society's perspective and seeks to understand the consequences of marketing actions and transactions in a society. Will more food or less be required to feed the population of a country in the future? If a tax cut is proposed, how will consumers spend such reductions? What policies would cause consumers to save more and spend less on current consumption? Should consumers be encouraged to buy remarketed homes, cars, clothing, and sports equipment instead of new products, thereby using less natural resources but diminishing the need for human workers in factories that manufacture new products?

In free markets of the world, people answer these questions and determine macroeconomic policies by voting in the polling booths and in the marketplace. Although the study of consumer behavior currently focuses mostly on micromarketing research (the marketing policies of profit and nonprofit organizations), its roots are in macromarketing; this topic is known today as psychological economics.[2]

Demographics and Industrial Demand

Consumer trend analysis affects both consumer-based marketing and industrial marketing or business-to-business marketing because *industrial demand is ultimately derived from consumer demand.* Consumer analysis can reveal industrial products and services needed by growth firms producing and marketing consumer goods. Firms such as Cisco Systems and EMC, for example, have produced fortunes for their investors and employees because they market industrial products that facilitate the Internet rather than products for consumers.

Changing Structure of Consumer Markets

Firms that fail to plan generally plan to fail. Planning, however, requires information about markets and their four main components—*people with needs, ability to buy, willingness to buy, and authority to buy.* Without understanding how many people there will be in the future, firms cannot adequately plan for product development or predict increasing or declining market demand. This chapter focuses on forecasting the number and nature of people throughout the world and their ability to buy products (with economic resources). It also discusses how peoples' needs relate to age and other demographic factors, as well as personality, values, lifestyles, and psychographic characteristics. Willingness to buy is affected by the many variables described throughout this book, and authority to buy is addressed in areas such as Chapter 12 on family and household influences.

People: Foundation of Market Analysis

Although the title of this book is *Consumer Behavior,* we are really studying *people* behavior. People are the foundation of markets and market analysis. Demographic analysis answers: How many will there be? What will be the age distribution? Where will they live? Combine demographics with data on purchasing power or wealth, and the result is **economic demographics,** the *study of the economic characteristics of a nation's population,* which will be examined later in this chapter.

Population trends are reliably predictable compared with many other variables in the study of consumer behavior. There are unknowns, however, such as natural calamities, wars, and medical problems like plagues in ancient times or AIDS in modern times, that might affect population projections unexpectedly. Ordinarily, though, three variables determine the size and nature of population—*births, deaths,* and *net migration.* Although births are usually the most important, they are also the most volatile and difficult to forecast.

How Many Babies Will Be Born?

Several terms are used to describe and project future populations. **Birthrate** is the *number of live births per 1,000 population in a given year.* The **fertility rate** is the *number of live births per 1,000 women of childbearing age* (defined as 15 to 44 years). **Total fertility rate** (TFR) is the *average number of children that would be born alive to a woman during her lifetime if she were to pass through all of her childbearing years conforming to the age-specific fertility rates of a given year.* It answers the simple question: How many children are women having currently? In many developing countries, the number is more than 6.0. Currently, in the United States, it is about 2.0. TFR is even lower in Europe and most other developed countries. This is significant because the replacement rate—the number of births required to maintain current population levels—is 2.1 children, allowing for infant mortality. Birthrates should not be confused with **natural increase**, which is the *surplus of births over deaths in a given period.*

Population momentum is crucial for understanding the dynamics of population growth. It refers to the fact that *the future growth of any population will be influenced by its present age distribution and is the reason that replacement level fertility does not immediately translate into zero population growth.* Even if fertility had fallen to that level in 2000, world population would continue to grow another 43 percent before stabilizing in about 60 years.

Future Fertility Scenarios   Forecasting births in future decades is difficult. Although fecundity, the physiologic capability of couples to reproduce, is fairly predictable, fertility, which is actual reproductive performance, is more difficult. The solution to the problem of forecasting babies—and thus, total population—is to provide several projections based on different fertility assumptions. The Census Bureau calls these Series I (highest), assuming 2.7 children per woman; Series II (middle), assuming 2.1 children; and Series III (lowest), assuming 1.7. Before 1993, fertility had been at the low level for about 15 years, but in the 1990s a dramatic increase occurred, to almost 2.1. Is this just a temporary move due to baby boomers' "last chance" to have babies, or is it a fundamental change toward higher fertility? The answer makes a big difference in projections of future population, as you can see in Figure 7.2.

What Causes Babies?   To predict how the population size will change, marketers must examine the variables that determine birthrates. First is *age distribution* of the population. Second is *family structure,* which involves facts such as proportion of people who are married, proportion of women employed outside the home, and average age when people get married. The third cause of births is *social attitudes* toward family and children. Finally, birthrates are affected by *technology,* such as availability and cost of contraception, as illustrated in Consumer in Focus 7.1.

Although the *number* of children in a family affects its buying and consumption patterns, *order effects* can affect consumption even when total births remain constant. First-order (firstborn) babies may generate $1,500 of retail sales, for

Figure 7.2 Projections of Resident Population 1950 to 2050

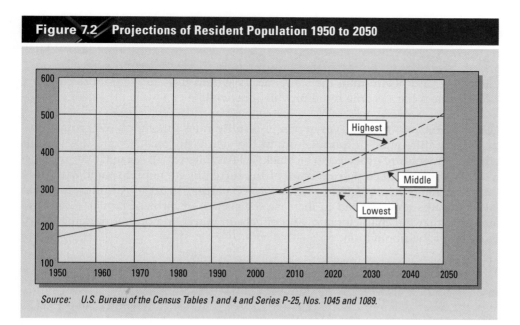

Source: *U.S. Bureau of the Census Tables 1 and 4 and Series P-25, Nos. 1045 and 1089.*

Consumer in Focus 7.1

Population Growth Fuels Birth Control Sales Efforts in India

In Mirazfari, a small village in the northern part of India, medicine man Sushil Bharati dispenses cough medicine and advice on karma from behind a small desk under a tree. In villages throughout India's poorest areas, Bharati and others like him are the center of life, and now, they have become the center of a marketing campaign for birth control called Butterfly. The program enlists the help of a network of medicine men to teach Indians about birth control pills and condoms, in exchange for free radio advertising, customer referrals, posters, and a percent of the profits from selling condoms. Although Mirazfari's 10,000 citizens are very poor and have on average eight children to feed, clothe, and house on an average income of $10 per month, the program is met with much skepticism.

The need to curb population growth is great in this country, whose population hit 1 billion in May 2000—surpassed only in size by China's 1.2 billion. In the past, the government tried to control growth with mandated sterilization; however, the government stopped this practice about three years ago owing in part to pressure from human rights groups. Now Butterflies can be found plastered on billboards and building walls around the state of Bihar, and even on Bharati's prescription pads.

Though the program is aimed to help quality of life in India, it is also admittedly about branding and making money. Similar ventures, some sponsored by the U.S. government and others by private funds, are trying to reach India's women through established networks of professionals. But networks of all types are having a difficult time convincing them to try some method of birth control. Some believe the pill causes cancer, whereas others leave it up to their husbands to decide all matters. One key in fighting this battle is literacy and education. Three southern states, in which literacy is much higher among women, have reached the replacement fertility rate of 2.1 children per couple. And signs do exist that even Bihar residents are beginning to try contraceptives.

Source: Miriam Jordan, *"Selling Birth Control to India's Poor,"* The Wall Street Journal *(September 21, 1999), B1-B4.*

example, compared with less than half of that for higher-order babies. One-child families are better able to afford nice restaurants and products such as personal computers, new clothing, and services such as private education, ballet school, and sports lessons. They have more resources to spend on a child's development, education, and health than the same family would if there were more children. Childlessness has become more prevalent as well.

Ethnic Variations ▶ Small variations in fertility rates among ethnic groups produce large differences in population. In the year 2010, fertility rates for various ethnic segments are expected to be black (2.44), white (2.05), Asian (1.95), and Hispanic (2.98).[3] About 66 percent of all births currently are non-Hispanic white, but that percentage is predicted to decline to 42 percent in 2050. All other race and ethnic groups are expected to increase their share of births. Chapter 11 will examine further the characteristics and effects on marketing of the changing ethnic makeup of the population.

How Long Will People Live?

Life expectancy has increased dramatically in most countries. Nearly a century ago, the average American died at age 47 years. Today, a newborn can expect to live 75 years. White females have the longest life expectancy at 79.3 years, and black males the shortest at 66 years. Black females have a life expectancy of 74.5 years, and white males a life expectancy of 72.6 years. As people live longer, the need for in-home healthcare, nursing home facilities, senior activity centers, and special products increases.

How Many People Will Immigrate?

Immigration represents 25 percent of annual growth in the United States. Legal net immigration was about 530,000 per year in the 1980s, increased to 700,000 during 1992 to 1994, and is projected to be about 880,000 thereafter. Undocumented migrants boost the numbers somewhat. Of significance here is the issue of culture—as people immigrate from other countries, how will their current cultures and values affect the new country, and how will they assimilate into the population? Again, many of these issues are covered in Chapter 11.

Most Likely Population Scenarios

No one knows exactly what number of consumers will exist in the future; however, the most likely scenario is shown in Table 7.1. This table serves as the basis for discussion of changing segments in the following pages.

The U.S. population is projected to grow from 260 million in 1994 to 274 million in 2000 and 382 million in 2050, based on middle series assumptions. If low fertility rates actually occur, the Census Bureau projects a population of 275 million in 2050.

What do you think will happen to fertility rates and population size? Will women begin having more babies than in recent decades, or will they have fewer? If you manage an organization, how do your assumptions influence your decision to invest money in new facilities and products? Those are the kinds of decisions that depend on your understanding of the population component of consumption.

Consumer analysts monitor several demographic trends when identifying domestic market opportunities. In addition to analyzing overall population growth or decline, marketers must understand how the age, geographic, and economic characteristics of the population are changing. Figure 7.3 summarizes some of the best resources for finding data to help marketers start their strategic marketing plans.

Table 7.1 Projections of the Population by Age, Sex, Race, and Hispanic Origin: 1995 to 2010 (in thousands as of July 1; includes Armed Forces overseas)

Age, Sex, Race, and Hispanic Origin	Lowest Series			Middle Series			Highest Series		
	1995	2000	2010	1995	2000	2010	1995	2000	2010
Total Population	260,715	268,108	278,078	262,754	274,815	298,109	264,685	281,306	317,895
Younger than 5 years old	19,165	17,438	16,356	19,553	18,908	19,730	19,949	20,448	23,640
5–19 years old	55,779	58,493	55,662	56,144	59,740	61,278	56,492	60,957	67,122
20–24 years old	17,672	17,647	20,118	17,885	18,161	21,061	18,091	18,660	21,974
25–34 years old	40,469	36,310	36,028	40,844	37,416	38,367	41,214	38,524	40,655
35–44 years old	42,296	43,995	36,782	42,500	44,662	38,853	42,726	45,461	41,191
45–54 years old	30,956	36,632	42,305	31,082	37,054	43,737	31,196	37,465	45,253
55–64 years old	21,042	23,626	34,134	21,153	23,988	35,378	21,238	24,257	36,260
65 years and older	33,335	33,968	36,694	33,594	34,886	39,705	33,778	35,534	41,790
16 years and older	199,881	207,677	222,829	201,294	211,976	234,650	202,602	216,006	245,437
White, total	216,151	220,092	223,922	217,511	224,594	237,412	218,811	229,063	251,352
Black, total	32,900	34,642	37,419	33,147	35,525	40,429	33,368	36,307	42,947
Hispanic, total	25,926	28,693	33,828	26,522	30,602	39,312	27,073	32,343	44,328
American Indian, Eskimo, and Aleut, total	2,241	2,383	2,658	2,247	2,409	2,772	2,250	2,422	2,833
Asian and Pacific Islander, total	9,422	10,991	14,079	9,849	12,287	17,496	10,257	13,514	20,763

Source: *U.S. Bureau of the Census,* Current Population Reports, *Series P-25, No. 1092.*

Changing Age Distribution in the United States

The changing age distribution in North America affects consumer behavior and effective marketing in many ways. Understanding market changes permits forecasting what kinds of products will be bought and consumed as well as related behaviors, attitudes, and opinions.[4] Take time to look at Table 7.1 and see how the various age segments are likely to either increase or decline in the next decade. What does this mean to you as a marketer of children's toys, low-end furniture, reading glasses, healthy foods, or wheelchairs? As you read the following pages, look for ways demographics affect a firm's current and future segmentation strategies.

Children as Consumers

The number of young children may decline during the 2000s, but their importance as consumers won't decline. Using the low and middle series of population projections, the number of children younger than 5 years and those between 5

Figure 7.3   Demographic Resource Guide

Census Data	Information
Bureau of the Census U.S. Department of Commerce (ww.census.gov).	Publications, newsletters, and databases that can be found in libraries or the U.S. Government Printing Offices, or accessed online
Statistics Canada	Complete resource guide to demographic statistics for Canada. Statistics Canada Daily also available
Population Reference Bureau www.prb.org	Collects and releases population statistics for all countries of the world
Survey of Current Business Bureau of Economics Analysis	Primary source for data on income, savings, and wealth

Private Data Firms	Information
Survey of Buying Power (SBP)	Published in July, it contains data on population, effective buying income, and retail sales for all metropolitan areas in the U.S. for most provinces, countries and cities in Canada.
American Demographics	Monthly magazine providing insight into demographic issues and marketing strategies. Also available is an annual directory of demographic resources

and 13 will decline by several million between 2000 and 2010, and the high series projects only a small increase. Under either assumption, however, the high proportion of first-order babies will generate high demand for quality products and services. In 1998, parents spent $4.86 billion on baby products.[5] In response to demand, companies are offering higher-quality children's products and more information about them. Parents probably will shop more at specialty stores, have higher expectations during usage of products, and pay for designer labels, as seen in Figure 7.4a. Chapter 12 discusses in detail the spending power of children in families. Their ability to buy mirrors their increased allowances and gives businesses a golden opportunity to encourage a retail–consumer bonding that could last for a lifetime of purchases.[6]

Communicating with children has become an important marketing tool for many companies, including Oilily, a Dutch clothier that sells bright, fun clothing for kids (and adults as well). Its Fan Club consists of more than 40,000 children and teens from around the globe. In addition to receiving birthday cards and a newsletter, they receive responses to all letters they write to the company—which total about 200 per day.[7] Oilily also gets ideas from its club members. A little girl wrote in that though she loved the bright clothing, her traditional eyeglasses were "cramping her style." Oilily responded by developing a line of brightly colored frames. The goal at Oilily is to connect with young consumers and keep them for life.

Rise of Teenagers

The number of teenagers increased during much of the 1990s and is expected to continue to rise, creating a growing market for clothing, music and entertainment, fast food, gasoline, and other products. Marketers are directing ads to teenagers, who are increasingly given the task of buying products for the family because they have more time and because they like shopping more than their parents do.[8]

Figure 7.4a   Ad for Baby Gap Appeals to Parents

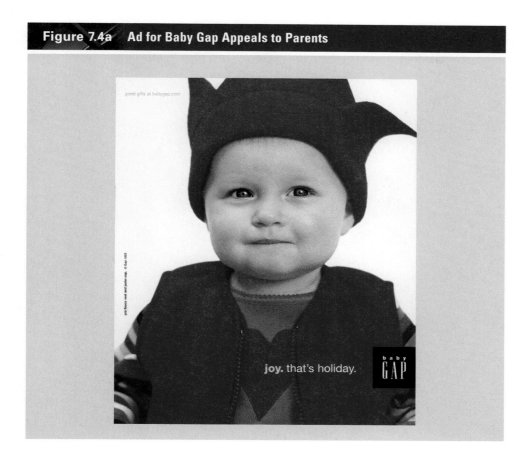

joy. that's holiday.

baby
GAP

But to get their attention, they expect marketers to be honest, use humor, be clear in message, and show them the product in ads.[9] Teen consumers tend to be fickle.[10] They are likely to switch brand preference quicker than other groups because of their high need to be accepted by their peers. Research indicates that what teens like best about shopping is being with their friends and that companies should focus some of their marketing efforts on opinion leaders within teen groups.[11]

The power of teen girls as consumers is on the rise. They have fueled the rise in popularity of celebrities such as the Spice Girls and Mia Hamm, the soccer mega-star. Teen girls search for products and ways to band together and relate to one another, and marketers address these needs. *Seventeen* magazine, the publication for teen girls for years, has a circulation of more than 2.5 million young readers. Although it features articles on issues of interest to young girls, the advertisers represent products that were traditionally not positioned to young girls, such as Lancome's Tresor perfume, Plymouth Neon, Clinique foundation, and Sears.[12]

Young Adults

During the late 1990s, the number of young adults between the ages of 18 and 24 increased, while the number of people between 25 and 34 years of age declined as a result of the baby bust of 1965 to 1980. The entire young adult segment, however, is expected to increase somewhat in the next decade. The younger portion of this segment views itself as too young to worry about "grown up" issues, such as health. In addition to adopting the habit of smoking, much of this group doesn't have health insurance or a regular doctor;[13] it lives life for the "now" more than

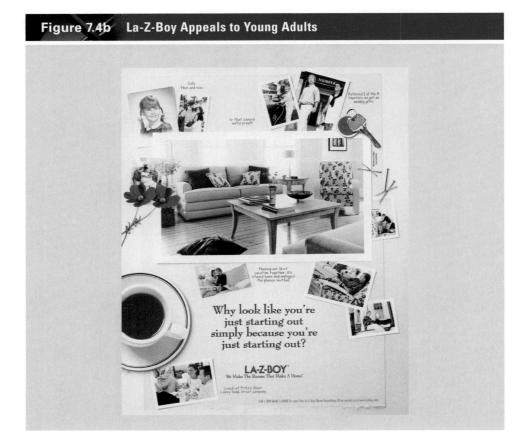

Figure 7.4b   La-Z-Boy Appeals to Young Adults

for the "later." The 25- to 34-year-olds will decline slightly during the first five years of the decade and then grow back to current levels by 2010.

Because age 25 to 34 years is the time when families usually form, have children, and buy their first home and new car, flat or declining sales of these and related products are to be expected. This age group is doing things later than their parents did, however. They live at home longer and graduate, marry, and start families later than their parents did.[14] When they do leave home, they use credit cards to support their "habit" of homes, microwaves, VCRs, and similar consumer goods, which they often buy from value-oriented retailers, such as Wal*Mart, Circuit City, and Best Buy. Despite their declining numbers, baby busters are an important market segment, as seen in the La-Z-Boy ad in Figure 7.4b.

Baby Boomers and Muppies

Perhaps one of the most important years of the decade was 1996—the year baby boomers started reaching age 50. "Baby boomers" refers to the large cohort of people born after World War II. The 74 million births that occurred by 1964 have affected markets, organizations, and all other aspects of society for decades. In the 1980s, marketers focused on yuppies—young urban professionals—because of their high discretionary incomes and influence on market trends. Today, yuppies have become muppies—middle-aged urban professionals—creating even more profitable markets. They are influencing everything from retailing and advertising to product development and the performance of the stock market.[15]

Baby boomers delayed getting married and having children to focus on their careers, the financial rewards of which created a permanent propensity to consume. They held much power in the marketplace because of their numbers, and marketers aimed to satisfy their wants—quality, aesthetically pleasing, personally satisfying, natural, and if possible, noncaloric products. Baby boomers buy more and save less than past generations, spending on products that past generations would have considered luxuries, such as consumer electronics, multiple cars, and household services.

The lifestyle decisions of baby boom consumers are influenced greatly by trends in marriage, divorce, and consumption during the 1980s and 1990s. They don't need a new car, but if they buy one, it will be higher quality than what they accepted as young adults. It may also be one that restores some of the "youth" they don't want to concede to the next generation. Porsche, Mercedes, and Lexus are auto brands that meet both criteria. When baby boomers buy homes or products for the home, they also face less immediacy and more ability to buy quality. Instead of a split-level preferred in younger years, they want a nicer but perhaps smaller home, along with a second home that might someday be used for retirement.[16]

The 45- to 55-year-old and 55- to 64-year-old age groups are projected to grow by six to ten million people by 2010. These age groups indulge in luxury travel, restaurants, and the theater, which often means they need more fashionable clothing and jewelry. Although they do not cook at home as often as their parents did, they remodel their homes to include gourmet kitchens (and large walk-in closets to store all of their "stuff").[17] They watch their waistlines and diets and are good prospects for spas, health clubs, cosmetics, beauty parlors, and healthier foods. And they are a prime prospect for financial products oriented toward asset accumulation and retirement income. They also have young attitudes, as shown in the ad for AARP in Figure 7.4c.

Figure 7.4c   AARP Appeals to Young Attitudes and Lifestyles

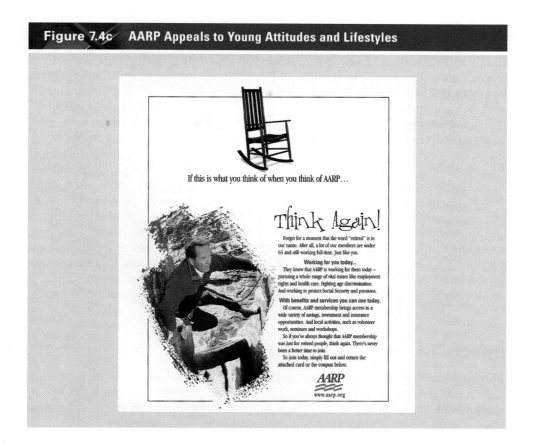

Young-Again Market

Another rapid growth segment is the "young-again" market, consumers who have accumulated lots of chronologic age but who feel, think, and buy young. Other terms to describe this segment include maturity market, seniors, and elderly.

Cognitive age is the *age one perceives one's self to be.* It is measured in terms of how people feel and act, express interests, and perceive their looks. Cognitively younger "older" women, for example, manifest higher self-confidence and greater fashion interests, are more work oriented, and have greater participation in entertainment and culturally related activities.[18] Cognitive age can be useful in conjunction with chronological age for better targeting of segments, more effective creative content, and more efficient media selections.

Older families have more to spend, but less *need* to spend. They are thrifty and careful with the money they do spend[19] because inflation causes prices to increase, but doesn't necessarily increase their income. They have experience with shopping and ability to wait to find good value. Consumption patterns vary substantially between the retired and those still working,[20] and therefore, some may respond more to coupons and be willing to shift their buying to off-peak times. Nevertheless, with home mortgages paid off or nearly so, no more college education to finance, and an inventory of appliances and furnishings, mature families are good prospects for luxury goods, travel-related products and services, healthcare, and a wide range of financial services.

Market segmentation is especially important in the mature market.[21] Most often, this is done on the basis of age, income, or work (retirement) status. Other segmentation variables are health, activity level, discretionary time, and engagement in society. Gender is also an important variable. Women greatly outnumber men because of greater life expectancy, and many (often widowed) typically cannot earn an income, have inadequate or dangerous housing, and suffer social and economic rejection.[22]

Communicating with older consumers requires alterations of traditional materials and messages. Many consumers in this age cohort have problems with the media because of declining sensory abilities.[23] Eyes don't see as well, creating the need for larger print and bright colors rather than pastels or earth tones, and TV commercials with visual changes every few seconds are annoying. Older consumers are likely to be newspaper readers and AM radio listeners and are more likely to shop department and traditional stores rather than discount stores, which they often find too big. They also tend to be more alert in the morning and therefore shop earlier than other consumers. This makes advertising and special services at stores more convenient for this segment when conducted in the morning.[24] Older consumers are pretty much like younger segments in their brand loyalty and shopping behavior[25] and respond equally well to young or older role models, at least for age-neutral products such as coffee.[26] But there is a sensitivity to revealing one's age. Therefore, an ad that blasts out in pictures or words that the product is for 60-year-olds won't work. Nor will advertising that is obviously directed to 30-year-olds. The most effective way to get around that problem is to create affinities between the product and some interest of the mature generation.

Effects of an Aging Population

The facts are that the populations of the United States, Japan, Canada, and Europe are becoming older; however, opportunities for products and services targeted toward all consumers will still exist. In addition to identifying new product lines, communication programs, and consumer segments, consumer analysts must understand what growth in this market means for labor and retirement policies, political elections, family structures, healthcare, and many other areas of life.

Changing Geography of Demand

The search for growing segments in a slow-growth society almost always leads to identifying domestic and global geographic areas of growth. *Where people live, how they earn and spend their money, and other socioeconomic factors*—referred to as **geodemography**—are critical to understanding consumer demand. The study of demand related to geographic areas assumes that people who live in proximity to one another also share similar consumption patterns and preferences.

Segmenting Geographically

Cities are the most important unit of analysis in most marketing plans as well as fundamental in determining the prosperity of nations.[27] Suburbs have grown rapidly, but today **exurbs**—*areas beyond the suburbs*—are experiencing the fastest growth. Fast-growing counties are often nonmetropolitan or rural but adjacent to suburban or metropolitan areas. Marketers must ask how the preferences and needs of consumers who live in the city versus in the exurbs differ, and how to address these differences in advertising and communication.

Cities are a fundamental unit of analysis in consumer research, especially in the design of promotional programs. Advertising media are usually bought on a geographic basis—many national magazines such as *Time* and *Business Week* sell regional advertising sections on a state or city basis. Print media are moving toward editions based on geographic areas as specific as zip codes. Cities are especially important for ethnic marketing. More than half of all Americans lived in the 50 largest metro areas in 1990, but more than 70 percent of Asians and Hispanics lived in those areas.

Which city do you believe is largest: San Jose or San Francisco? Columbus or Boston? If you picked San Jose and Columbus, you were correct because the question referred to cities. But San Francisco and Boston have larger metropolitan areas. The **metropolitan statistical area** (MSA) is defined as *a free-standing metropolitan area, surrounded by nonmetropolitan counties and not closely related with other metropolitan areas.* A **primary metropolitan statistical area (PMSA)** is a *metropolitan area that is closely related to another city. A grouping of closely related PMSAs* is a **consolidated metropolitan statistical area (CMSA).** More than one-third of the people in the United States live in the country's 22 megalopolises or CMSAs.

Which States Are Growing?

Market trends vary substantially between states. Projections about which states will grow the most in the next decades are shown in Table 7.2. California is expected to gain three million people from 1995 to 2005, while Florida is expected to gain more than two million. The states with the greatest percentage gains in population in the 1990s were Arizona, Colorado, Nevada, Utah, and Texas.

There are pitfalls associated with concentrating only on growth. Idaho is expected to grow by 20 percent in the next decade, and Nevada is expected to grow by almost 40 percent. Yet, these two states have much lower population. This illustrates the trap of chasing the trend but ignoring the substance. A 10 percent market share in a no-growth market such as Ohio or Michigan may be preferable to a high market share in a rapid-growth but minuscule state such as Alaska.

Table 7.2 Projections of the Total Population of States: 1995 to 2025

(Numbers in thousands. Resident population. For more detailed information, see Population Paper Listing #47, "Population Projections for States, by Age, Sex, Race, and Hispanic Origin: 1995 to 2025.")

Series A	July 1, 1995	July 1, 2000	July 1, 2005	July 1, 2015	% Δ 2005–2015
Alabama	4,253	4,451	4,631	4,956	7.0
Alaska	604	653	700	791	13.0
Arizona	4,218	4,798	5,230	5,808	11
Arkansas	2,484	2,631	2,750	2,922	6.3
California	31,589	32,521	34,441	41,373	20.2
Colorado	3,747	4,168	4,468	4,833	8.2
Connecticut	3,275	3,284	3,317	3,506	5.7
Delaware	717	768	800	832	4.0
District of Columbia	554	523	529	594	12.3
Florida	14,166	15,233	16,279	18,497	13.6
Georgia	7,201	7,875	8,413	9,200	9.4
Hawaii	1,187	1,257	1,342	1,553	15.7
Idaho	1,163	1,347	1,480	1,622	9.6
Illinois	11,830	12,051	12,266	12,808	4.4
Indiana	5,803	6,045	6,215	6,404	3.0
Iowa	2,842	2,900	2,941	2,994	1.8
Kansas	2,565	2,668	2,761	2,939	6.4
Kentucky	3,860	3,995	4,098	4,231	3.2
Louisiana	4,342	4,425	4,535	4,840	6.7
Maine	1,241	1,259	1,285	1,362	6.0
Maryland	5,042	5,275	5,467	5,862	7.2
Massachusetts	6,074	6,199	6,310	6,574	4.2
Michigan	9,549	9,679	9,763	9,917	1.6
Minnesota	4,610	4,830	5,005	5,283	5.6
Mississippi	2,697	2,816	2,908	3,035	4.4
Missouri	5,324	5,540	5,718	6,005	5.0
Montana	870	950	1,006	1,069	6.3
Nebraska	1,637	1,705	1,761	1,850	5.1
Nevada	1,530	1,871	2,070	2,179	5.3
New Hampshire	1,148	1,224	1,281	1,372	7.1
New Jersey	7,945	8,178	8,392	8,924	6.3
New Mexico	1,685	1,860	2,016	2,300	14.1
New York	18,136	18,146	18,250	18,916	3.6

Low growth ● >4%
High growth < 10%

North Carolina	7,195	7,777	8,227	8,840	7.5
North Dakota	641	662	677	704	4.0
Ohio	11,151	11,319	11,428	11,588	1.4
Oklahoma	3,278	3,373	3,491	3,789	8.5
Oregon	3,141	3,397	3,613	3,992	10.5
Pennsylvania	12,072	12,202	12,281	12,449	1.4
Rhode Island	990	998	1,012	1,070	5.7
South Carolina	3,673	3,858	4,033	4,369	8.3
South Dakota	729	777	810	840	3.7
Tennessee	5,256	5,657	5,966	6,365	6.7
Texas	18,724	20,119	21,487	24,280	13.0
Utah	1,951	2,207	2,411	2,670	10.7
Vermont	585	617	638	662	3.8
Virginia	6,618	6,997	7,324	7,921	8.2
Washington	5,431	5,858	6,258	7,058	12.8
West Virginia	1,828	1,841	1,849	1,851	—
Wisconsin	5,123	5,326	5,479	5,693	3.9
Wyoming	480	525	568	641	13.0

Projections of the Total Population of States: 1995 to 2025.

Economic Resources

As you saw in Chapter 5, the three primary resources that consumers spend when purchasing are economic, temporal, and cognitive. Economic resources, or ability to buy, is a key demographic variable in explaining why, what, and when people buy. The combination of age and income is the most frequently used demographic variable to define segments.

Economic resources can be measured in various ways. **Income** is defined as *money from wages and salaries as well as interest and welfare payments.* Official measures do not include other kinds of compensation such as employer or government benefits. Although income determines what consumers *can* buy, it does not determine what they *want* to buy—most consumers would *want* a new Porsche, but few can afford to buy one. Market research questionnaires often ask about an individual's behavior, but also ask about household income because it is a better determinant of the buying behavior of a household unit, as discussed in Chapter 12.

The median household income rose 3.5 percent in 1998—to reach a record annual income of $38,885 per year.[28] At the same time, the poverty rate decreased to 12.7 percent, the lowest it has been since 1979. While the rich are getting richer, the poor are getting richer as well, but at a much lower rate, leading to what is termed income inequality. The income for the poorest families rose less than 1 percent between 1988 and 1998, but rose 15 percent for the richest quintile.[29] The top 5 percent of households (those making $132,199 or more) accounted for 21.4 percent of all U.S. income in 1998.[30]

Consumer Confidence

Consumers drive the economy, accounting for more than two-thirds of all economic activity in the United States and Canada. Consumption is heavily *influenced by what consumers think will happen in the future,* referred to as **consumer confidence.** It influences whether consumers will increase their debt or defer spending to pay off debt. Measures of consumer confidence are important to marketers making decisions about inventory levels, staffing, or promotional budgets. During late summer, for example, retailers closely examine consumer confidence about future economic conditions to place inventory orders for holiday selling. If consumer confidence is high, holiday spending is usually strong.

Two organizations are known for their consumer confidence surveys. The Conference Board mail survey of 5,000 households asks respondents to look 6 months ahead and focuses on availability of jobs. The University of Michigan Survey, which tends to be less volatile, questions 500 households per month by telephone about such things as family finances and overall business conditions.

Wealth

Wealth is a *measure of a family's net worth or assets in such things as bank accounts, stocks, and a home, minus its liabilities.* Net worth influences willingness to spend, but not necessarily ability to spend, since much wealth is not liquid and cannot be spent easily. There is a correlation between income and net worth, but how much people accumulate over the years is more a function of how much they save than how much they earn.[31] In the latter 1990s, wealth for most Americans rose substantially, due to the rise in the stock market. The typical family's net worth rose 17.6 percent to $71,600 in 1998, up from $60,900 in 1995. Although consumers are segmented primarily on income rather than wealth, wealth has recently become more important to consumer analysts because of this significant increase, which has increased consumer confidence and brought spending to new levels.[32]

Wealthy consumers spend their money on services, travel, and investments more than others. Since they place a premium on time, superior customer service, immediate availability, trouble-free operation of products, and dependable maintenance and repair services are highly valued. They are targets for products that enhance the physical self, restore youthfulness (expensive cosmetics, skin care, cosmetic surgery, and spas), and protect and secure their property and themselves (security systems, security guards, and insurance).

Targeting the Up Market

The up market, often referred to as the "superaffluents," represents the top quintile of consumers in terms of income. These households often consist of two income earners who place high value on time because for them, time is scarcer than money. They value extra services that some retailers provide to capture new customers.[33] They are good targets for jewelry; electronics and home entertainment systems; upscale cars, including SUVs and sports models; art and entertainment. But just because this segment makes more money than other groups, marketers must not assume that they will spend all that they make and shop only at upscale stores and shopping centers. For many individuals in this group, accumulating money is as important as spending it. They shop discount stores,[34] use coupons, and wait for sales to buy products. Even down-scale or bargain stores such as Aldi, Odd Lots, and "dollar stores" are frequented by individuals with above average net worth.

Communicating to the up market is more print oriented than to other market segments. Readership of local weekday and Sunday newspapers and news magazines is higher, but television viewership is lower—although this segment has a higher concentration subscribing to cable television and listening to public radio. Appealing to consumers with simple ads that promote image often works well. This market also places more importance on credibility of the source selling or promoting the product—that is why product reviews or news articles talking about a product or service sometimes influence this group more than paid ads.

Targeting the Down Market

Throughout the world, the majority of consumers are low income. Although the United States, Canada, and other industrialized countries have a vast middle class, the number of lower-income consumers is high. Wal*Mart has found success by providing good products at reasonable prices to lower-income segments. It focuses on offering attractive stores, stylish and up-to-date products, and friendly service that treats customers with respect. Consequently, Wal*Mart has attracted a substantial portion of the up market into its stores as well as the down market. Closeout stores, such as Odd Lots, TJ Maxx, and Tuesday Morning, make it possible for all income-level consumers to buy brand name products at low prices. These firms specialize in buying product overruns from manufacturers or products from stores that are liquidating. They offer other firms' inventory to consumers at deep discounts.

Consumers' income situations may change depending on inflation, recessions, or personal situations, such as changes in health, job, or marital status. Astute marketers can react to economic changes, such as a recession, by promoting value. For example, Campbell Soup noticed consumers shifting from higher-priced foods such as ready-to-serve soups to cheaper products. It took cream of broccoli soup out of the expensive Gold Label can, cut the price, packed it in the familiar red-and-white can, promoted it as a base for homemade meals, and watched sales grow to 55 million cans to become the most successful new soup since 1935.[35]

Poverty

Poverty exists around the world, including in the most advanced and industrialized nations. Although poor people in the United States are making more income than in the past, the rate of increase is much lower than in the upper income levels, thereby creating a widening of the gap between rich and poor. Consumer behavior is concerned about the consumption patterns of homeless people and consumers with few economic resources. In addition to understanding how best to market to this group, consumer analysts are concerned with the effect of various educational policies, value systems, and economic policies on this segment.

Global Market Opportunities: Reacting to Slow-Growth Market Conditions

Countries experiencing slow or no population growth often turn to global markets to find growth markets. If you work for a U.S.-based firm and are charged with growing sales by 20 percent, you have several options. You can increase market share in the United States—but your traditional markets are declining in size and you have already expanded nationally—or you can choose to expand to global markets.

The world population is approximately 6.1 billion and growing at the rate of about 1.4 percent annually. That represents a decline from 2.04 percent in the 1960s and reversal of two centuries of increasing growth rates. The number of people added to the world population each year is projected to decline during the 21st century but will still produce a world population of 10.2 billion by 2090, when population in absolute numbers should begin to decline.

Fast-Growth Populations

The fastest growing country in the world is India. If current trends continue, India will surpass China as the most populous country sometime before 2025. Kenya is the fastest growing country by percentage increase, rising approximately 4.2 percent annually. Kenya is a land of economic potential because of its abundance of export commodities such as coffee and tea. However, as a consumer market, it does have some problems. With the average woman bearing eight children in her lifetime, just keeping up with the basic needs of a surging population will strain already limited resources.

The dramatic effect of the growth rates of developed and developing countries is indicated in Figure 7.5. In 1950, only 8 of the 15 most-populated countries were developing countries, and by the year 2050, it is projected to be 13—only 3 of the 30 most-populated countries will be industrialized countries. From a marketing perspective, the greatest challenge for the "rich" countries that hope to have growing markets for their products in the future is to assist "poor" countries in developing to where they are rich enough to be economically strong markets.

Global Market Demographics and Attractiveness

The most attractive markets are countries that are growing both in population and in economic resources. Two relevant indicators of market attractiveness are natural increase (percentage increase in population each year considering births and deaths) and life expectancy (indicating overall quality of life), as seen in Figure 7.6.

The search for both population growth and ability to buy increasingly takes consumer analysts to the Pacific Rim. Hong Kong, Singapore, Malaysia, and South Korea have much higher population growth rates than Europe and relatively high incomes. China and India are attracting the interest of world marketers because of the size of the population bases and the rapidity of their growth. Although low GNP is a disadvantage when selling in these countries, it is an advantage to those firms sourcing in these countries. Further, there are pockets of consumers who are able to buy many products, even in the poorest countries of the world. With large population size, the percentage of middle- to upper-income consumers does not have to be as high as in countries with smaller populations.

The following market summaries illustrate the facts a consumer analyst should consider when evaluating the attractiveness of a market. In general, a thorough analysis extends beyond demographics to include market preferences.

Consumer Behavior in Developing Countries

What are the most important attributes of developing countries? In addition to high birthrates and strong population growth, low annual income is a reality in

Figure 7.5 Top 25 Countries Measured by Population

1950	2000	2025	2050
1. China	1. China	1. India	1. India
2. India	2. India	2. China	2. China
3. Soviet Union	3. United States	3. United States	3. United States
4. United States	4. Indonesia	4. Indonesia	4. Nigeria
5. Japan	5. Brazil	5. Pakistan	5. Indonesia
6. Indonesia	6. Russia	6. Brazil	6. Pakistan
7. Brazil	7. Pakistan	7. Nigeria	7. Brazil
8. United Kingdom	8. Bangladesh	8. Bangladesh	8. Bangladesh
9. West Germany	9. Japan	9. Mexico	9. Congo (Kinshasa)
10. Italy	10. Nigeria	10. Russia	10. Mexico
11. Bangladesh	11. Mexico	11. Phillipines	11. Ethiopia
12. France	12. Germany	12. Japan	12. Phillipines
13. Nigeria	13. Phillipines	13. Congo (Kinshasa)	13. Russia
14. Pakistan	14. Vietnam	14. Vietnam	14. Vietnam
15. Mexico	15. Egypt	15. Ethiopia	15. Egypt
16. Spain	16. Turkey	16. Egypt	16. Iran
17. Vietnam	17. Iran	17. Iran	17. Turkey
18. Poland	18. Thailand	18. Turkey	18. Japan
19. Egypt	19. Ethiopia	19. Germany	19. Saudi Arabia
20. Phillipines	20. United Kingdom	20. Thailand	20. Sudan
21. Turkey	21. France	21. Burma	21. Uganda
22. South Korea	22. Italy	22. Sudan	22. Burma
23. Ethiopia	23. Congo (Kinshasa)	23. United Kingdom	23. Tanzania
24. Thailand	24. Ukraine	24. Colombia	24. Afghanistan
25. Burma	25. Burma	25. France	25. Yemen

Note: Data updated 12-29-99.
Source: U.S. Census Bureau, International Database.

many of these markets. Youthfulness is apparent, with large numbers of babies and children and lower life expectancy. Even though most developing countries are rural, consumers are usually dependent on other countries for food supplies and education. In fact, marketers might find themselves having to teach consumers about products we use in everyday life, such as deodorant. Though the goal is to create brand awareness (because there will always be competitors entering the market as well), stimulating product trial is often the overriding objective. Although in many parts of the world, television has been blamed for contributing to societal problems, studies indicate that attention should be focused on the pro-social effects of entertainment television programs in developing countries.[36]

Johnson & Johnson uses the strong appeal of the mother-child relationship in the South African ad shown in Figure 7.7. The photograph communicates the love and concern of a mother for her baby without the need for words. The copy, however, features an economy appeal by saving 20 cents. Moreover, the company has positioned itself as concerned about all children by donating 20 cents from each purchase to the Child Welfare Fund. This ad provides a useful example of effective strategy based on an understanding of the economic and cultural realities of the African market.

Southern Africa has received much attention in recent years. Botswana boasts great economic growth and advancement in education for all its citizens, making

Figure 7.6   World Populations of Selected Countries

	Population Mid-1999 (millions)	Total Fertility Rate	Life Expectancy at Birth (years)			GNP Per Capita 1997 (US$)
			Total	Male	Female	
Africa						
Egypt	66.9	3.3	65	67	69	1,500
Nigeria	113.8	6.2	54	53	55	280
Ethiopia	59.7	7.0	42	41	42	110
Kenya	28.8	4.7	49	48	49	340
Zimbabwe	11.2	4.0	40	40	40	720
Botswana	1.5	4.1	40	40	41	3,310
South Africa	42.6	3.3	58	55	60	3,210
Latin America						
Mexico	99.7	3.0	72	69	75	3,700
Cuba	11.2	1.6	75	73	78	–
Argentina	36.6	2.6	73	70	77	8,950
Brazil	168.0	2.3	67	63	70	4,790
Chile	15.0	2.4	75	72	78	4,820
Colombia	38.6	3.0	69	65	73	2,180
Peru	26.6	3.5	68	65	71	2,610
Venezuela	23.7	2.9	73	70	76	3,480
Asia						
Israel	6.1	2.9	78	76	80	16,180
Saudi Arabia	20.9	6.4	71	70	73	7,150
India	986.6	3.4	60	60	61	370
Indonesia	211.8	2.8	63	61	65	1,110
Philippines	74.7	3.7	67	66	69	1,200
Singapore	4.0	1.6	77	75	79	32,810
China	1,254.1	1.8	71	69	73	860
Japan	126.7	1.4	81	77	84	38,160
Korea, South	46.9	1.6	74	70	77	10,550
Europe						
Denmark	5.3	1.7	76	73	78	34,890
Switzerland	7.1	1.5	79	76	82	43,060
United Kingdom	59.4	1.7	77	74	80	20,870
Belgium	10.2	1.5	77	74	81	26,730
France	59.1	1.7	78	74	82	26,300
Germany	82.0	1.3	77	73	80	28,280
Netherlands	15.8	1.5	78	75	80	25,830
Hungary	10.1	1.3	71	66	75	4,510
Poland	38.7	1.5	73	69	77	3,590
Russia	146.5	1.2	67	61	73	2,680
Greece	10.5	1.3	78	75	80	11,640
Italy	57.7	1.2	78	75	81	20,170
Oceania						
Australia	19.0	1.7	78	76	81	20,650
North America						
Canada	30.6	1.5	79	76	82	19,640
United States	272.5	2.0	77	74	79	29,080

Source: World Population Data Sheet, Population Reference Bureau (1999).

it an attractive market to target. For many developing countries throughout Africa, including Botswana and South Africa, tourism plays a significant role in economic growth and market awareness. South Africa, known globally for its changed political system and lavish safari and vacation destinations, is in many ways both a developing and a developed nation. The home of open-heart surgery, digital

Figure 7.7   Advertising Appeal Based on African Culture

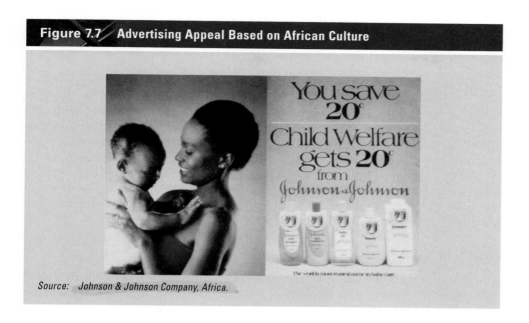

Source: Johnson & Johnson Company, Africa.

reattachment, and other medical breakthroughs, this country consists of sophisticated markets in which the most advanced marketing strategies are applicable
for specific segments. Internet usage has soared, with 42 percent of users between
18 and 24 years coming from the highest income groups, made up primarily of
white South Africans.[37] Other segments, however, need to be addressed at the
most basic marketing level—sometimes with visual language and personal network contacts, as described in Consumer in Focus 7.1.

Consumer Behavior in the Pacific Rim

The Pacific Rim provides some of the most attractive markets for growth-oriented
firms. The area includes many low-income but fast-growing population bases in
Southeast Asia, as well as some of the most affluent markets in the world, such
as Japan, Singapore, and Australia.

India

As a country projected to become the largest in the world, India is attracting worldwide interest among marketers. Although poor by Western standards, the attractiveness of India is based on its infrastructure; well-developed legal system; and
large numbers of well-educated doctors, engineers, and others needed for growth
of a thriving middle class. India is a country with growth in national income and
productivity but major problems caused by its large debt, shortage of foreign exchange, and unsettling coalitions of government.[38]

   The middle class is the key to understanding India's consumer markets and
why firms such as McDonald's have entered.[39] Although the government does
not publish statistics on this politically sensitive subject, some economists estimate the number at 7 to 12 percent of the population or a market range from 60
million to 100 million, larger than that of France.[40] Consequently, the demand for
consumer goods is rising rapidly, with dramatic increases in annual sales of cars,
motorbikes, scooters, and other durables, which on average are rising at the rate
of 20 percent annually. The middle-class family with a yearly income of about

$1,400 does not live in luxury but may be buying a television, a radio, appliances such as an electric iron and clocks, and a respectable wardrobe of shoes, jewelry, and silk saris.

South Korea

Ability to buy has increased at an astounding rate in South Korea, as has the desire to buy a variety of consumer products. Increasing income, plummeting birthrates, good healthcare, a high regard for religious values, and a young, well-educated population make South Korea an attractive market for many firms.

A key element in the success of Korea has been export capabilities, strongly assisted by government policies. Many large Korean firms, such as Daewoo and Hyundai (the most successful car ever imported to North America) are succeeding in the United States and other industrialized markets.

Australia

Australia is a market similar in characteristics to European and North American markets—high income and an older population.[41] It has a well-developed infrastructure and plenty of room to grow, with a majority of its population clustered around major cities, such as Melbourne, Sydney, and Perth. At one time, immigration was mostly European, but in recent years, nearly 50 percent of immigration has been Asian. Marketers find the nation attractive because it also has a well-developed advertising and marketing research system, which can support new product and brand development with sophisticated strategies and execution, as well as excellent retailers such as Coles-Meyer and Woolworth. *Crocodile Dundee,* Mel Gibson, and Outback Steakhouse fans alike can attest to the influence of Australian "image" on American movies and tastes.

China

China is the planet's largest nation. The pent-up demand of 1.2 billion consumers excites marketers all over the world. In the past, most of China's imports have been industrial goods, but new government priorities caused marketers to consider the potential for consumer markets. China is creating a market-based economy from one that had been a planned Communist country for decades, and currently runs a significant trade surplus with the United States.[42]

With increasing salaries of urban workers and the rise of new entrepreneurs in China's special economic areas, more people can buy a broader array of consumer goods.[43] What do Chinese consumers want to buy most? Refrigerators top the list in a study made in two of China's largest cities, Beijing (population 9.5 million) and Guyangzhou (population 7 million), with washing machines close behind. Televisions are the most often owned electrical appliances. Roughly 9 million people use the Internet, a 324 percent increase from the 1998 figure of 2.1 million.[44] With 79 percent of those online being male and 75 percent under age 30, reaching young, affluent, and educated Chinese men on the Internet is an efficient marketing method for many international firms.

In recent years, more than one million Chinese have become *dakuan,* or dollar millionaires, with approximately 5 percent of the population declared as affluent by Chinese standards. There exist many examples of individuals who have been able to develop their careers and live in lavish surroundings with luxury products, yet most citizens still live in crowded cities or poor farming villages. The shift to more of a market-driven system is producing enormous change and conflict in China, which raises major questions about the proper role of marketing activities. It also brings about changes in culture. A young, career-oriented generation of men and women exists today in China; their focus is on independence and themselves.[45] Chinese teenagers are also challenging authoritarian rules, even when it comes to music. The Flowers, a popular pop band, is playing to crowds of young girls and boys, and confronting the traditional view that rock and roll is not good for China's situation.[46]

Japan

Although Japan is smaller in land area than California, its 127 million people consume more goods and services than any other country in the world, except the United States. Land is perhaps the most scarce and valuable natural resource in Japan, which also lacks petroleum and other natural resources. Yet its main assets are its culture and people, which have contributed to the development of its powerhouse economy.

Japanese people love their culture. Although some young adults are questioning the strict work and family ethics of their elders, there still exists a very strong Japanese traditional lifestyle and aesthetic sense. The Japanese have integrated high technology into their traditional lives. Studies conclude that the fundamental philosophy for product designing and marketing in Japanese enterprises is to adapt high-tech products to the culture of the countries in which they are sold.[47]

In terms of marketing, the great majority of Japanese TV commercials are directed toward affective rather than cognitive components of attitude. Japanese consumers react more to beautiful background scenery, a star of the entertainment world, or the development of a story than to product recommendations. Japanese viewers dislike argumentative sales talk; product information should be short and conveyed with a song that sets a mood. This is an important point for foreign manufacturers accustomed to American hard-sell ads. Japanese advertising is more likely to develop a story, describe the expression of people, and enhance the mood of the product. The message usually comes at the end of the commercial, almost as an afterthought to the rest of the ad.

Latin America

As U.S. companies become more familiar with trading with Mexico and understanding the Mexican markets because of NAFTA, there is an increasing interest in Central and South American countries. The most attractive market segments include those of Brazil, Venezuela, Colombia, Argentina, and Chile.

Although most Latin American countries have high population growth rates and large markets of young consumers, some have promising income growth rates as well. Brazil is the tenth largest country in the world but has one of the largest rich–poor gaps; around 10 percent of its 170 million people belong to the high-income segment. American culture is becoming very popular in Brazil with the arrival of more American newspapers, magazines, automobiles, and fast-food restaurants. The acceptance of American culture is occurring in Chile as well, with brands and stores (such as Hallmark and Liz Claiborne) appearing frequently in shopping malls. Some grocery stores in Chile and Peru rival the biggest and best found in North America or Europe, with more than 50 checkout registers and oversized snack food aisles. In fact, one of the most significant changes in the last decade has been the effect that Latin American culture has had on other countries, including the United States—discussed in detail in Chapter 11.

Consumer analysts note that low reported per capita income levels often hide substantial market segments with high income levels. Although most consumers in Latin American countries might not be able to afford luxury or even mass market items, intermarket segmentation helps identify existing segments that can afford many items such as appliances, cars, designer clothing, travel, and specialty food items.

Eastern Europe

Eastern European economies opened up for trade with the rest of the world in the 1990s. Some have had more success than others. Hungary and Poland have both received much interest from global marketers and from consumers (in the form of tourism). The attractiveness of Eastern European markets for global marketers is the similarity with preferences of Western consumers. The most desired durable products in Eastern Europe are Western cars, video recorders, and microwaves, and the most wanted nondurables are perfume, athletic shoes, and fashionable clothing. Television viewing is the most frequent leisure-time activity, making TV advertising viable. Because fewer consumers have cars and they have limited storage space at home, 85 percent of East Europeans shop every day for food or other items.[48]

Companies such as Procter & Gamble are now significant marketers in countries such as Hungary, Poland, and Yugoslavia. Products include Pampers disposable diapers, Blend-a-Med toothpaste, Vidal Sassoon shampoo, Ariel laundry detergents, and a host of brands with proven track records in Western Europe. With assistance from international advertising agencies, P&G entered the market with culturally sensitive ads, which featured the P&G logo to emphasize corporate identity and develop credibility for future product introductions. Other successful Western European brands adapted their strategies slightly and found market adoption in the East. Today, with the influence of television, movies, and products, tastes in this part of the world have become quite similar to those found in Western Europe and in North America.

European Single Market

The European Union (EU) is a market larger than the United States. Its common currency, the euro, facilitates trade across national boundaries and throughout the market. People, money, and goods move across borders without passports, exchange controls, or customs.

As you saw earlier in this chapter, population growth has become nonexistent in Europe. In turn, countries unified economically in an attempt to develop efficiencies and growth in the 1990s in a way that became the pattern for the North American Free Trade Agreement (NAFTA). In Europe, factories become more efficient as they serve a market of 344 million people expected to purchase $4 trillion in goods and services. Greater efficiencies in the physical movement of goods and the financial movement of funds were additional goals of the single-market system. The result is also tougher competition for many firms as each takes a Europe-wide approach to marketing.

Borders between European countries may have only a sign noting the country and featuring the EU symbol prominently. In addition to national identity, even firms are identifying themselves with the EU symbol in advertising and point-of-purchase displays.[49] However, national identity and cultures have not disappeared. In fact, some argue that as the push for a single market occurs, the more likely individuals are to cling to their identities.

The largest market in the world today is the EU, and the dominant force in that market is Germany. It has been able to capitalize on trade opportunities with

Eastern Europe and is beginning to experience the returns for its investments in unification with former East Germany. Although Brussels is the capital city of the EU, from a marketing perspective, Berlin has arguably become the capital of all of Europe.

Germany has undergone drastic changes in almost every measurable area, including population, average income, average age, even geographic size of the country. Consumer analysts forecast growth in other countries; reunification achieved it almost instantly. The German form of capitalism is somewhere between the Japanese form, which promotes business, and the American form, which regulates business. The blend of business, government, and unions based on a structured value system has created a standard of living that is among the highest in the world. Germans do not have as high per capita income as Japanese, but they do have nice homes, world-class cars, good healthcare, fast highways, environmentally concerned cities ringed by green forests, and very good beer!

Canada

Although Canada is the world's largest country at 3.9 million square miles, about 80 percent of all Canadians live within 200 kilometers of the United States–Canada border. This geography creates a market about 4,000 miles long and 125 miles wide. The fact that Canadian consumers are in a horizontal string in contrast to U.S. population clusters is a logistics problem in Canada. Many of these U.S. clusters, which are oriented to urban centers, circle over major Canadian markets, especially Ontario. It often is more efficient to supply Canadian markets from those efficient high-volume distribution circles than from Canada's thin linear supply line. As a consequence, Canadian firms that operate in the northern United States and use those cities as distribution points to Canada may have lower costs than firms operating solely in Canada.[50]

The Influence of Individual Differences on Consumer Behavior

The effects of variables such as age, income, and geography are important to understanding consumer behavior and developing marketing plans. Additional understanding can be obtained by analyzing individual differences such as personality, values, and lifestyles and how they affect consumer behavior. These influences are shown at the right side of the Consumer Decision Process model featured throughout this text.

Personality and Consumer Behavior

Although consumer analysts can't look into the eyes of consumers, as the Swiss guide in Consumer in Focus 7.2 does, and tell if they will buy Fords or Chevrolets, they can analyze variables such as personality, values, and psychographics to predict the effects of individual variables on purchase and consumption. These individual differences pick up where demographics leave off and provide understanding of characteristics more determinant of behavior.

Everyone is different—just look at any fingerprint. Effective marketing and advertising programs are achieved with products and messages that have an

Consumer in Focus 7.2

From the Swiss village of Zermatt, a first glance of the Matterhorn is chilling. There are higher peaks nearby, but none stands so stark, so imposing as the defiant 14,692-foot granite pyramid, whispering "I dare you" to on-lookers.

As many as 2,000 people a year climb the Matterhorn during a short summer season from mid-July to mid-September. A corps of 75 expert guides makes the two-day adventure relatively safe for adults in good physical condition. Guides say men and women from 30 to 45 years are the best candidates because they have greater combined mental and physical strength than younger people. But there's no upper age limit—one man made the climb at 90. The climb itself takes 2 days, starting with a hike to the base camp. "Going down was very tough. I ran out of energy. Mental strength got me down," says Patricia Ruiz, a former IBM executive based in Paris who prepared by jogging up the steps to the top of the Eiffel Tower every day for six months.

The Matterhorn can be unforgiving. Each year, the mountain claims 10 to 20 lives of those who failed to respect the safety rules. The worst candidates, guides say, are those who seek to prove something to others. The best are those who are driven by awe of the mountain and a reverence for nature. Ask any mountain guide to take you to the top, and he'll first look into your eyes and see which type you are. A guide explains, "I can usually tell standing in the office if someone can make it or not."

Source: Excerpted from Gail Schares, "A Peak Experience," Business Week (June 1, 1992), 118.

especially strong appeal and cause consumers to think, "That product or message fits what I believe (values), the way I normally behave (personality), and my situation in life (lifestyle)." These variables are not more important than others you will study—knowledge, motivation, and attitudes—but lifestyles and the underlying personality they reflect are frequently more visible. When marketing communication is successful, a person feels the communicator understands him or her and respects his or her individuality.

Personality

Personality has many meanings. In consumer studies, **personality** is defined as *consistent responses to environmental stimuli.*[51] It is *an individual's unique psychological makeup, which consistently influences how the person responds to his or her environment.* Why do some people like to go to a movie or take a walk during free time and others like to run marathons or go skydiving? We often say it is because of personality. Consumer analysts approach the answer by employing three major theories: psychoanalytic, socio-psychological, and trait factor.[52]

Psychoanalytic Theory

Psychoanalytic theory recognizes that the human personality system consists of the *id, ego,* and *superego.*[53] The id is the source of psychic energy and seeks immediate gratification for biological and instinctual needs. The superego represents societal or personal norms and services as an ethical constraint on behavior. The ego mediates the hedonistic demands of the id and the moralistic prohibitions of the superego. The dynamic interaction of these elements results in *unconscious motivations* that are manifested in observed human behavior. Sigmund Freud believed that personality is derived from the conflict between the desire to satisfy physical needs and the need to be a contributing member of society.

Psychoanalytic theory served as the conceptual basis for the motivation research movement described briefly in Chapter 1 and was the forerunner of lifestyle studies. According to the philosophy of motivation researchers such as Dr. Ernest Dichter, consumer behavior is often the result of unconscious consumer motives, which can be determined through indirect assessment methods such as projective and related psychological techniques. The motivation research movement produced some extraordinary findings such as these often related examples: A man who buys a convertible sees it as a substitute mistress, and men want their cigars to be odoriferous to prove their masculinity.[54] Similarly, consumers buy gourmet foods, foreign cars, vodka, and perfume to express individuality.[55] These examples are subject to serious questions of validity and provide little more than a starting place for marketing planning. A consumer's personality is a result of much more than subconscious drives. Yet, a great deal of advertising is influenced by the psychoanalytic approach to personality, especially its heavy emphasis on sexual and other deep-seated biological instincts.

Socio-Psychological Theory

Socio-psychological theory recognizes the interdependence of the individual and society. The individual strives to meet the needs of society, whereas society helps the individual to attain his or her goals. The theory is therefore a combination of sociological and psychological elements.[56] Socio-psychological personality theory differs from psychoanalytic theory in two important respects. First, social variables rather than biological instincts are considered to be the most important determinants in shaping personality. Second, behavioral motivation is directed to meet those needs. For example, a person may buy a product that symbolizes an unattainable or socially unacceptable goal. Although the person might not admit why he or she bought the product, the acquisition fulfills the "forbidden desire" the consumer subconsciously has.

An example of socio-psychological personality theory is the Horney paradigm (based on theory developed by Karen Horney), which suggests that human behavior results from three predominant, interpersonal orientations: compliant, aggressive, and detached. Questions designed to measure these variables are referred to as a CAD scale.[57] Compliant people are dependent on others for love and affection, and are said to move toward others. Aggressive people are motivated by the need for power and move against others. Detached people are self-sufficient and independent, and move away from others.[58]

Trait-Factor Theory

Trait-factor theory is a quantitative approach to personality, which postulates that an individual's personality comprises predispositional attributes called traits. A **trait** is *any distinguishable, relatively enduring way in which one individual differs from another.* Examples of such traits might be sociability, relaxed style, amount of internal control, or other individual difference variables.[59] Consumer analysts might find traits such as risk taking, self-consciousness, and need for cognition[60] most useful in marketing planning.

Three assumptions delineate the trait-factor theory. It is assumed that traits are common to many individuals and vary in absolute amounts among individuals, and therefore, can be used to segment markets. It is also assumed that these traits are relatively stable and exert fairly universal effects on behavior regardless of the environmental situation. It follows then that they can predict a wide variety of behaviors. The final assumption asserts that traits can be inferred from the measurement of behavioral indicators.

Several standard psychological measures exist to inventory traits, such as the California Psychological Inventory and the Edwards Personal Preference Scale (EPPS). Widely used for psychological testing, these tests are sometimes applied to marketing[61] but often produce mixed results. Modified tests are more likely to be useful for consumer research.[62]

Perhaps one of the greatest applications of trait theory in marketing is in developing **brand personality**—the *personality consumers interpret from a specific brand.* Brands may be characterized in a variety of ways, such as old-fashioned, modern, fun, provocative, masculine, or glamorous. Some advertising addresses the tendencies of some consumers to buy and own products that are an extension of themselves or a reflection of who they would like to be.

Predicting Buyer Behavior

Trait-factor theory has been the primary basis of marketing personality research. The typical study attempts to find a relationship between a set of personality variables and assorted consumer behaviors such as purchases, media choice, innovation, fear and social influence, product choice, opinion leadership, risk taking, and attitude change. In early research, personality was found to relate to specific attributes of product choice.[63] Research also indicated that people could make relatively good judgments about other people's traits and how they relate to automobile brands, occupations, and magazine choices.[64]

Predicting consumer behavior was often the objective of personality research in the early years. Studies attempted to predict brand or store preference and other buyer activity, but usually found only very small amounts of variance in product choice explained by personality.[65] Looking back from today's vantage point, these results are not surprising. After all, personality is but one variable in the consumer decision-making process. If any relationship were to be established, dependent variables such as intention would be better candidates than behavior. Even if personality traits were found to be valid predictors of intentions or behavior, they are difficult to use in marketing strategy because:

1. People with common personalities can represent wide variations in demographic variables, and mass media is primarily segmented on a demographic basis.
2. Measures that isolate personality variables often don't demonstrate adequate reliability and validity.

Personality has been able to explain only about 10 percent of variance in behavior. Procter & Gamble conducted many studies several decades ago using personality as a segmentation variable. After three years of effort, the attempt was abandoned because the brand and advertising managers could not generate results that allowed them to develop marketing strategies any more effectively than with other methodologies.

The failure of personality measures to predict consumer behavior has stimulated development of more recent approaches. One approach is to relate personality measures to mediating variables or stages within the decision process, such as need recognition, and to understand the role of personality in information processing. Another incorporates personality data with information about individuals' social and economic conditions. And another approach is to use broader concepts such as values and psychographics.

Personal Values

Another way to understand why consumers vary in their individual decision making is values. Like attitudes, values represent consumer beliefs about life and acceptable behavior. Unlike attitudes, values transcend situations or events and are more enduring because they are more central in the personality structure. Values represent three universal requirements of human existence: biological needs, requisites of coordinated social interaction, and demands for group survival and functioning.[66] They express the goals that motivate people and appropriate ways to attain those goals. Because people hold the same values but differ only in the importance they place on them and because values play such a central role in cognition, values provide a powerful basis for understanding consumer behavior within and across cultures.[67] The enduring nature of values and their central role in personality structure have caused them to be applied to understanding many aspects of consumer behavior, including advertising cognitions, product choice, brand choice, and market segmentation.

Marketers may focus on individual or group values. When the importance of a value is so widely held that it becomes almost stereotypical of a market segment or group, we refer to it as a *social value*.[68] When we study culture in Chapter 11, the focus will be on social values. **Social values** *define "normal" behavior for a society or group.* **Personal values** *define "normal" behavior for an individual,* the focus here. Remember as you read the next few pages, however, that the values of groups to which you belong (social values) will have a major influence on your personal values.

Personal values reflect the choices an individual makes from the variety of social values or value systems to which that individual is exposed. Your values concerning work ethic and social interaction, for example, may determine how much time you spend studying this text, and thus the grade you may get in this course, and more important, your achievements throughout life. Although people are influenced by family, peer, and cultural values, individuals pick and choose from social values to develop their own personal values.

Rokeach Value Scale

Early research concerning values was influenced most by Milton Rokeach and his Rokeach Value Scale (RVS), although Burgess has shown that the concept of values is implicit or explicit in many of the psychological theories of Freud, Jung, Fromm, Adler, Horney, Erikson, Dichter, and others.[69] Rokeach believed values are concerned both with the *goals (end-state or terminal elements)* and the *ways of behaving (instrumental components) to obtain goals* as seen in Figure 7.8. His major contribution was to define values as enduring beliefs that specific modes of conduct or end states of existence are personally or socially preferable to opposing modes of conduct or end states of existence.[70] The RVS asks people to rank the importance of a series of goals and ways of behaving, which can be analyzed by gender, age, ethnicity, or whatever variable might be of interest in consumer analysis.

Several studies have linked personal values to brand choice, product usage, market segmentation, and innovative behavior.[71] In a study of car buying, researchers found consumption-related variables are related to family-oriented core values that stimulate motivation.[72] With low-involvement products such as deodorants, studies found that individuals who preferred Right Guard to Arrid, for

Figure 7.8	Rokeach Value Scale

Terminal (Desirable End States)	Instrumental (Modes of Conduct)
A comfortable life	Ambition
An exciting life	Broad-minded
A sense of accomplishment	Capable
A world at peace	Cheerful
A world of beauty	Clean
Equality	Courageous
Family security	Forgiving
Freedom	Honest
Happiness	Imaginative
Inner harmony	Independent
Mature love	Intellectual
National security	Logical
Pleasure	Loving
Salvation	Obedient
Self-respect	Polite
Social recognition	Responsible
True friendship	Self-controlled
Wisdom	

example, were consumers with high importance on the RVS measuring "mature love."[73] Most of the applications in the past used the RVS to describe the differences between segments defined *a priori* on demographic or other variables. More recently, consumer analysts are using values as the criterion for segmenting the population into homogeneous groups of individuals who share a common value system.[74]

Schwartz Value Scale

The work of psychologist Shalom Schwartz has become most influential on values research in marketing and other behavioral sciences. Schwartz's research has focused on identifying a universal set of values and determining the structure of their relations. His Schwartz Value Scale (SVS) and Portraits Questionnaire (PQ) were designed to measure a comprehensive set of values thought to be held by nearly everyone.[75] Based on empirical studies of more than 100,000 people in more than 60 countries, the Schwartz theory proposes that *values are trans-situational goals that serve the interest of individuals or groups and express one of ten universal motivations or value types*, thereby challenging the simple Rokeach classification of instrumental and terminal values.[76] Schwartz argues that the meaning of an individual value is reflected in the pattern of its relations with other values, usually determined using an analytical technique called smallest space analysis (SSA). These relations of the ten value types, and the four higher-order value domains that contain them, represent a continuum of related motivations that give rise to a circular structure (see Figure 7.9). The pursuit of a specific value may be compatible or in conflict with other values. For example, caring for one's family (benevolence) is compatible with caring for the environment (universalism) but in conflict with placing one's own needs before those of others in order to achieve personal goals (achievement).

These motivations or value types are the guiding principles in consumers' lives. Table 7.3 defines the ten motivational value types and gives some exem-

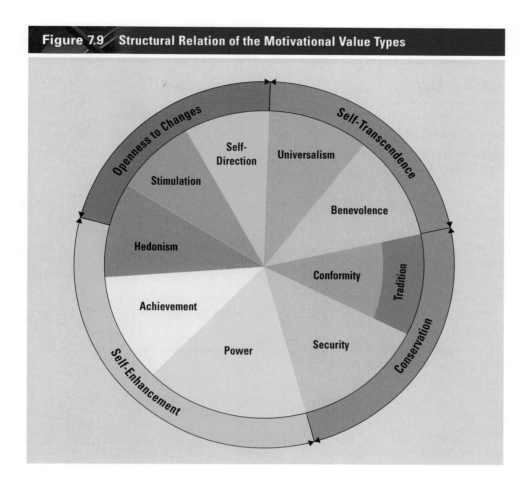

Figure 7.9   Structural Relation of the Motivational Value Types

plary values for each.[77] The SVS has been used to understand why some consumers prefer banks to competitive financial institutions as well as to compare brand preferences between market segments.[78]

Values and Consumer Decision Process

Personal values help explain how we answer the question, "Is this product for me?" Values are particularly important in the need recognition stage of consumer decision making but affect consumers in determining evaluative criteria, answering the question, "Is this brand for me?" Values influence the effectiveness of communications programs as consumers ask, "Is this situation (portrayed in the ad) one in which I would participate?" Values are enduring motivations or the "ends" people seek in their lives. In a sense, marketing often provides the "means" to reach these ends.

Laddering

Understanding how values determine market demand can be facilitated by a technique called **laddering**. Laddering refers to *in-depth probing directed toward uncovering higher-level meanings at both the benefit (attribute) level and the value level.* Laddering seeks to uncover the *linkages between product attributes, personal outcomes (consequences), and values* that serve to structure components of the cognitive network in a consumer's mind.[79]

Table 7.3 Definitions of the Ten Motivational Value Types in Terms of Their Goals and Specific Values That Represent Them

Value Type	Definition	Exemplary Values
Power	Social status and prestige, control or dominance over people and resources	Social power, authority, wealth
Achievement	Personal success through demonstrating competence according to social standards	Successful, capable, ambitious
Hedonism	Pleasure and sensuous gratification for oneself	Pleasure, enjoying life
Stimulation	Excitement, novelty, and challenge in life	Daring, varied life, an exciting life
Self-direction	Independent thought and action— choosing, creating, exploring	Creativity, curious, freedom
Universalism	Understanding, appreciation, tolerance, and protection for the welfare of *all* people and for nature	Broadminded, social justice, equality, protecting the environment
Benevolence	Preservation and enhancement of the welfare of people with whom one is in frequent personal contact	Helpful, honest, forgiving
Tradition	Respect, commitment, and acceptance of the customs and ideas that traditional culture or religion provide	Humble, devout, accepting my portion in life
Conformity	Restraint of actions, inclinations, and impulses likely to upset or harm others and violate social expectations or norms	Politeness, obedient, honoring one's parents or elders
Security	Safety; harmony; and stability of society, of relationships, and of self	Social order, clean

Source: Excerpted from Shalom H. Schwartz; "Are There Universal Aspects in the Structure and Contents of Human Values?" Journal of Social Issues 50, 4 (1994), 19–45.

Figure 7.10 shows the *attributes* provided by wine coolers (carbonation, crisp, expensive, label, bottle, less alcohol, filling, smaller size) and how the consequences of those *benefits* (refreshing, thirst quenching, more feminine, avoid negatives of alcohol, impress others, and so on) relate to the *values* (self-esteem, accomplishment, belonging, family life) of varying market segments. Any of these perceptual maps of the value structures could lead to developing alternative marketing strategies. Although the attributes might be the same, the image that should be developed for those with the self-esteem value would emphasize impressing others, perhaps with a sophisticated image. However, the other image would be developed for the family-life value, emphasizing socializing without the negatives of alcohol. Additional analysis may indicate the size of segments, the degree of overlap between segments, appeals that can be used to appeal to the widest number of consumers, and the level of abstraction that should be used in advertising and other elements of advertising strategy.[80] Recent advances in laddering theory focus on extending laddering to research on a wider range of goal-directed behaviors and on new statistical techniques to aid in interpretation.[81]

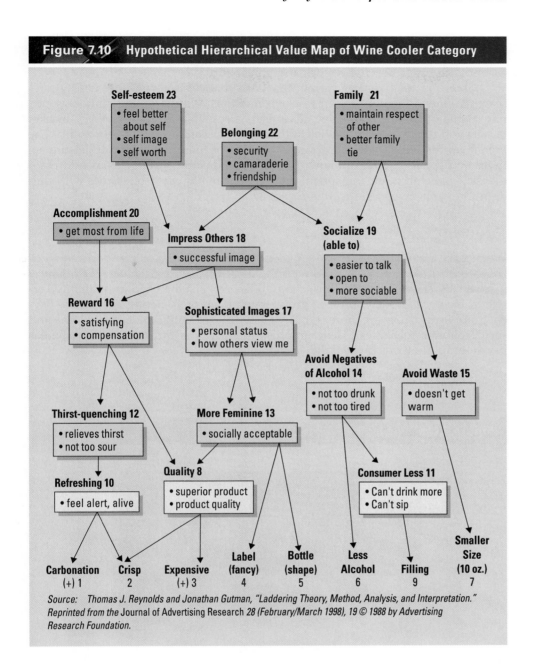

Figure 7.10 Hypothetical Hierarchical Value Map of Wine Cooler Category

*Source: Thomas J. Reynolds and Jonathan Gutman, "Laddering Theory, Method, Analysis, and Interpretation."
Reprinted from the* Journal of Advertising Research *28 (February/March 1998), 19 © 1988 by Advertising
Research Foundation.*

Lifestyle Concepts and Measurement

Lifestyle is a popular concept for understanding consumer behavior, perhaps because it is more contemporary than personality and more comprehensive than values. Lifestyle marketing attempts to relate a product, often through advertising, to the everyday experiences of the market target.

Lifestyle is a summary construct defined as *patterns in which people live and spend time and money,* reflecting a person's activities, interests, and opinions (AIOs), as well as demographic variables discussed earlier. People use constructs such as lifestyles to construe the events happening around them and to interpret, conceptualize, and predict events as well as to reconcile their values with events. This type of construct system is personal but also continually changes in response to a person's need to conceptualize cues from the changing environment to be consistent with his or her own values and personality.[82]

Values are relatively enduring; lifestyles change more rapidly. Lifestyle researchers must, therefore, keep research methods and marketing strategies current. Some of the most effective advertisers track lifestyle trends of key market targets and reflect those lifestyles in their ads, as seen in Figure 7.11a and b. The French ad for Vittel water shows consumption of the product during leisure activity and sport. The Australian ad for Clarion dashboard televisions addresses the issue of commuting and spending more time in our cars (sometimes with children forever asking, "Are we there yet?").

Psychographics

Psychographics is an *operational technique to measure lifestyles;* it provides quantitative measures and can be used with the large samples needed for definition of market segments. In contrast, psychographics can also be used in qualitative research techniques such as focus group interviews or in-depth interviews. Psychographic measures are more comprehensive than demographic, behavioral, and socioeconomic measures—demographics identify *who* buys products, whereas psychographics focus on *why* they buy.

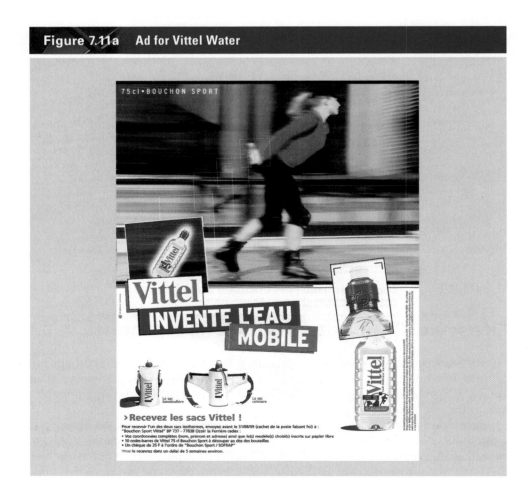

Figure 7.11a   Ad for Vittel Water

Figure 7.11b   Ad for Clarion Car Audio

The term *psychographics* is often used interchangeably with **AIO measures**— *statements that describe the activities, interests, and opinions of consumers.* AIO components are defined as:

- **Activity:** an action such as bowling, shopping in a store, or talking on the telephone. Although these acts are usually observable, the reasons for the actions are seldom subject to direct measurement.

- **Interest:** the degree of excitement that accompanies both special and continuing attention to an object, event, or topic.

- **Opinion:** a spoken or written "answer" that a person gives in response to a "question." It describes interpretations, expectations, and evaluations—such as beliefs about other people's intentions or anticipations concerning future events.[83]

Examples of each category are shown in Figure 7.12.

Market Segmentation

Psychographic studies are used to develop an in-depth understanding of market segments and sometimes to define segments—for example, single women between age 25 and 30 who actively participate in outdoor sports and care about nutrition. In order to identify significant lifestyle trends, researchers often ask

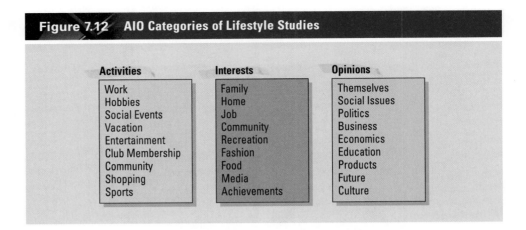

Figure 7.12   AIO Categories of Lifestyle Studies

Activities	Interests	Opinions
Work	Family	Themselves
Hobbies	Home	Social Issues
Social Events	Job	Politics
Vacation	Community	Business
Entertainment	Recreation	Economics
Club Membership	Fashion	Education
Community	Food	Products
Shopping	Media	Future
Sports	Achievements	Culture

consumers to answer AIO statements using a Likert scale. In one popular approach, consumers choose from five possible responses, ranging from strongly agree (scored +2) to strongly disagree (scored −2). Consumer responses can be analyzed by cross-tabulating each statement on the basis of variables believed important for market segmentation strategies, such as gender and age, or by looking at the mean response within these categories. If too many AIO statements are included in the research, it may become difficult to understand the basic structure of consumer lifestyles influencing purchase and consumption behavior. Thus, researchers often use techniques such as multidimensional scaling, principal components analysis, or exploratory factor analysis to reduce the number of related "dimensions" or "factors," based on their covariance or intercorrelations.[84]

Taking a psychographic approach, Procter & Gamble identified a core consumer insight into why people like to drink coffee and turned that into a brand appeal for Folgers coffee. In its ads, Folgers appealed to consumers' memories of smelling coffee brewing in their homes when they were young. For this generation, Folgers meant returning home to the safety and comfort of family. In the 1990s, however, a younger, more mobile group of coffee drinkers was born—the Starbucks generation. Coffee didn't mean a return to home (which for many meant divorce and unhappy childhoods)—Starbucks, rather, became a status symbol and icon for freedom and success. It also meant that a majority of coffee consumption was occurring outside the home. How could P&G compete with the fresh ground coffee and new image of Starbucks? It created Millstone, a fresh-ground gourmet coffee (in gourmet flavors) positioned to reach this new coffee-shop lifestyle segment. It packaged the coffee in bags rather than cans, offered more flavors, and let consumers bring coffee-shop coffee and aroma home with a grocery store brand.

With psychographic analysis, marketers can understand their core customers' lifestyles better and develop packaging and communication programs that position products to their various lifestyle attributes. How does the marketer of a new pasta dinner kit want to show the product in an ad? Should it show how easy it is to make the pasta (showing the man of the house preparing it without making a mess in the kitchen), or should it show how delicious it is (having people consume it at an elegant dinner table with candlelight and flowers)? The idea is to go beyond standard demographics to position the product in line with the activities, hopes, fears, and dreams of the product's best customers.

Marketers should beware, however, of recognizing certain AIOs and lifestyles and ignoring others, which sometimes represent a backlash to what has become popular. In the late 1980s, there was a dramatic rise in America's desire to be healthy and lose weight, which gave rise to the "healthy" lifestyle segment. Fat-free, low-sugar, and meatless products found their way into mainstream America with a plethora of marketers introducing everything from fat-free potato chips to cholesterol-free egg substitutes. Although these products are still popular, other marketers focused on the "rest of the population." Häagen-Dazs and Ben & Jerry's ice creams continue to satisfy the taste buds of the not-so-health-conscious consumer as well as health-conscious consumers who decide to "splurge." Just because consumers may belong to a particular lifestyle segment does not mean that they don't exhibit some "cross-over" behaviors.

Similarly, many consumers are living stressful, hectic lives—they have families, careers, and many obligations that prevent them from enjoying everyday activities like taking a walk or being with friends. Some people caught in this hectic sort of lifestyle are making drastic changes. They are leaving the big cities and two-hour commutes to and from work, and opting for a simpler lifestyle. They are willing to live on less in order to enjoy more time with their families, activities like gardening, and less stress.[85]

VALS™

A widely used approach to lifestyle marketing is the Values and Lifestyle System (VALS)™ developed at SRI International. The original program, based on how consumers agreed or disagreed with various social issue statements, identified nine American lifestyles, shown in Figure 7.13. The problem was that most consumers fell into only two of the categories, leaving the others too small to be significant to marketers. Further, as more consumers began to agree with the social issues measured, the results were less indicative of behavior.

As a result, VALS2™ was formulated in 1989. It captures consumers' attitudes and values by measuring how strongly they agree or disagree with phrases such as "I like a lot of excitement in my life" and "I like being in charge of a group." How consumers respond leads to classification of their self-orientations, which signify the goals and behaviors to which they will aspire. These self-orientations can be described as:

- **Principle oriented:** they make purchase decisions based on their beliefs and principles rather than what others think.
- **Status oriented:** these consumers are heavily influenced by the beliefs, opinions, and views of others.
- **Action oriented:** these individuals buy products to affect their environment and seek activity, variety, and risk taking.

In addition to self-orientation, the other dimension of the VALS2™ typology is resources, which refers to the physical, psychological, material, and demographic resources consumers have available to pursue their self-orientations.

VALS2™ defines eight categories of lifestyles. Marketers can use these descriptions and how many consumers fall into each category to help guide advertising and positioning statements.

- **Actualizers:** successful, active, sophisticated consumers with many re sources and high self-esteem. They place importance on their image.
- **Fulfilleds:** satisfied, mature, comfortable, reflective people who tend to be practical and look for functionality, value, and durability in the products they buy.

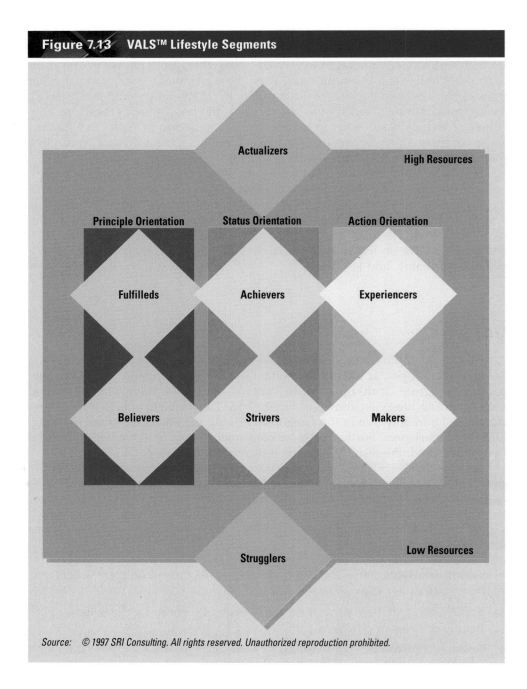

Figure 7.13   VALS™ Lifestyle Segments

- **Believers:** also principle oriented. They are conservative, with beliefs based on the established codes of church, community, family, and nation. They tend to buy proven brands and products made in the United States.

- **Achievers:** career-oriented people who like to feel in control of their lives and prefer predictability to risk and self-discovery. Their social lives revolve around family, church, and career. They prefer prestige brands that signal success to their peers.

- **Strivers:** concerned about the approval of others and seek self-definition, security, and the image of success. Although they emulate those they strive to be like, they lack the resources to attain their goals at that time.

- **Experiencers:** young, enthusiastic, impulsive consumers who like risk taking, variety, and excitement. They like new and off-beat products and activities. Because of their age, they have not formulated life values, behaviors, or political affiliation.

- **Makers:** focus on self-sufficiency, live within the context of family and work, and pay little attention to issues outside that realm. They can be found fixing cars and canning foods, and envy only material possessions that are functional, such as new tools or trucks.

- **Strugglers:** poor and usually poorly educated, have no social bonds, and are concerned with issues of the moment, such as obtaining food and healthcare. They are cautious consumers and seek security and safety.

Advertising agencies and marketing organizations use VALS to segment markets and communicate more effectively with segments. Mountain Dew has targeted effectively the Experiencers with their bold, loud, action-oriented ads that feature young people jumping out of airplanes and doing other extreme sports. It has become *the* drink for consumers in this group. Wal*Mart has positioned itself to the Maker market, appealing to the "Made in America" sentiment of this group and offering them products they need to take care of their families and be self-sufficient.

VALS™ and LOV

Although VALS gained rapid acceptance and widespread usage in marketing, it has its limitations. First, consumers are not "pure" in their type of lifestyle. Second, because VALS is a proprietary database, academic researchers may not feel comfortable with the reliability and validity of information reported. Fully identifying the variables used in the analysis, confirmatory factor analyses of the various scales used, the number of statistical relations that were tested, and the exact significance of test statistics would do much to allay these concerns.

An alternative to VALS is the List of Values (LOV) approach.[86] The LOV asks consumers to rate seven statements that were derived from the RVS. Although neither the RVS nor the LOV measures the comprehensive set of the universal values identified by Schwartz, both have proved useful in marketing research.[87] Researchers[88] compared VALS with LOV and found that when used with demographic data, the LOV approach predicted consumer behavior better than VALS.[89] When LOV is augmented with measures of more general values—such as materialism—the predictive power is further improved.[90]

Global Lifestyles

Increased globalization of markets requires that marketing strategy increasingly be planned on a global basis. VALS and other approaches have been used to identify lifestyle segments across country borders,[91] and the VALS typology has been used successfully to segment Canadian markets.[92] One of the most comprehensive studies of values on a wide range of topics in Europe was published by Ashford and Timms,[93] and deserves careful study by anyone interested in the values of Europeans. This study shows how values vary between Western European countries as well as changes over time. The study shows that the overwhelming majority of people in each country say that they are happy. There are no significant differences between men and women in any of the countries surveyed, but some countries enjoy higher levels of happiness than others. Schwartz's values have been shown to be especially useful in fast-changing transitional economies, such as those in Asia, Eastern Europe, and southern Africa, for relating value differences to the demographic characteristics of consumers and for explaining differences in lifestyle interests, brand loyalty, and innovative consumer behavior.[94]

Multiple Measures of Individual Behavior

As you have seen in this chapter, several measures of individual behavior are used in the analysis of consumer behavior. Demographics, including economic resources, have a major effect on buying, but lifestyles, values, and personality provide even more understanding of why people buy and consume products. Using some or all of these measures provides a way of defining market segments and an understanding of the segments that will be growing in the future.

Summary

Many variables or bases can be used to segment a market. Some of these bases include (1) personality, (2) demographic, (3) psychographic, and (4) values. Demographics focus on how the populations of the world are changing by monitoring birth rates, death rates, immigration, and economic resources. Consumer behavior analysts are increasingly required to understand buying and consumption decisions on a global basis. The fastest growing country in the world in population is India. African countries such as Kenya and Nigeria have rapid population growth but low income. The search for markets that have both population growth and good or improving economic conditions often leads to the Pacific Rim.

Beyond demographics, consumer analysts need to examine personality, values, and lifestyles. Deciding what products to buy and use varies between individuals because of the unique characteristics possessed by each individual. Personality is defined as consistent responses to environmental stimuli. Three major theories or approaches to the study of personality include psychoanalytic, socio-psychological, and trait factor. Personal values also explain individual differences among consumers. Rokeach developed the RVS and identified values as terminal and instrumental, or the ends to which behavior is directed and the means of attaining those ends. Schwartz developed the SVS, which identifies the value system that underlies motivations, and appears to have broad generality across disparate cultures.

Lifestyles are patterns in which people live and spend time and money. They are the result of the total array of economic, cultural, and social life forces that contribute to a person's human qualities. Psychographics or AIOs measure the operational form of lifestyles. AIO stands for activities, interests, and opinions, and may be either general or product specific. VALS2 is a system used to segment American consumers into eight primary categories and can be helpful in guiding marketing communication and product positioning strategies.

Review and Discussion Questions

1. "Analysis of consumer trends is obviously important for firms marketing consumer products but of limited value to industrial marketers." Evaluate this statement.

2. Will there be more or fewer births in the future in the United States? What variables should be considered in answering this question?

3. Assume a marketer of major appliances is interested in the effects of the baby boomers on demand for the company's products. What are your conclusions, and what, if any, research should be conducted to answer the question more fully?

4. "Maturity markets are growing in number very rapidly, but they are of little interest to marketers because they have little money compared with younger markets." Analyze this statement.

5. Which countries of the world will provide the best consumer markets in the next 5 to 10 years? In the next 10 to 30 years? Why?

6. How do you reconcile the belief that India represents an attractive market when reports indicate such a low per capita GNP?

7. Assume that a manufacturer of shoes wishes a market analysis on how to enter the most profitable markets in Africa. What should be included in the report?

8. Clearly distinguish between the following terms: lifestyles, psychographics, AIO measures, personality, and values.

9. Using the VALS2™ categories of lifestyle, choose a product and two different segments, and describe how the positioning and communication strategies would differ for the two segments.

10. Describe the trait-factor theory of personality and assess its importance in past and future marketing research.

11. Assume that you are developing an advertising program for an airline. How would you use laddering to assist in the development of the program?

12. How might personal values be used to segment markets for financial services? Could similar approaches be used in less-developed countries as well as industrialized markets?

Endnotes

1. David K. Foot, *Boom Bust & Echo* (Toronto: Macfarlane Walter & Ross, 1996), 2.

2. George Katona, *Psychological Economics* (New York: Elsevier Scientific Publishing, 1975).

3. John Knodel, "Deconstructing Population Momentum," *Population Today* (March 1999), 1–2.

4. "Projected Fertility Rates," U.S. Department of Commerce, Bureau of the Census, No. 98, 79.

5. Joseph O. Rentz and Fred D. Reynolds, "Forecasting the Effects of an Aging Population on Product Consumption: An Age-Period-Cohort Framework," *Journal of Marketing Research* 28 (August 1991), 355–360.

6. James Heckman, "Say 'buy-buy,'" *Marketing News* (October 11, 1999).

7. James U. McNeal and Chyon-Hwa Yeh, "Born to Shop," *American Demographics* (June 1993), 34–39.

8. "Teens, Toddlers Intriguing Market," *Mass Merchandise Retailer* (October 19, 1998), 16.

9. Heather Chaplin, "The Truth Hurts," *American Demographics* (April 1999), 68.

10. Marcia Mogelonsky, "Product Overload?" *American Demographics* (August 1998), 65–69.

11. Dennis H. Tootelian and Ralph M. Gaedeke, "The Teen Market: An Exploratory Analysis of Income, Spending, and Shopping Patterns," *Journal of Consumer Marketing* 9 (Fall 1992).

12. Nina Munk, "Girl Power," *Fortune* (December 8, 1997).

13. Alison Stein Wellner, "The Young and The Uninsured," *American Demographics* (February 1999), 73–77.

14. Bob Losyk, "Generation X: What They Think and What They Plan to Do," *The Futurist* (March/April 1997), 39–44.

15. Harry Dent, *The Roaring 2000s* (New York: Simon & Schuster, 1998).

16. For additional examples, see Dale Blackwell and Roger Blackwell, "Yuppies, Muppies and Puppies: They Are Changing Real Estate Markets," *Ohio Realtor* (August 1989), 11–15; Roger D. Blackwell and Margaret Hanke, "The Credit Card and the Aging Baby Boomers," *Journal of Retail Banking* 9 (Spring 1987), 17–25.

17. Carlos Tejada and Patrick Barta, "Hey, Baby Boomers Need Their Space, OK?" *The Wall Street Journal* (January 7, 2000), A1–A6.

18. Robert E. Wilkes, "A Structural Modeling Approach to the Measurement and Meaning of Cognitive Age," *Journal of Consumer Research* 19 (September 1992), 292–301.

19. George Moschis, "Marketing to Older Adults," *Journal of Consumer Marketing* 8 (Fall 1991), 33–41.

20. Thomas Moehrle, "Expenditure Patterns of the Elderly: Workers and Nonworkers," *Monthly Labor Review* 113 (May 1990), 34–41.

21. Paula Fitzgerald Bone, "Identifying Mature Segments," *Journal of Consumer Marketing* 8 (Fall 1991), 19–32.

22. Benny Barak, "Elderly Solitary Survivors and Social Policy: The Case for Widows," in Andrew Mitchell, *Advances in Consumer Research* (1984), 27–30.

23. Ivan Ross, "Information Processing and the Older Consumer: Marketing and Public Policy Implications," in Mitchell, *Advances,* 31–39.

24. Carolyn Yoon, "Age Differences in Consumers' Processing Strategies: An Investigation of Moderating Influences," *Journal of Consumer Research* 24 (December 1997), 329–342.

25. Nark D. Uncles and Andrew S. C. Ehrenberg, "Brand Choice among Older Consumers," *Journal of Advertising Research* 30 (August/September 1990), 19–22.

26. Alan J. Greco and Linda E. Swayne, "Sales Response of Elderly Consumers to Point-of-Purchase Advertising," *Journal of Advertising Research* 32 (September/October 1992), 43–53.

27. Jane Jacobs, *Cities and the Wealth of Nations* (New York: Random House, 1984).

28. "Charting the Pain Behind the Gain," *The Wall Street Journal* (October 1, 1999), B1.

29. Shannon McCaffrey, "Income gap for families is widening, report says," *The Columbus Dispatch* (January 18, 2000), 1A–2A.

30. Jacob M Schlesinger, Tristan Mabry, and Sarah Lueck, "Charting the Pain Behind the Gain."

31. Thomas J. Stanley and William D. Danko, *The Millionaire Next Door* (New York: Pocket Books, 1998).

32. Wendy Zellner, Rob Hof, Larry Armstrong, and Geoff Smith, "Shop Till The Ball Drops," *Business Week* (January 10, 2000), 42–44.

33. Valarie A. Zeithaml, "Service Quality, Profitability, and Economic Worth of Customers: What We Know and What We Need to Learn," *Journal of the Academy of Marketing Science* 28, 1, 67–85.

34. Marcia Mogelonsky, "Those With More Buy for Less," *American Demographics* (April 1999), 18–19.

35. "Seizing the Dark Day," *Business Week* (January 13, 1992), 26–28.

36. William J. Brown, "The Use of Entertainment Television Programs for Promoting Prosocial Messages," *Howard Journal of Communications* 3 (Winter/Spring 1992), 253–266.

37. Nua Internet Surveys, Webchek: South African Teenagers Surge Online (December 17, 1999).

38. "Caged, a Survey of India," *The Economist* (May 4, 1991).

39. Valerie Reitman, "India Anticipates the Arrival of the Beefless Big Mac," *The Wall Street Journal* (October 20, 1993), B1.

40. Anthony Spaeth, "A Thriving Middle Class Is Changing the Face of India," *The Wall Street Journal* (May 19, 1988), 22.

41. Grame Hugo, *Australia's Changing Population: Trends and Implications* (Oxford: Oxford University Press, 1987).

42. Bruce W. Nelan, "Watch Out for China," *Time* (November 29, 1993), 36–39.

43. Jerry Stafford, "Vast China Market Just Waiting to Be Researched," *Marketing News* (September 12, 1986), 1.

44. Nua Internet Surveys, China Internet Network Information Center: Amount of Chinese Internet Users Explodes (January 21, 2000).

45. Sandra Burton, "A New Me Generation," *Time* (November 29, 1993), 39.

46. Leslie Chang, "Teenage Band Tries to Rock China," *The Wall Street Journal* (July 21, 1999), B1.

47. Tohru Nishikawa, "New Product Development: Japanese Consumer Tastes in the Area of Electronics and Home Appliances," *Journal of Advertising Research* 30, 2 (1990), 30.

48. "Perestroika: The Consumer Signals," *Euromarketing Insights,* 2 (February 1991), 4. For statistical information on the European Community, see sources such as Brian Morris, Klaus Boehm, and Maurice Geller, *The European Community* (Berlin: Walter DeGruyter & Co., 1991); Secretariat of The Economic Commission for Europe, *Economic Survey of Europe* (New York: United Nations Publication, 1991); Alan Tillier, *Doing Business in Today's*

Western Europe (Chicago: NTC Business Books, 1992).

49. Jim Engel, Roger Blackwell, and Paul Miniard, *Consumer Behavior*, 8th edition (Fort Worth: Harcourt, 1995) 124.

50. Randall Litchfield, "Competitiveness and the Constitution," *Canadian Business* (August 1991), 18.

51. H. Kassarjian, "Personality and Consumer Behavior: A Review," *Journal of Marketing Research* (November 1971), 409–418.

52. For descriptions of major personality theories, see Walter Mischel, *Introduction to Personality: A New Look* (New York: CBS College Publishing, 1986); and Larry Hjelle and Daniel Ziegler, *Personality Theories: Basic Assumptions, Research and Applications* (New York: McGraw-Hill, 1987).

53. For a marketing view of psychoanalytic theory, see W. D. Wells and A. D. Beard, "Personality and Consumer Behavior," in Scott Ward and T. S. Robertson, eds., *Consumer Behavior: Theoretical Sources* (Englewood Cliffs, NJ: Prentice-Hall, 1973).

54. The classic example of this literature is Ernest Dichter, *Handbook of Consumer Motivations* (New York: McGraw-Hill, 1964). For an example of motivation research by Dr. Dichter, see the "Swan Cleaners" case in Roger D. Blackwell, James E. Engel, and W Wayne Talarzyk, *Contemporary Cases in Consumer Behavior* (Chicago: Dryden, 1990), 135–142.

55. Jeffrey F. Durgee, "Interpreting Dichter's Interpretations: An Analysis of Consumption Symbolism in The Handbook of Consumer Motivations," in Hanne Hartvig-Larsen, David Glen Mick, and Christian Alstead, eds., *Marketing and Semiotics: Selected Papers from Copenhagen Symposium* (Copenhagen, 1991).

56. For a more complete explanation of this approach, see C. S. Hall and G. Lindzey, *Theories of Personality* (New York: John Wiley & Sons, 1970), 154–155.

57. J. B. Cohen, "An Interpersonal Orientation to the Study of Consumer Behavior," *Journal of Marketing Research* 4 (August 1967), 270–278; J. B. Cohen, "Toward an Interpersonal Theory of Consumer Behavior," *California Management Review* 10 (1968), 73–80. Also see Jon P. Noerager, "An Assessment of CAD: A Personality Instrument Developed Specifically for Marketing Research," *Journal of Marketing Research* (February 1979), 53–59.

58. J. B. Cohen, "An Interpersonal Orientation to the Study of Consumer Behavior," *Journal of Marketing Research* 4 (August 1967), 270–278; J. B. Cohen, "Toward an Interpersonal Theory of Consumer Behavior," *California Management Review,*

10 (1968), 73–80. Also see Jon P. Noerager, "An Assessment of CAD: A Personality Instrument Developed Specifically for Marketing Research," *Journal of Marketing Research* (February 1979), 53–59.

59. A good introduction to the theory and techniques of this approach is found in A. R. Buss and W. Poley, *Individual Differences: Traits and Factors* (New York: Halsted Press, 1976).

60. Curtis Haugtvedt, Richard E. Petty, and John T. Cacioppo, "Need for Cognition and Advertising: Understanding the Role of Personality Variables in Consumer Behavior," *Journal of Consumer Psychology* 1 (1992): 239–260.

61. Raymond L. Horton, "The Edwards Personal Preference Schedule and Consumer Personality Research," *Journal of Marketing Research* 11 (August 1974), 335–337.

62. Kathryn E. A. Villani and Yoram Wind, "On the Usage of 'Modified' Personality Trait Measures in Consumer Research," *Journal of Consumer Research* 2 (December 1975), 223–226.

63. Mark I. Alpert, "Personality and the Determinants of Product Choice," *Journal of Marketing Research* 9 (February 1972), 89–92.

64. Paul E. Green, Yoram Wind, and Arun K. Jain, "A Note on Measurement of Social-Psychological Belief Systems," *Journal of Marketing Research* 9 (May 1972), 204–208.

65. The classic study of this topic is E. B. Evans, "Psychological Objective Factors in the Prediction of Brand Choice: Ford Versus Chevrolet," *Journal of Business* 32 (1959), 340–369.

66. Shalom H. Schwartz, "Value Priorities and Behavior: Applying a Theory of Integrated Value Systems," in Clive Seligman, James M. Olson, and Mark P. Zanna, eds., *The Psychology of Values: The Ontario Symposium* 8 (Mahwah, NJ: Lawrence Erlbaum, 1996), 1–24.

67. Steven M. Burgess, and Jan-Benedict E. M. Steenkamp, "Value Priorities and Consumer Behavior in a Transitional Economy," in Rajeev Batra, ed., *Marketing Issues in Transitional Economies* (Norwell, MA: Kluwer Academic Press, 1999), 85–105.

69. Lynn R. Kahle, "Contemporary Research on Consumer and Business Social Values," *Journal of Business Research* 20, 2 (1990), 81–82; Lynn R. Kahle, "Social Values and Consumer Behavior: Research from the List of Values," in Clive Seligman, James M. Olson, and Mark P. Zanna, eds., *The Psychology of Values: The Ontario Symposium* 8 (Mahwah, NJ: Lawrence Erlbaum, 1996), 135–152.

69. Steven M. Burgess, "Personal Values and Consumer Research: An Historical Perspective," in Jagdish N. Sheth, ed., *Research in Marketing* 11 (Greenwich, CT: JAI Press, 1992), 35–80.

70. Milton Rokeach, *The Nature of Human Values* (New York: Free Press, 1973), 5; also see M. Rokeach and S. J. Ball-Rokeach, "Stability and Change in American Value Priorities," 1968–1981, *American Psychologist* 44 (May 1989), 773–784.

71. Klaus G. Grunert, Suzanne C. Grunert, and Sharon E. Beatty, "Cross-Cultural Research on Consumer Values," *Marketing and Research Today* (February 1989), 30–39; J. M. Munson and E. F. McQuarrie, "Shortening the Rokeach Value Survey for Use in Consumer Research," *Advances in Consumer Research* 15 (Association for Consumer Research, 1988), 381–386; S. W. Perkings and T. J. Reynolds, "The Explanatory Power of Values in Preference Judgments Validation of the Means-End Perspective," *Advances in Consumer Research* 15 (Association for Consumer Research, 1988), 122–126; G. Roehrich, Pierre Valette-Florence, and Bernard Rappachi, "Combined Incidence of Personal Values, Involvement, and Innovativeness on Innovative Consumer Behavior," in *Is Marketing Keeping Up with the Consumer? Lessons from Changing Products, Attitudes and Behavior* (Vienna, Austria: ESOMAR, 1989), 261–279; D. K. Tse, J. K. Wong, and C. T. Tan, "Towards Some Standard Cross-Cultural Consumption Values," *Advances in Consumer Research* 15 (Association for Consumer Research, 1988), 387–395; Pierre Valette-Florence and Alain Jolibert, "Social Values, A.I.O. and Consumption Patterns: Exploratory Findings," *Journal of Business Research* 20 (March 1990), 109–122. Jan-Benedict E. M. Steenkamp, Frenkel Ter Hofstede, and Michel Wedel, "A Cross-National Investigation into the Individual and Cultural Antecedents of Consumer Innovativeness," *Journal of Marketing Research* 36 (February 1999), 1–17.

72. Donald E. Vinson, Jerome E. Scott, and Lawrence M. Lamont, "The Role of Personal Values in Marketing and Consumer Behavior," *Journal of Marketing* 41 (April 1977), 44–50.

73. Robert E. Pitts and Arch G. Woodside, "Personal Values and Market Segmentation: Applying the Value Construct," in R. E. Pitts and A. G. Woodside (1984), 55–67.

74. Wagner A. Kamakura and Jose Alfonso Masson, "Value Segmentation: A Model for the Measurement of Values and Value Systems," *Journal of Consumer Research* 18 (September 1991), 208–218.

75. Shalom H. Schwartz, Sonia Roccas, and Lelach Sagiv, "Universals in the Content and Structure of Values: Theoretical Advances and Empirical Tests in 20 Countries," *Advances in Experimental Social Psychology* 25 (1992), 1–49; S. H. Schwartz, A. Lehmann, and S. Roccas, "Multimethod Probes of Basic Human Values," in J. Adamopoulos and Y. Kashima, eds., *Social Psychology and Cultural Context* (Newbury Park, CA: Sage Publications, 1999).

76. Shalom H. Schwartz and Lelach Sagiv, "Identifying Culture-Specifics in the Content and Structure of Values," *Journal of Cross-Cultural Psychology* 23 (1992).

77. Schwartz, Roccas, and Sagiv, "Universals in the Content and Structure of Values."

78. S. M. Burgess, and R. D. Blackwell, "Personal Values and South African Financial Services Brand Preference," *South African Journal of Business Management* 25, 1 (1994), 22–29.

79. Thomas J. Reynolds and Jonathan Gutman, "Advertising Is Image Management," *Journal of Advertising Research* 24 (February/March 1984), 27–36.

80. Thomas J. Reynolds and Jonathan Gutman, "Laddering Theory, Method, Analysis, and Interpretation," *Journal of Advertising Research* 28 (February/March 1988), 11–31.

81. Richard P. Bagozzi, and Pratiba A. Dabholkar, "Consumer Recycling Goals and Their Effect on Decisions to Recycle: A Means-End Chain Analysis," *Psychology & Marketing* 11 (July/August 1994), 313–340; Richard P. Bagozzi, and Pratiba A. Dabholkar, "Discursive Psychology: An Alternative Conceptual Foundation to Means-End Chain Theory," *Psychology and Marketing* 17 (2000); see also the special issue of *International Journal of Research in Marketing* 12, 3, which was devoted to laddering, especially R. Pieters, H. Baumgartner, and D. Allen, "A Means-End Chain Approach to Consumer Goal Structures," *International Journal of Research in Marketing* 12, 3 (1995), 227–244.

82. George A. Kelly, *The Psychology of Personal Constructs* (New York: W. W. Norton, 1955); also see Fred Reynolds and William Darden, "Construing Life Style and Psychographics," in William D. Wells, ed., *Life Style and Psychographics* (Chicago: American Marketing Association, 1974), 71–96.

83. Reynolds and Darden, "Construing Life Style," 87.

84. Introductions to these multivariate techniques are available in J. F. Hair Jr., R. E. Anderson, R. L. Tatham, and W. C. Black, *Multivariate Data Analysis with Readings,* 5th ed. (Englewood Cliffs, NJ: Prentice-Hall, 1998); and George H. Dunteman, *Introduction to Multivariate Analysis* (Beverly Hills, CA: Sage Publications, 1984).

85. Glen Thrush, *American Demographics* (January 1999), 67–72.

86. Lynn R. Kahle, *Social Values and Social Change: Adaptation to Life in America* (New York: Praeger, 1983).

87. Lynn R. Kahle, and Larry Chiagouris, eds., *Values, Lifestyles, and Psychographics* (Mahwah, NJ: Lawrence Erlbaum, 1997).

88. Lynn R. Kahle, Sharon E. Beatty, and Pamela Homer, "Alternative Measurement Approaches to Consumer Values: The List of Values (LOV) and Values and Life Styles (VALS)," *Journal of Consumer Research* 13 (December 1986), 405–409; see also Burgess, "Personal Values and Consumer Behavior: An Historical Perspective"; and Matthew Perri III "Application of the List of Values Alternative Psychographic Assessment Scale," *Psychological Reports* 66 (July 1990), 403–406.

89. Thomas P. Novak and Bruce MacEvoy, "On Comparing Alternative Segmentation Schemes: The List of Values (LOV) and Values and Life Styles (VALS)," *Journal of Consumer Research* 17 (June 1990), 105–109.

90. Kim P. Corfman, Donald R. Lehmann, and Sarah Narayanan, "Values, Utility, and Ownership: Modeling the Relationships for Consumer Durables," *Journal of Retailing* 67 (Summer 1991), 184–204.

91. Arnold Mitchell, "Nine American Lifestyles: Values and Societal Change," *The Futurist* 18 (August 1984), 4–13.

92. Ian Pearson, "Social Studies," *Canadian Business* 58 (1985), 67–73.

93. Sheena Ashford and Noel Timms, *What Europe Thinks: A Study of Western European Values* (Aldershot: Dartmouth Publishing Company Limited, 1992).

94. Burgess and Steenkamp, "Value Priorities and Consumer Behavior in a Transitional Economy"; Steven M. Burgess, and M. Harris, "Values, Optimum Stimulation Levels and Brand Loyalty: New Scales in New Populations," *South African Journal of Business Management* 29, 4 (1998), 142–157.

CHAPTER 8

Consumer Motivation

OPENING VIGNETTE

On the waterfront, America is split into two segments: One, a shrinking majority, still drinks its water from taps at a cost that rarely exceeds a penny a gallon. The other demands bottled water at a cost that routinely tops the cost of gasoline. Since 1976, America's taste for bottled water has grown more than tenfold, from 255 million gallons to 3 billion. In 1997, Americans drank about 12 gallons of bottled water per capita. By comparison, French consumers average around 25 gallons, thus suggesting that there is still ample room in America for even greater consumption.

Thanks to explosive growth in sales of half-liter bottles that seem to be issued with running shoes, bottled water is more portable, its consumption more visible, than ever. Demographically, it's most popular among Americans to whom appearance is very important: younger, better-educated singles in outdoorsy states like California, Texas, and Florida.

Why are Americans today drinking so much more bottled water than a generation ago? Health concerns are one reason. Consumers' fears about the quality of tap water have been fed by localized outbreaks of waterborne disease. A 1993 outbreak in Milwaukee affected over 400,000 people, 50 of whom died. Yet death by tap water is about as likely as death by lightning. Regardless, a 1997 Water Quality Association survey showed that 75 percent of adult Americans have concerns about their household water supply. That's up from 50 percent two years earlier. And 33 percent said they do not believe their water is as safe as it should be. For these consumers, bottled water is seen as a safer alternative.

Taste is another reason. Some consumers perceive bottled water as possessing a cleaner and more desirable taste than the chlorinated aftertaste of tap water.

Are there other reasons why consumers buy bottled water? Yes there are. Consumer behaviorists say one source of satisfaction from drinking bottled water is a refreshed affirmation that the drinker can afford it. Explains Laurie Ries, an Atlanta marketing consultant, "It shows you are well-off enough to pay for something you don't necessarily need." This symbolism is not limited to what consumption of bottled water indicates about one's wealth. Bottled water has become a global icon for health consciousness. It enables drinkers to project a healthy image to those present during consumption. In either case, it is the product's symbolic image that motivates purchase behavior.

Source: Excerpted in part from Frank Greve, "Bottled Water: A Sign of Health or Wealth?" Miami Herald *(May 20, 1998), 7A; "The Water We Drink: Bottled or from the Tap,"* Health & You *(Blue Cross/Blue Shield, 1998), 1.*

One of the most fundamental questions that companies must answer about consumer behavior is: "Why do people buy our product?" Answering this question requires understanding consumer motivation. **Consumer motivation** represents *the drive to satisfy both physiological and psychological needs through product purchase and consumption.*[1] Implementing the marketing concept of providing products that satisfy consumers' needs must first begin with an understanding of what these needs are.

As shown by the chapter opener, there are multiple reasons why many consumers are willing to pay for an otherwise free commodity. The need for a healthier consumption experience leads some to buy. Others are looking for a better-tasting consumption experience. And some buy and consume bottled water because they are motivated to project a certain image of themselves to other people.

Although it is not feasible to describe in this chapter all the different types of needs that drive consumer behavior, it is possible and worthwhile to discuss some of them. In the following section, we review some of the needs that shape what people buy and consume.

Types of Consumer Needs

During the past century, psychologists and marketers alike have tried their hand at identifying and classifying needs.[2] Sometimes needs are classified into very broad categories (e.g., utilitarian-functional versus hedonic-experiential needs). Sometimes a very detailed list of needs is provided. What follows falls somewhere in between these two extremes.

Physiological Needs

Physiological needs are the most fundamental type of consumer needs. Indeed, our very survival depends on satisfying these needs. We must have food and water. And it wasn't too long ago in the history of mankind that satisfying these needs absorbed substantial amounts of people's time and energy. Raising crops, scouring for wild fruits and berries, hunting and/or fishing were activities undertaken by nearly everyone.

Although satisfying their need for food and water remains omnipresent for millions of people on our planet, those more fortunate live in a time where these needs are fulfilled with relatively little effort. Entire industries have developed that cater to our physiological needs. Food producers and manufacturers, beverage makers, grocery stores, and restaurants have freed many consumers from worrying about where their next meal is coming from. And with home delivery, need fulfillment is only a phone call away.

Physiological needs involve more than what we eat and drink. Humans need to sleep, and many people will spend one-third or more of their lives sleeping. This need has given birth to many product categories, including beds, mattresses, sleeping bags, pillows, sheets, and various sleeping aids. Sexual needs are also part of our physiological needs. The recent runaway success of the anti-impotency drug Viagra, with sales reaching $1 billion in its first year on the market, provides strong testament to the importance of our sexual needs.[3]

Safety and Health Needs

Once upon a time, mankind constantly worried about becoming some predator's next meal. Fortunately, those days are long gone. Even so, threats to our safety abound. Mother Nature, terrorists, criminals, drunk drivers, diseases and ailments new and old, product malfunctions, and simple human error jeopardize our health and safety. Safety needs motivate the purchase of firearms and other personal protection devices, hurricane shutters, home security systems, and residences within gated communities. During the 1990s, safety concerns fueled the sales of over-sized sport utility vehicles, trucks, and vans that made their drivers feel less vulnerable and in greater control. Even when safety is not the primary motivation behind purchase, it can still be a deciding factor. Some avoid certain forms of transportation (e.g., flying) and entertainment (e.g., skydiving) because they worry about whether they'll survive the experience.

Given the centrality of consumers' need for safety, companies, even entire industries, have benefited from connecting their products to this need. As reflected by the ad shown in Figure 8.1, Michelin's advertising tries to win customers by appealing to consumers' safety needs. The steel industry has been upgrading its image by emphasizing the metal's safety in its recent advertising. To learn more about this, look at Consumer in Focus 8.1.

Similarly, the need to maintain or improve our health, both mental and physical, is the foundation upon which many goods and services have been built. Medicines, hospitals, vitamins, exercise clubs and equipment, health foods and numerous health-related books, magazines and television shows owe their existence to consumers' health needs. Prescription drug sales in America have increased nearly five-fold since 1989 and are projected to exceed $100 billion in 2000 (see Figure 8.2).

Figure 8.1   Michelin Appeals to Consumers' Safety Needs

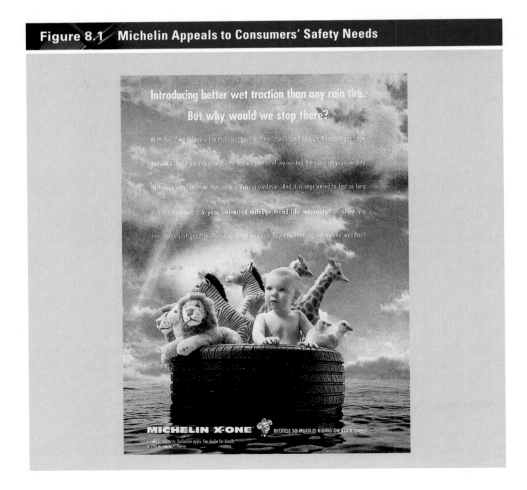

Consumer in Focus 8.1

The Steel Industry Connects with Consumers' Need for Safety

Throughout the 1980s, steelmakers invested roughly $50 billion to make steel lighter, cheaper, and higher quality. Their customers, including major appliance makers, recognized these innovations. But the end users—consumers who were driving the cars and loading the washing machines—didn't have a clue. If consumers didn't understand steel's benefits, they might not demand the material in the products they buy. And a drop in consumer demand would lead to a drop in orders from the industry's top clients.

The industry was particularly concerned about the low opinion of steel held by women. Women in U.S. households often decide or heavily influence purchases of the kinds of big-ticket items frequently made of steel. Research showed that their opinions stemmed more from a lack of awareness about steel than from negative feelings. Consequently, a na-

tional advertising campaign was launched in 1997 focusing on safety and environmental themes—major issues with women. Images that reflected the strength and reliability of steel were central elements of the commercials. One ad showed a diver in an underwater steel cage surrounded by menacing sharks.

Overall, viewers took from the ads that steel could protect them, which fed into their need for safety. Within the campaign's first year, public awareness of steel and its products jumped from 13 to 26 percent. People were thinking positive thoughts, too. By August 1998, positive mentions of the steel industry had risen to 78 percent, up from 24 percent in May 1997. The percentage of negative mentions fell to 1 percent from 37 percent.

Source: Excerpted from "Tough But Sensitive," American Demographics *(March 1999), 56.*

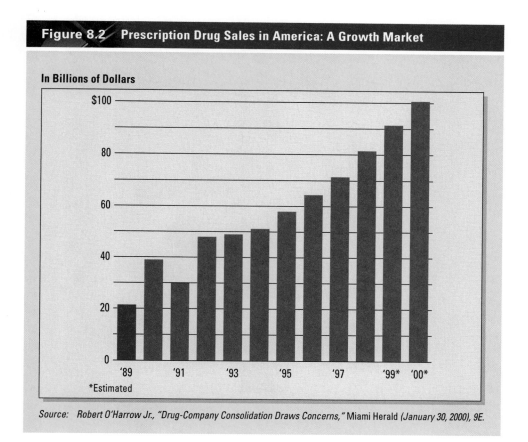

Figure 8.2   Prescription Drug Sales in America: A Growth Market

In Billions of Dollars

Source: Robert O'Harrow Jr., "Drug-Company Consolidation Draws Concerns," Miami Herald *(January 30, 2000), 9E.*

As we grow older, our health begins to deteriorate. Consequently, the health needs of older individuals are usually much more pressing than those of younger ones. And Americans, on average, are getting older. The tens of millions born during the population explosion following World War II through the mid-1960s (the baby boomer generation) are now moving into the 50-plus age category. The beginning of the 21st century will see an unprecedented increase in the number of Americans over 50. For this reason, industries and companies catering to consumers' health will reap the benefits that come from serving a growing market. You can expect many companies to jump on the health bandwagon when promoting their products. Two examples of this appear in Figure 8.3a and b.

The Need for Love and Companionship

By and large, humans are social creatures. Although the idea of being stranded all alone on a deserted island may appeal to some, most of us would prefer sharing the island with someone else. Most of us need love and companionship. Dating services, social clubs, bars, and vacation cruises and resorts catering to singles on the prowl thrive on this need. So do products that help us attract others during the dating game (from personal hygiene products to clothing to plastic surgery).

Moreover, products are often used as symbols of love and caring.[4] Flowers, candies, and greeting cards are often given as tokens of our affection for someone. This is also true for jewelry and diamonds. These industries have carefully cultivated their products' symbolic meaning. "Show her how much you care without saying a word" proclaims one jewelry advertisement. A brochure for

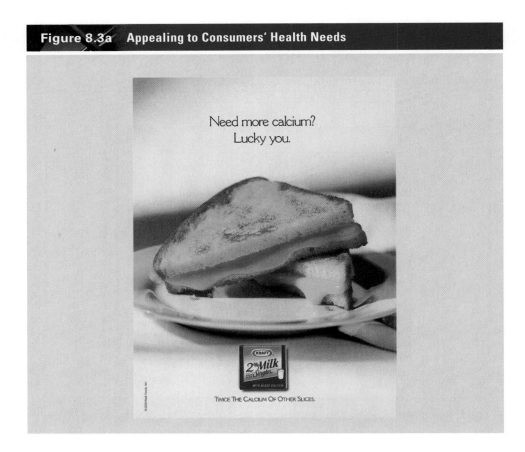

Figure 8.3a   Appealing to Consumers' Health Needs

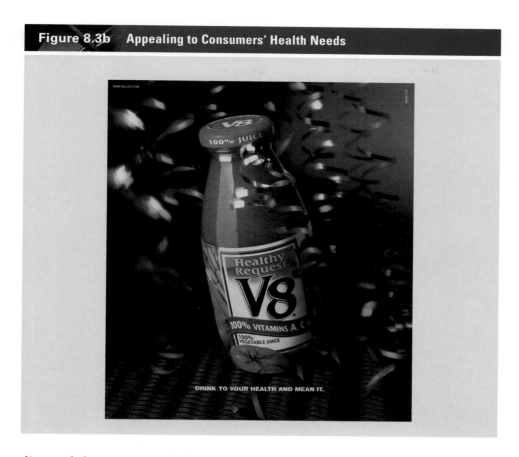

Figure 8.3b   Appealing to Consumers' Health Needs

diamonds begins with the statement, "All the ways to say 'I love you.'" And the diamond anniversary ring has become a symbol of one's continuing affections (see Figure 8.4). And as illustrated by the other ad in Figure 8.4, even rather ordinary products, such as those found at the grocery store, sometimes are positioned as symbols of our caring for someone else.

The need for love and companionship partly explains why Americans own so many pets. Do you know what the most popular pet is in America? Hint: It likes to say meow. Americans own 59 million cats. Fish are a close second at 55.6 million. Man's best friend ranks third, with Americans owning nearly 53 million dogs. Other popular pets include birds (12.6 million), rabbits and ferrets (5.7 million), rodents (4.8 million), horses (4 million), and reptiles (3.5 million).[5]

The Need for Financial Resources and Security

Money is the tool that the majority of us use for satisfying most of our needs. It can't buy love, but it sure can buy a lot of other things. The extent to which consumers can afford to satisfy their current needs depends primarily on their paycheck. But what about their future needs when they have left the work force and their paychecks behind? This is where the need for financial security comes in. It is the need to establish adequate financial resources so that one's "golden years" live up to their name.

In America, the government offers some financial support to retirees in the form of Social Security payments. But this alone does not come close to providing sufficient financial resources for most retirees wishing to maintain their pre-retirement lifestyle and consumption patterns. Without personal savings, life during the golden years will not be golden.

Figure 8.4   Symbols of Love

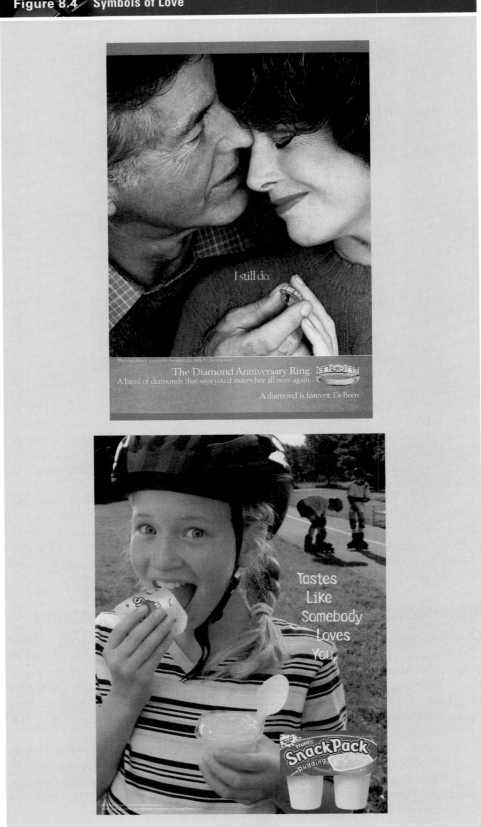

The need for financial security also extends to our important others. As long as I'm alive and working, my family will be taken care of. But what about when I'm no longer here? For this reason, I, along with millions of other consumers, buy life insurance. It satisfies our need to ensure the financial security of our loved ones, a need well recognized by the insurance industry.

The Need for Pleasure

There's a saying, "All work and no play makes Johnny a dull boy." Although some people may live for their work, most need pleasurable distractions. Without fun and excitement, life would be rather dull and boring indeed.

Consumers satisfy their need for pleasure in many different ways. Although our basic physiological requirements mandate the consumption of food, sometimes food consumption occurs even though we do not feel hungry. In such cases, we eat something simply because we wish to enjoy the consumption experience itself. A person who is feeling depressed may try to improve his or her mood by eating a favorite food. See how the coffee ad shown in Figure 8.5 appeals to consumers' need for pleasure by positioning product consumption as a way of achieving a good mood.

The entertainment industry is built on consumers' need for pleasure. Television, movies, music, Broadway plays, fictional books, sporting events, amusement parks, bowling alleys, ocean cruises, and nightclubs are popular because of the

Figure 8.5 Appealing to Consumers' Need to Feel Good

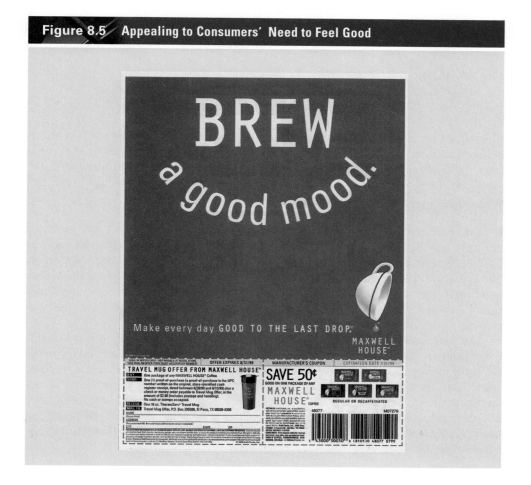

Consumer in Focus 8.2

Stickers That Send the Right Message

His mom is a retired Superior Court judge; dad's a prominent oral surgeon. What's a son to do? Why, grow up and sell stickers, of course. Colorful, in-your-face stickers whose slogans could make Dennis Rodman blush. "I come from a career family. My family just hasn't figured out my career yet," says Laurence Pokrasoff, 34, whose Huntington, California, company, Socially Hazardous, has rocketed from obscurity to more than $1 million in sales in four years.

Socially Hazardous is all about image, and the need for people to project images by slapping Socially Hazardous stickers on car bumpers, briefcases, skateboards—wherever. The oval stickers sell in about 20,000 stores worldwide, including surf and skate shops and large chains like Tower Records, Sam Goody, and Miller's Outpost. They come in two varieties—wild and mild—and sell for $2 to $3. Here are some (of the milder variety) of the 600 slogans on the glittery stickers:

- I Have a Black Belt in Shopping

- I Fear No Beer

- Normal People Worry Me

- Drama Queen

- Goddess

- Popularity Is a Socially Transmitted Disease

- We Are the People Our Parents Warned Us About

- I'm So Gothic, I'm Dead

Pokrasoff, who earned a bachelor's degree in 1990 from the New School of Architecture in San Diego, was noodling around with his drawings and working odd jobs when he hit upon the sticker idea. He had seen the familiar black-and-white stickers with the block letters advertising where a driver lives—LF for Lake Forest, for example—and decided to get to work. "Socially Hazardous is all about freedom of speech and being real, and expressing yourself in a world that isn't very loose and open-minded," says Pokrasoff. The company is branching out into clothing (it has more than 60 T-shirt designs) and novelty items like talking pillows. The $50 pillows come in a variety of "personalities" and talk when you squeeze them. Squeeze "The Attitude Chick" pillow and you'll hear, "I'm not in the mood to be stared at" as well as other things.

Source: Excerpted from Greg Hardesty, "Success Sticks to His Stickers," Sun-Sentinel *(January 2, 2000), 8G.*

pleasures they deliver. The same is true for the toy industry. In point of fact, many consumption activities are valued because of the fun and excitement they offer (e.g., skydiving, riding roller coasters, white water rafting, and hunting).

Social Image Needs

Do you care what your loved one and family thinks of you? Are you concerned about how you are perceived by your friends and co-workers? Nearly everyone is. We want our family to be proud of us. We want to be seen as a good person. Some want to be viewed as successful and, perhaps, rich; others want to be seen as attractive and hip. Social image needs are based on a person's concerns about how he or she is perceived by others. It is the need to project a certain image of oneself to our social environment.

As you well know, a person's social image depends, at least in part, on the products that the person buys and consumes. Where we live, what we drive, the clothing we wear, and the music we listen to contribute to our social image. Even something as mundane as the bottled water we drink (or, as described in Consumer in Focus 8.2, the stickers we buy and display) may be valued because it enables us to symbolically represent ourselves to others. The term **conspicuous consumption** is often used to describe *purchases motivated to some extent by the desire to show other people just how successful we are.*

Companies are continually reinforcing the notion that their products enable users to communicate their social image. "You can tell a lot about a man by his brand" announces an ad for Marlboro cigarettes. We are told, "Clothes may make the man but I prefer to see what's in his liquor cabinet" by one liquor ad. A jewelry ad shows a woman admiring another's engagement ring and saying, "What a big, beautiful diamond! Your fiancé must really be rich." Platinum and gold credit cards have been positioned as a way of gaining the respect of others. And carmakers often emphasize their products' ability to convey "who we are" by what we drive (see Figure 8.6).

The Need to Possess

Roper Starch Worldwide, a market research firm, has been surveying Americans about what they consider the "good life" to be for more than 20 years. In the 1970s, people defined the good life as including a steady job, a home, a good marriage, and a college education for their children. Today, the list is twice as long. It now includes a swimming pool, travel abroad, a second car, and money—lots of it.[6]

The need to possess is a hallmark characteristic of our consumer society. And, as reflected by the Starch surveys, it is a growing need. Consumers want more. Indeed, they expect more. They want and expect a better life, bigger and better products, and better service. Just look at the home. In 1970, new homes averaged 1,500 square feet; less than one-third had a fireplace. By 1996, nearly two-thirds had a fireplace and their average size increased 40 percent to 2,100 square feet. New houses became around three rooms bigger even though families were getting smaller.[7]

According to the American Moving and Storage Association, the average family carted 5,645 pounds of belongings when they moved in 1977. This average jumped to 7,262 pounds in 1995, an increase of nearly 30 percent.[8] What accounts for this increase? Certainly much of it can be attributed to consumers' need to acquire more and bigger products. Here's a quick inventory of one 29-year-old lawyer's possessions: "I've got a 61-inch TV, which, diagonally, is 1 inch bigger than my own mother. I've got an 11-speaker surround-sound system. I've got oversize plush couches and a monster-size kitchen with a huge bread maker and a commercial-size mixer. And I've got a large master bedroom with a walk-in closet that was the size of my bedroom in my old house."[9]

What is driving consumers' need to possess? For one, comfort. According to the lawyer with the oversized possessions: "It's nice when you're done with your day to be able to come home and soak in the big tub, grill in your big backyard, and watch your 61-inch TV. It allows you to escape the daily stress. You work hard; you want to enjoy your comforts."[10]

Although important, comfort is far from the only reason behind this need to possess. We may wish to possess some objects simply because of their historical significance. As an extreme example, consider Todd McFarlane, a comic book artist and creator. During a 1999 auction, he outbid all others and paid $3 million for a single baseball! Of course, it wasn't just any baseball. It was the 70th home-run ball hit by Mark McGwire when he established in 1998 the new major league record for home runs in a single season. "I blew my life savings on this," said McFarlane. "I'm not Donald Trump. I don't have a lot of cash."[11]

Collectors know full well the power of their need to possess. During my younger days, I was an avid coin collector. For many years, I spent part of my lunchtime looking through the school cafeteria's cash register for coins to be added to my collection. I visited local coin dealers and purchased (my budget was a bit more limited than Todd McFarlane's) certain coins that could no longer be found

Figure 8.6   The Product's Contribution to the Consumer's Social Image

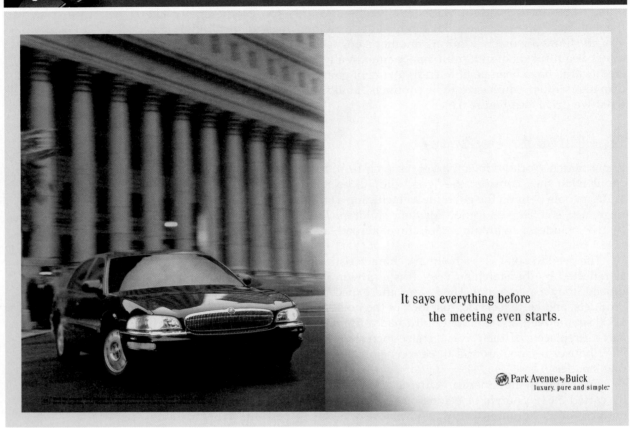

It says everything before
the meeting even starts.

Park Avenue by Buick
luxury, pure and simple.

in circulation. I routinely bought coin sets from the U.S. Mint. I even enlisted the help of my mother and sister. And the time I spent building my collection pales in comparison to the time I spent staring at my collection for no other reason than to admire its existence.

Objects may be valued because they make us feel connected to their prior owners. Consumers spent millions of dollars buying former possessions of famous individuals (Marilyn Monroe, Jacqueline Kennedy) during auctions held in the late 1990s. Possessions also play an important role in linking a person with his or her past. Objects may be acquired to preserve memories and to serve as a permanent nostalgic benchmark of a different time and place. Vacationers, for instance, often buy items (T-shirts, arts and crafts from local artists, and so on) to commemorate their travels.

At the extreme, possessions may become so important that we believe that they help define who we are. Have you ever heard the expression, "You are what you eat"? In this context, it's "You are what you own." It has even been suggested "That we are what we have is perhaps the most basic and powerful fact of consumer behavior."[12] From this perspective, consumers' **self-concept,** representing their *impressions of the type of person they are,* depends, at least in part, on what they possess.[13]

Finally, the need to possess plays an important role in impulse buying. **Impulse buying** occurs when *consumers unexpectedly experience a sudden and powerful urge to buy something immediately.*[14] Their need to possess is felt so strongly that it propels them to act quickly.

The Need to Give

How many times have you heard about someone making it big and feeling the need to give something back? Sometimes it's the college graduate who, after earning millions of dollars during a highly successful career, returns to his or her alma mater and provides the money necessary for student scholarships or a new building. Or it's the pro athlete who returns to the neighborhood where he or she grew up and funds a facility dedicated to keeping at-risk kids out of trouble. The story may differ in its details, but the underlying constant is the need to give.

Have you ever donated to charity? Most of us have, often for no more reason than to help others less fortunate than ourselves. Yet such altruism may be only one reason for giving. Sometimes we give because of its implications for our social image. We do not want to be seen as cheap or uncaring, especially when the request for a donation comes from a friend or co-worker. Donations, especially large ones, serve as symbols of the donor's wealth. Although wealthy donors often request anonymity, many do not. The success of charitable organizations' fund-raising activities heavily depends on their understanding the relative influence of these different reasons behind the need to give.

The need to give is not limited to money. It also encompasses products that are given to others as gifts. Gift giving is an essential part of many holidays. Valentine's Day, Mother's Day, Father's Day, and the granddaddy of them all, Christmas, are celebrated, at least in part, through gift-giving rituals. Birthdays, anniversaries, and graduations are also traditional gift-giving occasions.

Beyond giving to others, sometimes we feel the need to give to ourselves. We may do so in the form of **self-gifts.**[15] Self-gifts are *things that we buy or do as a way of rewarding, consoling, or motivating ourself.* The gift may be as small as eating a favorite snack. Or it may be as large as buying a new car or taking an expensive vacation. Notice how the ad in Figure 8.7 encourages consumers to buy the advertised product as a self-gift because they have been "very, very good this year."

The Need for Information

Making reasoned choices requires being informed. And being informed requires information. As discussed in previous chapters, consumer decision making heavily depends on the information, both internal (what you already know) and external (what you may learn while searching the environment), available to consumers at the time they make their choices. In the following chapter on consumer knowledge, we'll talk about the importance of internal information. But now we focus on how the need for information itself influences consumer behavior.

The purchase and consumption of many products can be attributed to consumers' need for information. Without it, there would be little reason to watch news programs on TV and even less reason to read the newspaper. How-to-do-it-yourself books and shows would disappear. Colleges and universities would be out of business. One reason the Internet has become so popular is it enables consumers to easily satisfy their informational needs although the results of a recent survey of Internet shoppers indicates considerable room for improvement. When asked what would make them click more often, the most frequent suggestion was to make the web site more informative.[16]

Consumers' need for information is also important because of its role in the persuasion process. Suppose you are planning to make a first-time purchase in a particular product category and encounter an advertisement for one of the brands in the category. Your need for relevant product information leads you to pay close attention to what the ad has to say.

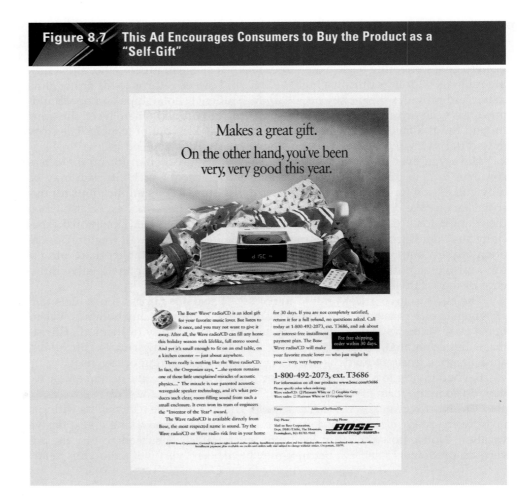

Figure 8.7   This Ad Encourages Consumers to Buy the Product as a "Self-Gift"

In contrast, suppose you encountered the ad at a time when you did not need the information it contains. In this case, there is obviously little reason for you to pay attention to the ad. And without attention, the ad has no chance of persuading you. Consequently, it is necessary for the advertiser to use some sort of attention-getting device (e.g., a pretty face, a well-known celebrity, a talking animal or reptile) as a way of attracting your attention. We will cover this topic in much greater depth in Chapter 14. In Chapter 15, we will discuss how the relative persuasiveness of different advertising elements (claims, pictures, music, and so on) depends on the need for information.

The Need for Variety

According to one saying, "Variety is the spice of life." How true this is! As you well know, too much of the same thing over and over again can quickly become rather boring. This certainly applies to product consumption. I usually drink Diet Coke. But every once in a while I'll buy a noncola-flavored soft drink at the grocery store just because I want something different tasting.[17] This need for variety is partly responsible for the recent popularity of musical mobile telephones in Japan. As one 21-year-old explains, "I think it is crazy for everyone to have the same or similar ringing tone." Over four million copies have been sold of a book that provides the numbers or symbols for programming the phone's ringing tone to produce a musical melody.[18]

Consumer in Focus 8.3

Greater Variety Spurs Coin Collectors' Interest

Starting in 1999, the U.S. Mint is issuing five new quarters every year through 2008, one designed for each of the 50 states in the order that they joined the union. Those initially released commemorated the first five states to ratify the Constitution—Delaware, Pennsylvania, New Jersey, Georgia, and Connecticut. Each state chose its own design for the back of the quarter, ranging from George Washington crossing the Delaware River on New Jersey's coin to an image of a beautiful tree on Connecticut's. The fronts of the quarters retain a portrait of Washington.

Emery Smith, 72, who has been collecting since he was a teenager, loves the new coins and thinks they are the spark coin collecting needed. "These quarters have helped more than anything else because they're so different," says Smith. "You see, all American coins are obsolete in design. They've all got dead presidents on them and nobody likes them."

And what a spark they have been. A 1999 study for the U.S. Mint estimated that 110 million Americans (around 40 percent of the entire population) are collecting the state quarters and that each collector has taken an average of 13 out of circulation. The quarter commemorating Connecticut, released in October 1999, helped the U.S. Mint sell a record $2 million worth of them in one day over its web site. Col-

lectors are buying them by the bag from the mint or going to banks and asking for rolls. "This is probably the hottest collectible of the decade," says Michael White of the U.S. Mint.

The mint makes a tidy profit on each quarter it produces, which is returned to the federal government's coffers. Each quarter costs five cents to make. The Federal Reserve Board pays full value. Collectors pay a premium on top of that for special editions.

The mint gave collectors and the public more coins to get excited about. Americans saw a new dollar coin in March 2000. It features an image of Sacagawea, the Shoshone Indian guide for the Lewis and Clark expedition of 1804–1806, toting her baby in a papoose. The coin is gold in color, not content. It is made of an alloy of manganese, brass, and copper. This new dollar coin has several features to avoid the problems with the Susan B. Anthony dollar coin introduced in 1979, which people complained was too similar to a quarter and unattractive. Its smooth edge and wider border, along with the gold coloring, distinguishes it from the quarter. And to facilitate consumer and retailer acceptance, the mint has negotiated with a major retailer to agree to use the new dollar in its registers, guaranteeing that Americans will receive it as change at some stores.

Source: Excerpted from Rafael Lorente, "Coin Collecting Gets Some Added Oomph," Sun-Sentinel *(January 9, 2000), 1A, 15A.*

Companies respond to consumers' need for variety in several ways. Food manufacturers may offer different versions of their original brand. They may also promote different ways for preparing and serving food products. As you can learn about in more detail in Consumer in Focus 8.3, the U.S. Mint is catering to collectors' need for variety by changing some of the coined money it produces. The need for variety is sometimes the focus of a product's positioning. An adventure tour may describe itself as offering vacationers something different and unique. The advertising for one steak sauce described the product as something "deliciously different."

Motivational Conflict and Need Priorities

Fulfilling one need often comes at the expense of another need. Money spent satisfying one need leaves less for the rest. The time allocated to one need means there's less time for fulfilling others. These *tradeoffs in our ability to satisfy various needs* cause **motivational conflict.**

Motivational conflict can take one of three basic forms. **Approach-approach** conflict occurs when the *person must decide between two or more desirable alternatives* (e.g., between buying new furniture and taking a cruise). **Avoidance-avoidance** conflict involves *deciding between two or more undesirable alternatives* (e.g., between mowing the yard and cleaning the pool). The last type, **approach-avoidance,** exists when *behavior has both positive and negative consequences.* Cigarette consumption satisfies smokers' need for nicotine but does so at the risk of their health. Working extra hours may further your career but maybe at the expense of your family.

Resolving motivational conflict requires people to prioritize their needs. Doing so means that they have to decide on the relative importance of each of their needs. These decisions will be of both a short-term (which needs to satisfy now) and long-term (which needs to satisfy in the future) nature. The rumblings in your stomach may motivate you to satisfy your need for food at that moment. Concerns about financial security during retirement may motivate years of saving money.

Like most things, consumers differ in the priorities they assign to their needs. What is vital to one person may be trivial to another. In a recent survey of women aged 20 to 50, 24 percent strongly agreed with the statement, "I am concerned about what others think of me."[19] For this group, the need to project a desirable social image will be very important, certainly more so than for those disagreeing with the statement. Those products perceived as better at fulfilling this need stand a much greater chance of being chosen and consumed, but only for those consumers for whom the need is an important priority.

One well-known approach to specifying the relative priority assigned to different needs is Maslow's hierarchy (see Figure 8.8). According to Maslow, some needs take precedence over other needs.[20] Physiological needs are the most basic in the hierarchy; they take top priority. Only after these needs have been fulfilled do people progress up the hierarchy to the next level of needs. In essence, then,

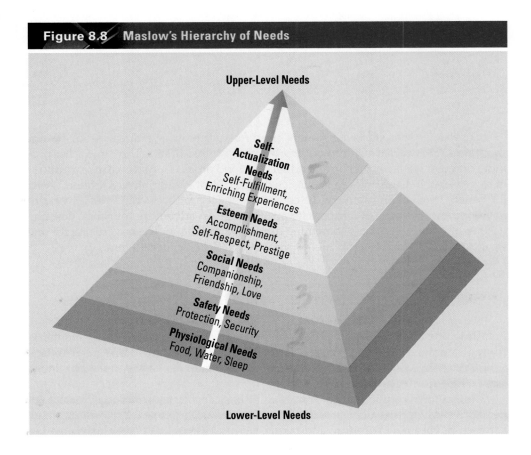

Figure 8.8   Maslow's Hierarchy of Needs

Maslow's hierarchy orders needs from most important (represented at the bottom of the hierarchy) to those least important (represented at the top of the hierarchy).

Maslow's hierarchy is a useful concept because it reminds us that people attach different priorities to their needs. Nonetheless, it should not be seen as providing a definitive specification of what these priorities may be. Although Maslow's ordering may correspond with the priorities of many, it certainly does not reflect everyone's priorities in all situations. Sometimes people ignore lower-order needs in pursuit of higher-order needs. A mother's love may lead her to disregard her own safety when the life of her child is at risk. Others pursue careers that satisfy their need for accomplishment at the expense of their love relationships.

Differences in the importance consumers attach to various needs ultimately affect how they evaluate products being considered for purchase and consumption. Different needs lead consumers to seek different product benefits. Car buyers that are strongly motivated by a desire to project a certain image are looking for a different benefit from those more concerned about safety. Consequently, the evaluative criteria (see Chapter 4) used during decision making may change depending on what benefits are desired and what needs are to be fulfilled. Those concerned with image will place greater importance on a car's styling and social standing. A car's safety features (e.g., airbags, anti-lock brakes) and safety record are accorded greater emphasis for those motivated by the need for safe transportation.

Because of these variations in consumers' motivational priorities, companies should find it useful to segment their markets along these lines. One way to do this is to use benefit segmentation. **Benefit segmentation** involves *dividing consumers into different market segments based on the benefits they seek (i.e., the needs they want fulfilled) from product purchase and consumption.* Companies can then tailor their marketing efforts more effectively and efficiently to a segment's needs. Obviously, the manner in which bottled water is positioned to the segment motivated by health needs should differ from how it's positioned to the segment that perceives bottled water as an appropriate way for conveying something about themselves to their social environment.

Motivational Intensity

Thus far we have ignored the issue of **motivational intensity,** which represents *how strongly consumers are motivated to satisfy a particular need.* Sometimes fulfilling a need preempts all else. At other times, motivational intensity is much more modest.

In Chapter 4, we noted that need recognition depends on the degree of discrepancy between one's current situation (where we are now) and one's ideal situation (where we want to be). As need deprivation increases, need recognition becomes more likely. Motivational intensity also grows stronger. Those who haven't eaten for 24 hours will experience a much greater sense of urgency to fill their stomachs. Motivational intensity also depends on the need's importance. The needs most important to consumers are pursued more intensively.

Another way of thinking about motivational intensity is through the concept of involvement. **Involvement** represents the *degree to which an object or behavior is personally relevant.*[21] To the extent some object or behavior is thought to satisfy important needs, the greater is its personal relevance. The more strongly motivated consumers are to satisfy their needs, the greater their involvement with potential sources of need satisfaction. Consumers motivated to project a favorable social image, for instance, will be more involved with products perceived as satisfying this need than those who are not so motivated. In the same way, products that evoke higher involvement (those that are more personally relevant to our needs) will increase consumers' motivation to acquire and consume these products.

Involvement and motivational intensity are important because they determine the amount of effort consumers exert when trying to satisfy their needs. As intensity and involvement increase, consumers try harder to fulfill their needs. They become more attentive to relevant information. They undertake more thinking and respond differently to persuasive communications (see Chapter 15). External search becomes greater.[22] Consumers may also consider a larger number of choice alternatives for attaining need satisfaction.

The Challenge of Understanding Consumer Motivation

Those interested in understanding consumer motivation must avoid the pitfall of believing that research is unnecessary because the reasons underlying purchase behavior are "obvious." To illustrate this point, we want to tell you a story about Mel Fisher. Mel searched for sunken treasure from a Spanish galleon that was sent to the bottom of the ocean by a hurricane in 1622. In 1985, after 15 years of searching and enduring many personal hardships, including the loss of a son who died when one of the search vessels capsized, another of Mel's sons found the treasure 41 miles off Key West. And what a treasure it was! Nearly $400 million in gems, gold, and silver. Almost overnight, Mel became a celebrity. He appeared as a guest on TV talk shows, was featured in National Geographic specials, and his life story was told in a made-for-TV movie.

Stop and think for a moment about what motivated Mel in his quest for sunken treasure. What would you guess to be his reasons for doing so? The most obvious explanation for why Mel searched so many years and sacrificed so much is that he was motivated by the wealth he would attain if his search were successful. Yet those who knew him say otherwise. According to Madeleine Burnside, executive director of the Mel Fisher Maritime Heritage Society, "It was never about the value of the gold. It was always about the hunt and the excitement. After they found the main pile, they all actually got terribly depressed. Because it was about the search." Pat Clyne, vice president of Treasure Salvors and Mel's friend for nearly 30 years, has a similar opinion. "He's not like other people. He wasn't interested in money. The whole thing was the expedition, the puzzle."[23]

The point that we're trying to make here is that obvious explanations for people's behavior may not always tell the whole story. Humans are complex creatures and engage in behaviors for reasons that sometimes are less than transparent. This also applies to consumer behavior. Indeed, the motivation for buying and consuming can be downright surprising sometimes, as the McCann-Erickson advertising agency learned when researching why Raid roach spray outsold Combat insecticide disks in certain markets. Most users agreed that Combat is a better product because it kills roaches with minimal effort by the user. So why did some of them still use roach spray? When the heaviest users of roach spray—low-income southern women—were asked to draw pictures of their prey, they portrayed roaches as men. "A lot of their feelings about the roach were very similar to the feelings they had about the men in their lives," says Paula Drillman, executive vice president at McCann-Erickson. The roach, like the man in their life, "only comes around when he wants food." Setting out Combat was easier, but it did not give them the satisfaction they derived from spraying roaches and seeing them die. "These women wanted control," Drillman explains. "They used the spray because it allowed them to participate in the kill."[24]

Understanding why people behave as they do is often a challenging endeavor. One reason this is so is that people may not be willing to disclose the real reasons behind their actions. Consumers may not feel comfortable divulging what makes them tick to others. The guy that buys a "muscle car" as a way of enhancing his own sense of masculinity may not wish to admit this. Similarly, how many charitable donors motivated by the need to display their wealth would be willing to admit this?

When people believe that their answers to a question may cast a less than favorable light on themselves, they may decide not to tell the truth. Rather, they provide answers that, to them, are socially acceptable. One compelling demonstration of this involves how consumers distort how much milk and alcohol they drink when asked to report on their consumption of these items. These self-reports are then compared with the empty milk and alcohol containers found in consumers' garbage cans. Many report drinking more milk than they actually do while underreporting their consumption of alcohol.

Another complicating factor is that people may not be able to tell us why they behave the way they do. Indeed, consumers spend millions of dollars each year hoping that psychologists can help them better understand the reasons for their feelings and actions. At the turn of the century, Sigmund Freud and his followers introduced the idea of **unconscious motivation,** in which *people are unaware of what really motivates their behavior.* According to Ernest Dichter, considered by many to be the father of motivational research, "Knowing one's own motivations is one of the most difficult things, because we try to rationalize. Most of us try to explain our behavior in an intelligent way, when very often it is not."[25]

Nonetheless, motivational researchers have been probing consumers' psyche for decades. Dichter proposed long ago that women were using Ivory soap to wash their sins away before a date. He also suggested that convertible automobiles serve as substitute mistresses for sexually frustrated men.[26] And many years ago, motivational researchers were posed the question, "Why do women bake cakes?" According to some, women baked cakes because of their unconscious desire to give birth. Perhaps it is for this reason that Pillsbury invented its famous "doughboy" character (see Figure 8.9).

Another challenge to understanding consumer motivation stems from the reality that it can change. What motivates purchase today may not be what motivates purchase in the future. Consider consumers' motivation for using soap. As one executive explains, "It used to be 'I'm trying to make myself presentable to you.' Now it's more about 'Hey, I've got to wash you off of me.'"[27] Students' motivations for attending college have also changed over time, according to an annual nationwide poll of college freshmen conducted by researchers at the University of California at Los Angeles. Three-fourths of those surveyed during the fall 1997 semester chose "being well-off financially" as an important goal for pursuing their education. Around 40 percent chose "developing a meaningful philosophy of life." In 1968, the numbers were almost the opposite. Back then, developing a philosophy was chosen by more than 80 percent; only 40 percent selected financial security.[28]

A change in consumer motivation can be good or bad news for business. If the change involves a particular need becoming more important to consumers, then businesses serving this need should benefit. Conversely, if a change is due to the need becoming less important, then businesses serving this need may suffer. In Japan, for example, female consumers' need to give "obligation chocolates" to their friends and co-workers for Valentine's Day (as opposed to "true-love" chocolates for their sweethearts) is declining, a trend that concerns both chocolate makers and retailers.[29]

Figure 8.9   Does the Pillsbury Doughboy Appeal to Consumers' Unconscious Needs?

Motivating Consumers

As should be apparent from the numerous examples presented throughout this chapter, companies often try to motivate consumer buying by linking their products to important needs. There are, however, other ways for motivating consumers. Some of these were discussed previously in Chapter 4's coverage of the need recognition stage of decision making (e.g., the motivational power of reminding consumers of their needs). We now turn to some others.

Overcoming Price Barriers

Not all of our needs are affordable. Sometimes a need goes unfulfilled or, if filled, with a less-than-desirable product (a cheaper product) because of costs. Many would love to experience the finer things in life. Unfortunately, only some of us are able and willing to pay the price to do so. Lowering a product's price overcomes the "I want it but I can't afford it" reason for not buying.

Companies use a variety of methods for overcoming the price barrier: price cuts, special sales, rebates (the earliest known rebate was offered in 1914 by the Ford Motor Co. for purchases of its Model T car), and coupons (supposedly the first grocery coupon, worth one cent, was offered by Grape Nuts cereal in 1895).[30] All try to motivate product purchase by reducing its cost. And usually they do, sometimes dramatically. When Southwest Airlines slashed the average price charged for a one-way ticket on a certain route by 62 percent, the number of tickets sold skyrocketed by more than 800 percent![31]

Nonetheless, motivating consumers through price is a dangerous proposition. One concern is that though sales may increase, profitability may not. After all, at least some of the consumers who buy at the reduced price would have done so even at the full price. According to one estimate, current users of a product account for more than 70 percent of coupon redemption.[32] For each of these, money is lost and profitability reduced. Consequently, unless the profit received from incremental customers (i.e., those who would not have purchased the product without the price reduction) is large enough to cover the losses incurred by selling to those who would have paid more, the company loses money.

Another concern with price reductions involves the type of customer they attract. Market research tests of rolling out new products with or without a coupon show that, of those who initially buy the product with a coupon, nearly one-fourth become repeat buyers. By comparison, nearly one-third of those who made their initial purchase without the coupon become repeat buyers.[33] As these findings suggest, consumers motivated today by price are less likely to become tomorrow's customers. Rather, they tend to give their business to whoever is offering the lowest price. Further, incentives based on price reductions have been found to increase the price sensitivity of both loyal and nonloyal consumers. As one of the researchers of the study showing this explains, "Over time, price promotions train consumers, particularly nonloyal ones, to look for deals in the marketplace instead of encouraging them to be loyal to a given brand based on attributes other than price."[34]

Despite these concerns, price reductions remain one of the most popular marketing tactics for motivating purchase behavior. Once the 1999 National Basketball Association players' strike ended, franchises slashed ticket prices for some seats in order to bring fans back to the arenas.[35]

Provide Other Incentives

Reducing a product's price is but one of the ways businesses can sweeten the deal. Another is to provide premiums (where one product is given freely for the purchase of another product), as illustrated by the advertisement shown in Figure 8.10. Think of the billions of children's meals that have been sold by fast-food restaurants because they included toys. When McDonald's decided to include miniature Beanie Babies in its Happy Meal, it produced nearly 100 million of the toys, its largest order ever for a promotion. Yet it still wasn't enough. Consumer demand was so overwhelming that McDonald's had to recommend to its restaurants to limit the sale to ten meals per customer after some began buying them by the caseload![36]

Sometimes the size of the incentives used to motivate potential customers is much larger than a free toy. Has a company wanted your business so much that it offered you a $25,000 shopping spree for free? Probably not—unless you're a whale. Whale is the term used by casinos for gamblers with lots of money and willing to wager hundreds of thousands, even millions, of dollars during their visit to the casino. Some casinos reserve their best penthouse suites, sometimes large enough to accommodate four average-sized homes, for whales only. Cost? There is none. In fact, virtually everything is free except, of course, the money wagered. Food, drinks, a butler for the suite who is available 24 hours a day, sightseeing trips to nearby attractions, and shopping sprees are used as bait during whale hunting.

Casinos are betting that they'll recoup more than enough money from a whale's losing wagers to offset the thousands of dollars in incentives given away. And a whale is much more valuable than a regular customer. According to one industry insider, a single whale can make more money for a casino than 1,000 regular customers over the long run. But beware. In the short run, catching a whale can be risky business. One major casino in Las Vegas lost $20 million during a whale's 40-minute visit to the blackjack table!

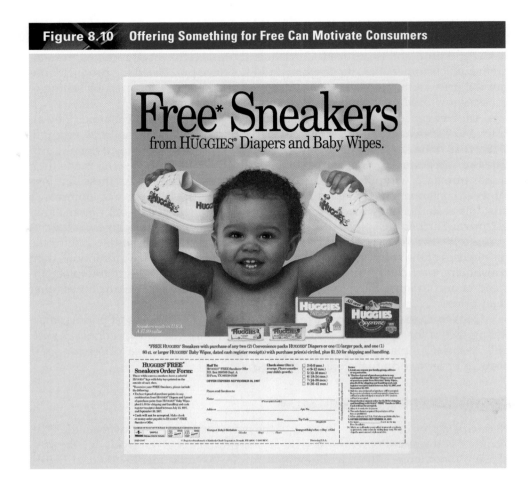

Figure 8.10   Offering Something for Free Can Motivate Consumers

Contests and sweepstakes are other types of incentives used to motivate consumers. The Toyota Corporation offered a contest in which visitors to its web site competed to win a pickup truck.[37] Publishers Clearing House has built its reputation and business (selling magazine subscriptions) through its famous sweepstakes drawing that gives consumers the chance of becoming an instant millionaire.

Implement a Loyalty Program

Beyond motivating initial or trial purchasing, companies are also interested in motivating repeat business. For example, health clubs have been successful at recruiting new members, but less so at retaining them since 30 percent of new members fail to renew their memberships.[38] Similarly, the number of bowlers holding membership in one of the industry's sanctioning bodies has declined from 8.5 million in 1976 to less than 4 million today.[39] Obviously, it's difficult for businesses to grow when their ability to retain customers is limited.

Loyalty programs try to *motivate repeat buying by providing rewards to customers based on how much business they do with a company.* The origins of loyalty programs can be traced to at least 1876 when a retailer began issuing S&H Green Stamps. The more the customer bought, the more stamps he or she received. Once the customer had accumulated enough stamps, the stamps could be redeemed for gifts.[40]

One of the most popular loyalty programs today is the airline industry's frequent-flyer program in which passengers earn credits toward future flights. Over

Consumer in Focus 8.4

Travelodge Hotels' Loyalty Program

Some have suggested that the economy lodging industry didn't need a loyalty program because the type of customer attracted to a budget hotel or motel was interested only in cost. But Travelodge Hotels thought otherwise. So in June 1997, it launched Travelodge Miles, a guest rewards program. Within five months, 30,000 people had signed on with around 200 new members joining their ranks daily.

The program thanks frequent Travelodge and Thriftlodge guests for their patronage with value-added rewards such as frequent-flyer miles, free hotel nights, free rental cars, and other travel perks. Guests earn one Travelodge Mile for each qualified lodging dollar spent at participating properties. Once they have accumulated 250 Miles, they can redeem them for Sleepy Bear dolls, T-shirts, or a road atlas. They can also save them as they work their way toward even

better rewards. Travelodge has also implemented several seasonal promotions that reward program members with everything from road maps to summer movie passes and prepaid long-distance calling cards.

An important feature of the program is its use of state-of-the-art swipe-card technology that automatically updates customers' accounts whenever they stay at a participating location. For management, the system makes it easy to track and gather data on the company's best customers, and has enabled the creation of a "Gold Level" for preferred customers. These Gold Level customers receive preferred room rates and free local phone calls. The enhanced level is already paying off with an increase in the average stay of preferred guests of almost a full night longer per each stay.

Source: Excerpted from Dorothy Dowling, *"Frequent Perks Keep Travelers Loyal,"* American Demographics *(September 1998), 32–36.*

32 million Americans have frequent-flyer accounts.[41] Free airline mileage is so enticing to consumers that it is featured in the loyalty programs of many different products, including hotels, rental cars, credit cards, and florists. Free airline mileage is a key element in Travelodge Hotels' loyalty program, described in Consumer in Focus 8.4.

Loyalty programs are becoming an important element in the marketing mix for Internet businesses. "You can expect that more and more businesses are going to be introducing loyalty programs of all sorts," says Irving Wladawsky-Berger, general manager of IBM's Internet division. "Over the Internet there is going to be a major push for businesses to differentiate themselves with loyalty programs."[42] And consumers are all for this. In a survey of online consumers, over half said they're more likely to buy from an e-commerce site if it offers a loyalty program.[43]

Enhance Perceived Risk

Another way of motivating consumers is to enhance the perceived risk of product purchase and consumption. **Perceived risk** represents *consumers' apprehensions about the consequences of their behavior.*[44] Consumers may have reservations about whether a product will live up to their expectations. They will be concerned when they think that purchase and consumption bring negative consequences. Ultimately, perceived risk depends on consumers' beliefs about the consequences of buying and consuming the product, whether the consequences are good or bad, and the consequences' importance to the consumer. If one is leery that an expensive vacation supposedly offering a unique consumption experience will turn out to be another ordinary but overpriced experience, perceived risk will be greater. The overwhelming medical evidence about the health risks of smoking has certainly increased the perceived risk of this consumption activity.

As you learned in Chapter 4, perceived risk influences consumer search. Greater risk causes more search. It does so because of its influence on consumer motivation. Usually, consumers are motivated not to put themselves at risk, especially when the outcomes are important. One way they try to reduce risk is by acquiring more information about the purchase decision. In essence, perceived risk affects the need for information. Depending on what is learned during search, consumers' choices may turn out differently than if less extensive search had been undertaken. Moreover, greater perceived risk may cause consumers to become more risk adverse when choosing products.

Educating consumers about their risks may motivate them to make more informed choices that reduce their exposure to risk. According to the headline of one car ad, "Most accidents happen in the showroom." The ad went on to describe the negative consequences (e.g., spending too much for too little) consumers might experience for doing a less than thorough search. Presumably, the ad tries to motivate consumers to undertake greater external search as a way of increasing the chances of the advertised carmaker being considered during decision making.

Similarly, the ad shown in Figure 8.11 emphasizes the health risk of choosing the wrong cold medicine for those with high blood pressure. Those to whom this ad would be personally relevant (those with high blood pressure and those who care about someone with this problem) may be motivated to respond although not necessarily in the same way. Those that unquestionably accept the ad's claims

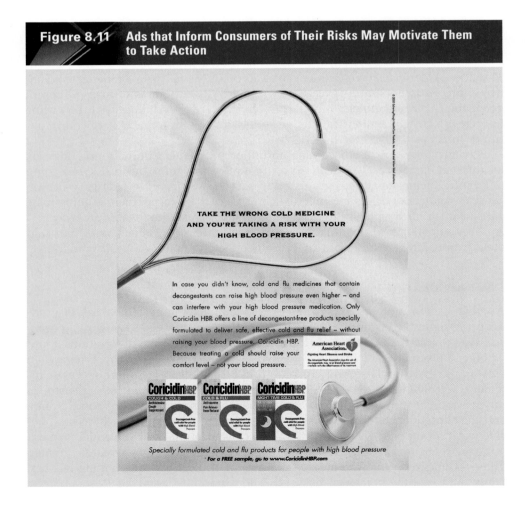

Figure 8.11 Ads that Inform Consumers of Their Risks May Motivate Them to Take Action

as true will recognize a need that the advertised brand can fill. This may lead them directly to purchase. More skeptical consumers may decide that additional information is needed and undertake external search, perhaps by talking to their doctors or pharmacists. Depending on what is learned, they may then decide to buy the advertised brand or a competitor's brand if during search it is discovered to be even better. It is even possible that purchase will not happen if consumers come to the conclusion that their need is not of sufficient magnitude to warrant such action.

Arousing Consumers' Curiosity

People, like cats, are curious creatures. Our curiosity often motivates us to learn more about what has aroused our interest. For new products (such as electrical cars, digital cameras, and web TVs) that need to educate potential customers about their benefits and attributes motivating consumers to acquire and learn product information is critical. Arousing consumers' curiosity may activate their need for information. One way of doing this is by advertising a benefit that is not normally associated with the product (such as a camera that allows the user to delete part of the picture).[45]

Summary

One of the most fundamental questions about consumer behavior is "Why do people buy?" The answer to this question is found in an understanding of consumer motivation. Consumers are motivated to purchase and consume products in order to satisfy their needs. As you have seen in this chapter, consumers have a variety of needs. Some (physiological, safety, and health, for instance) are fundamental to our survival. Others (such as financial security, pleasure, and giving to others) may be less essential for existing but are still critical to the consumer's sense of well-being. Those companies that better understand consumers' needs stand a greater chance of attracting and retaining customers.

Sometimes, consumers' purchase motivation is driven by a single need. Other times, motivation is more complex and fueled by multiple needs. Satisfying certain needs may come at the expense of others, thus leading to motivational conflict. In deciding which needs take precedence, consumers must prioritize them based on a need's importance at that particular moment in time.

Although essential, understanding consumer motivation is not easy. When asked why they buy, consumers may distort their answers. In the case of unconscious motivation, consumers themselves are not fully aware of why they behave the way they do. And because motivation can change over time, companies should continually monitor the reasons why people buy and consume.

Companies can enhance consumers' motivation to fill their needs through product purchase and consumption in several ways. Price reductions and other types of incentives—perhaps packaged in the form of a loyalty program—are important motivators for many. Messages that enhance perceived risk or arouse curiosity also hold the potential for motivating consumers.

Review and Discussion Questions

1. Why is it important for companies to understand consumer motivation?
2. Beyond understanding consumer motivation, what else does a company

need to know in order to fully appreciate the reasons that consumers buy specific products and brands?

3. A manufacturer of household cleaning products is interested in learning what motivates consumers to buy its products. What needs do you think consumers are trying to satisfy when buying and using these products?

4. What is Maslow's hierarchy of needs? How do differences in need priorities influence consumer behavior?

5. What are the potential advantages and disadvantages for a product that fulfills multiple needs?

6. Some suggest that it is important to distinguish between a need and a want. From this perspective, a need is something we must have, whereas a want represents something we desire but can live without. Do you think this is a meaningful distinction? Why or why not?

7. It has been suggested that products represent "symbols for sale." What does this mean to you?

8. A business is perplexed by the unexpected results of its recent advertising campaign and has turned to you for help in understanding what is going on. This new campaign was designed to increase the advertised product's personal relevance to consumers by emphasizing its ability to fill previously underappreciated needs. Yet, the campaign had no noticeable effect on sales of the advertised product. Rather, it appeared to stimulate the sales of a competitor. Why might this have occurred?

Endnotes

1. Harold W. Berkman, Jay D. Lindquist, and M. Joseph Sirgy, *Consumer Behavior* (Chicago: NTC Publishing Group, 1997).

2. See, for example, Ernest Dichter, *Handbook of Consumer Motivations: The Psychology of Consumption* (New York: McGraw-Hill, 1964); Jeffrey F. Durgee, "Interpreting Dichter's Interpretations: An Analysis of Consumption Symbolism in the Handbook of Consumer Motivations," in Hanne Hartvig-Larsen, David Glen Mick, and Christian Alstead, eds., *Marketing and Semiotics: Selected Papers from the Copenhagen Symposium* (Copenhagen, 1991); Morris B. Holbrook and Elizabeth C. Hirschman, "The Experiential Aspects of Consumption: Consumer Fantasies, Feelings, and Fun," *Journal of Consumer Research* 9 (September 1982), 132–140; Abraham H. Maslow, *Motivation and Personality* (New York: Harper & Row, 1970); David C. McClelland, *Personality* (New York: William Sloane, 1941); William J. McGuire, "Psychological Motives and Communication Gratification," in J. G. Blumer and C. Katz, eds., *The Uses of Mass Communications: Current Perspectives on*

Gratification Research (New York: Sage, 1974), 167–196; A. H. Murray, *Explorations in Personality* (New York: Oxford University Press, 1938).

3. Michele Chandler, "Viagra: A Drug-Business Boost, But No Cure-All," *Miami Herald's Business Monday* (July 13, 1998), 7.

4. For a classic article on the symbolic meaning of products, see Sidney J. Levy, "Symbols for Sale," *Harvard Business Review* (July/August 1959), 117–124. For an interesting history of the motivation research era, see Sidney J. Levy's comments in *ACR Newsletter* (March 1991), 3–6.

5. "Pet Popularity Race Has New No. 2," *Parade Magazine* (January 4, 1998), 16.

6. Brigid Schulte, "Big: It's Bigger Than Ever," *Miami Herald* (December 10, 1997), 1D, 2D.

7. Ibid.

8. June Fletcher, "Latest Sign of Status: Big Garage," *Miami Herald* (March 14, 1999), 1H, 8H.

9. Schulte, "Big: It's Bigger Than Ever."

10. Ibid.

11. "The People Column," *Miami Herald* (February 9, 1999), 2A.

12. Russell W. Belk, "Possessions and the Extended Self," *Journal of Consumer Research* 15 (September 1988), 139–168. Also see Joel B. Cohen, "An Over-Extended Self?" *Journal of Consumer Research* 16 (June 1989), 125–128; Russell W. Belk, "Extended Self and Extending Paradigmatic Perspective," *Journal of Consumer Research* 16 (June 1989), 129–132.

13. For additional information about the self-concept, see M. Joseph Sirgy, "Self-Concept in Consumer Behavior: A Critical Review," *Journal of Consumer Research* 9 (December 1982), 287–300; M. Joseph Sirgy, "Using Self-Congruity and Ideal Congruity to Predict Purchase Motivation," *Journal of Business Research* 13 (1985), 195–206.

14. Dennis W. Rook, "The Buying Impulse," *Journal of Consumer Research* 14 (September 1987), 189–199.

15. David Glenn Mick and Michelle DeMoss, "Self-Gifts: Phenomenological Insights from Four Contexts," *Journal of Consumer Research* 17 (December 1990), 322–332.

16. Elaine Walker, "From Browser to Buyer," *Miami Herald* (April 11, 1999), 1E, 4E.

17. For research on the need for variety, see Leigh McAlister, "A Dynamic Attribute Satiation Model of Variety Seeking Behavior," *Journal of Consumer Research* 12 (September 1982), 141–150.

18. "Japan's New Fad: Mobile Phones that Ring Musically," *Miami Herald* (March 15, 1999), 16A.

19. "Status Unconscious," *American Demographics* (March 1999), 28.

20. Abraham H. Maslow, *Motivation and Personality* (New York: Harper & Row, 1970).

21. Richard L. Celsi and Jerry C. Olson, "The Role of Involvement in Attention and Comprehension Processes," *Journal of Consumer Research* 15 (September 1988), 210–224.

22. Peter H. Bloch, Daniel L. Sherrell, and Nancy M. Ridgway, "Consumer Search: An Extended Framework," *Journal of Consumer Research* 13 (June 1986), 119–126; Judith Lynne Zaichkowsky, "Measuring the Involvement Construct," *Journal of Consumer Research* 12 (December 1985), 341–352.

23. Nancy Klingener, "Treasure Hunter Passes into Legend," *Miami Herald* (December 21, 1998), 1A, 18A.

24. Rebecca Piirto, "Beyond Mind Games," *American Demographics* (December 1991), 52–57.

25. Ibid. For those interested in learning more about Dichter's thinking, see Ernest Dichter, *Handbook of Consumer Motivations: The Psychology of Consumption* (New York: McGraw-Hill, 1964).

26. Ibid.

27. Tara Parker-Pope, "Dial Soap Aims at Soothing Fear of Germs," *The Wall Street Journal* (January 20, 1998), B7.

28. "It's What You Earn, Not What You Learn," *Miami Herald* (January 11, 1998), 3A.

29. "Women Say *Sayonara* to Valentine Chocolates," *Miami Herald* (February 13, 1999), 20A.

30. For a very interesting discussion of the history of promotions, see David Vaczek and Richard Sale, "100 Years of Promotion," *PROMO Magazine* (August 1998), 32–41, 142–145.

31. Tom Belden, "It's More Than Fare: Airlines Yield Key Data," *Miami Herald's Business Monday* (July 14, 1997), 12.

32. Vaczek and Sale, "100 Years of Promotion."

33. *Insights,* NPD Research, Inc., 1979–1982.

34. Katherine Zoe Andrews, "Do Marketing Policies Change Consumer Behavior in the Long Run?" *Insights from MSI* (Winter/Spring 1997), 1–2.

35. Mike Phillips, "NBA Learning Art of Self-Promotion," *Miami Herald* (February 5, 1999), 4D.

36. "McDonald's Runs Low on Teenie Beanie Toys," *Miami Herald* (April 16, 1997), 11B.

37. Jess McCuan, "Auto Companies Head Online in Search of Sales Leads," *The Wall Street Journal* (July 6, 1999), A20.

38. Michelle Chandler, "More Than Just Dumb Bells," *Miami Herald's Business Monday* (April 20, 1998), 18–20.

39. Dick Evans, "Strike Ten Just Not Generating Business," *Miami Herald* (June 13, 1999), 7C.

40. Vaczek and Sale, "100 Years of Promotion."

41. Dorothy Dowling, "Frequent Perks Keep Travelers Loyal," *American Demographics* (September 1998), 32–36.

42. David Poppe, "How Do Internet Retailers Foster Customer Loyalty?" *Miami Herald's Business Monday* (February 8, 1999), 13.

43. Jennifer Lach, "Carrots in Cyberspace," *American Demographics* (May 1999), 43–45.

44. James R. Bettman, "Perceived Risk and Its Components: A Model and Empirical Test," *Journal of Marketing Research* 10 (May 1973), 184–190; Raymond A. Bauer, "Consumer Behavior as Risk

Taking," in Robert S. Hancock, ed., *Dynamic Marketing for a Changing World* (Chicago: American Marketing Association, 1960), 389–398; Graham R. Dowling, "Perceived Risk: The Concept and Its Measurement," *Psychology and Marketing* 3 (Fall 1986), 193–210; Lawrence X. Tarpey and J. Paul Peter, "A Comparative Analysis of Three Consumer Decision Strategies," *Journal of Consumer Research* 2 (June 1975), 29–37.

45.   Katherine Zoe Andrews, "The Power of Curiosity: Motivating Consumers to Learn," *Insights from MSI* (Summer 1999), 1, 6.

CHAPTER 9

Consumer Knowledge

OPENING VIGNETTE

Endless Games is a small toy company that started out three years ago with the board game Six Degrees of Kevin Bacon. Sales were good. But two Christmases ago, it brought out Password, which had been off the shelves for 15 years. "When we resurrected that," says Brian Turtle, national sales manager, "it set off such a spark."

Since then, Endless Games has gone into the television board game archives and brought back The Newlywed Game, Beat the Clock, The Price is Right, Family Feud, and Concentration, which celebrated its 40th anniversary in 1999. No, Endless Games is not challenging Milton Bradley, yet. "But we're in the rear view mirror," says Turtle. "A lot of people can't say that after three years in business."

The success, says Turtle, is simply because of prior familiarity. "People know what's inside," he explains. "Selling a board game is so different than a toy because it's a closed box. People don't know much about it. But when you give them something they're familiar with, then they're interested."

Turtle thinks the sales come from all ages: people who played the game way back when and people who remember it on their parents' shelves. And, just as every generation grows up with *I Love Lucy*, today's kids know all the old game shows. The Game Show Network, a cable TV network, telecasts many of those classic game shows, dating as far back as the 1950s.

Source: Excerpted from Roger Bull, "Always in Style," The Times-Union (November 26, 1999), D1.

As illustrated in the opening vignette, prior familiarity with a product may determine whether we leave it sitting on the shelf or buy it and take it home. Product familiarity is a reflection of our knowledge about the product.[1] Have we heard of the product before? What do we know about the product's attributes, benefits, and uses? The answers to these questions can be critical inputs for evaluating purchase alternatives and deciding what to buy.

This chapter focuses on **consumer knowledge,** which can be defined as the *subset of the total amount of information stored in memory that is relevant to product purchase and consumption.* For example, what does the SPF number found on sunscreens represent? What differences are there between Rolex and Timex watches? "When you care enough to send the very best" is the slogan for which product? Should young children drink large quantities of juices? Should diabetics minimize consumption of foods containing salt or sugar? What product category contains a brand named Topol? What comes to mind when you think about Volvo automobiles?

Although these questions cover a broad range of topics, they share a common bond in that each taps into your consumer knowledge. SPF stands for "sun protection factor" and the number represents the product's strength in protecting skin from the harmful rays of the sun. Rolex and Timex watches differ in their prices, quality, and the prestige of product ownership. The slogan comes from Hallmark. Drinking 12 ounces or more of juice each day may cause children to be shorter and fatter.[2] Diabetics should avoid foods containing sugar. Topol is a brand of toothpaste. And only you can answer the question concerning Volvo automobiles.

What we know or don't know strongly influences our decision-making processes. Consider two individuals preparing to buy a used car. One person, an experienced buyer, is very knowledgeable about automobiles. The other is an inexperienced, first-time buyer possessing very limited product knowledge. These knowledge differences may lead each buyer down a different path. The knowledgeable individual feels confident in his ability to reasonably assess the strengths and weaknesses of the used cars he examines during search. The less knowledgeable individual does not. Given this inability to evaluate the product, he may elicit the aid of a "purchase pal," someone seen as being better equipped for evaluating the choice alternatives and willing to provide the necessary assistance.

Beyond affecting how a decision is made, consumer knowledge may also determine the final decision itself. Those used cars available for purchase but unknown to the buyer cannot be chosen. Or a telltale sign of engine problems, though undetected by a novice, may cause an expert to eliminate the car from further consideration. Knowledgeable consumers are more capable of evaluating a product's true merits,[3] which gives them a greater chance of choosing the better product.

Because of the pivotal role consumer knowledge plays during decision making and the many business and public policy implications derived from examining consumer knowledge (which we cover later in the chapter), understanding this knowledge is essential. In the following sections, we discuss five different types of consumer knowledge: (1) knowledge of the product's existence, (2) knowledge of the product's attributes and associations, (3) purchase knowledge, (4) consumption and usage knowledge, and (5) persuasion knowledge.

Types of Consumer Knowledge

Knowledge of the Product's Existence

One of the most fundamental aspects of consumer knowledge involves whether or not consumers are aware of a product's existence. In our earlier discussion of consumer decision making (Chapter 4), we noted that, before a product can enter the consideration set, it must gain entrance into the awareness set, which comprises those products known to the consumer. Until consumers learn about a product's existence, it is impossible to convert them into customers.

For this reason, gaining awareness among consumers is essential, especially for new products. A fundamental step when introducing a new product or store is to inform consumers of its existence. This is the case for the advertisement shown in Figure 9.1. Even established products often find themselves trying to create awareness, such as when they move into new markets. The Saturn Corp. is very familiar to American consumers as a supplier of automobiles. However, few Japanese consumers knew of the company when it entered Japan in 1997. Only 1 percent of Japanese surveyed even mentioned Saturn when asked to identify familiar automobile makers.[4] Enhancing Japanese consumers' awareness of Saturn will be critical to the company's future success.

Which brand names have the highest awareness levels among American consumers? According to one study, the top five, in order, were Campbell's soup, Hallmark greeting cards, UPS (United Parcel Service), Hershey's, and McDonald's.[5]

Figure 9.1   Advertising Aimed at Creating Store Awareness

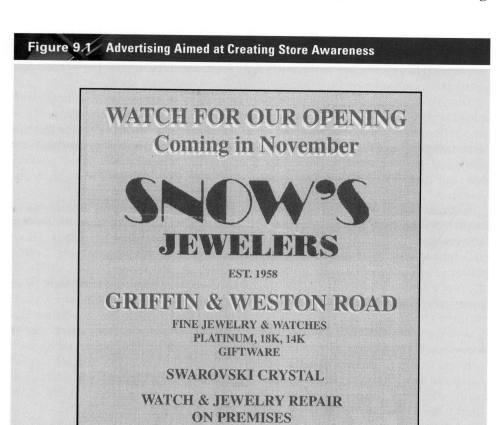

There are two basic approaches to assessing awareness. The first focuses on what consumers are able to *recall* from memory. Before reading past this sentence, stop and write down all the brands of toothpaste familiar to you. The percentage of people naming a particular brand would provide one indication of brand name awareness. In addition, we could also examine the particular brand named before any other brand name. The *percentage of people that name a given brand first* is known as **top-of-the-mind awareness.**

The second approach to measuring awareness focuses on name *recognition.* Rather than asking consumers to recall familiar names, consumers would be given a list of names and asked to identify the names familiar to them. Continuing our toothpaste example, consider the following set of toothpaste brands: Aim, AquaFresh, Check Up, Close Up, Colgate, Crest, Gleem, Pearl Drops, Pepsodent, Sensodyne, Topco, Topol, Ultrabrite, and Zact. It is probably a safe bet that you recognized at least one of these brand names but that you did not recall it when asked to do so in the preceding paragraph. For this reason, recall-based measures typically yield more conservative estimates of awareness than do recognition-based measures.

Knowledge of the Product's Attributes and Associations

Each product within the awareness set is likely to have a set of associations between itself and other information stored in memory. Crest may be strongly associated with fluoride protection. Rolex and Mercedes-Benz are likely to be linked with prestige. McDonald's is the home of the golden arches and Ronald McDonald. Goodyear has the blimp. And for many consumers, the name Nike activates the advertising slogan "Just do it."

Each of these products will possess additional associations beyond those mentioned. It is the entire array of associations that defines its **product image.** These associations may involve the *product's physical properties and attributes as well as the benefits and feelings that come from product consumption.* They may also include symbols (such as the drum-playing rabbit in the Energizer battery ads), persons (Michael Jordan and Gatorade), sponsorships (see Consumer in Focus 9.1), advertising campaigns and slogans, logos, and so on.

Image analysis involves *examining what consumers know about a product's attributes and associations.* The initial step of an image analysis is to identify the particular attributes and associations that determine a product's image. These associations can be revealed by consumers' responses to the question, "What comes to mind when you think about [brand or product name]?"

Not all associations are equally linked to a product. Some associations will be more salient and stronger than others. The Disney Co. has created numerous cartoon characters over the years. Yet few of them, if any, rival the association between the company and Mickey Mouse. The second step, then, of an image analysis is to assess the strength of a product's associations. This can be done in a couple of ways. One approach is to simply count how many consumers report a particular association when responding to the question about what comes to mind when they think about the product. The stronger the association, the more often it should be reported by consumers.

Another approach involves asking consumers to indicate the extent to which they perceive the product as being linked to particular attributes and associations. Computer companies, for example, might ask consumers to rate their products' reliability and the quality of their support service. We will defer further discussion of how this can be done until the next chapter where we describe multiattribute attitude models.

Consumer in Focus 9.1

And the Silver Medal Goes to . . . Nike?

Being an official sponsor of the Olympic games is not cheap these days. Most of the 11 main Olympics sponsors paid a minimum of $40 million each in cash and services for worldwide rights to market their names with the fabled five rings during the 1998 Winter Games and the 2000 Summer Games. So how successful have the companies been in establishing their Olympic connection?

To answer this question, the Leo Burnett ad agency surveyed consumers and asked them to pick the real Olympics sponsors from a list of big advertisers. McDonald's earned top honors with 85 percent correctly identifying it as an official sponsor. Next came Visa (70 percent), followed by Coca-Cola (68 percent), IBM (65 percent), and Kodak (63 percent).

Yet these numbers by themselves do not tell the full story. Particularly disturbing was that 11 of the 20 names most readily identified by consumers as official worldwide sponsors don't truly qualify. In fact, actual sponsor Coca-Cola—with 68 percent recognition—wasn't all that far ahead of nonsponsor Pepsi, which 55 percent of the survey identified incorrectly as a sponsor. Likewise, sponsor United Parcel Service, at 50 percent, had nonsponsor Federal Express hot on its heels, garnering 40 percent.

Particularly eye-popping is the number registered by Nike. Of those surveyed, 73 percent incorrectly named Nike as an official sponsor. This percentage exceeded that attained by all the bona fide sponsors except McDonald's.

Source: Excerpted from Sally Goll Beatty, "Olympic-Sponsor Recognition is Rivaled," The Wall Street Journal (February 18, 1998), B8.

A thorough understanding of a product's image often requires more than looking at the set of associations linked to the product. It may also be necessary to explore what a particular association represents in the consumer's psyche. Beyond knowing that Clydesdales are strongly associated with Budweiser, it is desirable to understand what Clydesdales symbolize to the consumer. For some, they may represent power, strength, and tradition: "They're working horses . . . that's the way they used to deliver beer." Others might view them as symbolizing the working-class man: "Strong, hard working, and proud." The end result of this type of probing is an enriched appreciation of the product's meaning to the consumer.[6]

Image analysis need not be limited to products alone. It can also be applied to the companies that produce the products. In 1999, *The Wall Street Journal* reported the findings of a study examining the corporate images of American companies.[7] Over 10,000 consumers rated the companies along 20 different attributes, including how much the company was respected and admired; the quality, innovation, value, and reliability of its products and services; and whether the company was a good citizen in its dealings with communities, employees, and the environment. These ratings were then combined to derive a "reputation quotient (RQ)," with higher ratings representing more favorable corporate images. And the winner is—Johnson & Johnson, the healthcare company famous for its baby powder and shampoo. For a complete listing of the 30 companies receiving the highest RQ ratings, see Table 9.1.

It's easy to see how consumers' image of a company's products would influence what they buy. But what about such things as whether the company itself is respected or is viewed as being environmentally responsible? Do consumers take these things into consideration when making their purchase decisions? According to *The Wall Street Journal* study, many do. Around 25 percent of consumers reported boycotting a company's products or urging others to do so during the past year when they disagreed with its policies and actions. Some of those surveyed indicated that they still harbor ill feelings toward Exxon because of the Alaskan oil spill. One woman reported that she wouldn't let her boyfriend stop at an Exxon gas station, "even for a pack of gum or to use the restroom."[8]

Table 9.1 Corporate Images: The Top 30

Rank and Company	RQ	Rank and Company	RQ	Rank and Company	RQ
1 Johnson & Johnson	83.4	11 Dell	78.4	21 FedEx	75.7
2 Coca-Cola	81.6	12 General Electric	78.1	22 Procter & Gamble	71.9
3 Hewlett-Packard	81.2	13 Lucent	78.0	23 Nike	71.3
4 Intel	81.0	14 Anheuser-Busch	78.0	24 McDonald's	71.2
5 Ben & Jerry's	81.0	15 Microsoft	77.9	25 Southwest Airlines	70.6
6 Wal*Mart	80.5	16 amazon.com	77.8	26 America Online	69.2
7 Xerox	79.9	17 IBM	77.6	27 DaimlerChrysler	69.1
8 Home Depot	79.7	18 Sony	77.4	28 Toyota	68.6
9 Gateway	78.8	19 Yahoo!	76.9	29 Sears	67.6
10 Disney	78.7	20 AT&T	75.7	30 Boeing	67.3

Source: Ronald Alsop, "The Best Corporate Reputations in America," The Wall Street Journal (September 23, 1999), B1, B22.

Purchase Knowledge

Purchase knowledge encompasses the *various pieces of information consumers possess about buying products.* This includes what consumers know about the product's price, whether it can be bought more cheaply at certain times, and where the product can be purchased.

How Much Does It Cost?

Certainly one of the most critical aspects of purchase knowledge involves the product's price because it can often make or break a sale. Such knowledge is important for a couple of reasons. First, think about how many times you have shopped around for the lowest price. Consumers unaware of the prices charged for the product of interest usually take the time and effort to acquire this information, particularly for more expensive products. In addition, knowledge about the typical range of prices within a product category may influence consumers' perceptions of whether the price charged by a single product is reasonable.[9] An exorbitant price may not seem unreasonable to the uninformed. Consequently, creating price knowledge is critical for companies offering consumers significant price savings. One example of this is illustrated in the ad shown in Figure 9.2, in which Buy.com communicates its lower prices relative to Amazon.com.

Managers' pricing decisions may depend on their perceptions of how well informed consumers are about prices.[10] Managers are more motivated to hold prices down and respond to competitors' price cuts when they believe consumers are

Figure 9.2 Creating Price Knowledge

knowledgeable about the prices charged by the market. Low levels of price knowledge, however, enable companies to be less concerned about price differences relative to the competition. If consumers are largely uninformed about relative price differences, companies may exploit this ignorance through higher prices. Accordingly, a key part of a product's image analysis involves understanding consumers' knowledge about its absolute price (the price of a 1-pound can of Maxwell House coffee) and its price relative to competition (whether this brand costs more or less than other brands).

When to Buy?

Consumers' beliefs about when to buy is another relevant component of purchase knowledge. Consumers who know that a product is traditionally placed on sale during certain times of the year may delay purchasing until such times.[11] Knowledge about when to buy can also determine when new innovations are purchased. Many consumers do not acquire new products immediately because they believe that prices will drop over time.

Where to Buy?

A fundamental issue consumers must address during decision making is where they should purchase the product. Many products can be acquired through different channels. Cosmetics may be purchased from a retail store, a catalog, a field representative of a cosmetic firm that uses a sales force (such as Avon or Mary Kay), or even the Internet. Because a channel may consist of multiple competitors, the consumer must decide which one to patronize. A consumer who has chosen to buy her cosmetics from a brick-and-mortar retailer can pick from several different department stores, mass merchandisers, and specialty stores.

Decisions about where to buy depend on purchase knowledge. A lack of awareness precludes purchase consideration. One of the biggest challenges facing Internet retailers is creating awareness of their existence. Ads such as the one shown in Figure 9.3 are intended to overcome this challenge. Similarly, the U.S. Postal Service recently mailed consumers a brochure informing them of the variety of ways for buying postage stamps, including by mail, over the phone, and through the Internet (www.usps.com).

For traditional brick-and-mortar retailers, another component of purchase knowledge involves where the product is located within the store. In one study, shoppers were shown floor plans of a supermarket and asked to identify the location of various products. Shoppers were more accurate for products placed on peripheral or exterior aisles than for those items located along central or interior aisles. Accuracy was also greater for smaller stores and for shoppers reporting higher levels of store patronage.[12]

Knowledge about a product's location within a store can affect buying behavior.[13] When consumers are unfamiliar with the store, they have to rely more heavily on in-store information and displays for identifying product locations. This increased processing of in-store stimuli may activate needs or desires previously unrecognized, thereby leading to unplanned purchases.

Consumption and Usage Knowledge

Consumption and usage knowledge encompasses the *information in memory about how a product can be consumed and what is required to actually use the product.* This knowledge is important for several reasons. First, consumers are unlikely to buy a product when they lack sufficient information about how to use it. Marketing efforts designed to educate the consumer about how to consume the product are

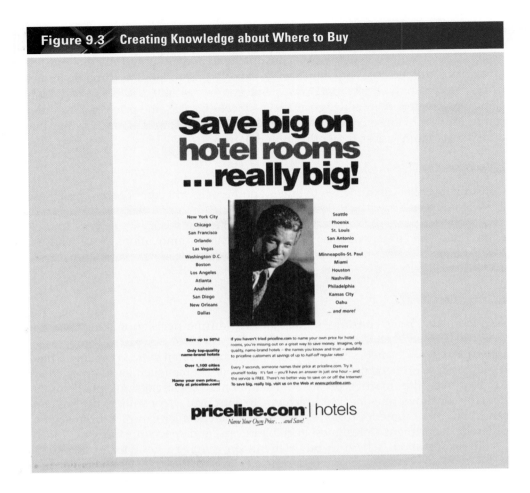

Figure 9.3   Creating Knowledge about Where to Buy

then needed. For example, some consumers avoid making conference calls simply because of a lack of knowledge about how to do so. One way of overcoming this barrier, shown in Figure 9.4, is to provide consumers with the necessary information on a plastic card that can be stored for future reference. Even when consumers possess usage knowledge, educational efforts might still be necessary. You might remember from Chapter 6 (see Consumer in Focus 6.2) the example of trying to teach Russians how to drink vodka "properly."

Another barrier to purchase occurs when consumers possess incomplete information about the different ways or situations in which a product can be consumed. Educational efforts are warranted again, as is the case for the Bounce ad presented in Figure 9.5. The ad describes how Bounce, traditionally found in clothes dryers, can be used throughout the home as a freshener. Such efforts are quite common, since businesses often identify and promote new product uses to enhance demand, particularly in the case of mature products.

Note, however, that care must be taken in selecting new uses. A major concern is that a new use may, in fact, lower a product's attractiveness to consumers. For example, Avon employed a multiple-usage positioning for its bath oil, Skin-So-Soft. In addition to describing its use as an after-shower moisturizer, Avon suggested that it could remove tar spots on automobiles. Some consumers may be less than enthusiastic about using a skin moisturizer that also removed tar from a car!

Figure 9.4 Creating Knowledge about How to Use a Service

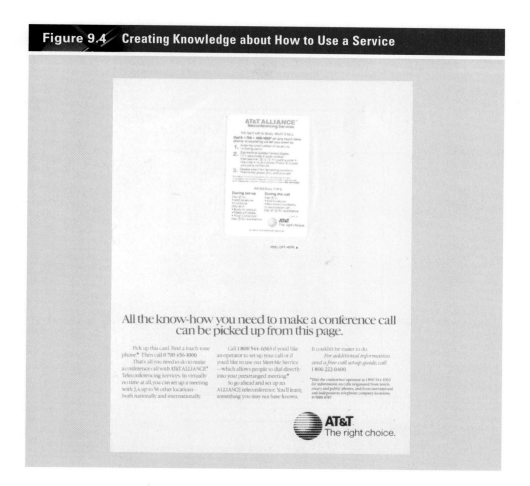

Even if inadequate consumption knowledge does not prevent product purchase, it can still have detrimental effects on consumer satisfaction. A misused product may not perform properly, causing customers to feel dissatisfied. Even worse, misuse may lead to bodily injury, such as accidents involving handheld power saws.[14]

Persuasion Knowledge

Persuasion knowledge represents what consumers know about the goals and tactics of those trying to persuade them.[15] Let's test your persuasion knowledge. Look at Figure 9.6, which reproduces a road sign posted by those supporting a candidate's election to the local school board. Can you identify the goals and tactics of this persuasion attempt?

If you have ever voted in an election where numerous candidates are competing for numerous positions, there is a very good chance that at least some of the names shown in the voting booth were unfamiliar to you. And sometimes you are forced to make a choice between two or more unknown individuals. Yet this choice might easily change if one of the candidates was familiar to you. As noted in the chapter opening vignette, such familiarity may be a deciding factor. Consequently, enhancing voters' familiarity with a candidate's name may tip the scales in the candidate's favor.

Figure 9.5   Expanding Consumers' Knowledge about Different Ways to Use a Product

One goal, then, of the road sign appearing in Figure 9.6 is to build awareness of the candidate's name. Most people probably recognize this. What may escape most people is the sign's use of visual imagery for increasing voters' memory of the candidate's name. In particular, the red heart provides a visual representation of the name. As we shall see in Chapter 16, visual representations of semantic concepts (e.g., the name of a person or product) can be a very effective tactic for enhancing memory.

The use of the red heart within the sign has another potential benefit, depending on whether the heart evokes particular feelings or associations that are favorable. If it does, then these feelings and associations may carry over to the candidate. By simply pairing the candidate with a liked stimulus, voters' liking of the candidate may be increased. Later in Chapter 15, we discuss how simply associating one object with another may influence consumers' beliefs, attitudes, and choices.

Persuasion knowledge is important because it influences how consumers respond to persuasion attempts. Knowledge about a particular persuasion tactic may not only eliminate its effectiveness, it may also reduce persuasion, such as when consumers resent being subjected to tactics perceived by them as manipulative.

Figure 9.6   Do You Recognize the Persuasion Tactics Used by This Sign?

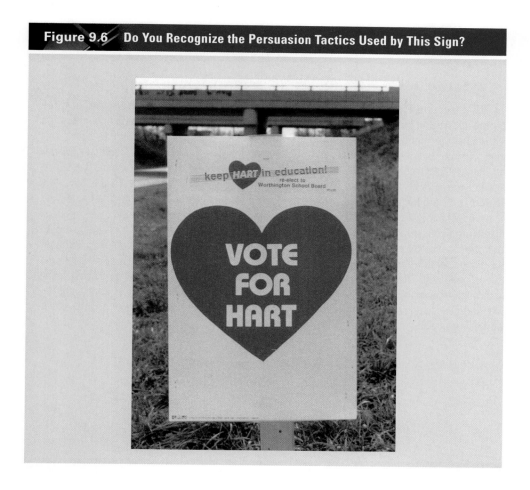

Sources of Consumer Knowledge

People acquire their consumer knowledge from a variety of sources. The opinions of others, especially those perceived to be more knowledgeable about the product in question, are valuable sources of information. Much of what we know as consumers can be traced to what we have learned from our family, friends, co-workers, and others (salespeople, pharmacists, teachers, and so forth).

Consumer knowledge is also acquired from nonpersonal sources of information. The media is filled with stories about consumers and products. Companies spend billions of dollars each year on advertising designed to educate consumers about their products (see Consumer in Focus 9.2). Magazines, such as *Consumer Reports,* are loaded with product ratings and tips on how to be a smarter shopper. The Internet has provided consumers with easy access to a wealth of information. Figure 9.7 contains an ad for an Internet company (CNET.com) that offers product-comparison information to consumers looking to buy a computer. And the Yellow Pages have been a valued source of information for decades. Even so, as described in Consumer in Focus 9.3, it's trying to enhance its image as a consumer resource book.

One of the most fundamental sources of consumer knowledge comes from experience itself. No matter what others may say, there's no substitute for the real thing. In most cases, we learn a considerable amount from buying and consuming.

Consumer in Focus 9.2

Magazine and Television Advertising as Sources of Information

A new study sponsored by the Magazine Publishers of America suggests that magazine advertising deserves a little more respect when it comes to delivering cost-effective brand recognition. Conducted by Millward Brown, the study surveyed some 500,000 consumers by telephone over a two-year period. Participants were asked to recall any of 113 brands across 22 product categories and how they learned of the brand. The total number of respondents who said that they were made aware of a certain product through a magazine ad was 64 percent—29 percent through magazines alone, and 35 percent when magazines and television were combined. The total number made aware of a brand through television was 71 percent—36 percent attributed awareness to television alone, and 35 percent to combined television and magazine ads.

The study also found that magazines were almost three times more cost-effective than television in generating brand awareness.

The results are better than expected, some say. Magazines have long been treated as a weak runner-up to television in terms of creating brand awareness. But in fact, little has been known on the subject. Until now, data quantifying how magazine ads measure up on the effectiveness index have been scarce, forcing publishers and media buyers to make do with conventional wisdom and ancillary information. "We'd use Simmons or MRI data to look at the target audience and their media habits, as well as at successful case studies like the 'got milk?' campaign," says Anita Peterson, group director of magazine strategy at DDB Needham/Optimum Media.

Source: Excerpted from Rachel X. Weissman, "Just Paging Through," American Demographics (April 1999), 28–29.

Consumer in Focus 9.3

The Yellow Pages Wants to Expand Its Image as a Source of Information

The familiar refrain "Let Your Fingers Do the Walking" is being scrapped as the Yellow Pages seeks to change its image from a mere listing of telephone numbers to a consumer resource book. The "walking fingers" logo was created in 1961 and became one of the most widely recognized advertising campaigns. Slightly more than half the directory publishers still use the logo today. But after nearly a 40-year run, the slogan and fingers have been given their walking papers.

"Everybody knows about the Yellow Pages. Everybody knows about the walking fingers, but candidly it's a little boring," says Jim Logan, president and CEO of the Denver-based Yellow Pages Publishers Association. "When we started thinking about it . . . you sort of quickly came to the idea that if you wanted to increase usage, you would have to do something different."

So this $12 billion-a-year industry kicked off a $24 million campaign, featuring comedian Jon Lovitz, in January 1999, its first since the breakup of AT&T in 1984. The campaign replaces the walking fingers with a light bulb, along with the phrase, "Get an Idea." According to Logan, the goal is to reshape the image of the Yellow Pages into a consumer resource book.

Yet not everyone is sure that the change from the walking fingers to a light bulb is such a bright idea. "People generally use the Yellow Pages for a predetermined range of things that they need. I think the idea of repositioning as a book where you get an idea . . . stretches the publication into an area where it probably can't deliver on that promise," says Jim Johnson, president and CEO of Enterprise IG, a corporate branding and identity consulting firm in New York City.

Source: Excerpted from Sandy Shore, "Yellow Pages Seeks to Expand, Enhance Its Image," Miami Herald (December 15, 1998), 41A.

Figure 9.7   Sources of Knowledge on the Internet

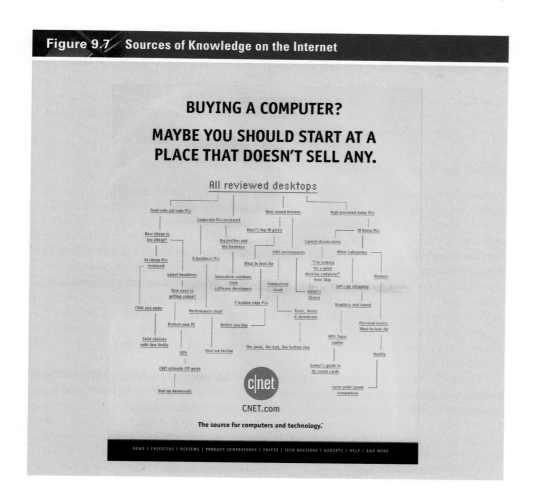

Sometimes purchase and consumption are chosen as a simple way of learning about the product rather than engaging in effortful information search. We may decide that the easiest way to learn about a new food item discovered at the grocery store is to take it home and try it.

Whether or not knowledge is based on direct experience is important. Actual experience typically makes us feel more confident about what we know.[16] Your mother may say that you're going to love her new recipe, but you really don't know until you actually taste it. Greater confidence, in turn, means that you are more likely to rely on this knowledge during decision making, thereby reducing external search. Finally, those interested in changing consumer knowledge face a greater challenge when this knowledge is based on direct experience. Compared to knowledge based on indirect experience (e.g., what you might learn from an ad or a friend), knowledge derived from actual experience is more resistant to change.[17]

Companies sometimes have to adjust their marketing strategies when targeting consumers lacking direct experience with the product. One example comes from the cruise line industry. Many consumers have never taken a cruise because they're apprehensive about whether they'll enjoy the consumption experience. To alleviate this concern, Carnival Cruise Lines offered a money-back guarantee for any unused portion of a cruise. During its first three months of existence, only 37 of the more than a quarter of a million passengers applied for the refund.[18]

The Benefits of Understanding Consumer Knowledge

Now that we have covered the main types and sources of consumer knowledge, let's turn our attention to the major business and public policy benefits offered by an analysis of consumer knowledge.

Lack of Knowledge

Perhaps the most basic benefit that can be derived from an examination of consumer knowledge is the identification of **knowledge gaps.** Knowledge gaps is the term we use to refer to *an absence of information in memory.* When consumers are unaware of the product's existence, an important knowledge gap exists. But knowledge gaps are not limited to simply whether consumers are familiar with what products and retailers are available. Even if the product's or retailer's existence is known, consumers still may have significant gaps in other aspects of their knowledge. Perhaps they are unaware of some important association or attribute, such as when consumers do not know which product charges the lowest price or which product offers the best warranty. Maybe they are ignorant of some valuable product use. There may be many different types of knowledge gaps in the minds of target consumers.

From a business perspective, the key is to identify gaps whose existence undermines the likelihood of consumers choosing the product when making their purchase decisions. Knowledge gaps are rampant for new products. A major hurdle for Web TV, in which consumers can gain access to the Internet through their television set instead of a computer, has been getting consumers to understand what Internet television really is.[19]

Knowledge gaps exist even for well-known products. Consider what happened when CBS's *60 Minutes* aired a segment that moderate consumption of red (but not white) wine reduces the risk of heart disease. Sales of red wine skyrocketed by 40 percent! One company later placed tags on its red wine bottles carrying excerpts from the program.[20] Similarly, Dannon hopes that educating consumers about the medical benefits of calcium consumption (see Figure 9.8) will enhance demand for its yogurt.

From a public policy perspective, knowledge gaps that undermine consumer welfare are the focal point. Governmental agencies such as the Federal Trade Commission may survey consumers about their knowledge to help guide policies aimed at protecting the "uninformed" consumer. When consumers are thought to lack sufficient information to make an "informed choice," policy makers may enact legislation that requires the disclosure of appropriate information. This was the motivation behind the government's requiring the cigarette industry to replace the original warning required by law ("The Surgeon General has determined that cigarette smoking is dangerous to your health"). Cigarette manufacturers are now required to rotate periodically a series of warning labels describing specific dangers (e.g., "Smoking causes lung cancer, heart disease, emphysema, and may complicate pregnancy"). Similarly, the Centers for Disease Control and the American Academy of Dermatology had been trying to educate consumers about the cancer risk of excessive exposure to the sun.[21]

Undesirable Knowledge

In addition to identifying knowledge gaps, businesses and public policy makers must also be sensitive to the possibility that consumers may possess knowledge

Figure 9.8 Dannon Wants to Educate Consumers About the Benefits of Product Consumption

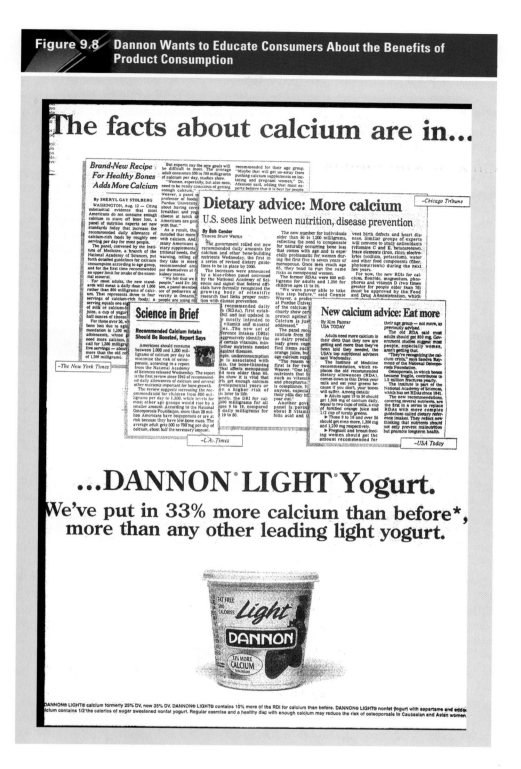

that is undesirable from the company's or policy maker's perspective. Analysis of a product's image, for instance, may reveal shortcomings that limit its sales potential. Mercedes-Benz has been very successful in developing a reputation for high-quality automobiles. Nonetheless, it also has certain associations that undermine its image. According to the chief creative officer of Mercedes' advertising agency, consumers view the brand as too "cold and Germanic."[22] Some people are put off by the company's snobby image. BMW has experienced similar problems. "Before, I think we were a little cold and aloof," says Jim McDowell, vice president of marketing for BMW's U.S. sales unit. "We have been working hard to project a more human side to BMW. We want it to be a smiling brand."[23]

Sometimes undesirable knowledge is the result of consumers being misinformed. They believe things that are not true. *This inaccurate knowledge,* typically referred to as **misperception,** may pose a major barrier to the success of a business. A retailer that charges the same prices as a competitor but is misperceived as being more expensive is at a disadvantage.

When misperceptions exist that undermine the product's attractiveness to consumers, corrective actions are necessary. Lever Brothers, the maker of Dove soap, identified several undesirable misperceptions about its product. It addressed this inaccurate knowledge by mailing target households a packet that contained, among other things, the brochure appearing in Figure 9.9. These misperceptions were listed inside the brochure, followed by an explanation as to why each was incorrect.

Figure 9.9   **One Company's Effort to Fight Product Misperception**

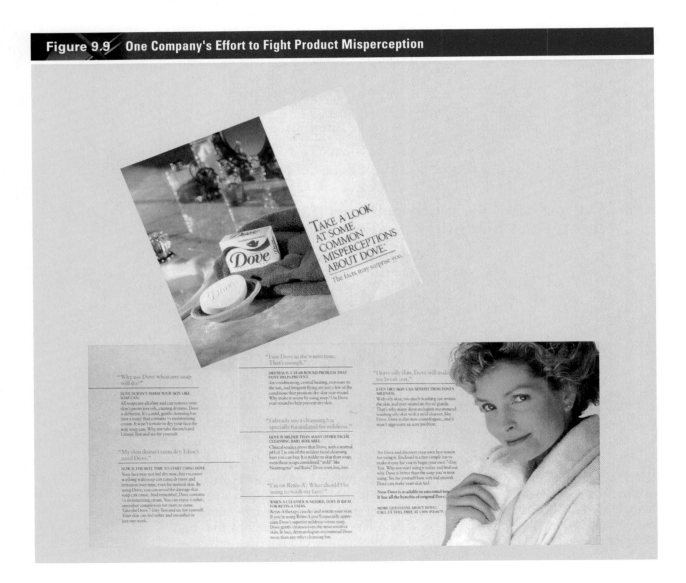

Another example comes from the lawn care industry. Consumers were asked to estimate the price of one company's service. Although customers gave very accurate estimates, this was not the case for nonusers. Their average price estimate was twice the actual price, and many nonusers exaggerated the price by a factor of 3 or 4. This discovery of nonusers' unfavorable price misperceptions resulted in a change in the company's advertising strategy. A new campaign centering on the theme "It's not as expensive as you might think" was soon launched. This same basic theme is reflected in the Mercedes ad shown in Figure 9.10. Consumer in Focus 9.4 describes Hallmark's recent efforts to change consumers' misperceptions about the prices of its greeting cards.

Thus, the detection of undesirable knowledge often triggers efforts to modify the product's image. Doing so requires changing consumers' opinions of the product. Later in the book is a chapter (Chapter 15) devoted to how this can be done.

Gauging the Product's Positioning Success

An understanding of consumer knowledge provides an acid test of a company's success in achieving its desired product positioning in the marketplace. A product trying to position itself as "cool" and "hip" can discover how successful it has been by examining the product's image among target consumers. The extent to which these desired associations is represented within consumers' product knowledge sends a clear signal of how well the company has created the desired mindset.

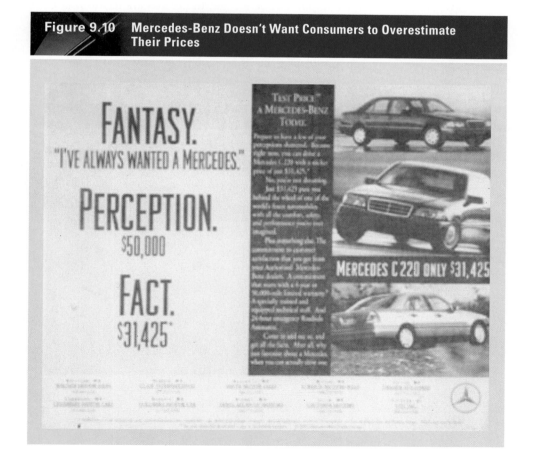

Figure 9.10   Mercedes-Benz Doesn't Want Consumers to Overestimate Their Prices

Consumer in Focus 9.4

Hallmark Tries to "Correct" Consumers' Price Knowledge

Never mind all those $3 and $4 Valentine's Day cards that you saw at the store. Hallmark Cards Inc. is trying to jump-start sales by arguing that its cards aren't as expensive as you think. In 1998, the greeting card company launched a $10 million advertising and marketing campaign plugging its lower-end cards that sell for less than $2. About 30 percent of the cards Hallmark sells costs more than that, and some cost as much as $4.75.

The new ads are a bit of a departure for a $175 million-a-year advertiser that is better known for urging consumers to buy by the label. "A lot of people think cards in general are too expensive," says Adrienne S. Lallo, a Hallmark spokeswoman. "We're out to correct that piece of misinformation." Hallmark is careful to note that it isn't lowering card prices, but trying to correct what it says is a misconception among customers. Some consumers believe that its cards are "50 percent higher than they really are," says Ms. Lallo.

Since 1990, total annual greeting card sales have been flat at about $7 billion. Hallmark, which holds about 42 percent of the greeting card market, says a major goal of the campaign is to strengthen the entire greeting card category, which has experienced stagnant sales for years.

One TV spot shows a can of soup with the caption "Feeds a cold." A caption under a card to a lover reads "Starts a fever." Another spot shows a bag of potato chips stamped "Greasy." A card addressed to the boss is tagged "Slick." In both commercials, the "cha-ching" sound of a cash register is followed by the card prices: $1.65 and $1.95, respectively.

Source: Excerpted from Calmetta Y. Coleman, "Hallmark Campaign Focuses on Card Costs," The Wall Street Journal (February 12, 1998), B6.

So how successful have companies been in getting teenagers to think of their products as "cool"? Each year, Teenage Research Unlimited, a market research company, surveys 2,000 teenagers about the three "coolest" brands at that time. What were the coolest brands among teenagers in 1998? Was there a change from 1997? Look at Table 9.2 for the answers to these questions.

Table 9.2   Cool Brands: Teenagers' Top 10

Top 1998 Brands (1997 rank)	Total 1998	1997	Males 1998	Females 1998
1. Nike (1)	38%	52%	42%	33%
2. Adidas (6)	19%	8%	15%	23%
3. Tommy Hilfiger (2)	18%	16%	18%	18%
4. Sony (4)	11%	9%	17%	5%
5. Gap (3)	10%	11%	5%	14%
6. Pepsi (8)	9%	7%	11%	8%
7. Coca-Cola (9)	8%	7%	9%	7%
8. Levi's (5)	7%	9%	7%	8%
9. Ralph Lauren/Polo (11)	7%	6%	6%	8%
10. Nintendo (7)	6%	7%	11%	2%

Source: Jennifer Lach, Like, "I Just Gotta Have It," American Demographics (February 1999), 24.

Note. Numbers represent the percentage of teenagers that identified the brand as one of three "coolest" brands.

Discovering New Uses

Consumers are often ingenious at coming up with new ways of using an old product. As such, they can be an invaluable source of ideas about new product uses. A classic example is Kimberly-Clarke's Kleenex tissue. It was sold originally as something to be used along with cold cream for removing makeup. Eventually, it was repositioned as a disposable handkerchief after the company had received numerous letters from consumers describing new uses for the product. At one point, the company included a package insert listing nearly 50 other uses that consumers had found.[24] By understanding usage knowledge, companies may discover new uses that can be promoted as a means of broadening their products' appeal.

Gauging the Severity of Competitive Threats

An assessment of consumer knowledge regarding competitors is useful for gauging competitive threats to one's business. To illustrate, suppose that a food company surveyed its customers about their opinions of the company's brand as well as competitors' brands. Now suppose that it found that competitor A is perceived as highly similar to the company's offering, while the rest of the competition is viewed as inferior. Consequently, the company should be much more concerned about competitor A's potential for stealing its customers and may wish to undertake activities that would help further differentiate its brand from competitor A's brand in the minds of its customers.

Enhancing the Effectiveness of Customer Recruitment Activities

Finally, an examination of consumer knowledge can assist in the development of customer recruitment activities. Consider attempts to steal a competitor's business. In this situation, it is necessary to focus on the brand images held by the competitors' customers. Ideally, this would be done for the customers of each separate competitor, because different competitive customers may hold very different images. Presumably, there are reasons why consumers decided to do business with the competition. These reasons should become apparent when you compare how a competitor's customers rate the product they currently buy and the product you want them to buy. Perhaps they think your product costs more. Maybe it is seen as possessing lower quality. Whatever the reason, you will have a better understanding of those deficiencies in your product that must be remedied in order to convert the competitor's customers into your customers.

Identifying what needs to be changed is only part of the story. You also need to identify how such changes might best be accomplished. Should the company rely on advertising to carry its message? If so, should the advertising target the customer, or would it be better to focus on a particular knowledge source such as the pharmacist? Maybe salespeople would be more successful in carrying the company's message. By understanding which knowledge sources consumers rely upon, companies can more effectively and efficiently direct their efforts in the proper direction.

The nature of consumer knowledge also carries implications concerning whether sales messages should focus on technical information regarding product attributes versus emphasizing product benefits that may be more easily understood by target consumers. Whereas knowledgeable consumers are able to use technical information when forming their product evaluations, unknowledgeable consumers are less able to do so. Instead, they may be more persuaded by messages conveying easily understood product benefits.[25] Finally, the nature of consumers' persuasion knowledge may suggest the need to avoid persuasion tactics that are blatantly obvious to the target market.

Summary

Consumer knowledge consists of the information stored within memory. This chapter discusses five major types of consumer knowledge: (1) knowledge of the product's existence (i.e., awareness), (2) knowledge of the product attributes and associations (i.e., its image), (3) purchase knowledge, (4) consumption and usage knowledge, and (5) persuasion knowledge. Awareness and image analyses help companies to better understand consumer knowledge. And this understanding may yield many benefits, such as the identification of knowledge gaps or undesirable knowledge (such as misperceptions) that undermine the odds of the product being chosen. Examining consumer knowledge sheds light on a product's positioning success. It may lead to the discovery of previously unappreciated product uses. And it is useful for gauging the severity of competitive threats and helps companies become more effective in their customer recruitment activities. Finally, companies should understand the sources of consumer knowledge and be especially attentive to whether this knowledge is based on direct experience.

Review and Discussion Questions

1. Why might a company care about top-of-the-mind awareness?

2. Consider the following set of results from an image analysis in which the customers of a competitive food product (brand A) rated their own brand, your brand (B), and another competitor (brand C). What conclusions can you draw from this information?

    good tasting <u>C</u>: <u>A</u>: <u>B</u>: __: __: __: __ poor tasting

    high in nutrition <u>C</u>: __: __: <u>A</u>: <u>B</u>: __: __ low in nutrition

    expensive <u>C</u>: __: __: <u>A</u>: __: <u>B</u>: __ inexpensive

    easy to cook __: <u>B</u>: <u>A</u>: __: __: __: <u>C</u> difficult to cook

3. What suggestions do you have for improving the informativeness of *The Wall Street Journal*'s study of corporate image discussed in the chapter?

4. Describe how advertising strategy may depend on consumer knowledge.

5. A grocer recently completed a study of consumers who patronize the store. One of the more intriguing findings was that the amount spent during a shopping trip depended on the number of times a consumer had shopped at the store. Consumers spent much more money when it was only their first or second trip. How can you explain this finding?

6. You are developing some brochures that describe a fairly sophisticated and technically oriented product. Results of market research indicate that the two primary target markets hold very different beliefs about how much product knowledge they possess. One segment perceives itself as very knowledgeable, whereas the other thinks it is quite ignorant about the product. What implications does this difference in perceived knowledge carry for developing the brochures?

7. A recent market study suggests that consumers have very limited knowledge about the prices charged by your product and competitors. When asked to give a specific price, most were unable to do so. Moreover, the average error of those giving a price was plus or minus 25 percent. What conclusions can you draw from these results about consumers' price sensitivity during decision making?

8. A recent survey of various target markets reveals important differences in both their level of product knowledge and use of friends' recommendations during decision making. Consumers having limited knowledge relied heavily on others' recommendations, whereas knowledgeable consumers did not. How can you explain this difference?

Endnotes

1. Joseph A. Alba and J. Wesley Hutchinson, "Dimensions of Consumer Expertise," *Journal of Consumer Research* 13 (March 1987), 411–454.

2. Fran Brennan, "Limit Kids' Juice Intake, Experts Say," *Miami Herald* (January 31, 1997), 1F.

3. Mita Sujan, "Consumer Knowledge: Effects on Evaluation Strategies Mediating Consumer Judgments," *Journal of Consumer Research* 12 (June 1985), 31–46.

4. Alan L. Adler, "Saturn Faces Difficult Launch in Japan," *Miami Herald* (May 15, 1997), 4G.

5. Diane Crispell and Kathleen Brandenburg, "What's in a Brand?" *American Demographics* (May 1993), 26–32.

6. For an interesting discussion of image analysis, see Sal Randazzo, "Build a BIP to Understand Brand's Image," *Marketing News* (September 16, 1991), 18.

7. Ronald Alsop, "The Best Corporate Reputations in America," *The Wall Street Journal* (September 23, 1999), B1, B22.

8. Ibid.

9. For research concerning the impact of prior knowledge on consumers' acceptance of a product's price, see Akshay R. Rao and Wanda A. Sieben, "The Effect of Prior Knowledge on Price Acceptability and the Type of Information Examined," *Journal of Consumer Research* 19 (September 1992), 256–270.

10. Joel E. Urbany and Peter R. Dickson, "Consumer Information, Competitive Rivalry, and Pricing in the Retail Grocery Industry" (working paper, University of South Carolina, 1988).

11. For research on how consumer knowledge about deals affects purchase behavior, see Aradhna Krishna, "The Effect of Deal Knowledge on Consumer Purchase Behavior," *Journal of Marketing Research* 31 (February 1994), 76–91.

12. Robert Sommer and Susan Aitkens, "Mental Mapping of Two Supermarkets," *Journal of Consumer Research* 9 (September 1982), 211–215.

13. C. Whan Park, Easwar S. Iyer, and Daniel C. Smith, "The Effects of Situational Factors on In-Store Grocery Shopping Behavior: The Role of Store Environment and Time Available for Shopping," *Journal of Consumer Research* 15 (March 1989), 422–433.

14. For an example of research concerning product safety knowledge, see Richard Staelin, "The Effects of Consumer Education on Consumer Product Safety Behavior," *Journal of Consumer Research* 5 (June 1978), 30–40.

15. Marian Friestad and Peter Wright, "The Persuasion Knowledge Model: How People Cope with Persuasion Attempts," *Journal of Consumer Research* 21 (June 1994), 1–31.

16. Lawrence J. Marks and Michael A. Kamins, "The Use of Product Sampling and Advertising: Effects of Sequence of Exposure and Degree of Advertising Claim Exaggeration on Consumers' Belief Strength, Belief Confidence, and Attitudes," *Journal of Marketing Research* 25 (August 1988), 266–281.

17. Chenghuan Wu and David R. Shaffer, "Susceptibility to Persuasive Appeals as a Function of Source Credibility and Prior Experience with the Attitude Object," *Journal of Personality and Social Psychology* 52 (1987), 677–688.

18. Dale K. DuPont, "Carnival Cruisers Just in Time for Money-back Offer," *Miami Herald* (November 21, 1996), 1C, 5C.

19. Michel Marriott, "Will Computers on TV Go the Way of the 8-Track?" *Miami Herald* (March 1, 1998), 16H.

20. Carole Sugarman, "Wine's Benefits, Risks Argued on Labels," *The State* (November 10, 1992), 4D.

21. Shannon Dortch, "There Goes the Sun," *American Demographics* (August 1997), 4–7.

22. Sally Goll Beatty, "Mercedes Hopes Duckie, Child Broaden Appeal," *The Wall Street Journal* (May 21, 1997), B1, B8.

23. Oscar Suris, "Now, BMW and Mercedes Seem Sensible," *The Wall Street Journal* (November 6, 1996), B1, B8.

24. The authors wish to thank Professor Jim Burroughs of Rutgers University for this example.

25. Joseph A. Alba and J. Wesley Hutchinson, "Dimensions of Consumer Expertise," *Journal of Consumer Research* 13 (March 1987), 411–454.

CHAPTER 10

Consumer Intentions, Attitudes, Beliefs, and Feelings

OPENING VIGNETTE

Americans' confidence in the economy surged in November 1999, boding well for retailers during the holiday shopping season. The Conference Board reported that its index of consumer confidence rose from 130.5 in October to an unexpectedly strong 135.8 in November. This increase ended a string of four straight months of decline and left the index only about four points below its peak of 139 in June 1999, which was the highest reading in more than 30 years.

The sharp rise comes after months of worry that confidence was swooning on fears that the economy was slowing. The Federal Reserve raised interest rates three times during the year to try to keep the economy from overheating and head off a resurgence of inflation. The rising interest rates shook Wall Street, sending stocks on a wild ride. But "consumers got over being pessimistic earlier in the fall and are feeling better now, particularly about the future," said Gary Thayer, chief economist at A. G. Edwards & Sons in St. Louis. Thanks to a sharp rebound on Wall Street, low unemployment rates and growth in personal income, consumers seem more certain that good economic times won't come screeching to a halt anytime soon.

Why are consumers' opinions about the future health of the economy important? Those optimistic about the future are more willing to spend their money, particularly when it comes to major purchases such as homes and automobiles. Consumer confidence is considered an important economic indicator because consumer spending accounts for two-thirds of the nation's overall economic activity.

So did this surging confidence show itself at the cash register? It certainly did. Americans went on a shopping spree during November 1999. Retail sales during this month increased by 0.9 percent and grew from across-the-board demand on everything from cars and clothing to hardware and furniture. By comparison, sales increased only 0.3 percent in October. "It looks like retailers are on track for one of the best, if not the best, Christmas buying seasons this decade," said Mark Zandi, economist with Regional Financial Associates.

Source: Excerpted from Jeannine Aversa, "Retail Sales Soar as Prices Hold," Miami Herald (December 15, 1999), 4C; Rachel Beck, "In Good News for Retailers, Consumer Confidence Spikes," Miami Herald (December 1, 1999), 7C.

Confidence in the economy's future health is but one of the countless opinions held by consumers. Consumers hold opinions about products, stores, companies, advertising, salespeople, shopping, consuming, other consumers, and the list goes on and on. Some of these opinions represent what we like and dislike. Other opinions represent what we believe and how we feel. And still other

281

opinions reflect our judgments about how we will behave in the future. This chapter focuses on these different types of opinions. We begin with a consideration of consumers' opinions about what they intend to do.

Consumer Intentions

One of the most important skills a company can possess is the ability to predict how people will act as consumers. Doing so helps them answer such fundamental questions as "How much of my existing product should be produced to meet demand?" and "How much demand will there be for my new product?" Yet answering these questions is far from easy. Businesses often lose money because they either underestimate or overestimate demand. The rather dramatic failure rate of new products (by some estimates, nearly 90 percent) provides compelling testimony to the difficulties of forecasting consumer behavior. And just about every Christmas there is at least one toy so popular that it quickly sells out, leaving frantic parents desperately searching in hope of finding just one more. The dissatisfaction that arose when consumers were unable to purchase a Furby toy advertised as available at Walgreens led this retailer to quickly apologize in writing (see Figure 10.1).

Beyond what consumers buy, companies are also interested in predicting where they'll buy, when they'll buy, and how much they'll buy. And this interest goes beyond just buying. Customer service departments must determine the number of personnel needed for handling consumer inquiries and complaints. Such determinations should be based at least partly on estimates of the number of consumers that will require daily attention. Industries that live off consumption

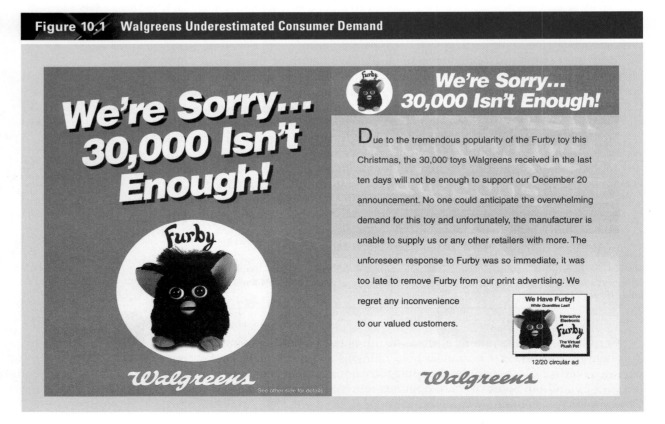

Figure 10.1   Walgreens Underestimated Consumer Demand

Consumer in Focus 10.1

Public Policy Makers Also Are Interested in Predicting Consumer Behavior

Government health officials predict that 3.5 million Americans would quit smoking—with the young and minorities leading the way—if tobacco opponents succeed with a plan to raise the price of a pack of cigarettes by half. A total of 2.4 million more would cut back on the number of cigarettes they smoke, according to a study released by the Centers for Disease Control and Prevention. Combined, those who would quit or cut back after a 50 percent price hike make up 13 percent of the nation's 47 million smokers. If the price rose just 25 percent, 6 percent of smokers would quit or cut back, the CDC said.

The CDC surveyed adults for 14 years for the study, breaking results down by race, age, income, and gender. Ninety-five percent of Hispanics would quit or cut back if prices rose 50 percent, compared with 16 percent of blacks and 2 percent of whites. Twenty-nine percent of smokers between the ages of 18 and 24 would quit or cut back, compared with

21 percent of those 25 to 39 and 5 percent of those at least 40 years old. The survey also found poorer people more likely to quit, with 15 percent of those earning the national median income of $33,106 or less quitting or cutting back, compared with 9 percent of those earning more than the median. Men were more likely to quit than women, 13 percent to 10 percent.

In June 1998, the U.S. Senate killed an antismoking bill that would have raised the price per pack, now an average $1.95 nationwide, by $1.10. Democrats have promised to revive the issue. "The tobacco industry in particular tried to make the case that increasing the price would be harmful to minority groups and low-income groups . . . but just the opposite is true," said Michael Eriksen, director of the CDC's Office of Smoking and Health. "That's good news because the same groups are the ones who bear the greatest burden from tobacco-related disease."

Source: Excerpted from "Many Would Quit Smoking If Prices Rose, U.S. Says," Miami Herald *(July 31, 1998), 14A.*

activities (e.g., television networks) are interested in predicting consumption behavior (e.g., whether a new show will attract a large enough audience to justify its being placed on the schedule). As described in Consumer in Focus 10.1, public policy makers may be interested in predicting the effects of a change in the marketplace (such as increasing the price of cigarettes) on consumption.

So how can we predict what people will do? A common practice is to rely on past behavior to forecast future behavior. If sales have increased steadily at a rate of 15 percent annually over the past few years, one might reasonably anticipate a similar increase next year. If a consumer has bought the same brand of coffee each of the last ten trips to the grocery store, it would seem a safe bet that the same brand will be purchased during the next trip.

But things change, and what happened in the past may become far less relevant than what is happening today. Sales of American flags soared like an eagle during the Gulf War of 1991 as a wave of patriotism flooded the country, a tidal wave that eventually subsided. Sales trends are sometimes erratic, jumping up and down. Cigar consumption in the United States peaked in 1973 at a little more than 11 billion cigars. In 1993, only 3.4 billion cigars went up in smoke. Sales then rebounded, especially among female consumers. Consumption rose to 5 billion cigars by 1997.[1] These fluctuations, unless of a regular nature, reduce the forecasting power of past behavior. And, of course, past behavior is not even available for forecasting first-time behaviors such as the purchase of a new product.

An alternative approach to predicting consumer behavior involves asking consumers what they intend to do. **Intentions** are *subjective judgments about how we will behave in the future.* There are many types of consumer intentions. **Purchase intentions** represent *what we think we'll buy.* A special type of purchase intentions is **repurchase intentions,** which *reflect whether we anticipate buying the same product or brand again.* **Shopping intentions** indicate *where we plan on making our prod-*

Figure 10.2   Measuring Different Types of Consumer Intentions

1. Purchase Intentions:

| Will you buy a Mercedes-Benz automobile during the next 12 months? | No chance 1 2 3 4 5 6 7 I definitely will |

2. Repurchase Intentions:

| The next time you purchase coffee, will you buy the same brand? | No chance 1 2 3 4 5 6 7 I definitely will |

3. Shopping Intentions:

| Will you shop at Wal*Mart during the next 30 days? | No chance 1 2 3 4 5 6 7 I definitely will |

4. Spending Intentions:

| Will you spend at least $1,000 on Christmas gifts this year? | No chance 1 2 3 4 5 6 7 I definitely will |

5. Consumption Intentions:

| Will you watch the next Super Bowl? | No chance 1 2 3 4 5 6 7 I definitely will |

---

uct purchases. **Spending intentions** represent *how much money we think we'll spend.* **Search intentions** indicate our *intentions to engage in external search,* a topic covered earlier in Chapter 4. **Consumption intentions** represent our *intentions to engage in a particular consumption activity* (e.g., watch TV, exercise). Figure 10.2 contains examples of how these different types of intentions might be measured.

People usually do what they intend to do. We imagine that you intend to read the rest of this chapter and you probably will. I expect to give my final exam tomorrow and hopefully I will (I did). Grocery shoppers intending to buy the items on their shopping list usually do. This is not to say that intentions are always fulfilled. One might travel to the local video store intending to rent a particular movie only to discover that they have all been checked out. Nonetheless, intentions have been shown repeatedly to provide a significant prediction of how people behave.[2]

As a demonstration, consider the 1992 presidential election. Two weeks prior to the election, voters reported whether they would vote for the incumbent, George Bush, or the challenger, Bill Clinton. Based on their answers, projections were made on a state-by-state basis. These projections appear in Figure 10.3. Note that some states are classified as "too close to call" because voters were evenly split between the candidates. The actual results of the presidential race are shown in Figure 10.4. Comparison of the two figures reveals that the polls accurately forecasted every state projected to go for Bush or Clinton.

Constraints on the Predictive Power of Intentions

Although intentions are a significant predictor of behavior, they are far from being a perfect predictor. We intended to have this textbook completed much earlier than it actually was. Have you kept all of your New Year's resolutions? Sometimes even the best intentions go unfulfilled.

Intentions can change. Unanticipated circumstances may cause them to change.[3] Suppose you fully intend at this moment to purchase a particular product.

Figure 10.3   Preelection Forecasts for the 1992 Presidential Race

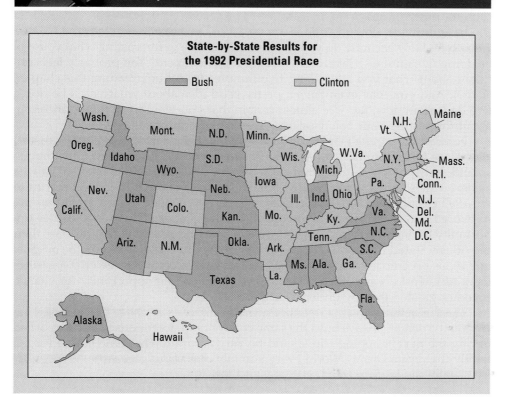

**Pre-election Forecasts for the 1992
Presidential Race**

☐ Bush   ☐ Clinton   ☐ Too close to call

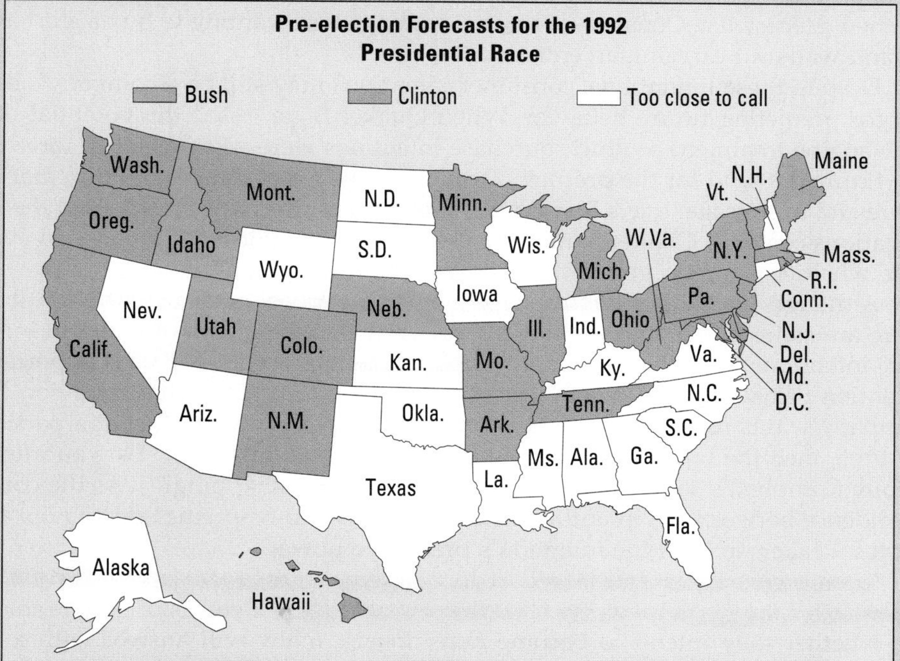

Source: American Political Network's weekly compilation of the latest data available from state polling.

Figure 10.4   State-by-State Results for the 1992 Presidential Race

**State-by-State Results for
the 1992 Presidential Race**

☐ Bush   ☐ Clinton

Yet later on during information search, you learn something that changes your intentions. Obviously, intentions measured prior to this change are unlikely to provide an accurate prediction of behavior. Similarly, you may not intend on buying a product yet end up doing so. Grocery shoppers often buy items that are not on their grocery list. Consumers enter a clothing store wanting to buy a shirt and tie and walk out carrying an entire suit.

Despite these limitations, consumer intentions may still be a company's best bet for predicting future behavior. When Quaker State tested the potential of a new engine treatment product, purchase intentions were a key factor in forecasting future demand for the product. "You can project that data into future market share and trial usage," says Bob Cohen, former executive vice president of the innovations center at Quaker State. "It's the best information you can have to evaluate whether or not to go forward and invest more money."[4]

Although we cannot control whether consumers act upon their intentions, there are some things that we can control or at least be aware of that will influence intentions' predictive accuracy. The measurement of intentions is important. Intention measures should fully correspond to the to-be-predicted behavior. If a company wants to predict whether consumers will buy its product at a particular time, then the intention measure should specify all this (e.g., "Do you intend to buy Campbell's soup the next time you go grocery shopping?"). As the correspondence between the intention measures and the to-be-predicted behavior becomes weaker, so does the intention's predictive power.[5]

Measuring what people intend to do may sometimes be less predictive of their future behavior than measuring what they expect to do.[6] If you ask cigarette smokers whether they intend to become nonsmokers, many will answer with a resounding "yes!" Yet fulfilling these intentions is far from easy. Sometimes habit is more powerful than willpower. A more realistic assessment might be obtained by measuring behavioral expectations. **Behavioral expectations** represent the *perceived likelihood of performing a behavior.* Although smokers may hold very strong intentions to quit, they may report more moderate expectations of doing so because of past failures.

In addition to how intentions are measured, when they're measured is also important. How accurate do you think you would be in forecasting what you will be doing five minutes, days, and years from this moment? You probably feel confident about what you'll be doing five minutes from now (reading this chapter, right?). And you may even have a pretty good idea about what you'll be doing five days from now. But it is almost certain that you would feel rather uncertain about forecasting your behavior five years into the future.

Forecasting accuracy depends on how far into the future one is trying to predict. If we ask consumers today what they intend to do tomorrow, our forecast should be right on target. Prediction of even more distant behavior can be achieved, as shown by how well voters' intentions measured two weeks prior to the 1992 election worked. But as the time interval between when intentions are measured and when the to-be-predicted behavior occurs, there is a greater opportunity for intentions to change. People may learn something that reverses their previously stated intentions. Whatever the reason, forecasts based on the original intentions become less accurate. Thus, as the time interval between the measurement of intentions and the behavior itself increases, the opportunity for change becomes greater, thereby undermining prediction.[7]

The predictive power of intentions further depends on the to-be-predicted behavior. If a person always buys the same coffee brand, intentions to buy this brand during the next shopping trip should be very accurate. The same is true for the family that visits Disney World every summer. Behaviors repeated with regularity usually can be forecasted with greater precision.

Also important is whether the behavior is under volitional control. **Volitional control** represents *the degree to which a behavior can be performed at will.* Many behaviors are under complete volitional control. For instance, you control whether you will continue to read the rest of this paragraph. Some behaviors, however, may not be under our complete control. You can't rent a video if it's not available. You may intend to get an A on your next exam, but whether you do depends at least somewhat on how difficult the professor makes the exam.

The existence of uncontrollable factors interferes with our ability to do what we intend to do. When this occurs, intentions become less accurate predictors of behavior. Consequently, **perceived behavioral control,** representing the *person's belief about how easy it is to perform the behavior,* is sometimes used along with intentions to predict behavior.[8]

Other Uses of Consumer Intentions

Consumer intentions are helpful as an indicator of the possible effects of certain marketing activities. In the hemp industry, for instance, there are conflicting opinions about the wisdom of reminding consumers about hemp's association with marijuana. Some emphasize this association when marketing their products; others avoid it. To determine whether this association helps or hinders, consumers were surveyed about whether they would be more or less likely to purchase a product made of hemp knowing it comes from the same plant as marijuana. For the results of the survey and more information about this situation, read Consumer in Focus 10.2.

Consumer in Focus 10.2

Purchase Intentions May Depend on What Consumers Know About Hemp

Marketers are getting hip to hemp, using it to make everything from burgers to bed linens. It nearly disappeared from the market during the past 70 years, and many consumers don't understand the difference between industrial hemp and its more familiar illegal cannabis cousin, marijuana. Though similar, the strains of hemp used to make the products contain only trace amounts of THC, the psychoactive chemical in marijuana.

Some marketers of hemp products, however, play up the plant's relationship to pot. One of the hemp skin care lines goes under the name Body Dope and is heralded in ads as "your daily dose." This has prompted a fierce debate in the hemp industry about whether marketers should "separate the rope from the dope." A study initiated by *Marketing News,* a publication devoted to its namesake, and conducted by Market Facts, a market research firm, indicates that companies would be wise to weed out any references to its relationship to marijuana. Less than 3 percent of the 1,000 consumers surveyed said they'd be more likely to buy a hemp product knowing that it was made from the same plant as marijuana. And although nearly 70 percent said it wouldn't affect their purchases, 25 percent said it would make them less likely to purchase a hemp product. Two percent said they didn't know how they'd be affected.

"That's a red flag," to marketers who play up the "anti-establishment message," says Thomas Mularz, vice president at Market Facts. "Advertising in *High Times* magazine may not have a lot of pull. Companies would be better off taking the high road to marketing, no pun intended." According to Kelly Wilhite, who owns the Austin Hemp Company, hemp's association with pot "is a definite minus, and a lot of companies are finding that out. We try to stay as far away from [pot] as we can. Otherwise, you'll be marketing to one kind of person" and alienating potential consumers "who are against marijuana but would be all for hemp."

Source: Excerpted from Cyndee Miller, "Hemp Is Latest Buzzword," Marketing News (March 17, 1997), 1, 6.

Similarly, consider a company contemplating a significant change in its product because it believes that doing so will lead to greater sales. Nonetheless, it recognizes that this change may not work and might even hurt sales. Before actually implementing this change, it could first explore whether the change influences consumers' intentions in the desired direction. This precaution could prevent a costly mistake. Evaluating the impact of potential marketing activities makes good business sense. Although no one knows for sure what will happen until something is implemented in the market, this does not eliminate the value of testing the waters. And given the strength of the intention–behavior relationship, intentions provide a reasonable test.

Intentions may also provide an informative indication of a company's likely success in retaining customers. You might remember from Chapter 6 that many satisfied customers still take their business elsewhere. Thus, customers who appear to be satisfied may report little intention of buying from the company again.

PC Magazine periodically surveys its subscribers about their opinions of different personal computers. Among other things, respondents are asked whether they would buy the same brand the next time they make a purchase. The results for repurchase intentions observed in one of the magazine's surveys are reported in Table 10.1. Although consumers' repurchase intentions were stronger than average for most computer makers, others were not so fortunate. Repurchase intentions clearly below the norm for the product category or industry reveal a competitive disadvantage in future customer retention.

Table 10.1 Some Consumers' Repurchase Intentions for Personal Computers

PC Vendor	Repurchase Intentions
Apple	Below average
Compaq	Above average
Dell	Above average
Gateway	Above average
Hewlett-Packard	Above average
IBM	Above average
Micron	Above average
MidWest Micro	Average
NEC	Above average
Packard Bell	Below average
Quantex	Above average
Sony	Above average

Note. The repurchase intentions column represents whether the proportion of respondents to PC Magazine's Service and Reliability Survey indicating that they would buy a new PC from the same vendor significantly differs from the average based on all vendors.

Source: Bruce Brown, "Home PCs," PC Magazine (December 15, 1998), 120.

Although much can be learned from understanding consumer intentions, the lesson is incomplete. To better understand why consumers hold the intentions that they do, we need to probe more deeply. Next stop: consumer attitudes.

Consumer Attitudes

The preceding discussion of intentions has ignored a fundamental question: What determines intentions? The answer: attitudes.[9] **Attitudes** represent *what we like and dislike.* Usually we do the things that we like to do while avoiding things that are disliked. If you don't like sushi, then it's unlikely that you intend to eat it. On the other hand, if you really do like sushi, you probably intend to consume it at some point in the future.

Holding a favorable attitude toward a product is almost always an essential prerequisite in order for consumers to hold a favorable purchase or consumption intention. If consumers don't like a product, they'll take their business elsewhere. At the same time, however, favorable attitudes toward a product do not automatically translate into favorable purchase intentions. A consumer may like one brand but intend to buy another brand that is liked even more. For this reason, attitudes are sometimes measured in the form of preferences. **Preferences** represent *attitudes toward one object in relation to another.* For example, which cola do you prefer, Coke or Pepsi?

Just because consumers prefer one product over its competitors' still doesn't mean that they intend to buy the preferred product. You can prefer a Jaguar automobile without intending to buy one. Maybe you don't need a new automobile. Maybe you do but can't afford the Jaguar's sticker price. And maybe you can afford it but refuse to spend that much money for a car.

The basic point is that having a favorable attitude toward a product is not the same as having a favorable attitude toward buying or consuming the product. Indeed, researchers distinguish between two types of attitudes: **attitude toward the object (A_o)** and **attitude toward the behavior (A_b).**[10] A_o represents an *evaluation of the attitude object* such as a product. A_b represents an *evaluation of performing a particular behavior involving the attitude object* such as buying the product. Given its focus on behavior, it is not surprising that A_b is related more strongly than A_o to intentions.[11] Examples of how to measure product attitudes and preferences are shown in Figure 10.5.

The Variety of Consumer Attitudes

So far our discussion of consumer attitudes has focused on whether a product is liked or disliked. Yet product attitudes represent only part of the attitudes that influence consumer behavior. As suggested by the coverage in Chapter 9 of corporate image, some consumers' attitudes toward a company affect whether they buy the company's products. Similarly, consumers' attitudes toward retailers influence where they shop. Attitudes are even important during the information search stage of decision making (see Chapter 4). External search becomes more likely as attitudes toward these activities become more favorable.

Attitudes toward a product's attributes are important. Do you prefer a cola or noncola soft drink? Do you like mint-flavored toothpaste? Do you like a sweet-tasting wine? Do you prefer furniture styled with a more traditional or modern look? Understanding these attitudes is essential for designing appealing products.

In addition to attitudes toward attributes, it's useful to understand attitudes toward other types of brand associations. These associations may include logos

Figure 10.5   Measuring Attitudes and Preferences

Attitude toward the behavior:

Buying an IBM personal computer would be:	Very good	1 2 3 4 5 6 7	Very bad
	Very rewarding	1 2 3 4 5 6 7	Very punishing
	Very wise	1 2 3 4 5 6 7	Very foolish

Attitude toward the object:

| How much do you like or dislike IBM personal computers? | Like very much | 1 2 3 4 5 6 7 | Dislike very much |

Preference:

| Compared to Apple personal computers, how much do you like IBM personal computers? | Like IBM much more than Apple | 1 2 3 4 5 6 7 | Like Apple much more than IBM |

(Do you like Nike's swoosh logo?), symbols (Do you like the drum-playing rabbit in the Energizer battery ads?), and product endorsers (Do you like Michael Jordan?). Whether these associations enhance or reduce consumers' product attitudes directly depends on whether they are liked or disliked.

Attitudes play a vital role in determining advertising effectiveness. A liked spokesperson can enhance persuasion; a disliked spokesperson can destroy it. More generally, consumers' attitudes toward the ad itself can strongly determine its effectiveness. A study by the Advertising Research Foundation indicates that viewers' liking of a TV commercial is an important predictor of the ad's success in the marketplace.[12] Attitudes toward the ad have been shown repeatedly to act as a significant determinant of the product attitudes held after viewing the ad.[13]

As you can see, there are many types of attitudes that must be considered when analyzing consumer behavior. Having acknowledged this diversity, we next turn to the fundamental issue of how attitudes are formed.

Attitude Formation

Suppose one evening while watching TV you see a commercial for a new restaurant that interests you. You give extra attention to the commercial, much more than you would normally. You carefully process the information presented in the ad about the restaurant's attributes (seafood cuisine, reasonable prices, relaxing atmosphere, waterfront location, and so on). You become even more interested. It looks as if it's a place that would provide a most enjoyable dining experience without taking a major bite out of your wallet. You make a mental note to yourself to dine at the restaurant the next time the opportunity presents itself.

In this example, you have formed an attitude toward the restaurant. Admittedly, this attitude may be held rather tentatively. At this point, all you have to go on is the commercial, not always the most reliable source of information. You haven't actually gone there yet. You haven't even talked to someone who has eaten at the restaurant. Nonetheless, you think that you would like it enough to warrant giving it a try.

Note that this attitude toward the restaurant is based on those beliefs formed about the restaurant. Your beliefs about the restaurant's cuisine, atmosphere, prices, and location led you to conclude that it is the type of place that you would like. The influence of beliefs about a product's attributes on attitude formation is considered in the following section.

The Role of Beliefs in Attitude Formation

Which brand of toothpaste is most effective in preventing cavities and tooth decay? Does high price indicate high quality? Are car salespeople trustworthy? Do you think the economy will be better, worse, or about the same a year from now? Do you believe that this book contains useful information?

Each of these questions focuses on your beliefs. **Beliefs** can be defined as *subjective judgments about the relationship between two or more things.* In Chapter 9, we discussed consumer knowledge. Beliefs are based on knowledge. What you have learned about a product determines what you believe about the product. Understanding a product's image requires understanding consumers' beliefs about the product.

According to multiattribute attitude models, beliefs about a product's attributes or characteristics are important because they determine the favorability of one's attitude toward the product. Two different multiattribute models are discussed next.[14]

The Fishbein Multiattribute Attitude Model   Fishbein's formulation has been used extensively by consumer researchers since its conception nearly 40 years ago.[15] Symbolically, it can be expressed as

$$A_o = \sum_{i=1}^{n} b_i e_i$$

where
A_o = attitude toward the object
b_i = the strength of the belief that the object has attribute i
e_i = the evaluation of attribute i
n = the number of salient or important attributes

The model proposes that attitude toward an object (such as a product) is based on the summed set of beliefs about the object's attributes weighted by the evaluation of these attributes. Attributes are not limited to simply product characteristics such as its price and features. They can include any of the associations mentioned in the Chapter 9 discussion of product image. Product endorsers, slogans, relationships with charitable organizations, and so on would also fall into the "attribute" category. It is only to simplify the presentation that the following example of the model's properties and operations uses product characteristics exclusively as the important attributes.

Suppose the model was used to understand consumers' attitudes toward three brands of running shoes. Doing so first requires identifying the important or salient attributes. Simply asking consumers which ones they use in evaluating brands in the product category usually is sufficient. Those attributes mentioned most frequently are considered to be the most salient. Suppose that the following attributes are identified:

- Whether the shoe is shock absorbent to permit running on hard surfaces
- Whether it is priced less than $50
- Durability of the shoe

- How comfortable it is to wear
- Whether it is available in a desired color
- Amount of arch support

Next, the appropriate b_i and e_i measures must be developed. The e_i component, representing the evaluation of an attribute, is measured on a 7-point evaluative scale ranging from "very good" to "very bad," such as

Buying running shoes priced at less than \$50 is
very good __ : __ : __ : __ : __ : __ : __ very bad
+3 +2 +1 0 −1 −2 −3

This would be done for each of the six salient attributes identified previously.

The b_i component represents how strongly consumers believe that a particular brand of running shoes possesses a given attribute. Beliefs usually are measured on a 7-point scale of perceived likelihood ranging from "very likely" to "very unlikely." For example,

How likely is it that brand A running shoes are priced at less than \$50?
very likely __ : __ : __ : __ : __ : __ : __ very unlikely
+3 +2 +1 0 −1 −2 −3

For each brand, it would be necessary to assess consumers' beliefs for each attribute. Given 3 brands and 6 attributes, a total of 18 belief measures would be necessary.[16]

A survey containing the b_i and e_i measures would then be administered to a sample of consumers. An average response would be calculated for each measure. A set of hypothetical results appears in Table 10.2. When interpreting the numbers in Table 10.2, it is important to keep in mind that the b_i and e_i scales range from a maximum score of +3 to a minimum score of −3.

The results for e_i indicate that durability and comfort are the most desirable product attributes, followed by shock absorbent and arch support, with color a relatively minor although still salient consideration. Unlike the remaining attributes,

Table 10.2 Hypothetical Results for Fishbein's Multiattribute Model

Attribute	Evaluation (e_i)	Beliefs (b_i) Brand A	Brand B	Brand C
Shock absorbent	+ 2	+ 2	+ 1	− 1
Price less than \$50	− 1	− 3	− 1	+ 3
Durability	+ 3	+ 3	+ 1	− 1
Comfort	+ 3	+ 2	+ 3	+ 1
Desired color	+ 1	+ 1	+ 3	+ 3
Arch support	+ 2	+ 3	+ 1	− 2
Total $\Sigma b_i e_i$ score		+ 29	+ 20	− 6

low price (less than $50) receives a negative score. This does not mean that price is unimportant. Rather, it indicates that low price is viewed as an undesirable characteristic. This result is to be expected when consumers perceive a price–quality relationship and are willing to pay a little more for extra quality.

The results for b_i indicate that brand A is viewed favorably because it receives positive belief ratings on all desired attributes. It attains maximum ratings on both durability and arch support. Nor is brand A believed to cost less than $50. Given that low price is undesirable, this belief works in favor of brand A.

As a rule of thumb, companies want consumers to perceive their products as (1) possessing desirable attributes (when e_i is positive, b_i should be positive) and (2) not possessing undesirable attributes (when e_i is negative, b_i should be negative). The Duracell ad in Figure 10.6 illustrates the former by touting that the battery's power enables it to last up to 50 percent longer. The Triaminic ad in Figure 10.7 illustrates the latter by talking about the absence of unnecessary medicine whose presence might lead to side effects.

Although brand B outperforms brand A on comfort and color in Table 10.2, it is perceived as inferior to brand A on the remaining attributes. Brand C is viewed as low priced, a belief that undermines attitude, given the negative evaluation of low price. The results further indicate that brand C is not believed to perform well in terms of absorbing shock, durability, and arch support. On the positive side, it is seen as somewhat comfortable and having a desired color.

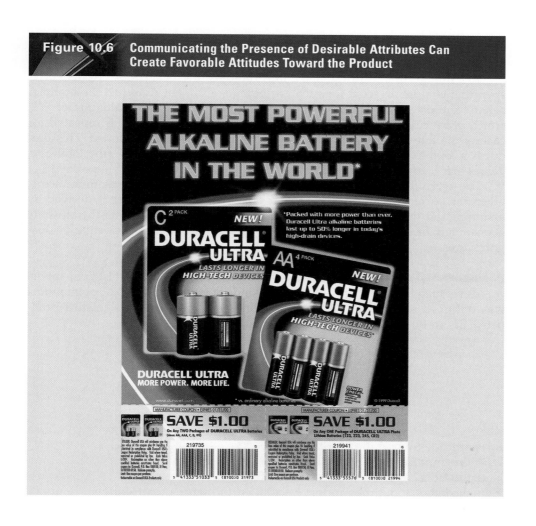

Figure 10.6 Communicating the Presence of Desirable Attributes Can Create Favorable Attitudes Toward the Product

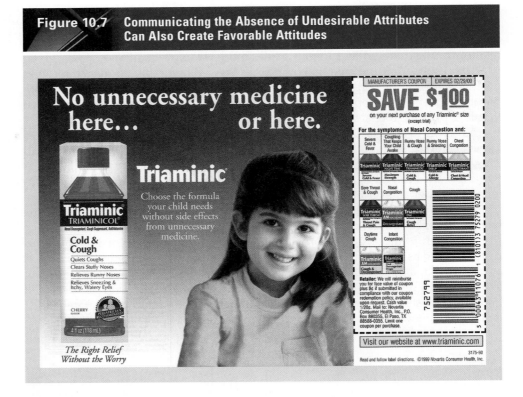

Figure 10.7   Communicating the Absence of Undesirable Attributes Can Also Create Favorable Attitudes

To estimate brand attitude, we first multiply the belief score by its corresponding evaluation score for each attribute ($b_i \times e_i$). For example, the brand A belief score of $+2$ for shock absorbency is multiplied by the evaluation of $+2$, which produces a value of $+4$ for this attribute. This procedure is repeated for each of the five remaining attributes. The $b_i e_i$ scores are then summed. This produces a total $\Sigma b_i e_i$ score of $+29$ for brand A. For brands B and C, the total $\Sigma b_i e_i$ values are $+20$ and -6, respectively.

The score for brand A is very good, considering that the maximum score, given the current set of evaluations, is $+36$. The maximum score is derived by assuming the "ideal" belief score ($+3$ or -3, depending on whether the attribute is positively or negatively evaluated) and combining it with the existing evaluation scores.

The Ideal-Point Multiattribute Attitude Model   Whereas the Fishbein model was developed to understand all different kinds of attitudes, the ideal-point model was designed specifically for understanding consumer attitudes toward products.[17] It can be represented symbolically as

$$A_p = \sum_{i=1}^{n} W_i \, | I_i - X_i |$$

where
A_p = attitude toward the product
W_i = the importance of attribute i
I_i = the "ideal" performance on attribute i
X_i = the belief about the product's actual performance on attribute i
n = the number of salient attributes

Under the ideal-point model, consumers indicate where they believe a product is located on scales representing the various degrees or levels of salient attributes. Consumers would also report where the "ideal" product would fall on these attribute scales. According to the model, the closer a product's actual rating is to the ideal rating, the more favorable the attitude.

As an illustration, suppose we applied the model to soft drinks and that the following attributes are identified as salient:

- Sweetness of taste

- Degree of carbonation

- Number of calories

- Amount of real fruit juices

- Price

Next, we would develop a scale representing various levels of each salient attribute. Using sweetness as an example, the scale could look like

very sweet taste __ : __ : __ : __ : __ : __ : __ **very bitter taste**
$$1 \quad 2 \quad 3 \quad 4 \quad 5 \quad 6 \quad 7$$

Consumers would report their ideal or preferred taste by placing an I in the appropriate response category (the I_i from the model equation). They'd also indicate their beliefs about where various brands fall along this taste continuum (the X_i from the model equation). Finally, consumers would provide ratings of attribute importance on a scale such as

not at all important __ : __ : __ : __ : __ : __ : __ **extremely important**
$$0 \quad 1 \quad 2 \quad 3 \quad 4 \quad 5 \quad 6$$

Suppose we found the results presented in Table 10.3. The first column specifies the attributes on which the ideal (the third column) and actual brand (the fourth and fifth columns) ratings were taken. Attribute importance ratings appear in the second column.

In this example, taste is the most important attribute; carbonation is the least important. The ideal-point ratings indicate that the ideal soft drink should be sweet tasting, somewhat carbonated, fairly low in calories, very high in fruit juices, and toward the low side on price. Brand A is perceived as matching or being very close to the ideal brand for all attributes. Brand B is thought to perform well on some attributes (calories) but not on others (carbonation).

Total brand attitude scores are estimated by first taking the difference between the ideal and actual brand ratings on an attribute. For taste, brand A has a difference of 0 (2 − 2), and the difference for brand B is −1 (2 − 3). This difference is converted to an absolute value, as indicated by the symbol surrounding $I_i − X_i$ in the model equation. This absolute value is multiplied by the importance score. This operation produces scores of 0 for brand A (0 × 6) and 6 for brand B (1 × 6) on the taste attribute. We would repeat this process for the remaining attributes and sum the scores. For brand A, the total score is 16; brand B's score is 29. Unlike Fishbein's multiattribute model, where higher scores indicate more favorable attitudes, lower scores are better under the ideal-point model. In fact, the best score a brand can receive is 0, indicating that the brand matches perfectly the ideal attribute configuration.

Table 10.3	Hypothetical Results for the Ideal-Point Multiattribute Attitude Model			
			Beliefs (X_i)	
Attribute	**Importance (W_i)**	**Ideal Point (I_i)**	**Brand A**	**Brand B**
Taste: sweet (1) – bitter (7)	6	2	2	3
Carbonation: high (1) – low (7)	3	3	2	6
Calories: high (1) – low (7)	4	5	4	5
Fruit juices: high (1) – low (7)	4	1	2	2
Price: high (1) – low (7)	5	5	4	3
Total $\Sigma W_i \mid I_i - X_i \mid$ score			16	29

Benefits of Using Multiattribute Attitude Models   A major attraction of these models is their substantial diagnostic power. Attitude measures tell us whether consumers like or dislike a product but are silent about *why* the product is liked or disliked. Such an understanding requires looking at what consumers believe about a product's attributes and the importance of these attributes.

One useful way of thinking about this is the simultaneous importance–performance grid shown in Figure 10.8. A brand's performance along a particular attribute is classified into one of eight cells. This classification depends on the attribute's importance (high versus low), the brand's performance on the attribute (good versus poor), and a competitive brand's performance on the attribute (good versus poor). Marketing implications are then drawn for each cell. For instance, when a company's brand is truly superior to competitors on an important attribute, this provides a competitive advantage that should be exploited, perhaps through a comparative advertising campaign.

Poor performance by all brands on an important attribute signals a "neglected opportunity." By enhancing our brand's performance on this attribute, we could turn this into a competitive advantage. Poor performance by all brands on an unimportant attribute, however, represents little opportunity. Improving the brand's performance would have little, if any, impact on product attitudes and choices as long as the attribute remained unimportant to consumers.

Multiattribute attitude models can also provide the information necessary for some types of segmentation. As an example, it might be useful to segment consumers based on the importance they place on various attributes. Marketing activities differ considerably when target consumers are primarily concerned with low price rather than high quality.

Another benefit of these models is their usefulness for new product development.[18] Discovering that current offerings fall short of the ideal brand reveals an opportunity for introducing a new product that more closely resembles the ideal. A multiattribute model has also been used successfully by the Lever Brothers Company to forecast the market shares of Tone moisturizing soap and Coast deodorant soap before their market introduction.[19]

Figure 10.8	The Stimulus Importance–Performance Grid		
Attribute Importance	**Our Performance**	**Competitor's Performance**	**Simultaneous Result**
High	Poor	Poor	Neglected Opportunity
		Good	Competitive Disadvantage
	Good	Poor	Competitive Advantage
		Good	Head-to-Head Competition
Low	Poor	Poor	Null Opportunity
		Good	False Alarm
	Good	Poor	False Advantage
		Good	False Competition

Source: Alvin C. Burns, "Generating Marketing Strategy Priorities Based on Relative Competitive Position," *Journal of Consumer Marketing 3 (Fall 1986)*, 49–56.

Finally, multiattribute attitude models provide guidance in the development of attitude change strategies. Shortly you will find a section devoted to attitude change that includes a discussion of the attitude change implications suggested by these models.

The Role of Feelings in Attitude Formation

Before our significant detour into the domain of multiattribute attitude models, we were exploring how attitudes are formed. As underscored by these models, beliefs about a product's salient attributes provide a cognitive foundation upon which attitudes may be built. But this is not the only way to build attitudes. Attitudes may also form as a result of our feelings about the attitude object.

Feelings can be defined as an *affective state* (such as the mood you currently are in) *or reaction* (such as the feelings experienced during product consumption or processing an advertisement). Feelings may be positive (e.g., feeling happy) or negative (e.g., feeling disappointed). They may be overwhelming (such as a near-death experience), or they may be virtually nonexistent (such as taking a vitamin pill).

Feelings take many forms. One study considered more than 60 different feelings that were grouped into three major categories: upbeat, negative, and warm.[20] Table 10.4 lists these different feelings. As discussed next, feelings can influence the attitudes formed during product consumption and the processing of persuasive messages.

Feelings as Part of the Consumption Experience In Chapter 6, we noted that consumption experiences often evoke feelings. Indeed, some experiences are liked primarily for their ability to induce certain feelings, whether it is the tranquility

Table 10.4   Types of Feelings

Upbeat	Negative	Warm
Active	Angry	Affectionate
Adventurous	Annoyed	Calm
Alive	Bad	Concerned
Amused	Bored	Contemplative
Attentive	Critical	Emotional
Attractive	Defiant	Hopeful
Carefree	Depressed	Kind
Cheerful	Disgusted	Moved
Confident	Disinterested	Peaceful
Creative	Dubious	Pensive
Delighted	Dull	Sentimental
Elated	Fed-up	Touched
Energetic	Insulted	Warm-hearted
Enthusiastic	Irritated	
Excited	Lonely	
Exhilarated	Offended	
Good	Regretful	
Happy	Sad	
Humorous	Skeptical	
Independent	Suspicious	
Industrious		
Inspired		
Interested		
Joyous		
Light-hearted		
Lively		
Playful		
Pleased		
Proud		
Satisfied		
Stimulated		
Strong		

Source: Julie A. Edell and Marian Chapman Burke, "The Power of Feelings in Understanding Advertising Effects," Journal of Consumer Research *14 (December 1987), 421–433.*

that comes from listening to the waves caress the shore at a tropical resort or the thrills of skydiving. Even for products whose consumption is relatively free of emotion (e.g., the plastic garbage bag), feelings in the form of frustration and regret may still be experienced if the product fails to perform properly (the garbage bag that bursts, leaving quite a mess to be cleaned up). Consequently, these feelings may influence consumers' post-consumption evaluations.[21] Consumers are more satisfied when consumption is accompanied by positive feelings and void of negative feelings. This, in turn, leads to more favorable product attitudes.

An example of measuring the feelings experienced during consumption (in this case, eating chocolate) appears in Figure 10.9. Note that this figure contains only a subset of the feelings from Table 10.4 that may be relevant to the consumption experience.

Feelings as Part of the Advertising Experience Beyond understanding the feelings experienced during product consumption, it is also necessary to understand the feelings experienced when consumers are processing advertising messages. Some ads may amuse us. The current advertising campaign for Budweiser beer uses all sorts of talking reptiles to entertain viewers. Other ads may annoy us, such as when they wear out their welcome because they have been repeated too often.[22]

Just as the feelings experienced during consumption determine consumers' post-consumption evaluations, so too do those experienced during ad processing determine consumers' post-message evaluations.[23] Attitudes toward the advertised product are more favorable after viewing an ad that evokes positive feelings. Conversely, ads that elicit negative feelings may cause consumers to hold less favorable product attitudes.

Mood State Thus far we have focused on the feelings experienced during product consumption and ad processing. But what about the feelings carried by consumers into these situations? That is, prior to consumption and processing, consumers already feel a certain way. How do you feel right now? Happy? Sad? Energized? Tired? Bored (we certainly hope not!)? *How people feel at a particular moment in time* is called their **mood state.**[24]

Figure 10.9 Measuring Feelings

How often, if at all, do you experience the following feelings as a result of *eating chocolate?*

Happy . . . never ___ very often
Excited . . . never ___ very often
Delighted . . . never ___ very often
Joyous . . . never ___ very often
Satisfied . . . never ___ very often
Proud . . . never ___ very often
Annoyed . . . never ___ very often
Depressed . . . never ___ very often
Guilty . . . never ___ very often
Regretful . . . never ___ very often

Mood states can be very influential during attitude formation.[25] Participants in one study listened to music that evoked a more or less favorable mood. They then tasted an unknown brand of peanut butter. Product attitudes became more positive when the mood during consumption was more favorable.[26] Similarly, mood states have been shown to influence the product attitudes formed as a result of ad processing.[27] One way companies can affect consumers' attitudes is to influence how they feel during attitude formation. A new store, for instance, might find it worthwhile to give shoppers a small gift when they enter the store as a way of enhancing their moods. Advertisers may benefit from placing their messages in television shows that evoke positive moods while avoiding those that may depress consumers' mood states.[28] Coca-Cola has avoided advertising during TV news programs because "there's going to be some bad news in there and Coke is an upbeat, fun product."[29]

Nonetheless, mood states need not always influence attitude formation. In the peanut butter study just described, mood's influence disappeared when either honey or baking soda was added to the peanut butter. Many loved the sweeter taste from using honey; nearly all hated the bitter taste produced by the baking soda. Presumably, these more intense feelings experienced during consumption overpowered any influence of consumers' pre-consumption mood states.

Attitude Change

Attitudes are not carved in stone. Indeed, they are often rather fickle. Today's craze may easily become tomorrow's has-been, as clothing and toy manufacturers know all too well.

Because of their dynamic nature, attitudes should not be taken for granted. Favorable product attitudes, if neglected, may gradually erode to a less favorable state, just like the name of a long forgotten acquaintance. Indeed, both positive and negative attitudes may become more neutral simply because of the passage of time.[30] **Attitude persistence** represents an *attitude's immunity to such corrosion.*

Often, however, attitudes change because we encounter something that warrants their revision. Remember the example used at the beginning of the "Attitude Formation" section in which the person forms a favorable attitude toward a restaurant based on its advertising? Suppose that the person dines at the restaurant and discovers that it's not anything like what she had anticipated. The attitude held prior to consumption would bear little resemblance to the attitude held after consumption. Advertising can work in the same way, such as when it informs us about another product that holds a significant advantage over the product we currently use.

Changing consumer attitudes is a frequent business objective. Converting nonusers into product users may require an attitude adjustment. Recruiting competitors' customers usually requires changing their preferences. One company's desire to change consumer attitudes is represented by the ad shown in Figure 10.10 and is discussed in Consumer in Focus 10.3.

Attitude Resistance

How easy is it to change consumer attitudes? It depends on their resistance.[31] **Attitude resistance** represents the *degree to which an attitude is immune to change.* Some attitudes are highly resistant to change; others are much more malleable. Ideally, companies want their customers' product attitudes to be highly resistant. This makes them less vulnerable to competitive attacks.[32] One indication of a company's

Figure 10.10   This Ad Wants to Change the Way You Think About Cadillac

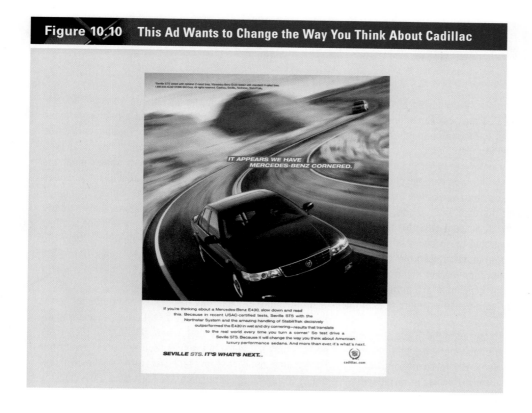

vulnerability to competitive attacks is the resistance of its customers' attitudes toward its product. Conversely, recruiting competitors' customers is much easier when doing so requires changing their attitudes, and these attitudes are less resistant to change.

So what determines attitude resistance? Ultimately, it depends on how strong a foundation the attitude is built upon. If consumers have eaten a food that, for them, has a repugnant taste, changing their attitudes toward this food may be virtually impossible. Direct experience with the attitude object often leads to firmly entrenched attitudes that are resistant to change. In contrast, attitudes based on indirect experience, such as those formed after seeing an advertisement or hearing what someone else has to say about the attitude object, are usually more susceptible to change.[33]

A strong foundation provides a basis for resisting counterattitudinal attacks. The salesperson for a competitor's offering may have some rather unflattering things to say about the product you currently prefer. Among other things, your ability to resist this attack depends on your product knowledge. To the extent that you are able to poke holes in the salesperson's arguments (e.g., by being knowledgeable about the weaknesses of the competitor's offering), your preference is less likely to change.

Attitude Change Implications from Multiattribute Attitude Models

From a multiattribute model perspective, there are three basic ways for changing consumer attitudes: (1) changing beliefs, (2) changing attribute importance, and (3) changing ideal points.[34]

Consumer in Focus 10.3

Cadillac Wants to Change Young Drivers' Attitudes

When something is described as the Cadillac of the class, people generally get the idea it's the best. But affluent young drivers haven't been making the same connection when it comes to buying luxury cars in recent years.

The brand had its heyday in the late 1950s and early 1960s when its powerful and stylish Eldorado with tail fins was the industry trendsetter. Cadillac's sales peaked in 1978 when it sold 350,813 cars. But over the past two decades, Cadillac sales have dropped nearly 50 percent (182,151 cars were sold last year) and are projected to go down this year as well. Considering the booming economy and the enormous wealth being created by the stock market these days, declining sales at a time when consumers are better able to afford the price of a luxury automobile is ample reason for concern.

Cadillac's troubles can be traced to the 1980s and 1990s when a number of luxury car challengers arrived from overseas, including Mercedes-Benz, BMW, Lexus, and Infiniti. Affluent young drivers often dismiss Cadillac as an older generation's status symbol. Indeed, the average age of a Cadillac owner is around 65 years old. Clearly, the automaker's future rests on its ability to attract a younger clientele. Doing so requires changing their brand attitudes.

So how is Cadillac trying to change younger drivers' brand attitudes? One approach involves a new advertising campaign suggesting that Cadillac is creating cars once again that combine the latest technological advances with stylish design. The cars offer the On-Star communications system that tracks where the car is by satellite and provides directions via cell phone, Night Vision technology that helps drivers see farther than the headlamps alone allow, and the StabiliTrak system for easier road handling. And ads such as the one shown in Figure 10.10, which describes how the Cadillac Seville STS outperformed the Mercedes-Benz E430 in recent road-handling tests, are carrying this message to consumers.

In addition, Cadillac has discovered the potential benefits of getting consumers to take a test drive. Advertising director Kim Kosak says that when BMW and Mercedes owners took a Cadillac for a spin, their attitudes toward the car became much more favorable. Accordingly, the ad in Figure 10.10 encourages consumers to "test drive a Seville STS. Because it will change the way you think about American luxury performance sedans."

Source: Excerpted from Skip Wollenberg, "Carmaker Hopes to Rejuvenate Image with New Ad Campaign," Marketing News (December 6, 1999), 29.

Changing Beliefs As illustrated by Consumer in Focus 10.3 and Figure 10.10, Cadillac wants to change "the way you think." And many other companies want the same thing. Mercedes-Benz pays for advertising that tells us "It's not as expensive as you might think" (see Figure 9.10 in Chapter 9). Hallmark wants to change beliefs about its cards being too expensive (see Consumer in Focus 9.3 in Chapter 9). In each case, the company is hoping that changing consumers' beliefs about their products will result in more favorable product attitudes that ultimately influence what consumers buy.

Returning to the prior soft drink example and Table 10.3, suppose we wanted to increase consumers' attitudes toward brand B relative to brand A. Changing the belief for brand B along any of the attributes except calories has the potential to improve attitudes. Because the belief for calories matches the ideal point, any change here would only hurt attitudes. For the remaining attributes, any belief change in the direction of the ideal point should make the brand more attractive to consumers.

Recognize that the need to modify the product offering to change consumers' beliefs will depend on the accuracy of these beliefs. When consumers hold undesirable beliefs because they have misperceived the offering (e.g., consumers who overestimate product price), efforts should focus on bringing these beliefs into harmony with reality. If, however, consumers are accurate in their perceptions of a product's limitations, it may be necessary to change the product itself.

Beyond enhancing consumers' beliefs about itself, brand B might also consider trying to reduce beliefs about the competition. Comparative advertising, by touting the advantages of the advertised brand over a competitor, can undermine beliefs about the competitor's brand.[35] Consequently, if feasible, brand B could undertake a comparative ad campaign to reduce consumers' perceptions of brand A.

Changing Attribute Importance   Another way of altering attitudes is to change the importance consumers attach to various attributes. Depending on how the brand is perceived, one might wish either to increase or to decrease an attribute's importance. Research has demonstrated the potential to enhance the salience of an attribute already viewed as somewhat important.[36] Nonetheless, as a general rule, changing an attribute's importance is more difficult to accomplish than changing beliefs.

For brand B in Table 10.3, what changes in attribute importance would you recommend? In answering this question, you need to consider how each brand is perceived relative to the ideal performance. When the beliefs for both brands match the ideal point, little is to be gained by altering the attribute's importance. No matter what importance is attached to fruit juices, the relative preference between brands A and B will not change given the current set of beliefs.

When, however, brand A is seen as closer to the ideal point for a particular attribute than brand B, decreasing the attribute's importance is to brand B's advantage. Such is the case for taste, carbonation, and price. Anything that can be done to make these attributes even less important to consumers helps reduce preferences for brand A relative to brand B.

Increasing attribute importance is desirable when the competitor's brand is farther from the ideal point than your offering. In Table 10.3, brand A is farther than brand B from the ideal point along the calories attribute. Consequently, enhancing the importance of calories would benefit brand B.

Another variant of changing attribute importance involves efforts to add a new attribute. That is, a company may try to create salience for an attribute that is currently unimportant. Flame broiling is unimportant to many consumers in selecting a fast-food burger restaurant although Burger King's advertising has attempted to alter this opinion. Adding a new attribute to the set of salient attributes essentially amounts to increasing the importance of something that previously was nonsalient.

Changing Ideal Points   Another option for changing attitudes suggested by the ideal-point model involves altering consumers' preferences about what the ideal product would look like. For example, would your ideal brand of mouthwash contain a lot of alcohol, some alcohol, or no alcohol? Based on the belief that alcohol increases the mouthwash's effectiveness, some people prefer this ingredient in their mouthwash. The ad for Rembrandt mouthwash shown in Figure 10.11, however, argues otherwise. It claims that though alcohol does kill bacteria, it may actually irritate a person's mouth. If believed, this ad would cause a change in the ideal point for many consumers.

There are several ideal-point changes in Table 10.3 that would help brand B. Attitudes toward brand B would become more favorable if consumers preferred either a more bitter taste, less carbonation, or a higher price. Such changes could also reduce attitudes toward brand A, depending on whether they broadened the gap between perceptions of brand A's performance and the ideal performance.

Changes for the remaining attributes, calories and fruit juices, would not be attractive to brand B. Given that brand B is seen as having the ideal number of

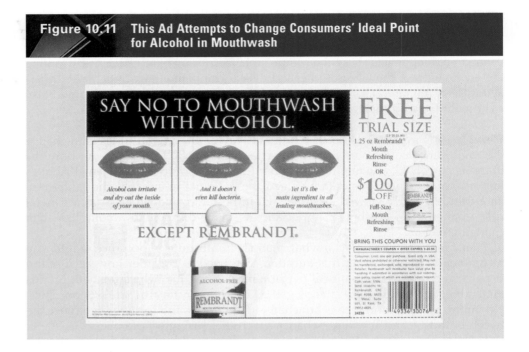

Figure 10.11   This Ad Attempts to Change Consumers' Ideal Point for Alcohol in Mouthwash

calories, altering the ideal point would be self-destructive. Although attitude toward brand B would improve if consumers preferred a little less fruit juice in their beverage, this change produces the same attitudinal impact for both brands. Given that the two brands are perceived as being the same on this attribute, any change in the preferred level of fruit juices cannot alter consumers' brand preferences.

Estimating the Attitudinal Impact of Alternative Changes   As you have seen, there are many alternative changes that one might consider implementing for increasing consumers' liking of brand B relative to its competitor. Decisions about which changes to pursue should depend on several considerations. Some changes will be discarded because they will require product modifications that are prohibitively expensive to implement or that are virtually impossible to accomplish (such as greatly improving product quality while maintaining a price lower than the competitor's).

Consumer resistance to change should also be considered because some changes may be more likely than others. A belief based on inaccurate product information about the brand's price can be corrected fairly easily. In the absence of an actual product change, it may be nearly impossible to change beliefs derived from actual consumption about the taste of Spam. Nor should one underestimate how difficult it can be to change attribute importance and ideal points. An airline with a poor safety record may wish that consumers place less importance on safety in selecting a carrier, but it is impossible for the company to accomplish this.

Another consideration in deciding which changes should be implemented is the potential attitudinal payoff that each change might deliver. Multiattribute attitude models help estimate this payoff. Let's go back to brand B in Table 10.3 one last time. Can you identify the single change that, if successful, would have the most favorable attitudinal impact from brand B's point of view?

Changing the ideal point for carbonation from 3 to 6 would be the single best change. The total multiattribute score for brand B would drop from 29 to 20 (remember, lower total scores are better for the ideal-point model). This same change would increase the total score for brand A from 16 to 25. This is the only single change that would give brand B a more favorable total score than brand A.

The next best change would involve shifting the ideal point for taste from 2 to 3. The new total scores for brands A and B would be 22 and 23, respectively. This process would continue for each of the possible changes, thus yielding information about their relative attitudinal impact. All else being equal, those changes offering the most favorable impact should be pursued.

Before closing, we should acknowledge that the preceding coverage of attitude formation and change is far from complete. In many ways, this chapter has only scratched the surface. We will return to these topics later in the book (see Chapter 15).

Summary

In many situations, anticipating how consumers will behave is important. One way of forecasting consumer behavior involves simply asking consumers what they intend to do. Under the right circumstances, these intentions may accurately predict future behavior.

It is also useful to understand what consumers like and dislike. Attitudes, representing these likes and dislikes, strongly influence intentions. These attitudes are formed from one's beliefs and feelings about the attitude object.

The chapter devoted considerable attention to multiattribute attitude models, which focus on consumers' beliefs about a product's attributes. Two types of multiattribute attitude models are the Fishbein and ideal-point models. A main advantage of the ideal-point model is that it identifies consumers' preferred or ideal configuration of product attributes. These models provide insight into the reasons that consumers hold the attitudes that they do. They also provide guidance when developing alternative attitude change strategies.

Review and Discussion Questions

1. A marketing research study undertaken for a major appliance manufacturer disclosed that 30 percent of those polled plan on purchasing a trash compactor in the next 3 months, and 15 percent plan on purchasing a new iron. How much confidence should be placed in the predictive accuracy of these intention measurements? More generally, will predictive accuracy vary across products? Why or why not?

2. You are interested in predicting whether a person will purchase a new Chrysler from the Bob Caldwell dealership in the next month. Someone suggests the following phrasing for the intention measure: "How likely is it that you will buy a new automobile soon?" Why is this measure unlikely to predict the behavior of interest?

3. In January 2000, before market introduction, Mr. Dickson conducted a survey of consumers' attitudes toward his new product. The survey revealed that 80 percent of those interviewed held favorable attitudes toward the product. The product was introduced in June 2001, and product sales have been very disappointing. What explanations can you offer for this discrepancy between the attitude survey and product sales?

4. Consider the following results for a TV set, based on Fishbein's multiattribute model:

Attribute	Evaluation	Brand Belief
Clear picture	+3	+2
Low price	+2	−1
Durable	+3	+1
Attractive cabinet	+1	+3

First, calculate the overall attitude score. Second, calculate the maximum overall score a brand could receive given the current set of attribute evaluations. Third, describe the product's strengths and weaknesses as perceived by consumers.

5. Using the multiattribute results presented in question 4, identify all possible changes that would enhance brand attitude. Which change would lead to the greatest improvement in attitude?

6. Discuss the tradeoffs between multiattribute attitude models, measures of attitude toward a product, and measures of purchase intentions in terms of (a) their relative predictive power and (b) their usefulness in understanding consumer behavior.

7. Assume a company is trying to decide which consumer segments represent its best bet for future expansion. To help in this decision, the research department has collected information about segment members' product attitudes. The results show the following average attitude scores on a 10-point scale ranging from "bad product" (1) to "good product" (10):

Segment A   8.2

Segment B   7.5

Segment C   6.1

Based on this information, segment A has been chosen as the best bet for expansion. Do you agree? What problems might exist with making this decision based on the current information?

Endnotes

1. Gregg Fields, "Blowing Smoke?" *Miami Herald* (January 25, 1998), 1F, 3F.

2. For research on the intention–behavior relationship, see Donald H. Granbois and John O. Summers, "Primary and Secondary Validity of Consumer Purchase Probabilities," *Journal of Consumer Research* 4 (March 1975), 31–38; Paul W. Miniard, Carl Obermiller, and Thomas J. Page, Jr., "A Further Assessment of Measurement Influences on the Intention–Behavior Relationship," *Journal of Marketing Research* 20 (May 1983), 206–212; David J. Reibstein, "The Prediction of Individual Probabilities of Brand Choice," *Journal of Consumer Research* 5 (December 1978), 163–168; Paul R. Warshaw, "Predicting Purchase and

Other Behaviors from General and Contextually Specific Intentions," *Journal of Marketing Research* 17 (February 1980), 26–33. Interestingly, research suggests that simply measuring behavioral intention may affect the likelihood of the behavior being undertaken. See Vicki G. Morwitz, Eric Johnson, and David Schmittlein, "Does Measuring Intent Change Behavior?" *Journal of Consumer Research* 20 (June 1993), 46–62.

3. Joseph A. Cote, James McCullough, and Michael Reilly, "Effects of Unexpected Situations on Behavior–Intention Differences: A Garbology Analysis," *Journal of Consumer Research* 12 (September 1985), 188–194.

4. Jennifer Lach, "Meet You in Aisle Three," *American Demographics* (April 1999), 41–42.

5. For an excellent discussion of the importance of measurement correspondence, see Icek Ajzen and Martin Fishbein, "Attitude–Behavior Relations: A Theoretical Analysis and Review of Empirical Research," *Psychological Bulletin* 84 (September 1977), 888–918. For an empirical demonstration, see James Jaccard, G. William King, and Richard Pomozal, "Attitudes and Behavior: An Analysis of Specificity of Attitudinal Predictors," *Human Relations* 30 (September 1977), 817–824.

6. Paul R. Warshaw and Fred D. Davis, "Disentangling Behavioral Intention and Behavioral Expectation," *Journal of Experimental Social Psychology* 21 (1985), 213–228.

7. Icek Ajzen and Martin Fishbein, *Understanding Attitudes and Predicting Social Behavior* (Englewood Cliffs, NJ: Prentice-Hall, 1980); E. Bonfield, "Attitude, Social Influence, Personal Norms, and Intention Interactions as Related to Brand Purchase Behavior," *Journal of Marketing Research* 11 (November 1974), 379–389.

8. Icek Ajzen, "From Intentions to Actions: A Theory of Planned Behavior," in J. Kuhland and J. Beckman, eds., *Action Control: From Cognitions to Behavior* (Heidelberg: Springer-Verlag, 1985), 11–39; Icek Ajzen, "The Theory of Planned Behavior," *Organizational Behavior and Human Decision Processes* 50 (1991), 179–211; Thomas J. Madden, Pamela Scholder Ellen, and Icek Ajzen, "A Comparison of the Theory of Planned Behavior and the Theory of Reasoned Action," *Personality and Social Psychology Bulletin* 18 (February 1992), 3–9.

9. Other factors beyond attitudes may also influence intentions. See Ajzen, "The Theory of Planned Behavior"; Ajzen and Fishbein, *Understanding Attitudes and Predicting Social Behavior*; Martin Fishbein and Icek Ajzen, *Belief, Attitude, Intention, and Behavior: An Introduction to Theory and Research* (Reading, MA: Addison-Wesley, 1975); Paul W. Miniard and Joel B. Cohen, "Mod-

eling Personal and Normative Influences on Behavior," *Journal of Consumer Research* 10 (September 1983), 169–180; Paul R. Warshaw, "A New Model for Predicting Behavioral Intentions: An Alternative to Fishbein," *Journal of Marketing Research* 17 (May 1980), 153–172.

10. Fishbein and Ajzen, *Belief, Attitude, Intention, and Behavior*.

11. Ibid.

12. Cyndee Miller, "Study Says 'Likability' Surfaces as Measure of TV Ad Success," *Marketing News* (January 7, 1991), 6, 14. Also see Cyndee Miller, "Researchers Balk at Testing Rough Ads for 'Likability,'" *Marketing News* (September 2, 1991), 2.

13. Scott B. MacKenzie, Richard J. Lutz, and George E. Belch, "The Role of Attitude toward the Ad as a Mediator of Advertising Effectiveness: A Test of Competing Explanations," *Journal of Marketing Research* 23 (May 1986), 130–143; Paul W. Miniard, Sunil Bhatla, and Randall L. Rose, "On the Formation and Relationship of Ad and Brand Attitudes: An Experimental and Causal Analysis," *Journal of Marketing Research* 27 (August 1990), 290–303; Andrew A. Mitchell and Jerry C. Olson, "Are Product Attribute Beliefs the Only Mediators of Advertising Effects on Brand Attitudes?" *Journal of Marketing Research* 18 (August 1981), 318–332.

14. Discussion of additional multiattribute models can be found in Frank A. Bass and W. Wayne Talarzyk, "Attitude Model for the Study of Brand Preference," *Journal of Marketing Research* 9 (February 1972), 93–96; Jagdish N. Sheth and W. Wayne Talarzyk, "Perceived Instrumentality and Value Importance as Determinants of Attitudes," *Journal of Marketing Research* 9 (February 1973), 6–9; Milton J. Rosenberg, "Cognitive Structure and Attitudinal Affect," *Journal of Abnormal and Social Psychology* 53 (November 1956), 367–372; Olli T. Ahtola, "The Vector Model of Preferences: An Alternative to the Fishbein Model," *Journal of Marketing Research* 12 (February 1975), 52–59.

15. Martin Fishbein, "An Investigation of the Relationships between Beliefs about an Object and the Attitude toward That Object," *Human Relations* 16 (August 1963), 233–240; Fishbein and Ajzen, *Belief, Attitude, Intention, and Behavior*; Ajzen and Fishbein, *Understanding Attitudes and Predicting Social Behavior*. For general reviews of multiattribute models in consumer research, see Richard J. Lutz and James R. Bettman, "Multi-Attribute Models in Marketing: A Bicentennial Review," in Arch G. Woodside, Jagdish N. Sheth, and Peter D. Bennett, eds., *Consumer and Industrial Buying Behavior* (New York: North-Holland, 1977), 137–149; William L. Wilkie and Edgar A. Pessemier, "Issues in Marketing's Use of

Multi-Attribute Models," *Journal of Marketing Research* 10 (November 1973), 428–441.

16. Evidence suggests that the order in which beliefs are measured (by attribute across brands versus by brand across attributes) can be important. See Eugene D. Joffee and Israel D. Nebenzahl, "Alternative Questionnaire Formats for Country Image Studies," *Journal of Marketing Research* 21 (November 1984), 463–471.

17. Examples of applying the ideal-point model can be found in James L. Ginter, "An Experimental Investigation of Attitude Change and Choice of a New Brand," *Journal of Marketing Research* 11 (February 1974), 30–40; Donald R. Lehmann, "Television Show Preference: Application of a Choice Model," *Journal of Marketing Research* 8 (February 1972), 47–55.

18. For research on the model's usefulness in new product development, see Morris B. Holbrook and William J. Havlena, "Assessing the Real-to-Artificial Generalizability of Multiattribute Attitude Models in Tests of New Product Designs," *Journal of Marketing Research* 25 (February 1988), 25–35.

19. "Lever Brothers Uses Micromodel to Project Market Share," *Marketing News* (November 27, 1981).

20. Julie A. Edell and Marian Chapman Burke, "The Power of Feelings in Understanding Advertising Effects," *Journal of Consumer Research* 14 (December 1987), 421–433.

21. Morris B. Holbrook and Elizabeth C. Hirschman, "The Experiential Aspects of Consumption: Consumer Fantasies, Feelings, and Fun," *Journal of Consumer Research* 9 (September 1982), 132–140; Haim Mano and Richard L. Oliver, "Assessing the Dimensionality and Structure of the Consumption Experience: Evaluation, Feeling, and Satisfaction," *Journal of Consumer Research* 20 (December 1993), 451–466; Richard L. Oliver, "Cognitive, Affective, and Attribute Bases of the Satisfaction Response," *Journal of Consumer Research* 20 (December 1993), 418–430; Robert A. Westbrook, "Product/Consumption-Based Affective Responses and Postpurchase Processes," *Journal of Marketing Research* 24 (August 1987), 258–270; Robert A. Westbrook and Richard L. Oliver, "The Dimensionality of Consumption Emotion Patterns and Consumer Satisfaction," *Journal of Consumer Research* 18 (June 1991), 84–91.

22. Arno J. Rethans, John L. Swasy, and Lawrence J. Marks, "Effects of Television Commercial Repetition, Receiver Knowledge, and Commercial Length: A Test of the Two-Factor Model," *Journal of Marketing Research* 23 (February 1986), 50–61.

23. Marian Chapman Burke and Julie A. Edell, "The Impact of Feelings on Ad-Based Affect and Cognition," *Journal of Marketing Research* 26 (February 1989), 69–83; Julie A. Edell and Marian Chapman Burke, "The Power of Feelings in Understanding Advertising Effects," *Journal of Consumer Research* 14 (December 1987), 421–433; Thomas J. Olney, Morris B. Holbrook, and Rajeev Batra, "Consumer Responses to Advertising: The Effects of Ad Content, Emotions, and Attitude toward the Ad on Viewing Time," *Journal of Consumer Research* 17 (March 1991), 440–453; Douglas M. Stayman and Rajeev Batra, "Encoding and Retrieval of Ad Affect in Memory," *Journal of Marketing Research* 28 (May 1991), 232–239.

24. For a general discussion of the role of mood in consumer behavior, see Meryl Paula Gardner, "Mood States and Consumer Behavior: A Critical Review," *Journal of Consumer Research* 12 (December 1985), 281–300.

25. Michael J. Barone, Paul W. Miniard, and Jean Romeo, "The Influence of Positive Mood on Consumers' Evaluations of Brand Extensions," *Journal of Consumer Research* 26 (March 2000), 386–400. Paul W. Miniard, Sunil Bhatla, and Deepak Sirdeshmukh, "Mood as a Determinant of Post-Consumption Evaluations: Mood Effects and Their Dependency on the Affective Intensity of the Consumption Experience," *Journal of Consumer Psychology* 1 (1992), 173–195.

26. Miniard, Bhatla, and Sirdeshmukh, "Mood as a Determinant of Post-Consumption Evaluations."

27. Rajeev Batra and Douglas M. Stayman, "The Role of Mood in Advertising Effectiveness," *Journal of Consumer Research* 17 (September 1990), 203–214; Gerd Bohner, Kimberly Crow, Hans-Peter Erb, and Norbert Schwarz, "Affect and Persuasion: Mood Effects Are the Processing of Message Content and Context Cues and on Subsequent Behaviour," *European Journal of Social Psychology* 22 (1992), 511–530; Daniel J. Howard and Thomas E. Barry, "The Role of Thematic Congruence Between a Mood-Inducing Event and an Advertised Product in Determining the Effects of Mood on Brand Attitudes," *Journal of Consumer Psychology* 3 (1994), 1–27; Richard E. Petty, David W. Schumann, Stephen A. Richman, and Alan J. Strathman, "Positive Mood and Persuasion: Different Roles for Affect Under High- and Low-Elaboration Conditions," *Journal of Personality and Social Psychology* 64 (1993), 5–20.

28. Marvin E. Goldberg and Gerald J. Gorn, "Happy and Sad TV Programs: How They Affect Reactions to Commercials," *Journal of Consumer Research* 14 (December 1987), 387–403; John P. Murry, Jr., John L. Lastovicka, and Surendra N. Singh, "Feelings and Liking Responses to

Television Programs: An Examination of Two Explanations for Media-Context Effects," *Journal of Consumer Research* 18 (March 1992), 441–451.

29. "GF, Coke Tell Why They Shun TV News," *Advertising Age* (January 28, 1980), 39.

30. An exception is the "sleeper effect" in which attitudes become more extreme over time. See A. R. Pratkanis, A. G. Greenwald, M. R. Leippe, and M. H. Baumgardner, "In Search of Reliable Persuasion Effects: III. The Sleeper Effect Is Dead. Long Live the Sleeper Effect," *Journal of Personality and Social Psychology* 54 (1988), 203–218.

31. For an excellent discussion and review of the literature concerning attitude resistance, see Alice H. Eagly and Shelly Chaiken, *The Psychology of Attitudes* (Fort Worth, TX: Harcourt Brace Jovanovich, 1993).

32. One way of enhancing resistance is suggested by inoculation theory. See William J. McGuire, "Inducing Resistance to Persuasion: Some Contemporary Approaches," in L. Berkowitz, ed., *Advances in Experimental Social Psychology* 1 (San Diego, CA: Academic Press, 1964), 191–229.

33. Russell H. Fazio and Mark P. Zanna, "On the Predictive Validity of Attitudes: The Roles of Direct Experience and Confidence," *Journal of Personality* 46 (June 1978), 228–243; Lawrence J. Marks and Michael A. Kamins, "The Use of Product Sampling and Advertising: Effects of Sequence of Exposure and Degree of Advertising Claim Exaggeration on Consumers' Belief Strength, Belief Confidence, and Attitudes," *Journal of Marketing Research* 25 (August 1988), 266–

281; Robert E. Smith and William R. Swinyard, "Attitude-Behavior Consistency: The Impact of Product Trial Versus Advertising," *Journal of Marketing Research* 20 (August 1983), 257–267.

34. For an empirical demonstration, see Richard J. Lutz, "Changing Brand Attitudes through Modification of Cognitive Structure," *Journal of Consumer Research* 1 (March 1975), 49–59.

35. Paul W. Miniard, Randall L. Rose, Michael J. Barone, and Kenneth C. Manning, "On the Need for Relative Measures When Assessing Comparative Advertising Effects," *Journal of Advertising* 22 (September 1993), 41–58; Paul W. Miniard, Randall L. Rose, Kenneth C. Manning, and Michael J. Barone, "Tracking the Effects of Comparative and Noncomparative Advertising with Relative and Nonrelative Measures: A Further Examination of the Framing Correspondence Hypothesis," *Journal of Business Research* 41 (February 1998), 137–143; Cornelia Pechmann and S. Ratneshwar, "The Use of Comparative Advertising for Brand Positioning: Association versus Differentiation," *Journal of Consumer Research* 18 (September 1991), 145–160; Randall L. Rose, Paul W. Miniard, Michael J. Barone, Kenneth C. Manning, and Brian D. Till, "When Persuasion Goes Undetected: The Case of Comparative Advertising," *Journal of Marketing Research* 30 (August 1993), 315–330.

36. Scott B. MacKenzie, "The Role of Attention in Mediating the Effect of Advertising on Attribute Importance," *Journal of Consumer Research* 13 (September 1986), 174–195.

Suggested Readings for Part III

Verne Gay, "Fill It Out and Be Counted: The U.S. Census Bureau Tries Paid Advertising to Raise Mail-In Response Rates for Census 2000," *American Demographics* (February 2000), 28–31.

Kendra Parker, "Pent-up Spending Energy," *American Demographics* (November 1999), 40–42.

Michael J. Weiss, "Parallel Universe" (Excerpt from his book, *The Clustered World*), *American Demographics* (October 1999), 58–63.

Dana L. Alden, Jan-Benedict E. M. Steenkamp, and Rajeev Batra, "Brand Positioning Through Advertising in Asia, North America and Europe: The Role of Global Consumer Culture," *Journal of Marketing* 63 (January 1999), 75–87.

Neeraj Arora and Greg M. Allenby, "Measuring the Influence of Individual Preference Structures in Group Decision Making," *Journal of Marketing Research* 36 (November 1999), 476–487.

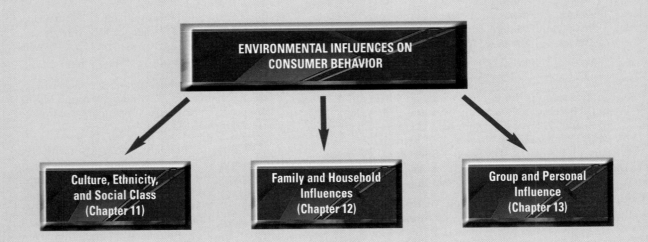

PART IV

Environmental Influences on Consumer Behavior

No person is an island. This statement certainly is true in the study of consumer behavior. Individuals come in all shapes, sizes, and colors, and behave in a variety of ways, as seen in the previous sections of this book. These characteristics are what make you unique as an individual. But what causes you to be the way you are? Is it genetic pre-disposition, the environment, or some combination thereof that has guided you in your evolution as a unique individual? Even scientists from many disciplines disagree on the answers to such basic questions.

One thing is clear—consumers are shaped to some extent by the environment in which they live, and they in turn affect their environments through their behaviors. The following chapters show you how this process takes place by addressing the impact of environmental influences on purchase and consumption decisions.

Fundamental to the discussion of environmental influences is the topic of culture. Chapter 11 focuses on the role of culture and ethnic influences on consumer behavior, including the roles of religion, values, and social class. Family and household influences are discussed in Chapter 12, including the changing roles of women and men in society and the changing makeup of the family unit. The final chapter in this section, Chapter 13, focuses on personal and group influences that shape the way we behave and live.

CHAPTER 11

Culture, Ethnicity, and Social Class

OPENING VIGNETTE

In today's global society, cultural icons and behaviors are transmitted from one nation to another through media and over the Internet. The result is a cultural swap-meet of sorts, in which products and fads popular in one culture are traded for those popular in another. Americans fell in love with Great Britain's Princess Diana, the late princess of Wales, who has appeared on the cover of the U.S. publication, *People* magazine, more than any other single person. American designers, such as Anna Sui and Marc Jacobs, capitalized on the transfer to the United States of *grunge* fashions popularized by England's youth market and seen often on MTV.

Many countries turn to the United States and England for new fads and cultural trends. The biggest tourist attraction in Romania today is not Dracula's castle or the painted monasteries of Bukovina. It is a $1 million replica of Southfork Ranch, the homestead featured in the American nighttime soap opera, *Dallas*, which still airs in syndication around the world. In its first year of operation, over two million people visited this iconic bridge to the West to revel in the luxurious surroundings, cars, and clothing that they had only been able to fantasize about until that point. Similar to the popularity of *Dallas* around the world has been the acceptance of McDonald's and the character of Ronald McDonald as an icon of the West. Chinese and Russian young adults alike save during the week so that they may take a date to McDonald's over the weekend, sometimes pausing to take pictures of each other standing alongside statues of Ronald himself.

But just as many fads or cultural icons flow from the United States to other countries, so are other cultures affecting life in the United States. Take music, for example. Ever since the Beatles invaded the United States in the 1960s, waves of other styles have affected American music. Most recently, Latin music has penetrated mainstream America's listening habits, with the rising popularity of groups such as Moloto and Ozomotli and mega-star Ricky Martin. Moloto and other Hispanic music actually represents rock en Español—a mix of rock, hip-hop, and elements of traditional Latin musical styles—and is a popular mix of sounds for Latin-based groups selling music in America. In fact, Latin music has become so popular in many pockets of the United States because of the increased Hispanic population, that WSKQ, a salsa radio station in New York, tied WLTW (a light music station) as one of the two most popular stations in the country's largest radio market.

Sources: Ira Matathia and Marian Salzman, "TransAtlantic Trend Tracking," Brandweek *(March 29, 1999), 27; Suein L. Hwang, "Salsa Radio Station Stirs Up New York,"* The Wall Street Journal *(September 10, 1998), B1; "Estas Preparado Para el Rock en Espanol?"* The Wall Street Journal *(April 29, 1999), B1.*

Many factors affect how we, as individuals and as societies, live, buy, and consume. External influences such as culture, ethnicity, and social class influence how *individual* consumers buy and use products, and help explain how *groups of consumers* behave.

The study of consumer behavior historically focused on individual differences and individual decision making, which remain important today because of the emphasis placed on communicating and attracting smaller segments of consumers. However, Markus and Kitayama[1] show that it is often more relevant to understand *the interdependent self* rather than *the independent self*, especially in a global economy, where 70 percent of the world's consumers live in a *collectivist* culture rather than in the *individualistic* culture of North America.[2] Influences such as culture and ethnicity not only affect how individuals make decisions, they also serve as a basis for segmentation strategies because they influence large groups of individuals.

What Is Culture?

Culture refers to a *set of values, ideas, artifacts, and other meaningful symbols that help individuals communicate, interpret, and evaluate as members of society.* It has been described as the "blueprint" of human activity, determining the coordinates of social action and productive activity.[3] Culture has also been defined as a set of socially acquired behavior patterns transmitted symbolically through language and other means to the members of a particular society.[4] Culture does not include instincts or idiosyncratic behavior occurring as a one-time solution to a unique problem. It does, however, reflect certain influences from factors such as ethnicity, race, religion, and national or regional identity, as seen in Figure 11.1. As some of these elements change within a society, so then does the culture change.

Culture includes both abstract and material elements, which allow us to describe, evaluate, and differentiate cultures. **Abstract elements** include *values, attitudes, ideas, personality types, and summary constructs, such as religion or politics.*

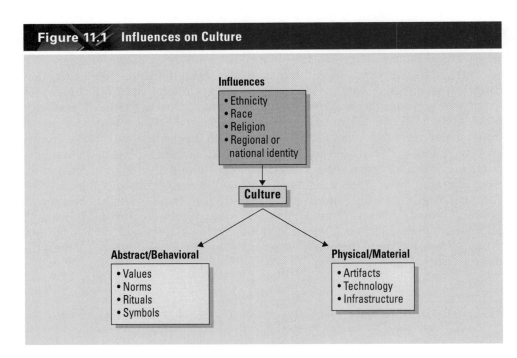

Figure 11.1   Influences on Culture

Influences
- Ethnicity
- Race
- Religion
- Regional or national identity

↓

Culture

Abstract/Behavioral
- Values
- Norms
- Rituals
- Symbols

Physical/Material
- Artifacts
- Technology
- Infrastructure

Some cultures also believe in myths or have superstitions, as seen in Consumer in Focus 11.1. A *symbol* might also evolve to represent a culture, such as the bald eagle, which represents the characteristics of courage and strength and the culture of the United States. This type of symbol, which embodies three central components—language, aesthetic styles, and story themes[5]—becomes short-hand for a culture, defining its characteristics and values in a way similar to how brands define the characteristics of a company or product.

Material components, sometimes referred to as **cultural artifacts,** include such things as *books, computers, tools, buildings, and specific products,* such as a pair of Levi's 501 jeans or the latest CD by Aerosmith or Garth Brooks. Computers, cellular phones, and Starbuck's coffee shops can all be considered American cultural artifacts of the last two decades of the 20th century, while business suits and air conditioners have become signs of global cosmopolitanism and modernity.[6] Products also provide *symbols of meaning* in a society[7] and often represent family relationships, as in the case of a special recipe handed down through generations, or are associated with one's national or ethnic identity. Products sometimes are used in *ritual behavior,* such as foods eaten during holidays or religious ceremonies. Occasionally, products become so much of a symbol in a society that they become *icons,* as in the case of brands such as McDonald's and Coca-Cola.

In Brazil, the belief in the mystical properties of guarana (a plant believed to enhance power, spirit, and sexual prowess) represents an abstract element of Brazilian culture, and guarana-based drinks available throughout Brazil are cultural artifacts. Even today, Brazilian consumers like Coke but love to drink guarana-based drinks.[8] Similarly, Unicum, a traditional Hungarian herb liqueur, has become part of the Hungarian culture and acts as a Hungarian cultural icon in the ad seen in Figure 11.2.

Culture provides people with a sense of identity and an understanding of acceptable behavior within society. Some of the more important characteristics influenced by culture are the following:[9]

Consumer in Focus 11.1

Superstition Can Affect Behavior in a Macroculture

Superstition has always had a big impact on human behavior, sometimes yielding macroeconomic effects for even the most industrialized societies. An example of the effects of superstition is the rate of Japanese births from 1960 to 1990. A general, steady decline is evident in recent decades. But what jumps out is the single-year 25 percent drop in 1966. Such a sudden dip and recovery in birthrates meant all kinds of problems for companies selling baby cribs in 1966 or bicycles in 1972, for colleges and universities in 1984, and for employers in 1988.

Why did the market plunge 25 percent for only one year? In much of Asia (where Chinese influences are strong), each year is associated with one of twelve animals. For example,

1996 was the year of the Rat. Both 1990 and 1978 were years of the Horse, as was 1966. In Japanese culture, there is a traditional belief about *heigo*, or the year of the *Fire* Horse, which occurs once every 60 years, the last time in 1966. According to this long-standing superstition, a female born in a year of the Fire Horse is destined both to live an unhappy life and to kill her husband if she marries. Judging by the birthrate that year in Japan, superstitions about the year of the Fire Horse deterred people from having children. The relevant point here is that superstitions can substantially affect behavior on a macroeconomic scale in industrialized countries.

Source: Excerpted from Cathy Anterasian, John L. Graham, R. Bruce Money, "Are U.S. Managers Superstitious about Market Share?" Sloan Management Review (Summer 1996), 67–77.

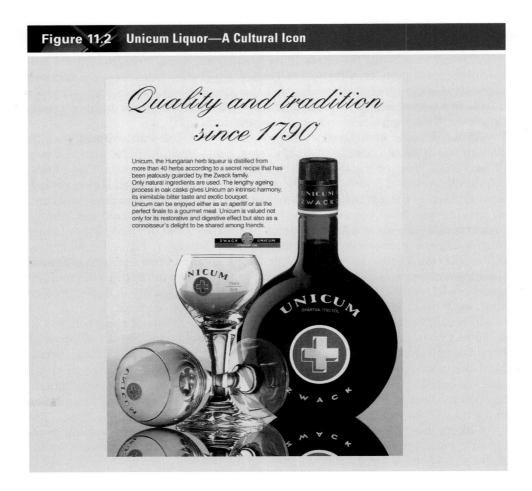

Figure 11.2   Unicum Liquor—A Cultural Icon

Quality and tradition since 1790

Unicum, the Hungarian herb liqueur is distilled from more than 40 herbs according to a secret recipe that has been jealously guarded by the Zwack family.
Only natural ingredients are used. The lengthy ageing process in oak casks gives Unicum an intrinsic harmony, its inimitable bitter taste and exotic bouquet.
Unicum can be enjoyed either as an aperitif or as the perfect finale to a gourmet meal. Unicum is valued not only for its restorative and digestive effect but also as a connoisseur's delight to be shared among friends.

1.   Sense of self and space
2.   Communication and language
3.   Dress and appearance
4.   Food and feeding habits
5.   Time and time consciousness
6.   Relationships (family, organizations, government, and so on)
7.   Values and norms
8.   Beliefs and attitudes
9.   Mental processes and learning
10. Work habits and practices

These characteristics can be used to define and differentiate one culture from another and identify cultural similarities. Marketers often use cultural characteristics to segment markets on a global basis or to advertise and sell products to different markets. For example, while expanding globally, McDonald's had to address food and eating habits of various cultures. Although research showed that the basic menu items would sell well in most markets, it had to add some foods to reflect the cultural preferences of local markets. In Japan, it added rice (the country's staple food) to the menu. In India, it addressed the sacred beliefs of the Hindu culture (that prohibit eating cows) by putting lamb-burgers on the menu.

In fact, such a large portion of this society is vegetarian that adding a veggie-burger to the menu would also have made sense.

Values and Norms

Two important elements of culture are values and norms. **Norms** are *rules of behavior held by a majority or at least a consensus of a group about how individuals should behave.* Cultural or social values are those shared broadly across groups of people, whereas personal values, as you read in Chapter 7, are the terminal (goals) or instrumental (behavior) beliefs of individuals.

Societal and personal values are not always the same; in fact, values may vary among people of the same culture. To illustrate this point, examine societal values about how we should treat others. Although societal values may condemn killing people, a terrorist's personal values might condone such behavior. Further, look at vegetarians around the globe. Vegetarians in the United States differ in behaviors from the cultural norms that say that eating animals and meat is acceptable, whereas in India, vegetarianism is the cultural norm and part of the value system of much of the country. These types of social values, described in this chapter, are closely related to the personal values described in Chapter 7 and can sometimes be measured with psychographic (AIO) or Rokeach (RVS) scales.[10]

Values and norms represent the beliefs of various groups within a society. **Macroculture** refers to *values and symbols that apply to an entire society or to most of its citizens.* **Microculture** refers to *values and symbols of a restrictive group or segment of consumers, defined according to variables such as age, religion, ethnicity, social class, or another subdivision of the whole.* Microcultures are sometimes called subcultures, but we use the term *microculture* to avoid concern that calling ethnic groups subcultures connotes inferiority.

Some countries, such as the United States, Switzerland, and Singapore, have national cultures made up of many microcultures, whereas other countries, such as Japan, tend to be more homogeneous. Countries like the United States reflect diverse ethnic components of their cultures, making them more dynamic and likely to change. U.S. marketers have to be ready to adapt to the changing needs of the market as influenced by the changes in the diverse ethnic groups and many microcultures. For example, hamburgers are a U.S. cultural icon, but the ethnic influences of the increasing Latino market have caused a change in what condiment is put on hamburgers—from ketchup to salsa. In contrast, a marketer in Tokyo can look out his corporate window and know that most Japanese consumers will have similar beliefs about honor, family, religion, education, and work habits, all important in understanding consumer behavior.

How Do People Get Their Values?

Unlike animals, whose behavior is more instinctive, humans are not born with norms of behavior. Instead, *humans learn their norms* through imitation or by observing the process of reward and punishment of people who adhere to or deviate from the group's norms. *The processes by which people develop their values, motivations, and habitual activity* are called **socialization** (the process of absorbing a culture). Parental practices, often directly related to cultural norms, can affect consumer socialization. For example, Japanese consumer socialization is characterized by benevolent dependence, which is consistent with a collectivist, interdependent society, whereas American consumer socialization is characterized by directed independence, which is consistent with an individualistic society.[11] Although some studies focus on how young people learn consumer skills, it is recognized that consumer socialization is a lifelong process.[12]

The process of how values are transferred from one generation to the next and where individuals get their values is summarized in Figure 11.3. The values transmission model shows how the values of a society are reflected in families, religious institutions, and schools, all of which expose and transmit values to individuals. These institutions and early lifetime experiences combine to affect which values individuals internalize and which ones they disregard.

Also important in the adoption process is the influence of peers and media. Media not only *reflects* societal values, but it can significantly *influence* the values of individuals. For example, a movie might portray taking drugs or driving drunk (values that society does not condone) as being acceptable or "cool," thereby potentially influencing the values of individuals. Media can also highlight cultural values important to a society and help pass them onto another generation or reinforce them in the society. European and German cultures emphasize the importance of children in families. Figure 11.4, featuring a German ad for Sparkasse Bank, reminds parents that there are a lot of reasons to build (a house), but none better or nicer than this one, referring to the picture of the baby.

Through the socialization process depicted in Figure 11.3, people adopt values that influence how they live, how they define right and wrong, how they shop, and what is important to them—such as pleasure, honesty, financial security, or ambition. These life forces produce preferences relating to color, packaging, convenience, hours of shopping, and characteristic interactions with salespeople and many others. Further, the values adopted by individuals shape the values of future societies. But just as individuals adopt certain values, they also abandon values when they no longer *meet the needs of society*. In fact, some

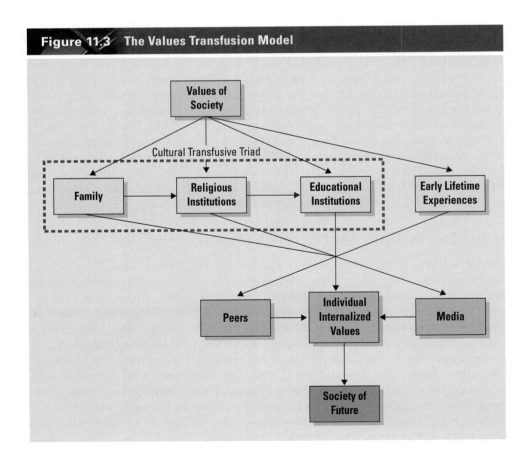

Figure 11.3   The Values Transfusion Model

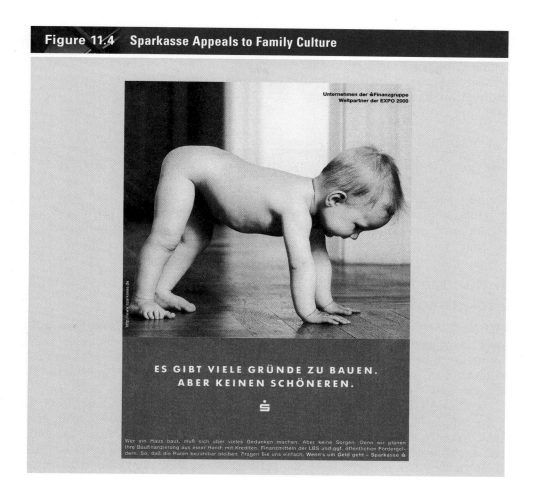

Figure 11.4 Sparkasse Appeals to Family Culture

anthropologists view culture as an entity serving humans in their attempts to meet the basic biological and social needs of society. When norms no longer provide gratification in a society, the norms are extinguished.

Adapting Strategies to Changing Cultures

Culture is *adaptive,* and marketing strategies based on the values of society must also be adaptive. When cultural changes occur, trends develop and provide marketing opportunities to those who spot the changes before their competitors do. As culture evolves, marketers may associate product or brand benefits with new values, or they may have to change the product if that value is no longer gratifying in society. For example, beef and other meats used to be staple breakfast, lunch, and dinner foods in the mass American culture. When most consumers worked on a farm or in strenuous manufacturing and labor jobs, high-energy and high-calorie foods were valued and gratifying. As those jobs were replaced by white-collar and other sedentary careers, the meat industry had to change its appeal to lean meats with fewer calories and less fat and cholesterol. Americans now consume more pounds of poultry per year than beef and pork.

Sometimes cultural norms change easily, and sometimes they remain the same for decades. Marketers must address **consumer socialization,** *the acquisition of consumption-related cognitions, attitudes, and behavior.* Norms learned early in life may be highly resistant to promotional efforts. When an advertiser is dealing with deeply ingrained, culturally defined behavior (about food, sex, basic forms of clothing, and so on), it is easier to change the marketing mix to conform to cultural values than to change the values through advertising. As an example, eating dogs, horses, sheep eyes, or even live fish is normal and healthy behavior in some cultures. Advertising would have great difficulty, however, in convincing typical North American consumers to buy these products.

How Culture Affects Consumer Behavior

Culture has a profound effect on why and how people buy and consume products and services. It affects the specific products people buy as well as the structure of consumption, individual decision making, and communication in a society.

Influence of Culture on Pre-Purchase and Purchase

Culture affects the need, search, and alternative evaluation stages of how individuals make purchase decisions in a variety of ways. Although marketers can influence these stages through point-of-purchase displays, advertising, and retailing strategies, certain cultural forces are difficult to overcome, at least in the short term.

Cultures view differently what is needed to enjoy a good standard of living. For example, North American households used to contain one television, around which family members gathered to watch shows. Now, consumers often buy several televisions for one household, and having a second television in the bedroom or the kitchen has become the cultural norm. Will computers experience the same increased importance? However, other cultures see this type of consumption as frivolous; their definition of *need* dictates that one television is adequate.

Culture also affects how consumers are likely to *search* for information. In some cultures, word-of-mouth and advice from a family member about product or brand choice are more important than information found in an advertisement. And some cultures are more likely to search the Internet for information. Regardless of method, marketers must understand which is valued more in a particular culture in order to formulate the most effective information strategy.

During *alternative evaluation,* some consumers place more weight on certain product attributes than on others, often due to the consumer's culture. For example, some wealthy consumers may think low price is the most important attribute, not because they lack money but because "thrift" (a cultural value) influences their choices. Conversely, a poor consumer may purchase an expensive pair of shoes because of personal or group values that persuade the individual to follow a fashion trend.

During *purchase* processes, the amount of price negotiation expected by both seller and buyer is culturally determined. In Greece and some Middle-Eastern countries, for instance, even the price of a physician's services is subject to negotiation, whereas in North American markets, a physician's fee is generally predetermined and non-negotiable. In Hong Kong, consumers are accustomed to walking through crowded marketplaces, in extreme heat, examining and buying freshly slaughtered meat that is hanging in the open air, as seen in Figure 11.5. North American consumers would be fearful of bacteria that might accumulate on the meat from exposure to the heat and insects.

Figure 11.5   Hong Kong Market

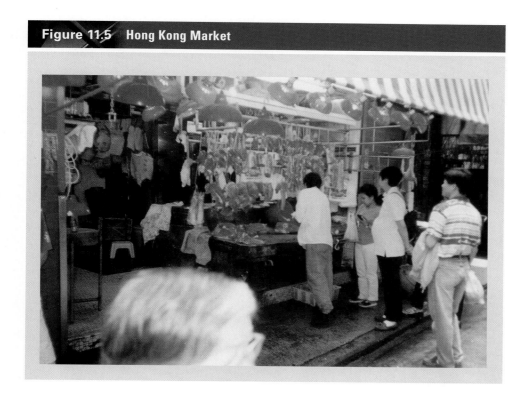

Influence of Culture on Consumption and Divestment

Culture also affects how consumers use or consume products. Consumers buy products to obtain function, form, and meaning, all of which marketers must address since they are defined by the cultural context of consumption.

When consumers use a product, they expect it to perform a *function*—to clean clothes in the case of washing machines. But consumers' expectations about function and form often vary between cultures. In European cultures, washing machines are expected to last for decades, "cook" the clothes to get them sanitary-clean, and be compact in size. Highly efficient, front-loading machines costing more than $1,000 are marketed successfully throughout Europe and Asia by firms such as Miele, a German-based manufacturer and supplier of household appliances (see Figure 11.6). Yet, when Miele introduced this product in North America, it found only limited success. Americans move more frequently than Europeans and do not want to "invest" in a machine they will have for only a few years; further, they expect the more convenient but less efficient cleaning ability of top-loading machines.[13]

Culture also influences how individuals *dispose* of products. Consequently, washing machines are almost a disposable product in the United States. When they break or if the consumer moves, they are often left behind or discarded. Some cultures promote reselling products after use, giving them to others to use, or recycling them and their packaging when possible, whereas others support throwing them away.

Figure 11.6   Product Function and Forms: $1,000 Washing Machines

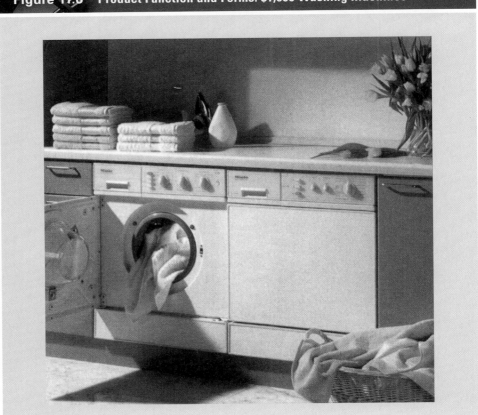

How Core Values Affect Marketing

Successful retailers know that a *basic group of products is essential to a store's traffic, customer loyalty, and profits.* These products are known as **core merchandise.** A group of values, called **core values,** also exists. These values are *basic to understanding the behavior of people and can be helpful to marketers in several ways.*

- *Core values define how products are used in a society.* Not only do core values determine what foods should be eaten, but they also determine with what other foods they are appropriate, how they are prepared, and the time of day to eat them.

- *Core values provide positive and negative valences for brands and communications programs.* Marketers may use celebrity athletes or musicians such as Tara Lipinski or Elton John to achieve positive valences to their brands, a successful strategy unless the image of the celebrity changes negatively.

- *Core values define acceptable market relationships.* A firm's native culture (and values) influences its business strategies, tactics, and practices in the global marketplace,[14] and it affects international buying practices as well.[15] For example, in Japan, a company will often do business with small suppliers or distribution companies owned by former employees, with whom they have a relationship or similar cultural backgrounds. But in the United

States, where the culture favors impersonal relationships and equality, it may be more difficult to develop the trust needed for effective relationship marketing.[16]

Core values define ethical behavior. The ethics of a particular firm are influenced by the values or ethics of the individuals it employs, just as the ethical climate of a country is influenced by the core values of its individuals and institutions. In recent years, the United States has been characterized as a "money culture" in which business executives operate principally on greed.[17] Depending on a person's own ethics, he or she might find various corporate goals incompatible with his or her own personal ethics,[18] causing stress and dissatisfaction. Sales managers can decrease the likelihood of ethical conflict by selecting and hiring individuals who have values and beliefs consistent with the organization's or who can learn the organization's values.[19]

Changing Values

Society's values change continuously even though the core values are relatively permanent. Marketers must pay special attention to values in transition because they affect the size of market segments. Changes in values may alter responses to advertising as well as responses to service offerings and preferred retailing formats. Some changes that have occurred during the 1990s have been identified in research at Young & Rubicam (see Table 11.1). They represent a paradigm shift or a fundamental reordering of the way we see the world around us.[20]

Changes in a society's values can be forecast on the basis of a **life-cycle explanation,** meaning that *as individuals grow older, their values change.* Therefore, the distinctive values seen now among young people will become like those of older ages in a few decades, and societal values in the future will be similar to today as younger people grow older and grow into the values of their parents. This is a theory of *behavioral assimilation.* **Generational change,** in contrast, suggests that *there will be gradual replacement of existing values by those of young people who form the* leading *generation in value terms.* When today's young people grow old, they will retain the values of their youth and replace societal values of today's older consumers.[21] What do you think? In 30 years, will you be more like your peers or your parents? Your answer will depend on how your values will be affected by the cultural transfusive triad (families, religious organizations, and schools) and early lifetime experiences.

Changing Family Influences

Family is the dominant transfusive agent of values in most cultures. Many changes are occurring in the family, examined more closely in Chapter 12, but some of the most significant are outlined here.

- *Less time for in-home or parent–child influence.* With many mothers working outside the home, about 60 percent of 3- to 4-year-olds attend preschool or daycare compared to 5.7 percent in 1965. Today, children are increasingly learning their values outside the family from babysitters, schools, and the media. The increase in single-mother births also diminishes potential parental influence on children.

- *Increasing divorce rates.* Most children are now raised part of their lives in single-parent households, contributing to decreased family influence. These

Table 11.1 Changing Values in Western Civilization	
Traditional Values	**New Values**
Self-denial ethic	Self-fulfillment ethic
Higher standard of living	Better quality of life
Traditional sex roles	Blurring of sex roles
Accepted definition of success	Individualized definition of success
Traditional family life	Alternative families
Faith in industry, institutions	Self-reliance
Live to work	Work to live
Hero worship	Love of ideas
Expansionism	Pluralism
Patriotism	Less nationalistic
Unparalleled growth	Growing sense of limits
Industrial growth	Information and service growth
Receptivity to technology	Technology orientation

Note: Developed Western societies are gradually discarding traditional values and are beginning to embrace emerging new values on an ever-widening scale.
Source: Joseph T. Plummer, "Changing Values," Futurist 23 (January/February 1989), 10.

children are often less likely to form and live in traditional families, influencing values of the future generation.

- *The isolated nuclear family.* Geographic separation of the nuclear family from grandparents and other relatives (due to increased mobility of jobs and education) contributes to lack of heritage or a yearning for roots.

Changing Religious Influences

The degree to which individuals attend religious institutions and believe in a "God" or "higher power" and the types of religious beliefs they have affect societal culture. Judeo-Christian religious institutions historically played an important role in shaping the values of Western cultures. In recent years, these institutions have changed substantially. Catholics have risen from tiny levels in 1776 to a quarter of the U.S. population largely because of European immigration in the early 1900s and current immigration from Hispanic countries. Baptists have replaced Anglicans (Episcopalians) as the dominant Protestant group.

The following summarizes some of the trends in religion occurring in the United States:

- *Decline in loyalty to traditional churches and religions.* The decline of institutionalized religion accelerated after World War II, with the spiritual seekers of the baby boomers. In 1958, 1 in 25 Americans had left the denomination in which they were raised, but by 1999, this number had jumped to 1 in 3. Religious groups declining in membership currently include moderate and liberal groups (Lutherans, Methodists, Presbyterians, Episcopalians, and others).

- *Increase in non-Christian religions.* With the increase in ethnic diversity has come an increased number of practicing Buddhists, Muslims, and others. These religions often promote conservatism and respect for family members.

- *Shift from traditional religion to spirituality.* Many Americans, especially aging baby boomers, are searching for experiential faith and spirituality rather than traditional religion. Spirituality is more personal and practical, involves stress reduction more so than salvation, and is about feeling good, not just being good.[22] Under this loose definition of faith and religion, millions of Americans have a sudden passion for spirituality,[23] and more people than ever are defining themselves as "religious," even if they rarely attend a church service.

- *Women becoming more religious.* Women tend to express their religious beliefs and spirituality more so than men and are joining more bible studies and women's groups to support each other in these efforts. Women are also more likely than men to define success in religious terms.[24] Figure 11.7 shows how women are keeping the faith in the United States.

- *Religion and spirituality are big business.* With the increase in spirituality has come an increase in the sales of religious books (on subjects from New Age practices to spiritual healing), spirituality retreats, apparel, alternative healthcare, spiritual education, religious broadcast stations, and religious gifts, especially those relating to angels. According to the Book Industry

---

Figure 11.7   Keeping the Faith

How important would you say religion is in your own life—very important, somewhat important, or not very important?

July 98		May 96
75%	Very important	69%
18	Somewhat important	21
7	Not very important	10

People practice their religion in different ways . . . Outside of attending religious services, do you pray several times a day, once a day, a few times a week, once a week, or never?

July 98		May 96
52%	Several times a day	38%
22	Once a day	25
13	A few times a week	18
9	Once a week or less	13
4	Never	5
*	Don't know/Refused	1

The latest numbers are from a national telephone poll of 1,000 adult women interviewed June 30–July 22, 1998, in a poll for the Center for Gender Equity conducted by Princeton Survey Research Associates. The May 1996 numbers are from the "May 1996 Religion and Politics Study," a national telephone survey of 1,975 adults age 18 or older conducted from May 31 through June 9, 1996, by The Pew Research Center for The People and The Press (PRC). The results here are based on the interviews only with the 1,034 female respondents.

Source: G. Evans Witt, "Women Show Their Spiritual Side," American Demographics (April 1999), 23.

Study group, in 1997, consumers spent $982 million on religious books, $268 million on inspirational books, and $27 billion[25] on alternative medicine (on treatments from massage to acupuncture).

Changing Educational Institutions

The third major institution that transmits values to consumers is education. The influence of education appears to be increasing, due partly to the increased participation of Americans in formal education and partly to the vacuum left by families and religious institutions. At the same time, there is concern about the nature of the increased influence.

- *A dramatic increase in formal education.* Today, one in four workers in the United States is a college graduate, up from about one in eight in 1970. Although fewer working women than men are college graduates currently, that might change since today more women are enrolled in colleges and universities than are men. Weekend and evening MBA programs and other innovations in university continuing education departments encourage higher levels of education, even among older individuals. The University of Phoenix is a for-profit corporation leading the way in many new, innovative methods of education and reaching nontraditional student groups.

- *Teaching: from memorization to questioning.* Previously, teaching often emphasized description and memorization of facts, with no latitude for questioning. The trend has been toward analytical approaches emphasizing questioning of the old and the formulation of new approaches and solutions. Consumers taught in this new environment may reject rigid definitions of right or wrong and practice aggressive consumerism. In turn, marketing organizations must revise sales programs and product information formats to provide answers when customers ask questions.

- *Internet teaching.* More students are experiencing some form of Internet learning, whether it be actual instruction from teachers through electronic sources or performing secondary research on the Internet. As young consumers, exposed early to computers and the Internet, become consuming adults, their expectations about how and for what to use electronic information and commerce will influence the marketing strategies of many firms and organizations.

The Influences of Age-Related Microcultures on Values

In addition to families, religious institutions, and educational institutions, culture and values are shaped by early life experiences. Consumer analysts employ **cohort analysis** to *investigate the changes in patterns of behavior or attitudes of groups called cohorts.* A **cohort** is *any group of individuals linked as a group in some way—* usually by age. Cohort analysis focuses on actual changes in the behavior or attitudes of a cohort, the changes that can be attributed to the process of aging, and changes that are associated with events of a particular period, such as the Great Depression or the Watergate scandal.[26] Though the 1960's counterculture brought with it an increase in feminist and immigrant values, some analysts say we have entered a post-modern era, in which cultural contradictions are celebrated and blended.[27] Although fads may change (flat-top haircuts in the 1950s and body piercing in the 1990s), the cultural dynamic is the same—minority groups will seek out these changes, and the majority will fall into the "I don't get it" category.[28]

Figure 11.8   Philips Gets Attention

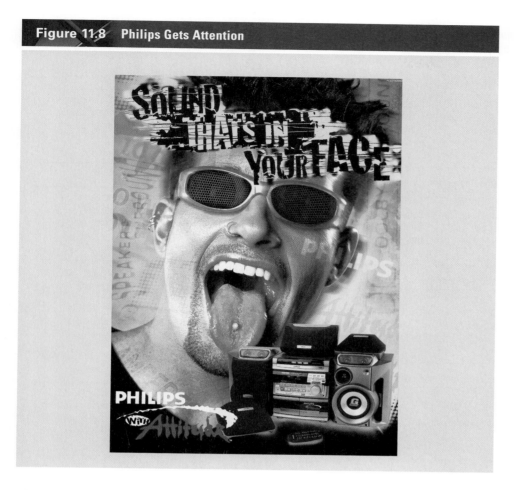

Philips developed an ad to try to connect with this latter cohort in the Australian ad for audio equipment in Figure 11.8.

Figure 11.9 highlights the various age-related cohorts into which consumers fall. Chapter 7 defined these groups even further and presented demographic descriptions of each. As you study these cohort descriptions, think about how their experiences might affect the values they have and how American culture will change as they become older.

National Culture

Culture has a profound impact on the way consumers perceive themselves, products they buy and use, purchasing processes, and the organizations from which they purchase. Marketers are giving more attention, however, to understanding macrocultures and how they affect consumer behavior. Hofstede[29] found four dimensions of culture that are common among 66 countries. These dimensions serve as a foundation for characterizing, comparing, and contrasting specific national cultures, and they are helpful in identifying environmentally sensitive segments of the market:[30]

- *Individualism versus collectivism.* Individualism describes the relationship between an individual and fellow individuals, or the collectivity that prevails in society. Figure 11.10 summarizes the attitudinal and behavioral differences associated with individualism and collectivism.

Figure 11.9   Consumer Age Cohorts

THE DEPRESSION COHORT (the G.I. generation)

BORN 1912–21 AGE IN '00: 79 to 80 **% OF ADULT POPULATION:** 7% (13 million) **MONEY MOTTO:** Save for a rainy day. **SEX MINDSET:** Intolerant **FAVORITE MUSIC:** Big band	People who were starting out in the Depression era were scarred in ways that remain with them today—especially when it comes to financial matters like spending, saving, and debt. The Depression cohort was also the first to be influenced by contemporary media: radio and especially motion pictures.

THE WORLD WAR II COHORT (the Depression generation)

BORN 1922–27 AGE IN '00: 73 to 78 **% OF ADULT POPULATION:** 6% (11 million) **MONEY MOTTO:** Save a lot, spend a little. **SEX MINDSET:** Ambivalent **FAVORITE MUSIC:** Swing	People who came of **age** in the 1940s were unified by the shared experience of a common enemy and a common goal. Consequently, this group became intensely romantic. A sense of self-denial that long outlived the war is especially strong among the 16 million veterans and their families.

THE POSTWAR COHORT (the silent generation)

BORN 1928–45 AGE IN '00: 55 to 72 **% OF ADULT POPULATION:** 21% (41 million) **MONEY MOTTO:** Save some, spend some. **SEX MINDSET:** Repressive **FAVORITE MUSIC:** Frank Sinatra	Members of this 18-year cohort, the war babies, benefited from a long period of economic growth and relative social tranquility. But global unrest and the threat of nuclear attack sparked a need to alleviate uncertainty in everyday life. The youngest subset, called the cool generation, was the first to dig folk rock.

THE BOOMERS I COHORT (the Woodstock generation)

BORN 1946–54 AGE IN '00: 46 to 54 **% OF ADULT POPULATION:** 17% (33 million) **MONEY MOTTO:** Spend, borrow, spend. **SEX MINDSET:** Permissive **FAVORITE MUSIC:** Rock & roll	Vietnam is the demarcation point between leading-edge and trailing-edge boomers. The Kennedy and King assassinations signaled an end to the status quo and galvanized this vast cohort. Still, early boomers continued to experience economic good times and want a lifestyle at least as good as that of their predecessors.

THE BOOMERS II COHORT (zoomers)

BORN 1955–65 AGE IN '00: 35 to 45 **% OF ADULT POPULATION:** 25% (49 million) **MONEY MOTTO:** Spend, borrow, spend. **SEX MINDSET:** Permissive **FAVORITE MUSIC:** Rock & roll	It all changed after Watergate. The idealistic fervor of youth disappeared. Instead, the later boomers exhibited a narcissistic preoccupation that manifested itself in things like the self-help movement. In this dawning **age** of downward mobility, debt as a means of maintaining a lifestyle made sense.

THE GENERATION X COHORT (baby-busters)

BORN 1966–76 AGE IN '00: 24 to 34 **% OF ADULT POPULATION:** 21% (41 million) **MONEY MOTTO:** Spend? Save? What? **SEX MINDSET:** Confused **FAVORITE MUSIC:** Grunge, rap, retro	The slacker set has nothing to hang on to. The latchkey kids of divorce and day care are searching for anchors with their seemingly contradictory "retro" behavior: the resurgence of proms, coming-out parties, and fraternities. Their political conservatism is motivated by a "What's in it for me?" cynicism.

Source: Faye Rice and Kimberly Seals McDonald, Making Generational Marketing Count, Fortune 131, 12 (June 26, 1995), 110.

- *Uncertainty avoidance.* Uncertainty avoidance concerns the different ways in which societies react to the uncertainties and ambiguities inherent in life. Some societies need well-defined rules or rituals to guide behavior, whereas others are tolerant of deviant ideas and behavior.

- *Power distance.* Power distance reflects the degree to which a society accepts inequality in power at different levels in organizations and institutions. It can affect preferences for centralization of authority, acceptance of differential rewards, and the ways people of unequal status work together.

Figure 11.10   Individualism Versus Collectivism

	Individualism (e.g., United States, Australia, Canada)	Collectivism (e.g., Hong Kong, Taiwan, Japan)
Self-construal	Defined by internal attributes, personal traits	Defined by important others, family, friends
Role of others	Self-evaluation (e.g., standards of social comparison, sources of appraisal regarding self)	Self-definition (e.g., relationships with others define self and affect personal preferences)
Values	Emphasis on separateness, individuality	Emphasis on connectedness, relationships
Motivational drives	Focus differentiation, relatively greater need to be unique	Focus on similarity, relatively greater need to blend in
Behavior	Reflective of personal preferences, needs	Influenced by preferences, needs of close others

- *Masculinity-femininity.* This factor defines the extent to which societies hold values traditionally regarded as predominantly masculine or feminine. Assertiveness, respect for achievement, and the acquisition of money and material possessions are identified with masculinity; and nurturing, concern for the environment, and championing the underdog are associated with a culture's femininity.

Geographic Culture

Although national cultural characteristics may exist for an entire nation, geographic areas within a nation sometimes develop their own culture. For example, the Southwest area of the United States is known for casual lifestyles featuring comfortable clothing, outdoor entertaining, and active sports. The Southwest may also appear to be more innovative toward new products, such as cosmetic surgery, when compared with conservative, inhibited attitudes that characterize other areas of the nation. Climate, religious affiliations of the population, nationality influences, and other variables are interrelated to produce a core of cultural values in a geographic area. Yet, research indicates that culture can cut across national, state, and provincial borders, and incorporate the culture, climate, institutions, business organizations, and resources of each region.[31]

Understanding the values of various regions may guide marketers' efforts to position products to various regions. For example, an advertisement promoting the capacity for self-fulfillment (e.g., "Set yourself free with Stouffer's") of a product may be more successful in the West than in the South. Security, on the other hand, may be a more successful appeal in the South than in comparably urbanized areas of the West (e.g., "Protect your home from break-ins with Electronic Touch Alarm").[32] For personal computers, an advertising campaign emphasizing how computers can help a person accomplish his or her goals or emphasizing the computer attributes that facilitate accomplishment will probably be more effective in the East than in the South.[33]

North American Core Values

Core values can be observed in Canada and the United States, even though both countries encompass values reflecting diverse national origins within their populations. Values are less rigid in North America because these countries are so young compared with most Asian and European countries.

The Foundation of American Values

The United States was an agrarian nation only two generations ago. Although it is now primarily urbanized and suburbanized, understanding its origin helps us analyze today's culture. Much of the religious and ethical tradition is believed to have come from Calvinist (Puritan) doctrine, with emphasis on individual responsibility and positive work ethic. "Anglo-Saxon civil rights, the rule of law, and representative institutions were inherited from the English background; ideas of egalitarian democracy and a secular spirit sprang from the French and American Revolutions. The period of slavery and its aftermath, and the European immigration of three centuries, have affected the American character strongly."[34] Even though most people are employees of large, complex organizations rather than farmers or shopkeepers, and goods are purchased rather than produced, many American values retain the agrarian base, emphasizing good work ethics, self-sufficiency, and the philosophy that an individual can make a difference.

American Values and Advertising

What are the core values that provide appeals for advertising and marketing programs? Eight of the most basic are described in Table 11.2. Sometimes advertisers are accused of appealing mostly to fear, snobbery, and self-indulgence, but after reviewing the values in Table 11. 2, you can see how such an approach would have limited appeal. Marketers are more successful when they appeal to core values based on hard work, achievement and success, optimism, and equal opportunity for a better material standard of living.

Advertisers must understand values to avoid violating standards. Benetton, the Italian apparel retailer, uses ads that reflect social issues. But most Americans never see some of Benetton's more provocative material. Figure 11.11 features some of these ads. In one, readers are presented with pastel-colored balloon-type images. A closer look reveals that they are condoms, part of a safe-sex blitz in which some stores gave away condoms. What some considered a religiously offensive ad ran throughout Europe, as did an ad designed to promote harmony among races, which was deemed as too provocative for the United States. Still another Benetton ad showed a black man and a white man chained together to promote the "united colors" theme. It was withdrawn in the United States after minority groups complained that the ad implied the black man was a criminal, and charged the company with racism.[35]

U.S. and Canadian Variations in Values

Canada and the United States are similar in many ways, but their values and institutions vary in important ways. For one, there is less of an ideology of Canadianism than there is one of Americanism. The emphasis on individualism and achievement can be traced to the American Revolution, an upheaval that Canada did not support. Canada presents a more neutral, affable face that distinguishes it from its more exuberant and aggressive neighbor. Canadians have greater awareness of American media and institutions than conversely.

Canada and the United States have different situations and different histories. For example, law and order enforced by the centrally controlled Northwest Mounted Police (now RCMP) tamed Canada's frontier much earlier than was the case in the United States. Seymour Lipset, one of the most prolific analysts of

Table 11.2	How Marketers Adapt to Core American Values

Material Well-Being

Achievement and success are measured mostly by the quantity and quality of material goods. There is display value in articles that others can see, such as designer clothing, luxury cars, and large homes. Although rebellion against such values is sometimes expressed, well-being is fundamental to the American value system. Americans believe in the marvels of modern comforts (good transportation, central heating, air conditioning, and labor-saving appliances) and believe in the "right" to have such things.

Twofold Moralizing

Americans believe in polarized morality, in which actions are either good or bad. Twofold judgments are the rule: legal or illegal, moral or immoral, and civilized or primitive. Consumers cast these judgments on public officials and companies, deeming them either ethical or unethical, not a little of both. Similarly, advertising that is "a little deceptive" is considered bad even if the overall message is largely correct. However, some conditions exist making the same behavior right or wrong depending on the situation. Gambling in many instances is illegal or "wrong," but when organized as a state lottery to benefit a good cause, it can be legal or "right."

Importance of Work over Play

Although work is associated in American values with purpose and maturity, play is associated with frivolity, pleasure, and children. In other cultures, festivals and holidays and children having fun are the most important events in society, whereas in the United States, even socializing is often work related.

Time Is Money

Americans view time differently from many other cultures. In the United States, time is more exact in nature, whereas in countries such as Mexico, time is approximate. Americans tend to be punctual, schedule activities at specific times, and expect others to keep appointments based on set times.

Effort, Optimism, and Entrepreneurship

Americans believe that problems should be identified and effort should be made to solve them. With proper effort, one can be optimistic about success. Europeans sometimes laugh at their American friends who believe that for every problem there is a solution. This attitude is based on the concept that people are their own masters and can control outcomes. In American culture, effort is rewarded, competition is enforced, and individual achievement is paramount. Entrepreneurship is one result of American values of effort, optimism, and the importance of winning.

Mastery over Nature

American core values produce a conquering attitude toward nature, which is different from Buddhism and Hinduism, in which people and nature are one and work with nature. Americans' conquering attitude stems from three assumptions: the universe is mechanistic, people are the masters of the earth, and people are qualitatively different from all other forms of life. American advertising depicts people who are in command of their natural environments when they show men fighting hair loss or women fighting wrinkles.

Egalitarianism

American core values support the belief that all people should have equal opportunities for achievement. Though some discrimination does occur, the core values, codified legislatively and judicially, favor equality of all people, especially those accepting the values and behaviors of the social majority.

Humanitarianism

American values support assistance of those less fortunate. Assistance expresses itself in the giving of donations to unknown individuals and groups needing aid because of natural disasters, disabilities, or disadvantages. Organizations such as the American Lung Association or the American Cancer Society benefit from Americans' beliefs in humanitarianism. For corporations, humanitarianism is not only a social responsibility but an important means through which to communicate with consumers.

Figure 11.11   How Social Values Affect Advertising

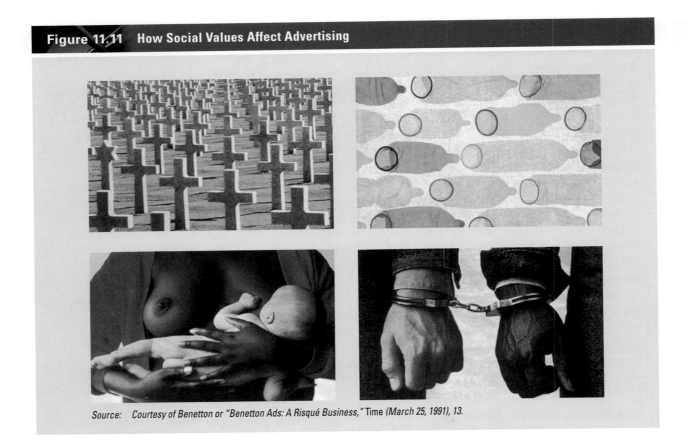

Source: *Courtesy of Benetton or "Benetton Ads: A Risqué Business," Time (March 25, 1991), 13.*

Canadian–U.S. relationships, believes this is the reason Canadians generally have more respect for law and order today than do U.S. citizens.[36] In Table 11.3, we summarize other differences between the values of the two countries based on Lipset's research.

Ethnic Microcultures and Their Influences on Consumer Behavior

Ethnicity is an important element in determining culture and predicting consumer preferences and behaviors. It is a process of group identification in which people use ethnic labels to define themselves and others. A "subjectivist" perspective reflects ascriptions people make about themselves. An "objectivist" definition is derived from sociocultural categories. In consumer research, ethnicity is best defined as some combination of these, including the strength or weakness of affiliation that people have with the ethnic group.[37] To the degree that people in an ethnic group share common perceptions and cognitions that are different from those of other ethnic groups or the larger society, they constitute a distinct ethnic group that may be useful to treat as a market segment.[38]

Specific consumers may not reflect the values of the ethnic group with which they are commonly identified. To believe that a given individual necessarily accepts the values of any specific microculture would make the observer guilty of stereotyping. Consumer behavior is a function of "felt ethnicity" as well as cultural identity, social surroundings, and product type.[39]

Table 11.3	Variations in Values Between Canada and the United States	
Canada		**United States**
More observance of law and order		Less observance
Emphasis on the rights and obligations of community		More emphasis on individual rights and obligations
Courts are perceived as an arm of the state		Courts perceived as a check on the powers of the state
Lawful society		Greater propensity to redefine or ignore rules
Use the system to change things		Employ informal, aggressive, and sometimes extra-legal means to correct what they think is wrong. "The greater lawlessness and corruption in the U.S. can also be attributed in part to a stronger emphasis on achievement"
Canadians find success in slightly bad taste		"Americans worship success"
Greater value of social relationships		Greater importance of work. Higher commitment to work ethic. Greater value of achievement (Goldfarb study)
Canadians more cautious		Americans take more risks
Corporate network denser in Canada. 1984—80% of companies on TSE controlled by 7 families; 32 families and 5 conglomerates control about 33% of all nonfinancial assets		One hundred largest firms own about 33% of all nonfinancial assets, few controlled by individuals
5 banks hold 80% of all deposits		Literally thousands of small banks in the United States
Anticombines legislation weakly enforced		Business affected by antielitist and anti–big business sentiments
Favor partial or total government ownership		Strong antitrust laws. Anti–big business, pro competition
Business leaders more likely to have privileged upbringing and less specialized education		Business leaders more likely to have a specialized education
Emphasis on social programs and government support		More laissez-faire
Canadian labor union density more than twice that of the American		
Fewer lobbying organizations in Canada even in proportion to smaller Canadian population. Since politicians toe party line, lobbying not as important		Seven thousand lobbying organizations registered with Congress—since Congresspersons can vote as they choose on a bill, lobbying can be effective

Source: Summarized from Seymour Martin Lipset, Continental Divide: The Values and Institutions of the United States and Canada *(New York: Routledge, 1990).*

America's Ethnic Microcultures

America, like countries such as Switzerland, Singapore, and South Africa, is a montage of nationality groups. Recent figures register 54 countries represented with 100,000 or more American residents. Figure 11.12 shows how immigration to the United States has changed over time, thus changing the makeup of the population and the influences on culture. Yet there do exist many similarities between immigration at the beginning and the end of the 20th century.[40] For example, the

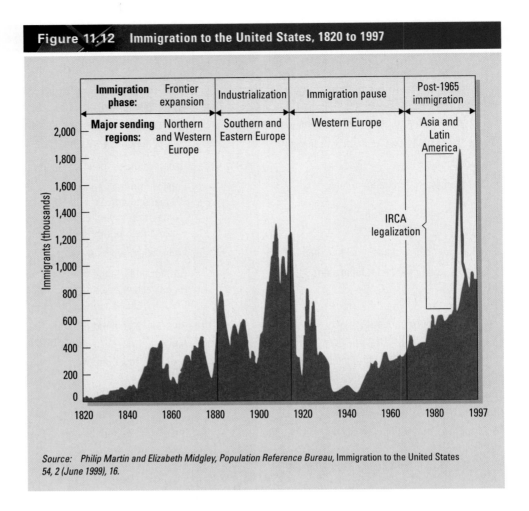

Figure 11.12   Immigration to the United States, 1820 to 1997

Source: Philip Martin and Elizabeth Midgley, Population Reference Bureau, Immigration to the United States 54, 2 (June 1999), 16.

number of immigrants (over one million) entering the United States during peak years is about the same, even though countries of origin are different in the early 1900s than in the late 1900s. However, during both periods, the economy was undergoing restructuring—with a shift from agriculture to industry in the beginning of the century and a shift from services to information in the 1990s.[41] In either case, immigrants arrived from countries and cultures different from the past, bringing with them new religions, cultures, and languages.

Some immigrants identify with much of their culture of origin; others do not. A variable closely associated with national ethnic identity is the language spoken at home. Two groups of Americans who often speak a language other than English are Chinese and Hispanics. Eighty-one percent of Chinese-Americans speak Chinese at home, whereas 43 percent of Hispanics speak Spanish at home, including Cuban-Americans at 92 percent and Mexican-Americans at 77 percent.[42] Their values, however, determine the degree to which immigrants embrace traditional American core values and how they contribute to the cultural diversity of North America. When an immigrant family becomes American, the members often manifest and reinforce the work ethic that is at the core of American values.[43]

As individuals are exposed to various ethnic subcultures, they often adapt to or take on characteristics of that culture. **Acculturation** measures the *degree to which a consumer has learned the ways of a different culture compared to how they were raised.* Individuals adapt to cultural changes in both social and professional situations—as they live among, befriend, and work with others. Managers and salespersons faced with the challenge of global business, find more success when they respond and adapt to the cultural differences of their business partners.[44]

Just as individuals adapt to cultural changes, so do companies and organizations operating in an increasingly global marketplace. A recent study of Latino, Asian, Middle Eastern, and Anglo retailers found that when they adapted to the cultures of their clients, changes occurred to themselves, their firms, their consumers, and ultimately, the marketplace.[45] Consumer in Focus 11.2 focuses on how Mony Life Insurance is adapting to a growing Indian-American market with new recruiting practices.

Euro-Descent Americans

More than 200 million Americans are of European descent; England is the background nation for 26.34 percent of Americans, followed closely by Germany with 26.14 percent and Ireland with 17.77 percent. In addition to the millions of second- and third-generation European-Americans, the increasing number of foreign-born European-Americans is attracting the attention of marketers, who recognize that Greek-Americans have different preferences than Swedish-Americans.

European immigration, which had been on a decline since the 1950s, increased dramatically from 1985 to 1995, experiencing a 155 percent increase over the period, to 161,000 persons in 1994.[46] According to the Immigration and Naturalization Service, over 1.2 million European immigrants came to the United States during those ten years, primarily stemming from the fall of Communism and the resulting freedom of Eastern Europeans. Recent immigrants and native-born Americans with close ties to their European heritage are defined as *Euro-American ethnics*.

Traditionally, European-American ethnics have displayed a "work hard, play hard" mentality and have been willing to work extended hours to save money for things like education, housing, and retirement. Their thriftiness is exhibited in

Consumer in Focus 11.2

Acculturation Leads to New Recruiting Practices

In efforts to tap into the growing market of Indian-Americans, Puneet Seth, managing director of Mony Life Insurance Co.'s New Jersey branch, is looking for new recruits in nontraditional places. In an age of electronic resumes and web-based recruiting, he is visiting Hindu temples in search of employees able to speak the language and specific dialect of the markets he is targeting. On a recent visit to the Bochasanwasi Akshar-Purshottam Sanstha temple in Edison, New Jersey, he encountered 400 worshipers, many of whom still speak Gujarati, the original language of the niche to which he is seeking to sell insurance. In this instance, his goal is to recruit a high-profile member of the community who would have influence in the market and understand the culture. Overall, he hopes to hire "a Punjabi, a Gujarati, and a Bihari" to reach other segments of the Indian-American market.

Indian-Americans, among the fastest growing ethnic cultures in the United States, have a median household income of $44,696 and perceive insurance to be the single most important investment tool to protect against unforeseen events. Yet, even with this desire for insurance, this ethnic market is more likely to buy from a salesperson who speaks the same language and understands their culture because of an implied, underlying level of trust. But finding a salesperson who can speak the language of the Indian-American customer can be tricky since 18 official Indian languages exist.

Source: Based on "Insurers Court Indian-American Market," The Wall Street Journal (October 12, 1999), B1.

their high coupon usage rate—75 percent versus 64 percent of all non-Hispanic whites—to reach their primary goal of creating security for themselves and their families. When asked about attitudes toward money, Russian-Americans cited the ability to make material purchases was more important than long-term security.[47] Although European ethnics like to save money, this does not mean they don't spend it on material items. According to Mediamark Research, 92 percent of this group owns VCRs and stereos, compared to 60 and 53 percent, respectively, of all non-Hispanic whites. Some of this conspicuous consumption is born from a desire to become "American," a status quickly attained through the acquisition of American symbols of success.

European-Americans tend to live in tight-knit communities, making them easy to reach with targeted advertising and promotions. However, they also tend to choose brands or products that reflect group preferences, making it difficult for a new brand to penetrate Euro-American ethnic groups.

One of those firms looking to attract European-American markets is AT&T. During the 1990s, the communications giant unleashed an ad campaign for the mass market featuring Whitney Houston singing "your true voice" and stressing sound quality. However, Russian-language-TV viewers instead saw a famous Russian comic in ads created by YAR, an ethnic marketing firm, because Whitney Houston had no meaning to this group. In fact, the issue of sound quality did not have much relevance to this group either. Russians were used to many failed attempts just to complete a call and then had to yell into the phone just to create enough sound to communicate. Further, "your true voice" translated into "the voice of Pravda"—the former Russian newspaper.

Native American Culture

In a sense, the truly "American" culture is that of Native Americans although marketers view Native Americans as a minority ethnic group in today's majority culture. After nearly a century of assimilation into white society, there is a resurgence of identification with Native American culture, both by Indians and *bahanas* (whites). Almost two million people in the United States identified themselves as American Indian in the 1990 census, and more than seven million claim some American Indian ancestry. Some American Indians dislike the idea of sharing their culture and spiritual practices with white people, but others welcome people of any race into their culture. The interest in Native American culture has increased consumer demand for products that reflect their ancient crafts and skills, which can be found in catalogs like Robert Redford's Sundance.

Multiethnic Microcultures

Increased ethnic diversity within a nation often leads to interracial relationships and marriages, resulting in children belonging to multiple ethnic subcultures. When this occurs, it is difficult to determine which of the influences will affect behavior and values more. For example, which is the greatest influence on golf superstar Tiger Woods's values and behaviors—his father's race (African-American) or his mother's race (Asian)? Knowing all of his ethnic and cultural influences allows marketers to reach him and other multiethnic consumers more effectively with diverse messages.

In 2000, the Bureau of the Census began collecting multiracial information on U.S. citizens for the first time in its history. When asked to describe one's race, individuals were allowed to mark multiple boxes, such as Asian, Black, and Native American, instead of being forced to select only one of the possible five categories. The difficulty is in tabulation—with the new format, 64 possible racial categories

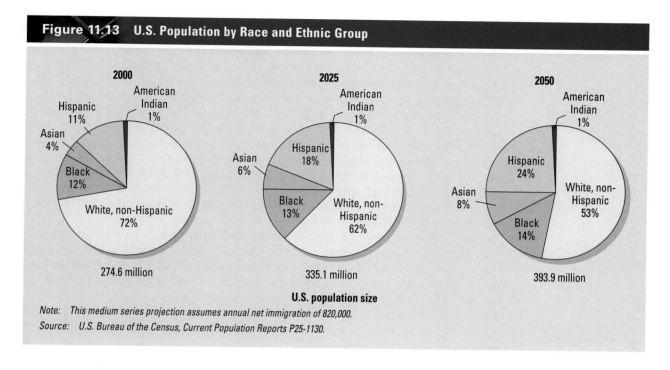

Figure 11.13   U.S. Population by Race and Ethnic Group

U.S. population size

Note: *This medium series projection assumes annual net immigration of 820,000.*

Source: *U.S. Bureau of the Census, Current Population Reports P25-1130.*

exist.[48] In spite of the complications, this information will yield more detailed and accurate data on specific racial groups, and identify needs for specialized advertising and market research.[49] *Interrace* magazine is an example of a product targeted toward multiethnic individuals.

Although marketers are interested in the estimated one to two million consumers classifying themselves as multiethnic, a majority of interest is focused on three ethnic groups: African-Americans, Hispanics (Latinos), and Asian-Americans. Figure 11.13 shows current and projected population breakdown by race and ethnicity, and Figure 11.14 shows the number of households and corresponding incomes for each major ethnic segment. These numbers explain why there is great interest in transcultural marketing among leading companies, such as Pepsi, McDonald's, and Coca-Cola.[50] Their interest is caused by two factors: *high projected growth rates* and *substantial buying power.* **Transcultural marketing research** is used to *gather data from specific ethnic groups and compare these data to those collected from other markets, usually the mass market.* The information identifies differences between groups, and guides effective communication and marketing strategies.

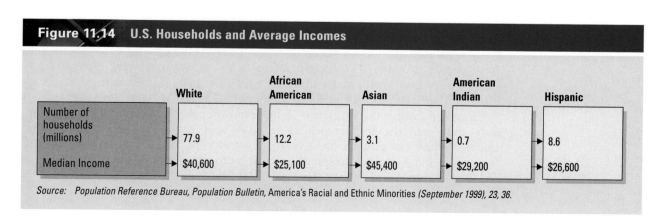

Figure 11.14   U.S. Households and Average Incomes

	White	African American	Asian	American Indian	Hispanic
Number of households (millions)	77.9	12.2	3.1	0.7	8.6
Median Income	$40,600	$25,100	$45,400	$29,200	$26,600

Source: *Population Reference Bureau, Population Bulletin, America's Racial and Ethnic Minorities (September 1999), 23, 36.*

Black or African-American Culture

African-American or black culture refers to a common heritage rather than to a skin color. In the United States, the black heritage is conditioned by a shared history beginning with slavery, discrimination and suffering, and segregation from the majority culture. Owing in part to this separation, a greater homogeneity among African-Americans than among whites has historically existed, although as the education level and corresponding income increases among segments of this group, the notion of homogeneity might be challenged.[51] Yet, when defining this market, controversy over proper terminology (black or African-American) still exists, even though more than 70 percent of black Americans prefer the term *black*, compared with 15 percent preferring African-American. Most marketers opt for the term *black/African-American*.[52]

Regardless of terminology, this market is worthy of serious marketing attention. It has a population base of more than 32 million people with substantial buying power, especially among the middle class.[53] Despite increased buying power, black consumers are underrepresented in advertisements and communication packages and often shown in stereotypical or menial roles.[54] That African-Americans compose 12.1 percent of the U.S. population and 11.3 percent of the readership of all magazines seems to support featuring black actors in ads for both black and mixed audiences.[55]

Structural Influences on Black/African-American Markets

The primary structural influences shaping African-American markets include income, education, families, and environment. All these factors when combined with personal situations and influences help predict consumer behavior of this market.

Income   About 21 percent of black households had incomes of $50,000 or more in 1997, up from just 9 percent in 1967.[56] Yet 33 percent of black families still live below the poverty level, as defined by the U.S. Department of Commerce, compared with 11 percent of white families and 29 percent of Hispanic families. Although a greater *number* of white families fall below the poverty level, the *percentage* of black families is larger.[57] Individual incomes for black men and women have risen in recent years, with 7.5 percent of men and 3.7 percent of women earning over $50,000 per year.[58] Depending on the study cited, the African-American market has a total purchasing power of between $450 billion and $533 billion.[59]

Two factors related to low income among black families are significant in the study of consumer behavior. First, there is the reality of low spending power for a large portion of this market. Consumers often buy from stores that compete on price and welcome food stamps, and they must spend a large portion of their income on staple products. Grocery stores such as Aldi and "dollar stores" benefit from their patronage. The second factor is the separation of the effects of low income versus ethnicity and culture on consumer behavior. Because many studies report only the consumption differences between black and white consumers without separating the influence of income differences, marketers may mistakenly minimize the importance of middle- and higher-income black market targets. When examined from a cultural standpoint, more similarities than differences in black and white spending exist, with a majority of the differences due to lower incomes and living in central cities.[60]

Education   The level of education among blacks varies greatly. A large number of children living below the poverty line or living in crime-ridden urban neighborhoods receive inferior education and lack the skills needed to get jobs, earn incomes, and acquire consumer skills. Many of them learn skills and behaviors on the streets rather than from teachers or parents. Yet, higher education has become a priority for a significant portion of this segment, as seen in the increase in the number of African-American college students over the last two decades.

Family Characteristics   The African-American culture is influenced by a variety of family characteristics. A high proportion of African-American families are headed by women, which is about twice as high as for white families. Only 38 percent of black children live with two parents compared with 77 percent of white children.[61] Therefore, black women influence many purchases traditionally purchased by male householders and have a great deal of authority in the family, which marketers must understand and portray correctly in ads. What's more, the average black family is younger than its white counterparts. The median age is about five years younger, a factor accounting for differences in preferences for clothing, music, shelter, cars, and many other products and activities.[62]

Research studies indicate that actors used in ads targeting this market should be consistent with the expectations of the market[63] and portrayed realistically if they are to influence the market. In the ad featured in Figure 11.15, Dove appeals to the inner strength associated with African-American women and their desire for beauty.

Discrimination   The effects of discrimination on the African-American culture are so massive and enduring that they cannot be ignored in the analysis of

Figure 11.15   Dove Appeals to Women's Strength

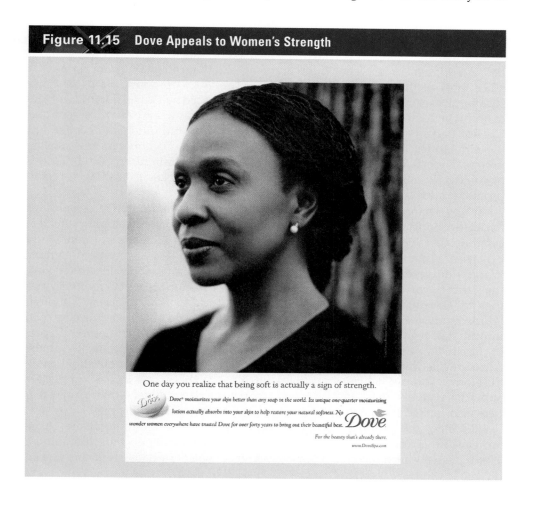

One day you realize that being soft is actually a sign of strength.

Dove® moisturizes your skin better than any soap in the world. Its unique one-quarter moisturizing lotion actually absorbs into your skin to help restore your natural softness. No wonder women everywhere have trusted Dove for over forty years to bring out their beautiful best. **Dove**

For the beauty that's already there.

www.DoveSpa.com

consumer behavior. Even after years of affirmative action programs, about which substantial controversy over effectiveness exists, employment parity for African-Americans has not been achieved. Some studies show that under-representation of minorities in higher- and lower-status occupations is still due to discrimination.[64]

As a result of years of discrimination, some black consumers have substantial skepticism toward white businesses—many of which supported segregated housing, limited employment opportunities, and restrained the use of blacks in the media until recent years. Today, firms that make a special effort to show sensitivity to the black culture, use black media wisely, and stand against discrimination may be able to turn a problem into an opportunity. In order to create better relationships with this segment, many companies create public relations programs and special promotions in conjunction with Black History month. For example, Kraft publishes a free booklet featuring African-American cooking, and Coca-Cola sponsors a "Share the Dream" scholarship program.[65]

It should not surprise you that black consumers like TV shows that portray blacks positively and are turned off by shows that feature embarrassing racial stereotypes and situations. Shows such as *ER* and *The Practice*, which are very popular among white viewers, have cast black actors in leading roles—in these cases, as doctors and attorneys. In its role to mirror societal changes and influence culture, television and other media have begun mainstreaming African-Americans (as well as other ethnic microcultures) into a variety of roles, shows, and ads designed to appeal to a variety of consumers.

African-American Consumption Patterns

How do African-Americans differ in their consumption patterns from other market segments? Consumer research has focused on this topic and on the similarities and differences between whites and blacks in the United States for decades.[66] Since most of these studies failed to control for socioeconomic status or other structural variables,[67] consumer researchers are faced with the dilemma of deciding which of the studies are still valid. But ask Ray Haysbert, president and CEO of Parks Sausage, and he'll probably tell you that differences do exist, but the similarities are even more pronounced, especially among middle-income groups. Parks Sausage, a black-owned firm based in Baltimore, achieved decades of success by selling products to all segments of the market *and* selling specialty products, such as chitterlings, to ethnic markets.

Many factors must be considered in developing marketing programs for African-Americans. Several studies provide guidelines for developing effective programs,[68] which consider both cultural and structural elements. A recent study by African American Markets Group (AAMG), a unit of Ketchem Public Relations Worldwide, reveals important insights into how to communicate effectively with the African-American market. Among magazines with the highest credibility ratings are *Essence*, *Ebony* (both black publications), and *Consumer Reports*. Although approximately 85 percent of those surveyed indicated that their leading source of information regarding products and companies is local television news, 82 percent said they look for information from magazines aimed specifically at the African-American market.[69] Respondents said they trust these publications more than other sources, which researchers attribute to their trust in black reporters and advice givers. Black-owned television news and local black-owned newspapers also ranked higher than other sources in terms of trustworthiness.[70]

Retailers and product manufacturers alike have become more aware of the African-American market. Retailers, such as J.C. Penney, Sears, and Montgomery Ward, have all introduced merchandise targeted specifically to black consumers.

Consumer in Focus 11.3

Microculture Goes Mainstream

Sometimes, what begins as a trend or style for an ethnic market segment can become a mainstream cultural norm or symbol. Take, for example, extra-baggy jeans that young people wear well below waistline level, showing off (ever-so-proudly) the tops of their underwear. What once was an urban style, found primarily in inner-cities, found its way into mainstream American fashion for teens in the 1990s. The trend began with urban youth who were trying to look "cool"—they began emulating young men recently released from prison. One of the first things taken from a man when he enters prison is his belt, causing his pants to bag. The uniforms in prison also tend to be baggy. The baggy look began to take on meaning outside prison walls, including a tough "don't mess with me" attitude.

Rap artists soon adopted the look, which today can be classified as "hip-hop," "urban," or "streetwear." Designers, such as Tommy Hilfiger, and labels, such as FUBU, have profited from the black- and Latino-inspired looks, which have found their way into mainstream American department stores.

Hip-hop represents a microculture, which evolved from an ethnic microculture and an age-based microculture—it derives its meaning from the experiences of young blacks living in cities. Its music, language, and fashions constantly change based on real-life experiences, making it a *real* culture that individuals can acquire, rather than a mere trend that teens adopt and quickly abandon. In fact, hip-hop has become so ubiquitous it has almost lost its racial connotation.

Though many suburban teens buy hip-hop music and fashions, researchers point out that many of them actually buy into the culture itself. They go beyond "rebellion" to claim to be part of black inner-city culture. Hilfiger and other designers actively market to urban youth (often through association with rap artists), hoping their brands will be accepted as real hip-hop symbols. Once this occurs, a significant portion of the white suburban teen segment is likely to follow.

Sears named its line of clothing Essence, and Spiegel Inc. launched "E Style" catalogs of women's clothing, geared toward readers of *Ebony* magazine. Tommy Hilfiger crossed ethnic market lines by making baggy pants and hip-hop styles mainstream, as seen in Consumer in Focus 11.3. Cosmetic giants such as Maybelline, Revlon, Procter & Gamble's Cover Girl, and L'Oreal are making special efforts to target women of color with products for dark skin tones. AM Cosmetics targets African-American women aged 18 to 34 with its Black Radiance line, which features colors, shades, and formulas suited for their skincare and makeup needs.[71] Cosmetic ads have also changed in recent years—they feature African-American models, rather than the blonde, blue-eyed beauties who dominated ads of the past.[73] Victoria's Secret incorporated into its marketing strategy a major role for black supermodel Tyra Banks.

Asian-American Culture

Asian-Americans have a strong give-and-take relationship with traditional American culture. Although they contribute to American culture (influencing everything from foods and tastes to values and education), they also adopt many Western philosophies into their own lifestyles and culture. Combine their willingness to adopt U.S. products (such as fashion apparel) with the fact that more than one-quarter of all immigrants to the United States in 1999 were from Asia, and you can see why Asian-Americans have become a desirable target for marketing organizations.

Asian-Americans are usually defined to include Chinese, Japanese, Koreans, Vietnamese, Cambodians, Laotians, Filipinos, Asian Indians, Pakistanis,

Hawaiians, Samoans, Guamanians, Fiji Islanders, and other Asians and Pacific Islanders living in the United States. As a whole, this market is expected to continue growing in size and percentage of U.S. population, perhaps reaching up to 20 million consumers early this century. Keep in mind as you read the following pages that there can be great variation in preferences and lifestyles among Asian-Americans of varied national backgrounds.

Structural Influences

Income   As you saw in Figure 11.14, Asian-Americans have higher incomes than the majority (white) markets in the United States and other ethnic microcultures. Fifty-three percent of Asian households have at least two income earners—with 74 percent of men and 59 percent of women in the work force. With purchasing power of between $101 billion and $188 billion,[74] marketers are reaching out to this segment.

Asian-Americans are also more likely to own a business than other minorities.[75] In fact, Koreans dominate entrepreneurial ventures, owning more than 113 businesses per 1,000 population, far more than any other minority or nonminority population group.[76] Koreans also have a higher rate of business success, due in part to their higher than average level of education and diligent work ethic. Interestingly, a major study of Korean immigrants concludes that the values of hard work and merchant ability have been developed as a result of coming to America, rather than because of their Korean background.[77]

Education   Asian-Americans believe strongly in education. They have the highest rate of education among any U.S. population category, with 83 percent having a high school diploma and 42 percent earning a college degree.[78] This group's higher income level is in direct correlation with its higher education level.

Family Characteristics   The Asian-American culture is characterized by hard work, strong family ties, appreciation for education, and other values that lead to success in entrepreneurship, technical skills, and the arts. Family is a priority for this ethnic group, and they tend to keep close ties with family members at home and abroad. Children are very important to the family structure. Some Asian-Americans tend to have more children than the majority culture, contributing to the rapid growth of this segment. From early ages, children are taught to respect elders, parents, and other family members. In turn, parents often sacrifice to provide the best possible education and opportunities for their children.

Family influences are also very strong among many Asian-Americans. For example, Chinese-American consumers often prefer shopping in large family groups for important purchases, with buying decisions approved by family elders. Though a product such as a car might be for a teenager or a middle-aged engineer, a successful sales approach might include communications directed to the grandfather or elderly uncle.

Asian-American Consumption Patterns

Among Asian-Americans, 54 percent shop as a leisure activity compared with 50 percent of the general population. Asians also think quality is more important than price when they choose a store. They are far more likely to use technology such as automated teller machines, and many more own VCRs, CD players, microwave ovens, home computers, and telephone answering machines.[79] Cultural sensitivity is key in marketing to Asian-Americans—sometimes firms need to look to multicultural marketing firms for advice. For example, a marketer might not know the importance of numbers to Asian-Americans, particularly the number 8, which symbolizes prosperity. Colors are also important (especially red), with different colors symbolizing different things. Many Asian-Americans believe that white envelopes should not be used around a holiday because white usually symbolizes death. Citibank varied one of its ads appearing during New Years by replacing corks from champagne bottles, which are considered inappropriate, with a dragon. Celebrities, especially those of Asian background, can also be very effective in appealing to this market. When Reebok featured tennis star Michael Chang in ads, shoe sales among Asian-Americans greatly increased.[80]

Marketers need to reach Asian-American consumers in different ways—not just through mass media, but also through cultural and foreign language publications. National- and language-oriented media may promote greater loyalty among readers and listeners, as well as provide excellent "cost-per-thousand" of concentrated market targets. For example, Vietnamese overwhelmingly prefer to read and hear ads in Vietnamese. They watch more native language television (about 9.5 hours per week) than other Asian-Americans, making it more important for a firm to communicate in their native tongue.[81] But not all Asian-Americans are the same. Recent immigrants from India may prefer to communicate with each other in Hindi, but prefer to read English. Marketers might find better results with English-language publications, such as *India Abroad*.[82]

Even with effective advertising and communication strategies, the sales process doesn't end with bringing consumers into the store. Some Asian-Americans, especially the Chinese, expect to bargain over price—to them it is a normal part of the business culture. But to someone more accustomed to American business—even a car salesperson—the exchange can seem downright cutthroat. One San Francisco Volkswagen dealer tells his salespeople, "When the guy comes in here and makes a ridiculous offer on a car, you don't get mad. You come back with something equally ridiculous and have a good laugh. Then start your real negotiation."[83]

Hispanic or Latino Culture

Although African-Americans are the largest ethnic microculture in the United States and Asian-Americans have the highest income, it is the Hispanic or Latino ethnic group that is receiving most of the attention from marketers and consumer analysts. The combination of rapid growth, size, and distinctive language is at the heart of the interest. Between the 1980 and 1990 census, the number of Hispanics increased from 14.6 million to 21.3 million. By 2015, experts believe Hispanics will outnumber African-Americans because of immigration and higher birthrates. The Hispanic market is 88 percent concentrated in cities, an attractive fact for media plans, distribution facilities, and other elements of marketing programs. Diversity in culture and other variables within this segment dictate it should be regarded as a heterogeneous set of wants and behaviors rather than the "Hispanic segment,"[84] and can be compared with other minority and majority segments using the Rokeach Value System (RVS).[85]

Who Is Hispanic?

Language and identity, rather than national origin, are the key elements in Hispanic culture, which may include any color or race. Which term, *Hispanic* or *Latino*, is more appropriate is a controversial question. The Census Bureau uses the term *Hispanic* to describe Americans whose origins are in the Spanish-speaking countries of the Western world, and new media and marketers typically use the same terminology. Outside Texas and the Southwestern United States, however, the term *Latino* is often preferred, and increasingly, country of origin, such as *Mexican-*, *Puerto Rican-*, or *Cuban-American*, is preferred. Academic groups and recent immigrants tend to prefer *Latino* to *Hispanic*, whereas affluent and older immigrants prefer the term *Hispanic*.[86] In this text, the term *Hispanic* is mostly used to reflect usage in government statistics and the media. *Latin* is also used increasingly to reflect, not only a music style, but a form of culture with appeal to many consumers beyond the Latino segment. Cable television, such as Univision, reaches many in the Hispanic market. Internet sites, such as **www.quepasa.com**, **www.miami.com**, and **www.el-mundo.es** provide up-to-date information of interest to the Hispanic market.

Hispanic consumers are often segmented into four groups: Mexicans, Puerto Ricans, Cubans, and others. Mexicans account for about 60 percent of all Hispanics (53 percent of whom were born in the United States), are concentrated in the Southwest states, and tend to be young with large families. Puerto Ricans account for 15 percent of Hispanics and are concentrated in the Northeast, especially in New York City. Most arrived in the United States during the past 25 years, and many are now in middle age, with young children born in the United States. Cubans make up about 7 percent of all Hispanics (7 percent of whom were born in the United States) and are concentrated in the Southeast. Cubans are the oldest group, have fewer children, and are the aristocracy in terms of occupation, education, and income. Other Hispanics (which constitute 18 percent) are primarily from Central America and are dispersed geographically. Ninety-three percent of them are foreign-born and are mostly young adults with few children.[87]

The diversity within the Hispanic market provides differences in values and motivations. Mexican-Americans are more likely to be assimilated into the U.S. culture. Although Cubans may not want to return to Cuba, they are more likely than are other Hispanics to think of themselves as Hispanic first and American second.[88]

Structural Influences

Income   Hispanics represent the fastest-growing ethnic market in the United States, with a buying power approaching $340 billion annually[89] and higher household incomes than blacks. Within the market, Cuban average income is much higher than that of any other Hispanic group and equal to or above the total American average, whereas Puerto Ricans have the lowest average of any Hispanic group.

Education   The number of Hispanics attending college and receiving bachelor's degrees has increased in recent years. In the early 1980s, Hispanic students made up 2.3 percent of the university population, and this number doubled to 4.7 percent by 1996.[90] It is likely that as this group's education level increases, so will its income level.

Family Characteristics   The family is extremely important in Hispanic culture and differs from non-Hispanic whites not only in values but also in size (larger) and age (younger).[91] It is estimated that by the year 2005, Hispanic youth will be the largest ethnic youth population in the United States, a figure that is expected to continue to increase because of higher fertility rates.[92]

Hispanic Consumption Patterns and Characteristics

Many firms have adapted product lines to meet the needs of the Latino segment. Pavion, which has a successful line of cosmetics for black consumers called Black

Radiance, added Solo Para Ti (Only For You) for Hispanic women. All aspects of Solo Para Ti (products, promotions, and even the name) were designed with the Latino culture in mind. The products are available in high-shine and in bright shades since these are the preferences of Hispanic women. To reach this market, Pavion advertises on Spanish-language TV and radio and features in-store promotions in both Spanish and English.[93] Similarly, Hispanic culture is affecting the tastes and preferences of the majority culture, causing companies to reformulate their product offerings.

Hispanics watch almost as much television as the average American, but they watch Spanish-language programming a majority of the time. According to Market Segment Research and Consulting (MSR), Hispanics watch, on average, 15.3 hours of Spanish programming per week and 10 hours of English programming.[94] Payless Shoes has experienced much success in reaching the Hispanic market during the show *Sabado Gigante* (Gigantic Saturday) on Univision's Spanish-language network. Even more effective than just airing an ad during the show, the anchors perform a skit about Payless Shoes and lead the audience in a song about the brand. Payless spokespersons say that some of their Hispanic customers (which account for 20 percent of their total customer base) enter the stores on Sundays singing the Payless jingle.[95]

Differences among segments of the Hispanic market affect purchase behavior in many ways, including the use of coupons. Proud that they are now making a better living, some Hispanic consumers are reluctant to use coupons that they believe are "for people who can't afford to pay the full price."[96] Webster found that Spanish-speaking Hispanics who identify closely with their microculture do not rely on printed sources of information as much as English-language Hispanics do, but do rely greatly on couponing, in-store point-of-purchase displays, and word-of-mouth.[97] However, as the Hispanic market is assimilated into an older non-Hispanic market, many characteristics of this microculture—such as higher brand loyalty, lower coupon usage, and more shopping enjoyment—are increasingly questionable.[98] Brand loyalty is increasingly questioned as typical behavior, although price, product quality, and shopping ease appear to be constant attributes of importance to Hispanics.[99]

Avoiding Marketing Blunders

Failure to understand the Hispanic culture can lead to marketing blunders. Humberto Valencia has identified three main types: translation blunders, culture misunderstandings, and Hispanic idiosyncrasies.[100]

Translation Blunders   Although most Hispanics are bilingual, about 94 percent speak Spanish in the home and think in Spanish—creating the need for marketers to communicate in Spanish.[101] This can lead to translation blunders. For example, one cigarette advertisement wanted to say the brand contained "less tar," but the translation actually said "less asphalt." Even market researchers can make a blunder when they ask for the *dama de la casa* (madam of the house) rather than the *senora de la casa* (lady of the house). In addition to conveying the wrong message, translation mistakes can offend and alienate an ethnic subculture.

Culture Misunderstandings   Serious misunderstandings occur when marketers use stereotypes of their own self-reference criteria for designing marketing and communication strategies. For example, a telephone company commercial portrayed a wife telling her husband to "run downstairs and phone Maria" and "tell her we'll be a little late." Two serious culture errors were committed. First, it is socially unacceptable for a Latin wife to give her husband orders. Second, Hispanics do not normally call to say they will not be on time; it is customary to arrive a little late. Misunderstandings about the meaning of time may be one of the reasons Mexican-Americans have more complaints about the delivery service of retailers than do other consumers.[102]

Hispanic Idiosyncrasies   Marketing blunders sometimes occur from failure to understand the idiosyncrasies of each segment of the total Hispanic market. A beer company filmed a Hispanic advertisement using the *Paseo del Rio* (Riverwalk) in San Antonio, Texas, as a background. The ad was well received among Hispanics living on the West Coast, who liked the Spanish atmosphere. In San Antonio itself, Hispanics did not like the ad because they considered the *Paseo del Rio* to be an attraction for non-Hispanic white tourists rather than for Hispanic residents.

French-Canadian Culture

One of the largest and most distinct cultures in North America is the French-Canadian area of Canada, mostly in Quebec. This might be considered a nationality group or a geographic culture. The province of Quebec accounts for more than 27 percent of the Canadian population and about 25 percent of income and retail sales.[103] For years, the French culture was somewhat ignored by English-oriented advertisers, thereby creating a social problem and limiting the potential effectiveness of communications to the French market. Some of the differential treatment may have been caused by different social class groupings compared with Anglo markets.[104]

Is advertising transferable between the French-Canadian (FC) culture and the English-Canadian (EC) culture? Some marketers believe that separate advertising material must be developed to be effective in the FC microculture. Others believe materials can be developed that are effective with both groups. A minimum of verbal material is used, with emphasis on the visual. Tamilia's research,[105] which compared communications with FC and EC consumers on a cross-cultural basis, indicated the potential for increasing effectiveness in advertising communications by targeting FCs with people-oriented ads and ECs with message-oriented ads.

Because of the size and importance of the FC market, it has attracted the attention of many marketers. The process of understanding communications in a cross-cultural setting, however, is applicable to other situations in which diverse ethnic groups are the target for marketing programs.

Social Class Microcultures

Microcultures can also be described in terms of social class. **Social class** is defined as *relatively permanent and homogeneous divisions in a society into which individuals or families sharing similar values, lifestyles, interests, wealth, status, education, economic positions, and behavior can be categorized.* Class membership exists and can be described as a statistical category whether or not individuals are aware of their common situation. Some of the concrete variables that define various social classes include occupation, education, friendships, ways of speaking, and possessions. Other perceived variables include power, prestige, and class.[106] Marketing research often focuses on social class variables since the mix of goods that consumers are *able* to buy is determined in part by social class.

For marketers and sociologists, status groups are of primary interest because they influence what people buy and consume.

Status groups reflect *a community's expectations for style of life among each class as well as the positive or negative social estimation of honor given to each class.* Simply stated, whereas "classes" are stratified based on their relations to the production and acquisition of goods, "status groups" are stratified according to lifestyles and the principles of the consumption of goods.[107] However, for practical purposes, it is usually adequate in the study of consumer behavior to treat the terms *status* and *class* interchangeably, recognizing that status may also be used in other contexts to describe differential respect given to an individual within a group.

If the 1980s were about greed and ostentation for upper social class groups and the 1990s were about value and self-fulfillment, what will be the legacy of the 2000s? The experts observe that in recent years, affluent tastes have run more toward the utilitarian. Range Rovers, Lincoln Navigators, or Ford Explorers, rather than Porsches, have been the vehicles of choice of upper income consumers,[108] prompting Mercedes and Lexus to develop and market SUVs to their "utilitarian, upper social class" consumers.

What Determines Social Class?

Your social class is influenced mostly by the family in which you were raised. Your father's occupation probably had a significant effect, since that has historically been the most important determinant, followed closely by the wife's occupation.[109] Variables that determine social class have been identified in social stratification studies since the 1920s and 1930s. Today, social class research includes thousands of studies dealing with the measurement of social class in large cities; movement between social classes; interactions of social class with gender, race, ethnicity, and education; and the effects of social class on poverty and economic policy. From extensive research, nine variables have emerged as most important in determining social class,[110] as shown in Figure 11.16.

For consumer analysts, six variables are especially useful in understanding a consumer's social class. These variables are occupation, personal performance, interactions, possessions, value orientations, and class consciousness.

Occupation   Occupation is the best single indicator of social class in most consumer research. The work consumers perform greatly affects their lifestyles and consumption patterns. For example, blue-collar workers spend a greater proportion of their income on food, whereas managers and professionals spend a higher share of their income on eating out, clothing, and financial services.[111]

Sometimes, people make the mistake of equating social class with income. Social class is not determined by income even though there may be a correlation due to the relationship between income and other variables that determine social class. A senior garbage collector, for example, might earn more than an assistant professor of history. The professor typically would be ascribed higher social class, however. You can probably think of more examples of how income and social class differ.

Personal Performance   A person's status can also be influenced by his or her success relative to that of others in the same occupation—that is, by an individual's

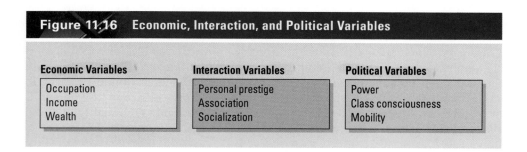

Figure 11.16   Economic, Interaction, and Political Variables

Economic Variables	Interaction Variables	Political Variables
Occupation Income Wealth	Personal prestige Association Socialization	Power Class consciousness Mobility

personal performance. Even though income is not a good indicator of overall social class, it may serve as a gauge of personal performance within an occupation. Personal performance also involves activities other than job-related pursuits. Perhaps your father has a lower-status occupation, but your family may still achieve more status if your father is perceived as one who helps others in need, is unusually kind and interested in fellow workers, or is a faithful worker in civic or religious organizations. A reputation as a good mother or a good father may contribute to one's status.

Interactions   People feel most comfortable when they are with people of similar values and behavior. Group membership and interactions are considered a primary determinant of a person's social class. The interaction variables of personal prestige, association, and socialization are the essence of social class. People have high **prestige** *when other people have an attitude of respect or deference to them.* **Association** is a *variable concerned with everyday relationships, with people who like to do the same things they do, in the same ways, and with whom they feel comfortable.* Social class behavior and values are clearly differentiated in children by the time they have reached adolescence, in variables that vary by social class such as self-esteem.[112] Social interactions ordinarily are limited to one's immediate social class even though opportunities exist for broader contact. Most marriages occur within the same or adjacent social classes.

Possessions   Possessions are symbols of class membership—not only the number of possessions, but also the nature of the choices. **Conspicuous consumption,** *people's desire to provide prominent visible evidence of their ability to afford luxury goods,* helps explain why different classes buy different products. Thus, a middle-class family may choose wall-to-wall carpeting, whereas an upper-class family is more likely to choose Oriental rugs, even if the prices are equal.[113]

Possessions and wealth are closely related. Wealth is usually a result of an accumulation of past income. In certain forms, such as ownership of a business or stocks and bonds, wealth is the source of future income that may enable a family to maintain its (high) social class from generation to generation. Thus, possessions that indicate a family's wealth are important in reflecting social class. Some products and brands are positioned as symbols of status, as the products used by upper middle or upper classes. For people who are striving to become associated with those classes, the purchase of such brands may be partially based on the desire for such affiliation or identification.

Value Orientations   Values indicate the social class to which one belongs. When a group of people share a common set of abstract convictions that organize and relate many specific attributes, it is possible to categorize an individual in the group by the degree to which he or she possesses these values. Some observers believe that in countries other than the United States, values are more important than possessions. Class is indicated more by merit derived from expressions in art, science, and religion and even in such mundane things as dressing and eating properly. In contrast, people in the United States are believed to make a religion of money.[114]

Class Consciousness   One of the important political variables of social class is class consciousness—the degree to which people in a social class are aware of themselves as a distinctive group with shared political and economic interests. To some extent, a person's social class is indicated by how conscious that person is of social class. Lower social class individuals may recognize the reality of social class but may not be as sensitive to specific differences. Thus, advertising for goods selling to upper-class market targets are often rich with social class symbols, but ads to middle and lower social class targets may not be well received if they use a direct class appeal.

Social Stratification

Have you noticed that in many contexts, for example, school or work, some people are ranked higher than others and are perceived to have more power or control? Americans may hope that everyone has the same opportunity to access products and services; however, the reality is that some people have either "more luck" or are better "positioned" to *attain* than others. **Social stratification** refers to the *perceived hierarchies in which consumers rate others as higher or lower in social status.* Those who *earn a higher status due to work or study* have **achieved status,** whereas those who are *lucky to be born wealthy or beautiful* achieve **ascribed status.**

Regardless of how status is achieved, social class can be classified into six distinct segments, as defined by W. Lloyd Warner in 1941: Upper upper, lower upper, upper middle, lower middle, upper lower, and lower lower. The Gilbert and Kahl definitions,[115] shown in Figure 11.17, provide generally accepted estimates on the size of various social classes, and emphasize economic distinctions, especially the recent emphasis on capitalism and entrepreneurship. The Coleman–Rainwater approach emphasizes how people interact with each other as equals, superiors, or inferiors, especially in their work relationships.

One complexity in measuring social class is the problem of *status inconsistency*—when people rate high on one variable but low on another. Highly paid athletes and popular musicians often fit this category. The other end of the spectrum of status inconsistency would include some professors who have average or lower income but much education and many cultural advantages. These people do not fit into many of the generalizations about social class.

Social Class Dynamics

Is it possible to change your social class? **Social mobility** refers to the process of *passing from one social class to another,* but includes more than just changing your occupation or income level. In England, citizens can rarely change class rapidly and cannot be royalty unless born into it. In India, the family never changes class, but individuals may do so through reincarnation. In countries such as Russia, China, and Hungary, consumers formerly subscribed to the common person ideology of Communism and Socialism. Today, there are new stirrings and the emergence of a consumer culture that is demonstrated in homes, electronic equipment, cars, number of bodyguards, and clothes that no longer reflect the stereotyped view of a person as a cog in the societal mechanism.[116]

Although in the United States it is possible to climb upward (upward mobility) in the social order, the probabilities of this actually happening are not very high.[117] Children's social class usually predicts their social class as adults,[118] ultimately limiting social mobility for men and women,[119] due to factors such as limited access to good education and racial prejudice.

Although individuals might not change their social status easily, they often display behaviors or symbols of other social classes. **Parody display** describes *the mockery of status symbols and behavior,* whereby an upper-class individual might wear blue jeans with holes in them to proclaim distaste for class or his or her own security in the social status system. Though some people think about upholding their social class, others rebel against it by becoming part of the counterculture, perhaps displaying their distaste for their class with body piercing or tattooing.

Figure 11.17   Social Classes in America

Two Recent Views of the American Status Structure

The Gilbert-Kahl New Synthesis Class Structure: A situations model from political theory and sociological analysis[a]	**The Coleman-Rainwater Social Standing Class Hierarchy: A reputational behavioral view in the community study tradition**[b]
Upper Americans	**Upper Americans**
Capitalist Class (1%) — Their investment decisions shape the national economy, income mostly from assets earned inherited, prestige university connections	Upper Upper (0.3%) — "Capital S society" world of inherited wealth, aristocratic names
Upper Middle Class (14%) — Upper managers, professionals, medium businessmen; college educated; family income ideally runs nearly twice the national average	Lower Upper (1.2%) — Newer social elite drawn from current corporate leadership
	Upper Middle (12.5%) — Rest of college graduate managers and professionals; lifestyle centers on private clubs, causes, and the arts
Middle Americans	**Middle Americans**
Middle Class (33%) — Middle-level white-collar, top-level blue-collar; education past high school typical; income somewhat above the national average	Middle Class (32%) — Average-pay white-collar workers and their blue-collar friends; live on "the better side of town," try to "do the proper things"
Working Class (32%) — Middle-level blue-collar; lower-level white-collar; income runs slightly below the national average; education is also slightly below	Working Class (38%) — Average-pay blue-collar workers; lead "working class lifestyle" whatever the income, school background, and job
Marginal and Lower Americans	**Lower Americans**
Working Poor (11–12%) — Below mainstream America in living standard but above the poverty line; low-paid service workers, operatives; some high school education	"A lower group of people but not the lowest" (9%) — Working not on welfare; living standard is just above poverty; behavior judged "crude," "trashy"
Underclass (8–9%) — Depend primarily on welfare system for sustenance; living standard below poverty line; not regularly employed; lack schooling	"Real lower lower" (7%) — On welfare, visibly poverty-stricken, usually out of work (or have "the dirtiest jobs"); "bums," "common criminals"

[a]*Abstracted by Coleman from Dennis Gilbert and Joseph A. Kahl, "The American Class Structure: A Synthesis," Chapter 11.* The American Class Structure: A New Synthesis *(Homewood, Ill.: The Dorsey Press, 1982).*

[b]*This condensation of the Coleman-Rainwater view is drawn from Chapters 8, 9, and 10 of Richard P. Coleman and Lee P. Rainwater, with Kent A. McClelland,* Social Standing in America: New Dimensions of Class *(New York: Basic Books, 1978).*

Social Class and Consumer Behavior

Social class affects consumer behavior in a variety of ways. Certain consumers read magazines, such as *Town & Country* and *Architectural Digest,* because the contents reflect the interests of the affluent social classes to which the readers belong or to which they aspire. The magazines advertise upscale products for affluent consumers and contain articles that reflect the themes and motivations of special significance to affluent social classes—articles about arts and craftsmanship, interior decoration, dominance of nature, the triumph of technology, fashions, and the ideology of affluence.[120]

Consumers associate brands of products and services with specific social classes. For instance, Heineken and Amstel Light are considered to be upper middle-class drinks, whereas Budweiser is perceived as a beer for "every person" and is consumed mainly by middle- and lower-class drinkers. In the United States early in this century, beer was perceived as a lower-class beverage, but today it is popular with all classes—perhaps as a result of marketing efforts and the introduction of up-scale micro-brews and imported beers.

Market Segmentation

Social class can be used to segment markets. The procedures for market segmentation include the following steps:

1. Identification of social class usage of product
2. Comparison of social class variables for segmentation with other variables (income, life cycle, and so on)
3. Description of social class characteristics identified in market target
4. Development of marketing program to maximize effectiveness of marketing mix based on consistency with social class attributes

Analysis of market segments by socioeconomic profile helps in the development of a comprehensive marketing program to match the preferences and behavior of the market target. This would include product attributes, media strategy, creative strategy, channels of distribution, and pricing.

Targeting various zip codes (or postal codes) facilitates social class segmentation. Zip codes estimate status without the need to collect additional data from respondents other than addresses. The marketing research firm Claritas uses zip code information to classify households into segments such as the "Suburban Elites" who live in Scarsdale (New York), Winnetka (Illinois), or similar locations. Each segment is described in terms of typical leisure time activities, frequently read publications, and favored brands.[121]

Positioning Based on Social Class Characteristics

Social class is an important concept in developing positioning strategies—the creation of perceptions in consumers' minds about the attributes of a product or organization. To accomplish positioning effectively requires a good understanding of the class characteristics of the target market and the class attributes desired for the product. As marketers, it is important to note that the number of consumers who aspire to higher social classes is much larger than those who are in them. Many of the middle class can buy products with the symbols and allure of higher social classes—and often do for products as diverse as those of Coach or Godiva. Market researchers at Grey Advertising estimate only a few million Americans have incomes that enable them to live affluent or rich lives. But far more—perhaps ten times as many—partake of the good life some of the time, treating themselves to Godiva chocolates (Figure 11.18), Armani cologne, or Hermes scarves. Wanting it all is a hallmark of the middle class. Buying the best on at least a few occasions is a way to set themselves apart and bolster their self-image. Ads for premium-priced products need to be sensual, provocative, and elegant for these products.[122]

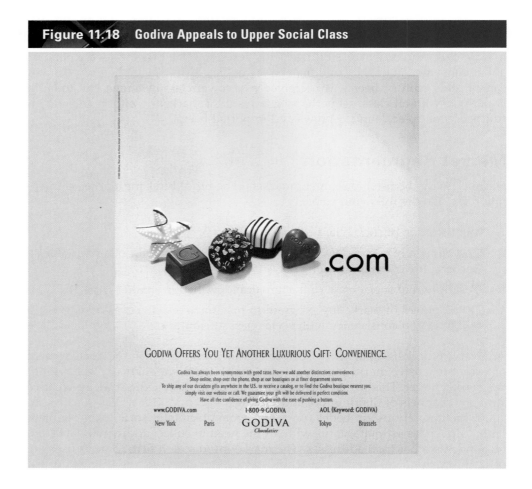

Figure 11.18   Godiva Appeals to Upper Social Class

GODIVA OFFERS YOU YET ANOTHER LUXURIOUS GIFT: CONVENIENCE.

Godiva has always been synonymous with good taste. Now we add another distinction: convenience.
Shop online, shop over the phone, shop at our boutiques or at finer department stores.
To ship any of our decadent gifts anywhere in the U.S. to receive a catalog, or to find the Godiva boutique nearest you,
simply visit our website or call. We guarantee your gift will be delivered in perfect condition.
Have all the confidence of giving Godiva with the ease of pushing a button.

www.GODIVA.com   1-800-9-GODIVA   AOL (Keyword: GODIVA)

New York   Paris   GODIVA   Tokyo   Brussels
                          Chocolatier

Summary

Culture is the complex of values, ideas, attitudes, and other meaningful symbols that allow humans to communicate, interpret, and evaluate as members of society. Culture and its values are transmitted from one generation to another, and individuals learn values and culture through socialization and acculturation. The core values of a society define how products are used, with regard to their function, form, and meaning. Culture also provides positive and negative valences for brands and for communication programs and defines the ideology of consumption.

The fundamental forces that form values are included in the cultural transfusive triad. In addition to the influences of the institutions of the family, religion, and schools, early lifetime experiences, such as depressions, wars, and other major events, also affect values.

North America is a multicultural society comprised of basic core values in the macroculture and many microcultures. With organizations striving to understand consumers better, many marketers are studying microcultures more closely, including how cultural icons and trends transcend from one microculture to another. These segments may be either age, religious, geographic, or ethnic microcultures.

Marketing to consumers in North America must be done in an environment of multicultural diversity. Ethnic groups may be formed around nationality, religion, physical attributes, or geographic location. Major microcultures in North America include Native Americans, Asian-Americans, African-Americans, Hispanics, and French-Canadians.

Another type of microculture is defined by social class. Social classes are relatively permanent and homogeneous groupings of people in society, permitting them to be compared with one another. For marketers, the most important determinants of social class are usually considered to be occupation, personal performance, interactions, possessions, value orientations, and class consciousness.

Social classes in the United States are traditionally divided into six groups: upper upper, lower upper, upper middle, lower middle, upper lower, and lower lower. Newer classification systems emphasize the enlarged capitalist or professional classes in the upper middle or lower lower classes. Each group displays characteristic values and behaviors that are useful to consumer analysts in designing marketing programs.

Review and Discussion Questions

1. What is meant by the term *culture?* Why does this term create confusion about its meaning?

2. Where do consumers get their values?

3. Examine the American core values described in this chapter. Consider how they are changing, what might influence them, and how they might influence a marketer of consumer electronics products.

4. Select the topic of family, religious institutions, or schools, and prepare a report documenting the changes that are occurring in the institution you chose.

5. Describe values of the various age cohorts. What appeals or methods of marketing are likely to be effective with various market segments?

6. Select one of the dimensions of culture identified by Hofstede, and describe how it might be used in market segmentation.

7. Are there really differences between black and white consumption patterns? Explain your answer.

8. Asian-Americans still represent a small proportion of the total population of the United States. Why should they be given much importance in marketing research and strategies? What types of adaptations in a marketing plan should be made to reach Asian-Americans?

9. Describe some of the influences on the American macroculture of the Latino culture.

10. Assume that the American Cancer Society wanted to target the Hispanic population with a campaign about the importance of early detection. What types of recommendations would you make for reaching this market effectively?

11. What variables determine an individual's social class? In what order of importance should they be ranked?

12. In what way does income relate to social class? Why is it used so little as an indicator of social class? What should be its proper value as an indicator?

13. A marketing researcher is speculating on the influence of the upper classes on the consumption decisions of the lower classes for the following

products: automobiles, food, clothing, and baby-care products. What conclusions would you expect for each of these products? Describe a research project that could be used to answer this question.

14. In what social class would you place professional athletes? Actors and actresses?

Endnotes

1. Hazel Rose Markus and Shinobu Kitayama, "Culture and the Self: Implications for Cognition, Emotion, and Motivation," *Psychological Review* 98 (1991), 224–253.

2. Harry C. Triandis, "Cross-Cultural Studies of Individualism and Collectivism," in John Berman, ed., *Nebraska Symposium on Motivation* (Lincoln: University of Nebraska Press, 1989), 41–133.

3. Grant McCracken, "Culture and Consumption: A Theoretical Account of the Structure and Movement of the Cultural Meaning of Consumer Goods," *Journal of Consumer Research* 13 (June 1986), 71–81.

4. Melanie Wallendorf and M. Reilly, "Distinguishing Culture of Origin from Culture of Residence," in R. Bagozzi and A. Tybout, eds., *Advances in Consumer Research* 10 (Association for Consumer Research, 1983), 699–701.

5. Dana L. Alden, Jan-Benedict E. M. Steenkamp, and Rajeev Batra, "Brand Positioning Through Advertising in Asia, North America and Europe: The Role of Global Consumer Culture," *Journal of Marketing* 63 (January 1999), 75–87.

6. Ibid.

7. James H. Leigh and Terrance G. Gabel, "Symbolic Interactionism: Its Effects on Consumer Behavior and Implications for Marketing Strategy," *Journal of Consumer Marketing* 9 (Winter 1992), 27–38.

8. Matt Moffett and Nikhil Deogun, "Brazilians Like Coke, But What They Love to Drink Is Guarana," *The Wall Street Journal* (July 8, 1999), A1.

9. Phillip R. Harris and Robert I. Moran, *Managing Cultural Differences* (Houston: Gulf Publishing Company, 1987), 190–195.

10. P. Valette-Florence and A. Jolibert, "Social Values, A.I.O., and Consumption Patterns," *Journal of Business Research* 20 (1990), 109–122.

11. Gregory M. Rose, "Consumer Socialization, Parental Style, and Developmental Timetables in the United States and Japan," *Journal of Marketing* 63, 3 (July 1999).

12. George P. Moschis, *Consumer Socialization* (Lexington, MA: Lexington Books, 1987), 9.

13. "Miele," in Roger D. Blackwell, Kristina S. Blackwell, and W. Wayne Talarzyk, *Contemporary Cases in Consumer Behavior* (Hinsdale, IL: Dryden Press, 1993), 452–462.

14. Johny Johansson and Ikujiro Nonaka, *Relentless, The Japanese Way of Marketing* (New York: HarperBusiness, 1996).

15. R. Bruce Money, Mary C. Gilly, and John L. Graham, "Explorations of National Culture and Word of Mouth Referral Behavior in the Purchase of Industrial Services in the United States and Japan," *Journal of Marketing* (October 1998), 76–87.

16. Angela da Rocha, Rebecca Arkader, and Antonio Barretto, "On Networks and Bonds: A Cultural Analysis of the Nature of Relationships," in David W. Cravens and Peter R. Dickson, eds., *Enhancing Knowledge Development in Marketing* (Chicago: American Marketing Association, 1993), 92–96.

17. William Taylor, "Crime? Greed? Big Ideas? What Were the '80s About?" *Harvard Business Review* (January/February 1992), 32–45.

18. Foo Nin Ho, Scott J. Vitell, James H. Barnes, and Rene Desborde, "Ethical Correlates of Role Conflict and Ambiguity in Marketing: The Mediating Role of Cognitive Moral Development," *Journal of the Academy of Marketing Science* (Spring 1997), 117–126.

19. Charles H. Schwepker, O. C. Ferrell, Thomas N. Ingram, "The Influence of Ethical Climate and Ethical Conflict on Role Stress in the Sales Force," *Journal of the Academy of Marketing Science* (Spring 1997), 99–108.

20. Joseph T. Plummer, "Changing Values," *Futurist* 23 (January/February 1989), 8–13.

21. Sheena Ashford and Noel Timms, *What Europe Thinks: A Study of Western European Values* (Aldershot: Dartmouth, 1992).

22. Richard Cimino and Don Lattin, "Choosing My Religion," *American Demographics* (April 1999), 62–65.

23. David B. Wolfe, "The Psychological Center of Gravity," *American Demographics* (April 1998), 16.

24. "A Measure of Success," *American Demographics* (April 1999), 9.

25. Ibid.

26. Norval D. Glenn, *Cohort Analysis* (Beverly Hills, CA: Sage Publications, 1977).

27. John Robinson and Nicholas Zill, "Matters of Culture," *American Demographics* (September 1997), 24.

28. Ibid.

29. Gert Hofstede, "Culture's Consequences: International Differences in Work-Related Values" (Beverly Hills, CA: Sage Publications, 1984).

30. Roger P. McIntyre, Martin S. Meloche, and Susan L. Lewis, "National Culture as a Macro Tool for Environmental Sensitivity Segmentation," in David Cravens and Peter Dickson, eds., *Enhancing Knowledge Development in Marketing* (Chicago: American Marketing Association, 1993), 153–159.

31. Joel Garreau, *The Nine Nations of North America* (Boston: Houghton Mifflin, 1981).

32. Lynn R. Kahle, "The Nine Nations of North America and the Value Basis of Geographic Segmentation," *Journal of Marketing* 50 (April 1986), 37–47.

33. Ibid.

34. Conrad M. Arensberg and Arthur H. Niehoff, "American Cultural Values," in James P. Spradley and Mihale A. Rykiewich, eds., *The Nacirema: Readings on American Culture* (Boston: Little, Brown and Company, 1980), 363–379. Table 17.1 builds on Arensberg and Niehoff.

35. "Benetton Ads: A Risque Business," *Time* (March 25, 1991), 13.

36. Seymour M. Lipset, *North American Cultures: Values and Institutions in Canada and the United States* (Orono, ME: Borderlands, 1990), 6.

37. Rohit Deshpande, Wayne D. Hoyer, and Naveen Donthu, "The Intensity of Ethnic Affiliation: A Study of the Sociology of Hispanic Consumption," *Journal of Consumer Research* 13 (September 1986), 214–219.

38. Elizabeth C. Hirschman, "An Examination of Ethnicity and Consumption Using Free Response Data," in AMA *Educators' Conference Proceedings* (Chicago: American Marketing Association, 1982), 84–88.

39. Johanna Zmud and Carolos Arce, "The Ethnicity and Consumption Relationship," in John F. Sherry, Jr., and Brian Sternthal, eds., *Diversity in Consumer Behavior* (Provo, UT: Association for Consumer Research, 1992), 443–449.

40. Philip Martin and Elizabeth Midgley, Population Reference Bureau, *Immigration to the United States* 54, 2 (June 1999), 16.

41. Ibid.

42. Edith McArthur, "What Language Do You Speak?" *American Demographics* (October 1984), 32–33.

43. Nathan Caplan, John K. Whitmore, and Marcella H. Choy, *The Boat People and Achievement in America: A Study of Family Life, Hard Work, and Cultural Values* (Ann Arbor, MI: University of Michigan Press, 1989).

44. Douglas W. LaBahn and Katrin R. Harich, "Sensitivity to National Business Culture: Effects on U.S.–Mexican Channel Relationship Performance," *Journal of International Marketing* 5, 4 (Winter 1997).

45. Lisa Penaloza and Mary C. Gilly, "Marketer Acculturation: The Changer and the Changed," *Journal of Marketing* 63, 3 (July 1999).

46. Shelly Reese, "When Whites Aren't a Mass Market," *American Demographics* (March 1997), 51–54.

47. Ibid.

48. William O'Hare, "Managing Multiple-Race Data," *American Demographics* (April 1998), 42–44.

49. Christy Fisher, "It's All In The Details," *American Demographics* (April 1998), 45–47.

50. Juan Faura, "Transcultural Marketing No Longer an Afterthought," *Marketing News* (January 4, 1999), 16.

51. Reynolds Farley and Suzanne M. Bianchi, "The Growing Gap between Blacks," *American Demographics* (July 1983), 15–18.

52. Jerome D. Williams, "Reflections of a Black Middle-Class Consumer: Caught between Two Worlds or Getting the Best of Both?" in Sherry and Sternthal, *Diversity in Consumer Behavior*, 850–855.

53. Cyndee Miller, "Research on Black Consumers," *Marketing News* (September 13, 1993), 1ff.

54. Mark Green, *Invisible People: The Depiction of Minorities in Magazine Ads and Catalogs* (New York: City of New York Department of Consumer Affairs, 1991).

55. Tommy E. Whittler, "The Effects of Actors' Race in Commercial Advertising: Review and Extension,"

Journal of Advertising 20 (1991), 54–60; Tommy E. Whittler and Joan DiMeo, "Viewers' Reactions to Racial Cues in Advertising Stimuli," *Journal of Advertising Research* 31 (December 1991), 37–46.

56. "Affluence Is at Record Level," *American Demographics Magazine Supplement* (1999), 8.

57. U.S. Department of Commerce, *Current Population Reports,* Series P-60-181 (Washington, DC: U.S. Government Printing Office, 1993).

58. Jennifer Lach, "The Color of Money," *American Demographics* (February 1999), 59–60.

59. Chris Sandlund, "There's a New Face to America," *Success* (April 1999), 40.

60. William O'Hare, "Blacks and Whites: One Market or Two?" *American Demographics* (March 1987), 44–48.

61. Nancy Ten Kate, "Black Children More Likely to Live with One Parent," *American Demographics* (February 1991), 11.

62. A collection of articles on this topic is found in Harriette Pipies McAdoo, ed., *Black Families* (Newbury Park, CA: Sage Publications, 1988).

63. William J. Qualls and David J. Moore, "Stereotyping Effects on Consumers' Evaluation of Advertising: Impact of Racial Difference between Actors and Viewers," *Psychology and Marketing* 7 (Summer 1990), 135–151.

64. Frank McCoy, "Rethinking the Cost of Discrimination," *Black Enterprise* 24 (January 1994), 54–59.

65. Marilyn K. Foxworth, "Celebrating Black History," *Public Relations Journal* 47 (February 1991), 16–21.

66. Raymond A. Bauer and Scott M. Cunningham, *Studies in the Negro Market* (Cambridge, MA: Marketing Science Institute, 1970). Also Donald Sexton, "Black Buyer Behavior," *Journal of Marketing* 36 (October 1972), 36–39.

67. Thomas E. Ness and Melvin T. Stith, "Middle-Class Values in Blacks and Whites," in Robert E. Pitts, Jr. and Arch G. Woodside, *Personal Values and Consumer Psychology* (Lexington, MA: Lexington Books, 1984), 255–270.

68. Parke Gibson, *$70 Billion in the Black* (New York: Macmillan, 1978); B. G. Yovovich, "The Debate Rages On: Marketing to Blacks," *Advertising Age* (November 29, 1982), M-10; David Astor, "Black Spending Power: $140 Billion and Growing," *Marketing Communications* (July 1982), 13–18; P. A. Robinson, C. P. Rao, and S. C. Mehta, "Historical Perspectives of Black Consumer Research in the United States: A Critical Review," in C. T. Tan and J. Sheth, eds., *Historical Perspectives in Consumer Research* (Singapore: National University of Singapore, 1985), 46–50.

69. Jake Holden, "The Ring of Truth," *American Demographics* (October 1998), 14.

70. Ibid.

71. Marc Spiegler, "Marketing Street Culture — Bringing Hip-Hop to the Mainstream," *American Demographics* (November 1996), 29.

72. "There's Room to Grow Ethnic, *Mass Merchandise Retailer* (May 3, 1999), 33.

73. Cyndee Miller, "Cosmetics Firms Finally Discover the Ethnic Market," *Marketing News* (August 30, 1993), 2.

74. Chris Sandlund, "There's a New Face to America," *Success* (April 1999), 40.

75. Wendy Manning and William O'Hare, "Asian-American Businesses," *American Demographics* (August 1988), 35–39.

76. William O'Hare, "Reaching for the Dream," *American Demographics* (January 1992), 32–36.

77. Ivan Light and Edna Bonacich, *Immigrant Entrepreneurs: Koreans in Los Angeles,* 1965–1982 (Los Angeles: University of California Press, 1988).

78. Cheryl Russell, *Racial and Ethnic Diversity,* 8.

79. Dan Fost, "California's Asian Market," *American Demographics* (October 1990), 34–37.

80. Cyndee Miller, "Hot Asian-American Market Not Starting Much of a Fire Yet," *Marketing News* (January 21, 1991), 12.

81. Marcia Mogelonsky, "Watching in Tongues," *American Demographics* (April 1998), 48–52.

82. Chris Sandlund, "There's a New Face to America," *Success* (April 1999), 44.

83. Joel Kotkin, "Selling to the New America," *Inc.* (July 1987), 46–47.

84. Geraldine Fennel, Joel Saegert, Francis Piron, and Rosemary Jimenez, "Do Hispanics Constitute a Market Segment?" in Sherry and Sternthal, *Diversity in Consumer Behavior,* 28–33.

85. Humberto Valencia, "Hispanic Values and Subcultural Research," *Journal of the Academy of Marketing Science* 17 (Winter 1989), 23–28; Van R. Wood and Roy Howell, "A Note on Hispanic Values and Subcultural Research: An Alternative View," *Journal of the Academy of Marketing Science* 19 (Winter 1991), 61–67.

86. "Quandry over One Term to Cover Myriad People," *The Wall Street Journal* (January 18, 1994), B1.

87. Daniel Yankelovich, *Spanish USA* (New York: Yankelovich, Skelly & White, Inc., 1981). Also see reports on a repetition in 1984 of the same study in "Homogenized Hispanics," *American Demographics* (February 1985), 16.

88. Yankelovich, *Spanish USA.*

89. "Soccer Plays to Growing Hispanic Market," *Population Today* (April 1999), 5.

90. *Statistical Abstract of the United States, 1998,* U.S. Department of Commerce, Bureau of the Census, Table No. 328, Degrees Earned by Level and Race/Ethnicity, 202.

91. Lisa Penaloza Alaniz and Marcy C. Gilly, "The Hispanic Family-Consumer Research Issues," *Psychology and Marketing* (Winter 1986), 291–303.

92. Helene Stapinski, "Generacion Latino," *American Demographics* (July 1999), 65.

93. Miller, "Cosmetics Firms Finally Discover the Ethnic Market."

94. Marcia Mogelonsky, "Watching in Tongues," *American Demographics* (April 1998), 48–52.

95. Barbara Matinez, "Dog Food, Toothpaste and Oreos Star on Popular Hispanic Television Programming," *The Wall Street Journal* (March 25, 1997), B1.

96. Luiz Diaz-Altertini, "Brand-Loyal Hispanics Need Good Reason for Switching," *Advertising Age* (April 16, 1979), SX–23.

97. Cynthia Webster, "The Effects of Hispanic Subcultural Identification on Information Search Behavior," *Journal of Advertising Research* 32 (September/October 1992), 54–62.

98. Robert E. Wilkes and Humberto Valencia, "Shopping-Related Characteristics of Mexican-Americans and Blacks," *Psychology and Marketing* 3 (Winter 1986), 247–259.

99. Joel Saegert, Robert J. Hoover, and Marye Tharp Hilger, "Characteristics of Mexican American Consumers," *Journal of Consumer Research* 12 (June 1985), 104–109.

100. Humberto Valencia, "Point of View: Avoid Hispanic Market Blunders," *Journal of Advertising Research* 23 (January 1984), 19–22.

101. Jim Sondheim, Rodd Rodriquez, Richard Dillon, and Richard Parades, "Hispanic Market: The Invisible Giant," *Advertising Age* (April 16, 1979), S–20. Also see Martha Frase-Blunt, "Who Watches Spanish Language TV?" *Hispanic* (November 1991), 26–27.

102. T. Bettina Cornewell and Alan David Bligh, "Complaint Behavior of Mexican-American Consumers to a Third-Party Agency," *Journal of Consumer Affairs* 25 (Summer 1991), I–18.

103. Clarkson Gordon, *Tomorrow's Customers in Canada* (Toronto: Woods Gordon, 1984).

104. Pierre C. Lefrancois and Giles Chatel, "The French-Canadian Consumer: Fact and Fancy," in J. S. Wright and J. L. Goldstrucker, eds., *New Ideas for Successful Marketing* (Chicago: American Marketing Association, 1966), 705–717; Bernard Blishen, "Social Class and Opportunity in Canada," *Canadian Review of Sociology and Anthropology* 7 (May 1970), 110–127.

105. Robert Tamilia, "Cross-Cultural Advertising Research: A Review and Suggested Framework," in Ronald C. Curhan, ed., *1974 Combined Proceedings of the AMA* (Chicago: American Marketing Association, 1974), 131–134.

106. Daniel W. Rossides, *Social Stratification* (Englewood Cliffs, NJ: Prentice-Hall, 1990).

107. Max Weber, in H. H. Gard and C. Wright Mills, eds., *From Max Weber: Essays in Sociology* (New York: Oxford University Press, 1946), 193.

108. Excerpts from Kenneth Labich, "Class in America," *Fortune* (February 7, 1994), 114–126.

109. Stephen L. Nock, "Social Origins as Determinants of Family Social Status" (paper presented to the Mid-South Sociological Association, 1980).

110. Reprinted with permission of Wadsworth, Inc. from Dennis Gilbert and Joseph A. Kahl, *The American Class Structure: A New Synthesis,* 3rd ed. (1982). Although not cited in each instance, this excellent book has influenced the content of this chapter in numerous other points.

111. Robert Cage, "Spending Differences across Occupational Fields," *Monthly Labor Review* 112 (December 1989), 33–43.

112. David H. Demo and Ritch C. Savin-Williams, "Early Adolescent Self-Esteem as a Function of Social Class," *American Journal of Sociology* 88 (1983), 763–773; Viktor Gecas and Monica A. Seff, "Social Class and Self-Esteem: Psychological Centrality, Compensation, and the Relative Effects of Work and Home," *Social Psychology Quarterly* 53 (1990), 165–173.

113. Hirschman, "Secular Immortality and the American Ideology of Affluence."

114. Michael Useem and S. M. Miller, "The Upper Class in Higher Education," *Social Policy* 7 (January/February 1977), 28–31.

115. The Gilbert–Kahl estimates are also accepted in Daniel W. Rossides, *Social Stratification* (Englewood Cliffs, NJ: Prentice-Hall, 1990), 406–408. Class publications that in the 1990s are still valuable reading for consumer analysts include Pierre Martineau, "Social Classes and Spending Behavior," *Journal of Marketing* 23 (October 1958), 121–130; Sidney Levy, "Social Class and

Consumer Behavior," in Joseph W. Newman, ed., *On Knowing the Consumer* (New York: John Wiley & Sons, 1966), 146–160; Richard R. Coleman and Bernice L. Neugarten, *Social Status in the City* (San Francisco: Jossey-Bass, 1971).

116. Natalya Prusakova, "Dress to Impress," *Business in the USSR* (December 1991), 90–93.

117. Andrea Tyree and Robert W. Hodge, "Five Empirical Landmarks," *Social Forces* 56 (March 1978), 761–769. Some of the methodological issues in these studies are discussed in C. Matthew Snipp, "Occupational Mobility and Social Class: Insights from Men's Career Mobility," *American Sociological Review* 50 (August 1985), 475–492.

118. John R. Snarey and George E. Vaillant, "How Lower- and Working-Class Youth Become Middle-Class Adults: The Association between Ego Defense Mechanisms and Upward Social Mobility," *Child Development* 56 (1985), 904–908.

119. Ivan D. Chase, "A Comparison of Men's and Women's Intergenerational Mobility in the United States," *American Sociological Review* 40 (August 1975), 483–505.

120. Elizabeth C. Hirschman, "Secular Immortality and the American Ideology of Affluence," *Journal of Consumer Research* 17 (June 1990), 31–42.

121. Kenneth Labich, "Class in America," *Fortune* (February 7, 1994), 114–126.

122. Jaclyn Fierman, "The High-Living Middle Class," *Fortune* (April 13, 1987), 27.

CHAPTER 12

Family and Household Influences

OPENING VIGNETTE

Had you asked Chris Demos ten years ago if she would be taking her dog to visit Santa Claus at Christmas time, the 35-year-old sales manager might have laughed in your face. But today, Demos, who's single but living with long-time beau Dimitri, stands outside PETsMART with Abbey, a three-year-old shar-pei, ready to take long-awaited holiday family photos. But the experience is just beginning. Abbey will go on to receive Christmas gifts from "mom and dad" and other family friends to rival those received by even the best children on Santa's list. The light of Demos's life, Abbey has brought fulfillment to her "parents'" lives.

Since they have no children, Chris and Dimitri parent their dog together (teaching her tricks and disciplining her when necessary) and take her places they might take children. For many young singles and couples today, a pet acts as a surrogate child for its owners. A generation ago, dogs slept outside the house in doghouses or on tattered blankets on the porch, but today, dogs that don't sleep with their owners sometimes sleep in specially constructed dog "palaces," furnished with satin pillows and linens to match those of their owners. Pet owners spend about $15 billion annually on products and services for their pets—from gourmet food to veterinary visits and animal psychologists (to counsel disturbed pets).

What has fueled the growth of retailers, such as PETsMART? Examining how families and households are changing lends insight into the reasons for the astounding growth experienced by the industry in recent years. PETsMART management took notice of the following household trends: delaying first marriages and living single longer, having fewer children and for some segments not having children at all, and the increasing number of older adults living alone. Hectic lifestyles also make it more difficult to socialize outside work and develop close relationships with other adults; pets fill that role well. By offering the right product mix and experience for consumers and their pets inside their stores, PETsMART is reaping the rewards of the increasing number of DINKs (dual income, no kids) who are becoming DIPs (dual income, pets). The company's tagline, "Where Pets Are Family," demonstrates its understanding of the needs and characteristics of its market.

According to the American Pet Products Manufacturers Association, Americans now own over 236 million dogs, cats, reptiles, birds, fish, and small animals, with 56 percent of all households owning a pet. However, it's interesting to note that 61 percent of all pet-owning households have no children at home. Demos concedes that the financial and time commitments of having Abbey are great, but the rewards are even greater.

The Importance of Families and Households on Consumer Behavior

If you are in charge of marketing breakfast cereal in the United States, India, Japan, or Brazil, to whom should you gear your marketing program and advertising campaign? After determining whether the cereal, muesli (in Europe), or mealies (in Africa) would be eaten hot or cold, you would ask who determines which brand of cereal will be purchased? Is it mothers, fathers, teens, children, or some combination of these? Kix cereal in the United States appeals to both children (tastes good) and mothers (is nutritious) with its tagline "Kid tested, mother approved." The importance of the family or household unit in consumer behavior arises for two reasons:

1. Many products are purchased by a family unit.
2. Individuals' buying decisions may be heavily influenced by other family members.

How families or households make purchase decisions depends on the roles of the various family members in the *purchase, consumption,* and *influence* of products. Household products like food and shampoo may be purchased by one person but consumed by many, whereas personal care items, such as cosmetics or shaving cream, might be purchased by an individual family member for his or her own consumption. Homes and cars, on the other hand, are often purchased by both spouses, perhaps with involvement from children or other members of the extended family. As Davis[1] explains, "A husband may buy a station wagon, given the reality of having to transport four children, despite his strong preference for sports cars," and a father may choose to ask his daughter and son about color and style before he and his wife purchase a car. Visits to shopping malls often involve multiple family members buying clothing and accessories, sometimes with a heavy dose of influence by family members—children may buy clothing paid for and approved of by parents, whereas teenagers may influence the clothing purchases of a parent.

Regardless of how many family members are present when items are being purchased, the other family members play an important role in the purchase. Just because Ling, wife and mother of two young children, is responsible for buying food for the family and acts as an individual in the market does not mean that her decisions are not influenced by the preferences and power of other family members. Even when people live single, they may prefer the same (or perhaps the opposite) style of furniture or brand of peanut butter as the family in which they were raised. Although marketing communications are usually directed to individuals, marketers should consider the consumption circumstances and the family structure before deciding on specific communication or advertising methods to attract their segment.[2]

What Is a Family?

A **family** is a group of two or more persons related by blood, marriage, or adoption who reside together. The **nuclear family** is the *immediate group of father, mother, and child(ren) living together.* The **extended family** is the *nuclear family, plus other relatives, such as grandparents, uncles and aunts, cousins, and parents-in-law.* The *family into which one is born* is called the **family of orientation,** whereas the *one established by marriage* is the **family of procreation.** As mentioned in the opening scenario, some consumers are stretching the definition of family to include family pets, as recognized in the tagline of the PETsMART logo and brand, shown in Figure 12.1.

What Is a Household?

The term **household** is used to describe *all persons, both related and unrelated, who occupy a housing unit.* There are significant differences between the terms *household* and *family* even though they are sometimes used interchangeably. It is important to distinguish between these terms when examining data.

The term household is becoming a more important unit of analysis for marketers because of the rapid growth in nontraditional families and nonfamily households. Among nonfamily households, the great majority consist of people living alone. The remaining nonfamily households include those consisting of elderly people living with nonfamily members, "Persons of Opposite Sex Sharing Living Quarters" (POSSLQs), friends living together, and same sex couples. Any of these households may or may not include children. Families are the largest category of households, but nonfamily households are growing faster. One way to avoid the problem of whether to study families or households is to simply use the term *consumer unit* (CU) or *minimal household unit* (MHU). It is easier and sometimes just as useful to avoid the distinctions between each group and refer to CU or MHU buying behavior.[3]

Figure 12.1 PETsMART Appeals to the Family

Structural Variables Affecting Families and Households

Family or household variables affect consumer purchasing. **Structural variables** include the *age of the head of household or family, marital status, presence of children, and employment status.* For example, consumer analysts have enormous interest in whether families have children and how many they have. Children increase family demand for clothing, food, furniture, homes, medical care, and education, while they decrease demand for many discretionary items, including travel, higher-priced restaurants, and adult clothing.

Other structural changes affect the types of products that are manufactured. For example, in Japan, high-tech companies have formed a consortium to standardize technology that has been developed to monitor and manage households. Consumer in Focus 12.1 focuses on how households in Japan may be run in the future.

Sociological Variables Affecting Families and Households

Marketers can understand family and household decisions better by examining the sociological dimensions of how families make consumer decisions. Three **sociological variables** that help explain how families function include *cohesion, adaptability, and communication.*

Consumer in Focus 12.1

Japanese "Smart" Homes

Have you ever woken up in the morning to wonder, "What's my blood sugar level today?" or gone to the store only to wonder whether you need milk or not. In Japan, home-owners will soon be able to run their homes, monitor their families, and measure the needs of the household with the touch of a button.

By the year 2003, the Matsushita Electrical Industry Group hopes to market HII—Home Information Infrastructure—to families and households throughout Japan. HII is a system that connects homes through fiber-optic cables to the vast world outside, including the Internet, cable TV, hospitals, and travel agents. The system revolves around an HII station—the central nervous system that serves as a depository for reams of information. Through screens in every room, occupants can monitor appliances throughout the house, check security cameras, and contact cyberspace. The bedroom, for example, contains a medical consultation kit through which consumers can type in their ailments and

call the doctor, who then makes a diagnosis based on the information submitted and electronic access to medical history from the household system.

At the heart of the system is a wireless terminal that permits remote access to the house. Consumers, therefore, can monitor household needs, such as what is in the refrigerator or in the pantry. These homes also feature smart toilets, which weigh individuals, monitor body fat, and measure sugar in the urine. And special high-tech perks inside the house cause lights to turn on when someone enters a room and allow family members to monitor each other's movements, activities, blood pressure, weight, and schedules inside the home.

For U.S. consumers, the nearest equivalent may be a home management system designed by IBM that allows people to operate all electronic devices using a universal remote control.

Source: *"Japanese 'Smart' Homes Know All, Tell All,"* The Columbus Dispatch *(April 28, 1999), 2F.*

- **Cohesion** is the *emotional bonding between family members.* It measures how close to each other family members feel on an emotional level. Cohesion reflects a sense of connectedness to or separateness from other family members.

- **Adaptability** measures the *ability of a family to change its power structure, role relationships, and relationship rules in response to situational and developmental stress.* The degree of adaptability shows how well a family can meet the challenges presented by changing situations.

- **Communication** is a *facilitating dimension, critical to movement on the other two dimensions.* Positive communication skills (such as empathy, reflective listening, supportive comments) enable family members to share their changing needs as they relate to cohesion and adaptability. Negative communication skills (such as double messages, double binds, criticism) minimize the ability to share feelings, thereby restricting movement in the dimensions of cohesion and adaptability. Understanding whether family members are satisfied with family purchases requires communication within the family.[4]

Family Celebrations and Gift Giving

Marketers have used sociological research on "resilient" families—those that are better able to negotiate their way through transitions and tragedies—because they affect consumer demand for many products. Families that place more importance on family celebrations, family time and routines, and family traditions are more likely to develop resilient families.[5] Though family celebrations help families survive crises, they also fuel retail sales. Hanukkah and Christmas generate about 50 percent or more of annual retail sales (and an even higher percentage of profits) for many retailers, making gift giving and family holidays an important area of study.[6] In recent years, Halloween has become the second most popular holiday in the United States in terms of retail sales of gifts and home decorations—two consumer behavior activities that convey a family's holiday spirit.[7] Other holidays that are being celebrated more frequently outside their countries of origin include Cinco de Mayo (Mexico), Kwanzaa (Africa), and Chinese New Year.

Some consumer analysts have been warning retailers about the dangers of relying too heavily on year-end holiday sales to meet their sales and profit forecasts. Traditionally, some retailers rely on Christmas, Kwanzaa, and Hanukkah to provide as much as half of their yearly sales.[8] But changes in family and household structures can be blamed in part for the decline in overall holiday spending. An increase in the number of divorced parents forces children to split holidays between two households, taking some of the joy out of the celebrations and making the physical movement of large gifts more difficult. With households in many industrialized countries having fewer children, fewer gifts need to be purchased. And families tend to buy the items they need when they want them rather than wait to receive them as gifts. This also makes it difficult for family members to buy gifts for one another because many consumers (especially 45- to 60-year-olds) already have what they want.[9]

There has been a shift among some consumers away from the commercialization of the holidays and toward the religious and familial meaning of traditions and celebrations. Advertisements attempt to relate a family's holiday celebrations to consumption as do in-store and shopping mall decorations. Figure 12.2 shows how Duracell relates to the holidays in an ad, whereas *egift* relates to consumers' needs to buy gifts throughout the year in Figure 12.3.

Figure 12.2   Appealing to Families' Holiday Celebrations

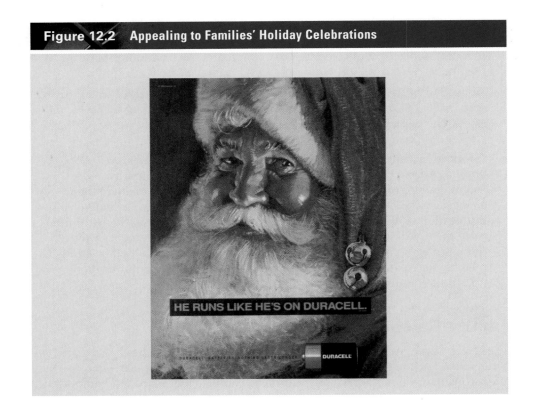

Figure 12.3   Appealing to Gift Giving Needs

Who Determines What the Family Buys?

Families use products even though individuals usually buy them. Determining what products should be bought, which retail outlet to use, how and when products are used, and who should buy them is a complicated process involving a variety of roles and actors.

Role Behavior

Families and other groups exhibit what sociologist Talcott Parsons called instrumental and expressive role behaviors. **Instrumental roles,** also known as functional or economic roles, involve *financial, performance, and other functions performed by group members.* **Expressive roles** involve *supporting other family members in the decision-making process and expressing the family's aesthetic or emotional needs, including upholding family norms.* How individual family members perform each of these roles may influence how they allocate family income to different types of products or retailers.

Individual Roles in Family Purchases Family consumption decisions involve at least five definable roles, which may be assumed by spouses, children, or other members of a household. Both multiple roles and multiple actors are normal.

1. *Initiator/gatekeeper:* Initiator of family thinking about buying products and gathering information to aid the decision.
2. *Influencer:* Individual whose opinions are sought concerning criteria the family should use in purchases and which products or brands most likely fit those evaluative criteria.
3. *Decider:* The person with the financial authority or power to choose how the family's money will be spent and on which products or brands.
4. *Buyer:* The person who acts as the purchasing agent by visiting the store, calling suppliers, writing checks, bringing products into the home, and so on.
5. *User:* The person or persons who use the product.

Marketers need to communicate with consumers assuming each of these roles, remembering that different family members will assume different roles depending on the situation and product. Children, for example, are *users* of cereals, toys, clothing, and many other products but may not be the buyers. One or both of the parents may be the *decider* and the *buyer,* although the children may be important as *influencers* and users. Parents may act as *gatekeepers* by preventing children from watching some TV programs or attempting to negate their influence. And those with the most expertise in an area may take on influencer roles.

Family marketing focuses on the *relationships between family members based on the roles they assume, including the relationship between purchaser and family consumer and between purchaser and purchase decision maker.* Family marketing identifies scenarios where some purchases might have more than one decision maker, whereas some have more than one consumer. Sometimes the purchaser and consumer are the same person; sometimes they are different people. The family marketing model, as seen in Figure 12.4, represents nine cells describing various purchaser-consumer relationships. Depending on where in the matrix various products fall, marketers can advertise and position products differently according to their purchaser-consumer relationships.

Figure 12.4   The Family Marketing Model

Family purchases fall into 9 categories, depending on who makes the purchase decision and who uses the item purchased.

A Consumer	A Purchase Decision Maker		
	One Member	**Some Members**	**All Members**
One Member	1	2 Tennis Racket	3
Some Members	4 Sugar Pops	5	6
All Members	7	8	9 Refrigerator

For Example:
1. Mom and Dad go to buy a new tennis racket for Mom. Dad advises Mom on her purchase. Some members are decision-makers and one member is a consumer: cell 2.
2. Mom goes to the grocery store to buy Sugar Pops cereal for her children. She'll never eat the stuff. One member is a decision-maker and some members are consumers: cell 4.
3. Mom, Dad, and the kids go to the department store to buy a refrigerator. All members are decision-makers and all are consumers: cell 9.

Source: Robert Boutilier, "Pulling the Family's Strings," American Demographics *(August 1993), 46.*

The family purchase decision-making process can be complex, but answering the following questions helps identify different purchaser-consumer relationships:

1. Who's buying for whom?
2. Who are the principal characters?
3. What's the plot for the purchase?
4. Who wants what when?
5. What can we assume?[10]

Although these answers may not identify all essential relationships marketers should consider, they do identify a family marketing plan, which creates a relationship between individuals and products based on the role each individual has in the influence or purchase of products.

In the restaurant industry, the trend has been to focus on marketing to the family as a single unit.[11] Although several decades ago, "going out for dinner" described a special night out for dating or married couples, today it describes a typical evening's solution for making and eating dinner for many American families. Though Boston Market led the pack of restaurants catering to home-style meals, other restaurant companies are creating fully integrated family marketing programs that include special advertising, menus, packaging, couponing, videos, and movie tie-ins. For example, KFC adopted a new mantra a few years ago— "take back the family." It focused on addressing *family needs* (such as convenience, quickness of service, affordability, and variety) from the mother's, father's, and children's perspectives. In addition to adding roasted chicken, chicken strips, and pot pies to its menu (much to the delight of its adult customers), KFC also developed a promotional program featuring Timon and Pumbaa characters from the Disney movie *The Lion King* (much to the delight of children).

Admittedly, the appeal to families arose from the restaurant industry's desire to grow sales and profits. At Burger King, the family market represents about one-third of its business. Children that come in and buy $1.99 Kids Club meals bring the entire family and boost the average check to approximately $9.00.

Restaurants are monitoring closely the changes occurring in the modern family. Kroger (a national grocery chain), Eatzies (a U.S. restaurant chain that focuses on take-home meals), and Wild Oats (a chain of mainstream healthy food stores) have made great strides in the home meal replacement (HMR) arena. HMR provides a solution to time-rushed families that don't have time to prepare meals and singles who don't want to cook for one person. They prepare a variety of main courses and numerous side dishes from which to choose, and they make it easy for either the male or female householder or teenager to "assemble" a well-balanced meal for the family.

Spousal Roles in Buying Decisions Which spouse is more important in family buying decisions? How does this vary by product category, stage of decision-making process, and individual household? Generally, the following role structure categories are used to analyze these questions:

1. *Autonomic:* an equal number of decisions is made by each spouse, but each decision is individually made by one spouse or the other
2. *Husband dominant:* the husband or male head-of-household makes a majority of the decisions
3. *Wife dominant:* the wife or female head-of-household makes a majority of the decisions
4. *Joint* (syncratic): most decisions are made by both husband and wife

These categories are sometimes simplified to "husband more than wife," "wife more than husband," "both husband and wife," or simply "husband only," "wife only," or "children only." The type of product, stage in the decision process, and nature of the situation surrounding the decision influences which situation exists. And, keep in mind, that the terminology *husband* and *wife* apply to roles performed by members of the household and are used even though the family members might not be married or may be same-sex couples.

Harry Davis and Benny Rigaux conducted a landmark study investigating husband-wife influences.[12] Their findings are usually presented in the familiar triangular configuration shown in Figure 12.5 and have greatly influenced thinking about the relative influence of husbands and wives on decision making and the extent of role specialization. Are there some roles in family decision making that one spouse typically performs? The study seems to indicate yes, but you can apply some of the information examined throughout this text to identify how the roles of household members are changing.

Influences on the Decision Process

How do husbands and wives perceive their relative influence on decision making across the decision stages? And what does this mean for marketers? Figure 12.5 shows how some product-service categories are traditionally wife dominant. They include women's clothing, children's clothing, and groceries. Two categories that are husband dominant include lawn mowers and hardware. Joint decisions tend to be made about vacations, televisions, refrigerators, and upholstered living room furniture. Autonomic decision making tends to be present in decisions about categories that include women's jewelry, men's leisure clothing, men's business

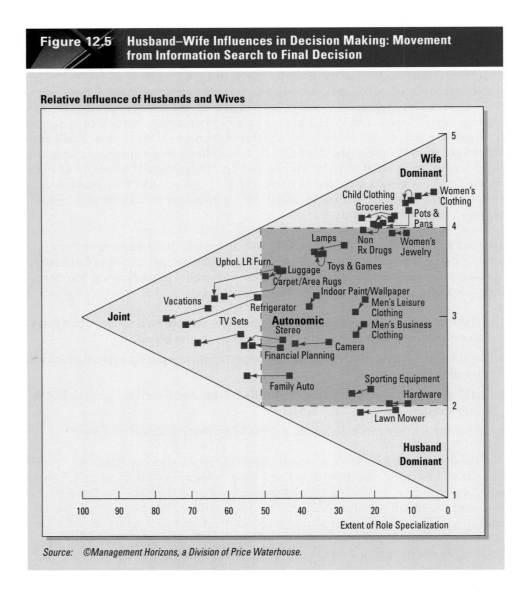

Figure 12.5 Husband–Wife Influences in Decision Making: Movement from Information Search to Final Decision

Relative Influence of Husbands and Wives

Source: ©Management Horizons, a Division of Price Waterhouse.

clothing, sporting equipment, lamps, toys and games, indoor paint and wallpaper, and luggage. By understanding where on this "map" the decisions to buy particular products fall, marketers can begin to determine which aspects of specific products to advertise to different household members and which media will reach the influential family member.

Influence by Decision Stage   Spouses exert different degrees of influence when passing through the different stages of the decision-making process. This is indicated in Figure 12.5 by the direction of the arrow, which shows movement from information search to final decision. This movement may be minimal in the case of many low-involvement goods but more pronounced for goods that are risky or have high involvement for the family. *The decision process tends to move toward joint participation and away from autonomic behavior as a final decision nears.* Movement is most pronounced for refrigerators, family autos, upholstered living room furniture, and carpets or rugs. Vacations are perhaps the most democratic of a family's purchase decisions.

The information search stage is more autonomic than joint when compared with final decisions. Marketing plans thus require specialized use of media, such as magazines or other media having a strong appeal to husbands or wives rather than both. Product or store design must reflect the evaluative criteria of both since consensus on these must be achieved in the final decision. Separate campaigns may be timed to coincide with specialized interests, especially for products with a long planning cycle.

Influence of Employment   In the past, marketers were able to refer to the traditional role structure categories to determine which family member was most likely to purchase a specific product. The high number of women working outside the home in recent years coupled with changing spousal roles has affected how couples divide their buying responsibilities.[13] Although traditional buying roles still apply, husbands in dual-income marriages may be willing to stop at the grocery store to pick up a few items, and working wives may drop the family car at the service station for an oil change. However, contemporary couples—many from the baby boomer segment—are not inclined to shift traditional joint buying responsibilities to only one spouse, but they are willing to shop jointly for major items that might have been the responsibility of one spouse in traditional families.

Influence of Gender   As the gender gap narrows, husband and wife decisions are increasingly made jointly (syncratically). Qualls[14] studied family decisions concerning vacations, automobiles, children's education, housing, insurance, and savings. Prior studies showed that decisions regarding these products were usually reported as wife or husband dominant. Qualls found overwhelmingly that joint decisions are now the norm for these products, with 80 percent of children's education and housing decisions made jointly. Increasing resources of women and shifts toward egalitarianism are producing more joint decision making in product and service categories of perceived high risk. In contrast, however, time pressures, brought about by larger numbers of dual-worker families, may produce more autonomic decisions in categories of perceived low risk.

Because of declining gender differences and the waning of gender identification of products, many marketers are researching how to transition gender-dependent products to a dual-gender positioning.[15] Easy-to-prepare foods, once targeted to women, are now marketed toward men and women, each of whom are tired when they get home from work and are looking for a way to decrease their time preparing the family meal. Yet consumer researchers must recognize that gender differences, despite movement away from sex role dominance, still exist for some products and in some situations,[16] such as personal care products. Literature reviews of these areas are available in Jenkins[17]; Bums and Granbois[18]; Gupta, Hagerty, and Myers[19]; and Roberts.[20] Although gender-related consumer behavior still exists, the roles are not determined by biological sex so much as the socialization experiences that teach men and women different consumer activities.[21]

Family Life Cycles

Families pass through a *series of stages that change them over time.* This process historically has been called the **family life cycle** (FLC). The concept may need to be changed to **household life cycle** (HLC) or **consumer life cycle** (CLC) in the future to reflect changes in society. However, we will use the term **FLC**[22] to show how the life cycle affects consumer behavior.[23]

Family Life Cycle Characteristics

The traditional FLC describes family patterns as consumers marry, have children, leave home, lose a spouse, and retire. These stages are described in Figure 12.6, along with consumer behaviors associated with each stage. But consumers don't necessarily have to pass through all these stages—they can skip multiple stages

Figure 12.6   Consumer Activities Occurring in Various Life Cycles

Young Singles

Young singles may live alone, with their nuclear families, or with friends, or they may co-habitate with partners—translating into a wide range of how much disposable income is spent on furniture, rent, food, and other living expenses in this stage. Although earnings tend to be relatively low, these consumers usually don't have many financial obligations and don't feel the need to save for their futures or retirement. Many of them find themselves spending as much as they make on cars, furnishings for first residences away from home, fashions, recreation, alcoholic beverages, food away from home, vacations, and other products and services involved in the dating game. Some of these singles may have young children, forcing them to give up some discretionary spending for necessities such as day care and baby products.

Newly Married Couples

Newly married couples without children are usually better off financially than they were when they were single, since they often have two incomes available to spend on one household. These families tend to spend a substantial amount of their incomes on cars, clothing, vacations, and other leisure activities. They also have the highest purchase rate and highest average purchases of durable goods (particularly furniture and appliances) and appear to be more susceptible to advertising.

Full Nest I

With the arrival of the first child, parents begin to change their roles in the family, and decide if one parent will stay home to care for the child or if they will both work and buy daycare services. Either route usually leads to a decline in family disposable income and a change in how the family spends its income. In this stage, families are likely to move into their first homes; purchase furniture and furnishings for the child; buy a washer and dryer and home maintenance items; and purchase new items such as baby food, cough medicine, vitamins, toys, sleds, and skates. These requirements reduce families' ability to save, and the husband and wife are often dissatisfied with their financial position.

Full Nest II

In this stage, the youngest child has reached school age, the employed spouse's income has improved, and the other spouse often returns to part- or full-time work outside the home. Consequently, the family's financial position usually improves, but the family finds itself consuming more and in larger quantities. Consumption patterns continue to be heavily influenced by the children, since the family tends to buy large-sized packages of food and cleaning supplies, bicycles, music lessons, clothing, sports equipment, and a computer. Discount department stores (such as Kohl's and Target), mass merchandisers (such as Wal∗Mart and Carrefour), and warehouse club stores (such as Costco and Sam's Club) are popular with consumers in this stage.

Full Nest III

As the family grows older and parents enter their mid-40s, their financial position usually continues to improve because the primary wage earner's income rises, the second wage earner is receiving a higher salary, and the children earn spending and education money from occasional and part-time employment. The family typically replaces some worn pieces of furniture, purchases another automobile, buys some luxury appliances, and spends money on dental services (braces) and education. Families also spend more on computers in this stage, buying additional PCs for their older children. Depending on where children go to college and how many are seeking higher education, the financial position of the family may be tighter than other instances.

Married, No Kids

Couples who marry and do not have children are likely to have more disposable income to spend on charities, travel, and entertainment than either couples with children or singles in their age range. Not only do they have fewer expenses, these couples are more likely to be dual-wage earners, making it easier for them to retire earlier if they save appropriately.

Figure 12.6 (cont.)

Older Singles

Singles, age 40 or older, may be *Single Again* (ending married status because of divorce or death of a spouse) or *Never Married* (because they prefer to live independently or because they co-habitate with partners), either group of which may or may not have children living in the household. *Single Again* families often find themselves struggling financially due to the high cost of divorce and the expense of having to raise a family on one income. They often have to set up a new household (usually not as big as their previous home); buy furnishings accordingly; pay alimony and/or child support; and sometimes increase travel expenditures if the children live in another city, state, or country. They also pay for clothing and leisure activities conducive to meeting a future mate. On the other hand, many *Never Married Single* households are well-off financially since they never had to pay child-related costs and often live in smaller homes than large families require. This group now has more available income to spend on travel and leisure but feels the pressure to save for the future, since there is no second income on which to rely as they get older.

Empty Nest I

At this stage, the family is most satisfied with its financial position. The children have left home and are financially independent allowing the family to save more. In this stage, discretionary income is spent on what the couple wants rather than on what the children need. Therefore, they spend on home improvements, luxury items, vacations, sports utility vehicles, food away from home, travel, second homes (or smaller but nicer homes than were needed to house large families), and products for their grandchildren. This group is also more educated than generations in the past and are looking for fun educational opportunities, including eco-tourism and computer-related skills.

Empty Nest II

By this time, the income earners have retired, usually resulting in a reduction in income and disposable income. Expenditures become health oriented, centering on such items as medical appliances and health, sleep and digestion medicines. They may also move to climates more suitable to their medical requirements. But many of these families continue to be active and in good health, allowing them to spend time traveling, exercising, and volunteering. Many continue working part time to supplement their retirement and keep them socially involved.

Solitary Survivor

Solitary survivors may be either employed or not employed. If the surviving spouse has worked outside the home in the past, he or she usually continues employment or goes back to work to live on earned income (rather than savings) and remain socially active. Expenditures for clothing and food usually decline in this stage, with income spent on health care, sickness care, travel, entertainment, and services, such as lawn care and house cleaning. Those who are not employed are often on fixed incomes and may move in with friends to share housing expenses and companionship, and some may choose to re-marry.

Retired Solitary Survivor

Retired solitary survivors follow the same general consumption patterns as solitary survivors; however, their income may not be as high. Depending on how much they have been able to save throughout their lifetimes, they can afford to buy a wide range of products. But for many, spending declines drastically due to lack of need for many new products and higher medical expenses. These individuals have special needs for attention, affection, and security.

based on their lifestyle choices. When reviewing this information, think about how contemporary developments such as divorce, smaller family size, and delayed age of marriage affect the consumption activities of these stages.[24]

The family lifecycle can be depicted graphically by using a curve similar to that of the product lifecycle. Figure 12.7 shows how income, on average, changes during life and how saving behavior affects income in latter stages. As household leaders enter their 30s and 40s, often their income levels increase (because they begin to reach higher earning positions and two adults are working), but so do their spending levels (especially if they have children). This decreases their disposable income during these life stages, making it more difficult for them to save money or splurge on luxury items. It is projected that between 1997 and 2002 the

Figure 12.7 Income Available to Spend by Life Cycle Stage

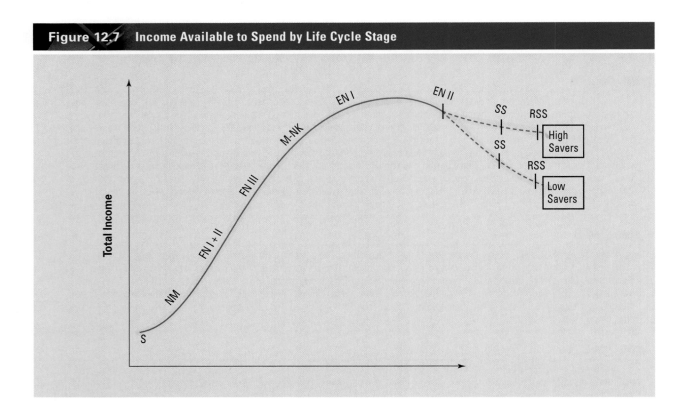

number of U.S. households headed by people between the ages of 25 and 44 will decline by 1.7 million, to 43 million, while householders between the ages of 45 and 64 will increase 5.5 million, to 37 million.[25] Changes in life stage and family life cycle will affect the demand for products from home furnishings to travel.

Marketers use the descriptions of these FLC stages when analyzing marketing and communication strategies for products and services, but they often add additional information about consumer markets to analyze their needs, identify niches, and develop consumer-specific marketing strategies. Marketers can add socioeconomic data (such as income, employment status, financial well-being, and activities) to family life stages to improve predictions about product choices and help explain further consumer activities.[26] Figure 12.8 shows how marketers might accomplish this task with a matrix of specific demographic or lifestyle factors, such as delaying having children or not having them at all.[27]

The data resulting from this type of analysis permit a quantitative analysis of market sizes. Additional data can be collected concerning preferences, expenditures, and shopping behaviors of each segment to identify and help attract core customers in the life stage most profitable to the firm. Keep in mind that life stage can be different for different consumers. For example, according to federal statistics, the number of older, second-generation fathers (men who remarry and have second families later in life) is growing.[28] Though these men may be in their 50s, their life stage is similar in many ways to that of a 30-year-old father—sometimes leaving them paying for one child's wedding while paying for another child's daycare. The FLC helps explain how families change over time; what's more, modified with market data, including individuals' life stages, it is useful in identifying core market targets.

Figure 12.8 Family Market Segmentation Analysis Matrix

FLC Stage	Age	Employment Status	Financial Well-Being	Activities Interests	Where Live	Income	How Active	Other Family in Household?
Young Singles Newly Married Couples Full Nest I Full Nest II Full Nest III Married, No Kids Older Singles Empty Nest I Empty Nest II Solitary Survivor Retired Solitary Survivor								

Family and Household Spending

Family life cycle stage is the most important predictor of family or household spending. The latter years of the 1990s brought with them economic growth and prosperity to many industrialized nations, including North America. At first glance, one might think that consumer spending must have sky-rocketed during this time—especially since the number of households grew and baby boomers had entered their peak spending years. But when examined from a household standpoint, the analysis revealed that the average American household spent cautiously during this time even though unemployment levels were down and wage rates were up. In fact, it wasn't until the last few years of the decade that spending by individual households was restored to the levels of 1987. The average household spent 13 percent less on food away from home, 25 percent less on major appliances, and 15 percent less on clothing in 1997 than in 1987.[29] Figure 12.9 shows how household spending changed for 12 major categories during the last decade of the 20th century. When examining these numbers, analyze why you think spending changed by thinking about demographic, lifestyle, and family issues.

Changing Family and Household Structure

The basic structure of families and households is changing in the United States, Canada, Europe, and other countries. Marketers and consumer analysts must understand how to evaluate how these changes can affect marketing strategy by asking questions like: What is the structure of contemporary families? How is that structure changing? How does structure affect the various stages of the consumer decision process? Are the developing realities of family structure a problem or an opportunity for our organization? For answers, marketers must analyze marriage patterns and living patterns, information on which can be found in census data from government agencies such as the Bureau of the Census or Statistics Canada and with primary research.

374   CHAPTER 12 *Family and Household Influences*

Figure 12.9   Family Spending Trends

Average annual spending of households by product and service category, 1987 to 1997; percent change, 1987–97; in dollars

Category	1997	1987	1987–97
Average annual spending	$34,819	$34,493	0.9%
FOOD	4,801	5,177	−7.3
Food at home	2,880	2,966	−2.9
Food away from home	1,921	2,211	−13.1
ALCOHOLIC BEVERAGES	309	408	−24.3
HOUSING	11,272	10,694	5.4
Shelter	6,344	5,869	8.1
Utilities, fuels, public services	2,412	2,361	2.2
Household services	548	524	4.5
Housekeeping supplies	455	482	−5.6
Household furnishings and equipment	1,512	1,458	3.7
APPAREL AND SERVICES	1,729	2,043	−15.4
Men, 16 and over	323	417	−22.5
Boys, 2 to 15	84	93	−9.9
Women, 16 and over	574	721	−20.3
Girls, 2 to 15	106	114	−7.4
Children under 2	77	82	−6.0
Footwear	315	260	21.2
TRANSPORTATION	6,457	6,499	−0.6
Cars and trucks, new	1,229	1,615	−23.9
Cars and trucks, used	1,464	1,215	20.5
Vehicle rental, leases, licenses, other	501	226	121.6
Public transportation	393	386	1.9
HEALTH CARE	1,841	1,604	14.8
Health insurance	881	554	59.1
Medical services	531	660	−19.5
Drugs	320	287	11.6
Medical supplies	108	103	4.7
ENTERTAINMENT	1,813	1,686	7.6
Fees and admissions	471	456	3.2
Television, radios, sound equipment	577	535	7.8
Pets, toys, playground equipment	327	308	6.2
Other entertainment products and services	439	386	13.8
PERSONAL CARE PRODUCTS & SERVICES	528	466	13.2
READING	164	201	−18.3
EDUCATION	571	476	19.9
TOBACCO PRODUCTS AND SUPPLIES	264	328	−19.5
MISCELLANEOUS	847	794	6.7
Cash contributions	1,001	1,047	−4.4
Personal insurance and pensions	3,223	3,073	4.9
Life and other personal insurance	379	415	−8.8
Pensions and Social security	2,844	2,658	7.0

Source: Cheryl Russell, "The New Consumer Paradigm," American Demographics *(April 1999), 52.*

To Marry or Not to Marry? That Is the Question

Marriage is in the cards for most people around the globe although many men and women are delaying the age of first marriage, opting to live single longer. In fact, the projected number of single 18- to 34-year-olds in 2005 in the United States is expected to be 35.4 million, and is expected to increase to 38.4 million by the year 2010.[30] In the United States, the average age at which men get married for the first time is nearing 27, whereas women get married just before they turn 25. The proportion of women in their early 30s who had never been married has also increased along with the number of co-habitating couples. However, by their early 40s, 72 percent of all men and 73 percent of all women have married.[31]

When consumers marry later, they usually have to buy fewer basic furnishings and products needed for housekeeping; in fact, they often have to consolidate two households, which means divesting of duplicate items. But what they *do* buy tends to be better quality. Delayed marriages also produce more extensive travel capabilities; a higher probability of owning two cars; and firmer preferences for styles, colors, and product designs.

Of those marriages that do occur, over half of them end in divorce. A recent study, however, indicates that the effects of divorce on children are not as great as in the past since divorce has become more socially acceptable.[32] Today's children of divorce are much more likely to marry than their counterparts of 20 years ago. Those that do divorce (or "single again" consumers) often carry with them preferences and shopping patterns learned in a family situation even though they are classified as single households. They may also have financial problems that restrict their ability to buy the things that married couples or never-married singles might buy.[33] But divorce does create markets, since one family becomes two, with two households that need furnishings, which is good news for mass retailers that sell household products at lower prices. Married couples of people that have been divorced are more likely, however, to divorce again, entering "single" status yet again. The resulting "blended families" make consumer analysis even more complex because of influences from stepchildren, siblings of the multiple families, and former spouses.

The Singles Boom

Individuals that delay marriage, get divorced, or lose a spouse are fueling the rise in the number of single households in industrialized countries. Nearly 73 million adult Americans are not in married relationships, according to Census Bureau reports, an increase of 35 million from just 20 years ago. This means that 69.3 percent of all adults are not married.

Individuals who choose not to marry often choose to co-habitate, either with opposite or same-sex partners. Legally composed of singles, but functioning more as families, co-habitating singles are the fastest growing segment of the singles market. The number of unmarried couples increased from 523,000 in 1970 to 1.6 million in 1980 to 4 million in 1997. Over one-half of these couples are between the ages of 25 and 44, and about one-third have at least one child living in the household.

Mature Singles Markets   When analyzing all individuals living single, we find that 61 percent are women with a median age of 66 years. For the men, the median age is 45 years. The demographics of single men and women are dramatically different because they are single for different reasons. Women live alone more because their husbands have died, and nearly half of all women older than

75 years are widows. Men live alone because they have not yet married or they are divorced. In the next 20 years, the wild and crazy single guys of the 1990s will become the tired and pudgy older guys.[34]

The time, money, and energy of women, especially elderly women, are creating a new kind of singles market, ripe with opportunities for firms focusing on travel, financial services, social activities, entertainment, and religious organizations. Consumer analysts will find most of this part of the "booming singles market" buying home-security devices, treatment for chronic health problems, congregate care facilities, and perhaps a sedate Caribbean cruise.

Younger Singles Markets   Specialized media and products are often directed to the younger portions of the singles market with magazines such as *Living Single* and products such as Stouffer's Singles, microwaveable single-serving meals. Home builders are also adapting because singles account for 36 percent of first-time home buyers.[35] Design changes include fewer bedrooms; less dining room space; and more kitchen space, which has become the "living room" for many in this segment. Master bedrooms are more luxurious, bathrooms more spa-like, and living space better equipped for high-tech entertainment.[36]

Gay and Lesbian Markets   Gay and lesbian consumers represent a segment of the market receiving more and more attention by marketers and organizations. Most are classified as singles (although some jurisdictions may recognize the married status of some homosexual households), sometimes living in traditional family settings at some point in their lives. Reliable data concerning the size of the market are scarce though it is estimated that as little as 6 percent or as much as 16 percent of adult Americans may be part of this market.[37] To add even more confusion to the subject, in 1993 the Alan Guttmacher Institute released findings of a recent study that only 1 percent of men considered themselves exclusively homosexual.[38] This raises the questions—is the market size 5 million or 18.5 million, and is the gay market purchasing power $394 billion or $514 billion?[39] According to Simmons Market Research, gay households have a median income of $55,670 and about 70 percent of gays have at least a college education and work in either professional or managerial jobs.[40]

Gays and lesbians are likely to be urban, travel extensively, spend considerable money on clothing, and express more interest in the arts. Often they are more aware of current social issues and more politically active than their heterosexual counterparts. But targeting all gay men is like targeting all heterosexual men. Although there are characteristics to define the homosexual market, as with all other markets, differences between individuals do exist. The issue for some marketers is how to target effectively the gay market without alienating heterosexual customers. Some firms are starting to do this with web sites designed especially for these markets.[41]

For the first time in history, the 1990 Census provided information on the number of same-sex couples and included a question in which gay couples had the opportunity to designate each other as an "unmarried partner" as opposed to "housemate/roommate." Although this does not directly measure sexual orientation, the National Gay and Lesbian Task Force hopes to use the data to influence policy making in the areas of corporate health benefits, probate, adoption law, and AIDS treatment and prevention. Some private companies, such as Overlooked Opinions, Inc., conduct ongoing panels reporting data on homosexual consumers.[42]

Targeting gay and lesbian markets can be accomplished in a variety of ways. Understanding their needs is the preface to each. Commercial research firms such as Overlooked Opinions have created a panel of more than 12,000 gay men, lesbians, and bisexuals, representing every state and all major markets. Research from this panel indicates that the gay market is not only very affluent but is very image conscious.

The primary marketing technique in reaching the gay market is simply to recognize that the market exists and be willing to establish a relationship with this segment. This can be done by participation in or sponsorship of activities considered important by gay consumers, such as sponsorship of AIDS research or community events relating to AIDS or gay rights. Corporations can also create considerable awareness among the gay community by sponsorship of operas, ballets, classical concerts, and museums that attract high participation among the gay community, while also reaching the wider community.

Marketers may also advertise in gay-oriented media that exist at both the local and national levels. Many publications, such as *The Advocate, Out, Overlooked Opinions, Genre,* and *Deneuve,* have become strong national advertising mediums and have attracted advertisers such as Banana Republic, Benetton, Benson & Hedges, and Calvin Klein. It is believed that advertisers generate high loyalty among gay readers for advertising in those media without alienating homophobic consumers who do not read such media. Carillon Importers began advertising Absolut vodka in *The Advocate* in 1979. After many years of clever Absolut ads and years of targeting the gay market in addition to its traditional straight market, patrons of gay bars tend to ask for Absolut rather than just vodka. Volkswagen and Diesel clothing both advertise to homosexual markets, but in different ways. A Volkswagen TV ad featuring two young men driving together, who stop to pick up a discarded chair, only to discard it themselves later, is recognized by gay men as a gay-oriented ad and perceived as straight by other consumers. Volkswagen uses straight media but designs ads with a sensitivity that attracts the gay market.[43] Diesel, on the other hand, features gay couples in its ads. Figure 12.10 shows a Visa ad targeted toward lesbian consumers.

Anheuser-Busch has been a supporter of various gay-oriented events and heavy advertiser in gay magazines. In April 1999, it ran an ad in *EXP* magazine, a St. Louis, Missouri, gay magazine, to announce that it would be the key sponsor for St. Louis's gay festival in June. Big controversy ensued because the ad showed two men holding hands, and the caption read, "Be Yourself and Make It a Bud Light." The ad was to run nationally, but Anheuser-Busch agreed to feature it in the local magazine first to promote the festival, much to the delight of festival organizers and attendees. The *St. Louis Post-Dispatch* ran a story on the ad, and the Associated Press picked up on the story, making it available to newspapers around the country. Festival organizers began e-mailing the gay community urging them to call Anheuser-Busch in support of the ad, whereas Conservative Christian leader Reverend Jerry Falwell contacted his supporters to do the opposite. Soon, the company was inundated with calls, and established separate telephone lines to take calls from consumers expressing their opinions.[44]

Household Characteristics

Average household size has fallen in most industrialized countries. In the United States, it dropped to 2.65 persons in 1996, down from 2.76 in 1980 and 3.14 in 1970. One-person households account for about 25 percent of the total, compared with 18 percent in 1970, and households with six or more persons dropped from 19.5 percent of all households to less than 6 percent today. Recent census surveys disclose that only 26 percent of American households consist of a married couple living with their own child(ren) younger than 18 years, compared with 31 percent in 1980 and 40 percent in 1970. Table 12.1 estimates changes in number of households by type in 2000 and 2010, and shows how rapidly the nonfamily households are increasing.

Figure 12.10   Visa Targets the Gay Market

Table 12.1   Projections of U.S. Households by Type: 2000 to 2010

	Number of Households		Percent Growth of Household Types (2000–2010)
	2000	2010	
All households	103.2	114.8	11.2
Family households			
Total	71.7	77.9	8.7
Married couples	55.5	59.3	6.5
Female householder	12.3	13.9	13.0
Male householder	3.9	4.7	20.5
Nonfamily households			
Total	31.6	36.9	16.8
Total female	17.1	19.7	15.2
Female living alone	15.0	17.3	15.3
Total male	14.5	17.2	18.6
Male living alone	11.2	13.4	19.6

Source: U.S. Bureau of the Census, Projections of the Number of Households and Families in the United States: 1995 to 2010, *P25–1129.*

Table 12.2 Median Income by Household Type		
	Median Income (1997)	**Percent Change in Real Income (1989–1997)**
All households	37,005	− 0.8
Family households	45,347	1.6
Married couples	51,681	3.5
Female householder (no husband present)	23,040	3.3
Male householder (no wife present)	36,634	− 6.3
Nonfamily households	21,705	− 2.3
Female householders	17,631	− 1.4
Male householders	27,592	− 5.0

Source: U.S. Bureau of the Census, Money Income in the United States: 1997, P60–200.

Marketers are increasingly interested in single-parent households. About 11 million of these are headed by a female with no husband present, and about 3 million by a male householder with no wife present. Women without husbands maintain 13 percent of all white family households, 44 percent of all black family households, and 23 percent of all Hispanic family households. The rate of increase in single black parenthood slowed during the past decade to 3.8 percent per year, but the rate for Hispanics more than doubled to 7 percent per year, the highest rate of increase for any ethnic group. About 26 percent of white children, 64 percent of black children, and 37 percent of Hispanic children live in a single-parent household.[45]

Median household income levels (in 1997 dollars) have increased from $31,583 in 1967 to $37,303 in 1989, but declined steadily until 1993 and began to rise thereafter, reaching $37,005 by 1997. Table 12.2 shows how the median income levels of various household types have changed during the last decade. Notice the significant decrease in real income among families and nonfamilies with male householders and nonfamily householder married couples. Nonfamily households grew substantially from 1980 to 1990, yet the annual incomes of families headed by single women or men barely changed.

Changing Roles of Women

Marketing managers have always been interested in lifestyle changes occurring among women because female consumers buy so many products—for themselves and for families. Women's lifestyles have changed dramatically during the last century, especially since Gloria Steinem made "feminist" a household word and singer Helen Reddy sang the 1970's smash hit, "I Am Woman." Those times brought with them a fight for equality between the sexes in terms of job opportunity, respect, and pay. And women never looked back. In fact, interest in female consumers continues to intensify because of greater numbers of women in the population, improved purchasing and employment status, and changed roles of women.

The female population is growing faster than the male population because women tend to live longer than men do. Some experts say this is due to genetic makeup, and others say it is stress related, speculating that as women move up the corporate ladder and manage households, they may begin to mirror the life expectancy of men. And women sometimes mirror the lifestyles of their male counterparts, especially as they take on similar roles in the work force or in social activities. Smoking trends as they relate to Asian women are highlighted in Consumer in Focus 12.2. Regardless of why women live longer than men, females now outnumber males by 6.5 million in the United States.

Feminine roles are of great concern today to consumer analysts and marketers. A **role** specifies *what the typical occupant of a given position is expected to do in that position in a particular social context.*[46] Consumer analysts are especially concerned with gender roles of women in the family and in their position as purchasing agents for the family. *One of the greatest challenges women face today is balancing their roles as wife or partner, mother, wage-earner, and consumer.*

Female Employment

Women in North America, Europe, and other countries today have much higher rates of employment outside the home than in past eras. Women have left hearth and home to bring home some of the bacon. Today, more than 59 percent of women in the United States are employed, in contrast to less than 25 percent in 1950. This trend is occurring on a global scale as well, with the percentages of women who work reaching 52 percent in Canada, 49 percent in Japan, 47 percent in Great Britain, 46 percent in Australia, and 39 percent in Western Germany.[47]

Women can choose to work full time or part time outside the home or stay at home, caring for the family and home full time. The greatest effect of work status is in family income, and therefore, family buying. Families in which the

Consumer in Focus 12.2

To Smoke or Not To Smoke?

Tobacco companies and lung disease experts alike see Asian women as a fertile market for their products—cigarettes and antismoking campaigns, respectively. Compared to American and European women, roughly 25 percent of whom smoke, only 4 to 8 percent of women living in Asia smoke. The Global Congress on Lung Health points out that 60 to 70 percent of Chinese, Japanese, and South Korean men already smoke. And although women begin smoking for different reasons than men (women tend to begin smoking to express maturity, independence, and sociability and to relax and ease stress) experts predict that the non-saturated female market will be targeted by tobacco companies soon.

Tobacco companies can approach this market from two different angles—by appealing to gender equality emotions or by appealing to feminine traits. As Asian women lag behind their U.S. counterparts in terms of job opportunities and advancement, some marketers speculate that some women will want to emulate the habits of men to fit into the work culture better and be viewed as more similar to professional Asian men. The other approach focuses on the fact that fewer women quit smoking because they think it will keep them thin. "This is the sort of connection that the tobacco industry is trying to make to every girl in the world," said Patricia White of Britain's National Health Service. Cigarette ads that portray smoking as a way to enhance beauty, confidence, and seductiveness will appeal to the feminine side of women.

The International Union Against Tuberculosis and Lung Disease classifies smoking in every country as an epidemic that starts off slowly, builds up and peaks, then declines as anti-smoking campaigns set in. Just as tobacco companies see this market as a means of increasing sales, so do health experts and social agencies see it as a market needing anti-smoking campaigns. The battle for gaining consumers' attention has begun.

Source: "Anti-smoking experts suggest ads targeted toward women," Marketing News (January 1999), 5.

female works full time average more than $14,000 additional income than households with only one person working. Today, the wife's work status is less of a determinant to how a family spends its income than is the total amount of net income the family has to spend.[48] Though employment might increase family income, working outside the home may increase family expenditures on items such as childcare, clothing, food away from home, gasoline, and motor oil. Families with two incomes also spend more on shelter than do one-earner families.[49]

Career Orientation

Employed individuals are sometimes classified by orientation toward their careers. Rena Bartos finds two groups of working women: those who think of themselves as having a career and those to whom work is "just-a-job." There are also housewives who prefer to stay at home and those who plan to work in the future. For marketers, this may be important because homemakers and just-a-job women are more likely to read traditional women's magazines, whereas professional women are more likely to read general interest and business-oriented magazines and newspapers.[50] As with other consumer classifications, working or nonworking wives should not be treated as homogeneous segments[51] because many differences exist and account for different purchasing behaviors within these groups. Figure 12.11 is an ad for Mercedes-Benz that is directed toward career women who have enough money to buy a Mercedes for the men in their lives. It appeals to and promotes equality in income and career between men and women.

Figure 12.11 Mercedes-Benz Targets Professional Women

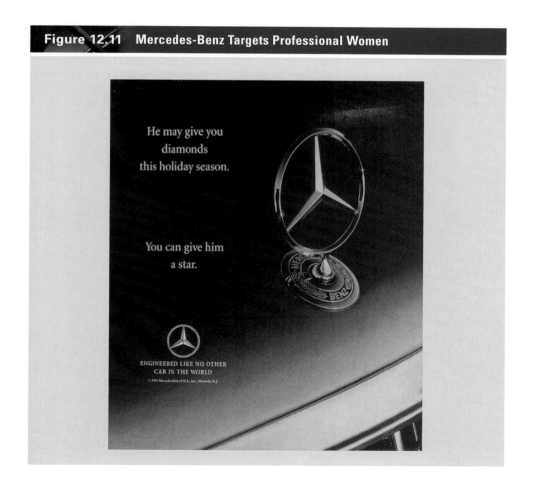

Women and Time

Married working women experience many time pressures. They often have two jobs: household responsibilities, including children, plus their jobs in the marketplace. Studies show they have significantly less leisure time than either their husbands or full-time homemakers.[52] This would suggest that working wives would buy more time-saving appliances, use more convenience foods, spend less time shopping, and so forth. Actually, research shows that working and non-working wives are similar in such behavior if income, life stage, and other situational variables are held constant,[53] and that working-wife families appear to spend more on food away from home, childcare, and some services.[54]

Role Overload

Role overload exists when the total demands on time and energy associated with the prescribed activities of multiple roles are too great to perform the roles adequately or comfortably.[55] Sex-role ideology, especially found in feminism, and other forces are creating pressures toward more equality in work-loads between men and women. Research shows that employed women work more hours each day than husbands who are employed and wives who are not employed, resulting in role overload for many women.[56] As women contribute more to the family income, they expect in return a more equal division of the household responsibilities.[57] There is evidence, especially among younger families, of a shift in attitudes toward work and housework that is causing a move toward more household equality between the sexes.[58]

Marketing to Women

Consumer researchers are interested in women's multiple roles, time pressures, and changing family structures in order to develop effective marketing and communication programs to reach them. With such information, marketers can look beyond the one-size-fits-all description of general segments of women to more descriptive and specific descriptions.

The "mother" category has been a relatively under-studied segment because of assumptions about this market segment. Leo Burnett, a U.S.-based advertising agency, studied the premise that "all mothers must be the same and can be reached through similar advertising because they are all concerned with the same issues (health and well-being of their children)." Through Leo*She*, its unit focusing on marketing to women, the company found four major groups of mothers, each with unique characteristics,[59] as described in Figure 12.12.

Different mom segments look at advertising, messages, products, time, and brands differently. For example, time-strapped Tug-of-War moms are the most brand conscious because they use recognized brands to save time and help simplify their shopping trips. Consumer products companies targeting these women should spotlight the values of their brands. But new brands or brands that are in trouble can benefit from targeting the emerging groups of Strong Shoulders moms (via inspirational television shows) and Mothers of Invention (via the web), according to Leo*She*. The key is not to treat all moms the same or expect to capture all of them with one single message.

Retailers and not-for-profit agencies can apply such information to existing strategies to better reach, keep, and service clients. For example, retailers are open longer hours than in years past because of conflicting work schedules. One study found that among mothers who work full time, 45 percent work different shifts than their spouse, and 57 percent of part-time working women work different

Figure 12.12 Multiple Moms: Four Strategies

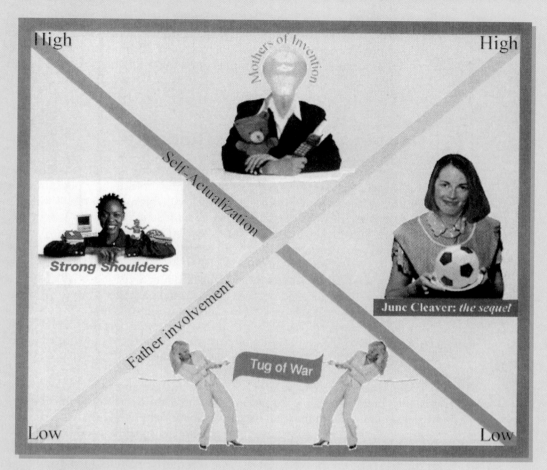

June Cleaver: The Sequel

These women believe in the traditional roles of "stay-at-home" moms and "bread-winner" dads. They tend to be white, highly educated, and from upscale backgrounds. Slightly more than half of them stay at home full time to care for their families, compared to the national average of 30 percent.

Tug of War Moms

They share some of the same traditional notions of motherhood, but are forced to work—and they aren't happy about that. These moms, 79 percent of whom work outside the home, are full of angst and anxiety.

Strong Shoulders

More than a third of this group are single mothers, who have a positive view of their lives, despite their lower income levels and little support from their children's dads. Thirty-four percent of these women are between 18 and 24 years old.

Mothers of Invention

These women enjoy motherhood, work outside the home, and have help with their child-rearing responsibilities from helpful husbands. Unlike the Tug-of-Wars, this group—a mix of gen xers and boomers—has developed new and creative ways to balance career with a happy home life.

shifts than their husbands.[60] Increased time pressures have also caused many retailers and agencies to create catalogs, Internet sites, and alternative shopping or access methods. Don Caster, a direct marketer of upscale women's clothing, adapts to women's busy schedules and hectic lifestyles by showing its products in the comfort of associates' homes. Clients can make appointments during their lunch hours, evening hours, or weekends to view and try on clothing in the comfort of a nice home. Or associates will bring samples of clothing to clients' homes or offices.

Changing Masculine Roles

Roles of men in families are changing substantially as well. It is not uncommon in the United States for the woman of the household to buy new tires for the car while the husband stays home to cook dinner or play with the kids. As men's share of family income decreases and as values shift in society, men are free to participate more fully in family functions and are taking on new roles in consuming and purchasing products.[61] In a survey of 1,000 American men by the advertising agency Cunningham & Walsh, more and more men could be observed as househusbands. The privately published survey disclosed that 47 percent of men vacuum the house, 80 percent take out the garbage, 41 percent wash dishes, 37 percent make beds, 33 percent load the washing machine, 27 percent clean the bathroom, 23 percent dust, 23 percent dry dishes, 21 percent sort laundry, 16 percent clean the refrigerator, and 14 percent clean the oven. More than 50 percent of men take part in regular shopping trips, suggesting that men are important targets for many types of household products.

Men not only participate in household and consumption activities but are increasing their rate of participation. Men now do one-fifth of the cooking, cleaning, and laundry, and married men now do more housework than unmarried men. Similarly, fathers are doing more (in the household) than they once did.[62]

Much literature has focused on the new roles of men.[63] Joseph Pleck, a leader in the field, notes that though the "new father" image is increasingly portrayed in the media, there *is*, in reality, substantive change in men's behaviors.[64] The new father is present at the birth, is involved with his children as infants (not just when they are older), participates in the actual day-to-day work of child-care, and is involved with his daughters as much as his sons.

Men in the 21st century see themselves as being more sensitive. Men remain interested in romance, but they also express a high interest in fitness, health, helping raise the children, helping out with household chores, and finding a better balance between work and leisure. These new roles appear to be creating a male market that is more interested in brands than in earlier decades. MassMutual, a financial services company, appeals to fathers' roles and responsibilities to their children in Figure 12.13.

As economic conditions and men's roles in the home change, men are redefining themselves. Whereas the man of the 1950s wanted a settled, stable, suburban existence, and the man of the 1970s cared more about power than fitting in, today's "organization man" carries a briefcase in one hand and pushes a baby carriage with the other. And although he considers his career important, he doesn't want to sacrifice time with his family.[65] Businesses will have to adapt to the changes that men are facing, such as having to stay home with a sick child. The compromises today's organization man is making are very similar to the ones made by working women, and firms that do not address these changing roles and needs could lose some of their best and brightest female and male employees.[66]

Figure 12.13   MassMutual Appeals to Male Roles

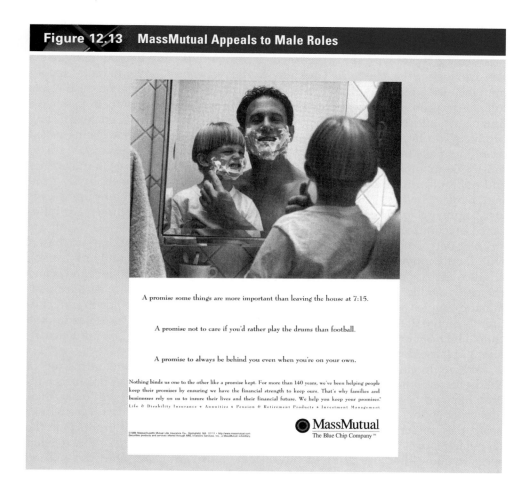

A promise some things are more important than leaving the house at 7:15.

A promise not to care if you'd rather play the drums than football.

A promise to always be behind you even when you're on your own.

Nothing binds us one to the other like a promise kept. For more than 140 years, we've been helping people keep their promises by ensuring we have the financial strength to keep ours. That's why families and businesses rely on us to insure their lives and their financial future. We help you keep your promises.

Life & Disability Insurance • Annuities • Pension & Retirement Products • Investment Management

◉ MassMutual
The Blue Chip Company℠

Children and Household Consumer Behavior

Children change dramatically how the family functions, in terms of relationships, employment, and purchases. Studies based on Canadian data indicate that young children cause less participation in the labor force, change how families spend their money, and reduce the amount of time and money available for leisure.[67]

Influence of Children

The children's market has captured the attention of marketers worldwide because of the increasing dollars, lira, and pounds they spend on products and because of the enormous influence they exert over spending power in a growing number of product categories, including footwear and clothing.[68] Children spent over $25 billion in 1998, buying confections, games, movies, and music from U.S. retailers. The fastest growing purchase category for children has been apparel, due in part to children assuming more responsibility for their own necessities.[69] Armed with money received from allowances, chores, and gifts from grandparents, children average just over 200 store visits per year, either alone or with parents. A typical 10-year-old goes shopping with parents two to three times per week (directly influencing about $188 billion of household purchases) and shops alone around once a week.

But their influence on household spending varies by product user and by degree.[70] Children tend to have greater influence in purchase decisions involving products for their own use,[71] whereas their influence is more limited on more expensive, higher risk products. Children exert *direct influence* over parental spending when they request specific products and brands. Direct influence also refers to joint decision making—actively participating with family members to make a purchase. Children's influence might also be *indirect,* occurring when parents buy products and brands that they know their children prefer, without being asked or told to make that specific purchase. These kinds of transactions account for almost $300 million in household spending. Automakers target kids in magazines and point-of-purchase displays because they indirectly influence about $17.7 billion in auto purchases.[72] And the influence of children on computer purchases is just beginning to blossom. Figure 12.14 shows how many purchases are influenced by children.

Not only do children influence choices, they are actually making purchases, with family money and with their own. Just as children affect family purchases, families affect young consumers' perception and evaluation of product and brand choices.[73] Children's consumer behavior is absorbed at very young ages from familial examples so that if parents exhibit brand loyalty to a specific brand, children perceive that brand and product to be good.[74] A family's influence upon a child's brand choices must be recognized by marketers because the influence affects purchase decisions later in life as well.

Where do children like to shop best? Convenience stores rank at the top of children's shopping lists because they sell a lot of candy and other products children like and because they are accessible. In fact, most children will make their first independent purchases at convenience stores. As children reach ages 8 to 10 years, they prefer mass merchandisers because of the breadth of products in the toy, snack foods, clothing, and school supplies categories. They also like to shop specialty stores because of the depth of toys, music, or shoes offered. Children usually have a favorite grocery store and recommend their mothers shop there when they shop together. Finally, children find drugstores and department stores cold and boring, and very adult oriented. Figure 12.15 shows the types of products children buy most often.

Figure 12.14 Mom, Buy a Jeep

Aggregate spending in millions of dollars influenced by children aged 4 to 12 on selected items, and per-child spending, 1997.

	Aggregate spending	Per-child spending
Food and beverages	$110,320	$3,131
Entertainment	25,620	727
Apparel	17,540	498
Automobiles	17,740	503
Electronics	6,400	182
Health and beauty	3,550	101
Other	5,570	158
Total	$187,740	$5,328

Source: James McNeal, *Tapping the three kid's market,* American Demographics *(April 1998), 39.*

Figure 12.15   Pizza, Pepsi, Beanie Babies

Aggregate spending in millions of dollars by children aged 4 to 12 on selected items, and per-child spending, 1997.

	Aggregate spending	Per-child spending
Food and beverages	$7,745	$220
Play items	6,471	184
Apparel	3,595	102
Movies/sports	1,989	56
Video arcades	1,326	38
Other	2,302	65
Total	$23,429	$665

Source: James McNeal, *Tapping the Three Kids' Market*, American Demographics *(April 1998), 40.*

Childhood Socialization

Much of consumer behavior is learned as a child.[75] Family communication about purchases and consumer behavior is the key in children's consumer socialization process. Children who buy Pepsi when they are young are more likely to buy Pepsi when they are older. They are also more likely to react negatively to product changes but are less affected by price increases. And single consumers tend to be more loyal to the brands they learned to buy as children.

So, how do children learn their consumer behaviors? They learn primarily from shopping with parents—known as co-shopping. Co-shoppers tend to be more concerned about their children's development as consumers, and they place more value on children's input in family consumer decisions, including decisions on products not encountered on typical co-shopping trips such as automobiles, major appliances, life insurance, and vacations.[76] Co-shoppers explain more to their children why they don't buy products and discuss the role of advertising, which to some extent may mediate the influence of advertising.

Different types of mothers communicate consumer skills and knowledge to their children in different ways. Researchers found that mothers who are restrictive and warm in their relationships with their children tend to monitor and control children's consumption activities more, whereas mothers who respect and solicit children's opinions use messages that promote purchasing and consumption decision-making abilities.[77]

Retailers can benefit from understanding the role of children in buying. Some retailers may consider children an interference with parents' shopping time. Retailers such as Ikea, the Swedish furniture firm with stores around the world, provide play areas for children while parents shop. A more proactive approach is found in Japanese department stores, which encourage children and parents, principally mothers, to interact with toys found in the store, making it a fun place for children to visit. This approach is shown in Figure 12.16.

Many changes in family structure directly affect how marketers communicate to children and their families. For example, delayed marriage and higher education are increasing the number of families with *only children* (who are accustomed to communicating with adults more than with siblings or peers). Their preferences may be much more "adult" than marketers traditionally expected. Effective communications must take into consideration the higher verbal and creative skills

Figure 12.16   Involving Children in Shopping in a Japanese Department Store

associated with only children. Further, families in which both parents are employed have less time to spend with children and may be willing to spend more money on consumer products for children to compensate.

Research Methodology for Family Decision Studies

When preparing an analysis of family influences on buying or the consumption decisions of families, most of the research techniques will be similar to other marketing research studies. However, a few unique aspects of family decisions should be considered.

The study of family consumer decisions is less common than that of individual consumer decisions because of the difficulty of researching and studying the family as a unit. Administering a questionnaire simultaneously to an entire family requires accessing all members (difficult in today's hectic environment), using language that has the same meaning to all family members (difficult with discrepancies in age or education), and interpreting results when members of the same family report conflicting opinions about family purchases or influences on decisions.

Measuring Influences

Role structure studies have often viewed purchasing as an act rather than a process and have based findings on questions such as "Who usually makes the decision to purchase?" or "Who influences the decision?" Yet, the role and influence of family members vary by stage in the decision process. The following questions might be useful for measuring family influence[78]:

1. Who was responsible for initial need recognition?
2. Who was responsible for acquiring information about the purchase alternatives?
3. Who made the final decision on which alternative should be purchased?
4. Who made the actual purchase of the product?

Husbands and wives are more likely to have similar perceptions about their relative influence on a given phase when questioning focuses on the decision stages.

The relevant role structure categories in a research project depend on the specific product or service under consideration, but in many product categories, only the husband or wife is involved. In other categories, it is useful to measure the amount of influence of different family members and other variables, such as family life cycle stage and lifestyles.[79]

Interviewer Bias

The gender of the interviewer or observer may influence the roles husbands and wives say they play in a purchase situation. To overcome this bias, either self-administered questionnaires (such as mail or Internet questionnaires) should be used or the observer should be randomly assigned to respondents, with an equal number of male and female interviewers.

Respondent Selection

In measuring family buying, it is necessary to decide which members of the nuclear family should be asked about the influence of family members. Results often vary considerably depending on which family members are interviewed. Most often, wives are the ones interviewed, but the percentage of couples whose responses agree is often so low that it makes interviewing only one member unacceptable. Some studies indicate that husbands' responses concerning purchase intentions are better predictors of total planned cost and number of items planned although wives predicted better for certain products such as appliances, home furnishings, and entertainment equipment plans.[80]

Summary

Families or households are consumer units of critical importance in the study of consumer behavior for two reasons. First, families or households are the unit of usage and purchase for many consumer products. Second, the family is a major influence on the attitudes and behavior of individuals. As consumers, we are the creation of our families to a large extent.

A family is a group of two or more persons related by blood, marriage, or adoption who reside together. A household differs from a family by describing all the persons, both related and unrelated, who occupy a housing unit. Thus, households outnumber families and are smaller in size; the average income is higher for families than households.

Family (or household) members occupy various roles, which include initiator (gatekeeper), influencer, decider, buyer, and user. The influence of spouses, children, or other family members varies depending on the resources of family members, the type of product, the stage in the family life cycle, and the stage in the buying decision. These variables are more important in understanding family decisions than traditional roles ascribed to one gender or the other.

The family life cycle describes how families change over time. Traditional approaches of analyzing the FLC have been updated with a consumer market matrix of life stages that emphasizes the relative income of a family in each stage. This matrix is built upon 11 stages: Young Singles; Newly Married Couples; Full Nest I, II, and III; Married, No Kids; Older Singles; Empty Nest I and II; Solitary Survivor; and Retired Solitary Survivor. Although not all individuals will go through each stage, they will progress through the process as suggested by the FLC model, which can be used to predict how much disposable income different families will have at different stages.

Families and households are changing in their structure and composition. Among more important recent changes are increases in the number of single households, smaller average family size, later marriages, divorce, remarriage and redivorce, co-habitating singles, and increased awareness of the gay market. The increasing number of employed women has created role overload for employed women who work more hours (combining paid work and family work) each week than their husbands or nonemployed women.

Marketers are concerned with the roles performed by women, men, and children. Advertising to women increasingly reflects themes of increasing income and responsibility and drives for self-fulfillment and self-enhancement. Masculine roles increasingly reflect shared performance of household activities. Children learn much of their consumption and buying behavior from parents and exert considerable influence on family purchases.

Marketing research techniques useful in studying families and households give special consideration to the decision process framework, questioning techniques, role structure categories and relative influence, interviewer bias, and respondent selection. A methodological problem is created because husbands and wives often differ in their responses to questions about how their families buy consumer goods and services.

Review and Discussion Questions

1. What is meant by the term *family*? What is the importance of studying families to the understanding of consumer behavior?

2. Some studies of consumer behavior maintain that the family rather than the individual should be the unit of analysis in consumer behavior. What are the advantages and disadvantages of using the family as the unit of analysis?

3. Do husbands or wives have the most influence on buying decisions? Outline your answer.

4. Explain the changes occurring in the home meal replacement (HMR) market, and describe why you think demand for these types of products will increase or decrease in the future.

5. Will there be more or fewer women employed outside the home in the future? What variables should be considered in answering this question? How does the answer affect demand for consumer products?

6. Analyze the statement, "Working women buy products and services essentially the same as nonworking women."

7. What is meant by the "singles" market? How would a travel company (such as an airline, resort, or cruise line) appeal to the singles market?

8. Assume that an airline has asked for a research project to understand how families make vacation decisions. You are asked to prepare a research design for the project. What would you suggest?

9. Assume that you are the marketing manager for a clothing firm that wishes to attract the gay market. How would you assess the size of this market? Outline the marketing program you would recommend.

10. Children do not have much purchasing power, relative to other markets. Yet, they are believed to be important in the understanding of consumer behavior. Why? What might firms do to be more profitable as a result of understanding the role of children in family buying?

Endnotes

1. Harry L. Davis, "Decision Making within the Household," *Journal of Consumer Research* 2 (March 1976), 241–260.

2. Terry Childers and Akshay Rao, "The Influence of Familial and Peer-based Reference Groups on Consumer Decisions," *Journal of Consumer Research* 19 (September 1992), 198–221.

3. For a discussion of these issues on a global perspective, see Nico Keilman, Anton Kuitsten, and Ad Vossen, eds., *Modeling Household Formation and Dissolution* (New York: Oxford University Press, 1988).

4. David H. Olson et al., *Families: What Makes Them Work?* (Beverly Hills, CA: Sage Publications, 1983).

5. Hamilton I. McCubbin and Marilyn A. McCubbin, "Typologies of Resilient Families: Emerging Roles of Social Class and Ethnicity," *Family Relations* 37 (July 1988), 247–254.

6. Russell Belk, "A Child's Christmas in America: Santa Claus as Deity, Consumption as Religion,"
Journal of American Culture 10 (Spring 1987), 87–100; David Cheal, *The Gift Economy* (London: Routledge, 1988); Elizabeth Hirschman and Priscilla LaBarbera, "The Meaning of Christmas," in Elizabeth Hirschman, ed., *Interpretative Consumer Research* (Provo, UT: Association for Consumer Research), 136–147.

7. Russell Belk and Gregory Coon, "Gift Giving as Agapic Love: An Alternative to the Exchange Paradigm Based on Dating Experiences," *Journal of Consumer Research* 20 (December 1993), 393–417.

8. Tibbett Speer, "Stretching the Holiday Season," *American Demographics* (November 1997), 43.

9. "Holiday Finale Disappoints Retailers—Again," *The Wall Street Journal* (December 26, 1997).

10. Robert Boutilier, "Pulling the Family's Strings," *American Demographics* (August 1993), 44–48.

11. Theresa Howard, "Family Marketing Values: Beyond Toys and Coloring Books," *Nation's Restaurant News* (April 1996).

12. Harry L. Davis and Benny R. Rigaux, "Perception of Marital Roles in Decision Processes," *Journal of Consumer Research* 1 (June 1974), 5–14.

13. Marilyn Lavin, "Husband-Dominant, Wife-Dominant, Joint: A Shopping Typology for Baby Boom Couples?" *Journal of Consumer Marketing* 10 (1993), 33–42.

14. William J. Qualls, "Changing Sex Roles: Its Impact upon Family Decision Making," in Andrew Mitchell, ed., *Advances in Consumer Research* 9 (Ann Arbor, MI: Association for Consumer Research, 1982), 267–270.

15. Joseph Bellizzi and Laura Milner, "Gender Positioning of a Traditionally Male-Dominated Product," *Journal of Advertising Research* 31 (June/July 1991), 72–79.

16. For research on this topic from a wide variety of disciplines, see Beth B. Hess and Myra Marx Ferree, *Analyzing Gender* (Newbury Park, CA: Sage Publications, 1987).

17. Roger Jenkins, "Contributions of Theory to the Study of Family Decision-Making," in Jerry Olson, ed., *Advances in Consumer Research* 7 (Ann Arbor, MI: Association for Consumer Research, 1980), 207–211.

18. Alvin Bums and Donald Granbois, "Advancing the Study of Family Purchase Decision Making," in Olson, *Advances in Consumer Research*, 221–226.

19. Sunil Gupta, Michael R. Hagerty, and John G. Myers, "New Directions in Family Decision Making Research," in Alice M. Tybout, ed., *Advances in Consumer Research* 10 (Ann Arbor, MI: Association for Consumer Research, 1983), 445–450.

20. Mary Lou Roberts, "Gender Differences and Household Decision-Making: Needed Conceptual and Methodological Developments," in Thomas C. Kinnear, ed., *Advances in Consumer Research* 11 (Provo, UT: Association for Consumer Research, 1984), 276–278.

21. Eileen Fischer and Stephen J. Arnold, "More than a Labor of Love: Gender Roles and Christmas Gift Shopping," *Journal of Consumer Research* 17 (December 1990), 333–343.

22. William D. Wells and George Gubar, "The Life Cycle Concept," *Journal of Marketing Research* 2 (November 1966), 355–363.

23. Fred D. Reynolds and William D. Wells, *Consumer Behavior* (New York: McGraw-Hill, 1977).

24. Patrick E. Murphy and William Staples, "A Modernized Family Life Cycle," *Journal of Consumer Research* 6 (June 1979), 12–22.

25. Brad Edmondson, "Do the Math," *American Demographics* (October 1999), 50–56.

26. Janet Wagner and Sherman Hanna, "The Effec-tiveness of Family Life Cycle Variables in Consumer Expenditure Research," *Journal of Consumer Research* 10 (December 1983), 281–291.

27. Mandy Putnam, Sharyn Brooks, and William R. Davidson, *The Expanded Management Horizons Consumer Market Matrix* (Columbus, OH: Management Horizons, a Division of Price Waterhouse, 1986).

28. Joanne Y. Cleaver, "Good Old Dad," *American Demographics* (June 1999), 59–63.

29. Cheryl Russell, "The New Consumer Paradigm," *American Demographics* (April 1999), 52–53.

30. Kendra Darko, "A Home of Their Own," *American Demographics* (September 1999), 35–38.

31. U.S. Bureau of the Census, No. 59, "Marital Status of the Population, 1997."

32. Jennifer Lach, "The Consequences of Divorce," *American Demographics* (October 1999), 14.

33. For a thorough analysis of the financial and other decision-making capabilities of these families, see Frank Furstenbert and Graham B. Spanier, *Recycling the Family* (Beverly Hills, CA: Sage Publications, 1984).

34. "The Future of Households," *American Demographics* (December 1993), 39.

35. Kendra Darko, "A Home of Their Own," *American Demographics* (September 1999), 35–38.

36. "Living Alone and Loving It," *U.S. News and World Report* (August 3, 1987).

37. W. Wayne Delozier and C. William Roe, "Marketing to the Homosexual (Gay) Market," in Robert L. King, ed., *Marketing: Toward the Twenty-First Century* (Richmond, VA: Southern Marketing Association, 1991), 107–109.

38. Felicity Barringer, "Sex Survey of American Men Finds 1% Are Gay," *New York Times* (April 15, 1993), A1.

39. Bradley Johnson, "The Gay Quandary," *Advertising Age* (January 18, 1993), 29–30.

40. Rachel X. Weissman, "Gay Market Power," *American Demographics* (June 1999), 32–33.

41. Ibid.

42. "Gay Community Looks for Strength in Numbers," *American Marketplace* (July 4, 1991), 134

43. Cyndee Miller, "Gays Are Affluent but Often Overlooked Market," *Marketing News* (December 24, 1990), 2.

44. Janet Kornblum, "Beer Ad in Gay Magazine Stirs Debate," *USA Today* (May 5, 1999), 12B.

45. U.S. Bureau of the Census, No. 75, "Family Groups with Children Under 18 Years Old, by Race and Hispanic Origin, 1997."

46. David Wilson, "Role Theory and Buying-Selling Negotiations: A Critical Review," in Richard Bagozzi, ed., *Marketing in the 1980s* (Chicago: American Marketing Association, 1980), 118–121.

47. Salah Hassan and Roger Blackwell, *Global Marketing Perspectives and Cases* (Fort Worth: Dryden Press, 1994), 122.

48. Rose M. Rubin, Bobye J. Riney, and David J. Molina, "Expenditure Pattern Differentials between One-Earner and Dual-Earner Households: 1972–1973 and 1984," *Journal of Consumer Research* 17 (June 1990), 43–52.

49. Eva Jacobs, Stephanie Shipp, and Gregory Brown, "Families of Working Wives Spending More on Services and Nondurables," *Monthly Labor Review* 112 (February 1989), 15–23.

50. Rena Bartos, *The Moving Target: What Every Marketer Should Know about Women* (New York: Free Press, 1982).

51. Charles Schaninger, Margaret Nelson, and William Danko, "An Empirical Evaluation of the Bartos Model of Wife's Work Involvement," *Journal of Advertising Research* 33 (May-June 1993), 49–63.

52. Marianne Ferber and Bonnie Birnbaum, "One Job or Two Jobs: The Implications for Young Wives," *Journal of Consumer Research* 8 (December 1980), 263–271.

53. Charles B. Weinberg and Russell S. Winer, "Working Wives and Major Family Expenditures: Replication and Extension," *Journal of Consumer Research* 7 (September 1983), 259–263.

54. Done Bellante and Ann C. Foster, "Working Wives and Expenditure on Services," *Journal of Consumer Research* 11 (September 1984), 700–707.

55. Patricia Voydanoff, *Work and Family Life* (Newbury Park, CA: Sage Publications, 1987), 83.

56. Alvin C. Burns and Ellen Foxman, "Role Load and Its Consequences on Individual Consumer Behavior," in Terence A. Shimp et al., eds., *1986 AMA Educators' Proceedings* (Chicago: American Marketing Association, 1986), 18.

57. Townsend and O'Neil, "American Women Get Mad."

58. F. Thomas Juster, "A Note on Recent Changes in Time Use," in R. Thomas Juster and Frank P. Stafford, eds., *Time, Goods, and Well-Being* (Ann Arbor, MI: Institute for Social Research, 1985), 313–332.

59. Cristina Merrill, "Mother's Work is Never Done," *American Demographics* (September 1999), 29–32.

60. Alan Otten, "People Patterns," *The Wall Street Journal* (June 14, 1988), 33.

61. Linda Jacobsen and Brad Edmondson, "Father Figures," *American Demographics* (August 1993), 22–27.

62. John P. Robinson, "Who's Doing the Housework," *American Demographics* (December 1988), 24–28ff.

63. Michael S. Kimmel, ed., *Changing Men: New Directions in Research on Men and Masculinity* (Newbury Park, CA: Sage Publications, 1987).

64. Joseph H. Pleck, "American Fathering in Historical Perspective," in Kimmel, *Changing Men*, 93.

65. Michael Kimmel, "What Do Men Want?" *Harvard Business Review* (November/December 1993), 50–63.

66. Ibid.

67. Robert E. Wilkes, "Husband-Wife Influence in Purchase Decisions: A Confirmation and Extension," *Journal of Marketing Research* 12 (May 1975), 224–227.

68. J. Gregan-Paxton and John Roedder, "Are Young Children Adaptive Decision Makers? A Study of Age Differences in Information Search Behavior," *Journal of Consumer Research* 21, 4 (March 1995), 567–580.

69. James McNeal, "Tapping the Three Kids' Markets," *American Demographics* (April 1998), 37.

70. Sharon Beatty and Salil Talpade, "Adolescent Influence in Family Decision Making: A Replication with Extension," *Journal of Consumer Research* 21 (September 1994), 332–341.

71. Chankon Kim and Hanjoon Lee, "Development of Family Triadic Measures for Children's Purchase Influence," *Journal of Marketing Research* (Summer 1997), 307.

72. James McNeal, "Tapping the Three Kids' Markets." *American Demographics* (April 1998), 37–41.

73. Margaret Hogg, Margaret Bruce, and Alexander Hill, "Fashion Brand Preferences among Young Consumers," *International Journal of Retail & Distribution Management* (August 1998), 293.

74. C. E. Hite and R. E. Hite, "Reliance on Brand by Young Children," *Journal of the Market Research Society* 37, 2 (1994), 185–193.

75. Scott Ward, "Consumer Socialization," in Harold Kassarjian and Thomas Robertson, eds., *Perspectives in Consumer Behavior* (Glenview, IL: Scott Foresman).

76. Sanford Grossbart, Les Carlson, and Ann Walsh, "Consumer Socialization and Frequency of Shopping with Children," *Journal of the Academy of Marketing Science* 19 (Summer 1991), 155–163.

77. Les Carlson, Sanford Grossbart, and J. Kathleen Stuenkel, "The Role of Parental Socialization Types on Differential Family Communication

Patterns Regarding Consumption," *Journal of Consumer Psychology.*

78. Robert E. Wildes, "Husband-Wife Influence in Purchase Decisions: A Confirmation and Extension," *Journal of Marketing Research* 12 (May 1975), 224–227.

79. Rosann L. Spiro, "Persuasion in Family Decision-Making," *Journal of Consumer Research* 9 (March 1983), 393–401.

80. Donald H. Granbois and John O. Summers, "Primary and Secondary Validity of Consumer Purchase Probabilities," *Journal of Consumer Research* 1 (March 1975), 31–38.

CHAPTER 13

Group and Personal Influence

OPENING VIGNETTE

Pikachu, Squirtle, Snorlax and hundreds of their best friends have invaded the lives of American children and their bewildered parents. The brain-children of Japanese outcast-turned-comic-creator, Satoshi Tajiri, Pokemon has fostered friendships in Japanese and U.S. schoolyards, started fights among even the best of friends, and created a buzz among managers of children's marketing and products companies. Pokemon has raised the bar for the power of word-of-mouth communication and diffusion among children.

Tajiri was a social outcast as a child; his friends were the many insects he collected from Japan's ponds and rice fields. His sadness in watching these pockets of nature give way to shopping malls and concrete roads fueled his desire to preserve the creatures of his childhood memories. Pokemon is his shrine to the fascinating world of insects, which attracts new worshippers each day. They pay homage by playing Pokemon Gameboy, collecting and swapping trading cards, watching Pokemon videos and movies, and talking about the unique powers of each of the creatures. In essence, the creatures are pitted against each other in "fights," with the goal being to kill your opponents' Pokemon before yours falls victim. Some Pokemon are more powerful than others, making some worth more than others in the eyes of kids.

The craze has affected school policies throughout the country—many of them banning the cards from school property, and others restricting the trading of cards during school hours. Not only do they distract children from schoolwork, the violent properties of the monsters have spawned similar behavior among overzealous children, who steal powerful cards from other kids or intimidate them into unfair trades.

Gavin, age 11, and his sister Anna, age 7, two bright elementary school students, have mastered the language, games, and lingo of the world of Pokemon. Their school also restricts use of the cards during the day, but has formed an after-school Pokemon league, which lets children wage war against each other with intense rounds of the card game. Aware of some of the problems brought about by the craze, they experience the positive aspects of the game. "I like to collect them and learn more about how each one evolves into a stronger Pokemon," says Gavin, who can recite the properties and special strengths of most of the creatures by heart. When asked how they learned about Pokemon, his sister adds, "I heard a few friends at school talk about it, and all of a sudden, everyone was collecting the cards and playing." They both have made new friends because of the cards, giving them something to talk about with kids they might not otherwise get to know.

Source: Howard Chua-Eoan and Tim Larimer, "PokeMania," Time (November 22, 1999), 81.

Group and Personal Influences on Individuals

Regardless of nationality, ethnicity, race, or gender, personal and group influences persuade human beings' actions and behaviors. Belonging to groups, trying to "fit in," and striving to please others affect the life choices and purchase decisions that individuals make. Input from people with whom we identify and aspire to emulate holds remarkable credibility. Indeed, it is common for group influences to be key factors in lifestyle trends, the acceptance of new fashions, and the trial and adoption of new products.

What Are Reference Groups?

A **reference group** is any "person or group of people that significantly influences an individual's behavior."[1] The values, attitudes, behaviors, and norms of this group are perceived to have relevance upon the evaluations, behaviors, and aspirations of another individual.[2] Reference groups might be individuals, such as celebrities, athletes, and political leaders, or they might be groups of individuals with similarities, such as musical groups, political parties, and sports teams. For example, research shows that most people are averse to behavior that contradicts group consensus.[3] Young people tend to seek approval of their peers more than older adults do. Wearing Abercrombie & Fitch (or similar brands, such as Old Navy and Tommy Hilfiger) decreases the risk they feel during the purchase process and increases their comfort level by helping them fit in with their friends. Figure 13.1 depicts the influence process, beginning with the source and type of influence, proceeding through the transmission of influence and degree of effect, and ending with the influence on behaviors, lifestyles, purchases, and consumption. This model can serve as a pictorial outline of the first half of this chapter.

Types of Reference Groups

Social groups can take many forms, and individuals can belong to a variety of groups. It is possible, for example, for a person to be part of a formal, primary

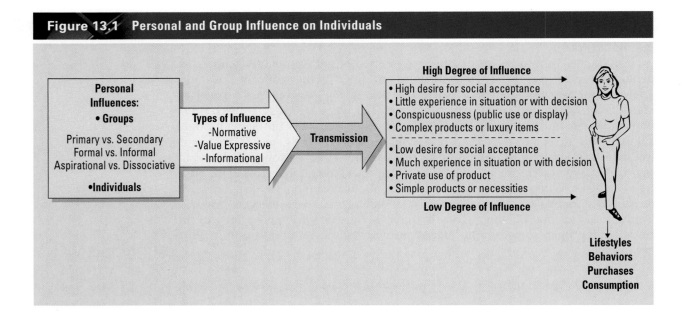

Figure 13.1   Personal and Group Influence on Individuals

group. Regardless of the type of reference group, input from others can be viewed as binding, in which case it is referred to as *normative* influence, or at other times, it can be viewed as *comparative,* which serves only as yet another source of information in decision making. These roles can occur in many types of groups, including:

- **Primary** The greatest influence and impact usually is exerted by primary groups—*a social aggregation that is sufficiently intimate to permit and facilitate unrestricted face-to-face interaction.* Because there exists cohesiveness and motivated participation, members exhibit marked similarities in beliefs and behavior.[4] The family is the most obvious example of a strongly influential primary group.

- **Secondary** Secondary groups also *have face-to-face interaction, but it is more sporadic, less comprehensive, and less influential in shaping thought and behavior.*[5] Examples are professional associations, trade unions, and community organizations.

- **Formal** Formal groups are *characterized by a defined structure* (often written) *and a known list of members and requirements for membership.* Examples are religious groups, fraternal bodies, and community service organizations. The influence exerted on behavior varies, depending on the motivation of the individual to accept and comply with the group's standards. Moreover, there are wide latitudes in the degree to which specific conformity is expected and enforced.

- **Informal** In contrast to formal groups, informal groups *have far less structure and are likely to be based on friendship or interests.* Though their norms can be stringent, they seldom appear in writing, but the effect on behavior can be strong if individuals are motivated by social acceptance. There also is a high degree of intimate, face-to-face interaction, which further strengthens the power with which expectations and sanctions are expressed and enforced.

- **Membership** When individuals are *recognized as members of a group, they have achieved formal acceptance status in the group.* Membership can be in informal groups of peers or family, or it can be in formal groups such as religious groups, fraternities and sororities, trade associations, or retail frequent buyer clubs. Formal membership groups are used increasingly in marketing efforts to target individuals with similar characteristics and behaviors. *Virtual* membership groups have evolved through chat-rooms and other "associations" on the Internet.

- **Aspirational** Aspirational groups *exhibit a desire to adopt the norms, values, and behavior of others with whom the individual aspires to associate.* On occasion, there is anticipation of acceptance into membership and motivation to behave accordingly, and at other times, there is no expectation of ever belonging to the group, which makes the aspiration symbolic. The influence of aspirational groups, though often indirect, can play a significant role in product choices. For example, a child training in soccer might wear the colors and emblems of her favorite soccer team, or a business student might wear suits similar to those worn by successful business leaders, especially during pre-graduation job recruiting.

- **Dissociative** Influence also can be exerted by dissociative groups—*groups from which an individual tries to avoid association.* This occurs when someone changes his or her social class by abandoning certain behaviors and brand choices for up-scale alternatives. Some teens also disassociate themselves from their peers and parents by dressing in counterculture clothing,

painting their hair purple, or tattooing their bodies. By disassociating themselves from one group, however, they associate themselves with another.

- **Virtual** Computers and the Internet have created a new form of group,
  based on virtual communities rather than geographic ones. Internet communities
  are based on "sets of social relations among people"[6] rather than face-to-
  face relationships. Chat-rooms allow individuals with similar interests to
  connect, interact with each other, and share information on topics from figure skating to deep-sea diving. The flow of information on the Internet is
  less inhibited than during other encounters since individuals don't actually
  meet face to face,[7] and individuals feel more comfortable writing things to
  one another that they would have difficulty saying in person.

Types of Group Influence

Three primary types of influence affect individuals' decisions, behaviors, purchases, and lifestyles. **Normative influence** occurs *when individuals alter their behaviors or beliefs to meet the expectations of a particular group.* In this instance, the
norms of the group influence factors, such as how an individual dresses or what
brand of car he or she drives. Often the goal of the individual is conformity. **Value-
expressive influence** occurs when *a need for psychological association with a group
causes acceptance of its norms, values, attitudes, or behaviors.* Even though there may
be no motivation to become a member, individuals often enhance their image in
the eyes of others, or achieve identification with people who are admired and respected. Since consumers often accept the opinions of others as providing credible and needed evidence about reality,[8] they often seek the advice of others before
making a purchase or life decision. **Informational influence** occurs *when people
have difficulty assessing product or brand characteristics by their own observation or contact.* In this instance, they will accept recommendations or usage by others as evidence about the nature of the product[9] and use the information in their own
product or brand decisions.

How Reference Groups Influence Individuals

Reference groups affect individual consumers in different ways and to different
degrees depending on individual characteristics and product purchase situations.
First, reference groups create *socialization of individuals.* Second, they are important in *developing and evaluating one's self-concept* and *comparing* oneself to others.
Third, reference groups are a device for *obtaining compliance* with norms in a
society.

Socialization

The process of socialization is accomplished through the influence of various reference groups, as discussed in Chapter 11. A company manual may explain dress
code to a new employee, for example, but informal work groups teach the person what is acceptable dress in different situations and for different occasions.
The process of socialization and acculturation permits an individual to know what
behavior is likely to result in stability both for the individual and for the group.

Self-Concept

People protect and modify their self-concept in their interactions with others in reference groups. What we think of ourselves is influenced in our social interactions by the reactions of others whose values we share or opinions we respect. One form of social interaction is the consumption of products. We communicate meaning to others when we buy and use products. Our clothing, cars, and careers make statements about us, and our behaviors and lifestyle are the presentation of ourselves (or an idealized view of ourselves) to our reference groups. By wearing a sports team's logo on a shirt, consumers blend their personal identities with the cultural milieu surrounding the product[10] and assume an altered social identity.

People also maintain their self-concept by conforming to *roles* they have learned. When individuals belong to many groups, they take on numerous roles, and feel pressure to act in certain ways expected by someone in that particular role.

Testimonial advertising is a direct application of understanding the social consequences of the self-concept. A child looks at sports mega-stars Tiger Woods and Michael Jordan wearing Nike apparel and either consciously or subconsciously attributes (at least in part) the respect and strength that he or she wants to the Nike brand. Testimonials from respected actors, politicians, or sports figures can be very effective if the self that is projected by the reference person in the testimonial is consistent with the idealized self of the consumer in the target audience.

Social Comparison

Most individuals have the need to assess themselves by comparing themselves to others. How successful, healthy, or wealthy a person perceives himself or herself to be often depends on how he or she fares in comparison to his or her peers or other reference group members. In addition to gaining information from groups, individuals use reference groups as benchmarks or yardsticks to measure their own behaviors, opinions, abilities, and possessions. But individuals select different comparison groups at different times. When the individual and group are similar, confidence in the accuracy of information received is greater;[11] however, we tend to value differing views only when we are very confident in our own opinions and abilities.[12]

Comparison is not limited to groups with which we have personal contact. Advertising and television can be sources of social comparison. In 1999, rumors and raised eyebrows were rampant in Hollywood, acknowledging the unusually thin group of young television stars, including Jennifer Aniston and Courteney Cox (*Friends*) and Calista Flockhart (*Ally McBeal*), who were being heralded as young, beautiful teen idols. Similarly, women are bombarded daily with airbrushed images of professional models gracing the pages of fashion magazines around the world. As women see these images, many of them feel increased dissatisfaction with their own bodies.[13] One effect of this social comparison has been a dramatic rise in the number of young women (14 to 25) suffering from anorexia and bulimia.

Conformity

The desire of an individual to fit in with a reference group often leads to **conformity**—*a change in beliefs or actions based on real or perceived group pressures.* Two types of conformity exist: *compliance* and *acceptance.* **Compliance** occurs *when an* *individual conforms to the wishes of the group without accepting all its beliefs or behaviors*, whereas **acceptance** occurs *when an individual actually changes his or her beliefs and values to those of the group.* Sometimes a consumer makes a conscious effort to emulate the behavior of others in the group or to be identified with the group's behavior to receive a reward (such as social acceptance). And sometimes the influence of the group is more subtle, occurring without the conscious effort of the individual being influenced. For example, some consumers might not know how to behave in a situation and use group norms as a guide on how to behave correctly.

When Are People Likely to Adhere to Norms?

Reference groups influence individuals to conform to group norms in varying degrees depending on the characteristics of the group, the individual, and the situation, as seen in Figure 13.1. The more cohesive a group is, the more influence it is likely to have on individual members, with much of the influence coming from loyal members of the group. Further, the size of the group affects its ability to influence; the old belief that there is "safety in numbers" holds true in many instances of group influence. An individual might turn to a group with expertise in a particular area to help him or her make product decisions, especially if the consumer has limited information available. A consumer is also more likely to conform to group norms if the person likes the group or possesses a strong desire to belong to the group. Individuals who have a high degree of desire for social acceptance might be more likely to be influenced by others than those who are more independent and do not place as much importance on social acceptance. Similarly, individuals who plan on using items publicly (displaying them) are more likely to be influenced by others so as to decrease the "risk" of choosing the "wrong" brand or product. Individuals are less swayed by group influences when purchasing necessity items to be used in private or items not requiring much thought or pre-purchase search. Yet normative influence can extend across many situations.[14]

Profits of Conformity   Conformity is most likely to occur when the rewards of compliance exceed its costs, concluded sociologist George Homans, who shed light on the dynamics of normative compliance and the relationship between its rewards and costs.[15] Rewards, such as self-esteem or approval, can reinforce behavior and encourage repetition, whereas costs can discourage certain behaviors. The degree of influence on final outcome is determined by an individual's perception of the "profit" inherent in the interaction (i.e., rewards minus costs). For example, if someone is asked to join another person for a cup of coffee, there will be rewards (companionship, coffee, esteem stemming from the invitation), but there may also be costs (lost time, perhaps missed opportunity to go with someone else). A marketing manager or salesperson may willingly assist dissatisfied customers even when they are verbally abusive because his or her future advancement is based on high customer retention.

Conspicuousness   Several studies over the years have demonstrated that conformity pressures are not sufficient to induce behavior unless the product or service is publicly conspicuous in its purchase and use.[16] Furthermore, luxuries are more susceptible to social influence than necessities.[17] Conspicuousness affects conformity in two primary ways. First, since the product will be seen by others, including group members, the desire to be accepted by the group causes many consumers to conform rather than risk public ridicule or embarrassment. Second, individuals (e.g., fashion-conscious consumers) receive clear signals from their peers about product alternatives, which make further information search unnecessary.[18]

Conformity is not a fixed product characteristic—it depends on the situation and the ways in which the product is used. For example, normative influence on brand choice is important when beer is to be served to friends but not when it is consumed privately.[19] Figure 13.2 explains how reference groups influence product and brand choice in different situations. In a study conducted by Bearden and Etzel,[20] over 800 respondents were asked to consider 16 products that differed along the private–public and necessity–luxury dimensions. For each product, they rated the extent of reference group influence on product category and brand choice. The study can be used to classify which types of product and brand choices are likely to be influenced more heavily by group influences than others. For example, a wristwatch is worn out of necessity, and it is of little consequence to what others do. But brand choice is quite different, an example being the high social acceptability in some quarters signified by wearing a Swatch or Rolex. As you examine Figure 13.2, you will gain helpful insights into the ways in which social influence becomes expressed.

Appealing to Normative Influence in Marketing Strategy

Marketers have learned the potency of appealing to the "in thing." The Pokemon phenomenon occurred because the target group's high susceptibility to normative influence and the product's high visibility interact to affect the buying action of the target group.

We cannot overlook the fact, however, that normative compliance seems to be declining in its impact in much of the Western world.[21] Various groups of consumers, including baby boomers, are putting personal needs ahead of group loyalty. A main factor in this decline, perhaps, is the worldwide growth of urbanization, which leads to greater social isolation and individualism. Grandparents, uncles, aunts, and other members of the extended family often have less face-to-face influence. Furthermore, urban living arrangements minimize the

Figure 13.2 Reference Group Influence on Product and Brand Purchase Decisions

	PRODUCT	
	Weak Reference Group Influence	**Strong Reference Group Influence**
Strong Reference Group Influences (+)	**Public Necessities** *Influence:* Weak Product and Strong Brand *Examples:* Wristwatch, automobile, suits	**Public Luxuries** *Influence:* Strong Product and Strong Brand *Examples:* Golf clubs, snow skis, sailboat
Weak Reference Group Influences (−)	**Private Necessities** *Influence:* Weak Product and Weak Brand *Examples:* Mattress, floor lamp, refrigerator	**Private Luxuries** *Influence:* Strong Product and Weak Brand *Examples:* TV or computer game, trash compactor, icemaker

(BRAND on left axis)

Source: William O. Bearden and Michael J. Etzel, " Reference Group Influence on Product and Brand Purchase Decisions," Journal of Consumer Research 9 (September 1982), 1985.

Figure 13.3   IBM Ad Appealing to Individuality

social interaction that takes place much more readily when living in rural communities. Finally, television and other mass media open windows to the world and thereby broaden horizons and interests beyond normal social circles. In fact, a case can be made that television and other media represent social reality with such power that the media themselves are becoming a major normative influence on beliefs and behavior.[22]

Another consideration leading to diminished normative compliance is a weakened respect for social norms, referred to by sociologists as *anomie*.[23] Some people feel an ambivalence that causes them to conform grudgingly or, in certain instances, fail to conform. Some marketers appeal to people who want to "be different" and express their individuality rather than be considered just "one of the group." The Chinese ad for IBM in Figure 13.3 speaks effectively to the man who wants to conform to the growing norm of owning a computer but wants to maintain a sense of personal identity.

Celebrities and Other Reference Group Appeals in Advertising

Celebrities, especially movie stars, television actors, entertainers, and sports figures, can be very powerful assets to any marketing and advertising campaign.

They help grab attention, create awareness, and communicate effectively with consumers who admire them or aspire to be like them. Consumers may relate to a common problem they share with the celebrity in the ad, or they may hope to emulate him or her by using the endorsed product. In either case, marketers hope that consumers will relate, in a positive light, the product to the celebrity endorser.

There are four primary ways celebrities can appear in advertisements. They can give *testimonials,* in which they tout the benefits of the product based on their personal usage, or *endorsements,* in which they lend their name or likeness to a product without necessarily being an expert in the area. A celebrity can also be an *actor* in a commercial or a company *spokesperson,* in which he or she represents the brand or company for an extended period. Michael Jordan does endorsements for Nike shoes and Hanes underwear. He lent his name and likeness to Jordan cologne (which features an artist's rendering of him on the bottle). He also serves as a dual actor and spokesperson for MCI in commercials, which feature him and Looney Toons cartoon characters from the hit movie *Space Jam.* After his 1998 presidential campaign, candidate Bob Dole endorsed VISA credit cards, and he began a testimonial campaign in which he promotes the new wonder drug Viagra.

Key to the success of any advertising campaign, even in the case of celebrity advertising, is credibility of the endorser—in this case, the celebrity. Most celebrities lose credibility with audiences when they promote multiple products because it seems they are motivated by financial incentives more than belief in the product. Yet Michael Jordan has maintained favorable reactions from audiences, despite his numerous contracts. Scandals in the personal lives of celebrities can also affect sales of brands that they endorse.

In addition to celebrities, other reference group appeals, including expert appeals and "common-man" appeals, are effective in reaching consumers. An **expert** is *any person who possesses unique information or skills that can help consumers make better purchase decisions than other types of spokespersons.* Doctors who sell pain relievers, service repairpersons who recommend one brand of appliance over another, or professional mountain guides who represent a particular brand of outdoor clothing are examples of expert appeals. In contrast, the **common-man appeal** *features testimonials from "regular" consumers with whom most individuals can relate.* Slice-of-life ads show how consumers use advertised products to solve everyday problems and make it easy for viewers to picture themselves in that specific purchase or usage situation.

Transmission of Influence Through Dyadic Exchanges

Group influences are transmitted to individuals in many ways. People often observe how a group behaves or dresses and emulate what they see. For example, children do this when they watch their older siblings and parents behave and consume products and copy what they see in order to be "older" or more like their parents. Television, movies, and music videos are a significant source for fashion trends, such as the Madonna-look of the 1980s or the short skirts and extreme thinness of TV lawyer Ally McBeal. They may also pick up new words and speech patterns (from TV shows like *Seinfeld*) and copy gestures, motions, or dances (such as the Macarena dance made popular around the world in 1997). Formal groups may communicate through publications such as newsletters and magazines and increasingly through online chat-rooms.

Of all these methods to transmit group influences, the most effective is often a person-to-person exchange. Not only do individuals receive personal communication from someone about behaviors and lifestyles, but they receive feedback on their own behaviors, which may further modify or reinforce behavior. Individuals may *choose to adopt a new behavior, and then decide to continue it or drop it based on the opinions of their peers and other primary reference groups.* These exchanges of resources (in this instance, opinions and comments) between two individuals represent **dyadic exchanges.** Two forms of dyadic exchanges, word-of-mouth communication and the service encounter are the focus of this section of the chapter.

Word-of-Mouth Communication

How often do you base a decision, at least in part, to go to a movie, try a new restaurant, or buy a new brand on what your friends or family have told you about it? When individuals hear about, observe, or experience things, they often tell others. This is **word-of-mouth (WOM) communication**—*the informal transmission of ideas, comments, opinions, and information between two people, neither one of which is a marketer.* For example, it is easy to imagine that, before widespread availability of television, radio, and other formalized means of communication, individuals relied heavily on the advice of their neighbors and families to choose a family physician. But even in today's age of e-commerce, advertising, and television, WOM is still a very powerful behavior and purchase influencer for many categories, including healthcare providers. The Internet, in fact, may be a powerful method of transmitting WOM communications.

In the WOM process, there exists a *sender* and a *receiver,* each of which gains something from the exchange. The **receiver** *gains information about behaviors and choices, which is valuable to the receiver in the decision process.* The receiver also receives feedback about current behaviors, which can be used to determine whether or not to continue them. Of particular value is the ability of WOM to reduce cognitive dissonance (doubts) after a major purchase decision.[24] Similarly, the **sender** *increases its confidence in its personal product or behavior choice by persuading others to do the same.* The sender also receives the psychological benefits of prestige, power, and helpfulness of supplying information and opinions that others accept in their decision process. The WOM process further increases the cohesion of the group by increasing the number of individuals adopting similar lifestyle, purchase, or behavior philosophies and actions. Figure 13.4 summarizes the benefits of WOM for both senders and receivers.

Opinion Leadership

The sender of information and opinions in the WOM process is often referred to as the **opinion leader.** This person, by definition, influences the decision of another person. But opinion leaders also change roles and seek advice from others when they do not have experience with or expertise in a specific area. Personal influence in the form of opinion leadership is most likely to occur when:

- *An individual has limited knowledge of a product or brand.* However, if internal search for information proves to be adequate, word-of-mouth has less impact on decision making.[25]
- *The person lacks ability to evaluate the product or service.*
- *The consumer does not believe or trust advertising and other sources of information.*
- *Other information sources have low credibility with the consumer.*
- *The individual has a high need for social approval.*

Figure 13.4	**Benefits of Word-of-Mouth**	
	HEDONIC BENEFITS	**FUNCTIONAL BENEFITS**
RECEIVER	• decrease *risk* of new behavior • increase confidence of choice • decreased cognitive dissonance • increase likelihood of acceptance by a desired group or individual	• more information about options • more reliable/credible information • less time spent on search • enhanced relationship with another individual
SENDER	• feeling of power and prestige of influencing others' behaviors • enhanced position within a group • decreased doubt about one's own behaviors	• potential reciprocity of exchange • increased attention and status • increase in number of individuals with similar behaviors • increased cohesion within group • satisfaction of verbal expression

- *Strong social ties exist between sender and receiver.*[26]
- *The product is complex.*
- *The product is difficult to test against objective criterion.* Therefore, the experience of others acts as a "vicarious trial."[27]
- *The product is highly visible to others.*

Generally speaking, people will not share their experience with products or services unless the conversation produces some type of gratification. In addition to the benefits and rewards of giving opinions shown in Figure 13.4, opinion leaders have additional reasons to offer opinions. Telling others about a new purchase can be pleasurable and exciting for the opinion leader, making him or her the center of attention during the discussion and often positioning the individual as having some expertise in a particular area. Through WOM, the opinion leader gains attention, shows connoisseurship, suggests status, and asserts superiority.[28] Although these motivations exist, often people just want to help a friend or relative make a better purchase decision, especially if they are very satisfied with a product or service of interest to another person.[29]

Characteristics of Opinion Leaders　Extensive research has been conducted over the years in many countries regarding the characteristics of opinion leaders.[30] Research indicates that opinion leaders and receivers often share similar demographic characteristics and lifestyles (i.e., they are *homophilous*),[31] yet they may have a greater social status within the same group as followers. This seems logical when you consider that individuals with similar characteristics might live in the same neighborhood or belong to the same clubs and have easy access to one another.

In general, researchers conclude that the most common characteristic of opinion leaders across categories is that they are very involved with a particular product category. They tend to read specialized publications about a specific category and actively seek information from mass media and other sources. They also possess greater self-confidence; are more outgoing and gregarious; and want to share information, talk with others, and seek their opinions.[32] Accordingly, their tendency to initiate conversations is directly proportional to the extent of interest or involvement in the topic under consideration.[33]

Similar to opinion leaders are **product innovators**—*individuals who are the first to try new products.* They are more adventurous than opinion leaders and are less concerned about deviating from group norms since they are less likely to be integrated into social groups. As you will see in the next section of this chapter, each of us has some degree of innovativeness and has over the course of our lives adopted some objects or ideas that we perceive as new.[34]

Overlapping Opinion Leadership   An individual may be classified as an opinion leader in one area, but not in another. For example, you may seek advice from a parent on which financial institution to establish checking and savings accounts, while your best friend might give better advice on fashion and clothing purchases. Individuals are deemed opinion leaders based on their perceived knowledge (or expertise) of a product category (or subject), and the greater the perceived expertise, the more likely that person's opinions are to influence decisions.[35] This influence may spill over to other related areas,[36] which is termed *opinion leadership overlap.* An electronics salesperson, for example, might sell stereo equipment, but might also be considered by some an opinion leader for televisions, speakers, VCRs, and DVDs, all of which are product categories that involve similar interests.

A recently identified source of personal influence possesses a large amount of information about a *variety* of products, categories, retail concepts, and markets. **Market mavens**[37] *gather much of their information from shopping experiences, openness to information* (including direct mail and the Internet), *and general market awareness, making them more aware of new products than other people.* Like opinion leaders, they have high levels of brand awareness and like to share their information with others. However, their knowledge base includes information on a vast variety of products (not just high-involvement items), allowing them to disseminate information on low- and medium-involvement items, such as shampoo and deodorant.[38]

Another new source of personal influence in the marketplace is the **surrogate consumer (or surrogate shopper)**—*an individual who acts as an agent to guide, direct, and/or conduct activities in the marketplace.*[39] Although expertise does lie in specific product and related categories, it also crosses over to various activities involving these related categories. For example, a new homeowner may hire an interior designer to source furniture and fixtures from Italy, coordinate wallpaper and paint from the United States with rugs and fabrics from Hong Kong, order all products, and deliver them when they arrive at their final destination. Surrogate consumers, such as car buyers or financial advisors, add an additional layer in the distribution process of high-involvement products, but they often increase the efficiency of the decision process by assuming some of the search, evaluation, and purchase activities. Firms that sell a large volume of product to surrogate consumers have to design and maintain relationships with them, which may differ from programs that foster relationships with consumers.[40]

Service Encounters

Consumers encounter marketers and salespeople every day, whether they visit a doctor, purchase a car, return a dress to a store, or take a camera in for repairs. Whenever there is *personal communication between a consumer and a marketer,* a **service encounter** occurs. A service encounter can be a consumption experience with a store and the various transactions and services that occur during a purchase or an experience with the specific service a consumer purchases.

During a service encounter, the buyer and the seller assume specific roles,[41] as if they had studied and are acting out parts in a play, with the store acting as the stage.[42] Deviation from expected roles can result in dissatisfaction with the purchase or service encounter, depending on when the interaction between the two parties occurs. Since this is a form of dyadic exchange, both parties gain something from the exchange and can therefore become dissatisfied with the process if expectations are not met.[43] For example, if an employee at the service counter is rude or underestimates how long a repair will take, the consumer is unhappy with the exchange. And if the consumer does not bring proper method of payment or yells at the employee for something out of his or her control, the employee becomes dissatisfied with the process.

One challenge for service providers is understanding the needs of different customers and matching the appropriate sales associate or sales approach to a particular type of customer. Some customers might desire a great deal of assistance with product evaluations and choice, whereas others prefer to have little interaction with the salesperson. Firms such as Wal*Mart, Home Depot, and Target are well known for training employees to be friendly and greet store guests, but they still may wait for a customer to ask for assistance or information. Since some departments within these mega-retailers contain low-involvement products while others sell high-involvement items, it can be expected that more assistance from outgoing associates will be required in departments selling high-involvement products. Smaller, specialty firms, such as Bath & Body Works, or apparel stores, such as Bloomingdale's, Nordstrom, and Canada's famed Harry Rosen, teach their employees to ask customers if they need assistance. They are trained to take cues from customers and assume an active role in product coordination and choice, if that is what the customer desires. However, some exclusive boutiques, such as Chanel or Escada, keep a respectable distance from their customers, who might include celebrities that want to be "left alone." Yet, these sales associates can quickly alter their strategies and become very involved in the service encounter depending on the cues they get from the customer.

The salesperson plays an important role in fostering a relationship between buyer and seller—which can include the retailer and the brand that is being sold. The extent of the relationship depends in part on *how* the salesperson communicates with the customer and what is communicated. Good sales associates listen to their customers, evaluate what is said and observed, and determine what products or services will satisfy their needs or desires best.[44] When a consumer develops a close relationship with a salesperson, a friendship may result, which can transform a mere marketing encounter into a social encounter[45] and motivate consumers to maintain relationships with these service providers.[46] For example, consumers are very loyal to their hairstylists—clients and hairstylists share personal information and see each other regularly over time, thereby creating a friendship that fosters loyalty and positive word-of-mouth.[47] Variations in the dyadic abilities of salespeople account for great variations in their effectiveness, especially for automobile, insurance, and other products in which the salesperson is a key component in the firm's marketing strategy.

How Personal Influences Are Transmitted

Several models theorizing how personal influence is transmitted between individuals and from groups to individuals have been developed. **Trickle-down,** the oldest theory, *alleges that lower classes often emulate the behavior of their higher-class*

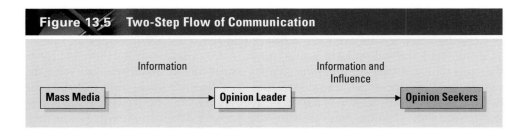

Figure 13.5   Two-Step Flow of Communication

counterparts.[48] Influence is transmitted vertically through social classes, especially in the area of new fashions and styles, where higher classes express wealth through conspicuous consumption, and lower social classes copy their behavior. But the trickle-down theory rarely occurs today because new fashions are disseminated overnight through mass media and quickly copied on a mass scale. And in reality, there is little direct, personal contact between social classes. It still occurs, however, in some developing economies where access to mass media is restricted or nearly absent. Even here, however, it is rapidly disappearing as media access increases.

Two-step Flow   At one time, it was accepted that advertisers and other commercial persuaders affected the masses through opinion leaders. The **two-step flow of communication** model, shown in Figure 13.5, *indicates that opinion leaders are the direct receivers of information from advertisements and that they interpret and transmit the information to others through WOM.*[49] But rarely does the opinion leader mediate the flow of mass media content as the two-step theory assumes. Current understanding shows that opinion leaders and seekers are both legitimate targets and are both affected by mass media. In fact, mass media can motivate the seeker to approach someone else for advice rather than vice versa.

Multistep Flow   With the recognition that mass media can reach anyone in a population and influence them directly, the **multistep flow of communication** model was developed. It *indicates that information can flow directly to different types of consumers, including opinion leaders, gatekeepers, and opinion seekers or receivers.* Gatekeepers, who neither influence nor are influenced by others, decide whether other group members should receive information or not. For example, a parent may monitor and restrict the television programs or web sites a child can access, thereby acting as a gatekeeper. Figure 13.6 shows how opinion leaders can receive information, pass it on to seekers, and receive feedback, and how information can reach seekers directly.

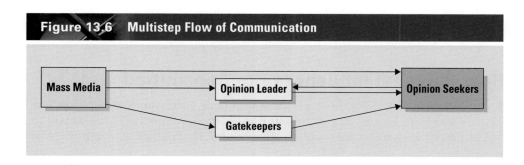

Figure 13.6   Multistep Flow of Communication

WOM and Opinion Leaders in Advertising and Marketing Strategy

How much advertising has Pokemon had to do to sell its cards, toys, and movies to children? Not much was spent on "formal" communication to fuel the rapid spread of Pokemon throughout U.S. and Japanese schoolyards because a majority of the "promotion" was word-of-mouth communication between children. In fact, WOM and personal influence can have a more decisive role in influencing behavior than advertising and other marketer-dominated sources.[50] At the heart of the issues are individuals' views that WOM is a more trustworthy and credible source of information. As a result, a large proportion of consumer buying decisions are influenced by direct (or personal) recommendations from others.[51] Although advertising provides information individuals might get from other sources, they don't always trust that the advertiser has his or her best interest in mind. Often they believe the advertiser will "stretch" the truth (puffing) or exaggerate the benefits of a product to benefit the company.

The Advertising–WOM Relationship

Advertising has a dual relationship with WOM. First, it can provide information to consumers about products and brands that they might seek from other sources (such as peers or families). If a consumer trusts a brand or product and its advertising, an individual's need for and receptiveness to WOM is decreased; however, if an ad or marketer is unfamiliar to a consumer or is not perceived as trustworthy, reliance on WOM increases. Second, advertising can create WOM among consumers and peer groups. Abercrombie & Fitch released a "magalog" (combination magazine and catalog) prior to the 1999 holiday season, which featured partially nude, young models, sometimes in suggestive poses. Because of its suggestiveness, it became a hot topic of conversation among teens and parents alike. When the media caught wind of the controversy, an adult radio station in Michigan phoned the Michigan attorney general's office to report the sale of inappropriate material to children. Within days, the company announced it would not sell the publication to anyone without identification that they were over 18 years of age. WOM created media exposure, which changed company policy. However, the same attention possibly made the publication even more popular and sought after by the target group of young adults.

Abercrombie & Fitch's WOM strategy seems negative at first glance—and may be for older adults who continue to shake their heads in disapproval over the company and its suggestive catalogs. But it has been positive for the teen and young adult markets, which want to separate themselves from the older adult population. In fact, the company doesn't really want traditional adult markets to "like" its styles and clothing—this would "turn off" much of its younger, independent market target.

Primary Reliance on Word-of-Mouth   On some occasions, it is possible to rely on word-of-mouth communication as a substitute for advertising. This was the strategy for Victoria's Secret for many years. It wasn't until the late 1990s that it undertook any formal advertising, which focused primarily on brand and image with its "Angels" campaign. Until then, it relied heavily on WOM among consumers and WOM occurring in dialog between actors in television shows. Admittedly, it is highly unusual to omit advertising and sales efforts entirely, and few would risk this step, but retailers as diverse as Wal*Mart Stores[52] and Victoria's Secret have demonstrated that advertising can be sharply reduced when word-of-mouth is strong.

Targeting Opinion Leaders   Opinion leaders are sensitive to various sources of information, including advertising,[53] and if they can be identified, it is theoretically feasible to market to them as a distinct segment. But this can be a challenge because of the similarity between sender and receiver, even in media exposure patterns. Hence, it may be difficult to mount strategies that reach only this segment, with the exception of when certain types of social or organizational leaders act as opinion leaders, such as coaches, physicians, pharmacists, and religious leaders. In addition to targeting their leadership roles and responsibilities through mass media, firms can target them through specialized media and association memberships with direct mail and publicity in trade or special interest magazines.

Stimulating Word-of-Mouth

There are several ways to stimulate WOM about a new product or service. For example, a company may lend or give opinion leaders a product to display and use. When it opened its U.S. dealerships, Lexus mailed invitations to known community leaders to test-drive a new model of their choice. Even though the number of immediate purchases was not great, individuals told their friends about the experience, created positive WOM, and stored the information for future purchase situations. Companies also give away free products for physicians and dentists to give to patients (e.g., Oral-B brand toothbrushes and dental floss) and for athletes to use when training and competing (e.g., Adidas clothing). In both cases, opinion leaders help foster relationships between sellers and consumers.

Another familiar option is to induce the opinion leader to open his or her home for product presentations. The classic example is the Tupperware party and its contemporary, a Longaberger Basket party. Not-for-profit organizations rely on this method of stimulating WOM to generate interest in fundraising events. They often ask community leaders to host events in their homes, hoping to capture interest and secure participation of potential patrons.

Creating Opinion Leaders

Organizations sometimes hire or d]irectly involve individuals who display characteristics of opinion leaders to influence consumers. The Gap, Banana Republic, and other clothing retailers often hire "popular" and attractive young people to work in their stores. They receive substantial discounts on clothing and are encouraged (sometimes required) to wear them when working, to promote the "in-ness" of the clothing.

Companies can also create opinion leaders by providing incentives for new customers to attract others to the store. They can offer attractive product premiums or even outright financial rebates for additional sales that new customers influence. Magazines sometimes offer customers a chance to submit the names and addresses of friends they think might purchase a subscription. If they do, within a specified time, the customer can receive a reduced rate or a year-long free subscription. E-trade.com gave United frequent flyer miles to individuals for referring friends to the web site.

At times, it also is possible to activate information search and dissemination through advertising that encourages word-of-mouth. An ad might use a phrase, such as "ask a person who owns one," to cause people to seek information from others, and a phrase, such as "tell a friend," to create opinion leaders. In addition to advertising, demonstrations, displays, and product trials can help generate WOM, consumer interest, and information search as well. For example, color television manufacturers sell their sets to hotels and motels at low prices partly because it causes trial usage with consumers. Similarly, automobile manufacturers make deals with rental companies on specific brands of cars, such as the Lincoln Continental featured at Budget Rent-a-Car.

Managing Negative WOM

"I would never buy a car from that dealer again. The salesperson was eager to sell me the car, but then he all but ignored me. He did a terrible job of helping me with my financial arrangements and never called to follow up on the sale. I've had some problems with the car, and it took the service department four days to tell me what was wrong with it. The people aren't friendly, and the service is terrible. . . . I'll never go back there." If your best friend were to relay these opinions to you, how likely would you be to buy a car from this dealer?

Just as positive word-of-mouth can be one of the marketer's greatest assets, the opposite can be true when the content is negative. More than a third of all word-of-mouth information is negative—which is usually given high priority and weighs heavily in decision making.[54] This occurs because marketer-dominated communication is uniformly positive, thus alerting the potential buyer to anything that provides a different perspective. Moreover, the dissatisfied buyer is more motivated to share information.[55]

Monitoring the Content of Word-of-Mouth   Although personal influence cannot be directly controlled by a business firm, its presence and impact can be monitored. For example, Coca-Cola examined the communication patterns of people who had complained to the company.[56] It found that more than 12 percent told 20 or more people about the response they had received from the company. Of those who were completely satisfied with the response, they told four to five others about their positive experience, whereas those who thought they were not treated adequately, told nine to ten people about their experience. Nearly one-third of those who thought their complaints were not dealt with adequately refused to buy any more company products, and another 45 percent reduced their purchases, showing how negative WOM can affect even low-involvement products. Manufacturers of high-involvement products, such as autos, evaluate dealers and customer satisfaction with extensive surveys.

Companies must also monitor *rumors* circulating about their brands and products. Usually not based at all on facts but rather fears and anxieties, rumors can change as they are transmitted from one person to another and take on lives of their own. The greater the degrees of anxiety and uncertainty, the more rapidly a rumor will spread throughout a population. Large and small firms around the world have been victims of rumors, including giants such as Procter & Gamble, Xerox, and McDonald's. During the 1980s, a rumor circulated that fast-food firms used worms in their hamburgers. McDonald's, Burger King, and Wendy's became aware of the rumor, but could not issue a statement that "they do not use worms in their hamburgers" because it would draw attention to the rumor and spread it to individuals who might not have heard it. Instead, Wendy's decided to do a promotional campaign touting the fact that Wendy's uses 100 percent pure beef in its hamburgers. The attention was focused on what the hamburgers contain rather than on what they didn't contain.

Curbing Negative Word-of-Mouth   Imagine you have just started your car and suddenly it surges, out of control, forward or backward. This is exactly what happened with the 1986 Audi 5000S, according to more than 500 complaints made to the National Highway Traffic Safety Administration. Audi management initially refused to acknowledge any culpability for this problem, even after a *60 Minutes* television exposition that activated public outrage. It took a drastic drop in sales to induce acknowledgment of a problem, product recall, and remedial repair.[57] It later turned out that Audi management was vindicated in their claims of innocence, but the company never fully recovered from this unfortunate attitude of insensitivity to its consumers.

What can be done in an instance like this? Certainly, stonewalling (denying the problem) is not the answer. The best strategy usually is an immediate acknowledgment of a problem by a credible company spokesperson. It is important to recognize that negative word-of-mouth rarely goes away by itself. If matters are not dealt with promptly, the financial results could be immediate and catastrophic.

Diffusion of Innovations

Just as influence diffuses between people, so do products and innovations diffuse through the marketplace. Marketers bombard consumers with thousands of new products each year. Compound that with new shopping outlet concepts, new product positioning, and new variations of existing products, and it is a wonder that consumers are able to make buying and consumption decisions at all. Some new products succeed, adopted by enough customers to achieve profitability, but most new products fail, often because the product satisfies needs or desires no better than existing products. The remainder of this chapter focuses on how products diffuse through the marketplace, why some are rejected and others are accepted, and the role of consumer insight.

Innovations and New Products

An **innovation** can be defined in a variety of ways, but the most commonly accepted definition is *any idea or product perceived by the potential adopter to be new.* It follows then that a **product innovation** or **new product** is *any product recently introduced to the market or perceived to be new when compared to existing products.* An organization may define a new product by the percentage of potential market that has adopted the product or the amount of time in the market, but consumers use *subjective* definitions of innovation, derived from the thought structure of a particular individual or entity.

Innovations can also be defined *objectively*, based on criteria external to the adopter. According to this definition, innovations are *ideas, behaviors, or things that are qualitatively different from existing forms.* But what constitutes a *qualitative difference* is not concrete. Marketers use the word *new* on packaging and in advertising to call attention to products recently introduced to the marketplace, but the Federal Trade Commission limits the use of the word *new* in advertising to products available in the marketplace for less than six months. Certainly, TV was qualitatively different from existing communication forms available at the time of its introduction to the market, but is Liquid Tide a new product compared with the existing form of Tide?

Innovation affects firms in many ways, including increased profits and enhanced shareholder value (ESV). But innovation is not limited to new products. Innovative ideas, innovative people, and innovative processes exist in thriving organizations throughout the world. Research indicates that winning firms generate "idea power" that provides the competitive advantage, not only in new products but also in new ideas in every area: better packaging, more efficient invoicing techniques, new planning systems, and lower-cost manufacturing.[58]

As significant as the effects on organizations, new products affect consumers' lives in many ways as well. Introducing new products may attempt to change consumers' behaviors beyond simply switching from one brand to another—it can change the way they live. Sometimes the changes have profound effects (both positive and negative) on the people who buy the new product. Though surgical breast implants have allowed cancer patients to regain positive self-image, they have jeopardized the lives of other patients whose implants ruptured and allegedly leaked into other areas of the body. Sometimes the changes have profoundly negative effects on the people who do not adopt them, as may be true for those who fail to adopt personal computers or vaccines. Perhaps more significant than any of these effects, the introduction of a new product can change how society is organized—as was the case with electricity and computers, and as is the case for cellular phones in Bangladesh, as described in Consumer in Focus 13.1.

Types of Innovations

One system of classifying innovations is based on the impact of the innovation on behavior in the social structure, which classifies innovations as continuous, dynamically continuous, and discontinuous.[59] They are presented in the order of least to most disruptive to existing behavior patterns.

A **continuous innovation** is the *modification of the taste, appearance, performance, or reliability of an existing product rather than the establishment of a totally new one.* Most new products fall into this category. Examples include adding baking soda or fluoride to Colgate toothpaste, the latest version of Microsoft's Powerpoint

Consumer in Focus 13.1

Diffusion of Cell Phones Changes Lives

From a small corrugated-metal and straw hut, in Bangladesh, Delora Begum, a 32-year-old entrepreneur and mother of two, reigns as her small village's "phone-lady" and connector to vast opportunities. In order to start her phone service, she secured a loan for 18,750 taka ($375) from Bangladesh's Grameen Bank and bought a Nokia cell phone. Known for its assistance to rural entrepreneurs, the bank is betting that connecting the country's 68,000 villages to each other and to the rest of the world will help its 120 million people jump into the digital age.

Although telephones have diffused throughout much of the world, they are just beginning to enter this country, in which only 3 in 1,000 people have a phone. With approximately 2,000 villages connected by the end of 1999, the goal is to spread the network nationwide within five years, putting every villager within two kilometers of a cell phone.

To date, the presence of phones has begun to boost personal income and quality of life. In addition to assisting in medical and emergency rescues, the phones have brought needed efficiency to local business. Store owners can *call in* orders for supplies rather than spend hours traveling to villages to place orders in person; farmers can learn fair market prices for their crops, cutting out middlemen who often exploit them; and craftsmen can price wood and supplies to ensure they are building enough margins into the prices they charge for their goods.

As for Mrs. Begum, "sales" of cell phone time are doing well. On average, she makes a $40 per month profit on the $215 worth of calling time she sells to villagers at the rate of 10 cents per minute. Her high income, which is twice the average gross monthly income, allows her to provide for her family, make payments on the phone Grameen sold to her at cost, and make deposits in her Grameen savings account. Life in Bangladesh is looking up for Mrs. Begum.

Source: Miriam Jordan, "It Takes a Cell Phone," The Wall Street Journal (June 25, 1999), B1.

software, reduced-calorie Amstel beer, or the new color versions of i-Mac computers and Gillette razors (as seen in Figure 13.7). A firm might also consider a product-line extension as a continuous innovation, as is the case with Gillette's addition of women's shaving cream.

A **dynamically continuous innovation** may involve *either the creation of a new product or a significant alteration of an existing one, but does not generally alter established purchase or usage patterns.* Examples include electric toothbrushes, compact disc players, organic foods, 3M's Post-it Notes, and recyclable food containers. General Electric and Bosch Siemens will introduce to the marketplace a new type of oven that cooks faster than a microwave and crisps and browns like a convection oven. Speed Cookers are expected to cost anywhere from $1,500 to over $5,000.[60]

A **discontinuous innovation** involves *the introduction of an entirely new product that significantly alters consumers' behavior patterns and lifestyles.* Examples include television, computers, cars, videocassette recorders, and the Internet. Some of the emerging forms of interactive media may prove to be discontinuous if they fundamentally change shopping behavior, transferring it from stores to homes.

Although these innovations are all product based, innovations might also be *usage based.* For many years, consumers bought Swanson's chicken broth to use as stock in soups and gravies. In order to increase sales, the company introduced an ad campaign showing consumers how to use Swanson broth, instead of oils

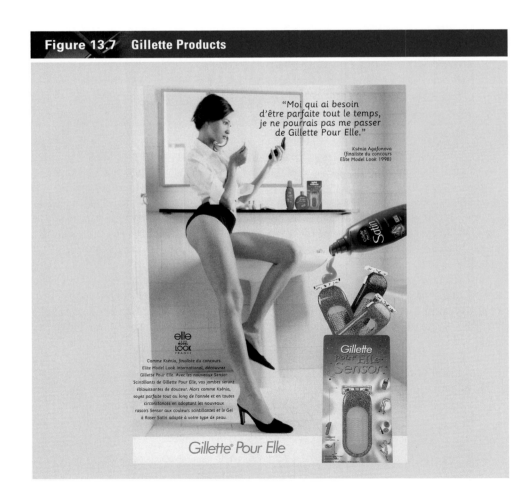

Figure 13.7   Gillette Products

and fats, in low-fat cooking. Individuals sometimes take the lead in this area and invent their own uses for existing products, as has been the case with duct tape, which is used by consumers not only for home repairs, but to tow cars, decorate dorm rooms, and even repair pet ducks!

Why Some Innovations Succeed and Others Don't

Some new products are winners in the marketplace and others are losers. For every success story such as compact discs or Nintendo, there are fizzles such as picture phones, quadraphonic audio systems, and home banking.[61] Successful products are those that become *culturally anchored*—so inextricably a part of a consumer's life and sociocultural surroundings that the person–product interface is an important part of the individual's self-concept.[62] Imagine doing without personal computers, fax machines, or microwave ovens with today's values and lifestyles. But why did these innovations succeed when others failed? Research by Rogers and others[63] indicate five main characteristics associated with successful new products: (1) relative advantage, (2) compatibility, (3) complexity, (4) trialability, and (5) observability.

Relative Advantage

The most important factor to examine when evaluating the potential success of a new product is its relative advantage—the degree to which consumers may *perceive* it to offer substantially greater benefits than the product they currently use. Analysts may ask to what degree the new product will be a substitute for existing ones or be complementary with the array of products already in consumers' inventories.

New products most likely to succeed are those that appeal to strongly felt consumer needs. In banking, automatic teller machines (ATMs), which gave consumers access to cash 24 hours per day, diffused through the social system quickly because of their high, perceived relative advantage over traditional banking. In contrast, debit cards, which act as cash or checks during the purchase process, have been slow to diffuse. Although they help consumers with credit problems manage their finances better and offer advantages to banks and retailers (such as decreased costs associated with handling cash), many consumers perceive little relative advantage of debit cards over checks or credit cards.

Compatibility

Compatibility refers to the degree to which a new product is consistent with an individual's existing practices, values, needs, and past experiences of the potential adopters. Many computer software and hardware product decisions are based on compatibility of the new product with an individual's existing system. The introduction of Mentadent's peroxide-based whitening toothpaste was well received by U.S. consumers looking for a way to brighten their teeth. The new toothpaste did not require any new equipment or new learning and was consistent with the norms that value white teeth. DVD, although quite different from videotapes in form, are very compatible in usage for consumers who already use a computer CD drive.

Similarly, Radio Shack was successful in introducing personal computers to America because of its existing distribution system of thousands of stores. Customers whose normal behavior favored technologically innovative products were already in the stores buying products. Computers, though technically different in function from the products Radio Shack once focused on, were related to consumers' product interests. The combination of distribution, personal service, and related product interests was compatible with the existing values and experiences of early adopters of computers.

Complexity

Complexity is the degree to which an innovation is perceived as difficult to understand and use. The more complex the new product, the more difficult it will be to gain acceptance. Microwave ovens diffused rapidly because they are easy to use. The complexity principle makes it advantageous to build products that are as simple as possible to use and understand, especially during initial introduction so that consumers can understand them. Instructions play an important role as well—the more complex the use or assembly instructions, the less likely the product will succeed. Complexity is a significant deterrent of trying new technology, including using computers and buying over the Internet.

Trialability

New products are more apt to succeed when consumers can experiment with or try the idea on a limited basis, with limited financial risk. For example, Procter & Gamble and General Foods give millions of new products away each year to make trial easy without economic risk to the consumer. Sampling, couponing, and trial-sized products all induce the trial of new soaps, foods, and perfumes (and other low-unit-value, consumer-packaged goods). But these methods also work for expensive, complex, high-involvement discontinuous innovations, even though a bit more creativity is required.

Leasing is a strategy widely used by auto manufacturers to introduce consumers to new car models. Auto manufacturers will sometimes make special offers to rental car companies on redesigned models or cars equipped with innovative features to give consumers an opportunity to try the new product or new feature. To the extreme, AOL mails free software to consumers that, when installed, gives them 250 hours of free Internet access.

Observability

Observability (and communicability) reflects the degree to which results from using a new product are visible to friends and neighbors. If consumers can see others benefiting from the use of a new product, it is more likely to be successful and diffuse faster. For instance, a young adult might see the social acceptance and compliments a peer receives when wearing a particular fashion, clothing brand, hairstyle, or fragrance, and choose to buy the product as well in order to receive the same benefit. The use of celebrities often enhances the visibility of products.

These five characteristics can be used to rate the likelihood of adoption in the marketplace. Innovations that rate high in multiple areas are more likely to diffuse through the desired market target than those that rate low. They can also be used to analyze competitive products, as seen in Consumer in Focus 13.2, which compares AOL and CompuServe on these variables. For further competitive analysis, you might want to review the product life cycle and examine the advantages and disadvantages of introducing a new product in the various stages.[64]

Consumer in Focus 13.2

AOL Versus CompuServe: How Consumers Evaluate Competitive Innovations

In the late 1970s, CompuServe began offering information on-line to technology- and information-based professionals. Scoring high on content and quality of service, CompuServe became a leader in its industry among technology-oriented individuals even though it was anything but user-friendly. America Online joined the cyber-race more than a decade later, but positioned its user-friendly service as a communication-based tool for the mass market. Although Compu-Serve expected its users to "figure out" how to navigate and use its products and services best, AOL made the technology easy for the mass market to use in everyday life. In head-to-head competition in the marketplace, which firm do you think fared best? This chart examines how consumers probably compared the two firms and what lead a majority of them to choose AOL.

Market Acceptance: Specialty vs. Mass Market

	Technology	Relative Advantage	Compatability	Complexity	Trialability	Observability
Compu-Serve (specialty)	A + for tech-oriented market— Others should just figure it out	Concise, extensive data access	Specialty: technology fit savvy market well and databases fit users	Difficult to use, even for tech-oriented consumers	Low	Limited to tech. areas and specialty markets
AOL (mass)	*Copy* Make technology easy for mass market to use in everyday life	Cheaper and time flexible way to communicate	Mass technology easy for those with existing computer	Easy to use for all consumers	High— free samples to mass market	Vast— consumers observe others through chat-rooms and through brand

The Diffusion Process

The most important contribution to the study of diffusion of innovations was a book of the same name, written by Everett Rogers in 1962, which has been continuously updated.[65] According to Rogers, **diffusion** is defined as the *process by which an innovation (new idea) is communicated through certain channels over time among the members of a social system.* Under this definition, a product might be around for a long time but still be perceived as new in a given market. Rogers's research identifies product characteristics and other variables that influence the diffusion process and explains how consumers individually adopt new products and innovations.

The diffusion of an innovation includes many stages, as seen in Figure 13.8:

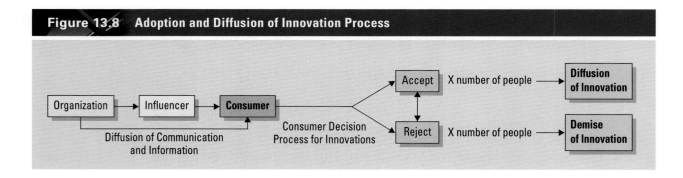

Figure 13.8   Adoption and Diffusion of Innovation Process

- Diffusion of information and communication—involves the communication between a consumer and an organization, a marketer, or a group or personal influencer

- Consumer decision process for an innovation—the process by which an individual consumer decides to adopt or reject an innovation

- Diffusion of innovation or demise of innovation—the cumulative effect of how many consumers either adopt or reject an innovation over time, leading to its diffusion or demise in the marketplace.

The model includes the diffusion process, which is societal in nature, and the adoption process, which is individual in nature, and shows their roles in the overall diffusion of innovation process.

The diffusion process is influenced by many factors, many of which have been identified in thousands of diffusion studies. From these studies, the primary success factors in the diffusion of innovations are:

- Innovation (new product, service, or idea, as discussed previously)
- Communication (through formal and informal channels)
- Time (for individuals' adoption decisions and rate)
- Social system (interrelated people, groups, or other systems)

Communication

Communication is critical in the diffusion process. How consumers learn about new products, either through consumer-marketer communication or consumer-consumer communication, influences the rate at which new products are identified and tried by consumers. As discussed earlier in this chapter, WOM plays an important role in product trial and diffusion.

In addition to interpersonal communication, marketers must also address the influence of advertising, Internet presence, salespersons, and opinion leaders in new product marketing strategy. Only when consumers become aware of a new product can trial be encouraged and the diffusion process initiated. Advertising can accelerate the diffusion process.[66] Optimal effects on profitability occur when a firm advertises heavily when the product is introduced and reduces advertising as the product moves through its life cycle and interpersonal communications take effect.

Time

Another factor influencing the diffusion process is time. How long it takes for an individual to move from product awareness to product purchase or rejection indicates how long it will take for a product to diffuse through the market. In this instance, time is dependent upon external factors (availability of product and economic resources) and internal factors (personality and adopter category). Some consumers will quickly decide a new product is not what they want, perhaps because of brand loyalty and satisfaction with current products. Other consumers may want a product but may not buy it for a variety of reasons.[67] Understanding the temporal process of adoption is very important. Otherwise, a firm might introduce a product, advertise it heavily, and commit large amounts of resources to the project only to see it "fail." In actuality, the firm may have underestimated the time required for the new product to diffuse through the market.

Social System

The social systems to which individuals belong often affect the adoption or rejection of a particular innovation. Marketers may refer to these systems as market segments or target markets, which they can describe in terms of innovativeness and openness to new products or ideas. The rate of diffusion varies between individuals and between societies based on cultural values, and the degree to which a society is futuristic, normal, or tradition oriented, timing and expectations of the diffusion can be modified for each market.[68] Although modern or contemporary social systems are more likely to try and accept new products, traditional societies are not.

As with any targeted marketing plan, communicating to consumers based on the characteristics and orientation of their social system is important in the adoption process. For example, the fitness craze that swept through the United States in the late 1990s created a climate ripe with opportunity for exercise equipment, health drinks, and exercise videotapes. Many aging baby boomers belong to this body-conscious segment, which was very willing to buy new products that promised better bodies and a younger appearance.

Speed of Diffusion

Although WOM is very important to the innovation diffusion process, marketers have little control over this variable. However, marketers have more control over some factors, such as product characteristics, pricing, and resource allocations, which contribute to the speed of diffusion. These and other variables that affect the speed of diffusion are represented in the following propositions.[69]

The greater the *competitive intensity* of the supplier, the more rapid the diffusion and the higher the diffusion level. Highly competitive firms have more aggressive pricing strategies and allocate greater resources to the product introduction. Intense competition frequently leads to price wars and an increase in demand due to the more price-sensitive customers entering the market. And the more innovative a new product is, the more likely a competitive firm is to retaliate with additional product-based innovations.[70]

The better the *reputation of the supplier* (breeding confidence among potential adopters), the faster the initial diffusion will be. A good reputation leads to source credibility, which in turn may reduce uncertainty and risk in the purchase decision.

Products diffuse more rapidly when *standardized technology* is used. Consumers may believe a purchase to be more risky if they are unsure which technology will become standard—perhaps this is why it takes from 5 to 15 years before new electronic technologies catch on among consumers.[71] When this risk is reduced or avoided, more consumers are likely to adopt the product.

Vertical coordination, a *high degree of dependence and interlocking relationships among channel members,* also increases the rate of diffusion. As coordination increases, the information flow from supplier to consumer increases and so, therefore, does diffusion.

Resource commitments, such as greater research and development expenditures, are positively related to innovations. As technologies become enhanced and more alternatives become available, diffusion becomes broader and more rapid. And as advertising, personal selling, sales promotion activities, and distribution support increases, diffusion also increases. Marketing research allocations can help guide R&D expenditures as well as develop a positioning strategy for the new technology, both of which are instrumental in the diffusion process. Some research shows that an increasing rate of adoption of innovations has resulted in a rapidly shortened product life cycle,[72] which translates into less time for management to approve moving to the next phase of product introduction.[73]

Consumer Decision Process for Innovations

Adoption of a new product is the result of a decision process, in many ways similar to the general decision process described throughout this book. But what makes the consumer decision process for new products different from that for other products? The main distinction lies in the emphasis on communications within the social structure rather than individual information processing. Examining diffusion variables represents a *relational approach,* which analyzes communication networks and how social-structural variables affect diffusion flows in the system, in contrast to a *monodic approach,* which focuses on the personal and social characteristics of individual consumers.

The most widely adopted model for understanding the adoption process of innovations is that of Everett Rogers, which includes knowledge, persuasion, decision, implementation, and confirmation, as seen in Figure 13.9. As you examine this model, keep in mind that not only does an individual consumer move through the stages of adopting or rejecting a new product, but other consumers also move through the process, the combined effects of which determine ultimate diffusion or demise.

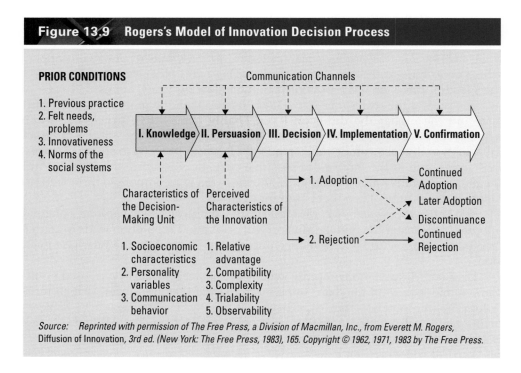

Figure 13.9   Rogers's Model of Innovation Decision Process

Source: Reprinted with permission of The Free Press, a Division of Macmillan, Inc., from Everett M. Rogers, Diffusion of Innovation, 3rd ed. (New York: The Free Press, 1983), 165. Copyright © 1962, 1971, 1983 by The Free Press.

Knowledge

The knowledge stage begins when a consumer receives physical or social stimuli that give exposure and attention to the new product and how it works. Knowledge of the new product is more likely to occur through media than in later stages, but can be influenced by opinion leaders as well. How a person receives and interprets the knowledge is affected by his or her personal characteristics.

Persuasion

Persuasion, in the Rogers paradigm, refers to the formation of favorable or unfavorable attitudes toward the innovation. If it is a new brand, consumers may attach attributes of the product category to it to persuade their evaluation.[74] The consumer may imagine how satisfactory the new product might be in some anticipated future-use situation, perhaps giving the product a "vicarious trial" in the consumer's mind.

Persuasiveness is related to perceived risks and consequences of adopting and using the new product. When an individual considers a new product, he or she must weigh the potential gains from adoption against the potential losses of switching from the product now used. If the new product is adopted, it may be inferior to a present product or cost more than the increased value gained by using the new product.

Decision

The decision stage involves a choice between adopting and rejecting the innovation. Some members of the social system are **adopters**—*people who have made a decision to use a new product*—whereas others are **nonadopters**—*people whose decision not to adopt may occur for many reasons.* Adoption involves both psychological and behavioral commitment to a product over time.[75] Ordinarily, this means *continued use of the product* unless situational variables (lack of availability, and so on) prevent usage. Consumers might also reject the innovation, and thus decide not to adopt. Active rejection involves the consideration of adoption, or perhaps even a trial, but a final decision not to adopt. Passive rejection consists of never really considering use of the innovation. Some will not be exposed to information about the product or will wait until other people have tried the product before doing so themselves.

Implementation

Implementation occurs when the consumer puts an innovation to use. Until the implementation stage, the process has been a mental exercise, but now behavioral change is required. The strength of the marketing plan may be the critical determinant in whether a good product that has been communicated effectively results in a sale.

Price, new product information, advertising, and communication play important roles in determining a sale. Post-it Notes is an example of a simple, new product consisting of notepaper with an adhesive strip on the back. The product, introduced by 3M, has diffused throughout the world as a replacement for paper clips, notepads, and loose pieces of paper. 3M gave away significant amounts of samples that office workers took to work and home. Family members began using them for many purposes, creating rapid diffusion of the product in the consumer as well as the business market.

Confirmation

During confirmation, consumers seek reinforcement for their innovation decision. Consumers sometimes reverse previous decisions, especially when exposed to conflicting messages about the innovation, causing dissonance. Those who adopt products can reject them after short or long periods, and vice versa. Discontinuance is a serious concern to marketers. Pringles, a potato snack similar to potato chips, was introduced by Procter & Gamble and was successful in attracting many adopters. The product eventually failed in its original form, however, because the degree of discontinuance was so high, a fact that went undetected until after the firm had invested millions of dollars in marketing and building additional manufacturing plants. Recently, Pringles gained new acceptance in the marketplace, with a "new, better-tasting" product and upbeat marketing campaign appealing to younger consumers. Similarly, many early purchasers of digital cameras found them so time consuming to use that they returned to analog (film) cameras, except for special uses in which the digital camera had advantages over film.

Consumers Most Likely to Buy New Products

In the development process, marketers need to determine who is most likely to buy the new product. Determinants include individuals' personalities, their aversion to or acceptance of risk, social status, and education level. In addition to individual characteristics, the role within the family also affects adoption behavior. Research studies indicate that there are times and situations in which wives' needs may be the driving factor behind much of the innovative behavior decision making that occurs in the family[76] for several product categories. These characteristics, combined with "degree of innovativeness," cause different adopter classifications to behave differently during the various decision process stages[77] and for new products and new brands.[78]

Consumers can be classified according to the time it takes for them to adopt a new product relative to other consumers. Figure 13.10 depicts the five major categories of consumers based on their adoption cycle time in relation to other adopters in their social system or market segment. **Innovators** are *the first consumer group to adopt products.* They tend to be venturesome, enjoy some risk, have an above-average education, and socialize with other innovators—sometimes being "experts" in the product category of the innovation. Innovators are less likely to seek solutions within the context of previous solutions to a problem.[79] Innovators often are the main market target for firms introducing new products since they influence additional potential adopters.[80] People may be innovators for some products but not for others. Consumers who are *innovators for many products* are said to be **polymorphic,** whereas those who are *innovators for only one product* are **monomorphic.**

Additional classifications of adopters are early adopters, early and late majority, and laggards. **Early adopters** tend to be *opinion leaders and role models for others, with good social skills and respect within larger social systems.* Some research indicates that early adopters use both mass media and interpersonal sources more than later adopters.[81] **Early majority** consists of *consumers who deliberate extensively before buying new products, yet adopt them just before the average time it takes the target population as a whole.* **Late majority** tends to be *cautious when evaluating innovations, taking more time than average to adopt them, and often at the pressure of peers.* **Laggards,** the last group to adopt innovations, tend to be *anchored in the past, are suspicious of the new, and exhibit the lowest level of innovativeness among adopters.* Some consumers may actively reject the new product from the very beginning. Rather than laggards, they might best be described as early rejectors. For that

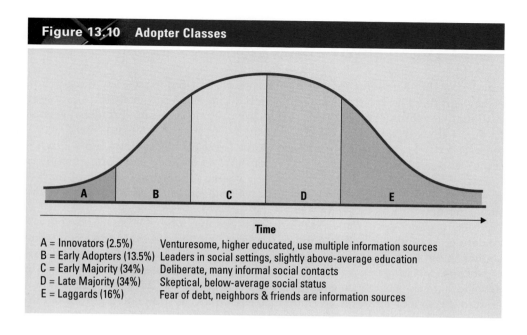

Figure 13.10   Adopter Classes

Time

A = Innovators (2.5%)   Venturesome, higher educated, use multiple information sources
B = Early Adopters (13.5%) Leaders in social settings, slightly above-average education
C = Early Majority (34%)   Deliberate, many informal social contacts
D = Late Majority (34%)   Skeptical, below-average social status
E = Laggards (16%)   Fear of debt, neighbors & friends are information sources

reason and others, adoption may be less than the 100 percent shown in Figure 13.10.

After some innovators have adopted a new product, others may follow, depending on the value of the innovation and other characteristics of the product. In fact, the rate of adoption increases as the number of adopters increases[82] causing the bell curve in Figure 13.10 to be taller and thinner. It is clear from this analysis that marketers must focus their attention on innovators and early adopters—if marketers do not succeed in winning adoption of the new product by these people, there is not much hope for the rest of the population.

Innovativeness is another benchmark to measure likelihood to adopt an innovation. **Innovativeness** is the *degree to which an individual adopts an innovation earlier than other members of a social system.* Degree of innovation can be measured based on time of adoption or based on how many prespecified new products an individual has purchased by a specific point in time. Innovators and early adopters have higher degrees of innovativeness than do late majority and laggards, which affects their brand loyalty, decision making, preference, and communication. Without characteristics such as innovativeness, consumer behavior would consist of a series of routine buying responses to a static set of products.

Innovators can be segmented into cognitive innovators and sensory innovators. **Cognitive innovators** *have a strong preference for new mental experiences,* whereas **sensory innovators** *have a strong preference for new sensory experiences.*[83] Some innovators prefer both. Advertising and other communication messages can be targeted accordingly. Communication aimed at cognitive innovators should emphasize the advantages of the innovation over other existing products and services. Communication targeted to sensory innovators should emphasize the uniqueness of the product and reduce its complexity, performance, and economic risks with long warranties, manufacturer-supported service centers, toll-free lines, and easy-to-read-and-understand instructions. Understanding the differences between these types of innovators allows marketers to select the media and tailor the messages to fit the attributes of the segment.[84]

Managerial Perspectives on Adoption and Diffusion of Innovation

Senior executives around the world understand that the successful introduction of new products is critical to their profitability and long-term financial success. Although development groups are producing primarily line and brand extensions or slight improvements to existing products, management teams need *breakthroughs* to fuel growth and profits. For some firms, these breakthroughs will not come because of their short-term focus on how to increase sales and customers today.[85] For others with long-term strategic vision, a poor track record of market acceptance is leaving even the best CEOs scratching their heads, wondering how to bolster new product development.

New product development requires the coordination between marketing, engineering, research, and other parts of the firm[86] along with extensive knowledge about the *end user*. This type of market knowledge is a strategic asset[87] and a core organizational competence.[88] As mentioned in Chapter 2, *consumer insight* is key to developing products that consumers are likely to adopt and decreasing the amount of time and money spent on failed new product trials, as shown in Figure 13.11. Intuition and information about a consumer need leads to the formation of an insight, which is analyzed through research of end users. For example, Figure 13.12 shows how Kodak has positioned a new technology based on the consumer insight that people want to turn special moments into memories. After interpretation of the research, the insight is either dismissed or confirmed—beginning product design and development.[89] Involving customers in the design process can lead to designs that customers find more appealing.[90] Implications of the insight and information about the diffusion and adoption processes are analyzed for existing products and potential products, which can lead to concept tests, depending on management's predictions about market adoption. Concept test results and additional research are again analyzed before resources are committed to full-scale production. Test market data and simulation models (as well as other mathematical models)[91] can help forecast future sales and profitability of new products as well as help marketing managers understand why consumers consider or reject them.[92]

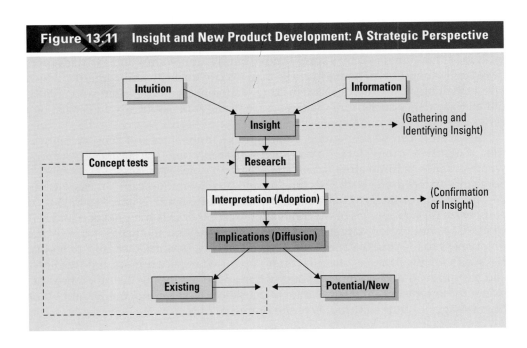

Figure 13.11   Insight and New Product Development: A Strategic Perspective

Figure 13.12 Kodak Positions Based on Insight Rather than Technology

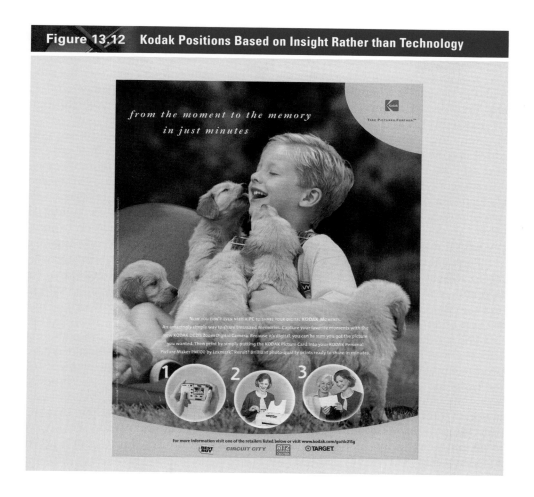

Important to the innovation development process is research. Studies indicate that a lack of research delays managers' decision-making process[93] and causes them to rely on what is already known about how new products are accepted, based on other products and theory. In addition to formal research, marketing managers need grass roots ways of understanding consumer reaction to new products. Silicon Graphics, Inc. turned to heavy graphics users for knowledge and used it in designing a new generation of (now very popular) graphics supercomputers.[94] Sony requires that its managers talk with dealers and consumers constantly to get their reactions to new products from Sony and its competitors, and Campbell Soup Co. insists that managers do their own grocery shopping.[95]

3M has taken the new product development process outside its walls and entered the minds, offices, and lives of its *lead* customers to discover what types of innovations they want to purchase. It has adopted a lead-user strategy, which focuses on collecting information from the leading edges of a company's target market rather than from its center.[96] In other words, they interview innovators rather than early adopters or early majority about either how they have "invented" their own solutions to a problem or how they have adapted existing products to meet their specific requirements. 3M's goal, also, is to target lead users from markets that face similar problems in a more extreme form. Development teams at 3M have found that some lead users had developed product innovations that were ahead of those available in the marketplace. Not only do they gain information and insight into what their customers' needs are, they develop closer relationships with them, which can only aid in the eventual sales process.

Summary

Personal and group influence often play an important role in consumer decision making, especially when there are high levels of involvement and perceived risk, and the product or service has public visibility. This is expressed both through reference groups and through word-of-mouth communication.

Reference groups are any type of social aggregation that can influence attitudes and behavior, including primary (face-to-face) groups, secondary groups, and aspirational groups. The influence occurs in three ways: (1) utilitarian (pressures to conform to group norms in thinking and behavior), (2) value-expressive (reflecting a desire for psychological association and a willingness to accept values of others without pressure), and (3) informational (beliefs and behaviors of others are accepted as evidence about reality). When there is motivation to comply with group norms, it is important to make this a feature in marketing appeals.

Personal influence also is expressed through what has traditionally been referred to as "opinion leadership." What this means is that a credible person, referred to as an "influential," is accepted as a source of information about purchase and use. The greater the credibility of the influential, the greater his or her impact on other people.

The diffusion of innovations deals with how a new product or innovation is adopted in a society. This is important to marketing organizations because new products must be brought out continuously for firms to survive. The elements of the diffusion process include the innovation, the communication of the innovation, time, and the social system. The diffusion process begins with the dissemination of information or communication to individuals, which leads them to make individual decisions about the adoption or rejection of an innovation. Finally, as more and more individuals adopt a new product, it diffuses throughout a given social system.

Everett Rogers, the most influential change agent in the area of diffusion, identified the types of consumers adopting a new product as innovators, early adopters, early majority, late majority, and laggards. If products are to be successful in the marketplace, they must be accepted by innovators and early adopters, and marketers increasingly research these groups for insights and target communication to them.

Review and Discussion Questions

1. For which of the following products would you expect personal and group influence to be a factor in buying decisions: soft drinks, motor oil, designer jeans, eyeliner, house paint, breakfast cereals, wine, carpeting, a dishwasher, and a digital camera? What are your reasons in each case?

2. Regarding each product listed in question 1, do you think there could be a variation between personal influence on product choice and on brand name? Why do you say this?

3. Recall the last time you volunteered information to someone about a brand or product that you purchased. What caused you to share in this way? How does your motivation compare with the motivations mentioned in the text?

4. Your company manufactures a full line of mobile homes in all price ranges. Several studies have indicated that word-of-mouth communication plays a role in the buying decision. Prepare a statement indicating the alternative strategies that can be used to harness and capitalize on this

source of consumer influence. Which strategy do you think would be most effective?

5. Assume that you are a public relations consultant for a state medical society concerned about public attitudes toward malpractice claims. The problem is to counteract a point of view, picked up through word-of-mouth monitoring, that filing a malpractice claim against a doctor is an easy way to pay medical bills or to get something for nothing. What can be done to attack this way of thinking?

6. Explain as precisely as possible the differences between continuous, dynamically continuous, and discontinuous innovations. Give some examples of each, other than those mentioned in the text.

7. What are the main competitive challenges facing firms in which understanding of diffusion of innovations might be helpful?

8. Prepare a short essay that explains how to pick winners from the many candidates for new product introduction.

9. The manufacturer of a new camera is attempting to determine who the innovators for the product might be. How would you describe the target market and influencers of this market? What would the communication strategy be in terms of WOM and advertising? What appeals would you suggest be used in promoting the product?

10. A large manufacturer of drug and personal grooming products wants to introduce a new toothpaste brand in addition to the three already marketed. Evaluate for the firm what information might be used for innovation studies to guide introduction of the product.

Endnotes

1. William O. Bearden and Michael J. Etzel, "Reference Group Influence on Product and Brand Purchase Decisions," *Journal of Consumer Research* 9 (September 1982), 184.

2. C. Whan Park and V. Parker Lewsig, "Students and Housewives: Differences in Susceptibility to Reference Group Influence," *Journal of Consumer Research* 4 (September 1977), 102–110.

3. For information on important studies in this area see: Solomon E. Asch, "Effects of Group Pressure on the Modification and Distortion of Judgments," in H. Guetzkow, ed., *Groups, Leadership, and Men* (Pittsburgh, PA: Carnegie Press, 1951); Lee Ross, Gunter Bierbrauer, and Susan Hoffman, "The Role of Attribution Processes in Conformity and Dissent: Revisiting the Asch Situation," *American Psychologist* (February 1976), 148–157; M. Venkatesan, "Experimental Study of Consumer Behavior Conformity and Independence," *Journal of Marketing Research* 3 (November 1966), 384–387.

4. Robert E. Witt and Grady D. Bruce, "Group Influence and Brand Choice," *Journal of Marketing Research* 9 (November 1972), 440–443.

5. James C. Ward and Peter H. Reingen, "Sociocognitive Analysis of Group Decision Making among Consumers," *Journal of Consumer Research* 17 (December 1990), 245–262.

6. Cara Okleshen and Sanford Grossbart, "Usenet Groups, Virtual Community and Consumer Behavior," in Joseph W. Alba and J. Wesley Hutchinson, eds., *Advances in Consumer Research* 25 (Provo, UT: Association of Consumer Research, 1998), 276–282.

7. Eileen Fischer, Julia Bristor, and Brenda Gainer, "Creating or Escaping Community? An Exploratory Study of Internet Consumers' Behaviors," *Advances in Consumer Research* 23 (Provo, UT: Association of Consumer Research, 1996), 178–182. Also see Siok Kuan Tambyah, "Life on the Net: The Reconstruction of Self and Community," *Advances in Consumer Research* 23 (Provo, UT: Association of Consumer Research, 1996), 172–177.

8. Robert Burnkrant and Alain Cousineau, "Informational and Normative Social Influence in Buyer Behavior," *Journal of Consumer Research* (December 1975), 206–215. Also see H. C. Kelman, "Processes of Opinion Change," *Public Opinion Quarterly* (1961), 57–78.

9. Bobby Calder and Robert Burnkrant, "Interpersonal Influence on Consumer Behavior: An Attribution Theory Approach," *Journal of Consumer Research* 4 (June 1977), 29–38.

10. Richard L. Oliver, "Whence Consumer Loyalty?" in George S. Day and David B. Montgomery, eds., *Journal of Marketing* 63 (Special Issue 1999), 33–44.

11. Abraham Tesser, Murray Millar, and Janet Moore, "Some Affective Consequences of Social Comparison and Reflection Processes: The Pain and Pleasure of Being Close," *Journal of Personality and Social Psychology* 54 (1988), 1, 49–61.

12. L. Wheeler, K. G. Shaver, R. A. Jones, G. R. Goethals, J. Cooper, J. E. Robinson, C. L. Gruder, and K. W. Butzine, "Factors Determining the Choice of a Comparison Other," *Journal of Experimental Social Psychology* 5 (1969), 219–232.

13. Marsha L. Richins, "Social Comparison and the Idealized Images of Advertising," *Journal of Consumer Research* 18 (June 1991), 71–83.

14. See William O. Bearden and Randall L. Rose, "Attention to Social Comparison Information: An Individual Difference Factor Affecting Consumer Conformity," *Journal of Consumer Research* 16 (March 1990), 461–472; and William O. Bearden, Richard G. Netemeyer, and Jesse E. Teel, "Measurement of Consumer Susceptibility to Interpersonal Influence," *Journal of Consumer Research* 15 (March 1989), 473–481.

15. George Homans, *Social Behavior: Its Elementary Forms* (New York: Harcourt, 1961).

16. Gwen Rae Bachmann, Deborah Roedder John, and Akshay R. Rao, "Children's Susceptibility to Peer Group Purchase Influence: An Exploratory Investigation," in Leigh McAllister and Michael L. Rothschild, eds., *Advances in Consumer Research* 20 (Provo, UT: Association for Consumer Research, 1992), 463–468; Stephen A. LaTour and Ajay K. Manrai, "Interactive Impact of Information and Normative Influence on Donations," *Journal of Marketing Research* 26 (August 1989), 327–335; Paul W. Miniard and Joel E. Cohen, "Modeling Personal and Normative Influences on Behavior," *Journal of Consumer Research* 10 (September 1983), 169–180; C. Whan Park and V. Parker Lessig, "Students and Housewives: Differences in Susceptibility to Reference Group Influence," *Journal of Consumer Research* 4 (September 1977), 102–109.

17. Bearden and Etzel, "Reference Group Influence."

18. David E. Midgley, Grahame R. Dowling, and Pamela D. Morrison, "Consumer Types, Social Influence, Information Search and Choice," in Srull, *Advances*, 137–143.

19. Miniard and Cohen, "Modeling Personal and Normative Influences."

20. William O. Bearden and Michael J. Etzel, "Reference Group Influence on Product and Brand Purchase Decisions," *Journal of Consumer Research* 9 (September 1982), 1985.

21. "31 Major Trends Shaping the Future of American Business," *The Public Pulse* 2 (1986), 1; Park and Lessig, "Students and Housewives"; and Robert E. Burnkrant and Alan Cousineau, "Informational and Normative Social Influence in Buyer Behavior," *Journal of Consumer Research* 2 (December 1975), 206–215.

22. L. J. Shrum, Thomas C. O'Guinn, Richard J. Semenik, and Ronald J. Faber, "Processes and Effects in the Construction of Normative Consumer Beliefs: The Role of Television," in Rebecca H. Holman and Michael R. Solomon, eds., *Advances in Consumer Research* 18 (Provo, UT: Association for Consumer Research, 1991), 755–763.

23. Emile Durkheim, *Suicide*, trans. by George Simpson (New York: Free Press, 1951). For a cultural perspective, see Robert Merton, "Anomie, Anomia, and Social Interaction: Contexts of Deviate Behavior," in M. B. Clinard, ed., *Anomie and Deviate Behavior* (New York: Free Press, 1964).

24. Hubert Gatignon and Thomas S. Robertson, "A Propositional Inventory for New Diffusion Research," *Journal of Consumer Research* 11 (March 1985), 849–867.

25. Paul M. Herr, Frank R. Kardes, and John Kim, "Effects of Word-of-Mouth and Product-Attribute Information on Persuasion: An Accessibility-Diagnosticity Perspective," *Journal of Consumer Research* 17 (March 1991), 458–462.

26. Jacqueline Johnson Brown and Peter H. Reingen, "Social Ties and Word-of-Mouth Referral Behavior," *Journal of Consumer Research* 14 (December 1987), 350–362.

27. William L. Wilkie, *Consumer Behavior* (New York: Wiley, 1986), 160.

28. Ernest Dichter, "How Word-of-Mouth Advertising Works," *Harvard Business Review* (November/December 1966), 147–166.

29. Paula Fitzgerald Bone, "Determinants of Word-of-Mouth Communications During Product Consumption," in John E. Sherry and Brian Sternthal, eds., *Advances in Consumer Research* 19 (Provo, UT: Association for Consumer Research, 1992), 579–583.

30. See, especially, Everett M. Rogers, *Diffusion of Innovations*, 3rd ed. (New York: Free Press, 1983). Also, most of the pertinent references have been cited in the first eight editions of this book.

31. See Brown and Reingen, "Social Ties and Word-of-Mouth Referral Behavior."

32. Laura J. Yale and Mary C. Gilly, "Dyadic Percep-

tions in Personal Source Information Search," *Journal of Business Research* 32 (1995), 225–237.

33. Meera P. Venkatraman, "Opinion Leadership: Enduring Involvement and Characteristics of Opinion Leaders: A Moderating or Mediating Relationship," in Marvin E. Goldberg, Gerald Gorn, and Richard W. Pollay, eds., *Advances in Consumer Research* 17 (Provo, UT: Association for Consumer Research, 1990), 60–67.

34. Elizabeth Hirschman, "Innovativeness, Novelty Seeking, and Consumer Creativity," *Journal of Consumer Research* (December 1980), 283–295.

35. Mary C. Gilly, John L. Graham, Mary Finley Wolfinbarger, and Laura J. Yale, "A Dyadic Study of Interpersonal Information Search," *Journal of the Academy of Marketing Science* 26, 2 (1998), 83–100.

36. Charles W. King and John O. Summers, "Overlap of Opinion Leadership Across Product Categories."

37. Lawrence F. Feick and Linda L. Price, "The Market Maven: A Diffuser of Marketplace Information," *Journal of Marketing* 51 (January 1987), 85.

38. Michael T. Elliott and Anne E. Warfield, "Do Market Mavens Categorize Brands Differently?" in Leigh McAlister and Michael L. Rothschild, eds., *Advances in Consumer Research* 20 (Provo, UT: Association for Consumer Research 1993), 202–208; and Frank Alpert, "Consumer Market Beliefs and Their Managerial Implications: An Empirical Examination," *Journal of Consumer Marketing* 10, 2 (1993), 56–70.

39. Charles W. King and John O. Summers, "Overlap of Opinion Leadership Across Product Categories," *Journal of Marketing Research* 7 (February 1970), 43–50.

40. Stanley C. Hollander and Kathleen M. Rassuli, "Shopping with Other People's Money: The Marketing Management Implications of Surrogate-Mediated Consumer Decision Making," *Journal of Marketing* 63 (April 1999), 2.

41. Michael R. Solomon, Carol Surprenant, John A. Czepiel, and Evelyn G. Gutman, "A Role Theory Perspective on Dyadic Interactions: The Service Encounter," *Journal of Marketing* 49 (Winter 1985), 99–111.

42. Stephen Grove and Raymond Fisk, "The Service Encounter as Theater," in John F. Sherry, Jr., and Brian Sternthal, eds., *Advances in Consumer Research* 19 (Provo, UT: Association for Consumer Research, 1992), 455–461.

43. Glenn B. Voss, A. Parasuraman, and Dhruv Grewal, "The Roles of Price, Performance, and Expectations in Determining Satisfaction in Service Exchanges," *Journal of Marketing* 62 (October 1998), 46–61.

44. Rosemary P. Ramsey and Ravipreet S. Sohi, "Listening to Your Customers: The Impact of Perceived Salesperson Listening Behavior on Relationship Outcomes," *Journal of the Academy of Marketing Science* 25 (Spring 1997), 2, 127–137.

45. Neeli Bendapudi, and Leonard L. Berry, "Customers' Motivations for Maintaining Relationships with Service Providers," *Journal of Retailing* 73, 1, (1997), 15–37.

46. Kevin P. Gwinner, Dwayne D. Gremler, and Mary Jo Bitner, "Relational Benefits in Service Industries: The Customer's Perspective," *Journal of the Academy of Marketing Science* 26, 2 (1998), 101–114.

47. Linda L. Price and Eric J. Arnould, "Commercial Friendships: Service Provider-Client Relationships in Context," *Journal of Marketing* 63 (October 1999), 38–56.

48. Thorstein Veblen, *The Theory of the Leisure Class* (New York: Macmillan, 1899); and George Simmel, "Fashion," *International Quarterly* 10 (1904), 130–155.

49. Paul E. Lazarsfeld, Bernard R. Berelson, and Hazel Gaudet, *The People's Choice* (New York: Columbia University Press, 1948), 151.

50. For a review of relevant research, see Herr, Kardes, and Kim, "Effects of Word-of-Mouth"; Linda L. Price and Lawrence F. Feick, "The Role of Interpersonal Sources and External Search: An Informational Perspective," in Thomas C. Kinnear, ed., *Advances* 11 (Provo, UT: Association for Consumer Research, 1984), 250–255; and Theresa A. Swartz and Nancy Stephens, "Information Search for Services: The Maturity Segment," in Kinnear, ed., *Advances,* 244–249.

51. Barbara B. Stern and Stephen J. Gould, "The Consumer as Financial Opinion Leader," *Journal of Retail Banking* 10 (Summer 1988), 43–52.

52. Christy Fisher, "Wal-Mart's Way," *Advertising Age* (February 18, 1991), 3.

53. Jonathan Gutman and Michael K. Mills, "Fashion Lifestyle and Consumer Information Usage: Formulating Effective Marketing Communications," in Bruce J. Walker et al., eds., *An Assessment of Marketing Thought and Practice* (Chicago: American Marketing Association, 1982), 199–203.

54. Herr, Kardes, and Kim, "Effects of Word-of-Mouth"; Marsha L. Richins, "Word of Mouth Communication as Negative Information," in Kinnear, ed., *Advances,* 697–702; and Richard W. Mizerski, "An Attribution Explanation of the Disproportionate Influence of Unfavorable Information," *Journal of Consumer Research* 9 (December 1982), 301–310.

55. John H. Holmes and John D. Lett, Jr., "Product

Sampling and Word of Mouth," *Journal of Advertising Research* 17 (October 1977), 35–40.

56. Measuring the Grapevine: Consumer Response and Word-of-Mouth. The Coca-Cola Co. (1981).

57. John E. Pluennecke and William J. Hampton, "Can Audi Fix a Dented Image?" *Business Week* (November 17, 1986), 81–82.

58. Rosabeth Moss Kanter, "Highlights," in Kanter, ed., *The Change Masters: Innovation and Entrepreneurship in the American Corporation* (New York: Free Press, 1987).

59. Thomas S. Robertson, "The Process of Innovation and the Diffusion of Innovation," *Journal of Marketing* (January 1967), 14–19.

60. Carl Quintanilla, "Forget Microwaves: 'Speed Cookers' Also Crisp and Brown," *The Wall Street Journal* (June 30, 1999), B1.

61. Thomas McCarroll, "What New Age?" *Time* (August 12, 1991), 44–45.

62. Michael S. Latour and Scott D. Roberts, "Cultural Anchoring and Product Diffusion," *Journal of Consumer Marketing* 9 (Fall 1991), 29–34.

63. Salah Hassan, "Attributes of Diffusion Adoption Decisions," Proceedings of the Academy of Marketing Science (1990).

64. For a good discussion on this, please see: Venkatesh Shankar, Gregory S. Carpenter, and Lakshman Krishnamurthi, "The Advantages of Entry in the Growth Stage of the Product Life Cycle: An Empirical Analysis," *Journal of Marketing Research* 36 (May 1999).

65. Everett M. Rogers, *Diffusion of Innovations*, 3rd ed. (New York: Free Press, 1983), 5.

66. Dan Horsky and Leonard S. Simon, "Advertising and the Diffusion of New Products," *Marketing Science* 2 (Winter 1983), 1–17.

67. John O'Shaugnessy, *Why People Buy* (New York: Oxford University Press, 1987), 25–38.

68. James Wills, A. C. Samli, and Laurence Jacobs, "Developing Global Products and Marketing Strategies: A Construct and a Research Agenda," *Journal of the Academy of Marketing Science* 19 (Winter 1991), 1–10.

69. Thomas S. Robertson and Hubert Gatignon, "Competitive Effects on Technology Diffusion," *Journal of Marketing* 50 (July 1986), 1–12.

70. Sabine Kuester, Christian Homburg, and Thomas S. Robertson, "Retaliatory Behavior to New Product Entry," *Journal of Marketing* 63 (October 1999), 90–106.

71. "New Technologies Take Time," *Business Week* (April 19, 1999), 8.

72. Richard Olshavsky, "Time and the Rate of Adop-

tion of Innovations," *Journal of Consumer Research* (March 1980), 425–428.

73. Milton D. Rosenau, Jr., "Speeding Your New Product to Market," *Journal of Consumer Marketing* 5 (Spring 1988), 23–35.

74. Thomas C. Boyd and Charlotte H. Mason, "The Link Between Attractiveness of 'Extrabrand' Attributes and the Adoption of Innovations," *Journal of the Academy of Marketing Science* 27 (Summer 1999), 306–319.

75. John M. Antil, "New Product or Service Adoption: When Does It Happen?" *Journal of Consumer Marketing* 5 (Spring 1988), 5–15.

76. David J. Bums, "Husband-Wife Innovative Consumer Decision Making: Exploring the Effect of Family Power," *Psychology and Marketing* 9 (New York: John Wiley & Sons, Inc., 1992), 175–189.

77. Gordon R. Foxall and Seema Bhate, "Cognitive Style and Personal Involvement as Explicators of Innovative Purchasing of 'Healthy' Food Brands," *European Journal of Marketing* 27 (1993), 5–16.

78. Gordon Foxall and Christopher G. Hawkins, "Cognitive Style and Consumer Innovativeness: An Empirical Test of Kirton's Adaption-Innovation Theory in the Context of Food Purchasing," *European Journal of Marketing* 20 (1986), 63–80.

79. M. J. Kirton, "Adaptors and Innovators: A Theory of Cognitive Style," in K. Gronhaug and M. Kaufman, eds., *Innovation: A Cross-disciplinary Perspective* (New York: John Wiley & Sons, 1986).

80. Vijay Mahajan and Eitan Muller, "When Is It Worthwhile Targeting the Majority Instead of the Innovators in a New Product Launch?" *Journal of Marketing Research* 35 (November 1998), 488–495.

81. Linda Price, Lawrence Feick, and Daniel Smith, "A Re-Examination of Communication Channel Usage by Adopter Categories," in Richard Lutz, ed., *Advances in Consumer Research* 13 (Provo, UT: Association for Consumer Research, 1986), 409–412.

82. Ram C. Rao and Frank M. Bass, "Competition, Strategy, and Price Dynamics: A Theoretical and Empirical Investigation," *Journal of Marketing Research* 24 (August 1985), 283–296.

83. Hirschman, "Innovativeness, Novelty Seeking, and Consumer Creativity"; and M. P. Venkatraman and L. P. Price, "Differentiating between Cognitive and Sensory Innovativeness: Concepts, Measurement and Their Implications," *Journal of Business Research* 20 (1990), 293–315.

84. Meera P. Venkatraman, "The Impact of Innovativeness and Innovation Type on Adoption," *Journal of Retailing* 67 (Spring 1991), 51–67.

85. Eric von Hippel, Stefan Thomke, and Mary

Sonnack, "Creating Breakthroughs at 3M," *Harvard Business Review* (September/October 1999), 47–57.

86. John P. Workman, Jr., "Marketing's Limited Role in New Product Development in One Computer Systems Firm," *Journal of Marketing Research* 30 (November 1993), 405–421.

87. Rashi Glazer, "Marketing in an Information-Intensive Environment: Strategic Implications of Knowledge as an Asset," *Journal of Marketing* 55 (October 1991), 1–19.

88. James M. Sinkula, "Market Information Processing and Organizational Learning," *Journal of Marketing* 58 (January 1994), 35–45. For more information, see: Gary Hamel and C. K. Prahalad, *Competing for the Future* (Boston: Harvard Business School Press, 1994).

89. Lisa Susanne Willsey, "Taking these 7 steps will help you launch a new product," *Marketing News* (March 29, 1999), 17.

90. Darren W. Dahl, Amitava Chattopadhyay, and Gerald J. Gorn, "The Use of Visual Mental Imagery in New Product Design," *Journal of Marketing Research* 36 (February 1999), 18–28.

91. Space does not permit more detailed discussion of these models. If you are interested, you will find them described, along with appropriate citations to source materials, in earlier editions of this text. See James Engel and Roger Blackwell, *Consumer Behavior,* 4th ed. (Homewood, IL: Dryden Press, 1982), 401–409. For a review of these

models, see C. Naqrasimhan and S. K. Sen, "Test Market Models for New Product Introduction," in Yoram Wind, Vijay Mahjan, and Richard Cardozo, eds., *New Product Forecasting—Models and Applications* (Lexington, MA: Lexington Books, 1981). Vijay Mahjan and Robert A. Peterson, *Innovation Diffusion: Models and Applications* (Beverly Hills, CA: Sage Publications, 1985). Also see Vijay Mahjan, Eitan Muller, and Frank M. Bass, "New Product Diffusion Models in Marketing: A Review and Directions for Research," *Journal of Marketing* 54 (January 1990), 1–26.

92. Glen L. Urban, John S. Hulland, and Bruce D. Weinberg, "Premarket Forecasting for New Consumer Durable Goods: Modeling Categorization, Elimination, and Consideration Phenomena," *Journal of Marketing* 57 (April 1993), 47–63.

93. *New Products Management for the 1980's* (New York: Booz-Allen & Hamilton, Inc., 1982).

94. Tiger Li and Roger J. Calantone, "The Impact of Market Knowledge Competence on New Product Advantage: Conceptualization and Empirical Examination," *Journal of Marketing* 62 (October 1998), 13–29.

95. Christopher S. Eklund, "Campbell Soup's Recipe for Growth: Offering Something for Every Palate," *Business Week* (December 14, 1984), 66–67.

96. Eric von Hippel, Stefan Thomke, and Mary Sonnack, "Creating Breakthroughs at 3M," *Harvard Business Review* (September/October 1999), 47–57.

Suggested Readings for Part IV

Roberto Suro, "Beyond Economics: Healthcare Adjusts to fit Ethnic Markets," *American Demographics* (February 2000), 48–55.

Lisa Penaloza and Mary C. Gilly, "Marketer Acculturation: The Changer and Changed," *Journal of Marketing* 63, 3 (July 1999), 84–104.

Gregory M. Rose, "Consumer Socialization, Parental Style, and Developmental Timetables in the United States and Japan," *Journal of Marketing* 63, 3 (July 1999), 105–119.

Roberto Suro, "Mixed Doubles," *American Demographics* (November 1999), 57–62.

Marnik G. Dekimpe, Philip M. Parker, and Miklos Sarvary, "Global Diffusion of Technological Innovations: A Coupled-Hazard Approach," *Journal of Marketing Research* 37 (February 2000), 47–59.

Lee G. Cooper, "Strategic Marketing Planning for Radically New Products," *Journal of Marketing* 64, 1 (January 2000), 1–16.

Jan-Benedict E. M. Steenkamp, Frenkel ter Hofstede, and Michel Wedel, "A Cross-National Investigation into the Individual and National Cultural Antecedents of Consumer Innovativeness," *Journal of Marketing* 63, 2 (April 1999).

Nancy Shepherdson, Alison Stein Wellner, Michelle Krebs, and Cristina Merrill, "Designated Drivers (A Special Report on the Auto Consumer of the Future)," *American Demographics* (January 2000), 43–59.

Brad Edmondson, "Buyers 'R' Us: Do the Math," *American Demographics* (October 1999), 50–56.

P. B. Seetharaman, Andrew Ainslie, and Pradeep K. Chintagunta, "Investigating Household State Dependence Effects Across Categories," *Journal of Marketing Research* 36 (November 1999), 488–500.

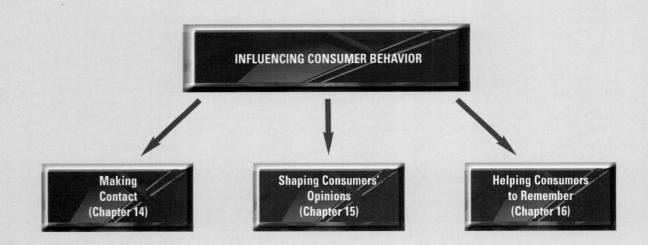

PART V

Influencing Consumer Behavior

In the prior sections of this text, we focused on those aspects of consumer behavior essential for building a basic understanding of consumers. But beyond understanding consumers, companies also need to know how to influence consumers. Companies try to influence what consumers buy, when they buy, and where they buy. Obviously, a company's long-term success heavily depends on its ability to influence consumer behavior.

The purpose of this section is to discuss the requirements that companies must satisfy if they are to be successful in their efforts to influence consumeers. We begin with the most fundamental prerequisite, making contact with potential buyers, the topic of Chapter 14. Making contact requires not only being at the right place at the right time, it also requires gaining that most valuable consumer resource: attention.

After making contact, companies typically try to shape the product opinions held by consumers. In Chapter 15 we focus on how this can be done. Finally, companies often find it in their best interests to help consumers remember things that increase the odds of them becoming customers. Chapter 16 deals with this topic.

CHAPTER 14

Making Contact

OPENING VIGNETTE

It's getting harder to avoid advertising. The refuges from commercialism are disappearing quickly. Snippets from a new movie flash on the cash machine screen while the automatic teller gets your money. A poster pitches skin cream from the inner door of the bathroom stall. Even elevators have been invaded with video screens carrying commercials. "I don't know if anything is sacred anymore," says Mike Swanson, who oversees client ad placements for the Minneapolis advertising agency Carmichael Lynch. "Everybody is looking for a way to stand out."

Advertisers are finding it harder and more expensive to be noticed in traditional media. Prime-time commercials can cost up to $500,000 for 30 seconds even though cable networks, videos, and the Internet have been drawing viewers away from the broadcast networks. So companies are allocating part of their advertising spending into new approaches. The choices seem boundless—ad space is being sold on video cases, parking lot tickets, golf scorecards, delivery trucks, gas pumps, and municipal garbage cans.

In the summer of 1998, ads began showing up in the sand of beaches along the New Jersey shore and made a return engagement the following year. Adman Patrick Dori designed a rubber-advertising mat that can be attached to a roller and leaves multiple impressions in the sand behind the tractor that rakes the beach every morning. On the average beach, about 5,000 mini-billboards measuring 12 by 4 feet are sculpted into the sand before the first beach goers arrive each day. Bestfoods Corp. used the new medium in 1998 for its Skippy peanut butter brand. Snapple soft drinks were first on the beach in 1999 (see Figure 14.1). Beach goers seem to like the sandy ads. "It's pretty cool," says Laura Nichols, a 20-year-old student from Jackson who said she noticed the ads as soon as she started walking on the beach.

Sources: Excerpted from Skip Wollenberg, "Advertisements Turn up on Beach, in Bathrooms," Miami Herald *(June 1, 1999), 8B, 10B. Also see Karen Jacobs, "Elevator Maker to Add Commercial Touch," The Wall Street Journal (December 7, 1999), B8; "Elevators Display News, Traffic, Stocks,"* Marketing News *(February 28, 2000), 57; John Grossman, "It's an Ad, Ad, Ad, Ad, World,"* Inc. *(March 2000), 23, 24, 26.*

Just as business must offer products that meet consumers' needs in order to succeed, so too must they make contact with their potential customers. Advertisements that are never seen cannot inform or persuade. Purchase incentives that get overlooked can't motivate buying. Products that sit unnoticed on the grocer's shelf will never know the joy of being scanned. Web sites ignored while traveling the information highway cannot prosper. Somehow, someway, companies must find a way of making contact. Doing so requires two things. The first is getting exposure.

Figure 14.1   Snapple Makes Contact with Beach Goers

Exposure

Exposure occurs when *there is physical proximity to a stimulus that allows one or more of our five senses the opportunity to be activated.* This activation happens when a stimulus meets or exceeds the **lower threshold:** *the minimum amount of stimulus intensity necessary for sensation to occur.* Given a stimulus of sufficient strength (e.g., a noise loud enough to be heard), sensory receptors are activated, and the encoded information is transmitted along nerve fibers to the brain.

Getting exposure essentially means entering the person's sphere of existence. I can't teach my students if I'm in the classroom and they're not. Similarly, television commercials that appear only in programs you never watch cannot influence you. Products offered at stores never entered can't be noticed either. Consequently, businesses must find a way of bringing their messages and products into sufficient physical proximity for consumers to have the opportunity to notice them.

A nice illustration of the importance of exposure comes from a company that discovered it could secure high placement in Internet search engines by changing how it listed itself. This, in turn, increases the number of potential customers exposed to the company's offering. Four months after changing its listing, monthly sales jumped from $25,000 to $65,000.[1] A similar demonstration is provided by a recent study of advertising sales flyers for supermarkets. Consumers exposed to the flyers spent more than twice as much on the products promoted in the flyers than did those not exposed.[2]

In seeking exposure, companies must identify those advertising media (see Consumer in Focus 14.1), promotional programs, and distribution channels that provide access to their target market. Which media yield sufficient numbers of target consumers at an affordable price? If television, what are the best days, times, and shows for broadcasting the commercial? How many target consumers will be exposed to the company's sponsorship of some promotional event? What channels of distribution do they use when buying the product? If through a brick-and-mortar retailer, how important is the product's location within the store? Answering such questions requires understanding target consumers' buying and consumption patterns.

Selective Exposure

Even if an advertiser is successful at getting its message to the right people at the right place at the right time, exposure still may not occur. This is because sometimes

Consumer in Focus 14.1

Making Contact with Teenagers

Teenagers spend $140 billion a year, and have yet to develop firm brand loyalties for many products. What's more, they're not yet making car or mortgage payments, so the majority of their income is discretionary. Teens have become a hot market, but one that marketers sometimes steer clear of because teens are also notoriously difficult to reach.

One book, *Wise Up to Teens,* by Peter Zollo, co-founder of the market research company Teenage Research Unlimited, gives companies clues about where to reach them. Among many other things, the book reports teenagers' opinions about which media they believe companies should use to reach them. Which media do you think teenagers suggested most often? It's not TV. It's the radio. Fifty-five percent recommended radio. Cable TV was a close second with 50 percent suggesting that advertisers use this medium for reaching them. In contrast, newspapers were rarely recommended, with fewer than one in ten suggesting this medium.

Teens invest a lot of time in listening to the radio. About 95 percent of the nation's teens listen to FM radio, averaging more than 10 hours each week. It's with them at home, in their cars, and outdoors, forging a relationship that is the basis of why they rate radio so highly. Many teens are intensely loyal to particular stations. Especially in small towns, radio connects local teenagers, informing them of coming events such as concerts, sports, school events, and so on. Radio also makes celebrities out of local disc jockeys. And,

in most markets, there are typically a few strong teen stations, allowing advertisers to efficiently reach large numbers of teens.

Radio allows teens to instantly select whatever music they prefer. And today, these preferences include many styles of music, leading to an extremely fragmented market. Teens might say their favorite music is hip-hop, rap, alternative, metal, techno, house, punk, reggae, or R&B. A few would even say country, classic rock, or swing. A preference for one type of music often excludes other styles. This difference goes far beyond musical preference. Teen language, fashion, style, activities, friends, and attitudes often correlate with taste in music.

Musical preferences vary across different teen segments that are defined along ethnic, gender, and geographic characteristics. African-American teens are the most efficiently targeted segment with radio since they gravitate to two formats: rap and R&B (often programmed together on a single urban station). Whereas white teens, in smaller numbers, also listen to these formats, they greatly prefer alternative and also listen to classic rock and country. Latino teens are the most musically adventurous, liking all the aforementioned formats. Selecting radio stations with the appropriate musical format helps advertisers make contact with their target segments.

Source: Excerpted from "Not Quite the TV Generation," American Demographics *(May 1999), 35–36. Also see Peter Zollo,* Wise Up to Teens: Insights into Marketing and Advertising to Teenagers, *2nd ed. (Ithaca, NY: New Strategist Publications, 1999).*

consumers deliberately try to avoid exposure. Rather than sit passively, they decide whether or not exposure happens. This is so for some Internet users of companies that offer free access in return for showering them with advertising. One user puts tape across her computer screen to block out the ads. Another tells how he and 15 co-workers used hacker software to eliminate advertisements.[3] A recent report from Forrester Research, a market research firm, indicates that over half of online consumers have never clicked on banner ads, leading some advertisers to question the long-term viability of this type of online advertising.[4]

The same sort of thing happens when consumers watch television. As shown in Figure 14.2, consumers usually find something else to do during the commercial break. Less than one out of five consumers report that they often watch commercials. Many get up and find something else to do. Others *grab the remote control and switch to another station.* This behavior, undertaken by millions of viewers, is called **zapping.**[5] It's similar to **zipping,** in which the person *fast-forwards through commercials when watching a VCR tape.* It's estimated that at least 50 percent of the ads are zipped.[6] And much to the chagrin of advertisers, VCR manufacturers offer models with a feature that edits commercials automatically during taping. Recognize that selective exposure essentially reduces the size of the audience being reached. The number of people watching a particular program typically is much greater than the number exposed to a commercial within the program.

The Danger of Overexposure

Though exposure is a good thing to have, too much of it may not be so good. New or novel stimuli typically command attention. However, as these stimuli

Figure 14.2   What Consumers Do During TV Commercial Breaks

Activity	Percent
Get up and do something else	45%*
Switch channels	39%
Talk to others in the room	34%
Sit and watch commercials	19%
Turn down sound on TV	19%
Read	11%
Use a computer	5%

*Numbers represent the percent of people who say they often do these activities when a TV commercial comes on.

Source: Jennifer Lach, "Commercial Overload," American Demographics (September 1999), 20.

become more familiar through repeated exposure, habituation sets in. **Habituation** occurs when a stimulus becomes so familiar and ordinary that it loses its attention-getting ability. Consider the couple who moves from a quiet, small town to an apartment in the middle of New York City. Initially, they'll find the noise levels very noticeable and disturbing. But before too long, they'll grow accustomed (i.e., become habituated) to the noise to the point that it's hardly noticed.

The same phenomenon occurs in advertising. In the beginning, a new ad may be very effective at grabbing attention. But after seeing the ad over and over again, consumers grow tired of it and stop paying attention. **Advertising wearout** is the term used to describe *ads that lose their effectiveness because of overexposure.*[7] One advertising researcher offers the following rule of thumb: commercials lose half their effectiveness after accumulating 1,000 gross rating points (the sum of all the ratings that a commercial gets based on the programs in which it appears). At the 1,000 mark, the ad has reached nearly half of all U.S. households with TV sets at least 10 times.[8]

Overexposure may not only cause ads to lose their ability to attract attention, it can have an even more detrimental impact. The tedium of seeing the same ad repeatedly sometimes causes consumers to become more critical and argumentative during ad processing. This, in turn, may result in consumers holding less favorable attitudes toward the ad and the product.[9]

One solution to the wearout problem involves using ads that differ in their executions but that carry the same basic message.[10] One ad campaign for Energizer batteries featuring the drum-banging pink bunny consisted of more than 20 commercials (see Figure 14.3). Not to be outdone, competitor Duracell developed more than 40 spots in which different battery-operated toys were shown to run longer when powered by a Duracell battery.[11] Although additional expenses are incurred from the production of multiple ad executions, this cost usually is a worthwhile investment for reducing the problem of advertising wearout.

Overexposure extends beyond advertising to the product itself. The successful Ron Jon surf shops recognize the potential payoff from increasing its stores and locations but is worried that, in so doing, it'll lose some of the mystique provided by its limited availability. The latest clothing fashions often become less appealing to trendsetters as the items become more commonplace. Overexposure may be one reason why the sales of Abercrombie & Fitch have slowed dramatically. As Megan Murray, a University of Michigan freshman, explains, "I hate the way it has its name all over everything. I guess the image is starting to wear off because it is everywhere."[12]

Although essential, exposure alone is insufficient for making contact. As noted earlier, simply because advertisers are successful in gaining exposure to their commercials does not necessarily mean that consumers are paying attention to them. The second requirement for making contact, then, is gaining attention.

Attention

According to Webster, attention is "the act of keeping one's mind closely on something or the ability to do this; mental concentration."[13] This definition reflects a fundamental element of attention—namely, its *focus* (i.e., the direction of attention). Right now your focus is here. If your phone or doorbell rings, or if somebody interrupts you, the focus of your attention will be redirected.

Yet focus is only part of attention. *Intensity* (i.e., the degree of attention) is the other. Sometimes we think about something as much as we possibly can. We give it our full and undivided attention. More often, we are less generous. Something may occupy our thoughts only for a fleeting moment. With all due respect to

Figure 14.3	Energizer Uses Multiple Ad Executions to Reduce Advertising Wearout

STONEHENGE, WILTSHIRE, ENGLAND. 7:53 A.M. STILL GOING. NOTHING OUTLASTS THE ENERGIZER.

MONUMENT VALLEY, UTAH. 5:32 P.M. STILL GOING. NOTHING OUTLASTS THE ENERGIZER.

Mr. Webster, we define **attention** as the *amount of thinking focused in a particular direction.*

Before companies can get consumers to pay their product's price, they must first get consumers to pay attention. Obviously, people don't buy products they have never thought about, even if only briefly. Do you remember the concept of the consideration set (those alternatives considered during decision making) from Chapter 4? Being in the consideration set means being thought about as a possible choice. Moreover, alternatives within the consideration set that become the focus of attention during decision making may stand a better chance of being chosen. When given the choice between frozen yogurt and a fruit salad, only 25 percent selected frozen yogurt when their attention was focused on the fruit salad. However, this percentage doubled when attention was focused on the yogurt.[14]

Similarly, before the messages companies transmit through their salespeople and advertising can work, consumers must pay attention. As the saying goes, a message that falls on deaf ears can't be heard. Ads and salespeople that are ignored can neither inform nor persuade.

The amount of attention or thinking is also important. Rather than undertaking the thinking necessary to carefully compare choice alternatives, consumers may opt for simpler decision strategies such as buying the cheapest or most familiar alternative. This may lead consumers to make different choices than if they had given more attention to the decision at hand. And as you'll learn in Chapters 15 and 16, the amount of thinking (as well as the content of this thinking) during information processing strongly influences how consumers respond to persuasive messages as well as what they remember.

Short-Term Memory: The Cognitive Resource for Attention

Understanding humans' mental capacity is the domain of the social science called cognitive psychology. Cognitive psychologists traditionally decompose mental capacity into three parts: sensory memory, short-term memory, and long-term memory. **Sensory memory** refers to *that part of capacity used when initially analyzing a stimulus detected by one of our five senses.* If the stimulus passes through this phase, it receives further processing using short-term memory. **Short-term memory** is *where thinking occurs.* Here the stimulus is interpreted and contemplated using concepts stored in long-term memory. **Long-term memory** is *the mental warehouse containing all of our knowledge* (which we discussed in Chapter 9). Depending on what occurs in short-term memory, new information may be passed along for storage into long-term memory. Later, in Chapter 16, you'll read about how companies try to implant information in consumers' long-term memory. But for now, we'll focus on short-term memory, for it's this part of mental capacity that's being allocated when something catches our attention.

Short-term memory is a limited mental resource. *The length of time it can be focused on a single stimulus or thought* (i.e., the **span of attention**) is not very long. You can demonstrate this to yourself by testing just how long you are able to concentrate on a particular thought before your mind begins to "wander." In advertising, the use of shorter commercials is one way to overcome consumers' limited attention spans.[15]

Nor can information survive very long in short-term memory without efforts to keep it activated. Suppose you were shown a phone number long enough to process it and then were prevented from rehearsing the number. How much time would elapse before the number faded away? Without rehearsal, information typically fades from short-term memory in 30 seconds or less.[16]

The size or capacity of short-term memory is also limited. We can process only a certain amount of information at a time. The size of short-term memory is often measured in terms of an informational chunk, which represents a grouping or combination of information that can be processed as a whole unit. Depending on which source one chooses to draw on, capacity varies from four or five chunks to as many as seven.[17]

Whereas consumer advocates usually urge businesses and regulators to disclose more product information so that consumers can make more informed (and presumably better) choices, some suggest that more information may actually have the opposite effect. Their concern is that consumers may become confused and make poorer choices when the amount of information processed during decision making exceeds cognitive capacity.[18] This may be particularly true for inexperienced buyers. According to Brian Wansink, professor of marketing and director of the Food and Brand Research Lab at the University of Illinois, "It depends on the consumer shopping cycle. At the start of the cycle, a shopper faced with too many products will not make a careful choice because he or she is too bewildered. It is not until the shopper is comfortable within the category that he or she can make good product choices."[19]

Grabbing Consumers' Attention

The world of the consumer is more cluttered than my 15-year-old daughter's bedroom. The average person is bombarded by hundreds of advertisements each and every day, a number that will only grow as advertisers find new ways to reach us.[20] Mailboxes are stuffed with catalogs and "junk mail" (see Figure 14.4 for some direct mail statistics by country). Telemarketers are constantly trying to reach us by phone although their ability to do so has been hampered greatly by answering machines and caller ID. One of the biggest complaints of Internet users is sorting through numerous unsolicited messages (called spam) that fill their e-mail address. Stores are stocked with thousands upon thousands of products crying for attention, with new ones arriving each day. In 1999, more than 25,000 new products were introduced to the marketplace.[21]

Figure 14.4   Is Your Mailbox Cluttered? It Depends on Where You Live

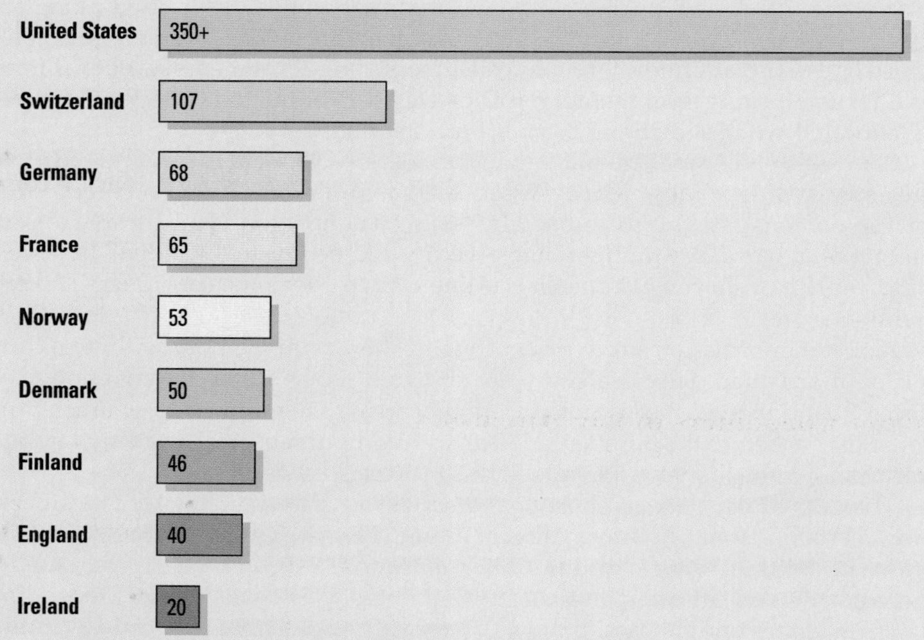

Country	Pieces
United States	350+
Switzerland	107
Germany	68
France	65
Norway	53
Denmark	50
Finland	46
England	40
Ireland	20

Note: Numbers represent the pieces of direct mail received annually per capita.

Source: Jennifer Lach, "Deutsche Delivers," American Demographics *(February 2000), 18, 20, 22.*

Even if consumers wanted to, it is simply impossible for them to pay attention to all the products and companies frantically waving their hands at them. They have to be selective in what receives their attention because, as was just pointed out, attention draws upon a limited cognitive resource. Some things gain entry into our thought processes; many do not. We drive by numerous retail establishments without noticing their existence. We rush past countless products during shopping trips oblivious to their presence. We ignore advertisements. We toss junk mail. Internet users delete e-mail without ever opening them up.

In the quest for consumers' attention, businesses face an uphill battle. Consumers have far more important things in their lives to be contemplating than the multitude of ordinary, low-involvement products that they buy and use with little thought. This partly explains why consumers, during an average shopping trip at the grocery store, spend less than three seconds looking at each product.[22]

For all these reasons, grabbing consumers' attention is one of the most formidable challenges facing business today. It's kind of like fishing when the lake is cluttered with fishermen and the fish aren't hungry—not the best circumstances for catching tonight's dinner. Yet despite these obstacles, it's still possible to catch something, especially if you use the right bait or lure and know where to cast it. The same is true for businesses trying to hook attention. They need to know what bait to use. And their options are numerous. Indeed, as described in the following pages, companies have an array of approaches at their disposal for grabbing attention.[23]

Connect with Consumers' Needs

Have you ever gone grocery shopping when you were extremely hungry? We imagine everybody has. You probably paid a lot more attention to products on the grocer's shelves than you might normally do. And you probably ended up with items in your shopping cart that otherwise would not have been purchased. In this instance, your heightened need for food made you allocate more cognitive resources to processing objects perceived as satisfying this need.

More generally, people are particularly attentive to stimuli perceived as relevant to their needs. Products and advertisements that do so will attract attention. And the better they are at delivering what the consumer wants, the more noticeable they become.

Connecting to consumers' needs may require reminding them of their needs before showing them how the product can satisfy these needs. A current TV commercial for Snickers candy bar starts with the question, "Hungry?" Viewers are then instructed to "grab a Snickers" as they watch the palm of a human hand voraciously devour the product. Sometimes making the connection requires educating consumers about their needs, something we talked about previously in Chapter 4.

Paying Consumers to Pay Attention

Recently, companies have begun to pay consumers for their attention. The Aristotle Publishing Company offers qualified web users between 50 and 75 cents for each piece of e-mail from political candidates that they read. More than one million voters have signed up for the service, a number expected to double within a year. Unlike a direct mailing that may be opened by only 2 or 3 percent of recipients, "you get a 98 percent open rate because you are by definition operating with permission," explains John Aristotle Phillips, the company's co-founder.[24]

The term **permission marketing** refers to *persuading consumers to volunteer their attention in return for some tangible benefit.*[25] One company, Broadpoint

Communications, offers customers 2 free minutes of long-distance calling for each 10- to 15-second commercial they listen to over the telephone. An average customer hears around 150 ads a month, which translates into 300 minutes of free long-distance time.[26]

Look! It Moves!

Thousands of years ago when humans had to worry about becoming some predator's next meal, the ability to detect something moving in the bushes was an essential survival skill. Although this threat has long since vanished, our sensitivity to movement has not. Stimuli in motion are more likely to attract attention than stationary objects. As described in Consumer in Focus 14.2, one company was happy to learn how the sales effectiveness of its point-of-purchase displays was enhanced greatly by including movement.

Even the suggestion or appearance of movement can draw attention. Advertisers often use quasi-motion in print advertisements for this purpose. An example of this appears in Figure 14.5.

Scene Changes

Another technique for capturing attention is the use of rapid-fire scene changes, which can cause an involuntary increase in brain activity.[27] In one advertising campaign for Pontiac automobiles, the commercials contained some scenes that lasted no longer than 1 1/2 seconds, some as short as 1/4 of a second. However, there is concern that quick-cut commercials may be less memorable and persuasive than slower-paced ads.[28]

Consumer in Focus 14.2

Gaining Attention with Movement

Point-of-purchase (POP) displays are often used by companies for attracting consumers' attention in a retail environment that is increasingly crowded with new products. The Olympia Brewing Company conducted a study to determine the effects of POP displays on purchase behavior. The research involved both food and liquor stores located within two California cities. Some of the stores received a display; others did not. These latter stores provided a baseline for determining whether the displays influenced sales. Further, two types of POP displays were tested: motion displays (those with some movement being generated by the display) and static displays (those without movement).

Sales in the stores were then monitored over a four-week period. The results (numbers represent the increase in sales over stores without displays) are presented here:

	Static Display	Motion Display
Food Stores	18%	49%
Liquor Stores	56%	107%

These findings clearly reveal the effectiveness of POP displays in generating sales. The presence of a display produced an average sales increase of more than 50 percent. The greater improvement in sales found for liquor stores suggests that POP displays become more effective when consumers are already inclined to purchase the product (it seems safe to believe that those visiting the liquor store were so inclined). Finally, including movement within the display substantially improved its effectiveness. The motion displaying generated nearly three times the sales of the static display in food stores and nearly twice the sales in liquor stores.

Figure 14.5   Attracting Attention with Quasimotion

Colors Are Nice

The attention-getting and holding power of a stimulus may be increased sharply through the use of color.[29] In a field study involving newspaper advertising, one-color ads produced 41 percent more sales than did their black-and-white counterparts.[30] Color ads cost more, so their incremental effectiveness must be weighed against the additional expense.

Moreover, some colors may be more attention getting than others. Did you know that red cars get more speeding tickets than cars of any other color? Although people who choose to drive a red car may be more inclined to speed, their odds of being noticed by police officers are heightened by the color of their car. Companies placing ads in the yellow pages telephone directories are encouraged to use this color as a way of attracting attention.

Make It Bigger

In general, the larger the stimulus, the more it tends to stand out and draw attention. Consequently, an easy way for companies to attract attention is to simply make things bigger. Larger print ads are more likely to grab attention than their smaller cousins. The same holds for the size of the illustrations or pictures within an ad.[31]

One demonstration of size's importance comes from the yellow pages. As consumers flip the pages, they're more likely to notice the bigger ads. It has been reported that doubling the size of a yellow pages' ad improved sales 500 percent. When the ad quadrupled in size, sales shot up 1,500 percent.[32] The effectiveness of FSIs (free-standing inserts) also depends on their size. FSIs are those ads containing coupons that are grouped together and inserted into the Sunday newspaper. In one advertisement sponsored by the industry's trade association, full-page FSIs are reported to be 20 percent more effective in generating trial and repeat purchasing than half-page FSIs.

Bigger may be better in the store as well. Products have a greater chance of being noticed as the size or amount of shelf space allocated to them increases. This can be especially important for impulse items, whose sales may depend partly on how much space they receive.[33]

Make It More Intense

Have you ever noticed that the volume of a commercial is sometimes much louder than the programming that preceded it? This is far from accidental. To the contrary, it's a deliberate attempt to get your attention by increasing stimulus intensity. Intense stimuli stand out relative to their weaker counterparts. Consequently, ads containing intense elements, such as loud sounds and bright colors, are more likely to be noticed. Radio and television commercials sometimes begin with a loud noise to attract attention.

Location! Location! Location!

There's an old real estate joke that goes something like this: "What are the three most important things to know about real estate? Location! Location! Location!" Though overstated (what about price?), the point being made is that location is critical. This is also true for attention. Stimuli may be more noticeable simply because of where they are located in the environment.

Grocery vendors know very well the importance of location. The sales for some products, especially those purchased more impulsively, are quite sensitive to where they are located in the retail environment. Many of the items at the grocery checkout would be bought far less frequently if displayed in more remote areas of the store. Products located at the end of the aisle or on shelves at eye level stand a better chance of being noticed as well.

An ad's location within a magazine influences attention. Greater attention is given to ads located in the front part than in the back part of the magazine, on right-hand pages than left-hand pages, and on the inside front, inside back, and outside back covers.[34] Presumably, this is because of the manner in which consumers typically flip through magazines. For smaller ads that do not occupy an entire page, attention may depend on where it is located on the page. A rule of thumb in advertising is that the upper left-hand corner of the page is the most likely to receive attention, whereas the lower right-hand corner is least likely.[35]

The Surprise Factor

In Chapter 6, we talked about the importance of consumers' expectations as a determinant of their post-consumption evaluations. Expectations are also important in the domain of attention. All of us have certain expectations about what we are likely to encounter during our daily routine. Stimuli congruent with our expectations may receive less attention than those that deviate from what's expected. Something that deviates from what we expect creates a mental incongruity. It's almost like a silent alarm in our head. Our attention is allocated to the source of the incongruity as we attempt to understand and resolve it.

The surprise factor is a popular tactic for gaining consumers' attention (see Consumer in Focus 14.3). It is an obvious aspect of the ads presented in Figure

Consumer in Focus 14.3

Shocking Advertising

An ad for AvMed prenatal care shows a smoking baby. Jenny McCarthy sits on the toilet in an ad for Candie's shoes. What's the message? Shock sells. Or at least attracts attention. Searching for new strategies to reach media-savvy consumers, advertisers increasingly are pushing the limits of taste and tolerance with shocking, titillating, and downright outrageous images to sell their products. From roadkill, to anorexic teens to beer-drinking seniors indulging in a little onscreen hanky-panky, in today's advertising, virtually anything goes.

"Over the last few years advertising has become more and more daring and research shows consumers have become increasingly concerned about it," says Walker Smith, managing partner of Yankelovich Partners, a consumer research firm. "A lot of this advertising is designed simply to break through the clutter. The question is whether it effectively positions your product in a way that is motivating and persuasive or just alienates the market."

It depends on whom that market is. Advertising that offends one consumer, experts agree, can be very appealing to another. Take the campaign for Candie's shoes. The fad pumps—they look like Dr. Scholl's with heels—have become this year's hallmark of hip teenagehood, thanks largely to racy print ads starring MTV-glam girl Jenny McCarthy. Aimed at Candie's core market of 12- to 24-year-old females, the ads feature McCarthy and her Candie's in a series of

provocative, bathroom-related poses. The most outrageous of the ads has her sitting on the toilet, newspaper in hand, panties around her ankles, and of course, a pair of bright orange Candie's on her feet.

"We did a lot of research for this campaign, and for the 12- to 17-year-old girl, Jenny McCarthy's popularity is off the charts," says David Conn, Candie's director of marketing. "Our audience finds the visuals cute and funny. Granted there's a fine line between what is gross and what is cute, but we care about how our customers react—not adults. And since we launched this campaign our sales are incredible."

Interestingly, complaints about racy commercials can be part of a strong marketing strategy, particularly if the product is aimed at young people eager to show off their independence. "Alienating the adult market creates a bond with younger consumers," notes Pippa Seichrist, vice president of the Miami Ad School. "That can be very good for business." Advertising for Calvin Klein jeans is a good example. In late 1995, a series of ads for the company's jeans showing child models in provocative poses created a national furor. The spots were compared with pornography films, lambasted by media experts and civic groups, and discussed at length in *The New York Times* and on morning talk shows. Nonetheless, jean sales went through the roof.

Source: Excerpted from Anne Moncreiff Arrarte, *"Now That We Have Your Attention,"* Miami Herald *(June 22, 1997), 1F, 2F.*

14.6. And it was considered an essential element in ads introducing Sea-Doo's new personal watercraft that showed the product in some unusual situations around the house (e.g., soaking in a bubble-filled bathtub, resting on satin bed sheets). According to one of the advertising executives in charge of the new campaign, "For Sea-Doo to perform in the market as expected, we have to create advertising that is unexpected. We need to surprise the reader. Intrigue him enough to stop turning pages, so he spends a few minutes learning about how great this product really is."[36]

In the same way, unusual product packaging helps the product stand out on the shelf. One manufacturer made a fortune selling hosiery in an oversized, plastic egg-shaped package that was very different from what women had grown accustomed to seeing in this product category.

Distinctiveness

Suppose you looked at a picture of five people dressed in suits. Four are wearing dark suits; the fifth has on a white suit. Which person do you think you would

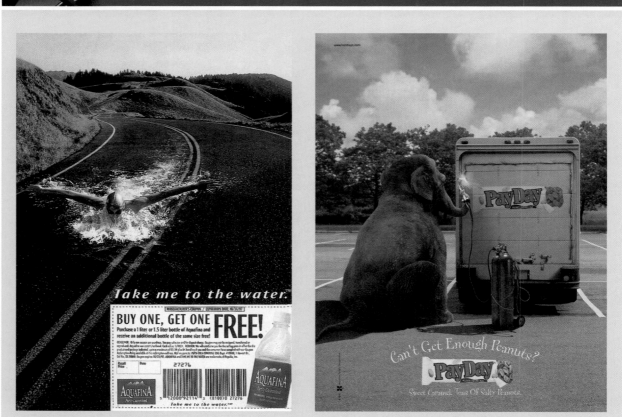

Figure 14.6   Unexpected Stimuli Are Effective at Getting Attention

look at first? Typically, the person dressed in white. Why? Because our attention is often drawn to those stimuli within a perceptual field that are distinctive. When everyone else wears dark colors, the white suit stands out. But dress everyone in the same color and this distinctiveness disappears.

As suggested by this example, one way to make an object appear distinctive is for it to contrast with other elements within the perceptual field in which the object appears. For example, if the packaging of competitors tends to be similar in its colors or shapes, then using different colors or shapes can help the company's package stand out.

The Human Attraction

In fishing, sometimes it's necessary to use one fish as bait for another. Similarly, companies often use people for catching consumers' attention. Famous individuals or celebrities are popular bait. Many companies hire celebrities to endorse their products. Certainly one of the most sought-after endorsers is basketball superstar Michael Jordan who has appeared as a spokesperson in advertising for numerous companies, including Nike, McDonald's, Quaker Oats, Sara Lee, General Mills, Wilson Sporting Goods, and MCI (see Figure 14.7). It's been estimated that, in one year alone, Michael Jordan earned $40 million for endorsing products.[37] Movie stars, even deceased ones, are used to attract attention. In an effort to break through the clutter of products on supermarket shelves, one company developed a line of common grocery products (cereal, trash bags, light bulbs) named Star

Figure 14.7 Celebrities Draw Attention

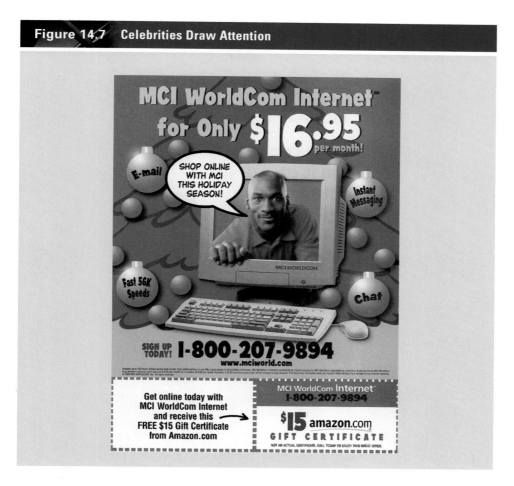

Pak, which features the faces of some very famous movie stars (Marilyn Monroe, Clark Gable) on the product packaging.[38]

As you well know, even noncelebrities, such as the woman in the ad shown in Figure 14.8, can grab attention, especially if they are attractive.[39] Good-looking individuals with toned bodies, especially if barely covered, usually attract a lot of attention. This is true on the beach, and it's also true in advertising. This is why advertisers use this attention-getting device so frequently. One study of advertising appearing in *Time, Newsweek, Cosmopolitan, Redbook, Playboy* and *Esquire* found that 40 percent of ads using adult models contained females dressed in a revealing manner.[40]

The Entertainment Factor

How many times have you watched a familiar television commercial simply because you enjoyed doing so? Probably more times than you even remember. Stimuli that entertain and amuse us draw our attention, even if they happen to come in the form of an advertisement.[41] The current Budweiser advertising campaign featuring Louie, the wisecracking lizard, effectively uses entertainment as an attention-getting device. One Internet company, Monster.com, which helps people find better jobs, relies on the entertainment factor in its commercial showing children reciting mundane career ambitions (e.g., one little girl saying, "I want to get paid less for doing the same job"). And believe it or not, some people watch the Super Bowl in eager anticipation of the commercials that appear during the broadcast. To learn more about this, read Consumer in Focus 14.4.

Figure 14.8   Attractive Noncelebrities Grab Attention Too

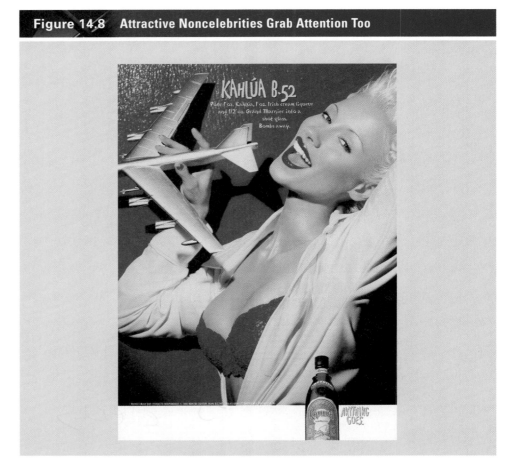

Consumer in Focus 14.4

Quiet Please, the Commercials Are Coming On!

Watching the Super Bowl has become a consumption ritual for millions of Americans. Roughly 125 million viewers are expected to tune in for this year's event. "Relatively speaking, the Super Bowl is an awesome event," according to Joe Mandese, editor of the *Meyers Report,* a television industry newsletter. "Nothing else comes close. For many advertisers, it's the only game in town." But it's a very expensive game to play. This year, companies will pay an average of $2.2 million for 30 seconds of airtime, nearly 40 percent higher than last year's $1.6 million. By comparison, the average 30-second spot on the highest rated weekly programs in prime-time television is "only" $500,000.

Beyond reaching so many people, the Super Bowl is attractive to advertisers because some viewers tune in to the game as much for the commercials as for the action on the field. Baltimore ad agency Eisner Communications recently released its annual survey of Super Bowl viewing habits and found that 8 percent of the viewing audience, an estimated 10 million people, will be watching the game solely for the ads. "The trend toward watching for the ads continues to inch up every year," says David Blum, an Eisner vice president.

Nonetheless, advertising during the Super Bowl poses its own set of unique challenges. "People expect high entertainment value, cutting-edge production and special effects," says Albert Sanchez, of the Donovan Consulting Group, who is working with Anheuser-Busch on its crop of Super Bowl ads. "People's bar for Super Bowl ads is much higher than for regular commercials. People expect to see the best of the best during Super Bowl Sunday."

Source: Excerpted from Cynthia Corzo, "Field of Ads," Miami Herald (January 25, 2000), 1C, 3C.

"Learned" Attention-Inducing Stimuli

Some stimuli attract our attention because we have been taught or conditioned to react to them. A ringing phone or doorbell, for example, typically elicits an immediate response from the person. Ringing phones or wailing sirens are sometimes included in the background of radio and TV ads to capture attention.

Certain words or phrases may also attract consumers' attention because they have learned that these words are associated with things they desire. The word *free* is a good example. Consumers love freebies; the ad in Figure 14.9 capitalizes on this with its bold headline "Is FREE Cheap Enough?" They also love saving money. Shoppers browsing through a store may be drawn to those products lying beneath signs proclaiming "Clearance Sale," "Special Sale," or "50% Off." A similar approach is used to grab consumers' attention as they sort through their junk mail for the day. On more than one occasion, I have been enticed to open a piece of mail that otherwise would have been deposited directly into the trash can because I saw the phrase "Pay to the order of" through the envelope's cellophane window.

Look for a Less Cluttered Environment

The likelihood that a particular stimulus receives attention is diminished as the number of stimuli competing for this attention increases. This is one reason (we'll talk about the other in Chapter 16) why clutter in the marketplace amplifies the

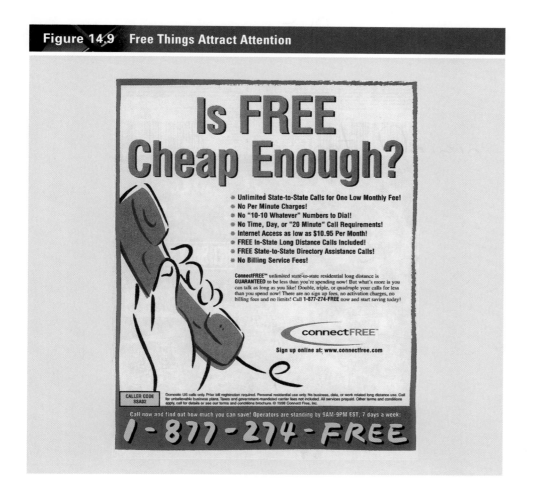

Figure 14.9   Free Things Attract Attention

challenge business faces in courting consumers' attention. By gaining exposure in less cluttered environments, a company can enhance its chances of being noticed.

Do you remember our discussion in the opening vignette about advertisers placing their ads in elevators and bathroom stalls? These locations are attractive to advertisers because they reach a "captive audience" at a place where there is little else to compete for their attention. "Being able to get into an environment where you're not competing with other advertising out there is important," counsels one businessman.[42]

For the same reason, advertising will soon be appearing on baggage carousels at major airports. Passengers typically wait 15 to 20 minutes for their baggage with little else to do. In this amount of time, an ad will appear eight or more times. Because of this repetition, the ad may be more memorable (see Chapter 16).[43]

Beyond where it advertises, when a company advertises may influence the amount of clutter it faces. Rather than face stiff competition during the 1999 holiday season, iVillage, a web site targeting women, decided to wait until after Christmas before resuming its $40 million advertising campaign. "Our strategy was to avoid the holiday clutter," explains a company spokesperson.[44]

Another way advertisers try to avoid clutter is to use isolation. **Isolation** involves *placing an object in a barren perceptual field.* Other objects that, if present, would compete for attention are eliminated. As illustrated by the ad appearing in Figure 14.10, advertisers use isolation by limiting the number of stimuli shown on an otherwise blank page.

Figure 14.10   This Ad Uses Isolation to Grab Attention

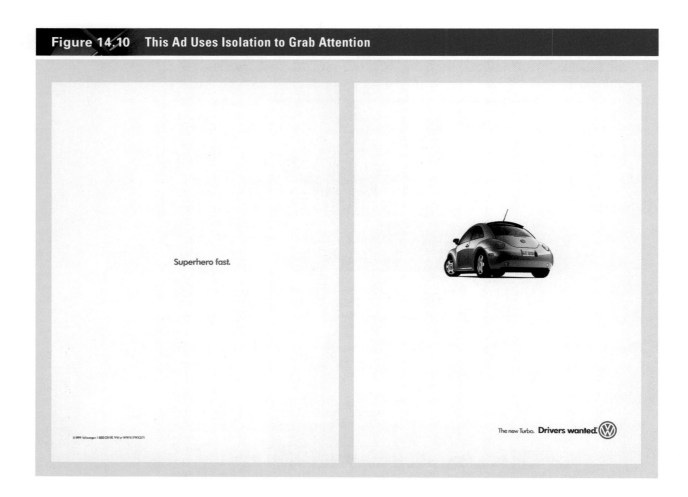

Superhero fast.

The new Turbo. **Drivers wanted.**

Attracting Attention: Some Additional Observations and Recommendations

In the preceding section, we reviewed a number of ways in which companies can try to get your attention. At the risk of stating the obvious, the need for using attention-getting stimuli depends on consumers' intrinsic motivation to pay attention. When consumers freely give their attention, the necessity of including stimuli that attract attention is diminished greatly. Given that such stimuli cost money and absorb precious ad space, they should be used only when necessary.

Moreover, the use of attention-getting stimuli carries some risk. For instance, suppose that a well-known celebrity is so effective at gaining attention that the remainder of the advertisement is ignored. When this occurs, advertising effectiveness suffers. Indeed, a stimulus that dominates viewers' attention, while leaving the remainder of the message ignored, is self-defeating. Companies must try to use stimuli that capture attention initially but that do not inhibit processing of the entire message.

Even if the attention-getting device does not cause the remainder of the ad to be ignored, it may still interfere with ad processing. Because short-term memory has limited capacity, allocating cognitive resources to one thing reduces the amount available for thinking about something else. If during class you start thinking about something that happened earlier in the day, you have reduced your mental capacity for processing what the instructor is saying. If your thoughts are fixated on the celebrity appearing in the commercial, there is less capacity for processing the rest of the ad (e.g., the advertised product and its claims).

To illustrate the adverse effects that may arise when attention is divided, consider the findings from so-called shadowing experiments.[45] In a typical experiment, subjects wear headphones and receive a different message in each ear. While listening to both messages, they are instructed to repeat out loud (i.e., shadow) the content of one of the messages. Despite hearing two different messages simultaneously, people can easily shadow one of them although doing so requires nearly all of their cognitive capacity. This means that little capacity remains for processing the message that is not shadowed. And this greatly impairs what is remembered about the nonshadowed message even though it is delivered directly into the person's ear. Indeed, recall of the nonshadowed message's content is virtually nonexistent. Even changes in the message from normal speech to a nonsense speech sound (e.g., normal speech played backwards) escape detection.

Interestingly, reducing the capacity available for processing an ad's claims does not mean necessarily that its persuasiveness is reduced. This will depend on whether the ad claims are strong (provide compelling reasons for buying the product) or weak (representing less than compelling reasons for purchase). A reduction in the processing of strong claims means that the consumer is less likely to appreciate just how strong they are. Consequently, persuasion is reduced. On the other hand, less processing of weak claims should be beneficial because consumers are less likely to think about their inadequacies. This, in turn, may improve the ad's persuasiveness.

Beyond interfering with the processing of advertising claims, attention-getting stimuli may affect an ad's persuasiveness in other ways. Rather than helping persuasion, such devices can actually backfire and reduce advertising effectiveness when consumers perceive the stimuli as a way to manipulate them.[46] Moreover, something used to attract attention may simply be disliked. A very famous endorser may serve as a powerful hook, but if this person is disliked, these negative feelings may rub off on consumers' product opinions. Models attired in bathing suits, although seen as appropriate endorsers for suntan products, may evoke unfavorable reactions when used to promote other types of products. For example, consider *Travel & Leisure Golf*'s use of supermodel Heidi Klum on its cover as a way of drawing younger males' attention to the magazine when sitting on the newsstand shelf. The cover shows a revealing and provocative picture of Heidi along with the cover line, "Playing with Heidi." Yet the average reader is a 52-year-old male. And females account for 39 percent of the magazine's readers. The cover runs the risk of alienating people in either group.[47]

Can Consumers Be Influenced if They Don't Pay Attention?

Thus far we have emphasized the importance of getting attention as a fundamental prerequisite for influencing consumer behavior. Nonetheless, some suggest that this may not be necessary. According to them, stimuli that are so weak that they cannot be perceived consciously may still be influential at an unconscious or subliminal level. *The notion that people are influenced by stimuli below our conscious level of awareness* is often referred to as **subliminal persuasion.**

Interest in subliminal persuasion can be traced to the late 1950s when Jim Vicary, the owner of a failing research business, claimed he discovered a way of influencing consumers without their conscious awareness. He reported Coca-Cola sales increased by 18 percent and popcorn sales grew by 52 percent when the words *DRINK COKE* and *EAT POPCORN* were flashed on a movie theater screen at speeds that escaped conscious detection. However, when an independent replication did not duplicate his findings, Vicary confessed to fabricating his results in the hope of reviving his business.[48]

For years, the subject lay dormant until Wilson Bryan Key contended in a popularized book that erotic subliminal cues are implanted in advertisements (e.g., the juxtaposition of ice cubes in a liquor ad) designed to appeal to subconscious sex drives.[49] Today, the use of subliminal stimuli is prevalent. Consumers spend millions of dollars each year on self-help tapes containing subliminal messages. Horror films occasionally include subliminal death masks and other scary images to enhance their ability to frighten viewers. Retailers sometimes embed subliminal messages within their in-store music in order to motivate employees and undermine shoplifting. Some resorts also have tried subliminal messages to help vacationers relax.[50]

Despite their prevalent use, the ability of subliminal stimuli to affect consumer behavior is highly questionable. Admittedly, some research does suggest that, in certain situations, subliminal stimuli may have modest effects.[51] Nonetheless, we are unaware of any research that provides a compelling demonstration of subliminal influences on actual behavior. As one writer on this subject observes:

> A century of psychological research substantiates the general principle that more intense stimuli have a greater effect on people's behavior than weaker ones. . . . Subliminal stimuli are usually so weak that the recipient is not just unaware of the stimulus but is also oblivious to the fact that he/she is being stimulated. As a result, the potential effects of subliminal stimuli are easily nullified by other ongoing stimulation in the same sensory channel.[52]

And even if the effects of subliminal stimuli were not nullified by the stimuli that are being processed consciously, we would wonder why someone would bother with, at best, a weak method of persuasion when much more effective methods can be used.

Summary

Making contact with consumers requires two things. The first requirement is exposure. Exposure is defined as the achievement of proximity to a stimulus such that an opportunity exists for activation of one or more of the five senses. For businesses, this means making sure that their messages and products are exposed to the right people at the right time and place. One obstacle to achieving this is that consumers are often selective in what they choose to be exposed to. Companies should also be alert to the dangers of overexposure.

The second requirement for making contact is attention. Attention represents the amount of thinking focused in a particular direction. Because attention draws upon our limited cognitive resources, we must be selective in what receives our attention. Unfortunately for business, products and advertising are rarely a top priority. Moreover, the competition for consumers' attention has created an extremely cluttered marketplace. These factors together makes gaining consumers' attention a most formidable business challenge.

Fortunately, companies have at their disposal an array of techniques and strategies for grabbing attention, many of which were covered in the chapter. Nonetheless, the use of such techniques and strategies can be risky. Ad stimuli that attract attention may interfere with consumers' processing of the rest of the advertisement.

Finally, we examined the potential to influence consumers without their attention. Subliminal persuasion refers to efforts to influence consumers with stimuli beneath their conscious level of awareness. The current consensus is that subliminal stimuli have, at best, minimal effects and that fears of their persuasiveness are largely unfounded.

Review and Discussion Questions

1. Consider the statement, "Exposure is a necessary but, by itself, insufficient condition for making contact." What does this mean?

2. What is the danger of overexposure? How can this danger be reduced?

3. What is meant by the expression, "a cluttered marketplace"? Why is this important to businesses? How has this influenced business strategy and tactics?

4. Listed below is a set of recommendations for designing yellow pages ads that appeared in *Link,* a trade magazine for the yellow pages industry:
   a. Use color wisely. Don't feel compelled to put every image or block of text into color. And don't just "colorize" your existing ad.
   b. Incorporate material from other media. If you advertise in other media, use the images from these ads in your yellow pages to create an integrated marketing approach.
   c. Beat the ho-hum pattern on the page. Use irregular borders to draw users away from your cookie-cutter competitors. And notice how copy is arranged in most ads and do the opposite.
   d. Use an illustration wherever appropriate. A visual image is an essential eye-catcher. Use something with a contemporary feel and avoid dated clip art.
   e. Use more "yellow space." Cluttered ads confuse and repel users. Words with a little space around them are more attractive and are more likely to be read.

   What principles for gaining attention are reflected in these recommendations?

5. Two consumers are exposed to the same ad. One is in the market for this product, but the other is not. How might these two consumers differ in their processing of this ad?

6. Suppose a company is considering one of two alternative attention-getting devices for use in its advertising. How should the company decide which to use?

7. Following the recommendation of its advertising agency, a company modified its current advertising campaign to include a famous celebrity as a way of enticing consumers to pay attention. Yet market research has challenged the wisdom of doing this since its advertising became less, not more, effective. Why might this have happened?

Endnotes

1. "Getting Good Listing Attracts Volumes," *Marketing News* (January 3, 2000), 9–10.

2. Scot Burton, Donald R. Lichtenstein, and Richard G. Netemeyer, "Exposure to Sales Flyers and Increased Purchases in Retail Supermarkets," *Journal of Advertising Research* 39 (September/October 1999), 7–14.

3. David E. Kalish, "Million Sign Up for Free Internet, But Not All Use It," *Miami Herald* (January 19, 2000), 7C.

4. Katherine Yung, "Advertisers Find the Net a Hard Nut to Crack," *Miami Herald's Business Monday* (July 12, 1999), 11.

5. "Background on Zapping," *Marketing News* (September 14, 1984), 36.

6. Michael G. Harvey and James T. Rothe, "Video Cassette Recorders: Their Impact on Viewers and Advertisers," *Journal of Advertising Research* (December 1984/January 1985), 10–19.

7. Margaret Henderson Blair and Michael J. Rabuck, "Advertising Wearin and Wearout: Ten Years Later—More Empirical Evidence and Successful Practice," *Journal of Advertising Research* 38 (September/October 1998), 7–18; Connie Pechmann and David W. Stewart, "Advertising Repetition: A Critical Review of Wearin and Wearout," *Current Issues and Research in Advertising* 11 (1988), 285–330; Douglas R. Scott and Debbie Solomon, "What Is Wearout Anyway?" *Journal of Advertising Research* 38 (September/October 1998), 19–28; David W. Stewart, "Advertising Wearout: What and How You Measure Matters," *Journal of Advertising Research* 39 (September/October 1999), 39–42.

8. Laura Bird, "Researchers Criticize Overuse of Ads," *The Wall Street Journal* (January 3, 1992), B3.

9. Richard E. Petty and John T. Cacioppo, "Effects of Message Repetition and Position on Cognitive Responses, Recall, and Persuasion," *Journal of Personality and Social Psychology* 37 (January 1979), 97–109; Arno J. Rethans, John L. Swasy, and Lawrence J. Marks, "Effects of Television Commercial Repetition, Receiver Knowledge, and Commercial Length: A Test of the Two-Factor Model," *Journal of Marketing Research* 23 (February 1986), 50–61.

10. Robert E. Burnkrant and Hanumantha R. Unnava, "Effects of Variation in Message Execution on the Learning of Repeated Brand Information," in Melanie Wallendorf and Paul F. Anderson, eds., *Advances in Consumer Research* 14 (Provo, UT: Association for Consumer Research, 1987), 173–176; H. Rao Unnava and Robert E. Burnkrant, "Effects of Repeating Varied Ad Executions on Brand Name Memory," *Journal of Marketing Research* 28 (November 1991), 406–416.

11. Bird, "Researchers Criticize Overuse of Ads."

12. Rebecca Quick, "Is Ever-So-Hip Abercrombie & Fitch Losing Its Edge With Teens?" *The Wall Street Journal* (February 22, 2000), B1, B4.

13. *Webster's New World Dictionary,* Second College Edition (Cleveland, OH: William Collins World Publishing Co., Inc., 1976).

14. Ravi Dhar and Itamar Simonson, "The Effect of the Focus of Comparison on Consumer Preferences," *Journal of Marketing Research* 29 (November 1992), 430–440.

15. For research on the effect of using shorter commercials, see Surendra N. Singh and Catherine A. Cole, "The Effect of Length, Content, and Repetition on Television Commercial Effectiveness," *Journal of Marketing Research* 30 (February 1993), 91–104.

16. Richard M. Shiffrin and R. C. Atkinson, "Storage and Retrieval Processes in Long-Term Memory," *Psychological Review* 76 (March 1969), 179–193.

17. Herbert A. Simon, "How Big Is a Chunk?" *Science* 183 (February 1974), 42–488; George A. Miller, "The Magical Number Seven, Plus or Minus Two: Some Limits on Our Capacity for Processing Information," *Psychological Review* 63 (March 1956), 81–97.

18. Jacob Jacoby, "Information Load and Decision Quality: Some Contested Issues," *Journal of Marketing Research* 15 (November 1977), 569–573; Jacob Jacoby, "Perspectives on Information Overload," *Journal of Consumer Research* 10 (March 1984), 432–435; Kevin Lane Keller and Richard Staelin, "Effects of Quality and Quantity of Information on Decision Effectiveness," *Journal of Consumer Research* 14 (September 1987), 200–213; Naresh K. Malhotra, "Information Load and Consumer Decision Making," *Journal of Consumer Research* 8 (March 1982), 419–430; Naresh K. Malhotra, "Reflections on the Information Overload Paradigm in Consumer Decision Making," *Journal of Consumer Research* 10 (March 1984), 436–440; Naresh K. Malhotra, Arun K. Jain, and Stephen W. Lagakos, "The Information Overload Controversy: An Alternative Viewpoint," *Journal of Marketing* 46 (Spring 1982), 27–37.

19. Marcia Mogelonsky, "Product Overload?" *American Demographics* (August 1998), 64–69.

20. For research on advertising clutter, see Tom J. Brown and Michael L. Rothschild, "Reassessing the Impact of Television Advertising Clutter," *Journal of Consumer Research* 20 (June 1993), 138–146; Raymond R. Burke and Thomas K. Srull, "Competitive Interference and Consumer Memory for Advertising," *Journal of Consumer Research* 15 (June 1988), 55–68; Kevin Lane Keller, "Memory and Evaluation Effects in Competitive Advertising Environments," *Journal of Consumer Research* 17 (March 1991), 463–476; Robert J. Kent and Chris T. Allen, "Competitive Interference Effects and Consumer Memory for Advertising: The Role of Brand Familiarity," *Journal of Marketing* 58 (July 1994), 97–105; Peter H. Webb, "Consumer Initial Processing in a Difficult Media Environment," *Journal of Consumer Research* 6 (December 1979), 225–236. Also see Michael L. Ray and Peter H. Webb, "Three Prescriptions for Clutter," *Journal of Advertising Research* 26 (February/March 1986), 69–77.

21: Caroline E. Mayer, "Scrambled, Fried or on a Stick?" *Miami Herald* (December 31, 1999), 1C, 3C.

22. Mogelonsky, "Product Overload?"

23. For an interesting discussion of how an ad's executional elements can affect attention, see Deborah J. MacInnis, Christine Moorman, and Bernard J. Jaworski, "Enhancing and Measuring Consumers' Motivation, Opportunity, and Ability to Process Brand Information," *Journal of Marketing* 55 (October 1991), 32–53.

24. Paul O'Donnell, "Read My Pitch! Earn Big Bucks!" *American Demographics* (November 1998), 13, 14, 18.

25. For a more detailed discussion by Yahoo!'s vice president of direct marketing, read Seth Godin, *Permission Marketing* (New York: Simon & Schuster, 1999).

26. Jennifer Lach, "First, a Word from Our Sponsor," *American Demographics* (January 1999), 39–41.

27. David H. Freedman, "Why You Watch Some Commercials—Whether You Mean To or Not," *TV Guide* (February 20, 1988), 4–7.

28. Michael J. McCarthy, "Mind Probe," *The Wall Street Journal* (March 22, 1991), B3.

29. Adam Finn, "Print Ad Recognition Readership Scores: An Information Processing Perspective," *Journal of Marketing Research* 25 (May 1988), 168–177.

30. Larry Percy, *Ways in Which the People, Words and Pictures in Advertising Influence Its Effectiveness* (Chicago: Financial Institutions Marketing Association, July 1984), 19.

31. Finn, "Print Ad Recognition Readership Scores."

32. W. F. Wagner, *Yellow Pages Report* (Scotts Valley, CA: Mark Publishing, 1988).

33. Keith K. Cox, "The Effect of Shelf Space upon Sales of Branded Products," *Journal of Marketing Research* 7 (February 1970), 55–58.

34. Finn, "Print Ad Recognition Readership Scores."

35. Sandra E. Moriarty, *Creative Advertising: Theory and Practice* (Englewood Cliffs, NJ: Prentice-Hall, 1986). For research indicating that changes in the position of elements within an ad can also influence the ad's persuasiveness, see Chris Janiszewski, "The Influence of Print Advertisement Organization on Affect toward a Brand Name," *Journal of Consumer Research* 17 (June 1990), 53–65.

36. Cynthia Corzo, "Centerfold Ad Campaign Makes Quite a Splash," *Miami Herald's Business Monday* (March 8, 1999), 11.

37. Dave Sheinin, "Tiger Has World by Tail," *Miami Herald* (May 20, 1997), 1A, 6A.

38. Joe Agnew, "Shoppers' Star Gazing Seen as Strategy to Slash Supermarket Shelf Clutter," *Marketing News* (January 16, 1987), 1, 16.

39. For research in this area, see M. Wayne Alexander and Ben Judd, Jr., "Do Nudes in Ads Enhance Brand Recall?" *Journal of Advertising*

Research 18 (February 1978), 47–50; Michael J. Baker and Gilbert A. Churchill, Jr., "The Impact of Physically Attractive Models on Advertising Evaluations," *Journal of Marketing Research* 14 (November 1977), 538–555; M. Steadman, "How Sexy Illustrations Affect Brand Recall," *Journal of Advertising Research* 9 (March 1969), 15–18; Lynn R. Kahle and Pamela M. Homer, "Physical Attractiveness of the Celebrity Endorser: A Social Adaptation Perspective," *Journal of Consumer Research* 11 (March 1985), 954–961; Penny M. Simpson, Steve Horton, Gene Brown, "Male Nudity in Advertisements: A Modified Replication and Extension of Gender and Product Effects," *Journal of the Academy of Marketing Science* 24 (1996), 257–262.

40. Lawrence Solely and Gary Kurzbard, "Sex in Advertising: A Comparison of 1964 and 1984 Magazine Advertisements," *Journal of Advertising* 15 (1986), 46–54, 64.

41. Thomas Madden and Marc Weinberger, "The Effect of Humor on Attention in Magazine Advertising," *Journal of Advertising* 22 (September 1982), 8–14; Marc G. Weinberger and Charles S. Gulas, "The Impact of Humor in Advertising: A Review," *Journal of Advertising* 32 (December 1982), 35–61.

42. Karen Jacobs, "Elevator Maker to Add Commercial Touch," *The Wall Street Journal* (December 7, 1999), B8.

43. Rodney Ho, "Baggage—Carousel Ad Business's Circuitous Launch," *The Wall Street Journal* (February 15, 2000), B2.

44. Jennifer Rewick, "iVillage Holds Ads Until After Christmas," *The Wall Street Journal* (December 23, 1999), B10.

45. E. C. Cherry, "Some Experiments on the Recognition of Speech with One and Two Ears," *Journal of the Acoustical Society of America* 25 (1953), 975–979.

46. Margaret C. Campbell, "When Attention-Getting Advertising Tactics Elicit Consumer Inferences of Manipulative Intent: The Importance of Balancing Benefits and Investments," *Journal of Consumer Psychology* 4 (1995), 225–254.

47. Heather Chaplin, "Fore, Baby!" *American Demographics* (October 1999), 64–65.

48. Walter Weir, "Another Look at Subliminal 'Facts'," *Advertising Age* (October 15, 1984), 46.

49. Wilson Bryan Key, *Subliminal Seduction: Ad Media's Manipulation of a Not-So Innocent America* (Englewood Cliffs, NJ: Prentice-Hall, 1972). Also see Wilson Bryan Key, *Media Sexploitation* (Englewood Cliffs, NJ: Prentice-Hall, 1976). Key's

claims have been strongly challenged. See Jack Haberstroh, "Can't Ignore Subliminal Ad Charges," *Advertising Age* (September 17, 1984), 3, 42, 44; Weir, "Another Look at Subliminal 'Facts'." Research continues in this area. See Ronnie Cuperfain and T. Keith Clark, "A New Perspective on Subliminal Advertising," *Journal of Advertising* 14 (July 1985), 36–41; Myron Gable, Henry T. Wilkens, Lynn Harris, and Richard Feinberg, "An Evaluation of Subliminally Embedded Sexual Stimuli in Graphics," *Journal of Advertising* 16 (1987), 26–31; Philip M. Merikle and Jim Cheesman, "Current Status of Research on Subliminal Perception," in Melanie Wallendorf and Paul Anderson, eds., *Advances in Consumer Research* 14 (Provo, UT: Association for Consumer Research, 1987), 298–302.

50. Jo Anna Natale, "Are You Open to Suggestion?" *Psychology Today* (September 1988), 28, 30.

51. Jon A. Krosnick, Andrew L. Betz, Lee J. Jussim, and Ann R. Lynn, "Subliminal Conditioning of Attitudes," *Personality and Social Psychology Bulletin* 18 (April 1992), 152–162; Robert B. Zajonc and Hazel Markus, "Affective and Cognitive Factors in Preferences," *Journal of Consumer Research* 9 (September 1982), 123–131. Also see Punam Anand and Morris B. Holbrook, "Reinterpretation of Mere Exposure or Exposure of Mere Reinterpretation," *Journal of Consumer Research* 17 (September 1990), 242–244; Punam Anand, Morris B. Holbrook and Debra Stephens, "The Formation of Affective Judgments: The Cognitive-Affective Model Versus the Independence Hypothesis," *Journal of Consumer Research* 15 (December 1988), 386–391; Timothy B. Heath, "The Logic of Mere Exposure: A Reinterpretation of Anand, Holbrook, and Stephens (1988)," *Journal of Consumer Research* 17 (September 1990), 237–241; Chris Janiszewski, "Preconscious Processing Effects: The Independence of Attitude Formation and Conscious Thought," *Journal of Consumer Research* 15 (September 1988), 199–209; Chris Janiszewski, "The Influence of Print Advertisement Organization on Affect toward a Brand Name," *Journal of Consumer Research* 17 (June 1990), 53–65; Carl Obermiller, "Varieties of Mere Exposure: The Effects of Processing Style and Repetition on Affective Response," *Journal of Consumer Research* 12 (June 1985), 17–31; Yehoshua Tsal, "On the Relationship between Cognitive and Affective Processes: A Critique of Zajonc and Markus," *Journal of Consumer Research* 12 (December 1985), 358–362.

52. Timothy E. Moore, "Subliminal Advertising: What You See Is What You Get," *Journal of Marketing* 46 (Spring 1982), 38–47.

CHAPTER 15

Shaping Consumers' Opinions

OPENING VIGNETTE

In the last few years, Mountain Dew has distributed pagers to thousands of youthful consumers and then beeped them with soft drink sales pitches from popular athletes and entertainers. The citrus-flavored drink with the caffeine kick has toured with the alternative music world's Warped Tour. And the brand signed on as a sponsor of the new Gravity Games extreme sports competition. The marketing of Mountain Dew, observers say, is a textbook example of how to reposition a brand.

As the 1980s dawned, owner PepsiCo was pitching the brand as a hillbilly drink with commercials that urged consumers to "tickle your innards." But during the 1980s, Pepsi and longtime ad agency BBDO New York created an image for the drink as an alternative for savvy youth. The dramatic growth was jumpstarted by the Do the Dew campaign that began in 1995. The campaign is aimed squarely at young males. Action-packed commercials revolve around four young males who have never met a mountain high enough to keep them from grabbing a snowboard. Mountain Dew's commercials are still populated by guys engaged in extreme sports. But the campaign's appeal has been broadened through the addition of urban-oriented commercials starring actor Jackie Chan, athlete Michael Johnson, and rapper Busta Rhymes.

"PepsiCo has done an extraordinary job of positioning Mountain Dew," says Peter Sealey, a marketing professor at the University of California and a former Coca-Cola executive. "It's probably Pepsi's most successful positioning since the Pepsi Generation."

America's fourth most popular soft drink (behind Coke Classic, Pepsi, and Diet Coke), Mountain Dew was the fastest growing top-10 soda brand last year with a 9.9 percent increase in cases sold, according to *Beverage Digest*. Coca-Cola's Sprite finished second with a 9 percent increase. Mountain Dew's 20-ounce bottle is the most popular soft drink sold in convenience stores.

Mountain Dew's marketers know that they can't afford to gloat about the brand's transformation from hayseed country cousin to a beverage of choice among savvy young consumers. Soft drink veterans are only too aware of the success enjoyed by Sprite that, 20 years ago, was a distant second to category leader 7 Up. Coke's marketing turned Sprite into the fifth-most popular soft drink, which currently has three times the market share of 7 Up, now relegated to the number 8 spot.

Source: Excerpted from Greg Johnson, "Dewing It," Miami Herald (October 22, 1999), 1C, 4C.

In Chapter 14, you learned about the exposure and attention requirements for making contact with target consumers. Yet even if contact is established, marketing's job is far from done. Beyond trying to get you to think about their products, companies also try to get you to think and feel about their products in a certain way. In other words, they want to shape your product opinions. This means influencing what you believe and how you feel about their products in order to achieve the desired product image and a favorable product attitude. As evidenced by Mountain Dew's successful repositioning of its image from the country to the city, companies that understand how to shape consumers' opinions will see the benefits on their bottom lines.

Though we have emphasized the importance of shaping consumers' opinions throughout the text (especially in Chapters 9 and 10), the question of how to do so has been relatively ignored. Until now, that is. The purpose of this chapter is to provide you with a better understanding of how this task can be accomplished. In building this understanding, we start at the beginning: opinion formation.

Opinion Formation

The first time we develop a belief, feeling, or attitude about something is called **opinion formation.** As discussed in Chapter 10, people's attitudinal opinions are based on their beliefs and feelings about the attitude object. To the extent the object is associated with favorable beliefs and feelings, attitudes become more positive. We did not discuss, however, what happens between exposure to some object or stimulus and the subsequent formation of beliefs, feelings, and attitudes. This is the domain of comprehension. **Comprehension** involves *the interpretation of a stimulus.* It's the point at which meaning is attached to the stimulus. This meaning depends on what occurs during stimulus processing. Different aspects of this processing are discussed next.

Stimulus Categorization

Initially, the person tries to answer the question, "What is it?" Answering this question involves **stimulus categorization** in which *the stimulus is classified using the mental concepts and categories stored in memory.* How a stimulus is categorized is important because the particular mental categories to which a stimulus is assigned affect the opinions formed about the stimulus.[1] Toro once introduced a lightweight snowblower named Snow Pup. But the name led many to categorize it as a toy. Even those who classified it into the proper product category often interpreted the brand name as indicating that it wasn't powerful enough for the job. Changing the name (first to Snowmaster and then simply Toro) eliminated these problems and helped sales.[2]

Unfortunately, consumers often make mistakes during stimulus categorization. The package used by Planters Fresh Roast peanuts looked so similar to the vacuum packaging used for coffee that many consumers miscategorized the product. Grocers were not happy with the mess shoppers made when they errantly poured the peanuts into coffee grinding machines.[3] When Frito-Lay introduced its new Cheetos Paws, a snack food in the shape of a cheetah's foot, in-store displays were located near the pet food aisle, leaving some consumers uncertain about the product category to which it belonged. In the words of one confused consumer, "Are Paws for my cat or for me?"[4] Nor is advertising immune to miscategorization. Early advertisements for Claritin, an antihistamine, used the tag line, "A clear day with Claritin." Yet many mistakenly categorized the product as an antidepressant.[5]

The Amount of Processing

Consider the advertisement containing a large amount of product information. To fully appreciate the product's benefits and competitive advantages, careful and extensive processing of the ad's contents is necessary. When consumers do so, the meaning derived from the ad should lead them to form very favorable product attitudes. But those that don't invest the cognitive effort to comprehend this information will remain ignorant about the product's benefits and advantages. Consequently, they'll have a different interpretation of what the ad conveys about the advertised product.

As this simple example illustrates, the amount of processing can shape comprehension and, consequently, opinion formation. Many stimuli, especially those categorized as an advertisement, may receive minimal processing. Having determined what it is, we decide to allocate our cognitive resources elsewhere. When this happens, there's little chance of the stimulus being influential.

At other times, we might pay enough attention to a commercial to follow what's happening and, perhaps, to notice what's being advertised, but that's about it. In so doing, we may *experience certain thoughts* (called **cognitive responses**) *and feelings* (called **affective responses**). We might think about how tired we are of seeing the same commercial over and over. Or maybe we'll feel amused by a commercial's humor. In any case, processing is far from extensive.

On some occasions, we allocate considerable amounts of our cognitive resources during processing. A commercial may be so engaging that we carefully follow everything it says and shows. The advertising campaign for Tasters' Choice coffee showcasing a budding relationship between a woman and the man living next door captivated the minds of many consumers. Or maybe we listen closely to what the commercial has to say about the product, perhaps because it's perceived as containing relevant information useful for a forthcoming and important purchase decision. Claims about the advertised product's benefits and competitive advantages are carefully scrutinized, with prior knowledge germane to the claims' validity being activated from long-term memory. Thinking may extend to product attributes beyond those discussed in the message. A direct mail advertisement emphasizing high product quality without mentioning price may lead consumers to infer that the price must be high; otherwise, why wouldn't it be shown?

Just how much processing is needed to derive meaning from a stimulus depends on how easily it can be processed. Some stimuli are processed easily; others are far more demanding, requiring much greater amounts of our cognitive resources. Look at the two ads shown in Figure 15.1. The Cracker Barrel ad can be comprehended quite easily in only a few seconds. This is not the case for the Claritin ad. Consumers must now engage in much more processing before they can grasp what it communicates. Given the reality that consumers are usually unwilling to invest much of their cognitive resources into processing advertising messages, advertisers often opt for simple messages that can be easily comprehended. Only when there is reason to believe that consumers will give the time and effort needed for processing more complex messages does it make sense to do so.

We do not wish to give the impression that extensive processing is necessary before a stimulus can affect comprehension and opinion formation. To the contrary, even relatively superficial processing may be sufficient for enabling a stimulus to be influential. According to **classical conditioning,** *simply pairing one stimulus that spontaneously evokes certain meanings and feelings with another can cause a transfer of these meanings and feelings from one to the other.*[6]

Classical Conditioning

For many, the term *classical conditioning* elicits thoughts of Pavlov and his dogs. Pavlov, the father of classical conditioning and winner of a Nobel Prize, showed how a stimulus acquires new meaning simply by its association with another stimulus. In his famous experiments with dogs, Pavlov started with *a stimulus* (called the **unconditioned stimulus**) *known to evoke automatically a particular response*

Figure 15.1   Which Ad Is Easier to Process?

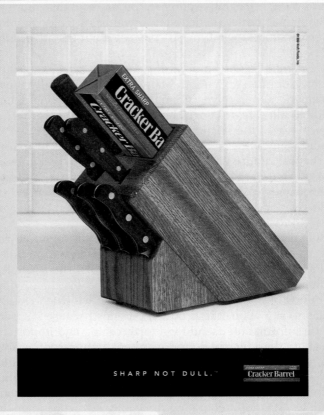

SHARP NOT DULL.™   Cracker Barrel

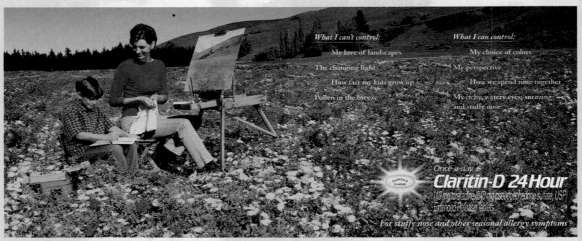

TAKE CLEAR CONTROL. TAKE CLARITIN.

What I can't control:
My love of landscapes
The changing light
How fast my kids grow up
Pollen in the breeze

What I can control:
My choice of colors
My perspective
How we spend time together
My itchy, watery eyes; sneezing; and stuffy nose

Once-a-day
Claritin-D 24 Hour
(10 mg loratadine/240 mg pseudoephedrine sulfate, USP)
Extended-Release Tablets

For stuffy nose and other seasonal allergy symptoms

Talk to your doctor about once-a-day, nondrowsy CLARITIN-D® 24 HOUR — for people ages 12 and up. CLARITIN-D® 24 HOUR is safe to take as prescribed: one tablet daily. In studies, dry mouth was the most commonly reported side effect. Other side effects including drowsiness and sleeplessness occurred about as often as they did with a sugar pill. *Some people should not take CLARITIN-D® 24 HOUR.* If you have a history of difficulty in swallowing tablets or any medical problems associated with swallowing abnormalities, you should not take CLARITIN-D® 24 HOUR. Due to pseudoephedrine (the decongestant in CLARITIN-D® 24 HOUR tablets and many over-the-counter allergy medications), you should not take CLARITIN-D® 24 HOUR if you have glaucoma (abnormally high pressure in your eyes), difficulty urinating, severe high blood pressure, severe heart disease, or are taking MAO inhibitors (certain prescription medications that treat depression).

Some people need to be especially careful using CLARITIN-D® 24 HOUR. Always take CLARITIN-D® 24 HOUR with a full glass of water. Also, the tablets must not be chewed or broken. Check with your healthcare provider before taking CLARITIN-D® 24 HOUR if you have high blood pressure; diabetes; heart disease; increased intraocular pressure (eye pressure); thyroid, liver, or kidney problems; enlarged prostate; or if you are pregnant, planning to become pregnant, or nursing a baby. You shouldn't take CLARITIN-D® 24 HOUR with any other antihistamines and decongestants, as too much pseudoephedrine sulfate can cause nervousness, sleeplessness, dizziness, and other related side effects. Please see next page for additional important information. *Available by prescription only.*

Call 1-888-833-0003 for more information and a $5.00 rebate certificate. Visit www.claritin.com

(called the **unconditioned response**). Specifically, food was used because it causes dogs to salivate. To show that this response could be transferred to a *new stimulus* (called the **conditioned stimulus**) *previously unassociated with this response,* he began ringing a bell whenever the dogs were given food. Eventually, simply hearing the bell caused the dogs to salivate. Because this response *arises from the conditioning that has taken place,* it's called the **conditioned response.**

Figure 15.2 shows the basic classical conditioning framework within a product context. In this example, based on the Cracker Barrel ad shown in Figure 15.1, knives, a symbol of sharpness, are paired with the product in the hope that this meaning can be conditioned to the product. If it does, the cheese will be perceived as having a sharper flavor. Obviously, before this can happen, consumers must undertake enough processing of the ad for this connection to be made. Nonetheless, as noted earlier, this requires relatively little processing, certainly far less than required by the Claritin ad shown in Figure 15.1.

One demonstration of meaning transfer comes from a study in which people processed an ad for a fictitious paper tissue. For some, the ad contained an explicit claim of softness. For others, the ad lacked this claim. Rather, it simply presented the picture of a cuddly little kitten. When asked about their opinions of the tissue's softness, participants reported more favorable beliefs when the product was paired with the kitten, thus reaffirming the power of classical conditioning for influencing consumers' opinions.[7]

Beyond a transfer of meaning, simple association may also cause a transfer of feelings and liking. Products are often paired with stimuli that, though devoid of product-relevant meaning, are well liked and evoke favorable feelings. Recent Budweiser commercials featuring Louie the wisecracking lizard are a good example. These commercials say nothing about why you might buy this product. Even so, Budweiser is betting millions of dollars that you'll like its product more (which, in turn, should enhance the likelihood of your buying it) simply because it has been associated with something that you feel good about.

The potential for product-irrelevant stimuli to affect product choice has been illustrated by research in which participants are given a choice between two similar pens. When one of the pens was paired with irrelevant but well-liked music, it was chosen most often. Yet when it was paired with disliked music, the other pen became the most popular choice.[8] Other research indicates that this effect may depend heavily on the nature of the choice set. When choosing among alternatives lacking a dominant brand (such as when choosing between two similar brands), association with a well-liked stimulus may tip the scales in favor of the brand making the association. Nonetheless, if a brand is clearly inferior to another

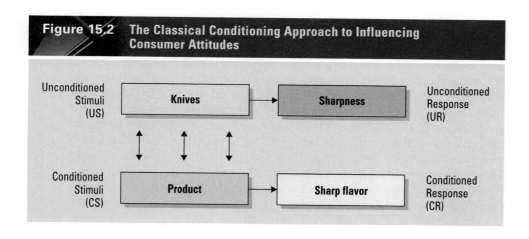

Figure 15.2   The Classical Conditioning Approach to Influencing Consumer Attitudes

Unconditioned Stimuli (US) — **Knives** → **Sharpness** — Unconditioned Response (UR)

Conditioned Stimuli (CS) — **Product** → **Sharp flavor** — Conditioned Response (CR)

brand in the choice set, it may not be able to offset this competitive disadvantage by pairing itself with some favorable but irrelevant stimulus.[9]

The power of association to shape consumers' opinions is invaluable to the marketing of products for at least two reasons. First, it frees companies from the constraints imposed by how well the product actually performs. Even if the product is inferior to a competitor, by selecting the appropriate stimuli for association with the product, favorable opinions can still be encouraged. As an example, consider Topol toothpaste. Although better than many of its competitors at removing stains, the most effective stain remover (at least during this particular time) was Zact HP, a competitive advantage heavily emphasized in Zact's advertising. For obvious reasons, Topol needed to stay away from talking about its relative performance. Instead, its advertising associated the product with stimuli designed to convey the idea that it removed stains and whitened teeth. Smiling male and female models decked out in all white clothing showing their pearly whites dominated Topol's advertising.

The other reason simple association is so attractive is that it works without requiring consumers to undertake extensive thinking during processing. As we have pointed out before, consumers usually have better things to think about than many of the products and advertisements that clutter the marketplace. Consequently, extensive thinking is more the exception than the rule. As a result, efforts to shape opinions that require less processing have a greater chance of succeeding.

The Content of Processing

In addition to the amount of processing, it's also important to understand the content of processing. A critical aspect of this content is the favorableness of the cognitive and affective responses that occur during processing. Favorable responses are a fundamental prerequisite for the formation of favorable product opinions. When these responses are unfavorable, companies will not be happy with the opinions that are formed. As a case in point, read Consumer in Focus 15.1.

Another key aspect of content is the extent to which processing involves product-relevant thinking. Differences in such thinking have led researchers to propose two different opinion formation processes: a central process and a peripheral process.[10]

The Central Process of Opinion Formation

Suppose an ad containing information about an important and forthcoming product purchase grabs your attention. Because of its personal relevance, you allocate considerable cognitive resources during processing. You carefully think about the ad claims, evaluating whether they provide compelling reasons for buying this product. These thoughts or cognitive responses become the foundation for building opinions. And depending on whether your cognitive responses are positive (e.g., thoughts that indicate acceptance of the ad claims) or negative (e.g., thoughts that indicate rejection of the ad claims), your opinions will be more or less favorable. In this instance, you followed a **central process** in which *opinions are formed from a thoughtful consideration of relevant information.*

Because of their reliance on relevant information, opinions formed through the central process are very sensitive to the strength or quality of this information. Ads describing compelling advantages of the advertised brand lead to more favorable opinions than ads that do not. This simple fact is well documented by research examining how the opinions formed after ad processing depend on the strength of the ad claims. In a typical study, some people process an ad containing strong, compelling claims; others process a similar ad in which the strong

Consumer in Focus 15.1

Centrum Silver's Ad Misses the Mark

With 13.6 percent of the market share for adult multivitamins, Centrum Silver, a product of one of American Home Products' divisions, is the second most popular brand in America, outflanking competitors like One-A-Day, Nature Made, and Geritol. Introduced in 1990, the product targets the 50-plus market that is 65 million strong and controls 55 percent of the country's discretionary income. Centrum Silver's sales have jumped 47 percent during the past two years.

Its current advertising campaign, "Still Exploring," features two handsome and healthy older adults bundled in khakis and denim who pull a canoe out of a lake, leap across a bubbling stream, and roast marshmallows over a crackling fire. An oversized bottle of vitamins rises from a silver pool, and a hearty male voice proclaims: "Life is an adventure, because you're over 50 and still exploring!" We hear a bit about "age-essential nutrients." The announcer says, "It's a great time to be silver!" And the 15 seconds are up.

Yet the campaign has its critics. Klaus Rohrich, president of Toronto-based Taylor/Rohrich Associates Inc., which specializes in marketing to 50-plusers, says the campaign is a good example of how companies often botch their attempts to attract older consumers. The imagery is hackneyed, he complains, and the camping scenario fatally flawed. Since the premise of the ad is that life can be an adventure after hitting 50, you think the company would be extra careful in what it chooses to represent its "adventure." Camping is neither a likely choice for people over 50 nor particularly adventuresome. Rohrich thinks a cruise would have been a better choice. The point is it should have been something older people are likely to do. Otherwise, the ad becomes irrelevant at best and offensive at worst.

Rohrich's sentiments are echoed by one of Centrum Silver's target customers. This 54-year-old, health-conscious woman changes the channel every time the commercial flashes across her TV screen. "How can they tell me what I need when they clearly don't know who I am," she explains. "They created an image of old people that's safe for young people, but has nothing to do with us. If it's aimed at me, they missed by a country mile." Most disconcerting is her comment, "The inauthenticity of the ad convinced me the product was bull."

Source: Excerpted from Heather Chaplin, "Centrum's Self-Inflicted Silver Bullet," American Demographics *(March 1999), 68–69.*

claims are replaced by weaker versions. If a central process is followed, those given the stronger claims should develop more favorable product opinions than those given the weaker claims. However, as product-relevant thinking decreases, the ad claims should become less influential. At some point, this thinking is so minimal that the opinions formed may be unaffected by the claims' strength.

Research findings demonstrating how the persuasiveness of an ad's claims depends on the thinking undertaken during processing are presented in Figure 15.3. In this study, subjects processed an advertisement for a fictitious product containing either strong or weak claims under conditions designed to influence the degree of product-relevant thinking.[11] Some subjects are told that they'll make a choice among various brands, including the advertised brand, and receive a free sample of whichever brand they choose. This should motivate more thinking about the product and its attributes during processing. Others were not informed about the forthcoming choice. Consequently, they had less incentive to think about the ad claims.

As shown in Figure 15.3, the extent to which opinions about the advertised product were affected by the ad claims depended on the amount of product-relevant thinking during processing. In the condition where such thinking was most likely to occur, those given the ad containing stronger claims formed much more favorable opinions than did those given the weaker claims. Yet the magnitude of this difference declines noticeably in the condition where product-relevant thinking was less likely to occur. In fact, the product opinions formed in this condition were essentially the same regardless of the ad claims.

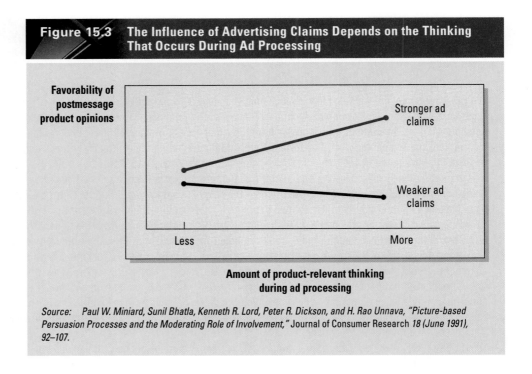

Figure 15.3 **The Influence of Advertising Claims Depends on the Thinking That Occurs During Ad Processing**

Source: *Paul W. Miniard, Sunil Bhatla, Kenneth R. Lord, Peter R. Dickson, and H. Rao Unnava, "Picture-based Persuasion Processes and the Moderating Role of Involvement,"* Journal of Consumer Research *18 (June 1991), 92–107.*

Although the preceding study focused on product-relevant information conveyed by advertising claims, such information can be communicated through other advertising elements. The type of people shown in an ad might be used to determine whether the product fits consumers' self-images. Think about how replacing the four young men in Mountain Dew's commercials with four elderly grandmothers would probably cause teenagers to form very different opinions about the soft drink.

The potential for nonclaim advertising elements to provide product-relevant information was demonstrated by a study that manipulated the type of picture included in an ad.[12] Some received an ad containing a picture designed to reinforce certain beliefs about the product's attributes; the ad given to others contained a picture devoid of product-relevant information. This study also manipulated the likelihood of product-relevant thinking in the same manner as the prior study. Following ad processing, subjects reported their product opinions, the results of which appear in Figure 15.4. Notice how the pattern of results strongly resembles those previously presented in Figure 15.3. When relatively little thinking about the product occurred during ad processing, opinions were unaffected by the picture manipulation. In contrast, the picture manipulation altered product opinions as such thinking became more prevalent. Those shown the ad with the picture providing relevant information formed more favorable opinions than did those shown the ad with a picture lacking relevant information.

The Peripheral Process of Opinion Formation

Whether extensive thinking about relevant information occurs during processing depends on both the person's motivation and ability to do so. If you're getting ready to spend thousands of dollars on something, you're probably very motivated (if not, you're probably very rich) to carefully evaluate relevant information. And if you're also able to do this (meaning that you have the knowledge necessary for understanding the information as well as the opportunity to do so),

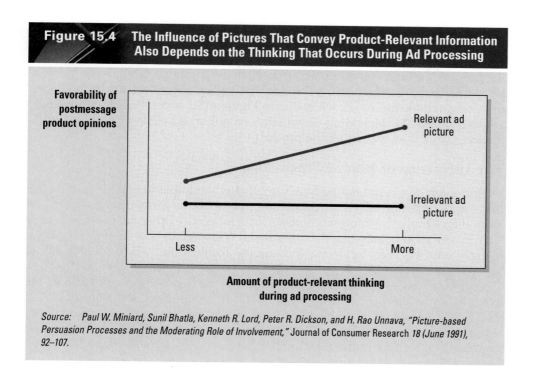

Figure 15.4   The Influence of Pictures That Convey Product-Relevant Information Also Depends on the Thinking That Occurs During Ad Processing

Favorability of postmessage product opinions

Relevant ad picture

Irrelevant ad picture

Less   More

Amount of product-relevant thinking during ad processing

Source: Paul W. Miniard, Sunil Bhatla, Kenneth R. Lord, Peter R. Dickson, and H. Rao Unnava, "Picture-based Persuasion Processes and the Moderating Role of Involvement," Journal of Consumer Research *18 (June 1991), 92–107.*

you probably will. But motivation or ability is often lacking. Just think of the countless commercials you have watched without trying to carefully evaluate the strengths and weaknesses of the advertised product. For whatever reason, you weren't motivated to undertake this type of thinking.

Nonetheless, limited thinking about relevant information does not preclude opinion formation. It simply means that opinions are formed through a different mental process. *Opinions that arise without thinking about relevant information* follow a **peripheral process.** For example, consumers may form opinions about the advertised product based on how much they like and enjoy the commercial itself. There's a considerable amount of research documenting the influence of consumers' attitude toward the ad as an important determinant of advertising effectiveness in shaping their opinions.[13] That a commercial's humor or entertainment value is irrelevant to evaluating the product's true merits doesn't matter when opinions are formed through a peripheral process. As emphasized in our earlier discussion about classical conditioning, simply activating favorable feelings in conjunction with the product can cause these feelings to be transferred over to the product.

To better illustrate the peripheral process of opinion formation, consider the study testing the effect of advertising pictures that served as peripheral cues.[14] **Peripheral cues** are *stimuli devoid of product-relevant information.* Because they lack relevant information, peripheral cues should not be influential when opinion formation follows a central process. Rather, any influence they exert is limited to when opinion formation follows a peripheral process.

In this study, some people received an ad containing a very attractive picture of a tropical beach at sunset. The ad given to others was identical except that the attractive picture was replaced with one of some ugly iguanas perceived as unattractive. As before, some subjects were informed about a forthcoming choice involving the advertised product as a way of encouraging more extensive thinking about the product.

Figure 15.5 displays the results involving the product opinions formed after ad processing. The attractive picture caused subjects to develop more favorable product opinions than did the unattractive picture, but only when thinking about the product's merits was minimal. When such thinking was more likely, opinions were unaffected by the pictures. Notice that the pattern of results in this figure differs from the patterns shown earlier in Figures 15.3 and 15.4. These differences are to be expected depending on whether or not an ad element provides information relevant to evaluating the product.

The Influence of Biased Processing

Even though a person may be highly motivated and able to engage in thoughtful consideration of relevant information, the opinions formed may depend on more than simply the information itself. This is because other factors may bias or alter information processing, thereby causing a change in how the information is interpreted. One such factor is expectations. To illustrate, take a look at Figure 15.6. What do you see?

Some perceive the stimulus (known as the "broken B") in Figure 15.6 as the letter B. Some interpret it as the number 13. It depends on how you look at it. And how you look at it can be altered by causing you to anticipate seeing either a letter or a number. Suppose that, prior to viewing the broken B, you first processed either four different capital letters or four pairs of digits. Doing so primes you to expect a letter or a number. This expectation, in turn, strongly affects your interpretation. Those expecting digits interpret the broken B as 13. Those anticipating letters interpret it as B.[15]

This same phenomenon takes place when consumers are forming their product opinions. We may interpret product information collected during search as being consistent with our prior expectations, especially if this information is ambiguous (i.e., open to multiple interpretations).[16] Expectations can even alter consumers' interpretations of their consumption experiences, a possibility acknowledged in Chapter 6.

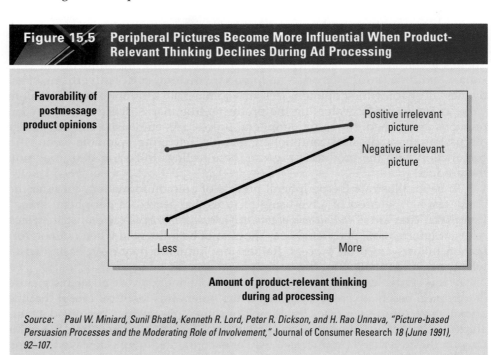

Figure 15.5   Peripheral Pictures Become More Influential When Product-Relevant Thinking Declines During Ad Processing

Favorability of postmessage product opinions

Positive irrelevant picture

Negative irrelevant picture

Less

More

Amount of product-relevant thinking during ad processing

Source: Paul W. Miniard, Sunil Bhatla, Kenneth R. Lord, Peter R. Dickson, and H. Rao Unnava, "Picture-based Persuasion Processes and the Moderating Role of Involvement," Journal of Consumer Research 18 (June 1991), 92–107.

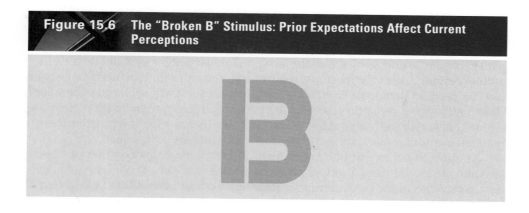

Figure 15.6   The "Broken B" Stimulus: Prior Expectations Affect Current Perceptions

Similarly, consumers' mood states at the time of information processing may also bias their interpretation and opinion formation in a mood-congruent manner (see Chapter 10). Consumers in a good mood may be more likely to interpret information more favorably than consumers in a less positive mood, thereby causing more favorable opinions to be formed.

How Businesses Influence Opinion Formation

Having covered the basics of comprehension and opinion formation, we now turn our attention to the variety of tactics used by businesses for influencing the opinions formed about their products.

Advertising's Role in Opinion Formation

As indicated by much of the preceding discussion, advertising can play a critical role in shaping the opinions formed by consumers. In this section, we talk about how various aspects of advertising contribute to this shaping process. In so doing, we decompose advertising into different parts, starting with the claims it makes about the advertised brand.

Advertising Claims

As demonstrated earlier, ads making stronger claims about the advertised brand's merits are better at creating favorable product opinions than those containing weaker claims, so long as consumers engage in sufficient thinking about product-relevant information during ad processing. But what makes a claim stronger or weaker? Let's start with its relevancy. Claims about things unrelated to the consumer's needs lack personal relevance. Relevant claims are those that connect with the person's life in some meaningful way. One industry study found that relevancy was the most important determinant of new product advertising's success in persuading consumers to try the product.[17]

The strength of an advertising claim also depends on what it conveys about the advertised product's characteristics and benefits. Consider the ad for Duracell Ultra claiming that it's "the most powerful alkaline battery in the world." If believed, consumers should form more favorable opinions about this product than would be the case when the ad contains more modest claims.[18] Similarly, the comparative ad that describes an important advantage over a well-known competitor represents a stronger advocacy for the advertised brand than a noncomparative ad that's silent about how the advertised brand stacks up relative to its competition. Consequently, comparative ads may lead consumers to form more favorable opinions about the advertised brand relative to the competitor used as a point of comparison.[19]

The extent to which advertising provides substantiation or support for its claims is important.[20] Product demonstrations are an effective way to substantiate claims. When St. Regis wanted to demonstrate the strength of its corrugated paper, it built a bridge of the material and showed a 2.5-ton Rolls Royce automobile driving over it. One study reports a significant relationship between the use of a product demonstration in TV commercials and their ability to persuade.[21] Testimonials from consumers about their consumption experiences with the product may also help reinforce advertising claims. Ads for weight-loss products often feature individuals telling us how many pounds they have lost.

Another characteristic of advertising claims that may affect consumers' opinions about the advertised product involves whether and when consumers can verify a claim's accuracy or truthfulness. **Search claims** are *those that can be validated before purchase by examining information readily available in the marketplace.* An ad claiming that the advertised product has the lowest price or best warranty can be verified by checking out the competition. **Experience claims** *can also be verified but require product consumption in order to do so.* If an ad for a new brand of salad dressing claims to have a better taste than the brand you currently use, you don't really know if this is true until you have tried it. Sometimes advertising claims are such that *verification of their accuracy is either impossible or unlikely because they require more effort than consumers are willing to invest.* Such claims are called **credence claims.** A good example of this is Tylenol's long-running claim, "Used by more hospitals than any other brand of pain reliever." We think it's a safe bet that no consumer has ever surveyed enough hospitals to determine the truthfulness of this claim. Perhaps because they believe that companies are more motivated to tell the truth when their claims can be verified prior to product purchase, consumers perceive search claims to be much more truthful than either experience or credence claims.[22]

Even the manner in which product claims are stated can affect the opinions formed from these claims. As a simple example of this, consider meat products. Because the percentage of lean meat plus the percentage of fat content always equals 100 percent, information about the percentage of one automatically provides information about the other. If meat is described as 80 percent lean, this means that it has a fat content of 20 percent. Conversely, if meat is described as 20 percent fat, then you know that it's 80 percent lean. Thus, descriptions about either the meat's leanness or fat percentage are equally informative. Even so, they're not equally influential. In one study, a meat product was described as either 80 percent lean or 20 percent fat. When asked their opinions of this product, those receiving the description of the meat's leanness formed much more favorable product opinions than those receiving the description of the meat's fat content.[23]

Whether a claim is stated in an objective or a subjective manner is also important. **Objective claims** *focus on factual information that is not subject to individual interpretations.* **Subjective claims,** however, are *ones that may evoke different interpretations across individuals.* Claims such as "low-priced" or "lightweight" would be considered subjective, inasmuch as what is low or light for one person may not be for the next. These same attributes could be expressed objectively by giving the actual price and weight. Because objective claims are more precise and more easily evaluated, they are perceived as more believable, they evoke more favorable thinking during processing, and they create more favorable beliefs and attitudes about the advertised product.[24]

Although the preceding discussion of how advertising claims can influence opinion formation presumes that a sufficient level of thinking about these claims will occur during ad processing, advertising claims may still be influential even if such thinking is rather minimal. This can occur when the sheer number of claims serves as a peripheral cue. Under the peripheral route, simply increasing the quantity (rather than quality or strength) of claims can lead to more favorable opinions, even if these additional claims are limited to unimportant information.[25]

Product Endorsers

As explained in Chapter 14, advertisers often use product endorsers for attracting attention. They also use endorsers for shaping consumers' product opinions. Omega watches, for instance, labels itself "Cindy Crawford's choice" (see Figure 15.7) in the hope of making itself more attractive in the eyes of many consumers.

Endorsers can help shape consumers' product opinions in several ways. First, their simple association with the product may be reason enough for buying it. Think of how many pairs of sneakers have been sold simply because they had Michael Jordan's name on them. His name alone transforms the product into a status symbol. So powerful is his appeal that retail sales for the Michael Jordan fragrance exceeded $75 million less than one year after its introduction.[26]

Endorsers can be a rich source of meanings that companies may wish to associate with their products. One reason the makers of Tic Tac breath mints chose actress Kimberly Quinn to serve as a spokeswoman in its new commercials was that she "reflects the attributes of the brand in terms of being friendly, approachable and trustworthy."[27] The makers of Slim Jim, on the other hand, enlisted professional wrestlers to create a particular meaning for its product. You can find out more about this in Consumer in Focus 15.2.

Consumer in Focus 15.2

Wrestling and Belching Convey the Right Meaning for Slim Jim

Anyone who has ever lived with, dated, or been a teenage boy knows nothing gets the attention of this demographic group better than a really good, really loud, really juicy belch. This is why, for six years, GoodMark Foods, a division of ConAgra, has associated its Slim Jim meat snacks with professional wrestler Macho Man Randy Savage and World Championship Wrestling, the entertainment industry's equivalent of audible indigestion. Wrestling evokes feelings of rebelliousness and irreverence, an in-your-face sort of humor that appeals to teenage boys.

Slim Jim's ties to wrestling are "brilliant," according to research experts, because the sport-o-tainment so appeals to the guttural instincts of teen boys. "The idea of the product as being not mom-endorsed is important," says Allison Cohen, president of PeopleTalk, a qualitative research agency in New York and Boston. "It appeals to the behavior teen boys exhibit all day when they are not under mom's thumb. They are enjoying themselves, having fun. The gross-out factor is perfect."

Nonetheless, GoodMark felt the campaign needed tweaking, so it recently launched new TV spots featuring "Slim Jim Guy," who, when ingested, causes eruptions in a teenage boy's stomach. Viewers can almost smell the pungent odor of the young man's burp. "We wanted to find a way of getting even more product identification in the advertisement, and not to make them so much a biography of Randy Savage or to be too distracted from the message of Slim Jim," says Jeff Slater, vice president of marketing at GoodMark. Barbara Coulon, director of trends at Youth Intelligence in New York City, believes the Slim Jim Guy commercials hit home with teen boys because they are irreverent and disgusting, qualities that appeal to the target's bathroom humor. "The character goes against society—he's very outspoken and gross. They like gross."

The effectiveness of the brand's advertising is showing up at the cash register. Slim Jim was the number 1 brand in the meat-snacks category with sales of nearly $35 million in the 52 weeks ending July 18, 1999 (the most recent period for which figures are available). Compared to the same period the year before, sales were up nearly 25 percent.

Source: Excerpted from Adrienne W. Fawcett, "Going for the Gross-Out," American Demographics (February 2000), 42–43.

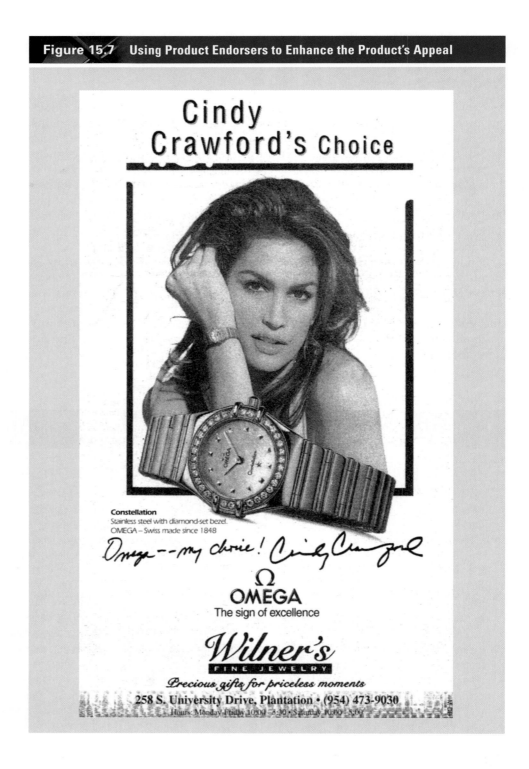

Figure 15.7   Using Product Endorsers to Enhance the Product's Appeal

One complicating factor in using product endorsers to convey meaning is that their effectiveness may depend on the particular product they endorse. According to the **match-up hypothesis,** *endorsers are most effective when they are perceived as appropriate spokespeople for the endorsed product.*[28] A supermodel may be a great choice for a cosmetics' manufacturer but less so for an investment company.

Similarly, endorsers may provide testimonies of the product's effectiveness. Ads for L'Oreal hair coloring use actress Heather Locklear as a product endorser.

One advantage of doing so is that Ms. Locklear and her beautiful blonde hair may be interpreted as visual evidence of the product's effectiveness.

Product endorsers may cause consumers to become more accepting of an ad's claims. A source's trustworthiness is critical here. Trusted sources evoke more favorable opinions than sources of questionable trustworthiness. The source's expertise is also important since consumers may be more accepting of claims supported by someone perceived as more knowledgeable although this influence may easily evaporate when questions exist about the source's trustworthiness.[29]

Finally, endorsers might serve as a peripheral cue. In this case, their attractiveness,[30] how much they are liked,[31] or their celebrity status,[32] regardless of how relevant any of this may be to evaluating the claims and advertised product, can lead to more favorable opinions being formed.

The Use of Free Product Samples

Giving consumers free product samples is one way companies encourage the formation of favorable product opinions. As shown in Figure 15.8, Internet providers such as America Online, CompuServe, and MCI offer hours of free access in the

Figure 15.8   Internet Providers Offer Hours of Free Access to Entice Potential Customers

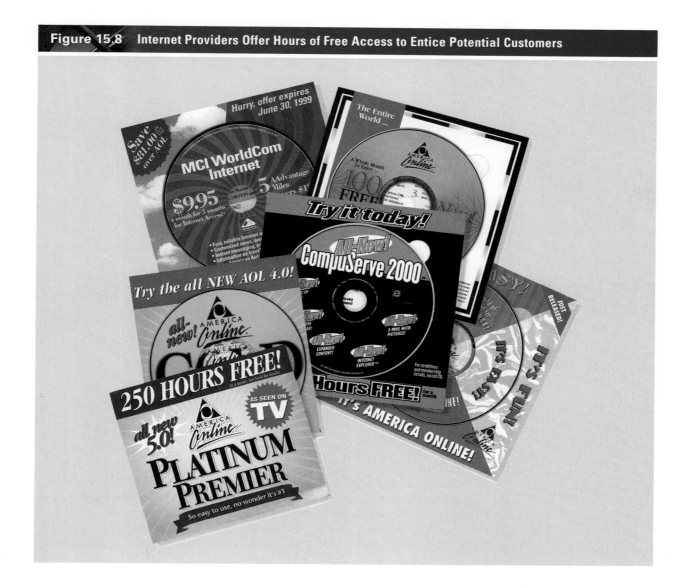

hope that potential customers will become actual customers. When Coca-Cola introduced its Surge soft drink to the marketplace, nearly seven million free samples were distributed.[33]

The effectiveness of providing free samples when rolling out a new product is documented by market research examining their impact on sales. Figure 15.9 summarizes the findings based on eight new product introduction tests conducted by National Panel Diary, a major market research firm, in which one group of consumers received a free sample whereas another group did not. The effect of free samples is revealed by a comparison of the two groups. The top graph in Figure 15.9 represents the results involving initial or trial purchasing. As can be seen, nearly 50 percent more households receiving a free sample made an initial purchase relative to "control" households (those not receiving a free sample). Moreover, as indicated by the bottom graph in Figure 15.9, those who purchased after receiving the free sample were slightly more likely to buy it again.

To estimate the impact of offering free samples on total market penetration, we simply multiply the trial rate times the repurchase rate for those who did or did not receive a free sample. Free samples yielded a total penetration of 5.7

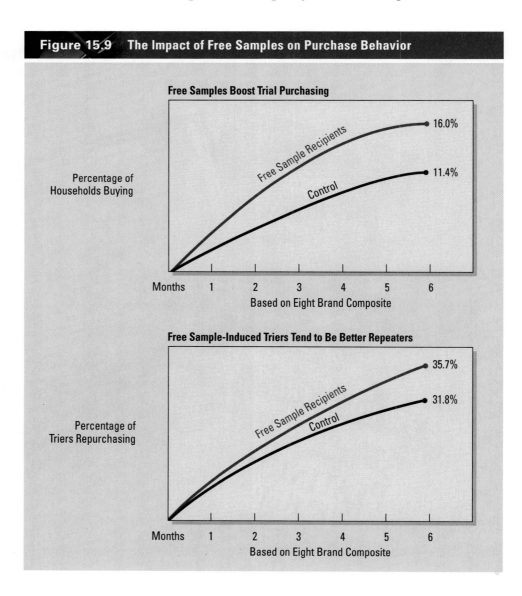

Figure 15.9   The Impact of Free Samples on Purchase Behavior

Free Samples Boost Trial Purchasing

Free Sample Recipients — 16.0%
Control — 11.4%

Percentage of Households Buying

Months   1   2   3   4   5   6

Based on Eight Brand Composite

Free Sample-Induced Triers Tend to Be Better Repeaters

Free Sample Recipients — 35.7%
Control — 31.8%

Percentage of Triers Repurchasing

Months   1   2   3   4   5   6

Based on Eight Brand Composite

percent after six months (trial rate of 16.0 percent times the repurchase rate of 35.7 percent). This compares to a level of 3.6 percent (11.4 percent times 31.8 percent) when free samples were not used. Free samples increased market penetration for these new products by nearly 60 percent ([5.7 − 3.6]/3.6). Accordingly, as long as the product delivers, providing consumers with a free product sample can be a very effective way of shaping their opinions.

The Product's Name

In the immortal words of William Shakespeare, "A rose by any other name would smell as sweet." But would consumers' perceptions of a product be the same regardless of its name? You might remember from Chapter 6 the beer-tasting study in which consumers rated the same beer much more favorably when they were informed of its brand name prior to consumption than when they were unaware of the name.[34] Moreover, when consumers were ignorant of a beer's brand name, all the tasted brands were rated the same. But once their identities were revealed, consumers reported significant differences in their ratings. Apparently, a beer by any other name doesn't taste the same.

One of our favorite stories illustrating the importance of a product's name comes from a company selling cricket manure as a fertilizer for gardeners and growers.[35] Initially, the product was named "CC-84." The CC stood for cricket crap; the 84 represented the year the product was first offered. Yet the name failed to convey the organic origins of the product. Rather, it was more likely to be viewed as a chemical than an organic fertilizer. Product sales went nowhere until its name was changed to "Kricket Krap," a name that better communicated the product's organic origins.

Thus, the meaning derived from a product's name may influence the opinions formed about the product. And when it conveys the wrong meaning, sales are likely to suffer. For this reason, Woolworth, a name strongly associated with its origins as a chain of five-and-dime stores, is searching for a new name better suited for a retailer with the largest chain of stores selling sneakers and sports clothes.[36]

Product Packaging

Sometimes a product's packaging influences consumers' opinions about what's inside the package. A grocery store discovered that its practice of prepackaging fresh fish with a plastic wrap caused consumers to believe that the fish was not fresh and had been frozen. When a seafood bar was added where unwrapped fish were displayed on crushed ice, sales nearly doubled.

Companies occasionally use packaging that's very similar to that of a leading competitor. This is the so-called me-too product that tries to create favorable opinions by using stimulus generalization. **Stimulus generalization** occurs when, *for an existing stimulus–response relationship, the more similar a new stimulus is to the existing one, the more likely it will evoke the same response.* By designing its packaging to resemble the packaging of a well-liked competitor, a company hopes that these favorable opinions will transfer, at least in part, to its product. The next time you are shopping at a grocery or drugstore, take a close look at the packaging of over-the-counter medicines. You'll find many examples of an established brand's packaging being imitated.

Different Colors Evoke Different Meanings

Because colors convey meaning, consumers' opinions may depend on a product's color. Suppose that we add chocolate coloring to vanilla pudding. Most who taste the pudding after being blindfolded so that they cannot see its color will report correctly that it has a vanilla flavor. Yet if consumers are allowed to see the pudding prior to tasting it, its color will cause many to think that it has a chocolate flavor.

Appliance makers have learned that consumers perceive their products as being lighter in weight when colored with pastel rather than darker tones. When Gateway computers updated its logo, a green color was added to "communicate growth, momentum and vitality."[37] Manufacturers of laundry soaps and cold capsules recognize the benefits of including colored granules as a visual cue of their products' effectiveness. To convey the idea that it sold inexpensive hot dogs, Wienerschnitzel, a 350-outlet hot dog chain, modified the colors of one outlet to include orange, a color often seen as connoting cheapness. When sales increased 7 percent, every outlet was redone using this color.[38]

Reference Pricing

In order to influence consumers' opinions about a product's price, companies often use reference pricing. **Reference pricing** involves *providing information about a price other than that actually charged for the product.* The price tags that a retailer places on the products it carries may list both the actual price charged by the retailer and a higher price, typically described as either the price recommended by the product manufacturer or the price previously charged (e.g., "Was $19.99. Now $14.99"). Similarly, companies that operate over the airwaves such as QVC and Home Shopping Network often list higher reference prices. This same tactic is employed by commercials that ask viewers, "How much would you be willing to pay for this fantastic product? $59? $79? $99? It can be yours for only $29.99!" Or maybe the commercial uses a much more expensive competitor's price as a point of reference. Regardless of the particular reference price used, the idea behind all this is to encourage consumers to form more favorable impressions about the actual price's reasonableness. And research documents the ability of reference pricing to do so.[39]

Opinion Change

Once an initial opinion has been formed, *any subsequent modification in it* represents **opinion change.** Businesses often find it in their best interests to try to change consumers' opinions. Take the healthcare system. Recent surveys of Americans' opinions do not paint a pretty picture. Nearly half of the respondents in one survey reported they didn't trust the healthcare system. In another survey, 63 percent believe traditional health insurance companies are more interested in their profitability than in the health of their patients. For HMOs, this percentage dropped slightly to 54 percent. Given such unfavorable opinions, it's not surprising that a growing number of consumers are opting for self-treatment, a trend that reduces the system's profitability.[40] The widespread existence of these negative opinions clearly indicates that the healthcare industry has an image problem. Eliminating this problem requires changing these existing opinions.

Similarly, consider the results reproduced in Figure 15.10 from a survey asking consumers their opinions about different providers of express parcel services. Each provider was rated in terms of its convenience, customer support, and reliability, with higher numbers indicating more favorable opinions. These results indicate that, on average, consumers have less favorable opinions about DHL relative to how they perceive the competition. To the extent that such perceived deficiencies

Figure 15.10   Consumers' Opinions of Express Parcel Services

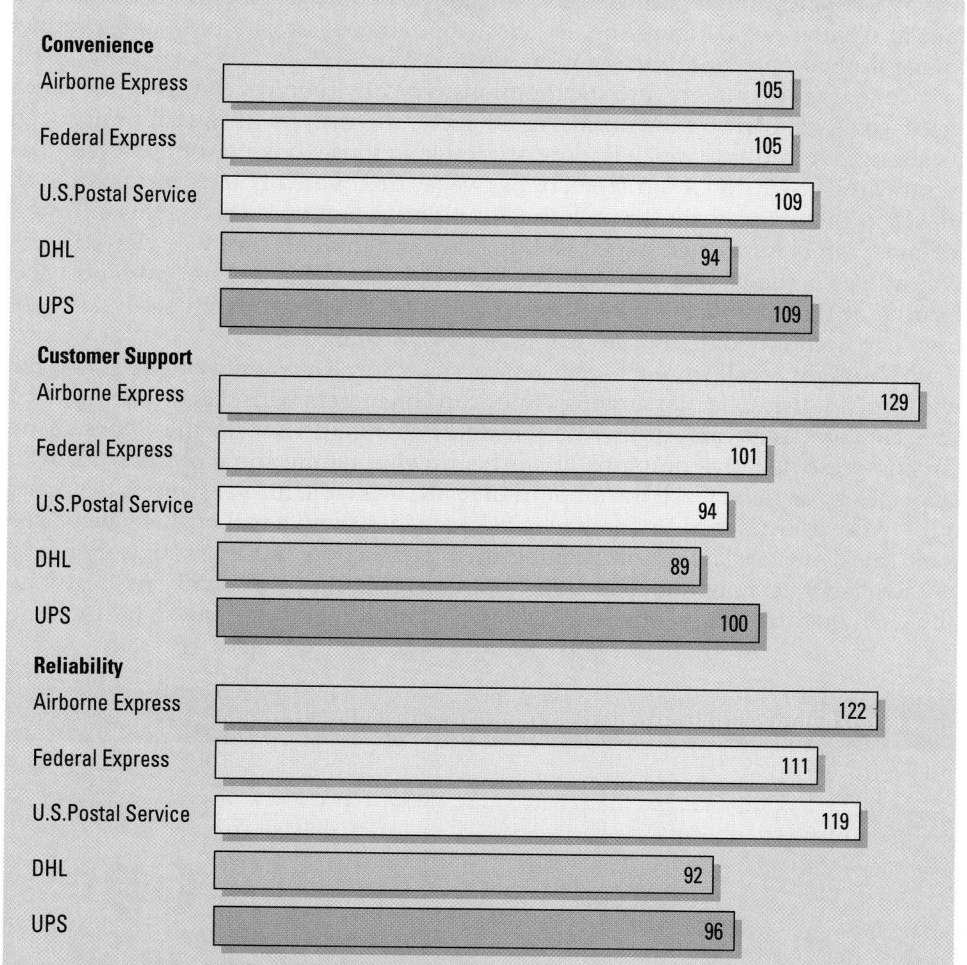

Convenience

Airborne Express — 105

Federal Express — 105

U.S.Postal Service — 109

DHL — 94

UPS — 109

Customer Support

Airborne Express — 129

Federal Express — 101

U.S.Postal Service — 94

DHL — 89

UPS — 100

Reliability

Airborne Express — 122

Federal Express — 111

U.S.Postal Service — 119

DHL — 92

UPS — 96

Note: Higher numbers indicate more favorable opinions.

Source: Jennifer Lach, "Rush Those Reindeer," American Demographics (December 1998), 23.

reduce the odds of consumers choosing DHL, increasing the favorableness of these opinions will enhance its chances of gaining a greater share of the market.

As suggested by these examples, the issue of opinion change becomes relevant whenever consumers hold opinions that reduce their chances of becoming customers. One approach for understanding these opinions is based on the multiattribute attitude model discussed in Chapter 10. By examining consumers' beliefs about a product's important attributes, we can determine which may be in need of repair. If, for instance, a brand's taste is a major reason why people buy from the competition, then improving its taste is essential for attracting these people.

The need for changing consumers' product opinions commonly occurs for mature products. Products that have been around for many years often need a facelift. Today's smashing success eventually becomes tired and worn out. Once upon a time, the Guess brand name, most well known for its jeans, was ranked third by teenagers in terms of its "coolness." Two years later, it had dropped to number 23.[41] Consequently, companies frequently attempt to revitalize their mature products. After Aurora Foods purchased Duncan Hines baking mixes from

Procter & Gamble in 1998, it modernized the packaging, raised its price, and rolled out a new advertising campaign.[42] Similarly, Rock City, a tourist attraction offering 14 acres of some of nature's most intriguing handiwork atop Lookout Mountain in Chattanooga, Tennessee, has been updating its positioning and product image in the hopes of attracting more visitors.[43]

Changing consumers' product opinions typically requires changing the product itself. As shown by the ad in Figure 15.11, the makers of Brawny improved its strength in order to make it more attractive to those looking for a stronger paper towel. The MGM Grand Hotel in Las Vegas discovered that its main entrance, in which customers walk through the mouth of a giant lion's head, was a turnoff for many of its Asian customers. Walking through this entrance was viewed symbolically as being devoured by the lion, a symbolism that did not portend good fortune at the gambling table. Consequently, MGM developed a secondary entrance to accommodate those wishing not to be eaten.

You might recall from Chapter 6 (see, especially, Consumer in Focus 6.4) the widespread dissatisfaction among American consumers with the airline industry. One carrier, American Airlines, is currently changing itself in the hopes of reversing these negative opinions. It has begun eliminating some of the seats in its airplanes so as to increase the amount of space available for passengers to spread out.[44] And, as described in Consumer in Focus 15.3, tequila makers have increased their sales substantially by improving their production and marketing methods.

Realize that changing consumers' opinions need not necessarily require actually changing the product itself. Often it will, but sometimes it doesn't. Mountain

Figure 15.11   Companies Often Improve Their Products to Improve Consumers' Opinions

Consumer in Focus 15.3

Tequila's Getting Better and So Are Sales

Once a key component of barroom brawls in spaghetti Westerns and monumental hangovers, the firewater that took its name from a small town just west of Guadalajara is now the preferred drink in Mexico's most exclusive restaurants and drawing rooms. Those who think Mexicans have a hereditary fondness for tequila or are constitutionally better equipped to handle it will be surprised to learn that, in fact, many Mexicans have long shunned the drink of revolutionary heroes and legendary hangovers. For more than a decade, far more tequila has flowed north of the Rio Grande than south of it.

But now, thanks to better production methods, glitzy marketing gimmicks, and its booming popularity abroad, Mexicans are renewing a long-lost love affair with their national drink. Longer aging in oak barrels, stringent quality controls, and packaging in fancy bottles have spawned a new breed of "designer" or "boutique" tequilas that are (dare it be said?) smooth and even silky.

"There was a time when tequila was a cheap product, drunk only by the lower classes when they had a fight with their sweetheart, downed a bottle of tequila, and got drunk listening to sad music," says Dionisio E. Baquedano, a top executive at Casa Pedro Domecq, which makes Sauza, the most popular tequila brand in Mexico. "The upper-class people wouldn't touch it. But it has become more refined, and now people drink it before lunch or dinner in the highest-class restaurants."

Last year, Mexicans drank an estimated 15.3 million gallons of tequila, up a whopping 51 percent from the previous year. The country is on the verge of overtaking the United States as the world leader in tequila consumption.

Ironically, the booming popularity of this most Mexican of liquors, first used in a rugged form hundreds of years ago by Aztecs in religious rituals, then refined by the Spanish through distillation, began outside Mexico. As rich Mexicans started sampling better tequilas abroad than at home, they returned to Mexico and demanded higher quality tequila. "Tequila used to be a drink of poor campesinos, but then all the foreigners started to drink it and Mexicans followed the trend," says Francisco Lopez, manager of Mexico City's Agave Azul restaurant, which has a 7-page menu offering 79 brands of tequila. And it owes perhaps its greatest debt to an Austrian entrepreneur who came up with a slick marketing gimmick: putting a tiny cactus inside a clear bottle of tequila and charging as much as $100 a bottle.

Source: Excerpted from John Ward Anderson, "Designer Tequila: Mexico's New Upscale Drink," Miami Herald (March 16, 1997), 9F.

Dew's repositioning described in the opening vignette was accomplished by changing the tone of its advertising while leaving the product untouched. Even if the to-be-changed opinion involves some tangible product characteristic (e.g., the product's price), actually changing this characteristic may be unnecessary. If, for example, consumers inaccurately perceive a product's price relative to the competition, changing this perception may only require educating consumers about their mistaken opinions. We acknowledged this possibility previously in Chapter 9's coverage of misperception.

Nonetheless, in those instances where it is necessary to actually modify the product itself, an important question involves how much change is necessary before consumers notice that a change has taken place. Suppose, for example, that a manufacturer wishes to cut its product's price just enough so that consumers perceive it as less expensive. How much of a price cut is necessary? Answering this question requires consideration of the differential threshold.

The Differential Threshold

The **differential threshold** represents the smallest change in stimulus intensity that will be noticed. This change is often referred to as the just noticeable difference (jnd). According to **Weber's law,** *activating the differential threshold or* *achieving the jnd depends on more than simply the absolute amount of change.* To illustrate, suppose that a product that normally sells for $2 is offered for $1. Most consumers would perceive this as a significant price savings. Now suppose that a product that normally sells for $200 is offered for $199. Although the absolute amount of price savings ($1) in this situation is the same as that in the prior situation, consumers are unlikely to hold the same opinions about the significance of the savings. This is because perceptions of change depend on the initial starting point before the change as well as the amount of change itself. In particular, Weber's law predicts that it's the absolute amount of change ($1) divided by the initial starting point (either $2 or $200) that ultimately determines people's perceptions of change. Mathematically, this can be expressed as $\Delta I / I$, where ΔI represents the absolute amount of change, and I represents the initial starting point.

Accordingly, in the first situation, the $1 price reduction is judged relative to the initial selling price of $2. In the second situation, however, the $1 price reduction is considered relative to the $200 selling price. The former represents a 50 percent price reduction; the latter represents a price reduction of less than 1 percent. Ultimately, whether each is perceived as representing a significant price reduction depends on the minimum percentage change needed for activating the differential threshold. One rule of thumb is that a price reduction of at least 15 percent is necessary for attracting consumers to a sale.[45] Consequently, the item costing $200 would need to be reduced by $30 in order to reach this 15 percent threshold. Of course, the size of the differential threshold can vary from one consumer to the next and from one product decision to another. Only through market research can companies determine the size of the differential threshold relevant to their particular situation.

Realize that companies are sometimes interested in changing their products or prices *without* consumers noticing such changes. In these situations, companies wish to stay beneath the differential threshold. Price increases and reductions in product size (such as a shrinking candy bar) are changes that, if possible, should be undertaken without activating the just noticeable difference.

The Difficulty of Changing Consumers' Opinions

Typically, it's much easier to influence opinions at the time they are being formed than to change pre-existing opinions, especially if these prior opinions are confidently held. Why? Because efforts to change opinions may face considerable resistance due to the original opinion, a potential roadblock that doesn't exist in opinion formation.

Nonetheless, the size of this roadblock changes from one opinion to the next. Some opinions are held so strongly that it is virtually impossible to change them. In America, opinions about the desirability of a democratic society are untouchable.

Other opinions, however, are much less resistant to change, as demonstrated by Mountain Dew's successful repositioning discussed earlier. Ultimately, it depends on their foundation. For example, a consumer might notice a new product on the grocer's shelf and decide to buy it and try it. The opinions held following consumption are based on direct or first-hand experience with the product. We know whether we liked the product's taste. And if we don't, nothing short of actually improving its taste is likely to change our opinion. No matter how much advertising claims otherwise, we'll hold on to those opinions founded in our actual experiences.

Suppose, however, that the first time you learn about this new product is during a conversation with another person describing how much he disliked its taste.

Any opinions formed from this conversation are based on indirect or secondhand experience. In this instance, we may be less confident in the veracity of our opinions, particularly if we're uncertain about whether our taste buds are similar to this person's. Consequently, we may be less resistant to efforts aimed at changing our opinions.

These differences in an opinion's resistance to change are documented by the following study. Some of the participants formed an initial opinion of a brand of peanut butter by actually tasting it. Others were not given this opportunity. Instead, they were simply given written information about the product. Everyone then processed a persuasive communication for the product that was delivered by a source possessing either high or low credibility. When initial opinions were based on indirect experience, the opinions held after message processing were significantly more favorable if the source was credible. Yet when initial opinions were based on direct experience, postmessage opinions were unaffected by the source's credibility, thus revealing that such opinions were more resistant to the persuasive communication.[46]

The Danger of Changing Consumers' Opinions

One complicating factor in the opinion change game is that making changes to improve the opinions of some can hurt the opinions of others, something politicians know all too well. Changing voters' opinions about a candidate's stance on a particular issue (e.g., abortion, gun control, protecting the environment) may be good news for those on one side of the issue but bad news for those on the other side.

This is also true for consumers' opinions about products. Revising a product's image may be necessary for attracting one segment but may alienate another segment. This was an important concern for Borden Foods when updating the look of Sailor Jack, the treasured mascot of its Cracker Jack's brand of snack food. This change was necessary for attracting today's youthful consumers, many of whom perceived the product as an "old" person's snack. At the same time, however, it was important not to alienate those who had been loyal customers for half a century or more.[47]

Similarly, changing a product's taste to please the taste buds of some may cause those preferring the original taste to look elsewhere. This was the case many years ago when the Coca-Cola Company decided to drop its original formula in favor of a new formulation. The wave of consumer protest that engulfed the company quickly caused it to bring back its original formula. Thus, when contemplating efforts to change consumers' opinions, it's important to consider the potential net effect of such efforts. Changes designed to attract some customers must be weighed against their potential for alienating other customers.

Summary

Shaping consumers' opinions is a fundamental business activity. Sometimes this requires encouraging consumers to form favorable product opinions, such as when introducing a new product or taking an established product into new markets and making contact with new customers. At other times, this requires changing previously formed opinions, such as when a product is actually modified or repositioned in order to enhance its appeal.

The product opinions formed by consumers heavily depend on what happens during the comprehension stage of information processing. The particular mental categories to which a product is assigned affect these opinions. So do the cognitive and affective responses that occur during processing.

One universal truth supported by decades of research on human judgment is that people's opinions are easily influenced during their formative stages. As you have seen in this chapter, even stimuli that convey nothing about the product and its attributes may be influential during opinion formation. Consistent with the concept of classical conditioning, simple association with the "right" stimuli can cause consumers to form favorable product opinions. And, of course, there are many other ways to encourage favorable opinions. A product's name, its price, its packaging, its advertising, even free samples, can be used to foster favorable product opinions.

Review and Discussion Questions

1. Explain how classical conditioning can be used for shaping consumers' opinions.

2. What are the central and peripheral processes of opinion formation?

3. Suppose you were faced with the choice between an ad that attempts to create favorable attitudes by making several strong claims about the product and an ad devoid of such claims but filled with attractive visuals and favorable music. How might your preference for using a particular ad depend on (a) consumer's involvement at the time of ad exposure, (b) consumer's product knowledge at the time of ad exposure, and (c) the product's performance relative to competition?

4. An advertiser wants to include some well-liked music in its commercials describing the results of independent laboratory tests that support the product's effectiveness. Do you think this music should occur prior to the product claims, after the product claims, or does it matter where it occurs during the commercial?

5. To determine which of two alternative celebrities should be used as the endorser for an upcoming ad campaign, a company assessed how much target consumers liked each celebrity. Based on these results, one of the celebrities was selected and the campaign was launched. Shortly thereafter, the campaign was withdrawn, for it proved ineffective. Interestingly, when the campaign was reintroduced using the celebrity who was liked less, it was quite effective. How can you explain the greater effectiveness of the less liked endorser?

6. Why is it usually easier to shape consumers' opinions while they are being formed than it is to influence pre-existing opinions?

7. A retailer of computer goods is puzzled by consumers' response to her recent fall sale. There was only one purchase of the $3,000 model (sale priced at $2,750). The $1,000 model (sale priced at $875), despite having only half the $250 savings offered by the more expensive model, sold out. How can you explain these results?

8. In an effort to enhance its product's appeal to younger consumers, a company replaces the celebrity used for many years as its product endorser with a much younger celebrity. To its surprise, product sales actually declined after the change was made. Why might this have happened?

Endnotes

1. Susan Fiske and Mark A. Pavelchak, "Category-Based Versus Piecemeal-Based Affective Responses: Developments in Schema-Triggered Affect," in Richard M. Sorrentino and E. Tory Higgins, eds., *The Handbook of Motivation and Cognition: Foundations of Social Behavior* (New York: Guilford, 1986), 167–203. For an application of categorization theory in the context of brand extensions, see Michael J. Barone, Paul W. Miniard, and Jean B. Romeo, "The Influence of Positive Mood on Brand Extension Evaluations," *Journal of Consumer Research* 26 (March 2000), 387–401.

2. J. Neher, "Toro Cutting a Wide Swath in Outdoor Appliance Marketing," *Advertising Age* (February 25, 1979), 21.

3. Robert M. McMath, "Chock Full of (Pea)nuts," *American Demographics* (April 1997), 60.

4. Robert Johnson, "In the Chips," *The Wall Street Journal* (March 22, 1991), B1–B2.

5. Rachel X. Weissman, "But First, Call Your Drug Company," *American Demographics* (October 1998), 27, 28, 30.

6. For research on classical conditioning in a product context, see Chris T. Allen and Thomas J. Madden, "A Closer Look at Classical Conditioning," *Journal of Consumer Research* 12 (December 1985), 301–315; Chris Janiszewski and Luk Warlop, "The Influence of Classical Conditioning Procedures on Subsequent Attention to the Conditioned Brand," *Journal of Consumer Research* 20 (September 1993), 171–189; Terence A. Shimp, Elnora W. Stuart, and Randall W. Engle, "A Program of Classical Conditioning Experiments Testing Variations in the Conditioned Stimulus and Context," *Journal of Consumer Research* 18 (June 1991), 1–12; Elnora W. Stuart, Terence A. Shimp, and Randall W. Engle, "Classical Conditioning of Consumer Attitudes: Four Experiments in an Advertising Context," *Journal of Consumer Research* 14 (December 1987), 334–349.

7. Andrew A. Mitchell and Jerry C. Olson, "Are Product Attribute Beliefs the Only Mediators of Advertising Effects on Brand Attitudes?" *Journal of Marketing Research* 18 (August 1981), 318–332.

8. Gerald J. Gorn, "The Effects of Music in Advertising on Choice Behavior: A Classical Conditioning Approach," *Journal of Marketing* 46 (Winter 1982), 94–101.

9. Paul W. Miniard, Deepak Sirdeshmukh, and Daniel E. Innis, "Peripheral Persuasion and Brand Choice," *Journal of Consumer Research* 19 (September 1992), 226–239. Also see Timothy B. Heath,

Michael S. McCarthy, and David L. Mothersbaugh, "Spokesperson Fame and Vividness Effects in the Context of Issue-Relevant Thinking: The Moderating Role of Competitive Setting," *Journal of Consumer Research* 20 (March 1994), 520–534.

10. Richard E. Petty and John T. Cacioppo, *Communication and Persuasion: Central and Peripheral Routes to Attitude Change* (New York: Springer-Verlag, 1986); and Richard E. Petty and John T. Cacioppo, "The Elaboration Likelihood Model of Persuasion," in Leonard Berkowitz, ed., *Advances in Experimental Social Psychology* 19 (New York: Academic Press, 1986), 123–205. A similar conceptualization is offered by Shelly Chaiken, "Heuristic Versus Systematic Information Processing and the Use of Source Versus Message Cues in Persuasion," *Journal of Personality and Social Psychology* 39 (November 1980), 752–766. Also see Alice H. Eagly and Shelly Chaiken, *The Psychology of Attitudes* (Fort Worth, TX: Harcourt Brace Jovanovich, 1993).

11. Paul W. Miniard, Sunil Bhatla, Kenneth R. Lord, Peter R. Dickson, and H. Rao Unnava, "Picture-based Persuasion Processes and the Moderating Role of Involvement," *Journal of Consumer Research* 18 (June 1991), 92–107.

12. Ibid.

13. Interest in attitude toward the ad was largely sparked by the following two articles: Mitchell and Olson, "Are Product Attribute Beliefs the Only Mediators of Advertising Effects on Brand Attitudes?" and Terence Shimp, "Attitude toward the Ad as a Mediator of Consumer Brand Choice," *Journal of Advertising* 10 (1981), 9–15. Also see Stephen P. Brown and Douglas M. Stayman, "Antecedents and Consequences of Attitude toward the Ad: A Meta-analysis," *Journal of Consumer Research* 19 (June 1992), 34–51; Scott B. MacKenzie, Richard J. Lutz, and George E. Belch, "The Role of Attitude toward the Ad as a Mediator of Advertising Effectiveness: A Test of Competing Explanations," *Journal of Marketing Research* 23 (May 1986), 130–143; Paul W. Miniard, Sunil Bhatla, and Randall L. Rose, "On the Formation and Relationship of Ad and Brand Attitudes: An Experimental and Causal Analysis," *Journal of Marketing Research* 27 (August 1990), 290–303.

14. Miniard, Bhatla, Lord, Dickson, and Unnava, "Picture-based Persuasion Processes and the Moderating Role of Involvement."

15. Jerome S. Bruner and A. Leigh Minturn, "Perceptual Identification and Perceptual Organization," *Journal of General Psychology* 53 (July 1955), 21–28.

16. Young-Won Ha and Stephen J. Hoch, "Ambiguity, Processing Strategy, and Advertising-Evidence Interactions," *Journal of Consumer Research* 16 (December 1989), 354–360.

17. David Olson, "The Characteristics of High-Trial New-Product Advertising," *Journal of Advertising Research* 25 (October/November 1985), 11–16.

18. Although stronger claims generally produce more favorable opinions than weaker claims, there may be situations in which weaker claims are actually better. For a demonstration of this, see Marvin E. Goldberg and Jon Hartwick, "The Effects of Advertiser Reputation and Extremity of Advertising Claim on Advertising Effectiveness," *Journal of Consumer Research* 17 (September 1990), 172–179.

19. Dhruv Grewal, Sukumar Kavanoor, Edward F. Fern, Carolyn Costley, and James Barnes, "Comparative Versus Noncomparative Advertising: A Meta-Analysis," *Journal of Marketing* 61 (October 1997), 1–15; Paul W. Miniard, Randall L. Rose, Michael J. Barone, and Kenneth C. Manning, "On the Need for Relative Measures when Assessing Comparative Advertising Effects," *Journal of Advertising* 22 (September 1993), 41–58; Paul W. Miniard, Randall L. Rose, Kenneth C. Manning, and Michael J. Barone, "Tracking the Effects of Comparative and Noncomparative Advertising with Relative and Nonrelative Measures: A Further Examination of the Framing Correspondence Hypothesis," *Journal of Business Research* 41 (February 1998), 137–143; Randall L. Rose, Paul W. Miniard, Michael J. Barone, Kenneth C. Manning, and Brian D. Till, "When Persuasion Goes Undetected: The Case of Comparative Advertising," *Journal of Marketing Research* 30 (August 1993), 315–330.

20. James M. Munch, Gregory W. Boller, and John L. Swasy, "The Effects of Argument Structure and Affective Tagging on Product Attitude Formation," *Journal of Consumer Research* 20 (September 1993), 294–302.

21. Cyndee Miller, "Demonstrating Your Point: Showing How the Product Works Adds Authenticity," *Marketing News* (September 13, 1993), 2.

22. Gary T. Ford, Darlene B. Smith, and John L. Swasy, "Consumer Skepticism of Advertising Claims: Testing Hypotheses from Economics of Information," *Journal of Consumer Research* 16 (March 1990), 433–441.

23. Irwin P. Levin and Gary J. Gaeth, "How Consumers Are Affected by the Framing of Attribute Information Before and After Consuming the Product," *Journal of Consumer Research* 15 (December 1988), 374–378.

24. See William K. Darley and Robert E. Smith, "Advertising Claim Objectivity: Antecedents and Effects," *Journal of Marketing* 57 (October 1993), 100–113; Julie A. Edell and Richard Staelin, "The Information Processing of Pictures in Print Advertisements," *Journal of Consumer Research* 10 (June 1983), 45–61; Ford, Smith, and Swasy, "Consumer Skepticism of Advertising Claims: Testing Hypotheses from Economics of Information;" and Morris B. Holbrook, "Beyond Attitude Structure: Toward the Informational Determinants of Attitude," *Journal of Marketing Research* 15 (November 1978), 545–556.

25. Richard E. Petty and John T. Cacioppo, "The Effects of Involvement on Responses to Argument Quantity and Quality: Central and Peripheral Routes to Persuasion," *Journal of Personality and Social Psychology* 46 (January 1984), 69–81. Also see Joseph W. Alba and Howard Marmorstein, "The Effects of Frequency Knowledge on Consumer Decision Making," *Journal of Consumer Research* 14 (June 1987), 14–25.

26. Robin Givhan, "$75 Million! Smell of Cash Rising Quickly from Jordan Fragrance," *Miami Herald* (May 22, 1997), 5F.

27. Suzanne Vranica, "Tic Tac Maker Hopes Fresh Face Breathes New Life into Campaign," *The Wall Street Journal* (December 13, 1999), B25.

28. Michael A. Kamins, "An Investigation into the 'Match-Up Hypothesis' in Celebrity Advertising: When Beauty Only May Be Skin Deep," *Journal of Advertising* 19 (1990), 4–13.

29. For a general review, see Brian Sternthal, Lynn Phillips, and Ruby Dholakia, "The Persuasive Effect of Source Credibility: A Situational Analysis," *Public Opinion Quarterly* 42 (Fall 1978), 285–314. Also see Danny L. Moore, Douglas Hausknecht, and Kanchana Thamodaran, "Time Compression, Response Opportunity, and Persuasion," *Journal of Consumer Research* 13 (June 1986), 85–99; S. Ratneshwar and Shelly Chaiken, "Comprehension's Role in Persuasion: The Case of Its Moderating Effect on the Persuasive Impact of Source Cues," *Journal of Consumer Research* 18 (June 1991), 52–62; Arch G. Woodside and J. William Davenport, Jr., "The Effect of Salesman Similarity and Expertise on Consumer Purchasing Behavior," *Journal of Marketing Research* 11 (May 1974), 198–202; Chenghuan Wu and David R. Shaffer, "Susceptibility to Persuasive Appeals as a Function of Source Credibility and Prior Experience with the Attitude Object," *Journal of Personality and Social Psychology* 52 (1987), 677–688. We should note that less credible sources on occasion induce more persuasion. See Robert R. Harmon and Kenneth A. Coney, "The Persuasive Effects of Source Credibility in Buy and Lease Situations," *Journal of Marketing Research* 19 (May

1982), 255–260; Brian Sternthal, Ruby Dholakia, and Clark Leavitt, "The Persuasive Effect of Source Credibility: Tests of Cognitive Response," *Journal of Consumer Research* 4 (March 1978), 252–260.

30. Michael J. Baker and Gilbert A. Churchill, Jr., "The Impact of Physically Attractive Models on Advertising Evaluations," *Journal of Marketing Research* 14 (November 1977), 538–555; Shelly Chaiken, "Communicator Physical Attractiveness and Persuasion," *Journal of Personality and Social Psychology* 37 (August 1979), 752–766; and Lynn R. Kahle and Pamela M. Homer, "Physical Attractiveness of the Celebrity Endorser: A Social Adaptation Perspective," *Journal of Consumer Research* 11 (March 1985), 954–961.

31. Kahle and Homer, "Physical Attractiveness of the Celebrity Endorser."

32. Richard E. Petty, John T. Cacioppo, and David Schumann, "Central and Peripheral Routes to Advertising Effectiveness: The Moderating Role of Involvement," *Journal of Consumer Research* 10 (September 1983), 135–146.

33. Nikhil Deogun, "Coca-Cola Plans Splashy Rollout of Citrus Soda," *The Wall Street Journal* (December 16, 1996), B1, B11.

34. Ralph I. Allison and Kenneth P. Uhl, "Influence of Beer Brand Identification on Taste Perception," *Journal of Marketing Research* 1 (August 1964), 36–39. For a demonstration of the importance of brand name in car buying, see Mary W. Sullivan, "How Brand Names Affect the Demand for Twin Automobiles," *Journal of Marketing Research* 35 (May 1998), 154–165.

35. "Fertilizer by Any Other Name Doesn't Sell as Well, by Jiminy," *The State* (September 28, 1991), 9A.

36. Yumiko Ono, "What's in a Name? Woolworth Seeks to Shed Dime-Store Image," *The Wall Street Journal* (March 20, 1998), B6.

37. Sally Beatty, "Gateway 2000 Plans Shorter Name, Longer Client Talks and No Cows," *The Wall Street Journal* (April 24, 1998), B6.

38. Randall Lane, "Does Orange Mean Cheap?" *Forbes* (December 23, 1991), 144–146.

39. See, for example, Joel E. Urbany, William O. Bearden, and Dan C. Weilbaker, "The Effect of Plausible and Exaggerated Reference Prices on Consumer Perceptions and Price Search," *Journal of Consumer Research* 15 (June 1988), 95–110.

40. Rachel X. Weissman, "But First, Call Your Drug Company," *American Demographics* (October 1998), 27, 28, 30.

41. Frederick Rose and John R. Emshwiller, "Guess, Coolness Fading, Plans Sultry Ads," *The Wall Street Journal* (November 19, 1997), B8.

42. Dana James, "Rejuvenating Mature Brands Can Be Stimulating Exercise," *Marketing News* (August 16, 1999), 16–17.

43. "Chattanooga Attraction Gets Revamped Image," *Marketing News* (September 14, 1998), 33.

44. Scott McCartney, "News for the Knees: AMR Will Expand Coach-Seat Legroom," *The Wall Street Journal* (February 4, 2000), A3.

45. Albert J. Della Bitta and Kent B. Monroe, "A Multivariate Analysis of the Perception of Value from Retail Price Advertisements," in Kent B. Monroe, ed., *Advances in Consumer Research* 8 (Ann Arbor, MI: Association for Consumer Research, 1980), 161–165.

46. Chenghuan Wu and David R. Shaffer, "Susceptibility to Persuasive Appeals as a Function of Source Credibility and Prior Experience with the Attitude Object," *Journal of Personality and Social Psychology* 52 (1987), 677–688. Also see Lawrence J. Marks and Michael A. Kamins, "The Use of Product Sampling and Advertising: Effects of Sequence of Exposure and Degree of Advertising Claim Exaggeration on Consumers' Belief Strength, Belief Confidence, and Attitudes," *Journal of Marketing Research* 25 (August 1988), 266–281; Robert E. Smith and William R. Swinyard, "Attitude-Behavior Consistency: The Impact of Product Trial Versus Advertising," *Journal of Marketing Research* 20 (August 1983), 257–267.

47. Ian P. Murphy, "All-American Icon Gets a New Look," *Marketing News* (August 18, 1997), 6.

CHAPTER 16

Helping Consumers to Remember

OPENING VIGNETTE

There's only so much milk any human being can reasonably consume in a given week. For most of us, a gallon should suffice perfectly well. So how to explain the unusual burst in "incremental gallon sales" (to use dairy-industry jargon) over a two-day period last fall? Some nine million *extra* gallons of milk poured out of stores nationwide. Nine million: That represented about a 10 percent boost in overall gallon sales for one week. In any mature industry, a 1 percent boost would be considered good news. In the milk business—staid, reliable, unaccustomed to dramatic leaps in sales—a 10 percent burst is virtually unheard of.

To what do America's dairy people and bovines owe their gratitude? A modest little magazine entitled *The Best of Nickelodeon* that appeared in stores across the country last October. Some 4.5 million copies of the magazine, packed with the usual assortment of games, puzzles, and articles—and nothing but ads for milk—also came wrapped with a belly band that read, "Buy Two Gallons of Milk, Get This Magazine Free." Just do the math.

But some attribute this surge in demand to more than using the magazine as an incentive for purchase. Peter Gardiner is a senior partner and media director at Bozell New York and architect of myriad integrated marketing plans for the Dairy Management and Milk Processor Education Program (MilkPEP), sponsored by the National Fluid Milk Processor Promotion Board. He explains, "What happened is that people would see the display in stores and say, 'Oh my gosh, I forgot to buy milk.'" And *voila!* Nine million extra gallons swept through checkouts nationwide.

Source: Excerpted from Verne Gay, "Milk, the Magazine," American Demographics (February 2000), 32–34.

Have you ever returned from grocery shopping and suddenly realized that you forgot to buy something that you needed and had intended to purchase? Hasn't everybody? Nor is this forgetting limited to supermarket products. Failure to remember is a recurring theme of consumer behavior. We often forget that it's time for our car's next oil change or our teeth's next cleaning. Each time a consumer forgets to buy something, some company has lost a sales opportunity.

This failure to remember encompasses both product consumption and product purchase. How many times have you forgotten to watch some television program that you wanted to see? Many taking medications often forget that it's time for their next pill.[1] The orange juice industry discovered that many purchasers forgot about it in the refrigerator.[2] The less often products such as medications and orange juice are consumed, the less often they need to be purchased. This means fewer sales at the cash register.

Even when consumers do remember to make purchase and consumption decisions, memory and what's remembered from it can still play an important role during the decision-making process. You might recall from Chapter 4 our coverage of the consideration set and how consumers' ability to remember choice alternatives (called the retrieval set) often determines whether these alternatives gain entry into the consideration set. Products that are not retrieved from memory won't be considered when making choices unless they're physically present during decision making.

Similarly, what's remembered about the alternatives receiving consideration initially may determine what receives consideration subsequently. Consider buying a home. Initially, people usually search a number of homes for sale prior to purchase. They may then narrow the field down to a handful of homes for a second round of visits. In many cases, whether a home makes the cut depends on what the person remembers about the home. For this reason, interior decorators recognize the importance of "memory points" when decorating a builder's model homes. These memory points help a model stand out and become memorable. One decorator, for instance, used a barnyard motif in a room with a sensor that triggered barnyard noises when someone entered the room.[3]

Unless consumers are judging choice alternatives using information physically in front of them, evaluations of the considered alternatives depends completely on what's retrieved from memory. Maybe overall evaluations previously formed about the choice alternatives are retrieved and compared when making the decision (see Chapter 4). Or maybe the decision is made based on what is remembered about the alternatives' attributes. In either case, what's remembered determines what's chosen.[4] Imagine two individuals looking to buy a TV. The first goes to the closest store and buys the TV judged best for the money. The other goes to the same store and buys nothing because he remembers seeing the TV most attractive to him at a lower price at a competitor's store. His evaluation of buying from the first retailer was reduced to the point where purchase did not occur because of what he remembered about another retailer.

Helping consumers remember is also useful for enhancing advertising effectiveness. To illustrate, consider the use of nostalgic advertising appeals that remind consumers of something from their good old days. Maybe it's their high school prom. Or maybe it's a romantic vacation. Whatever it is, the objective is to encourage consumers to remember some past favorable experience in their lives. The positive feelings attached to this past experience may then be transferred to the product opinions held after ad processing.[5]

In some cases, advertising may focus on activating the consumer's memory of past consumption experiences. The ad for Cap'n Crunch cereal shown in Figure 16.1 does so. In so doing, the company hopes that past users will recall favorable memories of eating the cereal and decide to try it again.

For these reasons, businesses' best interests usually (but not always, as described in Consumer in Focus 16.1) lie in helping consumers to remember. This chapter considers how this might be accomplished. But first, we need to cover some background material that will provide you with a better understanding of the task faced by businesses. Remembering consists of two basic processes: cognitive learning (getting information into memory) and retrieval (getting it back out).

Cognitive Learning

In Chapter 14, we talked about cognitive capacity and the distinction between short-term memory (where thinking and interpretation occurs) and long-term

Figure 16.1   Cap'n Crunch Cereal Wants Consumers (and Their Taste Buds) to Remember Previous Consumption Experiences

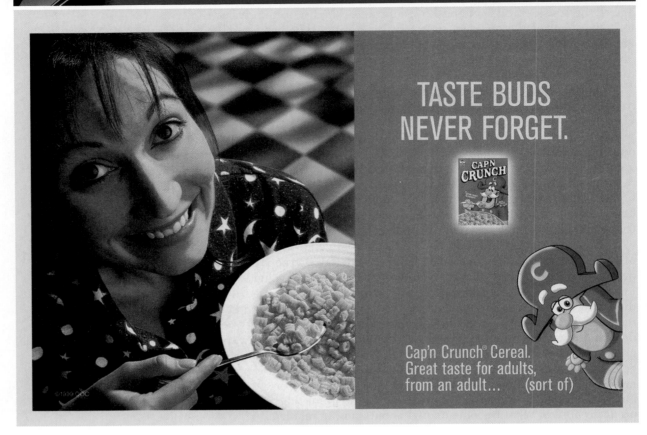

memory (the mental warehouse in which knowledge resides). **Cognitive learning** occurs *when information processed in short-term memory is stored in long-term memory.* Obviously, how well something can be remembered depends on how well it was learned to begin with. After all, you can't remember something you don't know! So what determines cognitive learning? Rehearsal and elaboration are two key factors.

Rehearsal

Rehearsal *involves the mental repetition of information or, more formally, the recycling of information through short-term memory.* Some describe it as a form of inner speech.

Rehearsal serves two main functions. First, it allows for the maintenance of information in short-term memory. An example is when we mentally repeat a telephone number that we looked up just long enough for us to dial the number. Rehearsal is undertaken to keep the information activated long enough for the person to dial the number. The second function of rehearsal involves the transfer of information from short-term memory to long-term memory. Greater rehearsal increases the strength of the long-term memory trace, thereby enhancing the likelihood that the trace can be later retrieved.

Consumer in Focus 16.1

We Hope You Forget About It

Back in 1914, the Ford Motor Company offered a $50 rebate on a Model T costing nearly $500. Since then, product rebates have become very popular for enticing consumers to buy everything from computers to dishwashers to baby seats to grocery items. Office Max, an office-supply chain, sells 217 different products that offer a rebate. Cox Direct, a direct-marketing company, says 76 percent of surveyed package-goods companies used money-back offers in 1996, up from 66 percent in 1995. NCH NuWorld, America's biggest coupon processor, says the use of traditional cents-off coupons is down, but its mail-in rebate business is increasing, especially for higher-priced items. And Young America says its business is growing 25 percent annually thanks to ever-more-complex rebate and premium programs. The company mails out 30 million rebate checks a year on behalf of companies like PepsiCo, Nestle, and Office Max.

Why are rebates so popular? Manufacturers like rebates because they let them offer price cuts to consumers directly. They can also be rolled out and shut off quickly. That allows manufacturers to fine-tune inventories or respond quickly to competitors without actually cutting prices. Because buyers fill out forms with names, addresses, and other data, rebates yield important information about customers.

But maybe the best reason of all to offer rebates is that many consumers never bother to redeem them, thereby enabling manufacturers to offer, in effect, phantom discounts. "The whole point behind rebates is to entice purchases and hope [consumers] don't remember to submit" their claims, says Charles Weil, president of Young America.

Sources: Excerpted from "Rebates Really Payoff—for the Manufacturers," Miami Herald (February 11, 1998), 17A. Also see David Vaczek and Richard Sale, "100 Years of Promotion," PROMO Magazine (August 1998), 32–41, 142–145.

Elaboration

The amount of **elaboration** *(representing the degree of integration between the stimulus and existing knowledge)* that occurs during processing influences the amount of learning that takes place. At low levels of elaboration, a stimulus is processed in much the same form in which it's encountered. For instance, a person wanting to remember a license plate numbered AJN268 might encode this stimulus without any elaboration by simply repeating "A-J-N-2-6-8."

A more elaborate encoding of this license plate number could involve rearranging the letters into the name JAN, adding the numbers (which total 16), and then visualizing a 16-year-old girl named Jan. This, in fact, was what a person reported doing in order to remember the license number of a car he witnessed leaving the scene of a bank robbery. After realizing he had seen the getaway car, he telephoned the police and gave them the license number. The suspects were apprehended, and he received a $500 reward.

Greater elaboration generally leads to greater learning.[6] The more a person elaborates on a piece of information (or the more "deeply" it is processed), the greater the number of linkages formed between the new information and information already stored in memory. This, in turn, increases the number of avenues or paths by which the information can be retrieved from memory. In essence, the memory trace becomes more accessible given the greater number of pathways (linkages) available for retrieval. Many of the techniques suggested by memory experts and performers for increasing one's ability to learn and remember new information rely on the benefits of elaboration.[7]

The amount of elaboration that occurs during information processing depends on the person's motivation and ability to do so.[8] Each is discussed next.

Motivation

A person's motivational state at the time of exposure to new information has a considerable influence on what's learned. Sometimes people *deliberately try to learn so that they can later remember* the information, as might be the case for the student reading this text in preparation for a forthcoming exam or someone trying to absorb and remember a salesperson's suggestions on what to look for when buying the product. Such learning is called **intentional learning.**

Of course, sometimes we learn even when we're not trying. If you read this morning's newspaper or watched the news on TV, you probably learned a thing or two even though this was not your intention. *Learning that occurs despite the absence of the intention to do so* is called **incidental learning.** As one would expect, learning is greater when it's intentional than incidental.[9]

Ability

Knowledge is an important determinant of learning because it enables the person to undertake more meaningful elaboration during information processing. In a classic study of how prior knowledge enhances learning, chess masters and novices were shown chess games in progress.[10] Masters generally held a substantial advantage over novices in remembering the board positions of the chess pieces. Interestingly, this superiority disappeared when subjects were exposed to games in which the pieces were organized randomly. Thus, the beneficial effect of knowledge materialized only when the information conformed to the expert's knowledge structures and expectations (i.e., when the pieces' placement "made sense").

Even when knowledge is high, ability may be low. This is because the ability to learn depends on both individual and environmental factors.[11] A knowledgeable person may be unable to engage in much elaboration of an ad appearing on TV if the room is filled with distractions (such as a crying baby). Similarly, the aging process reduces our ability to learn.[12]

Mental Representations

Mental representations refer to *the particular manner in which information is stored in long-term memory.* Sometimes a stimulus is stored in the same form in which it initially appears, as would be the case when consumers focus on learning the specific price of a product. Alternatively, it may be translated into a different form for storage. Rather than a product's specific price, consumers may store the price perceptions formed during processing (e.g., "too expensive," "cheap," "about average").[13]

The same piece of information may be represented within long-term memory in different forms. The concept of **dual coding** proposes that *information can be stored in both semantic* (i.e., its meaning) *and visual* (i.e., its appearance) *forms.*[14] Consider the child trying to learn state capitals. For Arkansas, it's Little Rock. Beyond presenting this information verbally, one could also represent it visually, as shown in Figure 16.2. Doing so enhances the chances of this information being stored semantically and visually.

The advantage of having multiple representations in memory is that it increases the number of possible mental pathways that can be traveled when trying to remember. The child who is shown the picture in Figure 16.2 has an additional way (the picture itself) for remembering the state capital of Arkansas. This, in turn, improves the odds of remembering. Later on, we'll talk about how companies can encourage multiple representations as a way of helping consumers to remember.

Figure 16.2   Pictures Evoke Visual Mental Representations That Increase Learning.

Little Rock, Arkansas

Another aspect of mental representations involves the manner in which they are organized in long-term memory.[15] Although there are many theories about memory organization, the literature favors the view of memory being organized in the form of an **associative network**.[16] This perspective proposes that *the information residing within memory is organized much like a spider's web.* Memory nodes containing bits of information are linked to other memory nodes in a series of hierarchical networks (e.g., networks representing specific brands of personal computers would be part of a broader network representing the entire product category that is part of an even broader network of computer-related products). Figure 16.3 displays a simplified (in that many other linkages that would exist are not shown) associative network for an IBM personal computer. In this figure, IBM represents the central node that is linked to other nodes (e.g., fast response time), of which some are linked further to additional nodes (e.g., ease of operation). Recognize that the image analysis discussed in Chapter 9 attempts to identify the various nodes (or associations, as they were called in that chapter) that are linked to the node representing the brand name.

Retrieval

Learning is but one part of remembering. It only addresses getting information from short-term memory into long-term memory. It ignores getting this information back out. The other part of remembering is retrieval. **Retrieval** involves the *activation of information stored in long-term memory that's then transferred into short-term memory.* Together, learning and retrieval are the two fundamental requirements for remembering (see Figure 16.4).

Figure 16.3 An Associative Network for the IBM Personal Computer

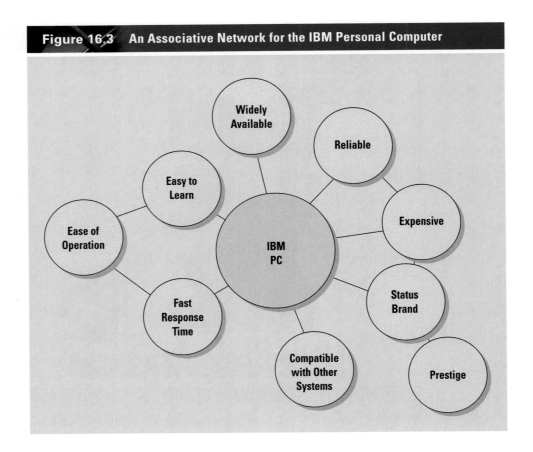

Figure 16.4 The Cycle of Remembering

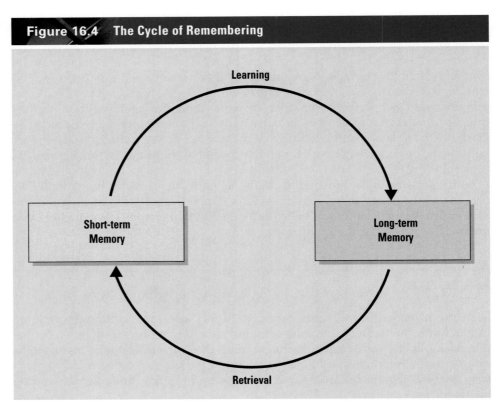

The likelihood that retrieval is successful depends on a couple of things. A key factor is the strength of the memory trace of the to-be-remembered information. Some information is so well known and strongly represented in memory that it can be recalled easily and spontaneously (e.g., the names of your family members). The memory trace for other information, however, may be much weaker. Greater effort and concentration is required before retrieval is successful. Sometimes the memory trace is so weak that retrieval may succeed only if helped by retrieval cues. A **retrieval cue** is a *stimulus that activates information in memory relevant to the to-be-remembered information.* For example, do you remember the name of your first-grade teacher? Many cannot without assistance. But if we show them a picture of their first-grade classroom, their classmates, or their teacher, this may stimulate their memory. Although still in their head, the to-be-remembered information was not accessible until activated by its linkage to the memory node activated by the picture. Later on, we'll talk more about retrieval cues and their usefulness in helping consumers remember.

Successful retrieval also depends on the number and strength of linkages between the to-be-remembered item and other memory nodes. According to the concept of **spreading activation,** *activating one memory node causes a ripple effect that spreads throughout its linkages to other nodes.*[17] This, in turn, increases the chances that other nodes are activated, depending on the strength of the linkages. Consequently, if the to-be-remembered node is strongly associated with another, then retrieving the latter may help in retrieving the former. Take the product that has forged a strong relationship with a celebrity spokesperson. Thinking about the celebrity will facilitate retrieval of the product (and vice versa). Moreover, as linkages become more prevalent, there's a greater opportunity for activating the to-be-remembered node while searching memory. Assume one memory node has five strong linkages. Activating any of the five linkages may lead to successful retrieval. Now suppose there's only one strong linkage. Obviously, the chances of remembering are much less.

Forgetting

As we know all too well, people's efforts at remembering are not always successful. The failure to retrieve something from memory is commonly known as **forgetting.**

Why does forgetting occur? According to **decay theory,** *memories grow weaker with the passage of time.* Just like the paintings of famous artists that have faded over the centuries, so too does information painted on the canvas of the brain. Unless information is reactivated after initial learning, decay sets in and the memory trace becomes weaker. At some point, the memory becomes so weak that retrieval may not be possible.

Yet forgetting also occurs even though the memory trace is far from being weak. This is because not everything stored in long-term memory is accessible for retrieval at a particular moment in time. All of us have experienced situations in which we tried unsuccessfully to remember something, only to have it "pop" into our mind at a later point in time (e.g., trying to remember someone's name or a song's title, the answer on a test, etc.). Research shows that information appearing to be forgotten was simply inaccessible at the time retrieval was attempted initially. Later on, with the help of retrieval cues, this previously inaccessible information was remembered.[18]

This failure to retrieve something that has not faded from memory is attributable to the effects of interference. **Interference theory** proposes that *the chances of retrieving a particular piece of information become smaller as interference from other information becomes larger.* To illustrate, suppose that we asked people to write down all the brands of toothpaste they can remember. Prior to doing this, some are shown an advertisement for one brand of toothpaste; the rest of them don't see the ad. Do you think there would be a difference in the number of brands remembered between those who did and didn't see the ad? There is. Those given the ad remember *fewer* brands beyond the one being advertised. Ad processing leads to activating the advertised brand's name in short-term memory. Doing so, in turn, interferes with the ability to retrieve other brand names from long-term memory.[19]

In Chapter 14, we talked about the notion of clutter and how the large number of products and advertisements in today's marketplace makes it all the more difficult to capture consumers' attention. Yet even if an advertisement is able to break through the clutter and gain attention, clutter can still be a problem by causing interference. Consumers are less able to remember the product message delivered by an advertisement when this ad is either preceded or followed by advertising for competitive products.[20] The proliferation of dot-com advertising scheduled to appear during the Super Bowl in 2000 raised concerns about how effective a dot-com company's advertising might be. You can learn more about this by reading Consumer in Focus 16.2.

Recognition and Recall

Beyond the strength of the memory trace, retrieval also depends on whether the to-be-remembered information requires recognition or recall. For recognition, we

---

Consumer in Focus 16.2

Interference Occurs in Advertising, Not Just in Football

Budweiser will be there, not far from Frito-Lay and Pepsi. But so will a record number of dot-coms, including some names you've likely never heard of. Sunday's big football game also is the Super Bowl of television advertising. Companies will be paying an average of $2.2 million for 30 seconds of airtime. Attracted by the roughly 125 million viewers, advertisers traditionally launch new campaigns or introduce new products during the Super Bowl.

This year, traditional advertisers such as Pepsi-Cola, Frito-Lay, Visa, and Anheuser-Busch will share commercial space with a host of Internet-related companies that includes well-known web sites such as DowJones.com, E*trade.com, HotJobs.com, Monster.com, and Pets.com, as well as relatively obscure sites such as OurBeginning.com, Computer.com, and KForce.com. Nearly 20 percent of the Super Bowl's 61 television spots had been taken up by dot-coms. That translates into more than a dozen Internet companies making their Super Bowl debuts this year. By comparison, there was just one dot-com spot in the 1997 and 1998 games, and only three in 1999.

"The real challenge this year is the dot-coms," says Albert Sanchez, of the Donovan Consulting Group, who is working with Anheuser-Busch on its crop of Super Bowl ads. "Are they all going to become a blur at the end of the day, or will they be able to distinguish themselves from the others and break away from the clutter?" Concerns about the ability to break through this clutter of dot-com advertising was one reason Angeltips.com decided to withdraw its scheduled appearance during the Super Bowl. Chief Executive Steve Fu didn't want to get lost among a bunch of dot-com commercials.

This clutter of dot-com advertising extends well beyond the Super Bowl. According to the latest figures, dot-coms spent $1.4 billion in traditional advertising media for the first three quarters of 1999. That's almost three times as much as a year earlier. It's gotten to the point that some pros are wondering whether viewers are experiencing dot-com overload. "There's just too much out there now," says Edward Boches of the Mullen advertising agency, which created the early commercials for Monster.com, an Internet job site whose current commercial depicts children reciting mundane career ambitions. "I don't see how people can remember them. It's like being introduced to 40 persons at a party."

Sources: Excerpted from Cynthia Corzo, "Field of Ads," Miami Herald (January 25, 2000), 1C, 3C; John Dortschner, "Ads!Are!Everywhere!.Com," Miami Herald (January 30, 2000), 1E, 2E.

simply need to identify whether we're familiar with something because we've seen it before. Students taking an exam, for example, would rely on recognition when answering multiple-choice questions. Similarly, consumers would rely on brand recognition when given a list of brand names and asked to indicate those names familiar to them. Or maybe they're shown an advertisement and asked whether they'd seen it before, thus representing ad recognition. Note, then, that recognition measures provide the strongest possible retrieval cue: the to-be-remembered information itself.

Recall, on the other hand, is more cognitively demanding than recognition. As you well know, it's usually easier to answer multiple-choice questions than short answer (e.g., the question asking you to define retrieval) and essay (e.g., the question asking you to describe the various ways in which companies can help consumers to remember) questions. This is also true when examining consumers' memory for ads and brands. Asking consumers to indicate those brands of toothpaste familiar to them from an exhaustive listing of these brands is not the same as asking them to write down all the brands they can think of (as you might remember from our example of this in Chapter 9). Typically, people appear to have a better memory of something when it's measured using recognition rather than recall.[21]

Recall measures come in two basic types. The first, called **unaided** or **free recall,** *does not contain any retrieval cues.* An example would be asking consumers to remember all the brands advertised during the Super Bowl. A second type is **aided** or **cued recall.** For instance, *after telling consumers that an ad appeared during the Super Bowl for a certain type of product* (e.g., soft drinks), *they'd be asked to recall the particular brand.* Given the beneficial effect of retrieval cues noted earlier, consumers remember more when they answer aided rather than unaided recall measures.

Product Awareness

Earlier in the text, we discussed product awareness and how it's an important prerequisite for gaining consideration during decision making (see Chapter 9). We also acknowledged that this awareness could be assessed using either brand recognition or brand recall measures. We didn't discuss, however, when recognition or recall is the most appropriate indicator of product awareness. We do so now.

Think about when consumers are forming their consideration sets and deciding which brands are worthy of purchase consideration. Sometimes these sets are developed using only internal search (covered in Chapter 4), in which case choice alternatives must be freely recalled from memory. In this instance, whether consumers can recognize a brand name is much less relevant than whether they can recall it. Because unless they do, it won't be considered, no matter how recognizable the name may be. Recall is the most appropriate indicator of product awareness for consideration sets generated inside the person's head.[22]

At other times, consideration sets are formed at the point of purchase. Indeed, purchase decisions involving grocery and health and beauty aid products are often made in the store.[23] Nonhabitual grocery shoppers may quickly scan the shelf to see what's available and what to consider further. In this case, they need only recognize rather than freely recall the product. Consequently, product awareness in the form of recognition is most relevant. The Adolph Coors Company tracked recognition of its Coors brand of beer as one indicator of its "Blast to Cash" promotional giveaway. "As a result of running this promotion, brand recognition of Coors has gone up for two years in a row, rising from the No. 3 spot to the No. 1 spot in brand awareness," explains an executive with SCA Promotions, a provider of assorted promotional games.[24]

Brand recognition should include more than simply the product's name because recognition of its packaging may also play an important part in gaining entry into the consideration set. One benefit of showing the product packaging in the ad appearing in Figure 16.5 is that it facilitates consumers' ability to recognize it on the grocer's shelf.

Determining whether recall or recognition is the most relevant measure of product awareness therefore requires understanding which type of retrieval is required for entering the consideration set. Making this determination is important to businesses for two reasons. First, dollars are likely to be wasted if only brand recognition is needed and brand recall is used as the advertising objective.[25] This is because it typically requires fewer ad and product exposures (and hence dollars) to achieve a certain level of recognition than is needed to reach the same level of recall. Second, the usefulness of certain business tactics may depend on whether the decision process is based on brand recognition or brand recall. Educating consumers about a product's packaging so that they can more easily recognize it should pay greater dividends for decisions that rely on brand recognition.[26]

Advertising Awareness

Companies are also interested in what consumers remember about their advertising messages. Sometimes this involves examining those advertisements consumers remember seeing. During the 1999 holiday season, online shoppers were asked to name the most memorable dot-com advertisement they'd seen. Despite

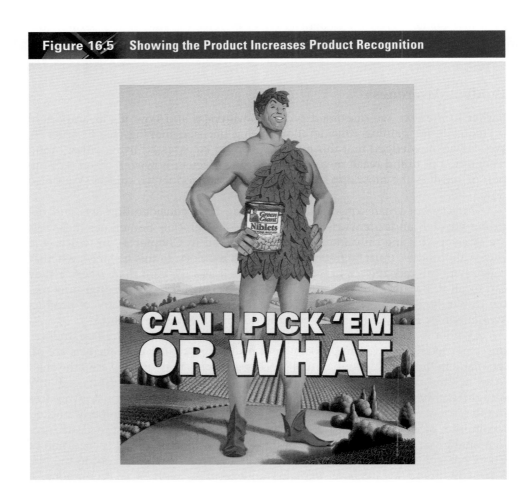

Figure 16.5   Showing the Product Increases Product Recognition

heavy spending by Internet companies on advertising during the holidays, nearly one-fourth couldn't recall even a single ad, leading some to question the value of such advertising.[27] Realize, however, that questioning an ad's effectiveness because consumers can't recall it implicitly assumes that memory of an ad's existence is necessary before it can be influential. Yet there's reason to wonder about the validity of this assumption. After processing an ad, someone might remember certain pieces of information about the product (e.g., what it looks like, how much it costs) without remembering the source of this information. And just because an ad is remembered need not mean that it's effective. Obnoxious or offensive ads can be very memorable, but the negative feelings they generate can also have a negative effect on consumers' product opinions.

Rather than being concerned about *how many* people remember seeing a company's ad, emphasis should be placed on *what* they remember about the ad. Do they remember the name of the advertised product? What, if anything, do they remember about the claims made in the ad? Questions such as these were asked by Kraft Foods when evaluating a new advertising campaign for its DiGiorno brand of frozen pizza. Copy tests revealed that 64 percent could recall the commercial's main message (an average commercial scored only 24 percent), and 52 percent could recall the brand name.[28] Contrast this with findings concerning what's remembered from the banner ads that appear on web sites. One market research firm reports that, of those online consumers who have bothered to click on a banner ad (which, by the way, is less than 50 percent), more than two-thirds couldn't remember what they saw.[29]

Whether consumers remember the particular brand being advertised and the claims made about it is important for the following reasons. If they don't remember the brand, then it's unlikely that anything else that's remembered will be linked to this brand in memory. Even worse, if consumers are confused about which brand was featured in the advertisement, they may mistakenly link the ad claims to a competitor's brand.[30] And because product information conveyed by an ad is intended to make the product more attractive to consumers, remembering this information should increase its chances of being chosen.

Nonetheless, the fact that consumers can remember an ad's claims does not mean that they *believe* the claims. And if they don't believe the claims, then they're unlikely to hold favorable product attitudes. For this reason, greater recall of the claims may not translate into more favorable attitudes.[31]

How Companies Can Help Consumers to Remember

Having discussed some of the basics concerning learning and retrieval, we now turn our attention to the ways in which companies can enhance the odds that consumers remember those things important to their becoming customers. Some of the following suggestions are effective because they facilitate the learning process, thereby leading to stronger memory traces. Others work by assisting the retrieval process. In either case, the ultimate outcome is an improvement in consumers' ability to remember.

Reminders

One obvious way to help consumers remember involves reminding them of what it is the company wants them to remember. This is the purpose of the ad shown in Figure 16.6 that asks consumers if they remembered to purchase the advertised product.

Figure 16.6   Using Reminders to Help Consumers Remember

Similarly, doctors and dentists send postcards to patients reminding them that it's time for their annual checkup. AT&T followed up its initial mail offering to potential customers, which included a check as a financial incentive for switching telephone companies, with a postcard reminding them of the prior offer (see Figure 16.6).

Another example involves consumers' fallible memory concerning when it's time to change the oil in their automobiles. Without being reminded, many would forget to change their oil until way past the time it was due. To reduce such forgetting, many automobile shops place a small sticker on the inside windshield that indicates when the next oil change is due (and those shops that don't have wasted an opportunity for increasing future sales).

Reminders in the form of retrieval cues at the point of purchase may also help advertising effectiveness.[32] Because of the typical delay between when an ad is processed and when a purchase is made, any relevant product information learned from the ad may not be readily accessible at the point of purchase.[33] One method for encouraging the activation of such information from memory is to place retrieval cues on the product's packaging. Such cues would consist of some image strongly associated with the advertising itself. A nice example of this is Energizer batteries and the drum-playing pink bunny featured in its commercials. Although these commercials were well received, many had difficulty remembering just what brand was being advertised. Consequently, the favorable feelings generated by the commercials were not linked very strongly to the Energizer name. To overcome this, the packaging was modified to include the pink bunny as a retrieval cue. Figure 16.7 shows the original packaging without the bunny, which was subsequently changed by including an insert with the bunny. Eventually, the bunny was stamped onto the package itself. One indication of the potential payoff of using advertising retrieval cues comes from the Campbell Soup Company. Its sales increased by 15 percent when point-of-purchase materials were related directly to television advertising.[34]

Companies sometimes include retrieval cues in one commercial that activate memories generated by a different commercial for the same product. The current advertising campaign for one maker of pre-mixed liquor drinks uses two different commercials, each emphasizing a different young couple enjoying themselves dancing at the same party. Each commercial briefly shows the couple featured in the other commercial. By doing this, the advertiser encourages reactivation of the memories supplied by the other commercial. This helps build a stronger memory trace. It also strengthens the linkages in memory between the mental representations held after processing each commercial.

Figure 16.7   Energizer Modified Its Packaging to Help Consumers Remember

Consumer in Focus 16.3

The Memory Value of Product Premiums

Product premiums have a long history in the United States. Back in the early 1800s, politicians began imprinting slogans on buttons, and commemoratives spread their name among the masses. Soon afterward, the American Manufacturing Concern started distributing rulers, yardsticks, paint stirrers, cribbage boards, and paperweights imprinted with advertising messages. By the middle of the 19th century, imprinted calendars were a common sight in the average home or business.

The first full-fledged marketing plan to use premiums as a centerpiece is attributed to Jasper Meek, an Ohio printer at the end of the 1800s. "He noticed that children's school books were always getting muddy, so he printed canvas bags with the slogan 'Buy Cantwell Shoes' and gave them out to families with a [shoe] purchase," says Margaret Kaeter, editor of *Potentials in Marketing,* a promotional products trade magazine. What better way to keep the Cantwell brand top of mind than putting it on something parents have to look at every day?

Premiums possess a number of advantages over tradi-tional advertising tools. First of all, they are tangible; they can be touched, handled, and used. They are also durable. A premium can be saved, and is often passed along from one person to another.

Another benefit of premiums is that they serve as sym-bols that remind people of memories past. You might forget how passionately you loved your high school sweetheart un-til you find the ten-year-old ticket stubs from a concert you attended together. "That tangible symbol will allow you to remember in great detail a whole range of memories and feelings that you couldn't possibly access otherwise," says Dan Bagley III, professor of mass communications at the Uni-versity of Florida and second-generation promotional prod-ucts pro. Although tokens from one's first love affair may evoke more tender emotions than a T-shirt from a radio-station promotion, both will stimulate memories. In its study of trade shows, Exhibit Surveys Inc. found that premiums boost the memorability of the occasion as well as increas-ing booth traffic, responses to invitations, and goodwill to-ward the company.

Source: Excerpted from Rebecca Piirto Heath, "An Engraved Invitation," Marketing Tools *(November/December 1997), 36–42.*

Product premiums (items offered for free or at a reduced rate as an incentive for some behavior, usually buying the product) also can help remind consumers of certain memories. Consumer in Focus 16.3 discusses this possibility.

Saying It Over and Over: The Value of Repetition

Earlier we noted that greater rehearsal leads to stronger memories. Although stu-dents preparing for an upcoming exam may be highly motivated to rehearse their notes, they're unlikely to do so when watching TV commercials. Usually our thoughts linger on the commercial for no longer than the time it appears on the screen before us. Only when we perceive the commercial as providing relevant information for an important purchase decision are we likely to take the time and effort to rehearse this information.

To overcome this lack of rehearsal, companies rely on repetition by showing their advertisements repeatedly. Consumers are "forced" into rehearsal each time they process the ad. Repetition essentially represents externally induced rehearsal.

The beneficial influence of repetition on learning has been well substanti-ated.[35] The standard finding is that learning grows with additional exposures, al-though at a diminishing rate (i.e., each successive exposure contributes less to memory than the preceding one), until it plateaus, at which point further repeti-tion is unproductive. Moreover, the effectiveness of repetition in building long-term memory is enhanced when repetitions are spread out rather than clustered closely together.[36]

Just how much repetition is necessary for maximizing learning depends on both the person and the to-be-learned information.[37] Those highly motivated to remember what the ad has to say may do so after a single exposure as long as the ad doesn't say too much. But if it conveys a large or complex set of information, consumers may be unable to fully comprehend and learn the ad information during a single exposure to the ad. Additional exposures to the ad would then be necessary for greater learning. This is also true for even simple messages when consumers lack the motivation for intentional learning.

Recognize that this beneficial influence of repetition on learning has its limits. Because learning plateaus after a certain number of repetitions, further repetition beyond this point is a waste of money. And, as you learned in Chapter 14, too many repetitions can cause advertising to wear out. The negative responses from seeing the same ad over and over again may hurt consumers' product opinions. It is for this reason that companies should develop multiple ad executions carrying the same basic message. Rather than, say, showing the same ad 20 times, the company is better off developing at least 2 different versions of the ad and showing each 10 times.

The potential benefits of repetition may also be limited by advertising clutter. One study reports that repetition enhanced recall when advertising for competitive products was minimal or nonexistent. Yet this increase disappeared under higher levels of competitive advertising.[38]

Beyond repeating the same ad over and over, repetition can also be used within a single ad. This occurs in a humorous commercial for AFLAC, an insurance company. The commercial shows a man trying to remember the company's name while oblivious to a helpful duck that repeatedly shouts AFLAC. When Kraft developed its DiGiorno brand of pizza, an Italian name was chosen in order to "lend authenticity to the product." But consumers had trouble pronouncing the name, which raised concerns about their ability to remember it. Consequently, Kraft made sure that the brand name was repeated several times in its commercials.[39]

Encourage Elaboration

Previously, we covered how elaborative processing, in which a stimulus is linked or related to various concepts in memory, promotes learning. By encouraging consumers to engage in elaboration during processing, companies can make it easier for consumers to remember. How can this be done? One example is the radio advertisement for an automotive parts supplier called Kar Part Outlet. The ad encouraged listeners to elaborate on the name by linking each word in the name to a different concept in memory. This was done by having the spokesperson say, "Kar, as in what you drive; Part, as in what you do to your hair; Outlet, as in what you stick a plug in."

Another way to encourage elaboration is through self-referencing. **Self-referencing** involves *relating a stimulus to one's own self and experiences.* Suppose some people are asked whether each word in a list describes them. In making this determination, they're likely to engage in self-referencing as they reflect on the type of person they are and whether their behaviors and experiences are consistent with the word's implications. Now suppose that others are given the same list of words but perform a different task (e.g., such as identifying a synonym for the word). If we later test everyone's memory for the words, those asked to self-reference have greater recall.[40]

This facilitating effect of self-referencing is attributed to a more elaborate encoding of the information. The representation of the self in memory is a complex, highly organized structure. The activation of this richer structure during encoding enhances the number and strength of potential linkages that can be made between the to-be-remembered information and other stored information that, in turn, increases the likelihood of retrieval.

Research supports the potential for encouraging self-referencing through advertising copy. By using the word *you* and ad copy that prompted the retrieval of prior relevant product experiences, recall of the ad information was enhanced.[41] We should point out, however, that some have found self-referencing reduces retrieval of information conveyed by advertising claims, at least in some circumstances.[42] Further research is needed to clarify when self-referencing helps or hurts.

Encourage Multiple Representations in Memory

Previously, we described that information stored in long-term memory may be represented in different forms, such as semantically and visually. Depending on how people typically represent the to-be-remembered information in memory, efforts to encourage additional forms of representation may be worthwhile. For example, consider a print ad containing copy that evokes visual imagery during processing. Because this visual imagery may be a part of the mental representation for any stored information, including actual pictures in the ad of the imagery suggested by the ad copy may not help much, if at all. If, however, the ad copy fails to evoke imagery, then including pictures will enhance the formation of visual representations and, consequently, improves retrieval.[43]

In the same way, providing consumers with a visual representation of the brand name can increase its memorability, especially if consumers don't spontaneously generate such representations on their own. Consider the fictitious names "Jack's Camera Shoppe" and "Arrow Pest Control." Visual representations of these names, perhaps along the lines of those shown in Figure 16.8, might help consumers remember the names. Similarly, consumers exposed to the ad for Curve perfume shown in Figure 16.9 may be better able to remember Curve because of the ad's visual elements that reinforce the name. And, in case you forgot, you encountered another example of encouraging visual representations earlier in the text (see Chapter 9, Figure 9.6).

Figure 16.8   Visual Representations Can Increase the Memorability of Brand Names

Figure 16.9   Encouraging Visual Representations in Advertising

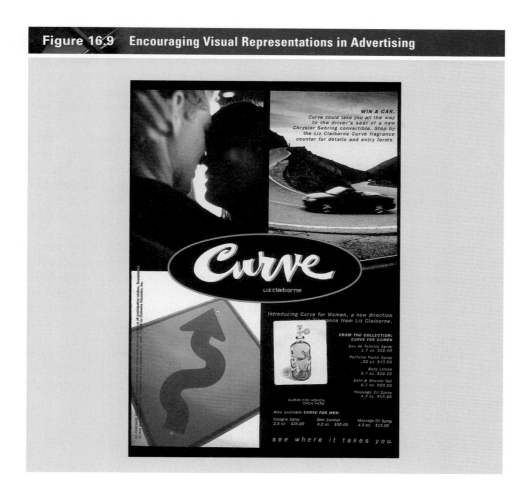

The Importance of Consistency

In a print ad for a brand of vodka, the copy reads, "SMOOTH AS ICE ... Icy cold. Icy clear. Imported Icy Vodka of Iceland. Why can't everything in life be this smooth?" The ad picture shows a bottle with the brand name ICY that appears to be made of smooth clear ice. In this ad, the brand name, the copy, and the picture convey the same meaning.

Consistency facilitates remembering. Greater consistency among elements within an advertisement, as in the just described vodka ad, increases what consumers remember about the ad and advertised product.[44] The product benefits described within an ad are better remembered when these benefits are consistent with those suggested by the advertised product's name. Similarly, pictures that convey a meaning similar to that attached to the brand name enhance memory of the name (as would be expected given our earlier discussion concerning dual coding and multiple representations). Moreover, when the ad copy also conveys the same meaning as the name and picture, brand name recall improves even further.

Use Easy-to-Remember Stimuli

Which phone number do you think would be the easiest for consumers to remember the next time they want to order some flowers: 1-800-356-9377 or 1-800-flowers? The answer's pretty obvious, isn't it? The latter phone number, by virtue of requiring consumers to remember a single word rather than seven digits, imposes significantly fewer demands on memory. As such, it's easier to remember.

Words themselves differ in how easily they are remembered. **Concrete words,** such as tree or dog, are *those that can be visualized rather easily.* In contrast, **abstract words,** such as democracy or equality, *are less amenable to visual representation.* Consequently, concrete words are more likely than abstract words to evoke a visual representation in memory, thereby providing an additional pathway for later retrieval. This is why people given a list of both concrete and abstract words will demonstrate greater memory for the concrete ones.[45]

The memory advantage held by concrete words should be considered when developing new brand names. Names using concrete words (e.g., Black Tie, Head and Throat, Sunburst) usually will be easier to remember than names using abstract or made-up words (e.g., Actifed, Advil, Encaprin, Nuprin). Unless this memory advantage is negated by other considerations (e.g., such as when an abstract brand name is more effective in shaping consumers' product opinions), concrete names may be the most sensible choice for a brand.

Stimuli that are distinctive or unique are also easier to remember. For example, suppose we gave people a few minutes to learn a list of 100 names. The list given to some contains only female names, including Jennifer as one of them. Others are given a list containing Jennifer's name along with 99 male names. When asked to remember the names on the list, more people will retrieve Jennifer's name when it was the only female name on the list. Its distinctiveness makes it stand out more and less susceptible to retrieval interference.

The more a company incorporates distinctiveness into its offering, the more memorable the offering becomes. Its name, packaging, positioning, and advertising can contribute to creating a distinctiveness that separates it from the competition, both in its image and in its memorability.

Put Consumers in a Good Mood

In Chapter 10, we introduced the concept of mood or how people feel at a particular moment in time, and discussed its significance during opinion formation. Another reason mood is important is it influences retrieval. In general, a positive mood increases retrieval. Moreover, the favorableness of retrieved memories depends on whether mood is positive or negative. Positive moods increase the chances of remembering favorable information; negative moods trigger the retrieval of unfavorable information.[46]

It follows, then, that putting consumers in a good mood increases their chances of remembering positive things about the product. Commercials that do so by, say, using humor or music will facilitate the retrieval of positive product information that, in turn, should make consumers more receptive to the commercial messages. Or think about the businessperson preparing to close the deal with a potential customer. Doing something that improves the prospect's mood (perhaps a free meal at a nice restaurant) should increase the retrieval of information that helps the businessperson accomplish his or her objective.

Summary

Remembering is a fundamental part of consumer behavior and decision making. We have to remember the particular purchase and consumption needs that must be filled. And the alternatives considered during decision making, as well as our opinions of them, may heavily depend on what we remember.

Before something can be remembered, it must be learned. Material processed in short-term memory is transferred to long-term memory given sufficient rehearsal or elaboration. But getting something into long-term memory is only half the requirements for remembering. The other half is getting it back out (retrieval). But retrieval is not always successful. Memories grow weaker as time passes since their last activation. Even if a memory has not decayed, other memories may interfere with its retrieval.

Thus, by influencing learning and retrieval, companies can help consumers to remember. This chapter identifies a number of ways for doing this, ranging from as obvious as using reminders to, perhaps less obvious, putting consumers in a good mood. Companies also need to understand which type of retrieval, recall or recognition, is most relevant during consumer decision making.

Review and Discussion Questions

1. What are the various ways in which companies can help consumers remember?

2. Consider the print ad for Isle of Capri casino, in which the copy says "Isle have fun. Isle get lucky. Isle get rich." Explain why this ad may increase memory of the casino's name.

3. The product manager for a new brand of skin softener is considering two possible names: Soft Skin versus Dickson's Skin Moisturizer. Which name would you recommend? Why?

4. A canned-goods manufacturer is interested in comparing the effectiveness of two very different commercials. The first commercial repeatedly shows pictures of the product sitting on the grocer's shelves, riding in the grocery cart, and being placed in the buyer's pantry. The second commercial briefly shows the product one time. Instead, it focuses on images that provide a visual representation of the brand name. When each commercial was examined in a market test, the second commercial was better at increasing brand name recall. Yet it was not as effective as the first commercial for increasing sales. Why might the commercial that's inferior in generating brand name recall prove superior in generating sales?

5. After learning about the potential benefits of including retrieval cues on a product's packaging for stimulating memory of its advertising, a company modified its packaging to include a scene from one of its current commercials. To its dismay, doing this didn't seem to help much because sales were unaffected. How might one explain the apparent ineffectiveness of this retrieval cue?

6. In Consumer in Focus 16.1, we gave an example of where companies hope consumers won't remember. Can you think of other situations where this would be true?

Endnotes

1. Kathryn Kranhold, "Drug Makers Prescribed Direct-Mail Pitch," *The Wall Street Journal* (December 16, 1999), B16.

2. Lynda Edwards, "Web Zine Claims Citrus Department Stole Its Ham Sandwich," *Miami Herald's Business Monday* (May 10, 1999), 7.

3. Alan J. Heavens, "Model Home Says, 'Buy Me.'" *Miami Herald* (May 30, 1999), 1H, 4H.

4. Gabriel Biehal and Dipankar Chakravarti, "Information Accessibility as a Moderator of Consumer Choice," *Journal of Consumer Research* 10 (June 1983), 1–14; Gabriel Biehal and Dipankar

Chakravarti, "Consumers' Use of Memory and External Information in Choice: Macro and Micro Perspectives," *Journal of Consumer Research* 12 (March 1986), 382–405; John G. Lynch, Jr., Howard Marmorstein, and Michael F. Weigold, "Choices from Sets Including Remembered Brands: Use of Recalled Attributes and Prior Overall Evaluations," *Journal of Consumer Research* 15 (September 1988), 169–184; Prakash Nedungadi, "Recall and Consumer Consideration Sets: Influencing Choice Without Altering Brand Evaluations," *Journal of Consumer Research* 17 (September 1990), 263–276.

5. Mita Sujan, James R. Bettman, and Hans Baumgartner, "Influencing Consumer Judgments Using Autobiographical Memories: A Self-Referencing Perspective," *Journal of Marketing Research* 30 (November 1993), 422–436.

6. Terry L. Childers and Michael J. Houston, "Conditions for a Picture-Superiority Effect on Consumer Memory," *Journal of Consumer Research* 11 (September 1984), 643–654; Fergus I. M. Craik and Endel Tulving, "Depth of Processing and the Retention of Words in Episodic Memory," *Journal of Experimental Psychology: General* 104 (September 1975), 268–294; Fergus I. M. Craik and Michael J. Watkins, "The Role of Rehearsal in Short-Term Memory," *Journal of Verbal Learning and Verbal Behavior* 12 (December 1973), 599–607; Meryl Paula Gardner, Andrew A. Mitchell, and J. Edward Russo, "Low Involvement Strategies for Processing Advertisements," *Journal of Advertising* 14 (1985), 4–12; Scott A. Hawkins and Stephen J. Hoch, "Low-Involvement Learning: Memory without Evaluation," *Journal of Consumer Research* 19 (September 1992), 212–225; Joel Saegert and Robert K. Young, "Comparison of Effects of Repetition and Levels of Processing in Memory for Advertisements," in Andrew A. Mitchell, ed., *Advances in Consumer Research* 9 (St. Louis: Association for Consumer Research, 1982), 431–434.

7. We should acknowledge that evidence exists that indicates too much elaboration may actually reduce learning. See David Glen Mick, "Levels of Subjective Comprehension in Advertising Processing and Their Relations to Ad Perceptions, Attitudes, and Memory," *Journal of Consumer Research* 18 (March 1992), 411–424.

8. Richard E. Petty and John T. Cacioppo, "The Elaboration Likelihood Model of Persuasion," in Leonard Berkowitz, ed., *Advances in Experimental Social Psychology* 19 (New York: Academic Press, 1986), 123–205.

9. Gabriel Biehal and Dipankur Chakravarti, "Information-Presentation Format and Learning Goals as Determinants of Consumers' Memory Retrieval and Choice Processes," *Journal of Consumer Research* 8 (March 1982), 431–441; James H. Leigh

and Anil Menon, "Audience Involvement Effects on the Information Processing of Umbrella Print Advertisements," *Journal of Advertising* 16 (1987), 3–12; Barry McLaughlin, "Intentional and Incidental Learning in Human Subjects: The Role of Instructions to Learn and Motivation," *Psychological Bulletin* 63 (May 1965), 359–376; Bernd H. Schmitt, Nader T. Tavassoli, and Robert T. Millard, "Memory for Print Ads: Understanding Relations Among Brand Name, Copy, and Picture," *Journal of Consumer Psychology* 21, 1, 55–81.

10. William G. Chase and Herbert A. Simon, "Perception in Chess," *Cognitive Psychology* 4 (January 1973), 55–81. For a more general discussion, see Joseph W. Alba and J. Wesley Hutchinson, "Dimensions of Consumer Expertise," *Journal of Consumer Research* 13 (March 1987), 411–454.

11. Rajeev Batra and Michael Ray, "Situational Effects of Advertising: The Moderating Influence of Motivation, Ability and Opportunity to Respond," *Journal of Consumer Research* 12 (March 1986), 432–445; Danny L. Moore, Douglas Hausknecht, and Kanchana Thamodaran, "Time Compression, Response Opportunity, and Persuasion," *Journal of Consumer Research* 13 (June 1986), 85–99; James M. Munch and John L. Swasy, "Rhetorical Question, Summarization Frequency, and Argument Strength Effects on Recall," *Journal of Consumer Research* 15 (June 1988), 69–76.

12. Catherine A. Cole and Michael J. Houston, "Encoding and Media Effects on Consumer Learning Deficiencies in the Elderly," *Journal of Marketing Research* 24 (February 1987), 55–63. Also see Gary J. Gaeth and Timothy B. Heath, "The Cognitive Processing of Misleading Advertising in Young and Old Adults," *Journal of Consumer Research* 14 (June 1987), 43–54.

13. For recent research on the mental representation of product information, see Terry L. Childers and Madhubalan Viswanathan, "Representation of Numerical and Verbal Product Information in Consumer Memory," *Journal of Business Research* 47 (February 2000), 109–120.

14. Allan Paivio, *Mental Representations: A Dual Coding Approach* (New York: Oxford University Press, 1986).

15. For research on how consumer-related knowledge is organized, see Gabriel Biehal and Dipankar Chakravarti, "Information-Presentation Format and Learning Goals as Determinants of Consumers' Memory Retrieval and Choice Processes," *Journal of Consumer Research* 8 (March 1982), 431–441; Eric J. Johnson and J. Edward Russo, "The Organization of Product Information in Memory Identify by Recall Times," in H. Keith Hunt, ed., *Advances in Consumer Research* 5 (Chicago: Association for Consumer Research,

1978), 79–86; J. Edward Russo and Eric J. Johnson, "What Do Consumers Know about Familiar Products?" in Jerry C. Olson, ed., *Advances in Consumer Research* 7 (Ann Arbor, MI: Association for Consumer Research, 1980), 417–423.

16. John R. Anderson, *The Architecture of Cognition* (Cambridge, MA: Harvard University Press, 1983).

17. A. M. Collins and E. F. Loftus, "A Spreading Activation Theory of Semantic Processing," *Psychological Review* (November 1975), 407–428. For a recent investigation of spreading activation in the context of brand extensions, see Maureen Morrin, "The Impact of Brand Extensions on Parent Brand Memory Structures and Retrieval Processes," *Journal Marketing Research* 36 (November 1999), 517–525.

18. Endel Tulving and Zena Pearlstone, "Availability Versus Accessibility of Information in Memory for Words," *Journal of Verbal Learning and Verbal Behavior* 5 (August 1966), 381–391.

19. Joseph W. Alba and Amitava Chattopadhyay, "Effects of Context and Part-Category Cues on Recall of Competing Brands," *Journal of Marketing Research* 22 (August 1985), 340–349; Joseph W. Alba and Amitava Chattopadhyay, "Salience Effects in Brand Recall," *Journal of Marketing Research* 23 (November 1986), 363–369. Also see Paul W Miniard, H. Rao Unnava, and Sunil Bhatla, "Investigating the Recall Inhibition Effect: A Test of Practical Considerations," *Marketing Letters* 2 (January 1991), 290–303.

20. Raymond R. Burke and Thomas K. Srull, "Competitive Interference and Consumer Memory for Advertising," *Journal of Consumer Research* 15 (June 1988), 55–68. Also see Carolyn L. Costley and Merrie Brucks, "Selective Recall and Information Use in Consumer Preferences," *Journal of Consumer Research* 18 (March 1992), 464–474; Kevin Lane Keller, "Memory and Evaluation Effects in Competitive Advertising Environments," *Journal of Consumer Research* 17 (March 1991), 463–476. Interference effects may depend on consumers' familiarity with the advertised brand. See Robert J. Kent and Chris T. Allen, "Competitive Interference Effects and Consumer Memory for Advertising: The Role of Brand Familiarity," *Journal of Marketing* 58 (July 1994), 97–105. The effects of advertising clutter also depend on whether memory is measured using recall or recognition. See Tom J. Brown and Michael L. Rothschild, "Reassessing the Impact of Television Advertising Clutter," *Journal of Consumer Research* 20 (June 1993), 138–146.

21. For research on recall and recognition measures, see Adam Finn, "Print Ad Recognition Readership Scores: An Information Processing Perspec-

tive," *Journal of Marketing Research* 25 (May 1988), 168–177; Surendra N. Singh and Gilbert A. Churchill, Jr., "Using the Period of Signal Detection to Improve at Recognition Testing," *Journal of Marketing Research* 23 (November 1986), 327–336; Surendra N. Singh and Catherine A. Cole, "Forced-Choice Recognition Tests: A Critical Review," *Journal of Advertising* 14 (1985), 52–58; Surendra N. Singh and Michael L. Rothschild, "Recognition As a Measure of Learning from Television Commercials," *Journal of Marketing Research* 20 (August 1983), 235–248; Surendra N. Singh, Michael L. Rothschild, and Gilbert A. Churchill, Jr., "Recognition Versus Recall As Measures of Television Commercial Forgetting," *Journal of Marketing Research* 25 (February 1988), 72–80.

22. James R. Bettman, *An Information Processing Theory of Consumer Choice* (Reading, MA: Addison-Wesley, 1979).

23. John A. Quelch and David Kenny, "Extend Profits, Not Product Lines," *Harvard Business Review* 72 (September/October 1994), 153–160.

24. Kathleen V. Schmidt, "Marketers Win Big in Giveaway Gamble," *Marketing News* (February 28, 2000), 7.

25. Surendra N. Singh, Michael L. Rothschild, and Gilbert A. Churchill, Jr., "Recognition Versus Recall as Measures of Television Commercial Forgetting," *Journal of Marketing Research* 25 (February 1988), 72–80.

26. For a discussion of advertising tactics to enhance brand recognition and recall, see John R. Rossiter and Larry Percy, "Advertising Communication Models," in Elizabeth C. Hirschman and Morris B. Holbrook, eds., *Advances in Consumer Research* 12 (Provo, UT: Association for Consumer Research, 1985), 510–524.

27. John Dorschner, "Ads!Are!Everywhere!.com," *Miami Herald* (January 30, 2000), 1E, 2E.

28. "Upper Crust," *American Demographics* (March 1999), 58.

29. Katherine Yung, "Advertisers Find the Net a Hard Nut to Crack," *Miami Herald's Business Monday* (July 12, 1999), 11.

30. For a demonstration of mistaken brand identity, see Cornelia Pechmann and David W. Stewart, "The Effects of Comparative Advertising on Attention, Memory, and Purchase Intentions," *Journal of Consumer Research* 17 (September 1990), 180–191.

31. Amitava Chattopadhyay and Joseph W. Alba, "The Situational Importance of Recall and Inference in Consumer Decision Making," *Journal of Consumer Research* 15 (June 1988), 1–12; Barbara

Loken and Ronald Hoverstad, "Relationships between Information Recall and Subsequent Attitudes: Some Exploratory Findings," *Journal of Consumer Research* 12 (September 1985), 155–168. Note, however, that the relationship between recall and attitude is stronger when attitudes are not formed during ad processing but are formed at a later time based on retrieval of the ad information. For a discussion of this issue, see Reid Hastie and Bernadette Park, "The Relationship between Memory and Judgment Depends on Whether the Judgment Task Is Memory-Based or On-Line," *Psychological Review* 93 (June 1986), 258–268; Meryl Lichtenstein and Thomas K. Srull, "Processing Objectives as a Determinant of the Relationship between Recall and Judgment," *Journal of Experimental Social Psychology* 23 (March 1987), 93–118.

32. Kevin Lane Keller, "Memory Factors in Advertising: The Effect of Advertising Retrieval Cues on Brand Evaluations," *Journal of Consumer Research* 14 (December 1987), 316–333. For additional research on retrieval cues, see Marian Friestad and Esther Thorson, "Remembering Ads: The Effects of Encoding Strategies, Retrieval Cues, and Emotional Response," *Journal of Consumer Psychology* 2 (1993), 1–24; Kevin Lane Keller, "Cue Comparability and Framing in Advertising," *Journal of Marketing Research* 28 (February 1991), 42–57; Kevin Lane Keller, "Memory and Evaluation Effects in Competitive Advertising Environments," *Journal of Consumer Research* 17 (March 1991), 463–476.

33. Cathy J. Cobb and Wayne D. Hoyer, "The Influence of Advertising at Moment of Brand Choice," *Journal of Advertising* (December 1986), 5–27.

34. Joseph O. Eastlack, Jr., "How to Get More Bang for Your Television Bucks," *Journal of Consumer Marketing* 1 (1984), 25–34.

35. Research on repetition effects can be found in Rajeev Batra and Michael Ray, "Situational Effects of Advertising: The Moderating Influence of Motivation, Ability and Opportunity to Respond," *Journal of Consumer Research* 12 (March 1986), 432–445; George E. Belch, "The Effects of Television Commercial Repetition on Cognitive Response and Message Acceptance," *Journal of Consumer Research* 9 (June 1982), 56–65; Arno J. Rethans, John L. Swasy, and Lawrence J. Marks, "Effects of Television Commercial Repetition, Receiver Knowledge, and Commercial Length: A Test of the Two-Factor Model," *Journal of Marketing Research* 23 (February 1986), 50–61; Surendra N. Singh and Catherine A. Cole, "The Effects of Length, Content, and Repetition on Television Commercial Effectiveness," *Journal of Marketing Research* 30 (February 1993), 91–104; Surendra N. Singh, Michael L. Rothschild, and Gilbert A. Churchill, Jr., "Recognition Versus Recall as Measures of Television Commercial Forgetting," *Journal of Marketing Research* 25 (February 1988), 72–80; Esther Thorson and Rita Snyder, "Viewer Recall of Television Commercials: Prediction from the Propositional Structure of Commercial Scripts," *Journal of Marketing Research* 21 (May 1984), 127–136.

36. Surendra N. Singh, Sanjay Mishra, Neeli Bendapudi, and Denise Linville, "Enhancing Memory of Television Commercials through Message Spacing," *Journal of Marketing Research* 31 (August 1994), 384–392.

37. Punam Anand and Brian Sternthal, "Ease of Message Processing as a Moderator of Repetition Effects in Advertising," *Journal of Marketing Research* 27 (August 1990), 345–353.

38. Burke and Srull, "Competitive Interference and Consumer Memory for Advertising."

39. "Upper Crust," *American Demographics* (March 1999), 58.

40. See, for example, T. B. Rogers, N. A. Kuiper, and W. S. Kirker, "Self-Reference and Encoding of Personal Information," *Journal of Personality and Social Psychology* 35 (September 1977), 677–688; Polly Brown, Janice M. Keenan, and George R. Potts, "The Self-Reference Effect with Imagery Encoding," *Journal of Personality and Social Psychology* 51 (November 1986), 897–906.

41. Robert E. Burnkrant and H. Rao Unnava, "Self-Referencing: A Strategy for Increasing Processing of Message Content," *Personality and Social Psychology Bulletin* 15 (December 1989), 628–638. Also see Kathleen Debevec, Harlan E. Spotts, and Jerome B. Kernan, "The Self-Reference Effect in Persuasion: Implications for Marketing Strategy," in Melanie Wallendorf and Paul Anderson, eds., *Advances in Consumer Research* 14 (Provo, UT: Association for Consumer Research, 1987), 417–420.

42. Sujan, Bettman, and Baumgartner, "Influencing Consumer Judgments Using Autobiographical Memories: a Self-Referencing Perspective."

43. H. Rao Unnava and Robert E. Burnkrant, "An Imagery-Processing View of the Role of Pictures in Print Advertisements," *Journal of Marketing Research* 28 (May 1991), 226–231.

44. Roberta L. Klatzky, *Human Memory: Structures and Processes* (San Francisco: W. H. Freeman, 1975), 230.

45. Kevin Lane Keller, Susan E. Heckler, and Michael J. Houston, "The Effects of Brand Name Suggestiveness on Advertising Recall," *Journal of Marketing* 62 (January 1998), 48–57; Schmitt, Tavassoli, and Millard, "Memory for Print Ads: Under-

standing Relations Among Brand Name, Copy, and Picture."

46. P. H. Blaney, "Affect and Memory: A Review," *Psychological Bulletin* 99 (1986), 229–246; Alice M. Isen, "Some Ways in Which Affect Influences Cognitive Processes: Implications for Advertising and Consumer Behavior," in Alice M. Tybout and P. Cafferata, eds., *Advertising and Consumer Psy-* *chology* (Lexington, MA: Lexington Books, 1989), 91–117; Patricia A. Knowles, Stephen J. Grove, and W. Jeffrey Burroughs, "An Experimental Examination of Mood Effects on Retrieval and Evaluation of Advertisement and Brand Information," *Journal of the Academy of Marketing Science* (Spring 1993), 135–143.

Suggested Readings for Part V

Erich Joachimstaler and Aaker, David A., "Building Brands without Mass Media," *Harvard Business Review* (January/February 1997).

Maureen Morrin, "The Impact of Brand Extensions on Parent Brand Memory Structures and Retrieval Processes," *Journal of Marketing Research* 36 (November 1999), 517–525.

Kevin Lane Keller, Susan E. Heckler, and Michael J. Houston, "The Effects of Brand Name Suggestiveness on Advertising Recall," *Journal of Marketing* 62, 1 (January 1998).

Cornelia Pechmann and Chuan-Fong Shih, "Smoking Scenes in Movies and Antismoking Advertisements Before Movies: Effects on Youth," *Journal of Marketing* 63, 3 (July 1999), 1–13.

Gerard J. Tellis, Fajesh K. Chandy, and Pattana Thaivanich, "Which Ad Works, When, Where, and How Often? Modeling the Effects of Direct Television Advertising," *Journal of Marketing Research* 37 (February 2000), 32–46.

Rik Pieters, Edward Rosbergen, and Michel Wedel, "Visual Attention to Repeated Print Advertising: A Test of Scanpath Theory," *Journal of Marketing Research* 36 (November 1999), 424–438.

Joan Raymond, "Kids Just Wanna Have Fun," *American Demographics* (February 2000), 57–61.

CASE 1

Pick 'n Pay

If you were asked to name countries where the world's top retailers could be found, would you think of South Africa? Perhaps not, but retail experts would, and chances are that they'd be thinking of Pick 'n Pay. Pick 'n Pay evolved from a chain of small upscale grocery stores in Cape Town to one of the largest portfolio retail organizations in the Southern Hemisphere. Its retail portfolio boasts a variety of retail concepts, including small discount-price stores (offering a limited assortment of basic food items for economically challenged consumers), neighborhood and family supermarkets and hypermarkets, and up-market stores (satisfying the sophisticated tastes of the urban elite with exclusive imported kitchen and home ware).

Although consumers see stores filled with tempting merchandise, a look behind the scenes of Pick 'n Pay reveals operating principles that focus on efficiency and continued growth and success. Its information backbone facilitates order processing, sales reporting, and stock management, while processing some 250,000 payments for third parties and 2 million monthly credit/debit card transactions. Yet even with superior information technology, Pick 'n Pay's most valuable operating strategy can be traced to founder Raymond Ackerman. Its guiding operating principles, which graphically describe everything from merchandising philosophies to human relationships, focus on Pick 'n Pay's unique *culture*—distinguishing it from others around the world.

Counterculture

Pick 'n Pay CEO Sean Summers summarizes the company's approach to satisfying customers and corporate culture. "We always ask: Are we doing things right? Are we doing the right things? We want to get the details right, every time and be the first to be what consumers want." Pick 'n Pay's *culture* is evident in its unyielding focus on *consumer value*, *social responsibility*, and its unique approach to *managing employees*.

Consumer Value

At a time when few people were courageous enough to question the Apartheid government's stifling regulatory policies, Pick 'n Pay developed a reputation for fighting cartels and monopolies on behalf of the consumer. These well-publicized fights, often conducted in the courts, demonstrated Ackerman's steely resolve to increase consumer value.

For Pick 'n Pay, consumer value means more than low prices, even though these may win consumer support and admiration. Pick 'n Pay is not satisfied with being the first to discount a price or having the lowest on-shelf prices—its goal is to "save you (consumers) time and money and simplify your life." To fulfill its goals, senior executives travel the world observing how the best retailers serve their customers, return to South Africa, and attempt to build something better than what they've seen abroad. As a result, Pick 'n Pay was the first in its market to introduce hypermarkets, in-store delicatessens and automated teller machines, on-floor customer services managers, baby change rooms, shopping carts for the disabled, house brands, branded financial services, and many other innovations.

Social Responsibility

In addition to promoting consumer value, Pick 'n Pay's culture promotes a social conduct dictated by Ackerman when he founded the company three decades ago. Pick 'n Pay supports self-help, feeding, and educational programs, environmental projects, and various fund-raising endeavors. Educational pamphlets about recycling, environmental concerns, and other social issues are printed and distributed in stores, and the board of directors monitors the firm's social actions closely.

Managing People at Pick 'n Pay

"Internal social responsibility" characterizes the firm's humanistic approach to people management. Although Ackerman located the first Pick 'n Pay stores in affluent suburbs (managers were normally white, English-speaking males), Pick 'n Pay was among the first to seek out South Africa's historically disadvantaged for management training and development. Ackerman once admitted, "I didn't stand up enough against Apartheid, but what I have done my whole business life is stand up for nondiscrimination." This is evident in Pick 'n Pay's new Vuselela program (a Xhosa/Zulu word that roughly translates as "process of renewal or rebirth") designed to "reaffirm Pick 'n Pay values of human dignity and mutual respect" and to stimulate employee motivation. Overseen by a black South African director, Issac Motaung, Vuselela is founded on a simple and powerful mission statement developed by the staff: "We serve. With our hearts we create a great place to be. With our minds we create a great place to shop."

Vuselela has resulted in a spirit of cooperation among individuals to contribute to the betterment of their stores and higher customer service and courtesy levels. Opportunities for self-improvement, including attending university-accredited courses at the Pick 'n Pay Institute, abound. In May 1997, a select group of achievers flew to Orlando, Florida, and attended the Walt Disney Institute. It was the most diverse group ever to participate, and the Disney staff described the initiative as "the most noble act they had ever seen from a company in its commitment to its people."

In addition to its humanistic approach to management, Pick 'n Pay fosters a hands-on culture, in which no manager, regardless of seniority, is above stocking store shelves if that's what's needed to satisfy customers. Every manager comes from within the organization—starting in "fruits and vegetables" and rotating through every area of operations before receiving any managerial responsibility. Even the most senior managers, clad in season-appropriate shirts sans ties, can be found in the stores listening to customers and staff or seated behind their raised desks located at the front of the store near the cash registers.

Serving Intermarket Segments in Emerging Economies

Emerging markets often are characterized by special problems that affect retail operations, including the formation of dual economies with great disparities in wealth between haves and have-nots. Further adding complexity to these markets are higher inflation, unemployment and crime rates, high costs of capital and indirect taxation that fuel growth in informal retail sectors, low labor costs, concentrated supplier power resulting in seller's markets, inefficient distribution channels, and limitation in product knowledge. These economic factors have pushed Pick 'n Pay to become a sophisticated, world-class portfolio retailer. Each company focuses on serving a specific segment of customers, with varying ethnic, economic, and lifestyle characteristics.

Score Supermarkets, which emphasizes efficiency, cleanliness, and easy shopping, moves big volumes of basic food and toiletry items through its stores and franchise outlets. Savings can be passed on to the lower-income segments served by these stores. Similarly, TM Supermarkets is a 25 percent held Zimbabwe chain of residential supermarkets that provides value to its customers. Rite Value convenience supermarkets operate from modern, attractive stores in finely targeted residential areas. Rite Value franchisees usually live within the communities they serve and contribute to their wealth and economic well-being.

Targeted to higher income segments than served by Score, Pick 'n Pay Family Supermarkets and Discount Supermarkets stock leading national food and toiletry brands and a limited range of clothing, hardware, and small kitchen appliances. Guided by research that shows that higher income consumers want better food labeling, extensive nutritional information, fresher foods, more pleasurable shopping experiences, and less crowded aisles, Pick 'n Pay Discount Supermarkets' store designs emphasize the shopping *experience* and offer more variety and product choices. Customers can buy fresh fish off ice and prepared foods, order special butcher's cuts, or select from a wide range of fresh fruit and vegetables in a village market walk-through deli (occupying more than one-third of the retail floor space).

Pick 'n Pay Hypermarkets offer an even more extensive range of products, including automotive goods, garden furniture, hardware, toys, major appliances, and electronics. Boardman's offers mainly European kitchen and home ware to discriminating clients with an emphasis on quality first and value second.

Product Mix Strategy: From Beans to Jeans

Pick 'n Pay's rapid growth and focus on a variety of segments has required constant attention to its product mix. Reflecting on its early years in the hypermarket business, one director once said, "we weren't that good in the beginning— clothing is not beans." Taking the consumer's perspective, Pick 'n Pay focuses on usage occasions and attempts to solve consumer problems so that it can manage, market, and sell a large product mix. Pick 'n Pay monitors the different criteria consumers use to determine purchase choices for different product and usage situations. For example, consumers might be willing to pay more for fresh, exotic fruits and vegetables used in salads and home-prepared desserts, but they may look for lower-priced canned vegetables to use in soups, or inexpensive children's T-shirts that will be worn for one season.

House Brands That Represent Value

All the stores that boast the Pick 'n Pay name keep on-shelf competition keen by offering five house brands, each targeted at a different economic stratum and backed by a "twice your money back guarantee." Suppliers who do not update their products to reflect international trends become vulnerable to the house brands. According to Summers, "We try to stay very close to customers and urge our suppliers to do the same. Over the past decade, people have become less trusting of brands, either because they promise something people don't want anymore or promise something they don't deliver, and manufacturers aren't always able to offer a range of quality products that we believe customers want."

Providing value (lower prices and high quality) to consumers with the Pick 'n Pay *brand* contributes to the chain's uncanny success in a wide range of product categories. Summers adds, "We earn nearly three times more gross profit on house brands than manufacturer name brands, but our real reason for offering house brands is to ensure that our customers get the quality they expect when they visit a Pick 'n Pay outlet." Today, consumers know that clothing bearing the Pick 'n Pay label often sells elsewhere at much higher prices when marketed under more up-market brand names.

Although he acknowledges the growing demands for convenience and pleasure in shopping, Summers believes that price and safety remain overriding factors for South African shoppers. "Most emerging economies have wealthy and economically challenged segments that live very different lifestyles. There is no doubt in our mind that price is very important to a larger proportion of South African shoppers than is the case in America or Europe. But we also have to look at the variety and quality of the goods we stock. South Africans don't always want all the bells and whistles people want overseas. Sometimes they want a well-made basic product, and we work hard to find it for them." Novelty also is important. Pick 'n Pay buyers were quick to get Teletubbies in-store and say they'll stock yo-yos again, if they become popular.

The Future

Pick 'n Pay is very different from the chain it was just ten years ago, and more change is on the horizon in the next decade. South Africa's miracle transition has not been without social problems that require management response. For example, security has become more important to most South Africans. Thinking about the financial and psychological price of shopping, managers monitor the local crime situation near their stores. Although Pick 'n Pay believes that social violence may be less severe than the international press suggests, Summers says that "violence in South Africa has risen to unacceptable levels." He adds, "People want to see a security guard in the parking lot and at the entrances of your store in many locations."

Growing spending power in South Africa's historically disadvantaged segments also requires careful thinking about the changing mix of consumers who walk through the doors at Pick 'n Pay. According to Summers, "It's really exciting to be part of a rapidly changing market. We're thinking about differences in culture and demographics that weren't very important a decade ago. If we get it right, we appeal to a wider range of preferences for food, clothing sizes, and the like. When we get it wrong, we sit with stock we have to move at discount prices. Our results suggest that we get it right a lot of the time, but I have no doubt it's going to keep us on our toes."

Focal Topics

1. What evaluative criteria would lead people to choose Pick 'n Pay over its competitors? How important are a firm's practices concerning social responsibility in consumer patronage decisions?

2. To what degree should Pick 'n Pay's marketing strategy vary between ethnic segments in South Africa?

3. What types of internal and external programs could Pick 'n Pay develop to communicate effectively with the various segments of employees and customers, respectively?

How would you position advertising or other public relations programs to its many customer segments?

4. Given the hypermarket approach, selling everything from "beans to jeans," how does the consumer decision process for clothing differ from that used to choose groceries?

5. Explain how firms that private-label such a wide variety of products extend a quality image to products from canned green beans to women's clothing.

Service Corporation International

"As inevitable as death and taxes," a familiar phrase to many, takes on special meaning when visiting the corporate offices of Service Corporation International (SCI). Dedicated to serving families in need, SCI has redefined the funeral industry by turning the challenges inherent to growing in a fragmented industry into profitable opportunities. SCI has become the world's largest provider of services and care relating to death—the one problem that faces every consumer in every country of the world.

SCI and the Death Care Industry

Robert L. Waltrip began as a funeral director in a single funeral home in Houston, Texas. In 1962, he founded SCI with three Houston funeral homes, and by 1999, it mushroomed into a $2.9 billion death care giant, serving more than 700,000 families through its 4,500 funeral service locations, cemeteries, and crematoria in 20 countries around the world, including Switzerland, Belgium, Italy, Czech Republic, and Singapore.

SCI operates *funeral homes* that provide all professional services relating to funerals, including the use of funeral facilities and motor vehicles. Consumers can buy caskets, coffins, burial vaults, cremation receptacles, flowers, and burial garments, while some locations operate crematoria. The company's *cemeteries* sell cemetery interment rights (including mausoleum spaces and lawn crypts) and merchandise (including stone and bronze memorials and burial vaults), and they perform burial services and manage and maintain cemetery grounds.

SCI also sells "pre-need"—prearranged funeral products and services—to consumers before the time they are needed. These products allow individuals to arrange their funerals "just the way they want" and pay for them before dying, locking-in today's prices for services performed later. They also relieve emotional decisions that families must make at difficult times. SCI's management believes pre-need increases stability to the funeral service industry and will stimulate future revenue growth in domestic and foreign markets.

Sales of these products have made SCI *the* global funeral care leader dedicated to providing a total approach to death. Its 40,000 professional and support personnel—united by the mission to ease the burden on families during the funeral process—uphold its leadership position using the cross-cultural marketing and management strategies SCI has perfected throughout the years.

Historically, family and friends of the deceased performed many death services, and in developing countries of the world, they still do. But in developed economies, families turn to their local funeral director and funeral home to take care of all the arrangements. Their choice of funeral home is often guided by family members and religious or ethnic groups, and often depends on the reputation of the firm in the community—how long the funeral firm has been in business and how trustworthy it is perceived to be.

In the United States today, there are over 22,000 funeral firms employing nearly 35,000 licensed personnel and about 89,000 personnel to handle the more than 2.3 million deaths that occur each year. Almost 78 percent of funeral homes are family owned and average 54 years in business, with the average firm handling approximately 159 funerals per year (about three per week), at an average price of $4,500 to $5,000. These firms are concentrated in rural areas and small towns, whereas SCI and its competitors are concentrated in metropolitan areas. Although SCI is the world's largest provider of death services, its total market share in any country is small compared to the number of independent firms. Its market share in North America is roughly 12 percent, whereas it is 28 percent in France, 24 percent in Australia, and 15 percent in the United Kingdom.

Lifestyles and Deathstyles

Critical to the growth of SCI is the understanding of consumer lifestyles and deathstyles. The more that is known about these factors, the better armed (with knowledge and therefore effective strategies) SCI locations will be to serve customers best. The funeral service industry monitors factors such as the changing demographic makeup of the world and the increase or decrease in popularity of specific products or service.

No one knows exactly how many people will die each year. Market demand is affected by factors such as natural disasters, intensity of weather, disease, and changes in life span that are difficult to predict. Historically, the number of deaths has increased by 1 percent annually, leaving death care companies little opportunity to grow based on natural increase. In fact, in 1997, the aggregate number of deaths actually declined from 1996 because of mild weather and a decrease in the number of AIDS-related deaths. At the same time, people are living longer—yet none have figured out how to elude death completely. According to the National Funeral Directors Association, the death rate has hovered between 8.5 and 8.8 deaths per 1,000 people since 1980 and is projected to maintain this rate until 2010. By the year 2020, the death rate could jump beyond the 10.0 rate if total population increases as projected.

In the next few decades, the number of people over 65 is expected to increase dramatically, translating into an increase in the need for death care services. To prepare for this demographically fueled increase in demand, SCI and its competitors are acquiring firms and expanding their resources. The first baby boomers, who represent the largest swell in total population numbers, will turn 65 in 2011. However, since people are living longer, predicting demand for at-need services is difficult. One answer to this unpredictable demand is marketing pre-need, which is becoming an increasingly popular choice with 60- to 70-year-old individuals who see it as an extension of estate planning. As more baby boomers deal with the death of their parents, they are also becoming more interested in pre-need, for their remaining parents and for themselves.

Changing deathstyles also relate to predictions about changes in demand for specific services. Cremation is becoming a popular alternative to interment, even in the United States. About one-third of the families served by SCI's North American funeral service locations selected cremation, substantially more than the 21 percent national average. And that number is expected to increase to 40 percent by the year 2010. A deciding factor for some consumers is cost—cremation is usually less expensive than the average burial, although the funeral can cost just as much with cremation as with burial. Based on industry studies published in *Pharos International* magazine, cremations account for over 98 percent of all dispositions of human remains in Japan, a country with limited land. Cremation memorialization has long been a tradition in Australian and U.K. markets—and in recent years, SCI has opened more than 20 cremation memorial gardens in North America.

Strategies for Success in the Death Care Industry

Consolidation of firms has become the strategy of choice across industries and around the globe, even in the cemetery and funeral business. Establishing new funeral and cemetery firms is very difficult because of high entry costs and the specific knowledge base and skills needed to operate effectively—not to mention the time required to build a loyal following and a relationship with a community. For more than 35 years, SCI has grown and prospered by implementing savvy globalization and acquisition strategies along with its cluster approach to expansion and operation.

Acquisition

SCI has achieved much of its growth with an aggressive, yet disciplined approach to acquisitions. Not wanting to reinvent the wheel or compete with the best-established firms in a community, SCI grows by identifying and acquiring premier firms in metropolitan areas, with the goal of not disrupting the external identity of the firm. Even after becoming a member of the SCI family, firms retain their local identity and many of their localized approaches to dealing with funeral customers, procedures, and internal management. SCI also builds new branches of well-known local firms in areas of suburban expansion.

SCI focuses heavily on "heritage" funeral home acquisitions in metropolitan areas with large segments of people aged 65 or above. A majority of heritage funeral firms were founded in the early to mid-20th century and passed down through generations of family owners. Rising labor costs, increasing government regulation, and declining interest among the sons and daughters to follow in their parents' footsteps have made independent ownership more difficult. Selling to SCI provides business owners who face such concerns an exit strategy. Though SCI operates the businesses under the firms' family names, it encourages former owners to remain involved as managers of or consultants to the firm. Thereby, the firm (as well as SCI) benefits from their public visibility, business expertise, and knowledge of local markets.

Cluster

The cluster concept, pioneered by SCI, has increased operating efficiency and responsiveness to consumers. Clusters generally consist of two to ten funeral homes or cemetery locations in a city or within a company-defined sector of a large metropolitan area. Elements, such as hearses and limousines, preparation facilities, administration, purchasing and personnel, are essentials in operating a funeral firm. In a fragmented industry, each firm must perform each function. In a typical cluster, one funeral home may maintain all vehicles, while another may provide preparation services, and a third may perform accounting and purchasing tasks. For example, though most funeral homes employ a few staff members to greet the public from day to day, the cluster concept allows firms to draw additional personnel from other firms if they have a heavy schedule on a particular day. This optimized use of equipment and personnel, along with merchandise discounts obtained through SCI's strong purchasing power, enables all cluster firms to reduce their overhead costs, reach their "breakeven" points earlier in the year than comparable independent firms, and earn more per dollar of revenue.

SCI has successfully implemented the cluster strategy in its North American, United Kingdom, and Australian operations and is proceeding with implementation in its French operations, which were acquired in August 1995. SCI has approximately 311 clusters in North America, the United Kingdom, and Australia, which range in size from 2 to 63 operations. There may be more than one cluster in a given metropolitan area, depending upon the level and degree of shared costs.

Global Deathstyles

In an age of global expansion, SCI's understanding of cultural sensitivities has made it successful globally. Although a myriad of industries are faced with this challenge, perhaps in no other industry are they more pronounced and ingrained than in death care and grief.

Even before its push for global expansion, SCI has cared for families of diverse national, religious, and cultural backgrounds—including those from Asian, Hispanic, Jewish, Native American, and Native Canadian communities. Experience with cultural and religious differences fueled SCI's success in other countries. Although the concept remains the same, the productivity and scope of operations achieved first in North America now extends throughout much of the world. Many of SCI's funeral service locations, cemeteries, and crematoria are increasingly found outside the United States. In fact, by the end of 1999, operations had expanded into 20 countries on 5 continents with acquisitions of firms that serve Muslim, Hindu, Sikh, Korean, Polish, Japanese, Vietnamese, and Kurdish families, just to name a few. Remaining true to its growth strategy, in most cases, these groups are served by SCI operations and dedicated professionals who are often friends of the families they serve.

Its recent acquisitions have made it the leading death care firm in Australia and the United Kingdom. It acquired the largest provider of funeral services in France (SCI now operates 950 funeral firms in France) with subsidiaries in other European countries and the Pacific Rim. Its success will depend not on how effectively SCI changes the behaviors of its clients, but on how well SCI adapts to the local customs.

In North America, SCI broadens its selection of products, expands the network of funeral business and puts additional effort into the sales programs for prearranged funerals wherever possible. In foreign markets, where funeral customers have sometimes remained unchanged for generations, SCI works internally to raise educational and professional standards among its staff. It also gradually introduces new service and merchandise options within the boundaries of cultural acceptance, which have been well received by consumers.

Critics concerned with future growth opportunities for the company should take note. In a world of over 6 billion people, more than 55 million are expected to pass away in the next year. Although SCI is the largest organization of its kind, it serviced just slightly more than *1 percent* of all the deaths worldwide in 1998—the remaining 53 million funeral services were performed by thousands of small businesses or government-owned operations in hundreds of communities. From a corporate standpoint, many of these enterprises represent future acquisition or management opportunities, and SCI is methodically contacting their owners to show them the advantages of affiliation with SCI.

Focal Topics

1. What will be the effect of demographic trends on the demand for funerals over the next decade? How do you expect this to vary between nations served by SCI?

2. Choose one ethnic or religious market segment and research its rituals and practices regarding the death of a family member. If you were serving this market segment, how would you best reach your segment, and what would your message be?

3. What should SCI's branding policy be in the future? Should it use a single brand for all its operations (either nationwide or globally or both), or should it continue with its current strategy?

4. Using the consumer decision process model, describe the typical process used to buy funeral services. How would the process vary for at-need and pre-need decisions? How should understanding the decision process affect SCI's sales and marketing strategies?

5. In addition to the basic services provided by SCI, what psychological or sociological services should SCI provide to families it serves? How would you justify, to senior management and shareholders, expenses incurred with these types of services if they do not provide additional revenue?

CASE 3

Amazon.com

In the massive jungle of retail concepts that appear around the globe, Jeff Bezos created a unique bookstore—both Amazon in proportion and significance. Command central for the "earth's biggest bookstore" is located in Seattle, Washington, a city known for being on the progressive edge in a variety of areas, including retail (the home of Starbuck's Coffee), computer software and graphics, and contemporary music.

Imagine entering a store that offers millions of titles, is open 24 hours a day, and can locate any book ever printed (although it may be used and expensive) for its customers. When you enter Amazon.com, you won't be able to sip coffee from the now commonplace bookstore café, and you won't be able to take books from the shelves and skim the pages. But you will be able to buy the book you want, when you want it, without ever leaving your home. This is no ordinary bookstore, and Mr. Bezos is no ordinary booksmith.

Business by the Book

Amazon.com was born as a result of Jeff Bezos's search for an entrepreneurial venture. His search began with a focus on the Internet, which was growing at 230 percent a year at that time. Mr. Bezos, a graduate of Princeton University in electrical engineering and computer science, did not start out specifically wanting to open a bookstore, but the impossibility of actually building a bookstore that could hold millions of books was the "clincher" that led to incorporating Amazon.com in 1994 and opening its doors for business in July 1995.

By January 2000, Amazon increased its offerings to 4.7 million book, music, and movie titles, and became the leading online retailer in all these categories. It has quickly become one of the most widely known, used, and cited commerce web sites, boasting an online auction house and free electronic greeting cards. It offers more than 18 million unique items in categories, including books, CDs, toys, electronics, videos, DVDs, home improvement products, software, and video games.

Customers enter Amazon.com through its web site (http://www.amazon.com). Customers simply click on a button to add books to their virtual shopping baskets (or subtract them if they change their mind) and then click on a "buy button," supply shipping and credit card details, select delivery services, and execute the order. But Amazon.com is not just a retailer—it is an information supplier. Consumers can enter the site and conduct targeted searches for specific titles or various topics, browse, read and submit title reviews, register for personalized services, participate in promotions, and check order status.

Marketing, Advertising, and Promotion

Bezos decided early on to leave the majority of the warehousing and physical distribution aspects of the business to his supply chain partners. Instead, his focus would be on the marketing side of the venture—undertaking a variety of marketing strategies, including advertising, alliances, and customer-interactive promotions to grow and maintain its customer base.

Because of Amazon.com's consumer appeal and the curiosity about electronic commerce, it has received, and may continue to receive, a high degree of media coverage. As a result of its public relations activities as well as unsolicited invitations, Amazon.com was featured in a wide variety of television shows, articles and radio programs, and as part of the "What's New" and "What's Cool" sections of Netscape and Yahoo!, respectively.

In the late 1990s, Amazon also engaged in a coordinated program of print advertising in specialized and general circulation newspapers and magazines, such as *The New York Times Book Review, The Wall Street Journal,* and *Wired.* It placed banner ads on more than 50 high-profile and high-traffic-count web sites, including C-Net, Yahoo!, Excite, Lycos, Quote.com, and CNN, encouraging readers to "click" through directly to the Amazon.com bookstore to shop or browse.

To increase its exposure among current Internet users, Amazon.com inked an agreement to provide its services to AOL members. AOL provides a "link" on its home page, accessed by all its members every time they log on, giving Amazon.com access to over 8.5 million Internet users. It also formed alliances with other online book retailers through its "Associates Program," which consists of several thousand enrolled members. The associate embeds a hyperlink to Amazon.com's web site with books recommended for that associate's targeted customer base. The customer is automatically connected to Amazon.com's site and may place his or her order. The associate company is able to offer enhanced services and recommendations, avoids the expenses associated with ordering and fulfillment (absorbed by Amazon), and receives a 15 percent commission for all orders.

Involving Consumers

Amazon.com's online community attracts and nurtures consumers. Readers, customers, authors, and publishers are invited to post book reviews, and the company sponsors review competitions and provides a forum for author interviews—all designed to entertain and engage readers, enhance the shopping experience, and encourage purchases. The goal is to make Amazon.com the one-stop-shopping stop for book, music, and video titles and related information.

Amazon.com has developed many methods for interacting with consumers. It provides book reviews from its editorial staff, consumers, and such sources as *The New York Times Book Review* and *The New Yorker* to help consumers make informed buying decisions. And company editors can suggest some of the very best books in more than 50 categories. The *Amazon.com Journal* section of the web site contains exclusive author interviews, feature articles, and columns. Numerous author interviews are presented on the site, along with reviews from professional sources and other customers. And it makes it possible for consumers to interact with authors who publish their e-mail addresses. And when customers don't come to Amazon.com, it goes to them. Its personal notification service, called "Eyes," will e-mail consumers a message when their favorite authors release new books, or "Editors" will notify them when new titles are released on their favorite subjects. "Editors" also provides sneak previews of new books, even before they are released, at no cost to consumers.

Pricing and Costs

Owing to increased competition, Amazon.com began slashing its prices. Initially, it discounted its *Amazon.com 500* (a list that features the books the company believes will become bestsellers) by a whopping 40 percent—that discount is still intact—while its standard discount on some 300,000 other titles was 10 percent. On June 10, 1997, Amazon.com announced it would extend its 40 percent discount to an undisclosed number of titles and offer a 30 percent discount on hardcover books and 20 percent off paperbacks on over 400,000 titles. This type of aggressive pricing policy was an obvious move to capture market share from its online and traditional competitors. Bezos boasts that these prices cause Amazon.com to offer "the lowest everyday book prices anywhere in the world."

After consumers see the price of the book they want to buy, they face the question of how much it will actually cost to receive the book. Amazon.com's normal shipping charge is $3.00 plus 95 cents for each book ordered, making it possible to realize significant savings only on multiple orders.

Electronic Competition

As Amazon.com was beginning to find substantial sales on the Internet, both Barnes & Noble and Borders (the largest U.S. bookstore chains) announced their intention to devote substantial resources to online commerce. Industry analysts debated possible cannibalization effects with the addition of online retailing options to location-based book companies. But Barnes & Noble bet that the electronic addition would complement well its current reach into the consumer marketplace. The giants and independents alike figure their stores may lose some business to electronic buying, regardless of which stores have a presence on the web. However, they are setting up virtual stores so that their consumers can still buy from them and won't be forced to go to a competitor. The assumption here is that when consumers choose to buy books electronically, they are choosing a different form of shopping and completing transactions—they are not necessarily looking to switch retailers.

Barnes & Noble launched BarnesandNoble.com (which it is billing as "the world's biggest bookstore online") in May 1997 and entered into a partnership with *The New York Times* web site, thereby presenting Amazon.com with its first serious competition. A virtual David-and-Goliath-style war began. BarnesandNoble.com continues to be Amazon's most fierce competitor.

Customer Service

Amazon.com relies heavily on its supply chain partners for accurate fulfillment and on-time delivery, thereby entrusting many components of customer satisfaction to its partners. But ultimately, it is Amazon.com that is responsible for the service that consumers experience. Although the company lists, and effectively advertises, millions of titles, consumers must read the fine print when it comes to fulfillment of orders. Some titles are available for shipment within 48 to 72 hours, and the remainder of in-print titles are generally available within 4 to 6 weeks; out-of-print titles generally are available in 2 to 6 months, but some of these may not be available at all.

Amazon.com's Financial Performance

Amazon.com's financial performance has been both rosy and murky. It recorded sales of $511,000 for the first six months of operation and has grown rapidly since first opening its virtual bookstore. From July 1995 through March 1997, Amazon.com had sales of more than $32 million with approximately 340,000 customer accounts in over 100 countries (during its first year, it sold 39 percent of its merchandise to international customers). Sales for the nine months ended September 30, 1999, increased from $357 million to $963 million. However, as sales continue to grow, profits remain illusive. In 1996, the company lost $5.8 million or 26 cents per share compared with a $300,000 loss in 1995 or 2 cents per share. During the first quarter of 1997 Amazon.com posted a net loss of $3.0 million ($0.13 per share) and a net loss of $6.7 million ($0.28 per share) for the second quarter. For the nine months ended September 1999, net losses rose from $78.1 million to $396.8 million.

The first chapter of Amazon.com's future has been written. It's a story of consumer enthusiasm and media attention. Only consumer lifestyles and the realities of the electronic marketplace can determine if that story will develop into a tragedy or if it will have a happy ending.

Focal Topics

1. Evaluate Amazon.com and two other e-tail web sites. Compare and contrast them based on five criteria you think are important in satisfying customers.

2. Consider Amazon's e-tail and Barnes & Noble's blended retail strategies. When and under which circumstances do consumers use the different formats and outlets? What are the advantages and disadvantages of having virtual *and* real "stores"?

3. Amazon has increased its product offerings substantially since its inception. What do you think should be its product mix in the future? Explain why you would expand or decrease product variety and which specific products you would offer.

4. Develop a customer loyalty (retention) program for Amazon. What should be the goals of the program, and what should it offer consumers as incentives?

5. How can traditional book or music stores compete with Amazon's strategy?

CASE 4

Avon

Avon is the world's largest direct seller of beauty and related products. Founded in 1886, Avon has blossomed during many changes occurring in the consumer marketplace. With $5.2 billion in annual revenue (1999), Avon is among the world's largest selling single brands of skin care, cosmetics, fragrances, and toiletries, including recognizable brands as Anew, Skin-So-Soft, Avon Color, Far Away, Rare Gold, Millennia, Starring, Avon Skin Care, and Women of Earth. It also markets an extensive line of fashion jewelry, apparel, gifts, and collectibles.

Avon has become a part of American culture and is on its way to influencing foreign cultures as well. With a history in championing women's rights, work opportunities, special health issues, and self-esteem, over 40 million women around the globe have sold Avon at one time or another. Its vision is to be the company that best understands and satisfies the product, service, and self-fulfillment needs of women—globally. The vision influences Avon's research, product development, marketing, and management practices.

Avon has more women (86 percent) in management positions than any other Fortune 500 company. Seventeen of Avon's 54 officers are women, including its CEO who was appointed in 2000, and 4 women sit on Avon's board of directors. Avon's Women of Enterprise Awareness program annually recognizes five women entrepreneurs for extraordinary business success, and the Avon Breast Cancer Awareness Crusade has raised over $25 million to support breast cancer education and access to early detection services. The Avon Worldwide Fund for Women's Health raises money for health-related problems of concern to women globally.

Beauty in the Eye of the Beholder

The world of beauty is a timeless world. Adornment of the face and body began before recorded history and persisted through the millennia. Egyptian women used an ancient eye shadow. The Greeks loved rouge and powder. Cosmetics were popular in Imperial Rome and the courts of 18th century Europe. Today, they are ubiquitous.

Throughout history and various cultures, beauty products have satisfied a profound and enduring human need—the desire to look one's best. The motivations of women around the world to use cosmetics have expanded over the years—beginning with the desire for outer beauty and then the desire for inner beauty and health. Fashions change, but the fundamental truth does not: When people look good, they feel good about themselves. One of Avon's goals is to help women around the world feel great about themselves, both in the way they feel and the way they look.

Reaching Customers

Avon is well known for its sales force of "Avon Ladies" who made famous the phrase, "Ding-dong, Avon calling." For many years, the door-to-door selling approach made sense for cosmetics—women were home during the day and were looking for inexpensive "luxuries" to give them beauty. Personal selling continues to work for Avon today; the company boasts 500,000 sales representatives in the United States alone, many of whom receive their total income as Avon salespersons. The difference is that they may no longer just ring doorbells of suburban homes. Today, they sell in the workplace, where management often encourages sales calls that keep employees on the premises rather than out shopping and away from work. Armed with effective sales brochures (600 million in 12 languages are printed each year), sales representatives can show their product lines without having to carry a case of products with them when they go to school or work.

Avon broke its direct-sales-only tradition in 1998 when it opened its first shopping mall kiosk in Atlanta's North Point Mall. Whereas Avon's traditional customers have an average household income of $35,000, the North Point Mall shopper has an average household income of $85,000.[1] A mall presence also allows Avon to reach a younger crowd with specific products, such as a $6 lipstick in bright colors. However, in order not to tread on the Avon lady's turf, only 400 of its 5,000 products will be available at retail locations. Retail analysts predict that each kiosk should gross between $200,000 and $450,000 per year, with a planned rollout to malls throughout the United States. Through its kiosks, Avon hopes to reach an additional 20 to 30 million women not buying its products today.

Avon has also expanded its sales effort to include online sales. The web site offers help to customers seeking a representative in their area, and it is also possible to order products online.

Avon Global

Avon products are marketed to women in 135 countries around the world through 2.8 million independent sales representatives. Avon's largest international companies are in Japan, Brazil, Mexico, and the United Kingdom. Other countries in which Avon has recently expanded include Poland, Hungary, the Czech Republic, and Slovakia.

China has been a successful market for Avon; professional women (including doctors) enjoy supplementing their income by selling Avon products and sometimes make more doing that than in their professional careers. Before Avon came to town, Chinese women found themselves with the money to buy things they wanted but nothing much to buy. Avon changed that when it began its march on China.

The Chinese joint venture operates differently from its U.S. counterparts in that it does not distribute its products to its representatives; they pick them up from branch depots to avoid communication and transportation problems. Chinese Avon ladies do not ring doorbells for cold-call sales as is done in the United

---

[1] Carolyn Edy, "Avon Malling," *American Demographics* (April 1999), 38–39.

States. Because the majority of them have other jobs, most sales occur in the work-place, among friends and family, and in schools. The most frequently sold items were skin care products, yet as Chinese women became more familiar with applying makeup, sales in this category increased.

One of the factors in Avon International's overall success was a strategic change in its organization. Individual countries have been given more decision-making responsibility, and area management has been moved closer to markets. The objective was increased sensitivity to consumers and market dynamics. The continuing change will put Avon International in an even better position to serve potential high-growth areas such as the Pacific Rim.

Another factor that is believed to be key for Avon International is the spreading of new ideas across national borders. When a new product or program proves successful in one country, it's then tested in other countries where market conditions are similar. Under this system, Avon companies often increase their chances of a successful innovation while decreasing product development costs. A good example of this process is lingerie, which began in Brazil in the mid-1980s and was then expanded to Mexico, Argentina, Venezuela, Japan, the United Kingdom, and Continental Europe.

In each case, the local Avon affiliate studied the market to learn what kind of lingerie their consumers wanted—lively and glamorous in Brazil but conservative in Japan. Local Avon companies are established for manufacturing and distributing the products to representatives. Avon studied the risk that lingerie sales might reduce sales of traditional Avon products. Tests showed that, in most cases, lingerie produces incremental sales, increasing average customer orders and winning Avon a larger share of total household budget. Avon lingerie is available in about two-thirds of Avon International markets.

Focal Topics

1. Which products or marketing methods of Avon are likely to be the most successful with African-American, Latino, and Asian-American markets in the United States? How do you recommend Avon expand sales to these market segments? What sorts of specialized programs, if any, should it develop to meet the specific needs of the segment?

2. Can Avon expect to use the same products and marketing programs in its International Division as its U.S. division? Why or why not?

3. Within the International Division, which countries do you recommend to target for maximum growth in the future? Identify which cultural characteristics would cause Avon to use similar or different sales and marketing strategies in those countries.

4. How has Avon adjusted its marketing plan to adapt to the changing roles of women in society in recent years, and what are these changes? How do you think the consumer marketplace will change in the next two decades, and how can Avon adapt its strategies even further? Your answers should address specific market segments based on demographic, psychographic, or geographic variables.

5. How have the motivations among consumers to achieve beauty changed in recent years? How would you adapt Avon's advertising campaigns to address these changes?

6. Analyze Avon's web site and online sales program. With an effective online strategy, analyze whether or not Avon will need its network of sales representatives in the future.

The Duck Company

Walk through most mass retailers throughout the United States and in select countries in South America, Canada, and Europe, and chances are that you will see a variety of household products bearing the picture of a cuddly duck. The Duck is the logo for Manco, an Avon, Ohio-based distributor that reached sales of around $300 million in 2000 by solving consumers' everyday household problems with an array of practical, consumer-friendly products. Among its best sellers are tapes; home insulation products; mailing and shipping supplies; office, school, and art supplies; shelf liners; and mats. Although Manco may not be a giant in the world of commerce, it is the dominant tape brand in the United States—beating out rival 3M for leading market share in duct tape and transparent tapes, and Rubbermaid in shelf liner and other competitive product categories.

The company stands as one of America's exemplars in demand-oriented management. Manco neither makes the products it sells nor sells its products to end consumers—it is a distributor. Yet it breaks the mold of the traditional wholesaler by taking over functions often performed by the manufacturer or the retailer. Its strength in the supply chain has been its ability to create a strong brand, listen to its customers and its customers' customers (end consumers), and develop products and packaging that meet the needs of both. In short, this wholesaler bases its business development on the study of consumer behavior.

The Customer Is King

How did Manco establish its leadership position in the tape and adhesives market? Chairman Jack Kahl will tell you it is due to the company's "customer-is-king" orientation. Armed with an unquenchable thirst for knowledge and an irrepressible entrepreneurial spirit, Kahl—who was named one of the ten "Most Admired CEOs in America" by *Industry Week* magazine in 1993—has set the tone for the company with his "whatever-it-takes" philosophy.

All company employees are focused on the customer and the end consumer. Sometimes that means that employees talk to consumers in their customers' retail stores to find out reactions to new products or new packaging. Sometimes that means driving all night long to a customers' headquarters with a product display that needs to be handled in a special way. And it always means recognizing the individuals within its customer organizations that make Manco work.

At first glance, consumer focus and customer service might seem far-fetched approaches for a company whose core products are basic consumables like duct tape and mailer envelopes. But that is what has taken the company from $800,000 in sales in 1971 (when Kahl bought it) to around $300 million in 2000. Kahl attributes his success to building "customers for life"—both among retailers who carry and promote Manco products and consumers who wouldn't buy anything else. Loyalty to Manco products is key to the continued success of all Manco products.

And the Duck Shall Lead Them

Manco's signature product is Duck® tape. Yes, Duck® tape—spelled the way Kahl heard most consumers pronounce *duct* tape, the generic name for the waterproof, all-purpose sealing tape invented by GIs during World War II from canvas and used for everything from bandaging wounds to patching pup tents. Kahl noticed that almost all of his customers had a duct tape story to tell, usually praising its remarkable strength and versatility, and they were eager to share their stories with the company.

In 1984, Kahl trademarked the name Duck® Tape, and designed and adopted a friendly yellow duck as a logo and company mascot. Known as the Manco Duck, it carries over to all Manco products the helpful, upbeat spirit of duct tape. Consumers love the cute, bug-eyed caricature. Indeed, the Disneyesque duck design was a conscious attempt to establish a memorable link in the minds of Manco customers with its products. Manco T. Duck appears on the packaging and display materials of all Duck brands and helps customers find fun and imaginative ways to solve life's little problems.

In addition to creating a consumer-friendly logo, it also markets its products under easy-to-understand brand names, which often tout a major product benefit. DraftBusters™, for example, is a product that consumers can use to insulate windows and doors to decrease drafts in a house. The combination of the name and the Manco Duck on packaging of such best-selling products as CareMail™, DraftBusters™, Softex™ Bath/Shower Mat, and Correct-It™ increase brand awareness among retail consumers.

Manco Duck also serves as an in-house morale booster. It appears at employee events and recognition ceremonies, including Duck Challenge Day, during which vendors, customers, special guests, and employees all gather to celebrate the accomplishments of the firm and its relationships. Manco Duck reminds employees that, though quality work is extremely important, they should always have fun at what they do and not take themselves too seriously. The duck is a constant reminder of Manco's commitment to be fun, friendly, imaginative, helpful, and resourceful in all the company does.

Consumer Knowledge

Expanding the mind of the employee to enter the mind of the customer is the end goal in Manco's continuous quest for knowledge. Kahl believes that he needs to know more about the customers than they know about themselves. Thus, the foundation of Manco's success and customer orientation is its continuous consumer research, including household and individual buying habits and trends. As a result, the company manages to stay not only one step but several steps ahead of where the market is going. The company uses a range of tools, including focus groups, expert advisory panels, and most important, a consumer hotline, to stay current. The 1-800-number, instituted in the early 1990s, is one of the most important ways to keep its finger on the pulse of the consumer marketplace.

The most common calls are inquiries: Where can I buy this tape? How do you apply weather-stripping? Manco operators are trained to dispense expert advice on the entire product line and have a database showing all outlets for the products nationwide. A second sizable group of callers makes suggestions for new uses for existing products or gives new product ideas. This information is systematically entered into the computer database. The complaints are also logged into the database for future reference, and each gets a callback, followed by a letter, and a refund if requested.

In addition to giving customers the personal attention they may not have received in the store (while building brand loyalty), the 1-800-line provides Manco with consumer insights. This information is compiled into a five-page monthly report, which summarizes trends, provides anecdotes, and presents graphs. And the department head is encouraged to pop into Kahl's office to relay timely, compelling, or especially poignant items that may come up between the monthly reports.

Solving Consumers' and Customers' Problems

Listening to a customer led to the creation of EasyLiner®, a nonadhesive, roll-out shelf liner that resembles rubber mesh and is easy to cut, place, and remove. For years, consumers had been lining their kitchen cabinet shelves and drawers with Contact® paper, a sticky-backed, vinyl paper made by Rubbermaid. Though sales were steady, Manco monitored customer reactions to and complaints about the product—even more closely than Rubbermaid did—and recognized an opportunity for an improved product.

The idea for a nonadhering shelf liner was presented to Kahl at a national housewares show in 1994 by a Wal*Mart merchandise manager. He indicated that consumers complained that Contact® paper was "hard to put down and even harder to take up." The Wal*Mart manager had the idea of adapting an existing product—nonskid carpet underliner—as a shelf liner. The two Manco executives recognized immediately the potential of the product and made an on-the-spot commitment to market the product.

Manco sprang into action with product design, consumer research, and packaging. The company tapped manufacturers already on its demand chain for help and consulted new ones. It took Manco just three months to bring the product from inception to market. EasyLiner® debuted on Wal*Mart's shelves in April 1994. Following on the heels of EasyLiner®, Manco introduced OfficeLiner® and ShopLiner® for use in the office and shop, respectively. OfficeLiner® is identical to EasyLiner® but in "office colors" like gray and almond, whereas ShopLiner® is a thicker product (used for such things as lining pickup truck beds for the hauling of tools).

A constant stream of consumer comments and requests continue to lead EasyLiner® product-line extension. One woman called the helpline and said EasyLiner® was great beside her swimming pool. A barrage of similar comments led to a flurry of research, both on the consumer side and the manufacturing side. In a fact-finding trip to Germany, Kahl discovered a similar product with a variety of applications already on the market, which led to the development of Manco's outdoor line. "Moonwalk" was introduced in the spring of 1997, which included 9-by-12-foot "rugs" and runners to put down by swimming pools or lay down on wooden decks to prevent children from getting splinters while playing.

More recently, the Duck brand has expanded into the home office and school products categories. Consumers complained about liquid typing correction products (such as Liquid Paper), which are "painted" over typed mistakes. They didn't like how the fluid dried-out, got lumpy, and took too long to dry. As a result, Manco conducted focus groups and developed a new tape-based correction product. Correct-It™ comes in a one-hand-required tape dispenser that, when rolled over paper, covers mistakes instantly and dryly. The same technology was used to create DryLighter™, a highlighter that does not bleed through paper and can actually be removed from the page if needed. Additional products in this category include FrameIt™ (a plastic frame that hangs on cloth cubicle walls), Easy-Stick™ (a roll-on nonpermanent glue), and OneTouch™ Disappearing Tape (transparent tape that can be rolled onto paper with one hand).

Manco Duck's Extended Family

In 1998, Manco joined The Henkel Group, the world's number-one consumer adhesives company. The union makes it possible for Manco to chase its dream of reaching new customers across the world and develop innovative new products.

Like Manco, Henkel began as a small, family-owned company, founded by Fritz Henkel in Aachen, Germany, in 1876. Henkel & Cie, a detergent company, was so successful that it expanded in 1878 and relocated to Duesseldorf. By the 1960s, Henkel had developed into a globally active group of companies under the leadership of Dr. Konrad Henkel, the grandson of Fritz Henkel.

Today, Henkel is the leading manufacturer of consumer detergents and household cleansers in Europe and is a world leader in adhesives, oleochemicals from natural fats and oils, surface pretreatment technologies, and industrial and institutional cleaners. It is in the global top ten of cosmetics and toiletries manufacturers. Worldwide, The Henkel Group has more than 56,000 employees, in more than 340 companies in 70 nations. Worldwide sales totaled DM 21.3 billion ($12 billion) in 1998.

In North America, Henkel is expanding its presence with many well-known consumer brands such as Duck brand tape, home, and office products; DEP® and LA Looks® hair-care products; Fa® hand soaps and body washes; and Loctite™ and Quicktite™ of Canada do-it-yourself and adhesives products. The company also entered into a joint venture with Dial to develop and market advanced laundry products in North America under Dial's Purex brand and an at-home dry-cleaning product under the Custom Cleaner brand.

The global presence, resources, and marketing support of Henkel is helping Manco take another step toward covering the earth in Duck® tape. But Manco is also helping Henkel in the areas of marketing and corporate culture. In addition to expanding the Duck brand globally, Manco has been charged with marketing the Loctite and LePage brands around the world as well. Its impressive array of customers, including Home Depot, Lowe's, Staples, OfficeMax, Ace Hardware, Target, Rite Aid, Sam's Club, and Wal*Mart, provides entrée to the consumer market for a variety of Henkel products. From a culture standpoint, Henkel sends management to study and learn how Manco develops long-lasting relationships with customers and consumers and how to incorporate many of the values supported by its corporate culture.

The Duck in Shades

Manco's acceptance in the consumer marketplace and its relationship with its customers make it a leader in its demand chain. Consequently, it has enjoyed rapid growth, even in highly competitive industries (and times)—challenging and beating some of the largest and most respected firms in the world, such as Rubbermaid and 3M. With continued focus on the consumer and brand development, the future looks so bright that the Manco Duck might have to wear shades.

Focal Topics

1. Describe how Manco uses consumer insight and consumer research in developing new products.

2. Choose an insight about a consumer household, office, or work need, and choose a product category that would fit the Manco Duck brand family. Develop a consumption analysis strategy for guiding product attributes.

3. For the product you developed in question 2, develop a brand name that would complement current Duck brand names. Discuss the important attributes of the brand to consumers and to retail customers.

4. Develop an Internet strategy for Manco. What would you include on the home page?

Address the issue of whether or not Manco should sell some of its products directly to consumers via the web.

5. Assume you are the product manager for either the Duck brand tape or office and school supplies. You have been asked to develop a strategy for introducing your product line throughout Europe. How would you gain attention for the brand? Develop a global advertising and promotions campaign that specifies which retailers would be your channel partners and which consumer segments you would target.

CASE 6

National Pork Producers Council

If the National Pork Producers Council (NPPC) had its way, retailers around the world would sell more pork, restaurants would increase their pork offerings, and consumers would buy and eat more pork. The NPPC, headquartered in Des Moines, Iowa, is the largest agricultural commodity organization in the United States. It is funded principally by a national collection of producers to support activities such as product research and promotion, market development, and producer education.

NPPC is responsible for category marketing or industrywide marketing—promoting the entire pork industry rather than a particular brand. As the association focuses its efforts on increasing the overall demand for pork, individual firms have to duke it out for market share of what the NPPC hopes will be a growing market. Category management strives to build relationships with retailers, a practice common among large, sophisticated packaged goods marketers.

The State of the Pork Industry

Pork producers find themselves in a worldwide growth industry. Meat consumption—which includes beef, pork, poultry, and other types of meat (including but not limited to mutton, buffalo, turkey, and venison)—has increased in recent years in the global marketplace. In 1998, domestic retail value of pork was $20.7 billion and food service was $15.3 billion, for a total supply chain production of $36 billion. The fresh pork industry is a smaller portion of sales than in the past—between 63 and 68 percent of the pork sold today is further processed, such as hotdogs and sausage.

In response to consumers' concerns, the pork industry increased production of lean pork by raising lean pigs in the 1990s for which it received premium prices. But as more producers produced lean pork, it became a commodity product and failed to yield the premium prices it did in the beginning. The beef industry is attempting to provide value-added items with more precooked beef products, as the poultry industry did in the 1990s. The broiler industry found a way to identify, create, and capture value. Whether it was Chicken McNuggets, chicken wings, rotisserie chicken, skinless chicken breasts, or any other product variations they have developed, the poultry industry has driven its supply chains to give the end users what they want.

The pork industry recognizes that it must do the same if it is to become the "meat of choice" in the next decade. In order to do this, pork producers need to tap the consumer market and figure out what types of pork products consumers want. Innovation and product development is key to the future of pork sales in domestic and foreign markets.

A key element in the advancement of pork sales throughout the United States and in international markets is Demand Enhancement—the NPPC department that acts as the industry's marketing department. It is made up of three principal program areas or areas of activity. These include:

- Consumer Marketing—which is made up of advertising and research, as well as the Pork Information Bureau (PIB), the public affairs and public relations operation
- Trade and Distribution Marketing—which involves retail marketing, food-service marketing, and new product support activities
- Foreign Market Development—which examines global markets in terms of consumer trends and potential trade relationships

The overriding goal of Demand Enhancement is to promote pork's acceptability and availability in the marketplace. Acceptability is defined as making the product desirable to consumers with advertising, public relations, promotion, direct and interactive marketing. Availability is moving the product through distribution, which is advanced with trade advertising, promotion, publicity, category management, national accounts programs, sales force, and trade show support.

The remainder of this case study will focus on the efforts of the NPPC in each of the marketing areas as they relate to acceptability and availability in the marketplace. Included will be consumer information provided by the NPPC to assist in developing your answers to the focal topics appearing at the end of the case.

Consumer Marketing

In the 1980s, the pork industry took on the challenge of changing the perception of pork in the minds of consumers and key distributors. At that time, total per capita consumption of pork had experienced growth as it rode the coattails of consumers' increase of total meat consumption. Though consumers were actually increasing the amount of meat they ate annually, pork's share of total meat protein had declined by almost 10 percent in the preceding 10 years. Pork had fallen out of favor with retailers and consumers alike. It was not featured regularly by retailers, food-service operators, the food press, or other publications. Pork's perception was dated; consumers thought of it as fatty and old fashioned, even though producers had spent much of their attention in the 1980s in developing leaner cuts and improved products.

The Other White Meat

In 1988, NPPC developed a new integrated marketing communication program to reposition and update pork in the minds of consumers, retailers, distributors, and the media under the theme of "The Other White Meat." Though you might remember the advertising appearing on television and in magazines, it also spawned programs through all three marketing programs described previously. The advertising began with a campaign showing a multitude of pork dishes in one ad—in effect, demonstrating the versatility of pork and providing examples of delicious entrees made with pork, which most consumers would think of making with other white meats such as chicken. The headline read, "We lead you to temptation, but deliver you from evil." These ads evolved over the years, never losing the focus on pork and "The Other White Meat" tagline. A more recent ad shows a picture and recipe for country pork skillet and features the headline: "Late Comers Can Always Fill Up On the Potatoes."

By 1997, people's association of pork to white meat had grown from 9 to 61 percent. Perhaps most interesting is the fact that pork has replaced both turkey and fish as the second most commonly recognized white meat in America. This is significant because consumers overwhelmingly prefer white meat to red—two to one. Before The Other White Meat campaign was released, it was projected that pork consumption would continue to decline in the late 1980s and 1990s, as it had during the preceding years. But rather than decline, the industry experienced a significant increase in demand. In fact, it performed 25 percent better than even the most optimistic projections.

Today, total recognition of the white meat message, on an aided and unaided basis, is now almost 90 percent. That means nine out of ten adults in America consider pork to be the other white meat. With the help of this campaign, pork is now showing up on menus and in meat and frozen-food cases across America.

Pork Information Bureau

The PIB is a comprehensive resource on the subject of pork, for consumer audiences as well as the food press, dieticians, nutritionists, other healthcare professionals, and educators. The overall orientation of the message and type of information the NPPC provides also changed to address issues broader than pork alone. PIB does provide recipes to consumers and the media, but its principal goal is to provide helpful, timely, and relevant information that consumers need. This might include information on how to read nutritional labels, dietary or nutrition information and cooking tips, or time-saving methods of cooking. PIB provides a 24-hour 1-800-number and online access with the answers to virtually any question that its audiences might have, including a database of approximately 1,000 recipes that can be cross-referenced by ingredient. It is designed so that editors can contact PIB and get information for publications quickly in a form ready to "drop" into their magazines. Years ago, it was virtually impossible to find information or recipes for pork in women's magazines or lifestyle publications.

Trade and Distribution Marketing

One of the goals of the Demand Enhancement program is to increase acceptability of pork in the marketplace and enhance the availability of the product (or the points of distribution). It concentrates on increasing the presence of pork in retail stores and restaurants.

The retail program designs specials and pork-related promotions for retailers to offer consumers. After conducting research among top retailers, NPPC learned that pork needed more than just promotions; it needed some excitement in the meat case. Unlike beef, pork didn't have truly premium cuts for the retailer to feature. As a result, America's Cut was born—a loin cut about 1½ inches thick. Retailers found that they could sell these cuts at a premium, sometimes as much as an additional $1.00 more per pound. This was a great example of value-added marketing.

Retailers also needed to learn more about the potential profitability of pork and merchandising versatility (the many ways pork can be featured in the meat case). NPPC can show retailers how to use category management models to increase their revenues. For example, NPPC helped a 100-plus store chain add between $5 million and $10 million per year to its bottom line, depending on the merchandising chosen.

On the food-service side, the goal has been to increase the number of dishes made with pork by providing restaurants and commercial kitchens with new recipes and presenting them with food trend information. Schools have also been a target market for NPPC efforts. Since the NPPC is limited in how it can reach the more than 700,000 food-service operators in America, the organization provides the roughly 35,000 sales representatives who work for food-service distributors with information and educational materials on pork. They are then better able to answer customers' questions about the use and preparation of pork. In recent years, restaurants such as TGI Friday and Hard Rock Café have increased the number of pork offerings on their menus.

Along these lines, a new program, Product Development Resource, was designed to act as a pork advocate working with food-service operations, food manufacturers, and processors to ensure consideration of pork when developing new products. In 1999, Healthy Choice increased its pork offerings, as did other frozen-food manufacturers such as Banquet, Patio, Stouffer's, and Lean Cuisine.

There has been a collision between the restaurant (food-service) organization and the retailer in recent years as they both vie for consumers' increased need and desire for prepared meals. In supermarkets, it is called Home Meal Replacement, and in restaurants it is called take-out. The NPPC must develop ways to help its customers in both arenas increase the number of pork-based meals consumers take home for consumption.

Foreign Market Development

Pork is the most widely consumed meat around the world today, representing about 44 percent of the world's total meat protein consumption. In 1990, pork represented 45 percent of all the meat protein consumed in the world. By 1999, that figure grew to 46 percent and is expected to reach 47 percent by the year 2007. At the same time, beef is expected to decline from 34 percent in 1990 and 28 percent in 1999 to roughly 24 percent in 2007.

The NPPC has shifted its foreign market focus in recent years from dealing with tariffs and restrictions to promotions and marketing. Today, U.S. pork producers export about 7 percent of their production to over 100 other countries, including Japan, Mexico, Canada, Russia, Hong Kong, Korea, Taiwan, and China. With the global popularity of pork, there seems to be opportunity for continued growth in exportation. However, the NPPC predicts poultry will compete heavily in all these areas, as it has in the United States in recent decades.

In order to compete effectively in these global markets, the U.S. Pork seal was developed to symbolize "the World's Best Pork" and act as a quality indicator. The NPPC hopes this seal will brand U.S. pork as being of superior quality and help establish its presence in global markets.

Throughout the United States, different ethnic groups have different food consumption characteristics. Among U.S. consumers, 37 percent of non-Hispanic whites buy pork once per week compared to 45 percent of Hispanics. More pork is purchased by Hispanic consumers on a weekly basis than any other sector of the U.S. population. As the NPPC taps into the taste preferences and special uses of pork in other cultures, marketers can begin to develop a better understanding of how to market to those cultures globally. Once the NPPC identifies areas of growth, it can tie into the tastes of that culture to increase average frequency of pork consumption among consumers around the world from once to twice per week.

Consumer Food Trends

Pork was the most consumed meat in the United States until the very early 1950s. In the United States today, almost nine out of ten consumers eat pork, in its many forms, making it the most consumed meat protein item in America. However, it is not the volume leader because much of this consumption is in the form of sausage, bacon, ham, and so forth, which often represent smaller portions than does a steak. But in any given day, more people in the United States will consume pork or meat from a hog in some form than any other meat in America. Table 1 shows how the consumption for chicken, beef, and pork have changed in recent years, and Table 2 shows when consumers typically eat various meats.

Consumers eat foods for different reasons. According to research conducted by the NPPC, consumers tend to eat pork because of its "emotional characteristics"—comfort serving to guests; something my family likes; a food I get a taste or craving for; it's popular; it's a good home-cooked food. These emotional characteristics of pork are even more determinant of consumption than other attributes such as calories, fat content, and nutritional value. Table 3 shows how pork ranks on a variety of attributes compared to beef and chicken. Note the lower scores pork receives compared to other meats. The attributes are ranked from highest score to lowest score in the pork category, yet other attributes may have ranked higher for the different meat categories. Table 4 summarizes consumers' perceptions about pork, chicken, and beef.

The NPPC has also conducted research focusing on changes in consumer food behaviors. It examined trends in meals prepared and eaten at home, meals eaten in restaurants, and meals prepared in restaurants but eaten at home. A summary of some of the general findings is included in Table 5.

Summary

As in many industries, the pork industry is experiencing consolidation at both the production and packing levels. Supply chain members are forming stronger relationships in order to focus on growing the entire market and addressing changing consumer demands, including an increased sensitivity to food safety and increased need for product versatility, variety, value, and nutrition. The NPPC sees the opportunity to be "something different" to consumers and is setting its sites on making pork the meat of choice in America once again.

Table 1	Changing Share of Meat and Poultry Markets		
	1986	**1998**	**Change**
Beef	40.2%	33.1%	− 7.1%
Pork	24.4%	25.1%	+ 0.7%
Chicken	20.2%	26.3%	+ 6.1%
Other	15.2%	15.5%	+ 0.3%

Source: NPPC.

Table 2 When Consumers Eat Pork, Beef, and Chicken

| | Average Day Incidence of Consumption | | | |
	Breakfast	Lunch	Snack	Dinner
Pork	33%	30%	5%	24%
Beef	1%	24%	3%	37%
Chicken	2%	23%	3%	28%

Source: NPPC.

In the next year, the NPPC must evaluate its marketing campaign and determine how The Other White Meat program should be updated. It needs to evaluate the success of the campaign in the consumer and retail markets, and identify areas to be addressed in the next decade.

Table 3 Consumer Evaluations of Meat Attributes (5 = highest)

	Pork	Chicken	Beef
Taste	3.9	4.3	4.3
Stands for home cooking	3.7	4.4	4.1
Ease of preparation	3.7	4.1	4.1
Prepare a variety of ways	3.7	4.6	4.4
Serve to guests	3.7	4.3	4.2
Versatility	3.6	4.5	4.2
Like to be seen eating	3.5	4.3	3.8
Nutritional value	3.4	4.2	3.6
Good value for the money	3.4	4.2	3.5
Amount of fat	3.4	2.5	3.7
Amount of calories	3.4	2.7	3.8
Food I get a taste for	3.3	4.0	4.0
Family favorite	3.3	4.2	4.1
Fits today's lifestyle	3.3	4.4	3.5
Popular food	3.3	4.5	4.3
Eat every week	3.2	4.3	3.8
Not too many calories	2.9	3.7	2.8
Not too much fat	2.9	3.7	2.8

Source: NPPC.

Table 4   Consumer Perceptions About Meat Categories

| | Percent of Consumers Agree/Strongly Agree | | |
	Pork	Chicken	Beef
Everyone in the family will eat	65%	84%	84%
Tastes great on the barbecue	57%	91%	87%
Is easy to prepare	49%	67%	70%
Is a favorite of your family	49%	73%	75%
You can easily feed a lot of people	42%	78%	79%
Provides good value for the money	34%	81%	57%
Is relatively inexpensive	27%	71%	42%

Source: NPPC.

Table 5   Selected Consumer Food Trends

- The number of meals prepared and eaten at home each year has fallen from 711 meals per person in 1992 to 672 in 1998.

- The number of meals purchased at a restaurant has steadily increased from 121 meals per person in 1990 to 137 meals in 1998.

- The number of take-out restaurant meals per person increased from 55 in 1990 to 69 in 1998.

- The top reasons people eat out are:
    "Didn't want to cook at home"   41%
    "Special occasion or holiday"   11%
    "Away or out on business"   11%
    "Out shopping"   8%

- Convenience is the most important reason homemakers choose one food over another to prepare and serve at home.

Source: NPPC.

Focal Topics

1. How would you measure the effectiveness of The Other White Meat program today? Develop the research methodology and also specific questions you would pose. What other information would you want to glean from such a research project? How would you present this type of information to council members so that it is most useful to them?

2. Do you think the NPPC should continue The Other White Meat campaign, or is it time to start a new campaign? Design an updated campaign using The Other White Meat tagline if you think it should be continued, or design a new promotional campaign if you think it should be changed. You might want to use some of the information from the

tables to address specific attributes in your campaign.

3. What type of appeal should NPPC use in foreign markets? Choose a particular foreign market, and research its pork consumption trends as well as other taste and food preferences. Adapt the message or positioning of the campaign you designed in question 2 to be most effective in that market.

4. How should the NPPC monitor the changing needs of consumers in ways that affect pork consumption? How are food preferences changing, and how can they be forecast to change in the future, based on your understanding of demographics, lifestyles, eating, and food preparation trends. What areas of food consumption in the home or away from the home are likely to change in the future? What types of research would help the NPPC identify these trends?

5. How should the NPPC monitor the changing needs of its members? Develop a survey to distribute to the various types of members (retailers, restaurants, distributors, and producers).

6. What type of Internet strategy should NPPC have? What type of information should it provide for and receive from consumers with this mechanism? You might want to begin by accessing and critiquing the NPPC web site—www.nppc.org.

CASE 7

Destroy-Your-Business.com

> *"At General Electric, the Internet is our priority #1, #2, #3 and #4."*
> *Jack Welch, CEO, General Electric*

Some of the best CEOs in the world are losing sleep at night pondering how to do business on the Internet effectively and cost-efficiently. Whether a person works in a firm the size of General Electric or Wal*Mart or in a small neighborhood store, business analysts hypothesize that there's a new firm fighting to put them out of business. Its name is dyb.com—destroy-your-business.com.

This case is designed to transform you from student to consumer analyst and marketing strategist. General Electric uses a similar format to help its managers understand better how to compete in the e-revolution and anticipate the potential strategies of its e-commerce competitors.

Imagine that you are the chief marketing officer (CMO) of dyb.com and have been charged with the task of creating marketing strategies to put your traditional bricks-and-mortar competitor out of business. The traditional firm, which has experienced steady growth throughout the 1980s and 1990s, does not have an e-commerce strategy yet, but you know it is developing one. However, you don't know the scope of its commitment to e-commerce—will the company have an informational web site or will it sell products to consumers online?

As CMO of dyb.com, you must analyze whether or not pursuing an e-tailing strategy will work for the industry and against the competitor you choose. The board of directors to which you must make your presentation expects you to take a consumer behavior approach to the analysis of market potential.

Focal Topics

1. Choose a consumer-based company from the following list to compete against, and define briefly the industry in which dyb.com will compete.

2. Describe, in terms of demographic, psychographic, and other variables, which key consumer segments the competitor targets.

3. Use the consumer decision process model to describe how consumers currently make decisions, buy, and evaluate either the product or retailer chosen.

4. Briefly describe the mission of dyb.com and the strengths of its e-tail strategy over the strategies of the competitor. How do target markets for dyb.com differ from the traditional segments?

5. Use the consumer decision process model to evaluate how consumers would make decisions, buy, and evaluate dyb.com (or its products). How do these processes fit consumers' lifestyles? Compare the advantages and disadvantages to consumers of dyb.com versus the traditional model.

6. According to your consumer analysis, does dyb.com have a long-term, viable business model?

7. If you answer yes, describe how you would attract customers. Describe which messages and communication strategies would be most effective in reaching and gaining consumers' attention.

8. Develop a retention strategy for loyal customers.

List of Competitors

Wal*Mart (mass retailer)

Ikea (retailer of furniture)

Gap (retailer of casual clothing)

Whirlpool (manufacturer of consumer appliances)

Nestle (food processor and marketer)

Godiva Chocolates (confectioner with retail stores)

Merrill-Lynch (international brokerage firm)

Kinko's (retailer of copying and related services)

Amway (direct marketer of consumer products)

Ford Motor Company (auto manufacturer)

Harry and David (cataloger of specialty foods and gifts)

L.L. Bean (cataloger of outdoor products)

Sony (consumer electronics)

9. Describe briefly how your competitor might compete against dyb.com once it enters the market. How difficult would it be for the traditional firm to address the advantages of the dyb.com model?

GLOSSARY

abstract elements The elements of culture that include values, attitudes, ideas, personality types, and summary constructs, such as religion or politics.

abstract words Words that are less likely to evoke a visual representation in memory.

acceptance The act of changing one's opinions.

accessibility The degree to which segments can be reached through advertising or methods of communication and retailing.

acculturation The degree to which consumers learn the ways of a different culture compared to ones in which they were raised.

achieved status A higher level of status achieved through work or study.

adaptability A measure of the ability of a family to change its power structure, role relationships, and relationship rules in response to situational and developmental stress.

adopters People who have made a decision to use a new product.

advertising wearout The loss of advertising effectiveness due to overexposure.

affective response Feelings that are experienced during processing.

AIO measures Statements that describe the activities, interests, and opinions of consumers.

anomie A weakened respect for social norms that leads to diminished normative compliance.

approach-approach conflict A conflict occurring when a consumer must decide between two or more desirable alternatives.

approach-avoidance conflict A conflict occurring when consumer behavior has both positive and negative consequences.

aspirational groups Social aggregations that exhibit a desire to adopt the norms, values, and behavior of others with whom the individual aspires to associate.

association A social class variable concerned with everyday relationships, with people who like to do the same things they do, in the same ways, and with whom they feel comfortable.

associative network The structure of information residing within memory that is organized much like a spider's web.

attention The amount of thinking focused in a particular direction.

attitude persistence An attitude's immunity to changing or becoming neutral over time.

attitude resistance The degree to which an attitude is immune to change.

attitude toward the behavior (A_b) An evaluation of performing a particular behavior that involves the attitude object.

attitude toward the object (A_o) An evaluation of the attitude object, such as a product.

attitudes Likes and dislikes of consumers that determine intentions.

attraction effect Where including a weak competitor in the consideration set makes the strong competitor more attractive.

avoidance-avoidance conflict A conflict occurring when consumers must decide between two or more undesirable alternatives.

back-translation The act of translating, using several translators, a message from its original language to the translated language and then back to the original.

behavioral expectations Consumers' perceived likelihood of performing a behavior.

beliefs Subjective knowledge-based judgments about the relationship between two or more things.

benefit segmentation Dividing consumers into different market segments based on the benefits they seek from purchasing and consuming products.

birthrate The number of live births per 1,000 population in a given year.

brand extensions The extension of a brand name that is well-known and respected in one product category to another product category for which it had not been known before.

brand personality The personality corresponding to use of a specific brand that consumers see as a reflection of themselves or think that they will develop by using that brand.

capacity The cognitive resources that an individual has available at any given time for processing.

categorization process The classification of a stimulus into mental categories.

central process A process of opinion formation in which opinions are formed from a thoughtful consideration of relevant information.

classical conditioning The act of pairing one stimulus that spontaneously evokes certain meanings and feelings with another, causing a transfer of these meanings and feelings from one to the other.

cognitive age The age at which one perceives oneself to be.

cognitive innovators Innovators who have a strong preference for new mental experiences.

cognitive learning The storing of information in long-term memory.

cognitive resources The mental capacity available for undertaking various information-processing activities.

cognitive response The thoughts that occur during processing.

cohesion The emotional bonding between family members.

comparative influence Input from others is compared with thoughts, beliefs, and behavior that an individual holds as the norm.

compliance The act of conforming to the wishes of a group without accepting all its beliefs or behaviors.

comprehension The interpretation of a stimulus, the point at which meaning is attached to it.

compulsive consumption Those buying and consumption behaviors that, though undertaken to bolster self-esteem, are inappropriate, excessive, and disruptive to the lives of those who are involved.

concrete words Those words that can be easily visualized.

conditioned response In Pavlov's theory of classical conditioning, the response arising from the conditioning that occurs to the unconditioned stimulus and response.

conditioned stimulus In Pavlov's theory of classical conditioning, the new stimulus to which the

unconditioned response can be transferred.

confirmation When a product's performance meets certain expectations.

conformity A change in beliefs or actions based on real or perceived group pressures.

congruity How similar members within the segment are in behaviors or characteristics that correlate with behavior.

conjunctive strategy An evaluation strategy employing a comparison of each brand to cutoffs that are established for each salient attribute of the brands.

consideration set Those alternatives considered during decision making.

consolidated metropolitan statistical area A grouping of closely related primary metropolitan statistical areas.

conspicuous consumption Consumption that is motivated to some extent by the desire to show one's successfulness to other people.

consumer behavior Activities people undertake when obtaining, consuming, and disposing of products and services. Also, a field of study that focuses on consumer activities.

consumer confidence The influence on the consumption process by what consumers think will happen in the future.

consumer decision process model (CDP mode) A model of the stages in the consumer decision process and of the factors that influence this process.

consumer insight An understanding of consumers' expressed and unspoken needs and realities that affect how they make life, brand, and product choices.

consumer knowledge The subset of the total amount of information stored in memory that is relevant to product purchase and consumption.

consumer life cycle The series of

stages that a consumer passes through during life which changes an individual's behavior over time.

consumer logistics The speed and ease with which consumers move through the retail and shopping process.

consumer motivation The drive to satisfy both physiological and psychological needs through product purchase and consumption.

consumer orientation A focus on how all organizations in a demand chain adapt to changing consumer lifestyles.

consumer socialization The acquisition of consumption-related cognitions, attitudes, and behavior.

consuming How, where, when, and under what circumstances consumers use products.

consumption analysis The study of why and how people consume.

consumption and usage knowledge The information in memory about how a product can be consumed and what is required to actually use it.

consumption intentions Indications of whether a consumer will engage in a particular consumption activity.

consumption norms Informal rules that govern consumption behavior.

consumption rituals Sequential, multiple consumption behaviors that tend to occur intensely, in a serious manner, and repeatedly, as a ritual.

continuous innovation The modification of the taste, appearance, performance, or reliability of an existing product rather than the establishment of a totally new one.

core merchandise A basic group of products that is essential to a store's traffic, customer loyalty, and profits.

cost versus benefit perspective A search for decision-relevant information when the perceived benefits of the new information are greater than the perceived costs of acquiring the information.

credence claims Advertising claims of which validation of accuracy is either impossible or unlikely because more effort is required than consumers are willing to invest.

cross-cultural analysis The act of comparing similarities and differences in behavioral and physical aspects of cultures.

cued recall The ability to remember information only after being given retrieval cues.

cultural artifacts Material components of a culture, including books, computers, tools, buildings, and specific products.

culture A set of values, ideas, artifacts, and other meaningful symbols that help individuals communicate, interpret, and evaluate as members of society.

cutoff A restriction or requirement for acceptable product performance.

data mining The creation of a database of names for developing continuous communications and relationships with the consumer.

decay theory A theory proposing that memories grow weaker with the passage of time.

demographics The size, structure, and distribution of a population.

differential threshold The threshold reflecting the smallest change in stimulus intensity that will be noticed.

diffusion The process by which an innovation is communicated through certain channels over time among the members of a social system.

direct selling Any form of face-to-face contact between a salesperson and a customer away from a fixed retail location.

discontinuous innovation The act of introducing an entirely new product that significantly alters consumers' behavior patterns and lifestyles.

discretionary time A time during which individuals feel no sense of economic, legal, moral, social, or physical compulsion or obligation.

disposing How consumers dispose of products and packaging.

dissociative groups Social aggregations with which an individual strives to avoid association caused by changing social class and abandoning certain behaviors.

dual coding A concept proposing that information can be stored in both semantic and visual forms.

dyadic exchanges Exchanges of resources between two individuals that influence these individuals' behaviors or beliefs.

dynamically continuous innovation The act of creating either a new product or a significant alteration of an existing one, but does not generally alter established purchase or usage patterns.

early adopters Opinion leaders and role models for others, with good social skills and respect within larger social systems, who adopt new innovations before the masses do.

early majority Consumers who deliberate extensively before buying new products, yet adopt them just before the average time it takes the target population as a whole.

economic demographics The study of the economic characteristics of a nation's population.

elaboration The degree of integration between the stimulus and existing knowledge.

elimination by aspects strategy An evaluation strategy resembling the lexicographic strategy but in which the consumer imposes cutoffs.

endorsements The act of a celebrity lending his or her name or likeness to a product without necessarily being an expert in the area.

evaluative criteria The standards and specifications used to com-

pare different products and brands.

expectancy disconfirmation model A model that proposes that satisfaction depends on the comparison of pre-purchase expectations with actual outcomes.

experience claims Advertising claims that can be verified following product consumption.

experimentation A research methodology that attempts to understand cause-and-effect relationships by manipulating independent variables to determine how these changes affect dependent variables.

expert One who possesses unique information or skills that can help consumers make better purchase decisions than other types of spokespersons.

exposure A physical proximity to a stimulus that allows one or more of our five senses the opportunity to be activated.

expressive roles Roles that involve the support of other family members in the decision-making process and the expression of the family's aesthetic or emotional needs.

extended family The nuclear family, plus other relatives, such as grandparents, uncles and aunts, cousins, and parents in-law.

extended problem solving Problem solving of a higher degree of complexity that influences consumers' actions.

external search The act of collecting information from one's environment.

exurbs Areas beyond the suburbs at which consumption may occur and at which population growth is rapidly increasing.

family A group of two or more persons related by blood, marriage, or adoption who reside together.

family life cycle The series of stages that a family passes through and that changes them over time.

family marketing Marketing based on the relationships between family members based on the roles they assume.

family of orientation The family into which one is born.

family of procreation The family established by marriage.

feelings An affective state or reaction that can be positive or negative and from which attitudes are developed.

fertility rate The number of live births per 1,000 women of child-bearing age.

field experiment An experiment occurring in a natural setting, such as a home or store.

focus groups Groups consisting of 8 to 12 people involved in a discussion led by a moderator who is skilled in persuading consumers to discuss a subject thoroughly.

forgetting The failure to retrieve something from memory.

formal groups Social aggregations characterized by a defined structure and a known list of members and requirements for membership.

free recall The ability to remember information without the use of any retrieval cues.

generational change The gradual replacement of existing values by those of young people who form the "leading" generation in terms of value.

generic need recognition The growth in size of the total market for a product.

geodemography Socioeconomic factors affecting consumption and purchase, including where people live and how they earn and spend their money.

household All persons, both related and unrelated, who occupy a housing unit.

household life cycle The series of states that a household passes through and that changes it over time.

hypermarket A market that incorporates breakthrough technology in handling materials from a warehouse-operating profile, providing both a warehouse feel for consumers and a strong price appeal.

image advertising The use of visual components and words to help consumers form expectations about what kind of experience they will have with a particular product, organization, or store.

image analysis An analysis that examines what consumers know about a product's attributes and associations.

impulse buying Buying that is unplanned and stems from an unexpected urge to purchase.

inbound telemarketing The use of a 1-800 number to place orders directly.

incidental learning Learning that occurs despite the absence of the intention to do so.

income Money from wages and salaries as well as interest and welfare payments.

informal groups Social aggregations that have far less structure than formal groups and are likely to be based on friendship or common interests.

information advertising A method of advertising that provides details about products, prices, hours of store operation, locations, and other attributes that might influence purchase decisions.

informational influence The act of accepting recommendations or usage by others as evidence about the nature of a product and using this information in making product or brand decisions.

in-home observation The act of placing marketers inside peoples' homes to examine exactly how products are consumed.

innovativeness The degree to which an individual adopts an innovation earlier than other members of a social system.

innovators Members of the first consumer group to adopt products.

instrumental roles Those functional or economic roles that involve financial, performance, and other functions performed by group members.

intentional learning Deliberate learning with the intent of later remembering what is learned.

intentions Subjective judgments about how individuals will behave in the future.

interference theory A theory proposing that the chances of retrieving a particular piece of information become smaller as interference from other information becomes larger.

intermarket segmentation The identification of a group of customers that are similar in a variety of characteristics which transcend geographic boundaries.

internal search The scanning and retrieval of decision-relevant knowledge from memory.

interviewer bias During an interview, the act of influencing responses by the interviewer or by an individual's desire to please the interviewer.

involvement The degree to which an object or behavior is personally relevant or of interest, evoked by a stimulus within a specific situation.

isolation When avoiding clutter in advertising, the act of placing an object in a barren perceptual field, eliminating other objects that may compete for attention.

knowledge gaps An absence of information in an individual's memory.

laboratory experiment An experiment occurring in a controlled setting, such as a laboratory or other research environment.

laddering In-depth probing directed toward uncovering higher-level meanings at both the benefit and value levels.

laggards Consumers who tend to be anchored in the past and suspicious of the new, and who are the last to adopt new innovations.

late majority Consumers who tend to be cautious when evaluating innovations, taking more time than average to adopt them, and often at the pressure of peers.

lexicographic strategy An evaluation in which brands are compared initially on their most important attribute.

life-cycle explanation The basis on which society's values are forecast, interpreting that society's values will change as individuals grow older and that individuals will tend to grow into the values that their parents now hold.

lifestyle Peoples' patterns of living and spending time and money that reflect their interests, activities, and opinions.

limited problem solving Problem solving of a lower degree of complexity that influences consumers' actions.

longitudinal studies Analysis of repeated measures of consumer activities over time to determine changes in their opinions, buying, and consumption behaviors.

lower threshold The minimum amount of stimulus intensity necessary for sensation to occur.

loyalty programs Programs that strive to motivate repeat buying by providing rewards to customers based on how much business they do with a company.

macroculture The values and symbols that apply to an entire society or to most of its citizens.

macromarketing The aggregate performance of marketing in society.

market aggregation The act of an organization to market and sell the same product or service to all consumers.

market analysis The process of analyzing changing consumer trends, current and potential competitors, company strengths and resources, and the technological, legal, and economic environments.

market mavens Individuals who serve as information sources about the marketplace because of their awareness of new products and other marketplace activities.

market segment A group of consumers with similar needs, behavior, or other characteristics, which are identified through the market segmentation process.

market segmentation The process of identifying groups of people who are similar in one or more ways, based on demographic, psychographic, behavioral, cultural, and/or other characteristics.

marketing The process of transforming or changing an organization so that it will have what people desire to buy.

marketing concept The process of planning and executing the conception, pricing, promotion, and distribution of ideas, goods, and services to create exchanges that satisfy individual and organizational objectives.

marketing era A time when productive capacity exceeded demand, causing firms to change their orientation away from manufacturing capabilities and toward the needs of consumers, thus adopting a marketing orientation.

marketing orientation A focus on how an organization adapts to consumers.

marketing strategy The allocation of resources to develop and sell products or services that consumers will perceive to be more valuable than competitive products or services.

mass customization The act of customizing goods or services for individual customers in high volumes and at relatively low costs.

match-up hypothesis In product endorsement, the use of endorsers is most effective when the endorsers are perceived as being the appropriate spokespeople for the product to be endorsed.

measurability The ability to obtain information about the size, nature, and behavior of a market segment.

membership The act of achieving formal acceptance status within a group.

mental representations The particular manner in which information is stored in long-term memory.

metropolitan statistical area A free-standing metropolitan area that is surrounded by nonmetropolitan counties and that is not closely related to other metropolitan areas.

microculture The values and symbols of a restrictive group or segment of consumers, defined according to variables such as age, religion, ethnicity, social class, or another subdivision of the whole.

midrange problem solving Problem solving that occurs along the middle of the continuum and that affects consumers' actions.

misperception Inaccurate knowledge that is obtained by a consumer as a result of being misinformed.

monochromic time The performance of only one activity at a time for the sole purpose of accomplishing one goal at a time.

monodic approach An approach to studying diffusion variables that focuses on the personal and social characteristics of individual consumers.

monomorphic Being an innovator for only one product.

mood state How the person currently feels.

motivation research The act of uncovering hidden or unrecognized motivations through guided interviewing.

motivational conflict Tradeoffs occurring when consumers fulfill one need at the expense of another need.

motivational intensity How strongly consumers are motivated to satisfy a particular need.

multi-channel retailing The act of reaching diverse consumer segments through a variety of formats based on consumers' lifestyles and shopping preferences.

multi-step flow of communication A model of communication in which information can flow directly to different types of consumers, including opinion leaders, gatekeepers, and opinion seekers or receivers, and in which the gatekeepers decide whether or not other group members should receive information.

natural increase The surplus of births over deaths in a given period.

need recognition A perception of a difference between the desired state of affairs and the actual situation that is sufficient to arouse and activate the decision process.

negative disconfirmation After purchasing, the product delivers less than what was originally expected.

negative reinforcement Product usage enables consumers to avoid negative outcomes.

nonadopters People whose decision not to adopt may occur for many reasons.

nondiscretionary time A feeling of physical, social, and moral obligations causing individuals to engage in time-consuming activities.

nonuser One who does not consume a particular product at a particular time.

normative influence The act of altering individuals' behaviors or beliefs to meet the expectations of a particular group.

nuclear family The immediate group of father, mother, and children living together.

objective claims Advertising claims focus on factual information that is not subject to individual interpretations.

observational approach The act of observing consumer behaviors in different situations.

obtaining The activities leading up to and including the purchase or receipt of a product.

ongoing search Information acquisition occurring on a relatively regular basis regardless of sporadic purchase needs.

opinion change Any subsequent modification of an opinion once it has been formed.

opinion formation The first time a belief, feeling, or attitude is developed about a particular product or item.

opinion leader In word-of-mouth communication, the sender of information and opinions who influences the decisions of others.

parody display The mockery of status symbols and behavior, whereby an individual from a higher class may act as one from a lower class to display dislike for the higher class.

perceived behavior control Consumers' beliefs about how easy it is to perform a behavior.

perceived risk Consumers' uncertainty about the potential positive and negative consequences of their purchase decisions.

peripheral cues In the peripheral process of opinion formation, those stimuli that are devoid of product-relevant information.

peripheral process A process by which opinions arise without thinking about relevant information.

permission marketing Persuading consumers to volunteer their attention in return for some tangible benefit.

personal values Values that define certain behaviors that become a norm for an individual.

personality Consistent responses to environmental stimuli that influence how individuals respond to their surrounding environment.

piecemeal process The evaluation of a choice alternative that is derived from consideration of the alternative's advantages and disadvantages along important product dimensions.

polychronic time The simultaneous combining of activities to accomplish several goals at the same time.

polymorphic Being an innovator for many products.

population momentum Theory based on the fact that the future growth of any population will be influenced by its present age distribution and is the reason that replacement level fertility does not immediately translate into zero population growth.

positive confirmation After consumption, the product delivers more than what was originally expected.

positive reinforcement Product usage provides some positive outcome to the consumer.

positivism The process of using rigorous empirical techniques to discover generalizable explanations and laws.

post-modernism The act of using qualitative and other research methods to understand consumer behavior.

preferences Consumers' attitudes toward one object in relation to another.

pre-purchase evaluation The manner in which choice alternatives are evaluated.

pre-purchase search Search motivated by an upcoming purchase decision.

prestige A feeling of pride in oneself that comes when other people have an attitude of respect or deference to them.

price The total bundle of disutilities given up by consumers in exchange for a product.

primary groups A social aggregation that is sufficiently intimate to permit and facilitate unrestricted face-to-face interaction.

product The total bundle of utilities obtained by consumers in the exchange process.

product image A product's physical properties and attributes as well as the benefits and feelings that come from this product's consumption.

product innovation Any product recently introduced to the market or perceived to be new as compared to existing products.

product innovators Individuals who are the first to try new products.

psychographics An operational technique of measuring lifestyles that can be used with the large samples needed for definition of market segments.

punishment Negative outcomes resulting from consumption of a product.

purchase intentions Indications of what consumers think they will purchase.

purchase knowledge The various pieces of information consumers possess about buying products.

receiver In word-of-mouth communication, one who gains the information about behaviors and choices, which is useful in the decision process.

reference group Any person or group of people that significantly affects or influences another individual's behavior.

reference pricing The act of providing information about a price other than that actually charged for the product.

relational approach An approach to studying diffusion variables that analyzes communication networks and how social-structural variables affect diffusion flows in the system.

repurchase intentions Indications of whether consumers anticipate buying the same product or brand again.

retail supply chain All the organi-

zations and processes involved in taking a product from inception to final consumption.

retrieval The activation of information stored in long-term memory.

retrieval cue A stimulus that activates information in memory relevant to the to-be-remembered information.

retrieval set The recall of choice alternatives from memory.

role What the typical occupant of a given position is expected to do in that position in a particular social context.

search The motivated activation of knowledge stored in memory or acquisition of information from the environment concerning potential need satisfiers.

search claims Advertising claims that can be validated before purchase by examining information readily available in the marketplace.

search intentions Indications of whether consumers will engage in external search.

secondary groups Social aggregation that has face-to-face interaction, but it is more sporadic, less comprehensive, and less influential in shaping thought and behavior than that of primary groups.

selective need recognition When the need for a specific brand within a product category is stimulated.

self-concept One's impressions of the type of person one is.

self gifts Purchases of items or services by consumers as a means of rewarding, consoling, or motivating themselves.

self-referencing A means of encouraging elaboration by relating a stimulus to oneself and one's experiences.

sender In word-of-mouth communication, one who relays information in an attempt to increase the confidence in a product or behavior choice.

sensory innovators Innovators who

have a strong preference for new sensory experiences.

service encounter The occurrence of a personal communication between a consumer and a marketer.

shadowing A method in which a researcher accompanies or "shadows" consumers through the shopping and consumption processes.

shopping intentions Indications of where consumers plan on making their product purchases.

signals Product attributes that are used to infer other product attributes.

simple additive An evaluation strategy by which the consumer counts or adds the number of times each alternative is judged favorably in terms of the set of salient evaluation criteria.

social class The relatively permanent and homogeneous divisions in a society into which individuals or families sharing similar values, lifestyles, interests, wealth, status, education, economic positions, and behavior can be categorized.

social mobility The process of moving from one social class to another due to changes in occupation, income level, and other factors.

social stratification The perceived hierarchies in which consumers rate others as higher or lower in social status.

social values Values held so highly that they almost become stereotypical of a market segment or group and define the behavior held as a norm for a society or group.

socialization The processes by which people develop their values, motivations, and habitual activity.

sociological variables (family) Three variables—cohesion, adaptability, and communication —that help explain how families function.

span of attention The length of time short-term memory can be focused on a single stimulus or thought.

spending intentions Indications of how much money consumers think they will spend.

spreading activation A concept proposing that activation of one memory node causes a ripple effect that spreads throughout its linkages to other nodes.

status groups Groups reflecting a community's expectations for style of life among each class as well as the positive or negative social estimation of honor given to each class.

stimulus generalization For an existing stimulus-response relationship, the more similar a new stimulus is to the existing one, the more likely it will evoke the same response.

store atmospherics The physical properties of the retail environment designed to create an effect on consumer purchases.

store image Consumers' overall perception of a store, which they rely on when choosing a store.

structural variables Variables that include the age of the head of household or family, marital status, presence of children, and employment status.

subjective claims Advertising claims that may be interpreted differently by different consumers.

subliminal persuasion The act of influencing people by stimuli below the conscious level of awareness.

substantiality The size of the market.

surrogate consumer An individual who acts as an agent to guide, direct, and/or conduct activities in the marketplace.

surveys The act of gathering information from a sample of consumers by asking questions and recording responses.

testimonials The act of a celebrity touting the benefits of a product based on that celebrity's positive experience with that product.

top-of-the-mind awareness In assessing consumer awareness, the ability of people to remember a given brand before any other brand name.

total fertility rate The average number of children that would be born alive to a woman during her lifetime if she were to pass through all of her childbearing years conforming to the age-specific fertility rates of a given year.

trait Any distinguishable, relatively enduring way in which one individual differs from another.

transcultural marketing research The act of gathering data from specific ethnic groups and comparing these data to those collected from other markets, usually the mass market.

trickle-down theory A theory that alleges that lower classes often emulate the behavior of their higher-class counterparts.

two-step flow of communication A model of communication in which the opinion leaders are the direct receivers of information from advertisements and interpret and transmit the information to others through word-of-mouth communication.

unconditioned response In Pavlov's theory of classical conditioning, the response evoked by the unconditioned stimulus.

unconditioned stimulus In Pavlov's theory of classical conditioning, the stimulus that automatically evokes a particular response.

unconscious motivation Being unaware of what really motivates one's behavior.

usage volume segmentation A form of segmentation that divides users into heavy, moderate, and light users.

user One who consumes a particular product at a particular time.

value The difference between what consumers give up for a product and the benefits they receive.

value-expressive influence The acceptance of a group's norms, values, attitudes, or behaviors to satisfy a need for psychological association with this group.

vertical coordination A high degree of dependence and interlocking relationships among channel members.

virtual groups Social aggregations based on virtual communities in which individuals from different geographic areas share information without face-to-face contact.

wealth A measure of a family's net worth or assets, including the value of bank accounts, stocks, and property, minus its liabilities.

Weber's law A theory holding that activating the differential threshold or achieving the just noticeable difference depends on the relative amount of change, not just the absolute amount of change.

word-of-mouth communication The informal transmission of ideas, comments, opinions, and information between two people, neither one of whom is a marketer.

zapping The act of switching viewing channels via remote control during commercials.

zipping The act of fast-forwarding through commercials when watching a VCR tape.

CREDITS

Chapter 1 Consumer in Focus 1.2, Vicki G. Morwitz, Eric A. Greenleaf, and Eric J. Johnson, "Divide and Prosper: Consumers' Reactions to Partitioned Prices," *Journal of Marketing Research* 35 (November 1998), 453–463; Consumer in Focus 1.3, Reprinted by permission of *The Wall Street Journal*. © 1999 Dow Jones & Company, Inc. All rights reserved worldwide.

Chapter 3 Figure 3.11, Hans C. M. Van Trijp, Wayne D. Hoyer, and J. Jeffrey Inman, "Why Switch? Product Category—Level of Explanations for True Variety-Seeking Behavior," *Journal of Marketing Research* (August 1996), 281–292.

Chapter 4 Table 4.1, John R. Hauser and Birger Wernerfelt, "An Evaluation Cost Model of Consideration Sets," *Journal of Consumer Research* 16 (March 1990), 393–408; Consumer in Focus 4.2, Excerpted from Maria A. Morales, "It Pays to Shop Around for Uniforms," *The Miami Herald* (July 20, 1997), 1B, 2B; Consumer in Focus 4.3, Excerpted from Maricris G. Briones, "And They're Off!" *Marketing News* (March 30, 1998), 1, 14; Consumer in Focus 4.4, "Washing Machines," Copyright 1991 by Consumers Union of U.S., Inc. Excerpted by permission from *Consumer Reports* (February 1991).

Chapter 5 Figure 5.1, Excerpted from Edward M. Tauber, "Why Do People Shop?" *Journal of Marketing* 36 (October 1972), 46–59; Figure 5.10, John P. Robinson and Franco M. Nicosia," Of Time, Activity, and Consumer Behavior: An Essay on Findings, Interpretations, and Needed Research," *Journal of Business Research* 22 (1991), 171–186.

Chapter 6 Table 6.1, Ronald B. Lieber, "Now Are You Satisfied? The 1998 American Customer Satisfaction Index," *Fortune* (February 16, 1998), 161–164; Consumer in Focus 6.1,

Excerpted from Lauran Neergaard, "Research Finds Internal Clock Important in Drug Effectiveness, Health," *The Miami Herald* (May 1, 1999), 11A; Consumer in Focus 6.2, Excerpted from Neela Baerjee, "Russia Learns to Savor Its 'Spirit'," *The Miami Herald* (June 5, 1999), 1C, 9C; Consumer in Focus 6.3, Excerpted from Don Oldenburg, "How Safe Is Toothpaste? FDA Orders Warning Labels with Chilling Message," *The Miami Herald* (June 20, 1997), 4F.

Chapter 7 Consumer in Focus 7.1, Reprinted by permission of *The Wall Street Journal*. © 1999 Dow Jones & Company, Inc. All rights reserved worldwide; Consumer in Focus 7.2, Excerpted from Gail Schares, "A Peak Experience," *Business Week* (June 1, 1992), 118; Table 7.3, Excerpted from Shalom H. Schwartz, "Are There Universal Aspects in the Structure and Contents of Human Values?" *Journal of Social Issues* 50, 4 (1994), 19–45; Figure 7.10, Thomas J. Reynolds and Jonathan Gutman, "Laddering Theory, Method, Analysis, and Interpretation," Reprinted from *Journal of Advertising Research* 28 (February/March 1988), 19. © 1988 by the Advertising Foundation; Figure 7.13, VALS lifestyle segments © 1997 SRI Consulting. All Rights Reserved.

Chapter 8 Consumer in Focus 8.1, Excerpted from "Tough But Sensitive," *American Demographics* (March 1999), 56; Figure 8.2, Robert O'Harrow, Jr., "Drug Company Consolidation Draws Concerns," *The Miami Herald* (January 30, 2000), 9E; Consumer in Focus 8.2, Excerpted from Greg Hardesty, "Success Sticks to His Stickers," *Sun Sentinel*, (January 2, 2000), 8G; Consumer in Focus 8.3, Excerpted from Rafael Lorente, "Coin Collecting Gets Some Added Oomph," *Sun Sentinel* (January 2, 2000), 1A, 15A; Consumer

in Focus 8.4, Excerpted from Dorothy Dowling, "Frequent Perks Keep Travelers Loyal," *American Demographics* (September 1998), 32–36.

Chapter 9 Opening Vignette, Excerpted from Roger Bull, "Always in Style," *The Times-Union* (November 26, 1999), D1; Table 9.1, Reprinted by permission of *The Wall Street Journal*. © 1999 Dow Jones & Company, Inc. All rights reserved worldwide; Table 9.2, Jennifer Lach, "Like, I Just Gotta Have It," *American Demographics* (February 1999), 24; Consumer in Focus 9.1, Reprinted by permission of *The Wall Street Journal*. © 1998 Dow Jones & Company, Inc. All rights reserved worldwide; Consumer in Focus 9.2, Excerpted from Rachel X. Weissman, "Just Paging Through," *American Demographics* (April 1999), 28–29; Consumer in Focus 9.3, Excerpted from Sandy Shore, "Yellow Pages Seeks to Expand, Enhance Its Image," *The Miami Herald* (December 15, 1998), 41A; Consumer in Focus 9.4, Reprinted by permission of *The Wall Street Journal*. © 1998 Dow Jones & Company, Inc. All rights reserved worldwide.

Chapter 10 Table 10.1, Bruce Brown, "Home PCs," *PC Magazine* (December 15, 1998), 120; Table 10.4, Julie A. Edell and Marian Chapman Burke, "The Power of Feelings in Understanding Advertising Effects," *Journal of Consumer Research* 14 (December 1987), 424, Table 1; Consumer in Focus 10.1, Excerpted from "Many Would Quit Smoking if Prices Rose, U.S. Says," *Miami Herald* (July 31, 1998), 14A; Consumer in Focus 10.2, Excerpted from Cyndee Miller, "Hemp Is Latest Buzzword," *Marketing News* (March 17, 1997), 1, 6; Consumer in Focus 10.3, Excerpted from Skip Wollenberg, "Carmaker Hopes to Rejuvenate Image with New Ad Campaign," *Marketing News* (December 6, 1999), 29; Figure 10.8,

Alvin C. Burns, "Generating Marketing Strategy Priorities Based on Relative Competitive Position," *Journal of Consumer Marketing* 3 (Fall 1986), 49–56.

Chapter 11 Table 11.1, Joseph T. Plummer, "Changing Values," *The Futurist* 23 (January/February 1989), 10; Consumer in Focus 11.1, Excerpted from: Are U.S. Managers Superstitious About Market Share? Cathy Anterasian, John L. Graham, R. Bruce Money, *Sloan Management Review* (Summer 1996), 67–77; Consumer in Focus 11.2, Reprinted by permission of *The Wall Street Journal*. © 1999 Dow Jones & Company, Inc. All rights reserved worldwide; Figure 11.9, Faye Rice and Kimberly Seals McDonald, "Making Generational Marketing Count," *Fortune* 131, 12 (June 26, 1995), 110; Figure 11.11, Courtesy of Benetton or "Benetton Ads: A Risqué Business," *Time* (March 25, 1991), 13; Figure 11.14, Population Reference Bureau, *Population Bulletin, America's Racial and Ethnic Minorities* (September 1999), 23, 36.

Chapter 12 Figure 12.4, Robert Boutilier, "Pulling the Family's Strings," *American Demographics* (August 1993), 46; Figure 12.5, © Management Horizons, a Division of Price Waterhouse; Figure 12.14, James McNeal, Tapping The Three Kid's Market, *American Demographics* (April 1998), 39; Figure 12.15, James McNeal, Tapping The Three Kid's Market, *American Demographics* (April 1998), 40; Consumer in Focus 12.1, "Japanese 'Smart' Homes Know All, Tell All," *The Columbus Dispatch* (April 28, 1999), 2F; Consumer in Focus 12.2, "Anti-Smoking Experts Suggest Ads Targeted Toward Women," *Marketing News* (January 1999), P.5.

Chapter 13 Opening Vignette, Howard Chua-Eoan and Tim Larimer, "PokeMania," *Time* (November 22, 1999), 81; Consumer in Focus 13.1, Reprinted by permission of *The Wall Street Journal*. © 1999 Dow Jones & Company, Inc. All rights reserved worldwide; Figure 13.2, William O. Bearden and Michael J. Etzel, "Reference Group Influence on Product and Brand Purchase Decisions," *Journal of Consumer Research* 9 (September 1982); Figure 13.9, Reprinted with permission of The Free Press, a Division of Macmillan, Inc, from Everett M. Rogers, *Diffusion of Innovation*, 3rd ed. (New York: The Free Press, 1983), 165. Copyright © 1962, 1971, 1983 by The Free Press.

Chapter 14 Figure 14.2, Jennifer Lach, "Commercial Overload," *American Demographics* (September 1999), 20; Figure 14.4, Jennifer Lach, "Deutsche Delivers," *American Demographics* (February 2000), 18, 20, 22; Consumer in Focus 14.1, Excerpted from "Not Quite the TV Generation," *American Demographics* (May 1999), 35–36; Consumer in Focus 14.3, Excerpted from Anne Moncrief Arrate, "Now That We Have Your Attention," *Miami Herald* (June 22, 1997), 1F, 2F; Consumer in Focus 14.4, Excerpted from Cynthia Corzo, "Field of Ads," *Miami Herald* (January 25, 2000), 1C, 3C.

Chapter 15 Opening Vignette, Excerpted from Greg Johnson, "Dewing It," *Miami Herald* (October 22, 1999), 1C, 4C; Figure 15.3, Paul W. Miniard, Sunil Bhatla, Kenneth R. Lord, Peter R. Dickson, and H. Rao Unnava, "Picture-Based Persuasion Processes and the Moderating Role of Involvement," *Journal of Consumer Research* 18 (June 1991), 92–107; Figure 15.4, Paul W. Miniard, Sunil Bhatla, Kenneth R. Lord, Peter R. Dickson, and H. Rao Unnava, "Picture-Based Persuasion Processes and the Moderating Role of Involvement," *Journal of Consumer Research* 18 (June 1991), 92–107; Figure 15.5, Paul W. Miniard, Sunil Bhatla, Kenneth R. Lord, Peter R. Dickson, and H. Rao Unnava, "Picture-Based Persuasion Processes and the Moderating Role of Involvement," *Journal of Consumer Research* 18 (June 1991), 92–107; Figure 15.10, Jennifer Lach, "Rush Those Reindeer," *American Demographics* (December 1998), 23; Consumer in Focus 15.1, Excerpted from Heather Chaplin, "Centrum's Self-Inflicted Silver Bullet," *American Demographics* (March 1999), 68–69; Consumer in Focus 15.2, Excerpted from Adrienne W. Fawcett, "Going for the Gross-Out," *American Demographics* (February 2000), 42–43; Consumer in Focus 15.3, Excerpted from John Ward Anderson, "Designer Tequila: Mexico's New Upscale Drink," *Miami Herald* (March 16, 1997), 9F.

Chapter 16 Opening Vignette, Excerpted from Verne Gay, "Milk, the Magazine," *American Demographics* (February 2000), 32–34; Consumer in Focus 16.1, Excerpted from "Rebates Really Payoff—for the Manufacturers," *Miami Herald* (February 11, 1998), 17A; Consumer in Focus 16.2, Excerpted from Cynthia Corzo, "Field of Ads," *Miami Herald* (January 25, 2000), 1C, 3C; John Dortschner, "Ads! Are! Everywhere! .Com," *Miami Herald* (January 30, 2000), 1E, 2E; Consumer in Focus 16.3, Excerpted from Rebecca Piirto Heath, "An Engraved Invitation," *Marketing Tools* (November/December 1997), 36–42.

Name Index

SUBJECT INDEX

Page numbers in *italics* denote figures; those followed by "t" denote tables.